LECTIONARY FOR·MASS

✛

SUNDAYS, SOLEMNITIES, FEASTS OF THE LORD AND THE SAINTS

STUDY EDITION

LTP

LITURGY
TRAINING
PUBLICATIONS

ACKNOWLEDGMENTS

Concordat cum originali: Reverend James P. Moroney
Executive Director, Secretariat for the Liturgy
National Conference of Catholic Bishops

Published by the authority of the Bishops' Committee on the Liturgy, National Conference of Catholic Bishops.

This study edition of the first volume of the *Lectionary for Mass for Use in the Dioceses of the United States* was edited by Gabe Huck with assistance from Theresa Pincich and Theresa Houston. Anna Manhart designed the inside and the cover using Linda Ekstrom's artwork from *The Lectionary for Mass*. Mark Hollopeter typeset this book using Goudy and Syntax. Katharine Weingart-Wolff created and arranged the letterforms in the title for Liturgy Training Publications. This book was printed in Canada by Webcom, Ltd.

05 04 03 02 01 00 99   5 4 3 2 1

ISBN 1-56854-335-2
RNABSE

CONTENTS

SOLEMNITIES OF THE LORD DURING ORDINARY TIME

THE CONTENT AND USE OF THE STUDY EDITION

This volume is intended for students, preachers, persons involved in the preparation of the Sunday liturgy, and anyone who uses the Sunday readings to prepare for Mass on Sunday or reflect on the liturgy afterward. The user will find here the readings for Sundays and some feast days in the translation approved by the United States bishops for use beginning in Advent of 1998. This constitutes Volume One of the revised edition of the lectionary. Volume Two will contain weekday readings, readings for other feasts and memorials of the saints, common texts for the saints, readings for ritual and occasional Masses.

Anyone using this book will find it most helpful to take time at the beginning for a careful look at the Table of Contents. The notes which follow are a guide to these contents.

Following the various decrees promulgating the lectionary, the book begins with the Introduction that accompanied the 1981 revision of the lectionary. It was the work of the Vatican office charged with liturgical renewal and is an important discussion of the liturgy of the word, the role of lector and other ministers, and the structure and principles of the lectionary in general. This Introduction is intended for all — preacher, lector, any baptized Catholic — who desire to understand better how the Bible has been and is the ground and the nourishment and the delight of Christian assemblies.

The Body of the Lectionary

For the most part, the order of the readings then follows the liturgical seasons: Advent, Christmas, Lent, Triduum, Easter. The Sundays of Ordinary Time, both the Sundays between Christmas and Lent and those following Pentecost, appear next. Whenever the lectionary provides three sets of readings, one for each year of the three-year cycle, these are found in order. For example: First Sunday of Advent, Year A, is followed by First Sunday of Advent, Year B, and then by First Sunday of Advent, Year C. A few Sundays, along with most of the great feasts, do not have complete sets of readings for each of the three years but use one or more of the same readings each year.

Following the Last Sunday in Ordinary Time (Christ the King) are several entries with which the user should be familiar:

• "Alleluia Verses for Sundays in Ordinary Time": These may be used as needed in place of the alleluia verse given before the gospel of each Sunday.

• "Solemnities of the Lord during Ordinary Time": These are the readings for the Sunday feasts of the Trinity and the Body and Blood of Christ, and the weekday feast of the Sacred Heart. The dates of these three feasts depend on the date of Pentecost.

• "Common Texts for Sung Responsorial Psalms": These refrains and psalms may be used, according to the proper season, in place of the psalm given for a specific Sunday.

• "Chrism Mass" and "Octave of Easter": The reading for these days are given here because of their importance in the liturgical year.

The final section of lectionary readings contains the scriptures assigned for days with the rank of "solemnity" and for those with the rank of "feast" that can replace Sundays of Ordinary Time. Any of the days in this section, except Saint Joseph and Annunciation (which always fall during Lent) and Immaculate Conception (which always falls in Advent), will replace a Sunday in Ordinary Time when their dates fall on Sunday. This includes the Commemmoration of All the Faithful Departed (November 2).

Appendices and Tables

The three appendices found in ritual editions of the lectionary are also included in this volume. They are:

• Appendix I: Latin texts of the sequences for Easter, Pentecost and the Body and Blood of Christ

• Appendix II: a listing of those books of scripture from which the readings of the entire lectionary (both Volume One and Volume Two) are taken, showing which verses are read and giving for each reading the lectionary number(s) where it will be found

• Appendix III: a listing of psalms which are used as responsorial psalms in Volume One or Volume Two of the lectionary, giving for each the lectionary number(s) where that psalm can be found. Note that any given responsorial psalm will usually not contain the whole text of the psalm. Thus the texts used from the same psalm on different days may be the same, may differ slightly, or may be entirely different.

This study edition concludes with seven tables (the first three are taken from the ritual edition of the lectionary, the others have been added by the publisher of this edition to help in the study and use of the lectionary):

• Table I gives the dates for Ash Wednesday, Easter, Ascension, Pentecost and the First Sunday of Advent for each year until the year 2025. It lists each given year as Year A, Year B or Year C in the lectionary cycle for Sundays, and as Year I or Year II in the lectionary cycle for weekdays.

• Table II also covers each year until 2025, giving the Sunday and week-day cycles followed by the number of weeks of Ordinary Time between the Christmas season and Lent. This table also indicates which week of Ordinary Time begins on the day after Pentecost.

• Table III is an overview of how the letters of the New Testament are read through the Sundays of Ordinary Time in all three years of the cycle.

• Table IV is an overview of how the Gospels of Matthew, Mark and Luke are read through the Sundays of Ordinary Time in all three years of the cycle. Tables III and IV are a great help in understanding how the Sunday readings take the church through the semi-continuous reading of the gospels and letters of the New Testament in the Sundays of Ordinary Time.

• Table V is an overview of the three Sunday readings in all three years of the lectionary cycle. Here the sequences of readings shown in Tables III and IV are joined with the First Readings for a complete overview of how the church reads scripture on Sundays and feasts.

• Table VI provides the date of every Sunday and feast from 1999 to 2013. This table is intended to help all who prepare the liturgy with an overview of how the feasts and seasons fall in a given calendar year.

• Table VII describes the use of the "Common Texts for Sung Responsorial Psalms" and lists the refrains and psalms by season and feast. This table can be used to carry forward what is suggested in #21 of the Introduction and then provided for beginning on page 441.

Features of This Study Edition

Because this edition is intended for study, use in preparation of the liturgy and the homily, and for private reading, it differs from the ritual edition of the lectionary in the following ways:

• though the "sense lines" of the ritual edition are retained, no efforts have been made to avoid page turns within readings

• when a reading has both a longer and shorter form, this is indicated with brackets around the verses in the shorter version, rather than by printing both forms separately

• when a reading is repeated exactly on another Sunday or feast, there is a reference only (the text itself is not repeated)

• when a responsorial psalm is repeated exactly, there is a reference only (the text itself is not repeated; the refrain, however, will always be given)

• the refrains of the responsorial psalm and of the alleluia verse are given only once in full, then their repetition is indicated by the use of "R."

• the words "A reading from . . . " and "The word/gospel of the Lord" are not included (but the biblical citations will always identify the book of scripture from which the reading is taken)

Each set of readings is assigned a "lectionary number" by the document which promulgated the revision of the lectionary in 1981. This is simply a device for quick reference. The lectionary number is found by the name of the Sunday or feast and is then used in several of the appendices and tables.

The Word of God in the Liturgy

The lectionary is the treasure of the church and so of every baptized person. The Introduction offers this concise invitation:

> The many riches contained in the one word of God are admirably brought out in the different kinds of liturgical celebrations and liturgical assemblies. This takes place as the unfolding mystery of Christ is recalled during the course of the liturgical year, as the Church's sacraments and sacramentals are celebrated, or as the faithful respond individually to the Holy Spirit working within them. For then the liturgical celebration, based primarily on the word of God and sustained by it, becomes a new event and enriches the word itself with new meaning and power. Thus in the liturgy the Church faithfully adheres to the way Christ himself read and explained the Scriptures, beginning with the "today" of his coming forward in the synagogue and urging all to search the Scriptures (Luke 4:16–21).

DECREES

SACRED CONGREGATION FOR DIVINE WORSHIP
Prot. n. 106/69

The Order of Readings from the Sacred Scriptures to be used at Mass was prepared by the Consilium for the Implementation of the Constitution on the Sacred Liturgy in accordance with the requirement of the Constitution that a more lavish table of the word of God be spread before the faithful, that the treasures of the Bible be opened up more widely, and that the more important part of the Holy Scriptures be read to the people over a prescribed number of years (art. 51). The Supreme Pontiff Paul VI approved it by the Apostolic Constitution *Missale Romanum*, on 3 April 1969.

Accordingly, this Sacred Congregation for Divine Worship, by special mandate of the Supreme Pontiff, promulgates this same Order of Readings for Mass, establishing that it enter into force on 30 November, the First Sunday of Advent, in the year 1969. However, in the coming liturgical year series B will be used for the Sunday readings and series II for the first reading on weekdays of Ordinary Time.

Since in the present Order of Readings only the references are given for the individual readings, the Episcopal Conferences will have complete texts prepared in the vernacular languages, observing the norms laid down in the Instruction on vernacular translations issued by the Consilium for the Implementation of the Constitution on the Sacred Liturgy on 25 January 1969. The vernacular texts may either be taken from translations of the Sacred Scriptures already lawfully approved for particular regions, and confirmed by the Apostolic See, or newly translated, in which case they should be submitted for confirmation to this Sacred Congregation.

All things to the contrary notwithstanding.

From the offices of the Sacred Congregation for Divine Worship, 25 May 1969, Pentecost Sunday.

+Benno Cardinal Gut   +A. Bugnini
  Prefect   Secretary

SACRED CONGREGATION FOR THE SACRAMENTS AND DIVINE WORSHIP
Prot. CD 240/81
REGARDING THE SECOND TYPICAL EDITION

The Order of Readings for Mass, first published in *editio typica* in 1969, was promulgated on 25 May of that year by special mandate of the Supreme Pontiff Paul VI, in accordance with the requirement of the Constitution on the Sacred Liturgy, in order to provide Bishops' Conferences with the references for the individual biblical readings at Mass with a view to the preparation of lectionaries in the vernacular languages in the different regions.

In that edition were lacking the biblical references of readings for celebration of the sacraments and other rites that have been published since May 1969. Moreover, following the issuing of the Neo-Vulgate edition of the Sacred Scriptures, it was laid down by the Apostolic Constitution *Scripturarum thesaurus* of 25 April 1979 that thereafter the text of the Neo-Vulgate must be adopted as the typical edition for liturgical use. Since the first *editio typica* is no longer available, it seemed opportune to prepare a second edition, having the following features with regard to the previous one:

1. The text of the Introduction has been expanded.

2. In compliance with the Apostolic Constitution *Scripturarum thesaurus*, the Neo-Vulgate edition of the Sacred Scriptures has been used in indicating the biblical references.

3. There have been incorporated all the biblical references to be found in the lectionaries for the celebration of sacraments and sacramentals that have been published since the first edition of the Order of Readings for Mass.

4. The biblical references have also been added for readings for certain Masses "for various needs" and for readings in other Masses which were inserted into the Roman Missal for the first time in its second edition of 1975.

5. As regards the celebrations of the Holy Family, the Baptism of the Lord, the Ascension, and Pentecost, references have been added for optional readings in such a way that biblical texts arranged for cycles A, B, and C in the Lectionary for Sundays and feasts are completed.

The Supreme Pontiff John Paul II has by his authority approved this second edition of the Order of Readings for Mass and the Sacred Congregation for the Sacraments and Divine Worship now promulgates it and declares it to be the *editio typica*.

The Episcopal Conferences will introduce the changes found in this second edition into the editions to be prepared in the vernacular.

All things to the contrary notwithstanding.

From the offices of the Sacred Congregation for the Sacraments and Divine Worship, 21 January 1981.

+James R. Cardinal Knox   +Virgilio Noè
   Prefect   Associate Secretary

CONGREGATION FOR DIVINE WORSHIP AND THE DISCIPLINE OF THE SACRAMENTS
Prot. 1667/97/L
THE UNITED STATES OF AMERICA

In response to the request of His Excellency Anthony M. Pilla, Bishop of Cleveland, President of the Conference of Bishops of the United States of America, made in a letter dated August 11, 1997, and in virtue of faculties granted to this Congregation by Pope John Paul II, we gladly confirm the first volume of the Mass Lectionary drawn up in English with the title *Lectionary for Mass for Use in the Dioceses of the United States of America*, and annexed to this decree.

In printed editions of the text there should be inserted in its entirety this Decree by which the Apostolic See accords the requested confirmation of the sole translation to be used in the celebration of Holy Mass in all the dioceses of the United States of America. Moreover, two copies of the printed text should be forwarded to this Congregation.

All things to the contrary notwithstanding.

From the offices of the Congregation for Divine Worship and the Discipline of the Sacraments, October 6, 1997.

+Jorge Medina E.   +Geraldo M. Agnelo
   Pro-Prefect   Archbishop Secretary

NATIONAL CONFERENCE OF CATHOLIC BISHOPS
UNITED STATES OF AMERICA

In accord with the norms established by decree of the Sacred Congregation of Rites in *Cum, nostra ætate* (January 27, 1966), this edition of the *Lectionary for Mass, Volume I: Sundays, Solemnities and Feasts of the Lord* is declared to be the vernacular typical edition of the *Ordo Lectionum Missae, editio typica altera* in the dioceses of the United States of America, and is published by authority of the National Conference of Catholic Bishops.

The first volume of the *Lectionary for Mass* was canonically approved for use by the National Conference of Catholic Bishops on June 20, 1992, and was subsequently confirmed by the Apostolic See by decree of the Congregation for Divine Worship and the Discipline of the Sacraments on October 6, 1997 (Prot. 1667/97/L).

On the First Sunday of Advent, November 29, 1998, the first volume of the *Lectionary for Mass* may be used in the liturgy. Upon promulgation of the second volume of the *Lectionary for Mass* a date for mandatory use will be established.

Given at the General Secretariat of the National Conference of Catholic Bishops, Washington D.C. on June 19, 1998, the Solemnity of the Sacred Heart of Jesus.

+Most Reverend Anthony M. Pilla
  Bishop of Cleveland
  President
  National Conference of Catholic Bishops

Reverend Monsignor Dennis M. Schnurr
General Secretary

INTRODUCTION

PREAMBLE

CHAPTER I: GENERAL PRINCIPLES FOR THE LITURGICAL CELEBRATION OF THE WORD OF GOD

1. Certain Preliminaries

a) The Importance of the Word of God in Liturgical Celebration

1. The Second Vatican Council,[1] the magisterium of the Popes,[2] and various documents promulgated after the Council by the organisms of the Holy See[3] have already had many excellent things to say about the importance of the word of God and about reestablishing the use of Sacred Scripture in every celebration of the Liturgy. The Introduction to the 1969 edition of the Order of Readings for Mass has clearly stated and briefly explained some of the more important principles.[4]

On the occasion of this new edition of the Order of Readings for Mass, requests have come from many quarters for a more detailed exposition of the same principles. Hence, this expanded and more suitable arrangement of the Introduction first gives a general statement on the essential bond between the word of God and the liturgical celebration,[5] then deals in greater detail with the word of God in the celebration of Mass, and, finally explains the precise structure of the Order of Readings for Mass.

b) Terms Used to Refer to the Word of God

2. For the sake of clear and precise language on this topic, a definition of terms might well be expected as a prerequisite. Nevertheless this Introduction will simply use the same terms employed in conciliar and postconciliar documents. Furthermore it will use "Sacred Scripture" and "word of God" interchangeably throughout when referring to the books written under the inspiration of the Holy Spirit, thus avoiding any confusion of language or meaning.[6]

c) The Significance of the Word of God in the Liturgy

3. The many riches contained in the one word of God are admirably brought out in the different kinds of liturgical celebration and in the different gatherings of the faithful who take part in those celebrations. This takes place as the unfolding mystery of Christ is recalled during the course of the liturgical year, as the Church's sacraments and sacramentals are celebrated, or as the faithful respond individually to the Holy Spirit working within them.[7] For then the liturgical celebration, founded primarily on the word of God and sustained by it, becomes a new event and enriches the word itself with new meaning and power. Thus in the Liturgy the Church faithfully adheres to the way Christ himself read and explained the Sacred Scriptures, beginning with the "today" of his coming forward in the synagogue and urging all to search the Scriptures.[8]

2. Liturgical Celebration of the Word of God

a) The Proper Character of the Word of God in the Liturgical Celebration

4. In the celebration of the Liturgy the word of God is not announced in only one way[9] nor does it always stir the hearts of the hearers with the same efficacy. Always,

however, Christ is present in his word,[10] as he carries out the mystery of salvation, he sanctifies humanity and offers the Father perfect worship.[11]

Moreover, the word of God unceasingly calls to mind and extends the economy of salvation, which achieves its fullest expression in the Liturgy. The liturgical celebration becomes therefore the continuing, complete, and effective presentation of God's word.

The word of God constantly proclaimed in the Liturgy is always, then, a living and effective word[12] through the power of the Holy Spirit. It expresses the Father's love that never fails in its effectiveness toward us.

b) The Word of God in the Economy of Salvation

5. When in celebrating the Liturgy the Church proclaims both the Old and New Testament, it is proclaiming one and the same mystery of Christ.

The New Testament lies hidden in the Old; the Old Testament comes fully to light in the New.[13] Christ himself is the center and fullness of the whole of Scripture, just as he is of all liturgical celebration.[14] Thus the Scriptures are the living waters from which all who seek life and salvation must drink.

The more profound our understanding of the celebration of the liturgy, the higher our appreciation of the importance of God's word. Whatever we say of the one, we can in turn say of the other, because each recalls the mystery of Christ and each in its own way causes the mystery to be carried forward.

c) The Word of God in the Liturgical Participation of the Faithful

6. In celebrating the Liturgy the Church faithfully echoes the "Amen" that Christ, the mediator between God and men and women, uttered once for all as he shed his blood to seal God's new covenant in the Holy Spirit.[15]

When God communicates his word, he expects a response, one that is, of listening and adoring "in Spirit and in truth" (John 4:23). The Holy Spirit makes that response effective, so that what is heard in the celebration of the Liturgy may be carried out in a way of life: "Be doers of the word and not hearers only" (James 1:22).

The liturgical celebration and the participation of the faithful receive outward expression in actions, gestures, and words. These derive their full meaning not simply from their origin in human experience but from the word of God and the economy of salvation, to which they refer. Accordingly, the participation of the faithful in the Liturgy increases to the degree that, as they listen to the word of God proclaimed in the Liturgy, they strive harder to commit themselves to the Word of God incarnate in Christ. Thus, they endeavor to conform their way of life to what they celebrate in the Liturgy, and then in turn to bring to the celebration of the Liturgy all that they do in life.[16]

3. The Word of God in the Life of the People of the Covenant

a) The Word of God in the Life of the Church

7. In the hearing of God's word the Church is built up and grows, and in the signs of the liturgical celebration God's wonderful, past works in the history of salvation are presented anew as mysterious realities. God in turn makes use of the congregation of the faithful that celebrates the Liturgy in order that his word may speed on and be glorified and that his name be exalted among the nations.[17]

Whenever, therefore, the Church, gathered by the Holy Spirit for liturgical celebration,[18] announces and proclaims the word of God, she is aware of being a new people in whom the covenant made in the past is perfected and fulfilled. Baptism and confirmation in the Spirit have made all Christ's faithful into messengers of God's word because of the grace of hearing they have received. They must therefore be the bearers of the same word in the Church and in the world, at least by the witness of their lives.

The word of God proclaimed in the celebration of God's mysteries does not only address present conditions but looks back to past events and forward to what is yet to come. Thus God's word shows us what we should hope for with such a longing that in this changing world our hearts will be set on the place where our true joys lie.[19]

b) The Church's Explanation of the Word of God

8. By Christ's own will there is a marvelous diversity of members in the new people of God and each has different duties and responsibilities with respect to the word of God. Accordingly, the faithful listen to God's word and meditate on it, but only those who have the office of teaching by virtue of sacred ordination or who have been entrusted with exercising that ministry expound the word of God.

This is how in doctrine, life, and worship the Church keeps alive and passes on to every generation all that she is, all that she believes. Thus with the passage of the centuries, the Church is ever to advance toward the fullness of divine truth until God's word is wholly accomplished in her.[20]

c) The Connection between the Word of God Proclaimed and the Working of the Holy Spirit

9. The working of the Holy Spirit is needed if the word of God is to make what we hear outwardly have its effect inwardly. Because of the Holy Spirit's inspiration and support, the word of God becomes the foundation of the liturgical celebration and the rule and support of all our life.

The working of the Holy Spirit precedes, accompanies, and brings to completion the whole celebration of the Liturgy. But the Spirit also brings home[21] to each person individually everything that in the proclamation of the word of God is spoken for the good of the whole gathering of the faithful. In strengthening the unity of all, the Holy Spirit at the same time fosters a diversity of gifts and furthers their multiform operation.

d) The Essential Bond between the Word of God and the Mystery of the Eucharist

10. The Church has honored the word of God and the Eucharistic mystery with the same reverence, although not with the same worship, and has always and everywhere insisted upon and sanctioned such honor. Moved by the example of its Founder, the Church has never ceased to celebrate his paschal mystery by coming together to read "what referred to him in all the Scriptures" (Luke 24:27) and to carry out the work of salvation through the celebration of the memorial of the Lord and through the sacraments. "The preaching of the word is necessary for the ministry of the sacraments, for these are sacraments of faith, which is born and nourished from the word."[22]

The Church is nourished spiritually at the twofold table of God's word and of the Eucharist:[23] from the one it grows in wisdom and from the other in holiness. In the word of God the divine covenant is announced; in the Eucharist the new and everlasting covenant is renewed. On the one hand the history of salvation is brought to mind by means of human sounds; on the other it is made manifest in the sacramental signs of the Liturgy.

It can never be forgotten, therefore, that the divine word read and proclaimed by the Church in the Liturgy has as its one purpose the sacrifice of the New Covenant and the banquet of grace, that is, the Eucharist. The celebration of Mass in which the word is heard and the Eucharist is offered and received forms but one single act of divine worship.[24] That act offers the sacrifice of praise to God and makes available to God's creatures the fullness of redemption.

FIRST PART: THE WORD OF GOD IN THE CELEBRATION OF MASS

CHAPTER II: THE CELEBRATION OF THE LITURGY OF THE WORD AT MASS

1. The Elements of the Liturgy of the Word and their Rites

11. "Readings from Sacred Scripture and the chants between the readings form the main part of the liturgy of the word. The homily, the profession of faith, and the universal prayer or prayer of the faithful carry it forward and conclude it."[25]

a) The Biblical Readings

12. In the celebration of Mass the biblical readings with their accompanying chants from the Sacred Scriptures may not be omitted, shortened, or, worse still, replaced by nonbiblical readings.[26] For it is out of the word of God handed down in writing that even now "God speaks to his people"[27] and it is from the continued use of Sacred Scripture that the people of God, docile to the Holy Spirit under the light of faith, is enabled to bear witness to Christ before the world by its manner of life.

13. The reading of the Gospel is the high point of the liturgy of the word. For this the other readings, in their established sequence from the Old to the New Testament, prepare the assembly.

14. A speaking style on the part of the readers that is audible, clear, and intelligent is the first means of transmitting the word of God properly to the congregation. The readings, taken from the approved editions,[28] may be sung in a way suited to different languages. This singing, however, must serve to bring out the sense of the words, not obscure them. On occasions when the readings are in Latin, the manner given in the *Ordo cantus Missae* is to be maintained.[29]

15. There may be concise introductions before the readings, especially the first. The style proper to such comments must be respected, that is, they must be simple, faithful to the text, brief, well prepared, and properly varied to suit the text they introduce.[30]

16. In a Mass with the people the readings are always to be proclaimed at the ambo.[31]

17. Of all the rites connected with the liturgy of the word, the reverence due to the Gospel reading must receive special attention.[32] Where there is an Evangeliary or Book of Gospels that has been carried in by the deacon or reader during the entry procession,[33] it is most fitting that the deacon or a priest, when there is no deacon, take the book from the altar[34] and carry it to the ambo. He is preceded by servers with candles and incense or other symbols of reverence that may be customary. As the faithful stand and acclaim the Lord, they show honor to the Book of Gospels. The deacon who is to read the Gospel, bowing in front of the one presiding, asks and receives the blessing. When no deacon is present, the priest, bowing before the altar, prays inaudibly, *Almighty God, cleanse my heart. . . .*[35]

At the ambo the one who proclaims the Gospel greets the people, who are standing, and announces the reading as he makes the sign of the cross on forehead, mouth, and breast. If incense is used, he next incenses the book, then reads the Gospel. When finished, he kisses the book, saying the appointed words inaudibly.

Even if the Gospel itself is not sung, it is appropriate for the greeting *The Lord be with you,* and *A reading from the holy Gospel according to . . . ,* and at the end *The Gospel of the Lord* to be sung, in order that the congregation may also sing its acclamations. This is a way both of bringing out the importance of the Gospel reading and of stirring up the faith of those who hear it.

18. At the conclusion of the other readings, *The word of the Lord* may be sung, even by someone other than the reader; all respond with the acclamation. In this way the assembled congregation pays reverence to the word of God it has listened to in faith and gratitude.

b) The Responsorial Psalm

19. The responsorial psalm, also called the gradual, has great liturgical and pastoral significance because it is an "integral part of the liturgy of the word."[36] Accordingly, the faithful must be continually instructed on the way to perceive the word of God speaking in the psalms and to turn these psalms into the prayer of the Church. This, of course, "will be achieved more readily if a deeper understanding of the psalms, according to the meaning with which they are sung in the sacred Liturgy, is more diligently promoted among the clergy and communicated to all the faithful by means of appropriate catechesis."[37]

Brief remarks about the choice of the psalm and response as well as their correspondence to the readings may be helpful.

20. As a rule the responsorial psalm should be sung. There are two established ways of singing the psalm after the first reading: responsorially and directly. In responsorial singing, which, as far as possible, is to be given preference, the psalmist, or cantor of the psalm, sings the psalm verse and the whole congregation joins in by singing the response. In direct singing of the psalm there is no intervening response by the community; either the psalmist, or cantor of the psalm, sings the psalm alone as the community listens or else all sing it together.

21. The singing of the psalm, or even of the response alone, is a great help toward understanding and meditating on the psalm's spiritual meaning.

To foster the congregation's singing, every means available in each individual culture is to be employed. In particular, use is to be made of all the relevant options provided in the Order of Readings for Mass[38] regarding responses corresponding to the different liturgical seasons.

22. When not sung, the psalm after the reading is to be recited in a manner conducive to meditation on the word of God.[39]

The responsorial psalm is sung or recited by the psalmist or cantor at the ambo.[40]

c) The Acclamation before the Reading of the Gospel

23. The *Alleluia* or, as the liturgical season requires, the verse before the Gospel, is also a "rite or act standing by itself."[41] It serves as the greeting of welcome of the assembled faithful to the Lord who is about to speak to them and as an expression of their faith through song.

The *Alleluia* or the verse before the Gospel must be sung and during it all stand. It is not to be sung only by the cantor who intones it or by the choir, but by the whole of the people together.[42]

d) The Homily

24. Through the course of the liturgical year the homily sets forth the mysteries of faith and the standards of the Christian life on the basis of the sacred text. Beginning with the Constitution on the Liturgy, the homily as part of the liturgy of the word[43] has been repeatedly and strongly recommended and in some cases it is obligatory. As a rule it is to be given by the one presiding.[44] The purpose of the homily at Mass is that the spoken word of God and the liturgy of the Eucharist may together become "a proclamation of God's wonderful works in the history of salvation, the mystery of Christ."[45] Through the readings and homily Christ's paschal mystery is proclaimed; through the sacrifice of the Mass it becomes present.[46] Moreover Christ himself is always present and active in the preaching of his Church.[47]

Whether the homily explains the text of the Sacred Scriptures proclaimed in the readings or some other text of the Liturgy,[48] it must always lead the community of the faithful to celebrate the Eucharist actively, "so that they may hold fast in their lives to what they have grasped by faith."[49] From this living explanation, the word of God proclaimed in the readings and the Church's celebration of the day's Liturgy will have greater impact. But this demands that the homily be truly the fruit of meditation, carefully prepared, neither too long nor too short, and suited to all those present, even children and the uneducated.[50]

At a concelebration, the celebrant or one of the concelebrants as a rule gives the homily.[51]

25. On the prescribed days, that is, Sundays and holydays of obligation, there must be a homily in all Masses celebrated with a congregation, even Masses on the preceding evening; the homily may not be omitted without a serious reason.[52] There is also to be a homily in Masses with children and with special groups[53]

A homily is strongly recommended on the weekdays of Advent, Lent, and the Easter season for the sake of the faithful who regularly take part in the celebration of Mass; also on other feasts and occasions when a large congregation is present.[54]

26. The priest celebrant gives the homily, standing either at the chair or at the ambo.[55]

27. Any necessary announcements are to be kept completely separate from the homily; they must take place following the prayer after Communion.[56]

e) Silence

28. The liturgy of the word must be celebrated in a way that fosters meditation; clearly, any sort of haste that hinders recollection must be avoided. The dialogue between God and his people taking place through the Holy Spirit demands short intervals of silence, suited to the assembled congregation, as an opportunity to take the word of God to heart and to prepare a response to it in prayer.

Proper times for silence during the liturgy of the word are, for example, before this liturgy begins, after the first and the second reading, after the homily.[57]

f) The Profession of Faith

29. The symbol, creed or profession of faith, said when the rubrics require, has as its purpose in the celebration of Mass that the assembled congregation may respond

and give assent to the word of God heard in the readings and through the homily, and that before beginning to celebrate in the Eucharist the mystery of faith it may call to mind the rule of faith in a formulary approved by the Church.[58]

g) The Universal Prayer or Prayer of the Faithful

30. In the light of God's word and in a sense in response to it, the congregation of the faithful prays in the universal prayer as a rule for the needs of the universal Church and the local community, for the salvation of the world and those oppressed by any burden, and for special categories of people.

The celebrant introduces the prayer; a deacon, another minister, or some of the faithful may propose intentions that are short and phrased with a measure of freedom. In these petitions "the people, exercising its priestly function, makes intercession for all men and women,"[59] with the result that, as the liturgy of the word has its full effects in the faithful, they are better prepared to proceed to the liturgy of the Eucharist.

31. For the prayer of the faithful the celebrant presides at the chair and the intentions are announced at the ambo.[60]

The assembled congregation takes part in the prayer of the faithful while standing and by saying or singing a common response after each intention or by silent prayer.[61]

2. AIDS TO THE PROPER CELEBRATION OF THE LITURGY OF THE WORD

a) The Place for the Proclamation of the Word of God

32. There must be a place in the church that is somewhat elevated, fixed, and of a suitable design and nobility. It should reflect the dignity of God's word and be a clear reminder to the people that in the Mass the table of God's word and of Christ's body is placed before them.[62] The place for the readings must also truly help the people's listening and attention during the liturgy of the word. Great pains must therefore be taken, in keeping with the design of each church, over the harmonious and close relationship of the ambo with the altar.

33. Either permanently or at least on occasions of greater solemnity, the ambo should be decorated simply and in keeping with its design.

Since the ambo is the place from which the word of God is proclaimed by the ministers, it must of its nature be reserved for the readings, the responsorial psalm, and the Easter Proclamation (the *Exsultet*). The ambo may rightly be used for the homily and the prayer of the faithful, however, because of their close connection with the entire liturgy of the word. It is better for the commentator, cantor, or director of singing, for example, not to use the ambo.[63]

34. In order that the ambo may properly serve its liturgical purpose, it is to be rather large, since on occasion several ministers must use it at the same time. Provision must also be made for the readers to have enough light to read the text and, as required, to have modern sound equipment enabling the faithful to hear them without difficulty.

b) The Books for Proclamation of the Word of God in the Liturgy

35. Along with the ministers, the actions, the allocated places, and other elements, the books containing the readings of the word of God remind the hearers of the presence of God speaking to his people. Since in liturgical celebrations the books too serve as signs and symbols of the higher realities, care must be taken to ensure that they truly are worthy, dignified and beautiful.[64]

36. The proclamation of the Gospel always stands as the high point of the liturgy of the word. Thus the liturgical tradition of both West and East has consistently made a certain distinction between the books for the readings. The Book of Gospels was always fabricated and decorated with the utmost care and shown greater respect than any of the other books of readings. In our times also, then, it is very desirable that cathedrals and at least the larger, more populous parishes and the churches with a larger attendance possess a beautifully designed Book of Gospels, separate from any other book of readings. For good reason it is the Book of Gospels that is presented to a deacon at his ordination and that at an ordination to the episcopate is laid upon the head of the bishop-elect and held there.[65]

37. Because of the dignity of the word of God, the books of readings used in the celebration are not to be replaced by other pastoral aids, for example, by leaflets printed for the preparation of the readings by the faithful or for their personal meditation.

CHAPTER III: OFFICES AND MINISTRIES IN THE CELEBRATION OF THE LITURGY OF THE WORD WITHIN MASS

1. THE FUNCTION OF THE PRESIDENT AT THE LITURGY OF THE WORD

38. The one presiding at the liturgy of the word communicates the spiritual nourishment it contains to those present, especially in the homily. Even if he too is a listener to the word of God proclaimed by others, the duty of proclaiming it has been entrusted above all to him. Personally or through others he sees to it that the word of God is properly proclaimed. He then as a rule reserves to himself the tasks of composing comments to help the people listen more attentively and of preaching a homily that fosters in them a richer understanding of the word of God.

39. The first requirement for one who is to preside over the celebration is a thorough knowledge of the structure of the Order of Readings, so that he will know how to work a fruitful effect in the hearts of the faithful. Through study and prayer he must also develop a full understanding of the coordination and connection of the various texts in the liturgy of the word, so that the Order of

Readings will become the source of a sound understanding of the mystery of Christ and his saving work.

40. The one presiding is to make ready use of the various options provided in the Lectionary regarding readings, responses, responsorial psalms, and Gospel acclamations;[66] but he is to do so in harmony[67] with all concerned and after listening to the opinions of the faithful in what concerns them.[68]

41. The one presiding exercises his proper office and the ministry of the word of God also as he preaches the homily.[69] In this way he leads his brothers and sisters to an effective knowledge of Scripture. He opens their minds to thanksgiving for the wonderful works of God. He strengthens the faith of those present in the word that in the celebration becomes sacrament through the Holy Spirit. Finally, he prepares them for a fruitful reception of Communion and invites them to take upon themselves the demands of the Christian life.

42. The president is responsible for preparing the faithful for the liturgy of the word on occasion by means of introductions before the readings.[70] These comments can help the assembled congregation toward a better hearing of the word of God, because they stir up an attitude of faith and good will. He may also carry out this responsibility through others, a deacon, for example, or a commentator.[71]

43. As he directs the prayer of the faithful and through their introduction and conclusion connects them, if possible, with the day's readings and the homily, the president leads the faithful toward the liturgy of the Eucharist.[72]

2. THE ROLE OF THE FAITHFUL IN THE LITURGY OF THE WORD

44. Christ's word gathers the people of God as one and increases and sustains them. "This applies above all to the liturgy of the word in the celebration of Mass, where there are inseparably united the proclamation of the death of the Lord, the response of the people listening, and the very offering through which Christ has confirmed the New Covenant in his Blood, and in which the people share by their intentions and by reception of the sacrament."[73] For "not only when things are read 'that were written for our instruction' (Romans 15:4), but also when the Church prays or sings or acts, the faith of those taking part is nourished and their minds are raised to God, so that they may offer him rightful worship and receive his grace more abundantly."[74]

45. In the liturgy of the word, the congregation of Christ's faithful even today receives from God the word of his covenant through the faith that comes by hearing, and must respond to that word in faith, so that they may become more and more truly the people of the New Covenant.

The people of God have a spiritual right to receive abundantly from the treasury of God's word. Its riches are presented to them through use of the Order of Readings, the homily, and pastoral efforts.

For their part, the faithful at the celebration of Mass are to listen to the word of God with an inward and outward reverence that will bring them continuous growth in the spiritual life and draw them more deeply into the mystery which is celebrated.[75]

46. As a help toward celebrating the memorial of the Lord with eager devotion, the faithful should be keenly aware of the one presence of Christ in both the word of God — it is he himself "who speaks when the Sacred Scriptures are read in the Church" — and "above all under the Eucharistic species."[76]

47. To be received and integrated into the life of Christ's faithful, the word of God demands a living faith.[77] Hearing the word of God unceasingly proclaimed arouses that faith.

The Sacred Scriptures, above all in their liturgical proclamation, are the source of life and strength. As the Apostle Paul attests, the Gospel is the saving power of God for everyone who believes.[78] Love of the Scriptures is therefore a force reinvigorating and renewing the entire people of God.[79] All the faithful without exception must therefore always be ready to listen gladly to God's word.[80] When this word is proclaimed in the Church and put into living practice, it enlightens the faithful through the working of the Holy Spirit and draws them into the entire mystery of the Lord as a reality to be lived.[81] The word of God reverently received moves the heart and its desires toward conversion and toward a life resplendent with both individual and community faith,[82] since God's word is the food of Christian life and the source of the prayer of the whole Church.[83]

48. The intimate connection between the liturgy of the word and the liturgy of the Eucharist in the Mass should prompt the faithful to be present right from the beginning of the celebration,[84] to take part attentively, and to prepare themselves in so far as possible to hear the word, especially by learning beforehand more about Sacred Scripture. That same connection should also awaken in them a desire for a liturgical understanding of the texts read and a readiness to respond through singing.[85]

When they hear the word of God and reflect deeply on it, Christ's faithful are enabled to respond to it actively with full faith, hope, and charity through prayer and self-giving, and not only during Mass but in their entire Christian life.

3. MINISTRIES IN THE LITURGY OF THE WORD

49. Liturgical tradition assigns responsibility for the biblical readings in the celebration of Mass to ministers: to readers and the deacon. But when there is no deacon or no other priest present, the priest celebrant is to read the Gospel[86] and when there is no reader present, all the readings.[87]

50. It pertains to the deacon in the liturgy of the word at Mass to proclaim the Gospel, sometimes to give the homily, as occasion suggests, and to propose to the people the intentions of the prayer of the faithful.[88]

51. "The reader has his own proper function in the Eucharistic celebration and should exercise this even though ministers of a higher rank may be present."[89] The ministry of reader, conferred through a liturgical rite, must be held in respect. When there are instituted readers available, they are to carry out their office at least on Sundays and festive days, especially at the principal Mass of the day. These readers may also be given responsibility for assisting in the arrangement of the liturgy of the word, and, to the extent necessary, of seeing to the preparation of others of the faithful who may be appointed on a given occasion to read at Mass.[90]

52. The liturgical assembly truly requires readers, even those not instituted. Proper measures must therefore be taken to ensure that there are certain suitable laypeople who have been trained to carry out this ministry.[91] Whenever there is more than one reading, it is better to assign the readings to different readers, if available.

53. In Masses without a deacon, the function of announcing the intentions for the prayer of the faithful is to be assigned to the cantor, particularly when they are to be sung, to a reader, or to someone else.[92]

54. During the celebration of Mass with a congregation a second priest, a deacon, and an instituted reader must wear the distinctive vestment of their office when they go up to the ambo to read the word of God. Those who carry out the ministry of reader just for the occasion or even regularly but without institution may go to the ambo in ordinary attire, but this should be in keeping with the customs of the different regions.

55. "It is necessary that those who exercise the ministry of reader, even if they have not received institution, be truly suited and carefully prepared, so that the faithful may develop a warm and living love for Sacred Scripture from listening to the sacred readings."[93]

Their preparation must above all be spiritual, but what may be called a technical preparation is also needed. The spiritual preparation presupposes at least a biblical and liturgical formation. The purpose of their biblical formation is to give readers the ability to understand the readings in context and to perceive by the light of faith the central point of the revealed message. The liturgical formation ought to equip the readers to have some grasp of the meaning and structure of the liturgy of the word and of the significance of its connection with the liturgy of the Eucharist. The technical preparation should make the readers more skilled in the art of reading publicly, either with the power of their own voice or with the help of sound equipment.

56. The psalmist, or cantor of the psalm, is responsible for singing, responsorially or directly, the chants between the readings — the psalm or other biblical canticle, the gradual and *Alleluia*, or other chant. The psalmist may, as occasion requires, intone the *Alleluia* and verse.[94]

For carrying out the function of psalmist it is advantageous to have in each ecclesial community laypeople with the ability to sing and read with correct diction. The points made about the formation of readers apply to cantors as well.

57. The commentator also fulfills a genuine liturgical ministry, which consists in presenting to the congregation of the faithful, from a suitable place, relevant explanations and comments that are clear, of marked sobriety, meticulously prepared, and as a rule written out and approved beforehand by the celebrant.[95]

SECOND PART: THE STRUCTURE OF THE ORDER OF READINGS FOR MASS

CHAPTER IV: THE GENERAL ARRANGEMENT OF READINGS FOR MASS

1. The Pastoral Purpose of the Order of Readings for Mass

58. On the basis of the intention of the Second Vatican Council, the Order of Readings provided by the Lectionary of the Roman Missal has been composed above all for a pastoral purpose. To achieve this aim, not only the principles underlying this new Order of Readings but also the lists of texts that it provides have been discussed and revised over and over again, with the cooperation of a great many experts in exegetical, liturgical, catechetical, and pastoral studies from all parts of the world. The Order of Readings is the fruit of this combined effort.

The prolonged use of this Order of Readings to proclaim and explain Sacred Scripture in the Eucharistic celebration will, it is hoped, prove to be an effective step toward achieving the objective stated repeatedly by the Second Vatican Council.[96]

59. The decision on revising the Lectionary for Mass was to draw up and edit a single, rich, and full Order of Readings that would be in complete accord with the intent and prescriptions of the Second Vatican Council.[97] At the same time, however, the Order was meant to be of a kind that would meet the requirements and usages of particular Churches and celebrating congregations. For this reason, those responsible for the revision took pains to safeguard the liturgical tradition of the Roman Rite, but valued highly the merits of all the systems of selecting, arranging, and using the biblical readings in other liturgical families and in certain particular Churches. The revisers made use of those elements that experience has confirmed, but with an effort to avoid certain shortcomings found in the preceding form of the tradition.

60. The present Order of Readings for Mass, then, is an arrangement of biblical readings that provides the faithful with a knowledge of the whole of God's word, in a pattern suited to the purpose. Throughout the liturgical year, but above all during the seasons of Easter, Lent, and

Advent, the choice and sequence of readings are aimed at giving Christ's faithful an ever-deepening perception of the faith they profess and of the history of salvation.[98] Accordingly, the Order of Readings corresponds to the requirements and interests of the Christian people.

61. The celebration of the Liturgy is not in itself simply a form of catechesis, but it does contain an element of teaching. The Lectionary of the Roman Missal brings this out[99] and therefore deserves to be regarded as a pedagogical resource aiding catechesis.

This is so because the Order of Readings for Mass aptly presents from Sacred Scripture the principal deeds and words belonging to the history of salvation. As its many phases and events are recalled in the liturgy of the word, it will become clear to the faithful that the history of salvation is continued here and now in the representation of Christ's paschal mystery celebrated through the Eucharist.

62. The pastoral advantage of having in the Roman Rite a single Order of Readings for the Lectionary is obvious on other grounds. All the faithful, particularly those who for various reasons do not always take part in Mass with the same assembly, will everywhere be able to hear the same readings on any given day or in any liturgical season and to meditate on the application of these readings to their own concrete circumstances. This is the case even in places that have no priest and where a deacon or someone else deputed by the bishop conducts a celebration of the word of God.[100]

63. Pastors may wish to respond specifically from the word of God to the concerns of their own congregations. Although they must be mindful that they are above all to be heralds of the entire mystery of Christ and of the Gospel, they may rightfully use the options provided in the Order of Readings for Mass. This applies particularly to the celebration of a ritual or votive Mass, a Mass in honor of the Saints, or one of the Masses for various needs and occasions. With due regard for the general norms, special faculties are granted concerning the readings in Masses celebrated for particular groups.[101]

2. The Principles of Composition of the Order of Readings for Mass

64. To achieve the purpose of the Order of Readings for Mass, the parts have been selected and arranged in such a way as to take into account the sequence of the liturgical seasons and the hermeneutical principles whose understanding and definition have been facilitated by modern biblical research.

It was judged helpful to state here the principles guiding the composition of the Order of Readings for Mass.

a) The Choice of Texts

65. The course of readings in the Proper of Seasons is arranged as follows. Sundays and festive days present the more important biblical passages. In this way the more significant parts of God's revealed word can be read to the assembled faithful within an appropriate period of time. Weekdays present a second series of texts from Sacred Scripture and in a sense these complement the message of salvation explained on festive days. But neither series in these main parts of the Order of Readings — the series for Sundays and festive days and that for weekdays — is dependent on the other. The Order of Readings for Sundays and festive days extends over three years; for weekdays, over two. Thus each runs its course independently of the other.

The sequence of readings in other parts of the Order of Readings is governed by its own rules. This applies to the series of readings for celebrations of the Saints, ritual Masses, Masses for various needs and occasions, votive Masses, or Masses for the dead.

b) The Arrangement of the Readings for Sundays and Festive Days

66. The following are features proper to the readings for Sundays and festive days:

1. Each Mass has three readings: the first from the Old Testament, the second from an Apostle (that is, either from a Letter or from the Book of Revelation, depending on the season), and the third from the Gospels. This arrangement brings out the unity of the Old and New Testaments and of the history of salvation, in which Christ is the central figure, commemorated in his paschal mystery.

2. A more varied and richer reading of Sacred Scripture on Sundays and festive days results from the three-year cycle provided for these days, in that the same texts are read only every fourth year.[102]

3. The principles governing the Order of Reading for Sundays and festive days are called the principles of "harmony" and of "semicontinuous reading." One or the other applies according to the different seasons of the year and the distinctive character of the particular liturgical season.

67. The best instance of harmony between the Old and New Testament readings occurs when it is one that Scripture itself suggests. This is the case when the doctrine and events recounted in texts of the New Testament bear a more or less explicit relationship to the doctrine and events of the Old Testament. The present Order of Readings selects Old Testament texts mainly because of their correlation with New Testament texts read in the same Mass, and particularly with the Gospel text.

Harmony of another kind exists between texts of the readings for each Mass during Advent, Lent, and Easter, the seasons that have a distinctive importance or character.

In contrast, the Sundays in Ordinary Time do not have a distinctive character. Thus the text of both the apostolic and Gospel readings are arranged in order of semicontinuous reading, whereas the Old Testament reading is harmonized with the Gospel.

68. The decision was made not to extend to Sundays the arrangement suited to the liturgical seasons mentioned, that is, not to have an organic harmony of themes devised with a view to facilitating homiletic instruction. Such an arrangement would be in conflict with the genuine conception of liturgical celebration, which is always the celebration of the mystery of Christ and which by its own tradition makes use of the word of God not only at the prompting of logical or extrinsic concerns but spurred by the desire to proclaim the Gospel and to lead those who believe to the fullness of truth.

c) The Arrangement of the Readings for Weekdays

69. The weekday readings have been arranged in the following way.

1. Each Mass has two readings: the first is from the Old Testament or from an Apostle (that is, either from a Letter or from the Book of Revelation), and during the Easter season from the Acts of the Apostles; the second, from the Gospels.

2. The yearly cycle for Lent has its own principles of arrangement, which take into account the baptismal and penitential character of this season.

3. The cycle for the weekdays of Advent, the Christmas season, and the Easter season is also yearly and the readings thus remain the same each year.

4. For the thirty-four weeks of Ordinary Time, the weekday Gospel readings are arranged in a single cycle, repeated each year. But the first reading is arranged in a two-year cycle and is thus read every other year. Year I is used during odd-numbered years; Year II, during even-numbered years.

Like the Order for Sundays and festive days, then, the weekday Order of Readings is governed by similar application of the principles of harmony and of semicontinuous reading, especially in the case of seasons with their own distinctive character.

d) The Readings for Celebrations of the Saints

70. Two series of readings are provided for celebrations of the Saints.

1. The Proper of Saints provides the first series, for solemnities, feasts, or memorials and particularly when there are proper texts for one or other such celebration. Sometimes in the Proper, however, there is a reference to the most appropriate among the texts in the Commons as the one to be given preference.

2. The Commons of Saints provide the second, more extensive group of readings. There are, first, appropriate texts for the different classes of Saints (martyrs, pastors, virgins, etc.), then numerous texts that deal with holiness in general. These may be freely chosen whenever the Commons are indicated as the source for the choice of readings.

71. As to their sequence, all the texts in this part of the Order of Readings appear in the order in which they are to be read at Mass. Thus the Old Testament texts are first, then the texts from the Apostles, followed by the psalms and verses between the readings, and finally the texts from the Gospels. The rationale of this arrangement is that, unless otherwise noted, the celebrant may choose at will from such texts, in view of the pastoral needs of the congregation taking part in the celebration.

e) Readings for Ritual Masses, Masses for Various Needs and Occasions, Votive Masses, and Masses for the Dead

72. For ritual Masses, Masses for various needs and occasions, votive Masses, and Masses for the dead, the texts for the readings are arranged as just described, that is, numerous texts are grouped together in the order of their use, as in the Commons of Saints.

f) The Main Criteria Applied in Choosing and Arranging the Readings

73. In addition to the guiding principles already given for the arrangement of readings in the individual parts of the Order of Readings, others of a more general nature follow.

1) The Reservation of Some Books to Particular Liturgical Seasons

74. In this Order of Readings, some biblical books are set aside for particular liturgical seasons on the basis both of the intrinsic importance of subject matter and of liturgical tradition. For example, the Western (Ambrosian and Hispanic) and Eastern tradition of reading the Acts of the Apostles during the Easter season is maintained. This usage results in a clear presentation of how the Church's entire life derives its beginning from the paschal mystery. The tradition of both West and East is also retained, namely the reading of the Gospel of John in the latter weeks of Lent and in the Easter season.

Tradition assigns the reading of Isaiah, especially the first part, to Advent. Some texts of this book, however, are read during the Christmas season, to which the First Letter of John is also assigned.

2) The Length of the Texts

75. A *middle way* is followed in regard to the length of texts. A distinction has been made between narratives, which require reading a fairly long passage but which usually hold the attention of the faithful, and texts that should not be lengthy because of the profundity of their doctrine.

In the case of certain rather lengthy texts, longer and shorter versions are provided to suit different situations. The editing of the shorter version has been carried out with great caution.

3) Difficult Texts

76. In readings for Sundays and solemnities, texts that present real difficulties are avoided for pastoral reasons. The

difficulties may be objective, in that the texts themselves raise profound literary, critical, or exegetical problems; or the difficulties may lie, at least to a certain extent, in the ability of the faithful to understand the texts. But there could be no justification for concealing from the faithful the spiritual riches of certain texts on the grounds of difficulty if the problem arises from the inadequacy either of the religious education that every Christian should have or of the biblical formation that every pastor of souls should have. Often a difficult reading is clarified by its correlation with another in the same Mass.

4) The Omission of Certain Verses

77. The omission of verses in readings from Scripture has at times been the tradition of many liturgies, including the Roman liturgy. Admittedly such omissions may not be made lightly, for fear of distorting the meaning of the text or the intent and style of Scripture. Yet on pastoral grounds it was decided to continue the traditional practice in the present Order of Readings, but at the same time to ensure that the essential meaning of the text remained intact. One reason for the decision is that otherwise some texts would have been unduly long. It would also have been necessary to omit completely certain readings of high spiritual value for the faithful because those readings include some verse that is pastorally less useful or that involves truly difficult questions.

3. Principles to be Followed in the Use of the Order of Readings

a) The Freedom of Choice Regarding Some Texts

78. The Order of Readings sometimes leaves it to the celebrant to choose between alternative texts or to choose one from the several listed together for the same reading. The option seldom exists on Sundays, solemnities, or feasts, in order not to obscure the character proper to the particular liturgical season or needlessly interrupt the semicontinuous reading of some biblical book. On the other hand, the option is given readily in celebrations of the Saints, in ritual Masses, Masses for various needs and occasions, votive Masses, and Masses for the dead.

These options, together with those indicated in the General Instruction of the Roman Missal and the *Ordo cantus Missae*,[103] have a pastoral purpose. In arranging the liturgy of the word, then, the priest should "consider the general spiritual good of the congregation rather than his personal outlook. He should be mindful that the choice of texts is to be made in harmony with the ministers and others who have any role in the celebration and should listen to the opinions of the faithful in what concerns them more directly."[104]

1) The Two Readings before the Gospel

79. In Masses to which three readings are assigned, all three are to be used. If, however, for pastoral reasons the Conference of Bishops has given permission for two readings only to be used,[105] the choice between the two first readings is to be made in such a way as to safeguard the Church's intent to instruct the faithful more completely in the mystery of salvation. Thus, unless the contrary is indicated in the text of the Lectionary, the reading to be chosen as the first reading is the one that is more closely in harmony with the Gospel, or, in accord with the intent just mentioned, the one that is more helpful toward a coherent catechesis over an extended period, or that preserves the semicontinuous reading of some biblical book.[106]

2) The Longer and Shorter Forms of Texts

80. A pastoral criterion must also guide the choice between the longer and shorter forms of the same text. The main consideration must be the capacity of the hearers to listen profitably either to the longer or to the shorter reading; or to listen to a more complete text that will be explained through the homily.

3) When Two Texts Are Provided

81. When a choice is allowed between alternative texts, whether they are fixed or optional, the first consideration must be the best interest of those taking part. It may be a matter of using the easier texts or the one more relevant to the assembled congregation or, as pastoral advantage may suggest, of repeating or replacing a text that is assigned as proper to one celebration and optional to another.

The issue may arise when it is feared that some text will create difficulties for a particular congregation or when the same text would have to be repeated within a few days, as on a Sunday and on a day during the week following.

4) The Weekday Readings

82. The arrangement of weekday readings provides texts for every day of the week throughout the year. In most cases, therefore, these readings are to be used on their assigned days, unless a solemnity, a feast, or else a memorial with proper readings occurs.[107]

In using the Order of Readings for weekdays attention must be paid to whether one reading or another from the same biblical book will have to be omitted because of some celebration occurring during the week. With the arrangement of readings for the entire week in mind, the priest in that case arranges to omit the less significant passages or combines in the most appropriate manner them with other readings, if they contribute to an integral view of a particular theme.

5) The Celebrations of the Saints

83. When they exist, proper readings are given for celebrations of the Saints, that is, biblical passages about the Saint or the mystery that the Mass is celebrating. Even in the case of a memorial these readings must take the place of the weekday readings for the same day. This Order of Readings makes explicit note of every case of proper readings on a memorial.

In some cases there are accommodated readings, those, namely, that bring out some particular aspect of a Saint's spiritual life or work. Use of such readings does not seem binding, except for compelling pastoral reasons. For the most part references are given to readings in the Commons in order to facilitate choice. But these are merely suggestions: in place of an accommodated reading or the particular reading proposed from a Common, any other reading from the Commons referred to may be selected.

The first concern of a priest celebrating with a congregation is the spiritual benefit of the faithful and he will be careful not to impose his personal preference on them. Above all he will make sure not to omit too often or without sufficient cause the readings assigned for each day in the weekday Lectionary: the Church's desire is that a more lavish table of the word of God be spread before the faithful.[108]

There are also common readings, that is, those placed in the Commons either for some determined class of Saints (martyrs, virgins, pastors) or for the Saints in general. Because in these cases several texts are listed for the same reading, it will be up to the priest to choose the one best suited to those listening.

In all celebrations of Saints the readings may be taken not only from the Commons to which the references are given in each case, but also from the Common of Men and Women Saints, whenever there is special reason for doing so.

84. For celebrations of the Saints the following should be observed:

1. On solemnities and feasts the readings must be those that are given in the Proper or in the Commons. For solemnities and feasts of the General Roman Calendar proper readings are always assigned.

2. On solemnities inscribed in particular calendars, three readings are to be assigned, unless the Conference of Bishops has decreed that there are to be only two readings.[109] The first reading is from the Old Testament (but during the Easter season, from the Acts of the Apostles or the Book of Revelation); the second, from an Apostle; the third, from the Gospels.

3. On feasts and memorials, which have only two readings, the first reading can be chosen from either the Old Testament or from an Apostle; the second is from the Gospels. Following the Church's traditional practice, however, the first reading during the Easter season is to be taken from an Apostle, the second, as far as possible, from the Gospel of John.

6) Other Parts of the Order of Readings

85. In the Order of Readings for ritual Masses the references given are to the texts already published for the individual rites. This obviously does not include the texts belonging to celebrations that must not be integrated with Mass.[110]

86. The Order of Readings for Masses for various needs and occasions, votive Masses, and Masses for the dead provides many texts that can be of assistance in adapting such celebrations to the situation, circumstances, and concerns of the particular groups taking part.[111]

87. In ritual Masses, Masses for various needs and occasions, votive Masses, and Masses for the dead, since many texts are given for the same reading, the choice of readings follows the criteria already indicated for the choice of readings from the Common of Saints.

88. On a day when some ritual Mass is not permitted and when the norms in the individual rite allow the choice of one reading from those provided for ritual Masses, the general spiritual welfare of the participants must be considered.[112]

b) The Responsorial Psalm and the Acclamation before the Gospel Reading

89. Among the chants between the readings, the psalm which follows the first reading is of great importance. As a rule the psalm to be used is the one assigned to the reading. But in the case of readings for the Common of Saints, ritual Masses, Masses for various needs and occasions, votive Masses, and Masses for the dead the choice is left up to the priest celebrating. He will base his choice on the principle of the pastoral benefit of those present.

But to make it easier for the people to join in the response to the psalm, the Order of Readings lists certain other texts of psalms and responses that have been chosen according to the various seasons or classes of Saints. Whenever the psalm is sung, these texts may replace the text corresponding to the reading.[113]

90. The chant between the second reading and the Gospel is either specified in each Mass and correlated with the Gospel or else it is left as a choice to be made from those in the series given for a liturgical season or one of the Commons.

91. During Lent one of the acclamations from those given in the Order of Readings may be used, depending on the occasion.[114] This acclamation precedes and follows the verse before the Gospel.

CHAPTER V: DESCRIPTION OF THE ORDER OF READINGS

92. It seems useful to provide here a brief description of the Order of Readings, at least for the principal celebrations and the different seasons of the liturgical year. With these in mind, readings were selected on the basis of the rules already stated. This description is meant to assist pastors of souls to understand the structure of the Order of Readings, so that their use of it will become more perceptive and the Order of Readings a source of good for Christ's faithful.

1. Advent

a) The Sundays

93. Each Gospel reading has a distinctive theme: the Lord's coming at the end of time (First Sunday of Advent), John the Baptist (Second and Third Sunday), and the events that prepared immediately for the Lord's birth (Fourth Sunday).

The Old Testament readings are prophecies about the Messiah and the Messianic age, especially from the Book of Isaiah.

The readings from an Apostle contain exhortations and proclamations, in keeping with the different themes of Advent.

b) The Weekdays

94. There are two series of readings: one to be used from the beginning of Advent until 16 December; the other from 17 to 24 December.

In the first part of Advent there are readings from the Book of Isaiah, distributed in accord with the sequence of the book itself and including the more important texts that are also read on the Sundays. For the choice of the weekday Gospel the first reading has been taken into consideration.

On Thursday of the second week the readings from the Gospel concerning John the Baptist begin. The first reading is either a continuation of Isaiah or a text chosen in view of the Gospel.

In the last week before Christmas the events that immediately prepared for the Lord's birth are presented from the Gospel of Matthew (chapter 1) and Luke (chapter 1). The texts in the first reading, chosen in view of the Gospel reading, are from different Old Testament books and include important Messianic prophecies.

2. The Christmas Season

a) The Solemnities, Feasts, and Sundays

95. For the vigil and the three Masses of Christmas both the prophetic readings and the others have been chosen from the Roman tradition.

The Gospel on the Sunday within the Octave of Christmas, Feast of the Holy Family, is about Jesus' childhood and the other readings are about the virtues of family life.

On the Octave Day of Christmas, Solemnity of the Blessed Virgin Mary, the Mother of God, the readings are about the Virgin Mother of God and the giving of the holy Name of Jesus.

On the second Sunday after Christmas, the readings are about the mystery of the Incarnation.

On the Epiphany of the Lord, the Old Testament reading and the Gospel continue the Roman tradition; the text for the reading from the Letters of the Apostles is about the calling of the nations to salvation.

On the Feast of the Baptism of the Lord, the texts chosen are about this mystery.

b) The Weekdays

96. From 29 December on, there is a continuous reading of the whole of the First Letter of John, which actually begins earlier, on 27 December, the Feast of St. John the Evangelist, and on 28 December, the Feast of the Holy Innocents. The Gospels relate manifestations of the Lord: events of Jesus' childhood from the Gospel of Luke (29–30 December); passages from the first chapter of the Gospel of John (31 December–5 January); other manifestations of the Lord from the four Gospels (7–12 January).

3. Lent

a) The Sundays

97. The Gospel readings are arranged as follows:

The first and second Sundays maintain the accounts of the Temptation and Transfiguration of the Lord, with readings, however, from all three Synoptics.

On the next three Sundays, the Gospels about the Samaritan woman, the man born blind, and the raising of Lazarus have been restored in Year A. Because these Gospels are of major importance in regard to Christian initiation, they may also be read in Year B and Year C, especially in places where there are catechumens.

Other texts, however, are provided for Year B and Year C: for Year B, a text from John about Christ's coming glorification through his Cross and Resurrection and for Year C, a text from Luke about conversion.

On Palm Sunday of the Lord's Passion the texts for the procession are selections from the Synoptic Gospels concerning the Lord's solemn entry into Jerusalem. For the Mass the reading is the account of the Lord's Passion.

The Old Testament readings are about the history of salvation, which is one of the themes proper to the catechesis of Lent. The series of texts for each Year presents the main elements of salvation history from its beginning until the promise of the New Covenant.

The readings from the Letters of the Apostles have been selected to fit the Gospel and the Old Testament readings and, to the extent possible, to provide a connection between them.

b) The Weekdays

98. The readings from the Gospels and the Old Testament were selected because they are related to each other. They treat various themes of the Lenten catechesis that are suited to the spiritual significance of this season. Beginning with Monday of the Fourth week of Lent, there is a semi-continuous reading of the Gospel of John, made up of texts that correspond more closely to the themes proper to Lent.

Because the readings about the Samaritan woman, the man born blind, and the raising of Lazarus are now assigned to Sundays, but only for Year A (in Year B and Year C they are optional), provision has been made for their use on weekdays. Thus at the beginning of the Third, Fourth, and Fifth Weeks of Lent optional Masses with these texts for the Gospel have been inserted and may be used in place of the readings of the day on any weekday of the respective week.

In the first days of Holy Week the readings are about the mystery of Christ's passion. For the Chrism Mass the readings bring out both Christ's Messianic mission and its continuation in the Church by means of the sacraments.

4. THE SACRED TRIDUUM AND THE EASTER SEASON

a) The Sacred Easter Triduum

99. On Holy Thursday at the evening Mass the remembrance of the meal preceding the Exodus casts its own special light because of the Christ's example in washing the feet of his disciples and Paul's account of the institution of the Christian Passover in the Eucharist.

On Good Friday the liturgical service has as its center John's narrative of the Passion of he who was proclaimed in Isaiah as the Servant of the Lord and who became the one High Priest by offering himself to the Father.

At the Vigil on the holy night of Easter there are seven Old Testament readings which recall the wonderful works of God in the history of salvation. There are two New Testament readings, the announcement of the Resurrection according to one of the Synoptic Gospels and a reading from St. Paul on Christian baptism as the sacrament of Christ's Resurrection.

The Gospel reading for the Mass on Easter day is from John on the finding of the empty tomb. There is also, however, the option to use the Gospel texts from the Easter Vigil or, when there is an evening Mass on Easter Sunday, to use the account in Luke of the Lord's appearance to the disciples on the road to Emmaus. The first reading is from the Acts of the Apostles, which throughout the Easter season replaces the Old Testament reading. The reading from the Apostle Paul concerns the living out of the paschal mystery in the Church.

b) The Sundays

100. The Gospel readings for the first three Sundays recount the appearances of the risen Christ. The readings about the Good Shepherd are assigned to the Fourth Sunday. On the Fifth, Sixth, and Seventh Sundays, there are excerpts from the Lord's discourse and prayer at the end of the Last Supper.

The first reading is from the Acts of the Apostles, in a three-year cycle of parallel and progressive selections: material is presented on the life of the early Church, its witness, and its growth.

For the reading from the Apostles, the First Letter of Peter is in Year A, the First Letter of John in Year B, the Book of Revelation in Year C. These are the texts that seem to fit in especially well with the spirit of joyous faith and sure hope proper to this season.

c) The Weekdays

101. As on the Sundays, the first reading is a semicontinuous reading from the Acts of the Apostles. The Gospel readings during the Easter octave are accounts of the Lord's appearances. After that there is a semicontinuous reading of the Gospel of John, but with texts that have a paschal character, in order to complete the reading from John during Lent. This paschal reading is made up in large part of the Lord's discourse and prayer at the end of the Last Supper.

d) The Solemnities of the Ascension and of Pentecost

102. For the first reading the Solemnity of the Ascension retains the account of the Ascension according to the Acts of the Apostles. This text is complemented by the second reading from the Apostle on Christ in exaltation at the right hand of the Father. For the Gospel reading, each of the three Years has its own text in accord with the differences in the Synoptic Gospels.

In the evening Mass celebrated on the Vigil of Pentecost four Old Testament texts are provided; any one of them may be used, in order to bring out the many aspects of Pentecost. The reading from the Apostles shows the actual working of the Holy Spirit in the Church. The Gospel reading recalls the promise of the Spirit made by Christ before his own glorification.

For the Mass on Pentecost day itself, in accord with received usage, the account in the Acts of the Apostles of the great occurrence on Pentecost day is taken as the first reading. The texts from the Apostle Paul bring out the effect of the action of the Spirit in the life of the Church. The Gospel reading is a remembrance of Jesus bestowing his Spirit on the disciples on the evening of Easter day; other optional texts describe the action of the Spirit on the disciples and on the Church.

5. ORDINARY TIME

a) The Arrangement and Choice of Texts

103. Ordinary Time begins on the Monday after the Sunday following 6 January; it lasts until the Tuesday before Lent inclusive. It begins again on the Monday after Pentecost Sunday and finishes before evening prayer I of the First Sunday of Advent.

The Order of Readings provides readings for thirty-four Sundays and the weeks following them. In some years, however, there are only thirty-three weeks of Ordinary Time. Further, some Sundays either belong to another season (the Sunday on which the Feast of the Baptism of the Lord falls and Pentecost Sunday) or else are impeded by a solemnity that coincides with that Sunday (e.g. The Most Holy Trinity or Christ the King).

104. For the correct arrangement in the use of the readings for Ordinary Time, the following are to be respected.

1. The Sunday on which the Feast of the Baptism of the Lord falls replaces the First Sunday in Ordinary Time. Therefore the readings of the First Week in Ordinary Time begin on the Monday after the Sunday following 6 January. When the Feast of the Baptism of the Lord is celebrated on Monday because

the Epiphany has been celebrated on the Sunday, the readings of the First Week begin on Tuesday.

2. The Sunday following the Feast of the Baptism of the Lord is the Second Sunday of Ordinary Time. The remaining Sundays are numbered consecutively up to the Sunday preceding the beginning of Lent. The readings for the week in which Ash Wednesday falls are interrupted after the Tuesday readings.

3. For the resumption of the readings of Ordinary Time after Pentecost Sunday:

· when there are thirty-four Sundays in Ordinary Time, the week to be used is the one that immediately follows the last week used before Lent;[115]

· when there are thirty-three Sundays in Ordinary Time, the first week that would have been used after Pentecost is omitted, in order to reserve for the end of the year the eschatological texts that are assigned to the last two weeks.[116]

b) The Sunday Readings

1) The Gospel Readings

105. On the Second Sunday in Ordinary Time the Gospel continues to center on the manifestation of the Lord, which is celebrated on the Solemnity of the Epiphany, through the traditional passage about the wedding feast at Cana and two other passages from the Gospel of John.

Beginning with the Third Sunday, there is a semicontinuous reading of the Synoptic Gospels. This reading is arranged in such a way that as the Lord's life and preaching unfold the doctrine proper to each of these Gospels is presented.

This distribution also provides a certain coordination between the meaning of each Gospel and the progress of the liturgical year. Thus after Epiphany the readings are on the beginning of the Lord's preaching and they fit in well with Christ's baptism and the first events in which he manifests himself. The liturgical year leads quite naturally to a conclusion in the eschatological theme proper to the last Sundays, since the chapters of the Synoptics that precede the account of the Passion treat this eschatological theme rather extensively.

After the Sixteenth Sunday in Year B, five readings are incorporated from John chapter 6 (the discourse on the bread of life). This is the natural place for these readings because the multiplication of the loaves from the Gospel of John takes the place of the same account in Mark. In the semicontinuous reading of Luke for Year C, the introduction of this Gospel has been prefixed to the first text (that is, on the Third Sunday). This passage expresses the author's intention very beautifully and there seemed to be no better place for it.

2) The Old Testament Readings

106. These readings have been chosen to correspond to the Gospel passages in order to avoid an excessive diversity between the readings of different Masses and above all to bring out the unity between the Old and the New Testament. The connection between the readings of the same Mass is shown by a precise choice of the readings prefixed to the individual readings.

To the degree possible, the readings were chosen in such a way that they would be short and easy to grasp. But care has been taken to ensure that many Old Testament texts of major significance would be read on Sundays. Such readings are distributed not according to a logical order but on the basis of what the Gospel reading requires. Still, the treasury of the word of God will be opened up in such a way that nearly all the principal pages of the Old Testament will become familiar to those taking part in the Mass on Sundays.

3) The Readings from the Apostles

107. There is a semicontinuous reading of the Letters of Paul and James (the Letters of Peter and John being read during the Easter and Christmas seasons).

Because it is quite long and deals with such diverse issues, the First Letter to the Corinthians has been spread over the three years of the cycle at the beginning of Ordinary Time. It also was thought best to divide the Letter to the Hebrews into two parts; the first part is read in Year B and the second in Year C.

Only readings that are short and readily grasped by the people have been chosen.

Table II at the end of this Introduction[117] indicates the distribution of Letters of the Apostles over the three-year cycle of the Sundays of Ordinary Time.

c) The Readings for Solemnities of the Lord during Ordinary Time

108. On the solemnities of Holy Trinity, Corpus Christi, and the Sacred Heart, the texts chosen correspond to the principal themes of these celebrations.

The readings of the Thirty-Fourth and last Sunday in Ordinary Time celebrate Christ the universal King. He was prefigured by David and proclaimed as king amid the humiliations of his Passion and Cross; he reigns in the Church and will come again at the end of time.

d) The Weekday Readings

109. The *Gospels* are so arranged that Mark is read first (First to Ninth Week), then Matthew (Tenth to Twenty-First Week), then Luke (Twenty-Second to Thirty-Fourth Week). Mark chapters 1 – 12 are read in their entirety, with the exception only of the two passages of Mark chapter 6 that are read on weekdays in other seasons. From Matthew and Luke the readings comprise all the material not contained in Mark. All the passages that either are distinctively presented in each Gospel or are needed for a proper understanding of its progression are read two or three times. Jesus' eschatological discourse as contained in its entirety in Luke is read at the end of the liturgical year.

110. The *First reading* is taken in periods of several weeks at a time first from one then from the other Testament;

the number of weeks depends on the length of the biblical books read.

Rather large sections are read from the New Testament books in order to give the substance, as it were, of each of the Letters.

From the Old Testament there is room only for select passages that, as far as possible, bring out the character of the individual books. The historical texts have been chosen in such a way as to provide an overall view of the history of salvation before the Incarnation of the Lord. But lengthy narratives could hardly be presented; sometimes verses have been selected that make for a reading of moderate length. In addition, the religious significance of the historical events is sometimes brought out by means of certain texts from the wisdom books that are placed as prologues or conclusions to a series of historical readings.

Nearly all the Old Testament books have found a place in the Order of Readings for weekdays in the Proper of Seasons. The only omissions are the shortest of the prophetic books (Obadiah and Zephaniah) and a poetic book (the Song of Songs). Of those narratives of edification requiring a lengthy reading if they are to be understood, Tobit and Ruth are included, but the others (Esther and Judith) are omitted. Texts from these latter two books are assigned, however, to Sundays and weekdays at other times of the year.)

Table III at the end of this Introduction[118] lists the way the books of the Old and the New Testament are distributed over the weekdays in Ordinary Time in the course of two years.

At the end of the liturgical year the readings are from the books that correspond to the eschatological character of this period, Daniel and the Book of Revelation.

CHAPTER VI: ADAPTATIONS, TRANSLATIONS AND FORMAT OF THE ORDER OF READINGS

1. ADAPTATIONS AND TRANSLATIONS

111. In the liturgical assembly the word of God must always be read either from the Latin texts prepared by the Holy See or from vernacular translations approved for liturgical use by the Conferences of Bishops, according to existing norms.[119]

112. The Lectionary for Mass must be translated integrally in all its parts, including the Introduction. If the Conference of Bishops has judged it necessary and useful to add certain adaptations, these are to be incorporated after their confirmation by the Holy See.[120]

113. The size of the Lectionary will necessitate editions in more than one volume; no particular division of the volumes is prescribed. But each volume is to contain the explanatory texts on the structure and purpose of the section it contains.

The ancient custom is recommended of having separate books, one for the Gospels and the other for the other readings for the Old and New Testament.

It may also be useful to publish separately a Sunday lectionary (which could also contain selected excerpts from the sanctoral cycle), and a weekday lectionary. A practical basis for dividing the Sunday lectionary is the three-year cycle, so that all the readings for each year are presented in sequence.

But there is freedom to adopt other arrangements that may be devised and seem to have pastoral advantages.

114. The texts for the chants are always to be adjoined to the readings, but separate books containing the chants alone are permitted. It is recommended that the texts be printed with divisions into stanzas.

115. Whenever a text consists of different parts, the typography must make this structure of the text clear. It is likewise recommended that even non-poetic texts be printed with division into sense lines to assist the proclamation of the readings.

116. Where there are longer and shorter forms of a text, they are to be printed separately, so that each can be read with ease. But if such a separation does not seem feasible, a way is to be found to ensure that each text can be proclaimed without mistakes.

117. In vernacular editions the texts are not to be printed without headings prefixed. If it seems advisable, an introductory note on the general meaning of the passage may be added to the heading. This note is to carry some distinctive symbol or is to be set in different type to show clearly that it is an optional text.[121]

118. It would be useful for every volume to have an index of the passages of the Bible, modeled on the biblical index of the present volume.[122] This will provide ready access to texts of the lectionaries for Mass that may be needed or helpful for specific occasions.

2. THE FORMAT OF INDIVIDUAL READINGS

For each reading the present volume carries the textual reference, the headings, and the *incipit*.

a) The Biblical References

119. The text reference (that is, to chapter and verses) is always given according to the Neo-Vulgate edition for the psalms.[123] But a second reference according to the original text (Hebrew, Aramaic, or Greek) has been added wherever there is a discrepancy. Depending on the decrees of the competent Authorities for the individual languages, vernacular versions may retain the enumeration corresponding to the version of the Bible approved for liturgical use by the same Authorities. Exact references to chapter and verses, however, must always appear and may be given in the text or in the margin.

120. These references provide liturgical books with the basis of the "announcement" of the text that must be read in the celebration, but which is not printed in this

volume. This "announcement" of the text will observe the following norms, but they may be altered by decree of the competent authorities on the basis of what is customary and useful for different places and languages.

121. The formula to be used is always: "A *reading* from the Book of . . . ," "A *reading* from the Letter of . . . ," or "A *reading* from the holy Gospel according to . . . ," and not: "The *beginning* of . . . ," (unless this seems advisable in particular instances) nor: "The *continuation* of. . . ."

122. The traditionally accepted titles for books are to be retained with the following exceptions.

1. Where there are two books with the same name, the title is to be: The first Book, The second Book (for example, of Kings, of Maccabees) or The first Letter, The second Letter.

2. The title more common in current usage is to be accepted for the following books:

· I and II Samuel instead of I and II Kings;

· I and II Kings instead of III and IV Kings;

· I and II Chronicles instead of I and II Paralipomenon;

· The Books of Ezra and Nehemiah instead of I and II Ezra.

3. The distinguishing titles for the wisdom books are: The Book of Job, Book of Proverbs, Book of Ecclesiastes, the Song of Songs, the Book of Wisdom, and the Book of Sirach.

4. For all the books that are included among the prophets in the Neo-Vulgate, the formula is to be: "A reading from the Book of the prophet Isaiah, or of the prophet Jeremiah or of the prophet Baruch" and: "A reading from the Book of the prophet Ezekiel, of the prophet Daniel, of the prophet Hosea, of the prophet Malachi," even in the case of books not regarded by some as being in actual fact prophetic.

5. The title is to be book of Lamentations and letter to the Hebrews, with no mention of Jeremiah or Paul.

b) The Heading

123. There is a *heading* prefixed to each text, chosen carefully (usually from the words of the text itself) in order to point out the main theme of the reading and, when necessary, to make the connection between the readings of the same Mass clear.

c) The "Incipit"

124. In this Order of Readings the first element of the *incipit* is the customary introductory phrase: "At that time," "In those days," "Brothers and Sisters," "Beloved," "Dearly Beloved," "Dearest Brothers and Sisters," or "Thus says the Lord," "Thus says the Lord God." These words are not given when the text itself provides sufficient indication of the time or the persons involved or where such phrases would not fit in with the very nature of the text.

For the individual languages, such phrases may be changed or omitted by decree of the competent Authorities.

After the first words of the *incipit* the Order of Readings gives the proper beginning of the reading, with some words deleted or supplied for intelligibility, inasmuch as the text is separated from its context. When the text for a reading is made up of non-consecutive verses and this has required changes in wording, these are appropriately indicated.

d) The Final Acclamation

125. In order to facilitate the congregation's acclamation, the words for the reader *The word of the Lord,* or similar words suited to local custom, are to be printed at the end of the reading for use by the reader.

NOTES

[1] Cf. especially Second Vatican Council, Constitution on the Sacred Liturgy, *Sacrosanctum Concilium*, nn. 7, 24, 33, 35, 48, 51, 52, 56; Dogmatic Constitution on Divine Revelation, *Dei Verbum*, nn. 1, 21, 25, 26; Decree on the Missionary Activity of the Church, *Ad gentes*, n. 6; Second Vatican Council, Decree on the Ministry and Life of Priests, *Presbyterorum Ordinis*, n. 18.

[2] Among the spoken or written statements of the Supreme Pontiffs, see especially: Paul VI, *Motu Proprio, Ministeria quaedam*, 15 August 1972, n. V: *Acta Apostolicae Sedis* [AAS] 64 (1972) 532; Apostolic Exhortation, *Marialis cultus*, 2 February 1974, n. 12: AAS 66 (1974) 125 – 126; Apostolic Exhortation, *Evangelii nuntiandi*, 8 December 1975, n. 28: AAS 68 (1976) 24 – 25, n. 43: *ibid.* pp. 33 – 34, n. 47: *ibid.* pp. 36 – 37; John Paul II, Apostolic Constitution, *Scripturarum thesaurus*, 25 April 1979 in *Nova Vulgata Bibliorum Sacrorum editione, Typis Polyglottis Vaticanis* 1979, pp. V – VIII; Apostolic Exhortation, *Catechesi tradendae*, 16 October 1979, nn. 23, 27, 48: AAS 71 (1979) 1296 – 1297, 1298 – 1299, 1316; Letter, *Dominicae Cenae*, 24 February 1980, n. 10: AAS 72 (1980) 134 – 137.

[3] Cf. Sacred Congregation of Rites, Instruction *Eucharisticum Mysterium*, 25 May 1967, n. 10: AAS 59 (1967) 547 – 548; Sacred Congregation for Divine Worship, Instruction *Liturgicae instaurationes*, 5 September 1970, n. 2: AAS 62 (1970) 695 – 696; Sacred Congregation for the Clergy, *Directorum catechesticum generale*, 11 April 1971: AAS 64 (1972) 106 – 107; n. 25: *ibid.*, p. 114; Sacred Congregation for Divine Worship, *Institutio Generalis Missalis Romani*, nn. 9, 11, 24, 33, 60, 62, 316, 320; Sacred Congregation for

Catholic Education, Instruction on liturgical formation in seminaries, *In ecclesiasticam futurorum sacerdotum*, 3 June 1979, nn. 11, 52; *ibid.*, Appendix, n. 15; Sacred Congregation for the Sacraments and Divine Worship, Instruction *Inaestimabile Donum*, 3 April 1980, nn. 1, 2, 3; AAS 72 (1980) 333–334.

[4] Cf. *Missale Romanum ex Decreto Sacrosancti Oecumenici Concilii Vaticani II instauratum auctoritate Pauli VI promulgatum, Ordo lectionum Missae*, (*Typis Polyglottis Vaticanis* 1969), pp. IX–XII (Praenotanda); Decree of promulgation: AAS 61 (1969) 548–549.

[5] Cf. Second Vatican Council, Constitution on the Sacred Liturgy, *Sacrosanctum Concilium*, nn. 35, 56; Paul VI, Apostolic Exhortation, *Evangelii nuntiandi*, 8 December 1975, nn. 28, 47: AAS 68 (1976) 24–25, 36–37; Letter, *Dominicae Cenae*, 24 February 1980, nn. 10, 11, 12: AAS 72 (1980) 134–146.

[6] For example, the terms "word of God," "Sacred Scripture," "Old" and "New Testament," "Reading (readings) of the word of God," "Reading (readings) from Sacred Scripture," "Celebration (Celebrations) of the word of God," etc.

[7] Thus one and the same text may be read or used for various reasons on various occasions and celebrations of the Church's liturgical year. This is to be recalled in the homily, in pastoral exegesis, and in catechesis. The indexes of this volume will show, for example, that Romans chapter 6 or Romans chapter 8 is used in various seasons of the liturgical year and in various celebrations of the sacraments and sacramentals.

[8] Cf. Luke 4:6–21; 24:25–35, 44–49.

[9] Thus, for example, in the celebration of Mass, for example, there is proclamation, reading, etc. (cf. *Institutio Generalis Missalis Romani*, nn. 21, 23, 95, 131, 146, 234, 235). There are also other celebrations of the word of God in the *Pontificale Romanum*, the *Rituale Romanum*, and the *Liturgia Horarum*, as restored by decree of Second Vatican Council.

[10] Cf. Second Vatican Council, Constitution on the Sacred Liturgy, *Sacrosanctum Concilium*, nn. 7, 33; Mark 16:19–20; Matthew 28:20; St Augustine, *Sermo* 85, 1: "The Gospel is the mouth of Christ. He is seated in heaven yet does not cease to speak on earth": *PL* 38, 520; cf. also *In Io. Ev. tract.* XXX, 1: *PL* 35, 1632; *CCL* 36, 289; *Pontificale Romano-Germanicum*: "The Gospel is read, in which Christ speaks by his own mouth to the people . . . the Gospel resounds in the church as though Christ himself were speaking to the people" (see C. Vogel & R. Elze, edd., *Le Pontifical romano-germanique du dixième siècle. Le Texte I, Ciottà del Vaticano*, 1963, XCIV, 18, p. 334); or "At the approach of Christ, that is the Gospel, we put aside our

staffs, because we have no need of human assistance" (*ibid.* XCIV, 23, p. 335).

[11] Cf. Second Vatican Council, Constitution on the Sacred Liturgy, *Sacrosanctum Concilium*, n. 7.

[12] Cf. Hebrews 4:12.

[13] Cf. St Augustine, *Quaestionum in Heptateuchum liber* 2, 73: *PL* 34, 623; *CCL* 33, 106; Second Vatican Council, Dogmatic Constitution on Divine Revelation, *Dei Verbum*, n. 16.

[14] Cf. St Jerome: "If, as St Paul says (1 Corinthians 1:24), Christ is the power of God and the wisdom of God, anyone who is ignorant of the Scriptures, is ignorant of the power of God and his wisdom. For ignorance of the Scriptures is ignorance of Christ" (*Commentarii in Isaiam prophetam, Prologus: PL* 24, 17A; *CCL* 73, 1); Second Vatican Council, Dogmatic Constitution on Divine Revelation, *Dei Verbum*, n. 25.

[15] Cf. 2 Corinthians 1:20–22.

[16] Cf. Second Vatican Council, Constitution on the Sacred Liturgy, *Sacrosanctum Concilium*, n. 10.

[17] Cf. 2 Thessalonians 3:1.

[18] Cf. *Collectae, Pro Sancta Ecclesia*, in *Missale Romanum ex Decreto Sacrosancti Oecumenici Concilii Vaticani II instauratum auctoritate Pauli VI promulgatum* (*Typis Polyglottis Vaticanis* 1975), pp. 786, 787, 790: St Cyprian, *De oratione dominica* 23: *PL* 4, 553; *CSEL* 3/2, 285; *CCL* 3A, 105; St Augustine, *Sermo* 71, 20, 33: *PL* 38, 463f.

[19] Cf. *Collecta, Dominica XXI* "per annum", in *Missale Romanum*, p. 360.

[20] Cf. Second Vatican Council, Dogmatic Constitution on Divine Revelation, *Dei Verbum*, n. 8.

[21] Cf. John 14:15–17, 25–26–16:15.

[22] Second Vatican Council, Decree on the Ministry and Life of Priests, *Presbyterorum Ordinis*, n. 4.

[23] Cf. Second Vatican Council, Constitution on the Sacred Liturgy, *Sacrosanctum Concilium*, n. 51; Decree on the Ministry and Life of Priests, *Presbyterorum Ordinis*, n. 18; also Dogmatic Constitution on Divine Revelation, *Dei Verbum*, n. 21; Decree on the Missionary Activity of the Church, *Ad gentes*, n. 6. Cf. *Institutio Generalis Missalis Romani*, n. 8.

[24] Second Vatican Council, Constitution on the Sacred Liturgy, *Sacrosanctum Concilium*, n. 56.

[25] *Institutio Generalis Missalis Romani*, n. 33.

[26] Cf. Sacred Congregation for Divine Worship, Instruction, *Liturgicae instaurationes*, 5 September 1970, n. 2: AAS 62 (1970) 695–696; John Paul II, Letter,

Dominicae Cenae, 24 February 1980, n. 10: *AAS* 72 (1980) 134–137; Sacred Congregation for the Sacraments and Divine Worship, Instruction, *Inaestimabile Donum*, 3 April 1980, n. 1: *AAS* 72 (1980) 333.

27 Second Vatican Council, Constitution on the Sacred Liturgy, *Sacrosanctum Concilium*, n. 33.

28 Cf. below, n. 111 of this Introduction.

29 Cf. *Missale Romanum ex Decreto Sacrosancti Oecumenici Concilii Vaticani II instauratum auctoritate Pauli VI promulgatum*, *Ordo cantus Missae, editio typica* 1972, Praenotanda, nn. 4, 6, 10.

30 Cf. *Institutio Generalis Missalis Romani*, n. 11.

31 Cf. *ibid.*, n. 272; and nn. 32–34 of this Introduction.

32 Cf. *ibid.*, nn. 35, 95.

33 Cf. *ibid.*, nn. 82–84.

34 Cf. *ibid.*, nn. 94, 131.

35 Cf. *Ordo Missae cum populo*, 11, in: *Missale Romanum ex Decreto Sacrosancti Oecumenici Concilii Vaticani II instauratum auctoritate Pauli VI promulgatum* (*Typis Polyglottis Vaticanis*, 1975), p. 388.

36 *Institutio Generalis Missalis Romani*, n. 36.

37 Paul VI, Apostolic Constitution, *Laudis canticum in Liturgia Horarum ex Decreto Sacrosancti Oecumenici Concilii Vaticani II instaurata auctoritate Pauli VI promulgata* (*Typis Polyglottis Vaticanis* 1971); cf. also Second Vatican Council, Constitution on the Sacred Liturgy, *Sacrosanctum Concilium*, nn. 24, 90; Sacred Congregation of Rites, Instruction, *Musicam sacram*, 5 March 1967, n. 39: *AAS* 59 (1967) 311; *Liturgia Horarum, Instituto Generalis*, nn. 23, 109; Sacred Congregation for Catholic Education, *Ratio fundamentalis*, n. 53.

38 Cf. below, nn. 89–90 of this Introduction.

39 Cf. *Institutio Generalis Missalis Romani*, nn. 18, 38.

40 Cf. *ibid.*, n. 272; and below, nn. 32ff of this Introduction.

41 Cf. *ibid.*, n. 39.

42 Cf. *ibid.*, nn. 37–39; *Missale Romanum ex Decreto Sacrosancti Oecumenici Concilii Vaticani II instauratum auctoritate Pauli VI promulgatum, Ordo cantus Missae*, Praenotanda, nn. 7–9; *Graduale Romanum*, 1974, Praenotanda, n. 7; *Graduale simplex, editio typica altera* 1975, Praenotanda, n. 16.

43 Second Vatican Council, Constitution on the Sacred Liturgy, *Sacrosanctum Concilium*, n. 52; Sacred Congregation of Rites, Instruction, *Inter Oecumenici*, 26 September 1964, n. 54: *AAS* 56 (1964) 890.

44 Cf. *Institutio Generalis Missalis Romani*, n. 42.

45 Second Vatican Council, Constitution on the Sacred Liturgy, *Sacrosanctum Concilium*, n. 35, 2.

46 Cf. Second Vatican Council, Constitution on the Sacred Liturgy, *Sacrosanctum Concilium*, nn. 6 and 47.

47 Cf. Paul VI, Encyclical, *Mysterium Fidei*, 3 September 1965, n. 36: *AAS* 57 (1965) 753; Second Vatican Council, Decree on the Missionary Activity of the Church, *Ad gentes*, n. 9; Paul VI, Apostolic Exhortation, *Evangelii nuntiandi*, n. 43: *AAS* 69 (1976) 33–34.

48 Cf. Second Vatican Council, Constitution on the Sacred Liturgy, *Sacrosanctum Concilium*, n. 35, 2; *Institutio Generalis Missalis Romani*, n. 41.

49 Second Vatican Council, Constitution on the Sacred Liturgy, *Sacrosanctum Concilium*, n. 10.

50 Cf. John Paul II, Apostolic Exhortation, *Catechesi tradendae*, 16 October 1979, n. 48: *AAS* 71 (1979) 1316.

51 Cf. *Institutio Generalis Missalis Romani*, n. 165.

52 Cf. *ibid.*, n. 42; and also Sacred Congregation of Rites, Instruction, *Eucharisticum Mysterium*, 25 May 1967, n. 28: *AAS* 59 (1967) 556–557.

53 Cf. Sacred Congregation for Divine Worship, Instruction, *Actio pastoralis*, 15 May 1969, n. 6 g: *AAS* 61 (1969) 809; *Directorium de Missis cum pueris*, 1 November 1973, n. 48: *AAS* 66 (1974) 44.

54 Cf. *Institutio Generalis Missalis Romani*, nn. 42, 338; *Rituale Romanum ex Decreto Sacrosancti Oecumenici Concilii Vaticani II instauratum, auctoritate Pauli VI promulgatum, Ordo celebrandi Matrimonium* (*Typis Polyglottis Vaticanis* 1969), nn. 22, 42, 57; *Ordo Exsequiarum* (*Typis Polyglottis Vaticanis* 1969), nn. 41. 64.

55 Cf. *Institutio Generalis Missalis Romani*, n. 97.

56 Cf. *ibid.*, n. 139.

57 Cf. *ibid.*, n. 23.

58 Cf. *ibid.*, n. 43.

59 Cf. *ibid.*, n. 45.

60 Cf. *ibid.*, n. 99.

61 Cf. *ibid.*, n. 47.

62 Cf. above, note 23 of this Introduction.

63 Cf. *Institutio Generalis Missalis Romani*, n. 272.

64 Cf. Second Vatican Council, Constitution on the Sacred Liturgy, *Sacrosanctum Concilium*, n. 122.

65 Cf. *Pontificale Romanum ex Decreto Sacrosancti Oecumenici Concilii Vaticani II instauratum auctoritate Pauli VI promulgatum, De Ordinatione Diaconi, Presbyteri et Episcopi* (*Typis Polyglottis Vaticanis* 1968), p. 28, n. 24; p. 68, n. 21; p. 85, n. 24; p. 70, n. 25; p. 100, n. 25.

66 Cf. below, nn. 78–91 of this Introduction.

67 Cf. *Institutio Generalis Missalis Romani*, nn. 318–320, 324–325.

68 Cf. *ibid.*, n. 313.

69 Cf. *ibid.*, n. 42; Sacred Congregation for the Sacraments and Divine Worship, Instruction, *Inaestimabile Donum*, n. 3: AAS 72 (1980) 334.

70 Cf. *Institutio Generalis Missalis Romani*, n. 11.

71 Cf. *ibid.*, n. 68.

72 Cf. *ibid.*, nn. 33, 47.

73 Second Vatican Council, Decree on the Ministry and Life of Priests, *Presbyterorum Ordinis*, n. 4.

74 Second Vatican Council, Constitution on the Sacred Liturgy, *Sacrosanctum Concilium*, n. 33.

75 Cf. *Institutio Generalis Missalis Romani*, n. 9.

76 Second Vatican Council, Constitution on the Sacred Liturgy, *Sacrosanctum Concilium*, n. 7.

77 Cf. *ibid.*, n. 9.

78 Cf. Romans 1:16.

79 Cf. Second Vatican Council, Dogmatic Constitution on Divine Revelation, *Dei Verbum*, n. 21.

80 Quoted *ibid.*

81 Cf. John 14:15–26; 15:26–16:4, 5–15.

82 Cf. Second Vatican Council, Decree on the Missionary Activity of the Church, *Ad gentes*, nn. 6 and 15; and also Dogmatic Constitution on Divine Revelation, *Dei Verbum*, n. 26.

83 Cf. Second Vatican Council, Constitution on the Sacred Liturgy, *Sacrosanctum Concilium*, n. 24; and also Sacred Congregation for the Clergy, *Directorium Catecheticum Generale*, 11 April 1971, n. 25: AAS 64 (1972) 114.

84 Cf. Second Vatican Council, Constitution on the Sacred Liturgy, *Sacrosanctum Concilium*, n. 56; see also Sacred Congregation for the Sacraments and Divine Worship, Instruction, *Inaestimabile Donum*, 3 aprilis 1980, n. 1: AAS 72 (1980) 333–334.

85 Cf. Second Vatican Council, Constitution on the Sacred Liturgy, *Sacrosanctum Concilium*, nn. 24 and 35.

86 Cf. *Institutio Generalis Missalis Romani*, n. 34.

87 Cf. *ibid.*, n. 96.

88 Cf. *ibid.*, nn. 47, 61, 132; Sacred Congregation for the Sacraments and Divine Worship, Instruction, *Inaestimabile Donum*, 3 aprilis 1980, n. 3: AAS 72 (1980) 334.

89 Cf. *Institutio Generalis Missalis Romani*, n. 66.

90 Cf. Paul VI, *Motu Proprio, Ministeria quaedam*, 15 August 1972, n. V: AAS 64 (1972) 532.

91 Cf. Sacred Congregation for the Sacraments and Divine Worship, Instruction, *Inaestimabile Donum*, nn. 2 and 18: AAS 72 (1980) 334; cf. also Sacred Congregation for Divine Worship, *Directorium de Missis cum pueris*, 1 November 1973, n. 22, 24, 27: AAS 66 (1974) 43.

92 Cf. *Institutio Generalis Missalis Romani*, nn. 47, 66, 151; cf. also *Consilium ad exsequendam Constitutionem de sacra Liturgia, De oratione communi fidelium* (Città del Vaticano 1966) n. 8.

93 Cf. *Institutio Generalis Missalis Romani*, n. 66.

94 Cf. *ibid.*, nn. 37a and 67.

95 Cf. *ibid.*, n. 68.

96 Cf, for example, Pope Paul VI, Apostolic Constitution, *Missale Romanum*, 3 April 1969, in *Missale Romanum ex Decreto Sacrosancti Oecumenici Concilii Vaticani II instauratum auctoritate Pauli VI promulgatum* (Typis Polyglottis Vaticanis 1975), p. 15, quoted in *Missale Romanum ex Decreto Sacrosancti Oecumenici Concilii Vaticani II instauratum auctoritate Pauli VI promulgatum, Ordo lectionum Missae, editio typica altera* (Typis Polyglottis Vaticanis, 1981), p. XXX.

97 Cf. Second Vatican Council, Constitution on the Sacred Liturgy, *Sacrosanctum Concilium*, nn. 35 and 51.

98 Cf. Pope Paul VI, Apostolic Constitution, *Missale Romanum*: in *Missale Romanum ex Decreto Sacrosancti Oecumenici Concilii Vaticani II instauratum auctoritate Pauli VI promulgatum* (Typis Polyglottis Vaticanis 1975), p. 15, quoted in *Missale Romanum ex Decreto Sacrosancti Oecumenici Concilii Vaticani II instauratum auctoritate Pauli VI promulgatum, Ordo lectionum Missae, editio typica altera* (Typis Polyglottis Vaticanis 1981), p. XXXI.

99 Cf. Second Vatican Council, Constitution on the Sacred Liturgy, *Sacrosanctum Concilium*, nn. 9 and 33; Sacred Congregation of Rites, Instruction, *Inter Oecumenici*, 26 September 1964, n. 7: AAS 56 (1964) 878; John Paul II, Apostolic Exhortation, *Catechesi tradendae*, 16 October 1979, n. 23: AAS 71 (1979) 1296–1297.

100 Cf. Second Vatican Council, Constitution on the Sacred Liturgy, *Sacrosanctum Concilium*, n. 35, 4; Sacred Congregation of Rites, Instruction, *Inter Oecumenici*, 26 September 1964, nn. 37–38: AAS 56 (1964) 884.

101 Cf. Sacred Congregation for Divine Worship, Instruction, *Actio pastoralis*, 15 May 1969, n. 6: AAS 61 (1969) 809; Sacred Congregation for Divine Worship, *Directorium de Missis cum pueris*, 1 November 1973, n. 41–47: AAS 66 (1974) 43; Paul VI, Apostolic

Exhortation *Marialis cultus*, 2 February 1974, n. 12:
AAS 66 (1974) 125 – 126.

[102] Each of the years is designated by the letter A, B, or
C. The following is the procedure to determine which
year is A, B, or C. The letter C designates a year whose
number is divisible into three equal parts, as though
the cycle had taken its beginning from the first year of
the Christian era. Thus the year 1 would have been
Year A; year 2, Year B; year 3, Year C, (as would years
6, 9, and 12). Thus, for example, year 1980 is Year C;
1981, Year A; 1982, Year B; and 1983, Year C again.
And so forth. Obviously each cycle runs in accord with
the plan of the liturgical year, that is, it begins with the
First Week of Advent, which falls in the preceding
year of the civil calendar.

The years in each cycle is marked in a sense by the
principal characteristic of the Synoptic Gospel used for
the semicontinuous reading of Ordinary Time. Thus
the first Year of the cycle is the Year for the reading of
the Gospel of Matthew and is so named; the second and
third Years are the Year of Mark and the Year of Luke.

[103] Cf. *Institutio Generalis Missalis Romani*, nn. 36 – 40;
*Missale Romanum ex Decreto Sacrosancti Oecumenici
Concilii Vaticani II instauratum auctoritate Pauli VI promulgatum, Ordo cantus Missae (Typis Polyglottis Vaticanis)*, nn. 5 – 9.

[104] Cf. *Institutio Generalis Missalis Romani*, n. 313.

[105] Cf. *ibid.*, n. 318; Sacred Congregation for the Sacraments and Divine Worship, Instruction, *Inaestimabile
donum*, n. 1: *AAS* 72 (1980) 333 – 334.

[106] For example: in Lent the continuity of the Old
Testament readings corresponds to the unfolding of
the history of salvation; the Sundays in Ordinary Time
provide the semicontinuous reading of one of the
Letters of the Apostles. In these cases it is right that
the pastor of souls choose one or other of the readings
in a systematic way over a series of Sundays, so that he
may establish a coherent plan for catechesis. It is not
right to read indiscriminately on one day from the Old
Testament, on another from the Letter of an Apostle,
without any orderly plan for the texts that follow.

[107] Cf. *Institutio Generalis Missalis Romani*, n. 319.

[108] Cf. *ibid.*, n. 316c; see Second Vatican Council,
Constitution on the Sacred Liturgy *Sacrosanctum
Concilium*, n. 51.

[109] Cf. *Institutio Generalis Missalis Romani*, n. 318.

[110] Cf. *Rituale Romanum ex Decreto Sacrosancti
Oecumenici Concilii Vaticani II instauratum, auctoritate
Pauli VI promulgatum, Ordo Paenitentiae (Typis
Polyglottis Vaticanis 1974)* Praenotanda, n. 13.

[111] Cf. *Institutio Generalis Missalis Romani*, n. 320.

[112] Cf. *ibid.*, n. 313.

[113] Cf. nn. 173 – 174, of this Order of Readings.

[114] Cf. n. 233, of this Order of Readings.

[115] So, for example, when there are six weeks before
Lent, the seventh week begins on the Monday after
Pentecost. The Solemnity of the Most Holy Trinity
replaces the Sunday of Ordinary Time.

[116] When there are, for example, five weeks before
Lent, the Monday after Pentecost begins with the
Seventh Week of Ordinary Time and the Sixth Week
is omitted.

[117] Cf. Table II at the end of this Introduction.

[118] Cf. Table III at the end of this Introduction. This
Table appears only in the Weekday volume.

[119] Cf. *Missale Romanum ex Decreto Sacrosancti
Oecumenici Concilii Vaticani II instauratum auctoritate
Pauli VI promulgatum, Ordo lectionum Missae, editio
typica altera (Typis Polyglottis Vaticanis, 1981)*, p. XLVII,
note 119.

[120] Cf. Sacred Congregation for Divine Worship,
Instruction *Liturgicae instaurationes*, 5 September 1970,
n. 11: *AAS* 62 (1970) 702 – 703; *Institutio Generalis
Missalis Romani*, n. 325.

[121] Cf. *ibid.*, nn. 11, 29, 68a, 139.

[122] Cf. Index of Readings, pp. 374 – 377, of this Order
of Readings.

[123] The references for the psalms follow the order
of the *Liber Psalmorum*, published by the Pontifical
Commission for the Neo-Vulgate (*Typis Polyglottis
Vaticanis*, 1969).

PROPER OF SEASONS
AND ORDINARY TIME

SEASON OF ADVENT

1A   FIRST SUNDAY OF ADVENT

FIRST READING

ISAIAH 2:1–5

THE LORD WILL GATHER
ALL NATIONS INTO
THE ETERNAL PEACE OF
THE KINGDOM OF GOD.

This is what Isaiah, son of Amoz,
    saw concerning Judah and Jerusalem.

In days to come,
the mountain of the Lord's house
    shall be established as the highest mountain
    and raised above the hills.

All nations shall stream toward it;
    many peoples shall come and say:
"Come, let us climb the Lord's mountain,
    to the house of the God of Jacob,
that he may instruct us in his ways,
    and we may walk in his paths."

For from Zion shall go forth instruction,
    and the word of the Lord from Jerusalem.
He shall judge between the nations,
    and impose terms on many peoples.
They shall beat their swords into plowshares
    and their spears into pruning hooks;
one nation shall not raise the sword against another,
    nor shall they train for war again.

O house of Jacob, come,
    let us walk in the light of the Lord!

**RESPONSORIAL
PSALM**

PSALM 122:1–2, 3–4, 4–5,
6–7, 8–9

R. Let us go rejoicing to the house of the Lord.

[This psalm is found on page 450 (lectionary number 174).]

SECOND READING

ROMANS 13:11–14

OUR SALVATION IS NEARER.

Brothers and sisters:
You know the time;
    it is the hour now for you to awake from sleep.
For our salvation is nearer now than when
        we first believed;
    the night is advanced, the day is at hand.
Let us then throw off the works of darkness
    and put on the armor of light;
        let us conduct ourselves properly as in the day,

not in orgies and drunkenness,
not in promiscuity and lust,
not in rivalry and jealousy.

But put on the Lord Jesus Christ,
and make no provision for the desires of the flesh.

ALLELUIA

SEE PSALM 85:8

R. Alleluia, alleluia.

Show us, Lord, your love;
and grant us your salvation.   R.

GOSPEL

MATTHEW 24:37–44

STAY AWAKE, THAT YOU
MAY BE PREPARED!

Jesus said to his disciples:
"As it was in the days of Noah,
so it will be at the coming of the Son of Man.
In those days before the flood,
they were eating and drinking,
marrying and giving in marriage,
up to the day that Noah entered the ark.
They did not know until the flood came
and carried them all away.
So will it be also at the coming of the Son of Man.
Two men will be out in the field;
one will be taken, and one will be left.
Two women will be grinding at the mill;
one will be taken, and one will be left.

"Therefore, stay awake!
For you do not know on which day your Lord will come.
Be sure of this: if the master of the house
had known the hour of night when the thief
was coming,
he would have stayed awake
and not let his house be broken into.
So too, you also must be prepared,
for at an hour you do not expect,
the Son of Man will come."

FIRST READING

ISAIAH 63:16b–17, 19b;
64:2–7

OH, THAT YOU WOULD
REND THE HEAVENS AND
COME DOWN!

You, LORD, are our father,
  our redeemer you are named forever.
Why do you let us wander, O LORD, from your ways,
  and harden our hearts so that we fear you not?
Return for the sake of your servants,
  the tribes of your heritage.

Oh, that you would rend the heavens and come down,
  with the mountains quaking before you,
while you wrought awesome deeds we could not hope for,
  such as they had not heard of from of old.
No ear has ever heard, no eye ever seen, any God but you
  doing such deeds for those who wait for him.

Would that you might meet us doing right,
  that we were mindful of you in our ways!

Behold, you are angry, and we are sinful;
  all of us have become like unclean people,
  all our good deeds are like polluted rags;
we have all withered like leaves,
  and our guilt carries us away like the wind.
There is none who calls upon your name,
  who rouses himself to cling to you;
for you have hidden your face from us
  and have delivered us up to our guilt.

Yet, O LORD, you are our father;
  we are the clay and you the potter:
  we are all the work of your hands.

**RESPONSORIAL
PSALM**

PSALM 80:2–3, 15–16,
18–19 (4)

R. Lord, make us turn to you; let us see your face
  and we shall be saved.

O shepherd of Israel, hearken,
  from your throne upon the cherubim, shine forth.
Rouse your power,
  and come to save us. R.

Once again, O LORD of hosts,
  look down from heaven, and see;
take care of this vine,
  and protect what your right hand has planted,
  the son of man whom you yourself made strong. R.

May your help be with the man of your right hand,
  with the son of man whom you yourself made strong.
Then we will no more withdraw from you;
  give us new life, and we will call upon your name. R.

SECOND READING

1 CORINTHIANS 1:3–9

WE WAIT FOR THE
REVELATION OF OUR
LORD JESUS CHRIST.

Brothers and sisters:
Grace to you and peace from God our Father
   and the Lord Jesus Christ.

I give thanks to my God always on your account
   for the grace of God bestowed on you in Christ Jesus,
   that in him you were enriched in every way,
   with all discourse and all knowledge,
   as the testimony to Christ was confirmed among you,
   so that you are not lacking in any spiritual gift
   as you wait for the revelation of our Lord Jesus Christ.

He will keep you firm to the end,
   irreproachable on the day of our Lord Jesus Christ.
God is faithful,
   and by him you were called to fellowship with his Son,
   Jesus Christ our Lord.

ALLELUIA

PSALM 85:8

R. Alleluia, alleluia.

Show us Lord, your love;
and grant us your salvation.   R.

GOSPEL

MARK 13:33–37

BE WATCHFUL! YOU DO
NOT KNOW WHEN THE
LORD OF THE HOUSE IS
COMING.

Jesus said to his disciples:
"Be watchful! Be alert!
You do not know when the time will come.

"It is like a man traveling abroad.
He leaves home and places his servants in charge,
   each with his own work,
   and orders the gatekeeper to be on the watch.
Watch, therefore;
   you do not know when the Lord of the house
     is coming,
   whether in the evening, or at midnight,
   or at cockcrow, or in the morning.
May he not come suddenly and find you sleeping.
What I say to you, I say to all: 'Watch!'"

FIRST READING

JEREMIAH 33:14–16

I WILL RAISE UP FOR
DAVID A JUST SHOOT.

The days are coming, says the LORD,
  when I will fulfill the promise
  I made to the house of Israel and Judah.

In those days, in that time,
  I will raise up for David a just shoot;
  he shall do what is right and just in the land.

In those days Judah shall be safe
  and Jerusalem shall dwell secure;
  this is what they shall call her:
  "The LORD our justice."

**RESPONSORIAL
PSALM**

PSALM 25:4–5, 8–9, 10,
14 (1b)

R. To you, O Lord, I lift my soul.

[This psalm is found on page 441 (lectionary number 174).]

SECOND READING

1 THESSALONIANS 3:12—4:2

MAY THE LORD
STRENGTHEN YOUR
HEARTS AT THE COMING
OF OUR LORD JESUS.

Brothers and sisters:
May the Lord make you increase and abound in love
  for one another and for all,
  just as we have for you,
  so as to strengthen your hearts,
  to be blameless in holiness before our God and Father
  at the coming of our Lord Jesus with all his holy ones.
    Amen.

Finally, brothers and sisters,
  we earnestly ask and exhort you in the Lord Jesus that,
  as you received from us
  how you should conduct yourselves to please God
  — and as you are conducting yourselves —
  you do so even more.
For you know what instructions we gave you
    through the Lord Jesus.

ALLELUIA

PSALM 85:8

R. Alleluia, alleluia.

Show us, Lord, your love;
and grant us your salvation.   R.

Jesus said to his disciples:
"There will be signs in the sun, the moon and the stars,
    and on earth nations will be in dismay,
        perplexed by the roaring of the sea and the waves.
People will die of fright
    in anticipation of what is coming upon the world,
        for the powers of the heavens will be shaken.
And then they will see the Son of Man
    coming in a cloud with power and great glory.
But when these signs begin to happen,
    stand erect and raise your heads
        because your redemption is at hand.

"Beware that your hearts do not become drowsy
    from carousing and drunkenness
        and the anxieties of daily life,
        and that day catch you by surprise like a trap.
For that day will assault everyone
    who lives on the face of the earth.
Be vigilant at all times
    and pray that you have the strength
        to escape the tribulations that are imminent
        and to stand before the Son of Man."

4A   SECOND SUNDAY OF ADVENT

FIRST READING

ISAIAH 11:1–10

HE SHALL JUDGE THE POOR
WITH JUSTICE.

On that day, a shoot shall sprout from the stump of Jesse,
    and from his roots a bud shall blossom.
The spirit of the Lord shall rest upon him:
    a spirit of wisdom and of understanding,
a spirit of counsel and of strength,
    a spirit of knowledge and of fear of the Lord,
    and his delight shall be the fear of the Lord.

Not by appearance shall he judge,
    nor by hearsay shall he decide,
but he shall judge the poor with justice,
    and decide aright for the land's afflicted.
He shall strike the ruthless with the rod of his mouth,
    and with the breath of his lips he shall slay the wicked.
Justice shall be the band around his waist,
    and faithfulness a belt upon his hips.

Then the wolf shall be a guest of the lamb,
    and the leopard shall lie down with the kid;
the calf and the young lion shall browse together,
    with a little child to guide them.

The cow and the bear shall be neighbors,
    together their young shall rest;
    the lion shall eat hay like the ox.
The baby shall play by the cobra's den,
    and the child lay his hand on the adder's lair.
There shall be no harm or ruin on all my holy mountain;
    for the earth shall be filled with knowledge of the Lord,
    as water covers the sea.

On that day, the root of Jesse,
    set up as a signal for the nations,
the Gentiles shall seek out,
    for his dwelling shall be glorious.

RESPONSORIAL PSALM

PSALM 72:1–2, 7–8, 12–13, 17 (SEE 7)

R. *Justice shall flourish in his time,*
    and fullness of peace for ever.   R.

O God, with your judgment endow the king,
    and with your justice, the king's son;
he shall govern your people with justice
    and your afflicted ones with judgment.   R.

Justice shall flower in his days,
    and profound peace, till the moon be no more.
May he rule from sea to sea,
    and from the River to the ends of the earth.   R.

For he shall rescue the poor when he cries out,
    and the afflicted when he has no one to help him.
He shall have pity for the lowly and the poor;
    the lives of the poor he shall save.   R.

May his name be blessed forever;
    as long as the sun his name shall remain.
In him shall all the tribes of the earth be blessed;
    all the nations shall proclaim his happiness.   R.

SECOND READING

ROMANS 15:4–9

CHRIST SAVES EVERYONE.

Brothers and sisters:
Whatever was written previously was written
        for our instruction,
    that by endurance and by the encouragement
        of the Scriptures
    we might have hope.

May the God of endurance and encouragement
    grant you to think in harmony with one another,
    in keeping with Christ Jesus,
    that with one accord you may with one voice
    glorify the God and Father of our Lord Jesus Christ.

Welcome one another, then, as Christ welcomed you,
    for the glory of God.

For I say that Christ became a minister of the circumcised
    to show God's truthfulness,
    to confirm the promises to the patriarchs,
    but so that the Gentiles might glorify God for his mercy.
As it is written:
    Therefore, I will praise you among the Gentiles
    and sing praises to your name.

ALLELUIA

LUKE 3:4, 6

R. *Alleluia, alleluia.*

Prepare the way of the Lord, make straight his paths:
all flesh shall see the salvation of God.   R.

GOSPEL

MATTHEW 3:1–12

REPENT, FOR THE KINGDOM
OF HEAVEN IS AT HAND!

John the Baptist appeared, preaching in the desert
    of Judea
    and saying, "Repent, for the kingdom of heaven
    is at hand!"
It was of him that the prophet Isaiah had spoken
    when he said:
    A voice of one crying out in the desert,
    Prepare the way of the Lord,
    make straight his paths.

John wore clothing made of camel's hair
    and had a leather belt around his waist.
His food was locusts and wild honey.
At that time Jerusalem, all Judea,
    and the whole region around the Jordan
    were going out to him
    and were being baptized by him in the Jordan River
    as they acknowledged their sins.

When he saw many of the Pharisees and Sadducees
    coming to his baptism, he said to them,
        "You brood of vipers!
Who warned you to flee from the coming wrath?

"Produce good fruit as evidence of your repentance.
And do not presume to say to yourselves,
    'We have Abraham as our father.'
For I tell you,
    God can raise up children to Abraham
        from these stones.
Even now the ax lies at the root of the trees.
Therefore every tree that does not bear good fruit
    will be cut down and thrown into the fire.

"I am baptizing you with water, for repentance,
  but the one who is coming after me is mightier than I.
I am not worthy to carry his sandals.
He will baptize you with the Holy Spirit and fire.
His winnowing fan is in his hand.
He will clear his threshing floor
  and gather his wheat into his barn,
  but the chaff he will burn with unquenchable fire."

5B SECOND SUNDAY OF ADVENT

FIRST READING

ISAIAH 40:1–5, 9–11

PREPARE THE WAY
OF THE LORD.

Comfort, give comfort to my people,
  says your God.
Speak tenderly to Jerusalem, and proclaim to her
  that her service is at an end,
  her guilt is expiated;
indeed, she has received from the hand of the LORD
  double for all her sins.

A voice cries out:
In the desert prepare the way of the LORD!
  Make straight in the wasteland a highway for our God!
Every valley shall be filled in,
  every mountain and hill shall be made low;
the rugged land shall be made a plain,
  the rough country, a broad valley.
Then the glory of the LORD shall be revealed,
  and all people shall see it together;
  for the mouth of the LORD has spoken.

Go up onto a high mountain,
  Zion, herald of glad tidings;
cry out at the top of your voice,
  Jerusalem, herald of good news!
Fear not to cry out
  and say to the cities of Judah:
  Here is your God!

Here comes with power
  the Lord GOD,
  who rules by his strong arm;
here is his reward with him,
  his recompense before him.
Like a shepherd he feeds his flock;
  in his arms he gathers the lambs,
carrying them in his bosom,
  and leading the ewes with care.

RESPONSORIAL PSALM

PSALM 85:9–10, 11–12, 13–14 (8)

*R. Lord, let us see your kindness,
    and grant us your salvation.*

[This psalm is found on page 441 (lectionary number 174).]

SECOND READING

2 PETER 3:8–14

WE AWAIT NEW HEAVENS
AND A NEW EARTH.

Do not ignore this one fact, beloved,
    that with the Lord one day is like a thousand years
    and a thousand years like one day.
The Lord does not delay his promise,
    as some regard "delay,"
    but he is patient with you,
    not wishing that any should perish
    but that all should come to repentance.

But the day of the Lord will come like a thief,
    and then the heavens will pass away with a mighty roar
    and the elements will be dissolved by fire,
    and the earth and everything done on it
        will be found out.

Since everything is to be dissolved in this way,
    what sort of persons ought you to be,
    conducting yourselves in holiness and devotion,
    waiting for and hastening the coming of the day of God,
    because of which the heavens will be dissolved
        in flames
    and the elements melted by fire.
But according to his promise
    we await new heavens and a new earth
    in which righteousness dwells.

Therefore, beloved, since you await these things,
    be eager to be found without spot or blemish
        before him, at peace.

ALLELUIA

LUKE 3:4, 6

R. Alleluia, alleluia.

*Prepare the way of the Lord, make straight his paths:
All flesh shall see the salvation of God.   R.*

GOSPEL

MARK 1:1–8

MAKE STRAIGHT THE
PATHS OF THE LORD.

The beginning of the gospel of Jesus Christ the Son
    of God.

As it is written in Isaiah the prophet:
*Behold, I am sending my messenger ahead of you;
    he will prepare your way.*

A *voice of one crying out in the desert:*
   "Prepare the way of the LORD,
   make straight his paths."

John the Baptist appeared in the desert
   proclaiming a baptism of repentance for the forgiveness
      of sins.
People of the whole Judean countryside
   and all the inhabitants of Jerusalem
   were going out to him
   and were being baptized by him in the Jordan River
   as they acknowledged their sins.

John was clothed in camel's hair,
   with a leather belt around his waist.
He fed on locusts and wild honey.

And this is what he proclaimed:
"One mightier than I is coming after me.
I am not worthy to stoop and loosen the thongs
   of his sandals.
I have baptized you with water;
   he will baptize you with the Holy Spirit."

6C SECOND SUNDAY OF ADVENT

FIRST READING

BARUCH 5:1–9

JERUSALEM, GOD WILL
SHOW YOUR SPLENDOR.

Jerusalem, take off your robe of mourning and misery;
   put on the splendor of glory from God forever:
Wrapped in the cloak of justice from God,
   bear on your head the mitre
   that displays the glory of the eternal name.
For God will show all the earth your splendor:
   you will be named by God forever
   the peace of justice, the glory of God's worship.

Up, Jerusalem! stand upon the heights;
   look to the east and see your children
gathered from the east and the west
   at the word of the Holy One,
   rejoicing that they are remembered by God.
Led away on foot by their enemies they left you:
   but God will bring them back to you
   borne aloft in glory as on royal thrones.

For God has commanded
   that every lofty mountain be made low,
and that the age-old depths and gorges

be filled to level ground,
that Israel may advance secure in the glory of God.
The forests and every fragrant kind of tree
have overshadowed Israel at God's command;
for God is leading Israel in joy
by the light of his glory,
with his mercy and justice for company.

RESPONSORIAL
PSALM

PSALM 126:1–2, 2–3, 4–5,
6 (3)

R. *The Lord has done great things for us; we are filled with joy.*

When the LORD brought back the captives of Zion,
we were like men dreaming.
Then our mouth was filled with laughter,
and our tongue with rejoicing.   R.

Then they said among the nations,
"The LORD has done great things for them."
The LORD has done great things for us;
we are glad indeed.   R.

Restore our fortunes, O LORD,
like the torrents in the southern desert.
Those who sow in tears
shall reap rejoicing.   R.

Although they go forth weeping,
carrying the seed to be sown,
they shall come back rejoicing,
carrying their sheaves.   R.

SECOND READING

PHILIPPIANS 1:4–6, 8–11

SHOW YOURSELVES PURE
AND BLAMELESS FOR THE
DAY OF CHRIST.

Brothers and sisters:
I pray always with joy in my every prayer for all of you,
because of your partnership for the gospel
from the first day until now.

I am confident of this,
that the one who began a good work in you
will continue to complete it
until the day of Christ Jesus.

God is my witness,
how I long for all of you with the affection
of Christ Jesus.
And this is my prayer:
that your love may increase ever more and more
in knowledge and every kind of perception,
to discern what is of value,
so that you may be pure and blameless
for the day of Christ,
filled with the fruit of righteousness
that comes through Jesus Christ
for the glory and praise of God.

R.Alleluia, alleluia.

Prepare the way of the Lord, make straight his paths:
All flesh shall see the salvation of God.   R.

GOSPEL

LUKE 3:1–6

ALL FLESH SHALL SEE
THE SALVATION OF GOD.

In the fifteenth year of the reign of Tiberius Caesar,
   when Pontius Pilate was governor of Judea,
   and Herod was tetrarch of Galilee,
   and his brother Philip tetrarch of the region
      of Ituraea and Trachonitis,
   and Lysanias was tetrarch of Abilene,
   during the high priesthood of Annas and Caiaphas,
   the word of God came to John the son of Zechariah
      in the desert.

John went throughout the whole region of the Jordan,
   proclaiming a baptism of repentance
      for the forgiveness of sins,
   as it is written in the book of the words
      of the prophet Isaiah:
   A voice of one crying out in the desert:
   "Prepare the way of the LORD,
   make straight his paths.
   Every valley shall be filled
   and every mountain and hill shall be made low.
   The winding roads shall be made straight,
   and the rough ways made smooth,
   and all flesh shall see the salvation of God."

7A   THIRD SUNDAY OF ADVENT

FIRST READING

ISAIAH 35:1–6a, 10

GOD HIMSELF WILL
COME TO SAVE US.

The desert and the parched land will exult;
   the steppe will rejoice and bloom.
They will bloom with abundant flowers,
   and rejoice with joyful song.
The glory of Lebanon will be given to them,
   the splendor of Carmel and Sharon;
they will see the glory of the Lord,
   the splendor of our God.

Strengthen the hands that are feeble,
   make firm the knees that are weak,
say to those whose hearts are frightened:
   Be strong, fear not!
Here is your God,
   he comes with vindication;

with divine recompense
    he comes to save you.
Then will the eyes of the blind be opened,
    the ears of the deaf be cleared;
then will the lame leap like a stag,
    then the tongue of the mute will sing.

Those whom the Lord has ransomed will return
    and enter Zion singing,
    crowned with everlasting joy;
they will meet with joy and gladness,
    sorrow and mourning will flee.

RESPONSORIAL PSALM

PSALM 146:6–7, 8–9, 9–10
(SEE ISAIAH 35:4)

R. Lord, come and save us.
*   or:*
R. Alleluia.

The Lord God keeps faith forever,
*   secures justice for the oppressed,*
*   gives food to the hungry.*
The Lord sets captives free.   R.

The Lord gives sight to the blind;
*   the Lord raises up those who were bowed down.*
The Lord loves the just;
*   the Lord protects strangers.   R.*

The fatherless and the widow he sustains,
*   but the way of the wicked he thwarts.*
The Lord shall reign forever;
*   your God, O Zion, through all generations.   R.*

SECOND READING

JAMES 5:7–10

MAKE YOUR HEARTS FIRM,
BECAUSE THE COMING
OF THE LORD IS AT HAND.

Be patient, brothers and sisters,
    until the coming of the Lord.
See how the farmer waits for the precious fruit
        of the earth,
    being patient with it
    until it receives the early and the late rains.
You too must be patient.
Make your hearts firm,
    because the coming of the Lord is at hand.

Do not complain, brothers and sisters, about one another,
    that you may not be judged.
Behold, the Judge is standing before the gates.
Take as an example of hardship and patience,
        brothers and sisters,
    the prophets who spoke in the name of the Lord.

R. Alleluia, alleluia.

The Spirit of the Lord is upon me,
because he has anointed me
to bring glad tidings to the poor.   R.

GOSPEL

MATTHEW 11:2–11

ARE YOU THE ONE WHO
IS TO COME OR SHOULD
WE LOOK FOR ANOTHER?

When John the Baptist heard in prison of the works
      of the Christ,
   he sent his disciples to Jesus with this question,
   "Are you the one who is to come,
   or should we look for another?"
Jesus said to them in reply,
   "Go and tell John what you hear and see:
   the blind regain their sight,
   the lame walk,
   lepers are cleansed,
   the deaf hear,
   the dead are raised,
   and the poor have the good news proclaimed to them.
And blessed is the one who takes no offense at me."

As they were going off,
   Jesus began to speak to the crowds about John,
   "What did you go out to the desert to see?
A reed swayed by the wind?
Then what did you go out to see?
Someone dressed in fine clothing?
Those who wear fine clothing are in royal palaces.
Then why did you go out? To see a prophet?
Yes, I tell you, and more than a prophet.
This is the one about whom it is written:
   Behold, I am sending my messenger ahead of you;
   he will prepare your way before you.

"Amen, I say to you,
   among those born of women
   there has been none greater than John the Baptist;
   yet the least in the kingdom of heaven
      is greater than he."

8B   THIRD SUNDAY OF ADVENT

FIRST READING

ISAIAH 61:1–2a, 10–11

I REJOICE HEARTILY
IN THE LORD.

The spirit of the Lord GOD is upon me,
   because the LORD has anointed me;
he has sent me to bring glad tidings to the poor,
   to heal the brokenhearted,

to proclaim liberty to the captives
  and release to the prisoners,
to announce a year of favor from the LORD
  and a day of vindication by our God.

I rejoice heartily in the LORD,
  in my God is the joy of my soul;
for he has clothed me with a robe of salvation
  and wrapped me in a mantle of justice,
like a bridegroom adorned with a diadem,
  like a bride bedecked with her jewels.

As the earth brings forth its plants,
  and a garden makes its growth spring up,
so will the Lord GOD make justice and praise
  spring up before all the nations.

RESPONSORIAL
PSALM

LUKE 1:46–48, 49–50, 53–54
(ISAIAH 61:10b)

R. My soul rejoices in my God.

My soul proclaims the greatness of the LORD;
  my spirit rejoices in God my Savior,
for he has looked upon his lowly servant.
  From this day all generations will call me blessed.   R.

The Almighty has done great things for me,
  and holy is his Name.
He has mercy on those who fear him
  in every generation.   R.

He has filled the hungry with good things,
  and the rich he has sent away empty.
He has come to the help of his servant Israel
  for he has remembered his promise of mercy.   R.

SECOND READING

1 THESSALONIANS 5:16–24

MAY YOU ENTIRELY,
SPIRIT, SOUL AND BODY,
BE PRESERVED BLAMELESS
FOR THE COMING OF
OUR LORD JESUS CHRIST.

Brothers and sisters:
Rejoice always. Pray without ceasing.
In all circumstances give thanks,
  for this is the will of God for you in Christ Jesus.

Do not quench the Spirit.
Do not despise prophetic utterances.
Test everything; retain what is good.
Refrain from every kind of evil.

May the God of peace make you perfectly holy
  and may you entirely, spirit, soul and body,
  be preserved blameless for the coming
    of our Lord Jesus Christ.
The one who calls you is faithful,
  and he will also accomplish it.

R. Alleluia, alleluia.

*The Spirit of the Lord is upon me,
    because he has anointed me
    to bring glad tidings to the poor.   R.*

GOSPEL

JOHN 1:6–8, 19–28

THERE IS ONE AMONG
YOU WHOM YOU DO NOT
RECOGNIZE.

A man named John was sent from God.
He came for testimony, to testify to the light,
    so that all might believe through him.
He was not the light,
    but came to testify to the light.

And this is the testimony of John.
When the Jews from Jerusalem sent priests and Levites
        to him
    to ask him, "Who are you?"
    he admitted and did not deny it,
    but admitted, "I am not the Christ."

So they asked him,
    "What are you then? Are you Elijah?"
And he said, "I am not."
"Are you the Prophet?"
He answered, "No."

So they said to him,
    "Who are you, so we can give an answer to those
        who sent us?
What do you have to say for yourself?"
He said:
    "I am *the voice of one crying out in the desert,*
    make straight the way of the LORD,
    as Isaiah the prophet said."

Some Pharisees were also sent.
They asked him,
    "Why then do you baptize
    if you are not the Christ or Elijah or the Prophet?"
John answered them,
    "I baptize with water;
    but there is one among you whom you do not recognize,
    the one who is coming after me,
    whose sandal strap I am not worthy to untie."

This happened in Bethany across the Jordan,
    where John was baptizing.

9C THIRD SUNDAY OF ADVENT

FIRST READING

ZEPHANIAH 3:14–18a

THE LORD WILL
REJOICE OVER YOU
WITH GLADNESS.

Shout for joy, O daughter Zion!
    Sing joyfully, O Israel!
Be glad and exult with all your heart,
    O daughter Jerusalem!
The LORD has removed the judgment against you,
    he has turned away your enemies;
the King of Israel, the LORD, is in your midst,
    you have no further misfortune to fear.

On that day, it shall be said to Jerusalem:
    Fear not, O Zion, be not discouraged!
The LORD, your God, is in your midst,
    a mighty savior;
he will rejoice over you with gladness,
    and renew you in his love,
he will sing joyfully because of you,
    as one sings at festivals.

**RESPONSORIAL
PSALM**

ISAIAH 12:2–3, 4, 5–6 (6)

R. Cry out with joy and gladness,
    for among you is the great and Holy One of Israel.

God indeed is my savior;
    I am confident and unafraid.
My strength and my courage is the LORD,
    and he has been my savior.
With joy you will draw water
    at the fountain of salvation.   R.

Give thanks to the LORD, acclaim his name;
    among the nations make known his deeds,
    proclaim how exalted is his name.   R.

Sing praise to the LORD for his glorious achievement;
    let this be known throughout all the earth.
Shout with exultation, O city of Zion,
    for great in your midst
    is the Holy One of Israel!   R.

SECOND READING

PHILIPPIANS 4:4–7

THE LORD IS NEAR.

Brothers and sisters:
Rejoice in the Lord always.
I shall say it again: rejoice!

Your kindness should be known to all.
The Lord is near.
Have no anxiety at all, but in everything,
    by prayer and petition, with thanksgiving,
    make your requests known to God.

Then the peace of God that surpasses all understanding
will guard your hearts and minds in Christ Jesus.

ALLELUIA

ISAIAH 61:1 (CITED IN
LUKE 4:18)

R. Alleluia, alleluia.

The Spirit of the Lord is upon me,
because he has anointed me to bring glad tidings to the poor.   R.

GOSPEL

LUKE 3:10–18

WHAT SHOULD WE DO?

The crowds asked John the Baptist,
  "What should we do?"
He said to them in reply,
  "Whoever has two cloaks
  should share with the person who has none.
And whoever has food should do likewise."

Even tax collectors came to be baptized
    and they said to him,
  "Teacher, what should we do?"
He answered them,
  "Stop collecting more than what is prescribed."
Soldiers also asked him,
  "And what is it that we should do?"
He told them,
  "Do not practice extortion,
  do not falsely accuse anyone,
  and be satisfied with your wages."

Now the people were filled with expectation,
    and all were asking in their hearts
    whether John might be the Christ.
John answered them all, saying,
  "I am baptizing you with water,
  but one mightier than I is coming.
I am not worthy to loosen the thongs of his sandals.
He will baptize you with the Holy Spirit and fire.
His winnowing fan is in his hand
    to clear his threshing floor
    and to gather the wheat into his barn,
    but the chaff he will burn with unquenchable fire."
Exhorting them in many other ways,
    he preached good news to the people.

FIRST READING

ISAIAH 7:10–14

BEHOLD, THE VIRGIN
SHALL CONCEIVE.

The LORD spoke to Ahaz, saying:
Ask for a sign from the LORD, your God;
  let it be deep as the netherworld, or high as the sky!
But Ahaz answered,
  "I will not ask! I will not tempt the LORD!"

Then Isaiah said:
  Listen, O house of David!
Is it not enough for you to weary people,
  must you also weary my God?
Therefore the Lord himself will give you this sign:
  the virgin shall conceive, and bear a son,
  and shall name him Emmanuel.

**RESPONSORIAL
PSALM**

PSALM 24:1–2, 3–4, 5–6
(7c, 10b)

R. Let the Lord enter; he is king of glory.

The LORD's are the earth and its fullness;
  the world and those who dwell in it.
For he founded it upon the seas
  and established it upon the rivers.

Who can ascend the mountain of the LORD?
  or who may stand in his holy place?
One whose hands are sinless, whose heart is clean,
  who desires not what is vain.

He shall receive a blessing from the LORD,
  a reward from God his savior.
Such is the race that seeks for him,
  that seeks the face of the God of Jacob.

SECOND READING

ROMANS 1:1–7

JESUS CHRIST, DESCENDED
FROM DAVID, IS THE SON
OF GOD.

Paul, a slave of Christ Jesus,
  called to be an apostle and set apart for the gospel
    of God,
  which he promised previously through his prophets
    in the holy Scriptures,
the gospel about his Son, descended from David
    according to the flesh,
  but established as Son of God in power
  according to the Spirit of holiness
  through resurrection from the dead, Jesus Christ
    our Lord.

Through him we have received the grace of apostleship,
  to bring about the obedience of faith,
    for the sake of his name, among all the Gentiles,

among whom are you also, who are called to belong
    to Jesus Christ;
to all the beloved of God in Rome, called to be holy.

Grace to you and peace from God our Father
    and the Lord Jesus Christ.

ALLELUIA

MATTHEW 1:23

R. Alleluia, alleluia.

*The virgin shall conceive, and bear a son,
and they shall name him Emmanuel.   R.*

GOSPEL

MATTHEW 1:18–24

JESUS WILL BE BORN OF MARY,
THE BETROTHED OF JOSEPH,
A SON OF DAVID.

This is how the birth of Jesus Christ came about.
When his mother Mary was betrothed to Joseph,
    but before they lived together,
    she was found with child through the Holy Spirit.

Joseph her husband, since he was a righteous man,
    yet unwilling to expose her to shame,
    decided to divorce her quietly.

Such was his intention when, behold,
    the angel of the Lord appeared to him in a dream
        and said,
    "Joseph, son of David,
    do not be afraid to take Mary your wife into your home.
For it is through the Holy Spirit
    that this child has been conceived in her.
She will bear a son and you are to name him Jesus,
    because he will save his people from their sins."

All this took place to fulfill what the Lord had said
        through the prophet:
    *Behold, the virgin shall conceive and bear a son,
    and they shall name him Emmanuel,*
    which means "God is with us."
When Joseph awoke,
    he did as the angel of the Lord had commanded him
    and took his wife into his home.

FIRST READING

2 SAMUEL 7:1–5, 8b–12,
14a, 16

THE KINGDOM OF DAVID
SHALL ENDURE FOREVER
BEFORE THE LORD.

When King David was settled in his palace,
   and the LORD had given him rest from his enemies
      on every side,
he said to Nathan the prophet,
   "Here I am living in a house of cedar,
   while the ark of God dwells in a tent!"
Nathan answered the king,
   "Go, do whatever you have in mind,
   for the LORD is with you."

But that night the LORD spoke to Nathan and said:
   "Go, tell my servant David, Thus says the LORD:
   Should you build me a house to dwell in?

"It was I who took you from the pasture
   and from the care of the flock
   to be commander of my people Israel.
I have been with you wherever you went,
   and I have destroyed all your enemies before you.
And I will make you famous like the great ones
      of the earth.

"I will fix a place for my people Israel;
   I will plant them so that they may dwell in their place
   without further disturbance.
Neither shall the wicked continue to afflict them
      as they did of old,
   since the time I first appointed judges
      over my people Israel.
I will give you rest from all your enemies.

"The LORD also reveals to you
   that he will establish a house for you.
And when your time comes and you rest
      with your ancestors,
   I will raise up your heir after you, sprung from your loins,
   and I will make his kingdom firm.

"I will be a father to him,
   and he shall be a son to me.
Your house and your kingdom shall endure forever
      before me;
   your throne shall stand firm forever."

RESPONSORIAL PSALM

PSALM 89:2–3, 4–5, 27, 29 (2a)

R. For ever I will sing the goodness of the Lord.

*The promises of the L*ORD *I will sing forever;*
*   through all generations my mouth shall proclaim your faithfulness.*
For you have said, "My kindness is established forever";
*   in heaven you have confirmed your faithfulness.   R.*

"I have made a covenant with my chosen one,
*   I have sworn to David my servant:*
forever will I confirm your posterity
*   and establish your throne for all generations."   R.*

"He shall say of me, 'You are my father,
*   my God, the rock, my savior.'*
Forever I will maintain my kindness toward him,
*   and my covenant with him stands firm."   R.*

SECOND READING

ROMANS 16:25–27

THE MYSTERY KEPT SECRET FOR LONG AGES HAS NOW BEEN MANIFESTED.

Brothers and sisters:
To him who can strengthen you,
    according to my gospel and the proclamation
        of Jesus Christ,
    according to the revelation of the mystery kept secret
        for long ages
    but now manifested through the prophetic writings and,
    according to the command of the eternal God,
    made known to all nations to bring about
        the obedience of faith,
    to the only wise God, through Jesus Christ
    be glory forever and ever. Amen.

ALLELUIA

LUKE 1:38

R. Alleluia, alleluia.

Behold, I am the handmaid of the Lord.
May it be done to me according to your word.   R.

GOSPEL

LUKE 1:26–38

BEHOLD, YOU WILL CONCEIVE IN YOUR WOMB AND BEAR A SON.

The angel Gabriel was sent from God
    to a town of Galilee called Nazareth,
    to a virgin betrothed to a man named Joseph,
    of the house of David,
    and the virgin's name was Mary.

And coming to her, he said,
    "Hail, full of grace! The Lord is with you."
But she was greatly troubled at what was said
    and pondered what sort of greeting this might be.

Then the angel said to her,
    "Do not be afraid, Mary,
    for you have found favor with God.

Behold, you will conceive in your womb and bear a son,
and you shall name him Jesus.

"He will be great and will be called Son of the Most High,
and the Lord God will give him the throne of David
his father,
and he will rule over the house of Jacob forever,
and of his kingdom there will be no end."

But Mary said to the angel,
"How can this be,
since I have no relations with a man?"
And the angel said to her in reply,
"The Holy Spirit will come upon you,
and the power of the Most High will overshadow you.
Therefore the child to be born
will be called holy, the Son of God.

"And behold, Elizabeth, your relative,
has also conceived a son in her old age,
and this is the sixth month for her who was
called barren;
for nothing will be impossible for God."
Mary said, "Behold, I am the handmaid of the Lord.
May it be done to me according to your word."
Then the angel departed from her.

12C FOURTH SUNDAY OF ADVENT

FIRST READING

MICAH 5:1–4a

FROM YOU SHALL COME
FORTH THE RULER OF
ISRAEL.

Thus says the LORD:
You, Bethlehem-Ephrathah,
too small to be among the clans of Judah,
from you shall come forth for me
one who is to be ruler in Israel;
whose origin is from of old,
from ancient times.

Therefore the Lord will give them up, until the time
when she who is to give birth has borne,
and the rest of his kindred shall return
to the children of Israel.
He shall stand firm and shepherd his flock
by the strength of the LORD,
in the majestic name of the LORD, his God;
and they shall remain, for now his greatness
shall reach to the ends of the earth;
he shall be peace.

RESPONSORIAL PSALM

PSALM 80:2–3, 15–16, 18–19 (4)

R. *Lord, make us turn to you; let us see your face and we shall be saved.*

[This psalm is found on page 4 (lectionary number 2).]

SECOND READING

HEBREWS 10:5–10

BEHOLD, I COME TO DO YOUR WILL.

Brothers and sisters:
When Christ came into the world, he said:
   "Sacrifice and offering you did not desire,
      but a body you prepared for me;
   in holocausts and sin offerings you took no delight.
   Then I said, 'As is written of me in the scroll,
      behold, I come to do your will, O God.'"

First he says, "Sacrifices and offerings,
   holocausts and sin offerings,
      you neither desired nor delighted in."
These are offered according to the law.
Then he says, "Behold, I come to do your will."
He takes away the first to establish the second.

By this "will," we have been consecrated
   through the offering of the body of Jesus Christ
      once for all.

ALLELUIA

LUKE 1:38

R. *Alleluia, alleluia.*

Behold, I am the handmaid of the Lord.
May it be done to me according to your word. R.

GOSPEL

LUKE 1:39–45

AND HOW DOES THIS HAPPEN TO ME, THAT THE MOTHER OF MY LORD SHOULD COME TO ME?

Mary set out
   and traveled to the hill country in haste
   to a town of Judah,
   where she entered the house of Zechariah
   and greeted Elizabeth.

When Elizabeth heard Mary's greeting,
   the infant leaped in her womb,
   and Elizabeth, filled with the Holy Spirit,
   cried out in a loud voice and said,
   "Blessed are you among women,
   and blessed is the fruit of your womb.
And how does this happen to me,
   that the mother of my Lord should come to me?
For at the moment the sound of your greeting
      reached my ears,
   the infant in my womb leaped for joy.

Blessed are you who believed
    that what was spoken to you by the Lord
    would be fulfilled."

SEASON OF CHRISTMAS

13ABC   THE NATIVITY OF THE LORD
DECEMBER 24 | AT THE VIGIL MASS

FIRST READING

ISAIAH 62:1–5

THE LORD DELIGHTS
IN YOU.

◆

*These readings are used at Mass
celebrated on the evening of
December 24, either before or after
Evening Prayer I of Christmas.*

*The texts that follow may
also be used for Masses on
Christmas Day, with the option
of choosing from one or another
of the three sets of readings
according to the pastoral needs
of each congregation.*

For Zion's sake I will not be silent,
    for Jerusalem's sake I will not be quiet,
until her vindication shines forth like the dawn
    and her victory like a burning torch.

Nations shall behold your vindication,
    and all the kings your glory;
you shall be called by a new name
    pronounced by the mouth of the LORD.
You shall be a glorious crown in the hand of the LORD,
    a royal diadem held by your God.

No more shall people call you "Forsaken,"
    or your land "Desolate,"
but you shall be called "My Delight,"
    and your land "Espoused."
For the LORD delights in you
    and makes your land his spouse.

As a young man marries a virgin,
    your Builder shall marry you;
and as a bridegroom rejoices in his bride
    so shall your God rejoice in you.

**RESPONSORIAL
PSALM**

PSALM 89:4–5, 16–17, 27,
29 (2a)

R. For ever I will sing the goodness of the Lord.

*I have made a covenant with my chosen one,
    I have sworn to David my servant:
forever will I confirm your posterity
    and establish your throne for all generations.   R.*

*Blessed the people who know the joyful shout;
    in the light of your countenance, O LORD, they walk.
At your name they rejoice all the day,
    and through your justice they are exalted.   R.*

He shall say of me, "You are my father,
my God, the rock, my savior."
Forever I will maintain my kindness toward him,
and my covenant with him stands firm.   R.

SECOND READING

ACTS 13:16–17, 22–25

PAUL BEARS WITNESS
TO CHRIST,
THE SON OF DAVID.

When Paul reached Antioch in Pisidia and entered
the synagogue,
he stood up, motioned with his hand, and said,

"Fellow Israelites and you others who are God-fearing,
listen.
The God of this people Israel chose our ancestors
and exalted the people during their sojourn
in the land of Egypt.
With uplifted arm he led them out of it.

"Then he removed Saul and raised up David as king;
of him he testified,
'I have found David, son of Jesse,
a man after my own heart;
he will carry out my every wish.'

"From this man's descendants God,
according to his promise,
has brought to Israel a savior, Jesus.
John heralded his coming by proclaiming
a baptism of repentance
to all the people of Israel;
and as John was completing his course, he would say,
'What do you suppose that I am? I am not he.
Behold, one is coming after me;
I am not worthy to unfasten the sandals of his feet.'"

ALLELUIA

R. Alleluia, alleluia.

Tomorrow the wickedness of the earth
will be destroyed:
the Savior of the world will reign over us.   R.

GOSPEL

LONGER FORM
MATTHEW 1:1–25

THE GENEALOGY OF JESUS
CHRIST, THE SON OF DAVID.

SHORTER FORM
MATTHEW 1:18–25

MARY WILL GIVE BIRTH
TO A SON, AND YOU ARE
TO NAME HIM JESUS.

The book of the genealogy of Jesus Christ,
   the son of David, the son of Abraham.

Abraham became the father of Isaac,
   Isaac the father of Jacob,
   Jacob the father of Judah and his brothers.
Judah became the father of Perez and Zerah,
   whose mother was Tamar.
Perez became the father of Hezron,
   Hezron the father of Ram,
   Ram the father of Amminadab.
Amminadab became the father of Nahshon,
   Nahshon the father of Salmon,
   Salmon the father of Boaz,
   whose mother was Rahab.
Boaz became the father of Obed,
   whose mother was Ruth.
Obed became the father of Jesse,
   Jesse the father of David the king.

David became the father of Solomon,
   whose mother had been the wife of Uriah.
Solomon became the father of Rehoboam,
   Rehoboam the father of Abijah,
   Abijah the father of Asaph.
Asaph became the father of Jehoshaphat,
   Jehoshaphat the father of Joram,
   Joram the father of Uzziah.
Uzziah became the father of Jotham,
   Jotham the father of Ahaz,
   Ahaz the father of Hezekiah.
Hezekiah became the father of Manasseh,
   Manasseh the father of Amos,
   Amos the father of Josiah.
Josiah became the father of Jechoniah and his brothers
   at the time of the Babylonian exile.

After the Babylonian exile,
   Jechoniah became the father of Shealtiel,
   Shealtiel the father of Zerubbabel,
   Zerubbabel the father of Abiud.
Abiud became the father of Eliakim,
   Eliakim the father of Azor,
   Azor the father of Zadok.
Zadok became the father of Achim,
   Achim the father of Eliud,
   Eliud the father of Eleazar.

Eleazar became the father of Matthan,
   Matthan the father of Jacob,
   Jacob the father of Joseph, the husband of Mary.
Of her was born Jesus who is called the Christ.

Thus the total number of generations
   from Abraham to David
   is fourteen generations;
   from David to the Babylonian exile,
   fourteen generations;
   from the Babylonian exile to the Christ,
   fourteen generations.

[Now this is how the birth of Jesus Christ came about.
When his mother Mary was betrothed to Joseph,
   but before they lived together,
   she was found with child through the Holy Spirit.

Joseph her husband, since he was a righteous man,
   yet unwilling to expose her to shame,
   decided to divorce her quietly.
Such was his intention when, behold,
   the angel of the Lord appeared to him in a dream
     and said,
   "Joseph, son of David,
   do not be afraid to take Mary your wife into your home.
For it is through the Holy Spirit
   that this child has been conceived in her.
She will bear a son and you are to name him Jesus,
   because he will save his people from their sins."

All this took place to fulfill
   what the Lord had said through the prophet:
   Behold, the virgin shall conceive and bear a son,
   and they shall name him Emmanuel,
   which means "God is with us."

When Joseph awoke,
   he did as the angel of the Lord had commanded him
   and took his wife into his home.
He had no relations with her until she bore a son,
   and he named him Jesus.]

14ABC THE NATIVITY OF THE LORD

DECEMBER 25 | MASS AT MIDNIGHT

FIRST READING

ISAIAH 9:1–6

A SON IS GIVEN US.

The people who walked in darkness
   have seen a great light;
upon those who dwelt in the land of gloom
   a light has shone.
You have brought them abundant joy
   and great rejoicing,
as they rejoice before you as at the harvest,
   as people make merry when dividing spoils.

For the yoke that burdened them,
   the pole on their shoulder,
and the rod of their taskmaster
   you have smashed, as on the day of Midian.

For every boot that tramped in battle,
   every cloak rolled in blood,
   will be burned as fuel for flames.
For a child is born to us, a son is given us;
   upon his shoulder dominion rests.
They name him Wonder-Counselor, God-Hero,
   Father-Forever, Prince of Peace.
His dominion is vast
   and forever peaceful,
from David's throne, and over his kingdom,
   which he confirms and sustains
by judgment and justice,
   both now and forever.
The zeal of the LORD of hosts will do this!

RESPONSORIAL PSALM

PSALM 96:1–2, 2–3, 11–12, 13
(LUKE 2:11)

R. Today is born our Savior, Christ the Lord.

Sing to the LORD a new song;
   sing to the LORD, all you lands.
Sing to the LORD; bless his name. R.

Announce his salvation, day after day.
Tell his glory among the nations;
   among all peoples, his wondrous deeds. R.

Let the heavens be glad and the earth rejoice;
   let the sea and what fills it resound;
   let the plains be joyful and all that is in them!
Then shall all the trees of the forest exult. R.

They shall exult before the LORD, for he comes;
   for he comes to rule the earth.
He shall rule the world with justice
   and the peoples with his constancy. R.

Beloved:
The grace of God has appeared, saving all
    and training us to reject godless ways
        and worldly desires
    and to live temperately, justly, and devoutly in this age,
    as we await the blessed hope,
    the appearance of the glory of our great God
    and savior Jesus Christ,
    who gave himself for us to deliver us
        from all lawlessness
    and to cleanse for himself a people as his own,
    eager to do what is good.

ALLELUIA

LUKE 2:10–11

R. Alleluia, alleluia.

I proclaim to you good news of great joy:
today a Savior is born for us,
Christ the Lord.

GOSPEL

LUKE 2:1–14

TODAY A SAVIOR HAS
BEEN BORN FOR YOU.

In those days a decree went out from Caesar Augustus
    that the whole world should be enrolled.
This was the first enrollment,
    when Quirinius was governor of Syria.
So all went to be enrolled, each to his own town.
And Joseph too went up from Galilee
    from the town of Nazareth
    to Judea, to the city of David that is called Bethlehem,
    because he was of the house and family of David,
    to be enrolled with Mary, his betrothed,
        who was with child.

While they were there,
    the time came for her to have her child,
    and she gave birth to her firstborn son.
She wrapped him in swaddling clothes and laid him
        in a manger,
    because there was no room for them in the inn.

Now there were shepherds in that region
        living in the fields
    and keeping the night watch over their flock.
The angel of the Lord appeared to them
    and the glory of the Lord shone around them,
    and they were struck with great fear.
The angel said to them,
    "Do not be afraid;

for behold, I proclaim to you good news of great joy
    that will be for all the people.
For today in the city of David
    a savior has been born for you who is Christ and Lord.
And this will be a sign for you:
    you will find an infant wrapped in swaddling clothes
    and lying in a manger."

And suddenly there was a multitude of the heavenly host
    with the angel,
    praising God and saying:
    "Glory to God in the highest
    and on earth peace to those on whom his favor rests."

15ABC   THE NATIVITY OF THE LORD

DECEMBER 25 | MASS AT DAWN

FIRST READING

ISAIAH 62:11–12

BEHOLD, YOUR
SAVIOR COMES!

See, the LORD proclaims
    to the ends of the earth:
say to daughter Zion,
    your savior comes!
Here is his reward with him,
    his recompense before him.

They shall be called the holy people,
    the redeemed of the LORD,
and you shall be called "Frequented,"
    a city that is not forsaken.

**RESPONSORIAL
PSALM**

PSALM 97:1, 6, 11–12

R. *A light will shine on us this day: the Lord is born for us.*

The LORD is king; let the earth rejoice;
    let the many islands be glad.
The heavens proclaim his justice,
    and all peoples see his glory. R.

Light dawns for the just;
    and gladness, for the upright of heart.
Be glad in the LORD, you just,
    and give thanks to his holy name. R.

SECOND READING

TITUS 3:4–7

BECAUSE OF HIS MERCY,
HE SAVED US.

Beloved:
When the kindness and generous love
    of God our savior appeared,
not because of any righteous deeds we had done
    but because of his mercy,

he saved us through the bath of rebirth
  and renewal by the Holy Spirit,
whom he richly poured out on us
  through Jesus Christ our savior,
so that we might be justified by his grace
  and become heirs in hope of eternal life.

ALLELUIA

LUKE 2:14

R. Alleluia, alleluia.

Glory to God in the highest,
and on earth peace to those
on whom his favor rests.

GOSPEL

LUKE 2:15–20

THE SHEPHERDS FOUND
MARY AND JOSEPH
AND THE INFANT.

When the angels went away from them to heaven,
  the shepherds said to one another,
  "Let us go, then, to Bethlehem
to see this thing that has taken place,
  which the Lord has made known to us."

So they went in haste and found Mary and Joseph,
  and the infant lying in the manger.
When they saw this,
  they made known the message
  that had been told them about this child.
All who heard it were amazed
  by what had been told them by the shepherds.

And Mary kept all these things,
  reflecting on them in her heart.
Then the shepherds returned,
  glorifying and praising God
  for all they had heard and seen,
  just as it had been told to them.

16ABC   THE NATIVITY OF THE LORD
DECEMBER 25 | MASS DURING THE DAY

FIRST READING

ISAIAH 52:7–10

ALL THE ENDS OF THE
EARTH WILL BEHOLD THE
SALVATION OF OUR GOD.

How beautiful upon the mountains
  are the feet of him who brings glad tidings,
announcing peace, bearing good news,
  announcing salvation, and saying to Zion,
  "Your God is King!"

Hark! Your sentinels raise a cry,
  together they shout for joy,

for they see directly, before their eyes,
  the LORD restoring Zion.

Break out together in song,
  O ruins of Jerusalem!
For the LORD comforts his people,
  he redeems Jerusalem.
The LORD has bared his holy arm
  in the sight of all the nations;
all the ends of the earth will behold
  the salvation of our God.

RESPONSORIAL PSALM

PSALM 98:1, 2–3, 3–4, 5–6 (3c)

R. *All the ends of the earth have seen the saving power of God.*

[This psalm is found on page 442 (lectionary number 174).]

SECOND READING

HEBREWS 1:1–6

GOD HAS SPOKEN TO US THROUGH THE SON.

Brothers and sisters:
In times past, God spoke in partial and various ways
  to our ancestors through the prophets;
  in these last days, he has spoken to us through the Son,
  whom he made heir of all things
  and through whom he created the universe,
  who is the refulgence of his glory,
  the very imprint of his being,
  and who sustains all things by his mighty word.

When he had accomplished purification from sins,
  he took his seat at the right hand
    of the Majesty on high,
    as far superior to the angels
    as the name he has inherited is more excellent
      than theirs.

For to which of the angels did God ever say:
  "You are my son; this day I have begotten you"?
Or again:
  "I will be a father to him, and he shall be a son to me"?
And again, when he leads the firstborn into the world,
  he says:
  "Let all the angels of God worship him."

ALLELUIA

R. *Alleluia, alleluia.*

A holy day has dawned upon us.
Come, you nations, and adore the Lord.
For today a great light has come upon the earth. R.

GOSPEL

LONGER FORM
JOHN 1:1–18

SHORTER FORM
JOHN 1:1–5, 9–14

THE WORD BECAME FLESH
AND MADE HIS DWELLING
AMONG US.

[In the beginning was the Word,
    and the Word was with God,
    and the Word was God.
He was in the beginning with God.
All things came to be through him,
    and without him nothing came to be.
What came to be through him was life,
    and this life was the light of the human race;
    the light shines in the darkness,
    and the darkness has not overcome it.]

A man named John was sent from God.
He came for testimony, to testify to the light,
    so that all might believe through him.
He was not the light,
    but came to testify to the light.

[The true light, which enlightens everyone,
        was coming into the world.
He was in the world,
    and the world came to be through him,
    but the world did not know him.
He came to what was his own,
    but his own people did not accept him.

But to those who did accept him
    he gave power to become children of God,
    to those who believe in his name,
    who were born not by natural generation
    nor by human choice nor by a man's decision
    but of God.

And the Word became flesh
    and made his dwelling among us,
    and we saw his glory,
    the glory as of the Father's only Son,
    full of grace and truth.]

John testified to him and cried out, saying,
    "This was he of whom I said,
    'The one who is coming after me ranks ahead of me
    because he existed before me.'"

From his fullness we have all received,
    grace in place of grace,
    because while the law was given through Moses,
    grace and truth came through Jesus Christ.
No one has ever seen God.
The only Son, God, who is at the Father's side,
    has revealed him.

17A   THE HOLY FAMILY OF JESUS, MARY, AND JOSEPH

SUNDAY WITHIN THE OCTAVE OF CHRISTMAS

FIRST READING

SIRACH 3:2–6, 12–14

THOSE WHO FEAR THE
LORD HONOR THEIR
PARENTS.

♦

*When a Sunday does not occur
between December 25 and
January 1, this feast is celebrated
on December 30 with only
one reading before the Gospel.*

God sets a father in honor over his children;
  a mother's authority he confirms over her sons.
Whoever honors his father atones for sins,
  and preserves himself from them.
When he prays, he is heard;
  he stores up riches who reveres his mother.
Whoever honors his father is gladdened by children,
  and, when he prays, is heard.
Whoever reveres his father will live a long life;
  he who obeys his father brings comfort to his mother.

My son, take care of your father when he is old;
  grieve him not as long as he lives.
Even if his mind fail, be considerate of him;
  revile him not all the days of his life;
kindness to a father will not be forgotten,
  firmly planted against the debt of your sins
  —a house raised in justice to you.

**RESPONSORIAL
PSALM**

PSALM 128:1–2, 3, 4–5
(SEE 1)

R. Blessed are those who fear the Lord and walk
    in his ways.

Blessed is everyone who fears the LORD,
  who walks in his ways!
For you shall eat the fruit of your handiwork;
  blessed shall you be, and favored.   R.

Your wife shall be like a fruitful vine
  in the recesses of your home;
your children like olive plants
  around your table.   R.

Behold, thus is the man blessed
  who fears the LORD.
The LORD bless you from Zion:
  may you see the prosperity of Jerusalem
  all the days of your life.   R.

SECOND READING

LONGER FORM
COLOSSIANS 3:12–21

SHORTER FORM
COLOSSIANS 3:12–17

FAMILY LIFE IN THE LORD.

[Brothers and sisters:
Put on, as God's chosen ones, holy and beloved,
  heartfelt compassion, kindness, humility, gentleness,
    and patience,
  bearing with one another and forgiving one another,
  if one has a grievance against another;
  as the Lord has forgiven you, so must you also do.
And over all these put on love,
  that is, the bond of perfection.

And let the peace of Christ control your hearts,
the peace into which you were also called in one body.
And be thankful.

Let the word of Christ dwell in you richly,
as in all wisdom you teach and admonish one another,
singing psalms, hymns, and spiritual songs
with gratitude in your hearts to God.
And whatever you do, in word or in deed,
do everything in the name of the Lord Jesus,
giving thanks to God the Father through him.]

Wives, be subordinate to your husbands,
as is proper in the Lord.
Husbands, love your wives,
and avoid any bitterness toward them.
Children, obey your parents in everything,
for this is pleasing to the Lord.
Fathers, do not provoke your children,
so they may not become discouraged.

ALLELUIA

COLOSSIANS 3:15a, 16a

R. Alleluia, alleluia.

Let the peace of Christ control your hearts;
let the word of Christ dwell in you richly.   R.

GOSPEL

MATTHEW 2:13–15, 19–23

TAKE THE CHILD AND
HIS MOTHER, AND FLEE
INTO EGYPT.

When the magi had departed, behold,
the angel of the Lord appeared to Joseph in a dream
and said,
"Rise, take the child and his mother; flee to Egypt,
and stay there until I tell you.
Herod is going to search for the child to destroy him."
Joseph rose and took the child and his mother by night
and departed for Egypt.
He stayed there until the death of Herod,
that what the Lord had said through the prophet
might be fulfilled,
Out of Egypt I called my son.

When Herod had died, behold,
the angel of the Lord appeared in a dream
to Joseph in Egypt and said,
"Rise, take the child and his mother and go
to the land of Israel,
for those who sought the child's life are dead."
He rose, took the child and his mother,
and went to the land of Israel.

But when he heard that Archelaus was ruling over Judea
in place of his father Herod,
he was afraid to go back there.
And because he had been warned in a dream,
he departed for the region of Galilee.
He went and dwelt in a town called Nazareth,
so that what had been spoken through the prophets
might be fulfilled,
He shall be called a Nazorean.

17B   THE HOLY FAMILY OF JESUS, MARY, AND JOSEPH
SUNDAY WITHIN THE OCTAVE OF CHRISTMAS

FIRST READING

GENESIS 15:1–6; 21:1–3

YOUR OWN ISSUE SHALL
BE YOUR HEIR.

◆

*The First Reading from Year A
and/or the Second Reading from
Year A may be used.*

◆

*When a Sunday does not occur
between December 25 and
January 1, this feast is celebrated
on December 30 with only one
reading before the Gospel.*

The word of the LORD came to Abram in a vision, saying:
"Fear not, Abram!
I am your shield;
I will make your reward very great."
But Abram said,
"O Lord GOD, what good will your gifts be,
if I keep on being childless
and have as my heir the steward of my house, Eliezer?"
Abram continued,
"See, you have given me no offspring,
and so one of my servants will be my heir."
Then the word of the LORD came to him:
"No, that one shall not be your heir;
your own issue shall be your heir."

The LORD took Abram outside and said,
"Look up at the sky and count the stars, if you can.
Just so," he added, "shall your descendants be."
Abram put his faith in the LORD,
who credited it to him as an act of righteousness.

The LORD took note of Sarah as he had said he would;
he did for her as he had promised.
Sarah became pregnant and bore Abraham a son
in his old age,
at the set time that God had stated.
Abraham gave the name Isaac to this son of his
whom Sarah bore him.

**RESPONSORIAL
PSALM**

PSALM 105:1–2, 3–4, 5–6,
8–9 (7a, 8a)

R. The Lord remembers his covenant for ever.

*Give thanks to the LORD, invoke his name;
make known among the nations his deeds.*

Sing to him, sing his praise,
proclaim all his wondrous deeds. R.

Glory in his holy name;
rejoice, O hearts that seek the LORD!
Look to the LORD in his strength;
constantly seek his face. R.

You descendants of Abraham, his servants,
sons of Jacob, his chosen ones!
He, the LORD, is our God;
throughout the earth his judgments prevail. R.

He remembers forever his covenant
which he made binding for a thousand generations
which he entered into with Abraham
and by his oath to Isaac. R.

SECOND READING

HEBREWS 11:8, 11–12, 17–19

THE FAITH OF ABRAHAM,
SARAH, AND ISAAC.

Brothers and sisters:
By faith Abraham obeyed when he was called to go
    out to a place
that he was to receive as an inheritance;
he went out, not knowing where he was to go.

By faith he received power to generate,
even though he was past the normal age
— and Sarah herself was sterile —
for he thought that the one who had made the promise
    was trustworthy.
So it was that there came forth from one man,
himself as good as dead,
descendants as numerous as the stars in the sky
and as countless as the sands on the seashore.

By faith Abraham, when put to the test, offered up Isaac,
and he who had received the promises was ready
    to offer his only son,
of whom it was said,
Through Isaac descendants shall bear your name.
He reasoned that God was able to raise
    even from the dead,
and he received Isaac back as a symbol.

ALLELUIA

HEBREWS 1:1–2

R. Alleluia, alleluia.

In the past God spoke to our ancestors through the prophets;
in these last days, he has spoken to us through the Son. R.

GOSPEL

LONGER FORM
LUKE 2:22–40

SHORTER FORM
LUKE 2:22, 39–40

THE CHILD GREW
AND BECAME STRONG,
FILLED WITH WISDOM.

[When the days were completed for their purification
according to the law of Moses,
they took him up to Jerusalem
to present him to the Lord,]
just as it is written in the law of the Lord,
*Every male that opens the womb shall be consecrated
to the Lord,*
and to offer the sacrifice of
a pair of turtledoves or two young pigeons,
in accordance with the dictate in the law of the Lord.

Now there was a man in Jerusalem whose name
was Simeon.
This man was righteous and devout,
awaiting the consolation of Israel,
and the Holy Spirit was upon him.
It had been revealed to him by the Holy Spirit
that he should not see death
before he had seen the Christ of the Lord.

He came in the Spirit into the temple;
and when the parents brought in the child Jesus
to perform the custom of the law in regard to him,
he took him into his arms and blessed God, saying:
"Now, Master, you may let your servant go in peace,
according to your word,
for my eyes have seen your salvation,
which you prepared in sight of all the peoples,
a light for revelation to the Gentiles,
and glory for your people Israel."

The child's father and mother were amazed
at what was said about him;
and Simeon blessed them and said to Mary his mother,
"Behold, this child is destined
for the fall and rise of many in Israel,
and to be a sign that will be contradicted
— and you yourself a sword will pierce —
so that the thoughts of many hearts may be revealed."

There was also a prophetess, Anna,
the daughter of Phanuel, of the tribe of Asher.
She was advanced in years,
having lived seven years with her husband
after her marriage,
and then as a widow until she was eighty-four.
She never left the temple,
but worshiped night and day with fasting and prayer.

And coming forward at that very time,
  she gave thanks to God and spoke about the child
  to all who were awaiting the redemption of Jerusalem.

[When they had fulfilled all the prescriptions
  of the law of the Lord,
  they returned to Galilee,
  to their own town of Nazareth.
The child grew and became strong, filled with wisdom;
  and the favor of God was upon him.]

17C   THE HOLY FAMILY OF JESUS, MARY, AND JOSEPH
SUNDAY WITHIN THE OCTAVE OF CHRISTMAS

FIRST READING

1 SAMUEL 1:20–22, 24–28

SAMUEL, AS LONG AS
HE LIVES, SHALL BE
DEDICATED TO THE LORD.

◆

*The First Reading from Year A
and/or the Second Reading from
Year A may be used.*

◆

*When a Sunday does not occur
between December 25 and
January 1, this feast is celebrated
on December 30 with only one
reading before the Gospel.*

In those days Hannah conceived,
  and at the end of her term bore a son
whom she called Samuel, since she had asked
  the Lord for him.
The next time her husband Elkanah was going up
  with the rest of his household
  to offer the customary sacrifice to the Lord
    and to fulfill his vows,
  Hannah did not go, explaining to her husband,
"Once the child is weaned,
I will take him to appear before the Lord
  and to remain there forever;
I will offer him as a perpetual nazirite."

Once Samuel was weaned, Hannah brought him up
    with her,
  along with a three-year-old bull,
  an ephah of flour, and a skin of wine,
  and presented him at the temple of the Lord in Shiloh.
After the boy's father had sacrificed the young bull,
  Hannah, his mother, approached Eli and said:
  "Pardon, my lord!
As you live, my lord,
  I am the woman who stood near you here,
    praying to the Lord.

"I prayed for this child, and the Lord granted my request.
Now I, in turn, give him to the Lord;
  as long as he lives, he shall be dedicated to the Lord."
Hannah left Samuel there.

RESPONSORIAL PSALM

PSALM 84:2–3, 5–6, 9–10
(SEE 5a)

R. Blessed are they who dwell in your house, O Lord.

How lovely is your dwelling place, O LORD of hosts!
  My soul yearns and pines for the courts of the LORD.
My heart and my flesh cry out for the living God.   R.

Happy they who dwell in your house!
  Continually they praise you.
Happy the men whose strength you are!
  Their hearts are set upon the pilgrimage.   R.

O LORD of hosts, hear our prayer;
  hearken, O God of Jacob!
O God, behold our shield,
  and look upon the face of your anointed.   R.

SECOND READING

1 JOHN 3:1–2, 21–24

WE ARE CALLED CHILDREN
OF GOD. AND SO WE ARE.

Beloved:
See what love the Father has bestowed on us
  that we may be called the children of God.
And so we are.
The reason the world does not know us
  is that it did not know him.
Beloved, we are God's children now;
  what we shall be has not yet been revealed.
We do know that when it is revealed we shall be like him,
  for we shall see him as he is.

Beloved, if our hearts do not condemn us,
  we have confidence in God and receive from him
    whatever we ask,
  because we keep his commandments
    and do what pleases him.
And his commandment is this:
  we should believe in the name of his Son, Jesus Christ,
  and love one another just as he commanded us.
Those who keep his commandments remain in him,
  and he in them,
  and the way we know that he remains in us
  is from the Spirit he gave us.

ALLELUIA

SEE ACTS 16:14b

R. Alleluia, alleluia.

Open our hearts, O Lord,
to listen to the words of your Son.   R.

GOSPEL

LUKE 2:41–52

HIS PARENTS FOUND JESUS
SITTING IN THE MIDST
OF THE TEACHERS.

Each year Jesus' parents went to Jerusalem for the feast
     of Passover,
   and when he was twelve years old,
   they went up according to festival custom.

After they had completed its days, as they were returning,
   the boy Jesus remained behind in Jerusalem,
   but his parents did not know it.
Thinking that he was in the caravan,
   they journeyed for a day
   and looked for him among their relatives
      and acquaintances,
   but not finding him,
   they returned to Jerusalem to look for him.

After three days they found him in the temple,
   sitting in the midst of the teachers,
   listening to them and asking them questions,
   and all who heard him were astounded
   at his understanding and his answers.
When his parents saw him,
   they were astonished,
   and his mother said to him,
   "Son, why have you done this to us?
Your father and I have been looking for you
      with great anxiety."
And he said to them,
   "Why were you looking for me?
Did you not know that I must be in my Father's house?"
But they did not understand what he said to them.

He went down with them and came to Nazareth,
   and was obedient to them;
   and his mother kept all these things in her heart.
And Jesus advanced in wisdom and age and favor
   before God and man.

18ABC   THE BLESSED VIRGIN MARY, MOTHER OF GOD

JANUARY 1 | THE OCTAVE DAY OF CHRISTMAS

FIRST READING

NUMBERS 6:22–27

THEY SHALL INVOKE
MY NAME UPON THE
ISRAELITES, AND
I WILL BLESS THEM.

The Lord said to Moses:
"Speak to Aaron and his sons and tell them:
   This is how you shall bless the Israelites.

"Say to them:
   The Lord bless you and keep you!
   The Lord let his face shine upon you,
      and be gracious to you!

The LORD look upon you kindly
and give you peace!

"So shall they invoke my name upon the Israelites,
and I will bless them."

RESPONSORIAL PSALM

PSALM 67:2–3, 5, 6, 8 (2a)

R. May God bless us in his mercy.

May God have pity on us and bless us;
   may he let his face shine upon us.
So may your way be known upon earth;
   among all nations, your salvation.   R.

May the nations be glad and exult
   because you rule the peoples in equity;
   the nations on the earth you guide.   R.

May the peoples praise you, O God;
   may all the peoples praise you!
May God bless us,
   and may all the ends of the earth fear him!   R.

SECOND READING

GALATIANS 4:4–7

GOD SENT HIS SON,
BORN OF A WOMAN.

Brothers and sisters:
When the fullness of time had come, God sent his Son,
   born of a woman, born under the law,
   to ransom those under the law,
   so that we might receive adoption as sons.

As proof that you are sons,
   God sent the Spirit of his Son into our hearts,
   crying out, "Abba, Father!"
So you are no longer a slave but a son,
   and if a son then also an heir, through God.

ALLELUIA

HEBREWS 1:1–2

R. Alleluia, alleluia.

In the past God spoke to our ancestors
   through the prophets;
in these last days, he has spoken to us
   through the Son.   R.

GOSPEL

LUKE 2:16–21

THEY FOUND MARY AND
JOSEPH AND THE INFANT.
WHEN THE EIGHT DAYS
WERE COMPLETED,
HE WAS NAMED JESUS.

The shepherds went in haste to Bethlehem
   and found Mary and Joseph,
   and the infant lying in the manger.
When they saw this,
   they made known the message
   that had been told them about this child.

All who heard it were amazed
   by what had been told them by the shepherds.

And Mary kept all these things,
   reflecting on them in her heart.
Then the shepherds returned,
   glorifying and praising God
   for all they had heard and seen,
   just as it had been told to them.

When eight days were completed for his circumcision,
   he was named Jesus, the name given him by the angel
   before he was conceived in the womb.

19ABC   SECOND SUNDAY AFTER CHRISTMAS

FIRST READING

SIRACH 24:1–2, 8–12

THE WISDOM OF GOD
LIVES IN HIS PEOPLE.

Wisdom sings her own praises and is honored in God,
   before her own people she boasts;
in the assembly of the Most High she opens her mouth,
   in the presence of his power she declares her worth;
in the midst of her people she is exalted,
   in holy fullness she is admired;
in the multitude of the chosen she finds praise,
   and among the blessed she is blessed.

"The Creator of all commanded and said to me,
   and he who formed me chose the spot for my tent,
saying, 'In Jacob make your dwelling,
   in Israel your inheritance,
   and among my chosen put down your roots.'

"Before all ages, in the beginning, he created me,
   and through all ages I shall not cease to be.
In the holy tent I ministered before him,
   and in Zion I fixed my abode.

"Thus in the chosen city I have rested,
   in Jerusalem is my domain.
I have struck root among a glorious people,
   in the portion of the LORD, his heritage;
   and in the company of the holy ones do I linger."

**RESPONSORIAL
PSALM**

PSALM 147:12–13, 14–15,
19–20 (JOHN 1:4)

R. The Word of God became man and lived among us.
   or:
R. Alleluia.

Glorify the LORD, O Jerusalem;
   praise your God, O Zion.

For he has strengthened the bars of your gates;
 he has blessed your children within you.   R.

He has granted peace in your borders;
 with the best of wheat he fills you.
He sends forth his command to the earth;
 swiftly runs his word!   R.

He has proclaimed his word to Jacob,
 his statutes and his ordinances to Israel.
He has not done thus for any other nation;
 his ordinances he has not made known to them. Alleluia.   R.

SECOND READING

EPHESIANS 1:3–6, 15–18

GOD DESTINED US FOR
ADOPTION TO HIMSELF
THROUGH JESUS CHRIST.

Blessed be the God and Father of our Lord Jesus Christ,
   who has blessed us in Christ
   with every spiritual blessing in the heavens,
   as he chose us in him, before the foundation
      of the world,
   to be holy and without blemish before him.
In love he destined us for adoption to himself
      through Jesus Christ,
   in accord with the favor of his will,
   for the praise of the glory of his grace
   that he granted us in the beloved.

Therefore, I, too, hearing of your faith in the Lord Jesus
   and of your love for all the holy ones,
   do not cease giving thanks for you,
   remembering you in my prayers,
   that the God of our Lord Jesus Christ,
      the Father of glory,
   may give you a spirit of wisdom and revelation
   resulting in knowledge of him.

May the eyes of your hearts be enlightened,
   that you may know what is the hope that belongs
      to his call,
   what are the riches of glory
   in his inheritance among the holy ones.

ALLELUIA

SEE 1 TIMOTHY 3:16

R. Alleluia, alleluia.

Glory to you, O Christ, proclaimed to the Gentiles;
Glory to you, O Christ, believed in throughout the world!

GOSPEL

LONGER FORM
JOHN 1:1–18

SHORTER FORM
JOHN 1:1–5, 9–14

THE WORD BECAME FLESH
AND MADE HIS DWELLING
AMONG US.

[This reading is found on page 36 (lectionary number 16).]

20ABC   THE EPIPHANY OF THE LORD
JANUARY 6

FIRST READING

ISAIAH 60:1–6

THE GLORY OF THE LORD
SHINES UPON YOU.

Rise up in splendor, Jerusalem! Your light has come,
   the glory of the LORD shines upon you.
See, darkness covers the earth,
   and thick clouds cover the peoples;
but upon you the LORD shines,
   and over you appears his glory.

Nations shall walk by your light,
   and kings by your shining radiance.
Raise your eyes and look about;
   they all gather and come to you:
your sons come from afar,
   and your daughters in the arms of their nurses.

Then you shall be radiant at what you see,
   your heart shall throb and overflow,
for the riches of the sea shall be emptied out before you,
   the wealth of nations shall be brought to you.
Caravans of camels shall fill you,
   dromedaries from Midian and Ephah;
all from Sheba shall come
   bearing gold and frankincense,
   and proclaiming the praises of the LORD.

**RESPONSORIAL
PSALM**

PSALM 72:1–2, 7–8, 10–11,
12–13 (SEE 11)

R. Lord, every nation on earth will adore you.

[This psalm is found on page 442 (lectionary number 174).]

EPHESIANS 3:2–3a, 5–6

NOW IT HAS BEEN
REVEALED THAT THE
GENTILES ARE COHEIRS
OF THE PROMISE.

Brothers and sisters:
You have heard of the stewardship of God's grace
   that was given to me for your benefit,
      namely, that the mystery was made known to me
         by revelation.

It was not made known to people in other generations
   as it has now been revealed
   to his holy apostles and prophets by the Spirit:
   that the Gentiles are coheirs,
      members of the same body,
   and copartners in the promise in Christ Jesus
      through the gospel.

R. Alleluia, alleluia.

We saw his star at its rising
and have come to do him homage.   R.

GOSPEL

MATTHEW 2:1–12

WE SAW HIS STAR AT ITS
RISING AND HAVE COME
TO DO HIM HOMAGE.

When Jesus was born in Bethlehem of Judea,
   in the days of King Herod,
      behold, magi from the east arrived in Jerusalem, saying,
      "Where is the newborn king of the Jews?
We saw his star at its rising
   and have come to do him homage."

When King Herod heard this,
   he was greatly troubled,
   and all Jerusalem with him.
Assembling all the chief priests and the scribes
      of the people,
   he inquired of them where the Christ was to be born.
They said to him, "In Bethlehem of Judea,
   for thus it has been written through the prophet:
   And you, Bethlehem, land of Judah,
   are by no means least among the rulers of Judah;
   since from you shall come a ruler,
   who is to shepherd my people Israel."

Then Herod called the magi secretly
   and ascertained from them the time
      of the star's appearance.
He sent them to Bethlehem and said,
   "Go and search diligently for the child.
When you have found him, bring me word,
   that I too may go and do him homage."

After their audience with the king they set out.
And behold, the star that they had seen at its rising
  preceded them,
    until it came and stopped over the place
      where the child was.
They were overjoyed at seeing the star,
    and on entering the house
      they saw the child with Mary his mother.

They prostrated themselves and did him homage.
Then they opened their treasures
    and offered him gifts of gold, frankincense, and myrrh.

And having been warned in a dream not to return
    to Herod,
    they departed for their country by another way.

21A   THE BAPTISM OF THE LORD
SUNDAY AFTER JANUARY 6 | FIRST SUNDAY IN ORDINARY TIME

FIRST READING

ISAIAH 42:1–4, 6–7

BEHOLD MY SERVANT
WITH WHOM I AM
WELL PLEASED.

◆

*In dioceses where the Epiphany is
transferred to a Sunday that falls
on January 7 or 8, the Baptism of
the Lord is transferred to the
Monday immediately following.
Only one reading before the
Gospel is used.*

Thus says the LORD:
Here is my servant whom I uphold,
    my chosen one with whom I am pleased,
upon whom I have put my spirit;
    he shall bring forth justice to the nations,
not crying out, not shouting,
    not making his voice heard in the street.
A bruised reed he shall not break,
    and a smoldering wick he shall not quench,
until he establishes justice on the earth;
    the coastlands will wait for his teaching.

I, the LORD, have called you for the victory of justice,
    I have grasped you by the hand;
I formed you, and set you
    as a covenant of the people,
    a light for the nations,
to open the eyes of the blind,
    to bring out prisoners from confinement,
    and from the dungeon, those who live in darkness.

**RESPONSORIAL
PSALM**

PSALM 29:1–2, 3–4, 3,
9–10 (11b)

R. *The Lord will bless his people with peace.*

*Give to the LORD, you sons of God,
    give to the LORD glory and praise,
Give to the LORD the glory due his name;
    adore the LORD in holy attire.   R.*

The voice of the Lord is over the waters,
the Lord, over vast waters.
The voice of the Lord is mighty;
the voice of the Lord is majestic.   R.

The God of glory thunders,
and in his temple all say, "Glory!"
The Lord is enthroned above the flood;
the Lord is enthroned as king forever.   R.

SECOND READING

ACTS 10:34–38

GOD ANOINTED HIM
WITH THE HOLY SPIRIT.

Peter proceeded to speak to those gathered
in the house of Cornelius, saying:

"In truth, I see that God shows no partiality.
Rather, in every nation whoever fears him
and acts uprightly
is acceptable to him.
You know the word that he sent to the Israelites
as he proclaimed peace through Jesus Christ,
who is Lord of all,
what has happened all over Judea,
beginning in Galilee after the baptism
that John preached,
how God anointed Jesus of Nazareth
with the Holy Spirit and power.
He went about doing good
and healing all those oppressed by the devil,
for God was with him."

ALLELUIA

SEE MARK 9:7

R. Alleluia, alleluia.

The heavens were opened and the voice
of the Father thundered:
This is my beloved Son, listen to him.   R.

GOSPEL

MATTHEW 3:13–17

AFTER JESUS WAS
BAPTIZED, HE SAW THE
SPIRIT OF GOD COMING
UPON HIM.

Jesus came from Galilee to John at the Jordan
to be baptized by him.
John tried to prevent him, saying,
"I need to be baptized by you,
and yet you are coming to me?"

Jesus said to him in reply,
"Allow it now, for thus it is fitting for us
to fulfill all righteousness."
Then he allowed him.

After Jesus was baptized,
he came up from the water and behold,

the heavens were opened for him,
and he saw the Spirit of God descending like a dove
and coming upon him.
And a voice came from the heavens, saying,
"This is my beloved Son, with whom I am
well pleased."

21B   THE BAPTISM OF THE LORD

SUNDAY AFTER JANUARY 6 | FIRST SUNDAY IN ORDINARY TIME

FIRST READING

ISAIAH 55:1–11

COME TO THE WATERS:
LISTEN, THAT YOU MAY
HAVE LIFE.

♦

*The First Reading from Year A
and/or the Second Reading from
Year A may be used.*

♦

*In dioceses where the Epiphany
is transferred to a Sunday that falls
on January 7 or 8, the Baptism
of the Lord is transferred to the
Monday immediately following.
Only one reading before the
Gospel is used.*

Thus says the LORD:
All you who are thirsty,
    come to the water!
You who have no money,
    come, receive grain and eat;
come, without paying and without cost,
    drink wine and milk!
Why spend your money for what is not bread,
    your wages for what fails to satisfy?
Heed me, and you shall eat well,
    you shall delight in rich fare.
Come to me heedfully,
    listen, that you may have life.
I will renew with you the everlasting covenant,
    the benefits assured to David.

As I made him a witness to the peoples,
    a leader and commander of nations,
so shall you summon a nation you knew not,
    and nations that knew you not shall run to you,
because of the LORD, your God,
    the Holy One of Israel, who has glorified you.

Seek the LORD while he may be found,
    call him while he is near.
Let the scoundrel forsake his way,
    and the wicked man his thoughts;
let him turn to the LORD for mercy;
    to our God, who is generous in forgiving.
For my thoughts are not your thoughts,
    nor are your ways my ways, says the LORD.
As high as the heavens are above the earth
    so high are my ways above your ways
    and my thoughts above your thoughts.

For just as from the heavens
    the rain and snow come down

and do not return there
     till they have watered the earth,
     making it fertile and fruitful,
giving seed to the one who sows
     and bread to the one who eats,
so shall my word be
     that goes forth from my mouth;
my word shall not return to me void,
     but shall do my will,
     achieving the end for which I sent it.

**RESPONSORIAL
PSALM**

ISAIAH 12:2–3, 4bcd, 5–6 (3)

R. *You will draw water joyfully from the springs of salvation.*

God indeed is my savior;
  I am confident and unafraid.
My strength and my courage is the LORD,
  and he has been my savior.
With joy you will draw water
  at the fountain of salvation.   R.

Give thanks to the LORD, *acclaim his name;*
  among the nations make known his deeds,
  proclaim how exalted is his name.   R.

Sing praise to the LORD *for his glorious achievement;*
  let this be known throughout all the earth.
Shout with exultation, O city of Zion,
  for great in your midst
  is the Holy One of Israel!   R.

SECOND READING

1 JOHN 5:1–9

THE SPIRIT AND THE
WATER AND THE BLOOD.

Beloved:
Everyone who believes that Jesus is the Christ
     is begotten by God,
     and everyone who loves the Father
     loves also the one begotten by him.
In this way we know that we love the children of God
     when we love God and obey his commandments.

For the love of God is this,
     that we keep his commandments.
And his commandments are not burdensome,
     for whoever is begotten by God conquers the world.
And the victory that conquers the world is our faith.

Who indeed is the victor over the world
     but the one who believes that Jesus is the Son of God?

This is the one who came through water and blood,
     Jesus Christ,
     not by water alone, but by water and blood.

The Spirit is the one who testifies,
 and the Spirit is truth.
So there are three that testify,
 the Spirit, the water and the blood,
 and the three are of one accord.
If we accept human testimony,
 the testimony of God is surely greater.
Now the testimony of God is this,
 that he has testified on behalf of his Son.

ALLELUIA

SEE JOHN 1:29

R. Alleluia, alleluia.

John saw Jesus approaching him, and said:
Behold the Lamb of God who takes away the sin of the world.   R.

GOSPEL

MARK 1:7–11

YOU ARE MY BELOVED SON;
WITH YOU I AM WELL
PLEASED.

This is what John the Baptist proclaimed:
 "One mightier than I is coming after me.
I am not worthy to stoop and loosen the thongs
  of his sandals.
I have baptized you with water;
 he will baptize you with the Holy Spirit."

It happened in those days that Jesus came from
  Nazareth of Galilee
 and was baptized in the Jordan by John.
On coming up out of the water he saw the heavens
  being torn open
 and the Spirit, like a dove, descending upon him.

And a voice came from the heavens,
 "You are my beloved Son; with you I am well pleased."

21C THE BAPTISM OF THE LORD
SUNDAY AFTER JANUARY 6 | FIRST SUNDAY IN ORDINARY TIME

FIRST READING

ISAIAH 40:1–5, 9–11

THE GLORY OF THE LORD
SHALL BE REVEALED AND
ALL PEOPLE SHALL SEE IT.

◆

*The First Reading from Year A
and/or the Second Reading from
Year A may be used.*

◆

*In dioceses where the Epiphany
is transferred to a Sunday that falls
on January 7 or 8, the Baptism
of the Lord is transferred to the
Monday immediately following.
Only one reading before the
Gospel is used.*

RESPONSORIAL PSALM

PSALM 104:1b–2, 3–4, 24–25,
27–28, 29–30 (1)

[This reading is found on page 10 (lectionary number 5).]

R. *O bless the Lord, my soul.*

*O Lord, my God, you are great indeed!
You are clothed with majesty and glory,
    robed in light as with a cloak.
You have spread out the heavens like a tent-cloth.* R.

*You have constructed your palace upon the waters.
    You make the clouds your chariot;
    you travel on the wings of the wind.
You make the winds your messengers,
    and flaming fire your ministers.* R.

*How manifold are your works, O Lord!
    In wisdom you have wrought them all —
the earth is full of your creatures;
    the sea also, great and wide,
in which are schools without number
    of living things both small and great.* R.

*They look to you to give them food in due time.
    When you give it to them, they gather it;
when you open your hand,
    they are filled with good things.* R.

*If you take away their breath,
    they perish and return to the dust.
When you send forth your spirit, they are created,
    and you renew the face of the earth.* R.

SECOND READING

TITUS 2:11–14; 3:4–7

JESUS CHRIST SAVED
US THROUGH THE BATH
OF REBIRTH AND RENEWAL
BY THE HOLY SPIRIT.

Beloved:
The grace of God has appeared, saving all
    and training us to reject godless ways
        and worldly desires
    and to live temperately, justly and devoutly in this age,
    as we await the blessed hope,
    the appearance of the glory of our great God
    and savior Jesus Christ,
    who gave himself for us to deliver us from all lawlessness
    and to cleanse for himself a people as his own,
    eager to do what is good.

When the kindness and generous love
    of God our savior appeared,
not because of any righteous deeds we had done
    but because of his mercy,
he saved us through the bath of rebirth
    and renewal by the Holy Spirit,
whom he richly poured out on us
    through Jesus Christ our savior,
so that we might be justified by his grace
    and become heirs in hope of eternal life.

ALLELUIA

SEE LUKE 3:16

R. Alleluia, alleluia.

John said: One mightier than I is coming;
he will baptize you with the Holy Spirit and with fire.   R.

GOSPEL

LUKE 3:15–16, 21–22

WHEN JESUS HAD BEEN
BAPTIZED AND WAS
PRAYING, HEAVEN WAS
OPENED.

◆

*The readings for the Sundays in
Ordinary Time (see n. 64) begin
on the Sunday following the feast
of the Baptism of the Lord.*

The people were filled with expectation,
    and all were asking in their hearts
        whether John might be the Christ.
John answered them all, saying,
    "I am baptizing you with water,
    but one mightier than I is coming.
I am not worthy to loosen the thongs of his sandals.
He will baptize you with the Holy Spirit and fire."

After all the people had been baptized
    and Jesus also had been baptized and was praying,
    heaven was opened and the Holy Spirit
        descended upon him
    in bodily form like a dove.
And a voice came from heaven,
    "You are my beloved Son;
    with you I am well pleased."

SEASON OF LENT

22A FIRST SUNDAY OF LENT

FIRST READING

GENESIS 2:7–9; 3:1–7

THE CREATION OF OUR
FIRST PARENTS, AND SIN.

The LORD God formed man out of the clay of the ground
    and blew into his nostrils the breath of life,
    and so man became a living being.
Then the LORD God planted a garden in Eden,
        in the east,
    and placed there the man whom he had formed.
Out of the ground the LORD God made various trees grow
    that were delightful to look at and good for food,
    with the tree of life in the middle of the garden
    and the tree of the knowledge of good and evil.

Now the serpent was the most cunning of all the animals
    that the LORD God had made.
The serpent asked the woman,
    "Did God really tell you not to eat
    from any of the trees in the garden?"
The woman answered the serpent:
    "We may eat of the fruit of the trees in the garden;
    it is only about the fruit of the tree
    in the middle of the garden that God said,
    'You shall not eat it or even touch it, lest you die.'"
But the serpent said to the woman:
    "You certainly will not die!
No, God knows well that the moment you eat of it
    your eyes will be opened and you will be like gods
    who know what is good and what is evil."
The woman saw that the tree was good for food,
    pleasing to the eyes, and desirable for gaining wisdom.
So she took some of its fruit and ate it;
    and she also gave some to her husband,
        who was with her,
    and he ate it.

Then the eyes of both of them were opened,
    and they realized that they were naked;
    so they sewed fig leaves together
    and made loincloths for themselves.

**RESPONSORIAL
PSALM**

PSALM 51:3–4, 5–6, 12–13, 17
(SEE 3a)

R. Be merciful, O Lord, for we have sinned.

[This psalm is found on page 443 (lectionary number 174).]

LONGER FORM
ROMANS 5:12–19

SHORTER FORM
ROMANS 5:12, 17–19

WHERE SIN INCREASED,
THERE GRACE INCREASED
ALL THE MORE.

[Brothers and sisters:
Through one man sin entered the world,
    and through sin, death,
    and thus death came to all men, inasmuch
        as all sinned] —
    for up to the time of the law, sin was in the world,
    though sin is not accounted when there is no law.

But death reigned from Adam to Moses,
    even over those who did not sin
    after the pattern of the trespass of Adam,
    who is the type of the one who was to come.

But the gift is not like the transgression.
For if by the transgression of the one, the many died,
    how much more did the grace of God
    and the gracious gift of the one man Jesus Christ
    overflow for the many.
And the gift is not like the result of the one who sinned.
For after one sin there was the judgment
        that brought condemnation;
    but the gift, after many transgressions,
        brought acquittal.

[For if, by the transgression of the one,
    death came to reign through that one,
    how much more will those who receive
        the abundance of grace
    and of the gift of justification
    come to reign in life through the one Jesus Christ.

In conclusion, just as through one transgression
    condemnation came upon all,
    so, through one righteous act,
    acquittal and life came to all.
For just as through the disobedience of the one man
    the many were made sinners,
    so, through the obedience of the one,
    the many will be made righteous.]

**VERSE BEFORE
THE GOSPEL**

MATTHEW 4:4b

*One does not live on bread alone,
but on every word that comes forth
    from the mouth of God.*

GOSPEL

MATTHEW 4:1–11

JESUS FASTED FOR FORTY
DAYS AND FORTY NIGHTS
AND WAS TEMPTED.

At that time Jesus was led by the Spirit into the desert
    to be tempted by the devil.
He fasted for forty days and forty nights,
    and afterwards he was hungry.
The tempter approached and said to him,
    "If you are the Son of God,
    command that these stones become loaves of bread."

He said in reply,
    "It is written:
    One does not live on bread alone,
    but on every word that comes forth
    from the mouth of God."

Then the devil took him to the holy city,
    and made him stand on the parapet of the temple,
    and said to him, "If you are the Son of God,
        throw yourself down.
For it is written:
    He will command his angels concerning you
    and with their hands they will support you,
    lest you dash your foot against a stone."
Jesus answered him,
    "Again it is written,
    You shall not put the Lord, your God, to the test."

Then the devil took him up to a very high mountain,
    and showed him all the kingdoms of the world
        in their magnificence,
    and he said to him, "All these I shall give to you,
    if you will prostrate yourself and worship me."
At this, Jesus said to him,
    "Get away, Satan!
It is written:
    The Lord, your God, shall you worship
    and him alone shall you serve."

Then the devil left him and, behold,
    angels came and ministered to him.

23B   FIRST SUNDAY OF LENT

FIRST READING

GENESIS 9:8–15

GOD'S COVENANT WITH
NOAH WHEN HE WAS
DELIVERED FROM THE
FLOOD.

God said to Noah and to his sons with him:
"See, I am now establishing my covenant with you
    and your descendants after you
    and with every living creature that was with you:

all the birds, and the various tame and wild animals
that were with you and came out of the ark.
I will establish my covenant with you,
that never again shall all bodily creatures be destroyed
by the waters of a flood;
there shall not be another flood to devastate the earth."

God added:
"This is the sign that I am giving for all ages to come,
of the covenant between me and you
and every living creature with you:
I set my bow in the clouds to serve as a sign
of the covenant between me and the earth.
When I bring clouds over the earth,
and the bow appears in the clouds,
I will recall the covenant I have made
between me and you and all living beings,
so that the waters shall never again become a flood
to destroy all mortal beings."

RESPONSORIAL PSALM

PSALM 25:4–5, 6–7, 8–9
(SEE 10)

R. Your ways, O Lord, are love and truth to those
who keep your covenant.

Your ways, O Lord, make known to me;
teach me your paths,
guide me in your truth and teach me,
for you are God my savior.   R.

Remember that your compassion, O Lord,
and your love are from of old.
In your kindness remember me,
because of your goodness, O Lord.   R.

Good and upright is the Lord,
thus he shows sinners the way.
He guides the humble to justice,
and he teaches the humble his way.   R.

SECOND READING

1 PETER 3:18–22

THE WATER OF THE FLOOD
PREFIGURED BAPTISM,
WHICH SAVES YOU NOW.

Beloved:
Christ suffered for sins once,
the righteous for the sake of the unrighteous,
that he might lead you to God.
Put to death in the flesh,
he was brought to life in the Spirit.
In it he also went to preach to the spirits in prison,
who had once been disobedient
while God patiently waited in the days of Noah
during the building of the ark,
in which a few persons, eight in all,
were saved through water.

This prefigured baptism, which saves you now.
It is not a removal of dirt from the body
   but an appeal to God for a clear conscience,
   through the resurrection of Jesus Christ,
   who has gone into heaven
   and is at the right hand of God,
   with angels, authorities and powers subject to him.

VERSE BEFORE THE GOSPEL

MATTHEW 4:4b

One does not live on bread alone,
but on every word that comes forth from the mouth of God.

GOSPEL

MARK 1:12–15

JESUS WAS TEMPTED BY
SATAN, AND THE ANGELS
MINISTERED TO HIM.

The Spirit drove Jesus out into the desert,
   and he remained in the desert for forty days,
      tempted by Satan.
He was among wild beasts,
   and the angels ministered to him.

After John had been arrested,
   Jesus came to Galilee proclaiming the gospel of God:
"This is the time of fulfillment.
The kingdom of God is at hand.
Repent, and believe in the gospel."

24C   FIRST SUNDAY OF LENT

FIRST READING

DEUTERONOMY 26:4–10

THE CONFESSION OF FAITH
OF THE CHOSEN PEOPLE.

Moses spoke to the people, saying:
   "The priest shall receive the basket from you
   and shall set it in front of the altar of the LORD,
      your God.

"Then you shall declare before the LORD, your God,
   'My father was a wandering Aramean
   who went down to Egypt with a small household
   and lived there as an alien.
But there he became a nation
   great, strong and numerous.
When the Egyptians maltreated and oppressed us,
   imposing hard labor upon us,
   we cried to the LORD, the God of our fathers,
   and he heard our cry
   and saw our affliction, our toil and our oppression.

"'He brought us out of Egypt
   with his strong hand and outstretched arm,

with terrifying power, with signs and wonders;
and bringing us into this country,
he gave us this land flowing with milk and honey.
Therefore, I have now brought you the firstfruits
of the products of the soil
which you, O Lᴏʀᴅ, have given me.'

"And having set them before the Lord, your God,
you shall bow down in his presence."

RESPONSORIAL PSALM

PSALM 91:1–2, 10–11, 12–13, 14–15 (SEE 15b)

R. Be with me, Lord, when I am in trouble.

[This psalm is found on page 443 (lectionary number 174).]

SECOND READING

ROMANS 10:8–13

THE CONFESSION OF FAITH OF ALL BELIEVERS IN CHRIST.

Brothers and sisters:
What does Scripture say?

The word is near you,
in your mouth and in your heart
— that is, the word of faith that we preach —
for, if you confess with your mouth that Jesus is Lord
and believe in your heart that God raised him
from the dead,
you will be saved.
For one believes with the heart and so is justified,
and one confesses with the mouth and so is saved.

For the Scripture says,
No one who believes in him will be put to shame.
For there is no distinction between Jew and Greek;
the same Lord is Lord of all,
enriching all who call upon him.
For *everyone who calls on the name of the Lord will be saved.*

VERSE BEFORE THE GOSPEL

MATTHEW 4:4b

One does not live on bread alone,
but on every word that comes forth from the mouth of God.

GOSPEL

LUKE 4:1–13

JESUS WAS LED BY THE SPIRIT INTO THE DESERT AND WAS TEMPTED.

Filled with the Holy Spirit, Jesus returned from the Jordan
and was led by the Spirit into the desert for forty days,
to be tempted by the devil.
He ate nothing during those days,
and when they were over he was hungry.

The devil said to him,
  "If you are the Son of God,
  command this stone to become bread."
Jesus answered him,
  "It is written, *One does not live on bread alone.*"

Then he took him up and showed him
  all the kingdoms of the world in a single instant.
The devil said to him,
  "I shall give to you all this power and glory;
  for it has been handed over to me,
  and I may give it to whomever I wish.
All this will be yours, if you worship me."
Jesus said to him in reply,
  "It is written:
  You shall worship the Lord, your God,
  and him alone shall you serve."

Then he led him to Jerusalem,
  made him stand on the parapet of the temple,
    and said to him,
  "If you are the Son of God,
  throw yourself down from here, for it is written:
    He will command his angels concerning you, to guard you,
  and:
    With their hands they will support you,
    lest you dash your foot against a stone."
Jesus said to him in reply,
  "It also says,
  You shall not put the Lord, your God, to the test."

When the devil had finished every temptation,
  he departed from him for a time.

25A   SECOND SUNDAY OF LENT

FIRST READING

GENESIS 12:1–4a

THE CALL OF ABRAHAM,
THE FATHER OF GOD'S
PEOPLE.

The LORD said to Abram:
"Go forth from the land of your kinsfolk
  and from your father's house to a land
    that I will show you.

"I will make of you a great nation,
  and I will bless you;
I will make your name great,
  so that you will be a blessing.
I will bless those who bless you
  and curse those who curse you.

All the communities of the earth
    shall find blessing in you."

Abram went as the LORD directed him.

R. Lord, let your mercy be on us, as we place
    our trust in you.

Upright is the word of the LORD,
    and all his works are trustworthy.
He loves justice and right;
    of the kindness of the LORD the earth is full. *R.*

See, the eyes of the LORD are upon those who fear him,
    upon those who hope for his kindness,
to deliver them from death
    and preserve them in spite of famine. *R.*

Our soul waits for the LORD,
    who is our help and our shield.
May your kindness, O LORD, be upon us
    who have put our hope in you. *R.*

SECOND READING

2 TIMOTHY 1:8b–10

GOD HAS SAVED US AND CALLED US TO BE HOLY.

Beloved:
Bear your share of hardship for the gospel
    with the strength that comes from God.

He saved us and called us to a holy life,
    not according to our works
    but according to his own design
    and the grace bestowed on us in Christ Jesus
        before time began,
    but now made manifest
    through the appearance of our savior Christ Jesus,
    who destroyed death and brought life and immortality
    to light through the gospel.

VERSE BEFORE THE GOSPEL

SEE MATTHEW 17:5

From the shining cloud the Father's voice is heard:
This is my beloved Son, hear him.

GOSPEL

MATTHEW 17:1–9

JESUS' FACE SHONE LIKE THE SUN.

Jesus took Peter, James, and John his brother,
    and led them up a high mountain by themselves.
And he was transfigured before them;
    his face shone like the sun
    and his clothes became white as light.
And behold, Moses and Elijah appeared to them,
    conversing with him.

Then Peter said to Jesus in reply,
  "Lord, it is good that we are here.
If you wish, I will make three tents here,
  one for you, one for Moses, and one for Elijah."

While he was still speaking, behold,
  a bright cloud cast a shadow over them,
  then from the cloud came a voice that said,
  "This is my beloved Son, with whom I am well pleased;
  listen to him."

When the disciples heard this, they fell prostrate
  and were very much afraid.
But Jesus came and touched them, saying,
  "Rise, and do not be afraid."
And when the disciples raised their eyes,
  they saw no one else but Jesus alone.

As they were coming down from the mountain,
  Jesus charged them,
  "Do not tell the vision to anyone
  until the Son of Man has been raised from the dead."

26B   SECOND SUNDAY OF LENT

FIRST READING

GENESIS 22:1–2, 9a, 10–13,
15–18

THE SACRIFICE OF ABRAHAM,
OUR FATHER IN FAITH.

God put Abraham to the test.
He called to him, "Abraham!"
"Here I am!" he replied.

Then God said:
"Take your son Isaac, your only one, whom you love,
  and go to the land of Moriah.
There you shall offer him up as a holocaust
  on a height that I will point out to you."

When they came to the place of which God had told him,
  Abraham built an altar there and arranged
    the wood on it.
Then he reached out and took the knife
  to slaughter his son.

But the LORD's messenger called to him from heaven,
  "Abraham, Abraham!"
"Here I am!" he answered.
"Do not lay your hand on the boy," said the messenger.
"Do not do the least thing to him.

I know now how devoted you are to God,
  since you did not withhold from me your own
    beloved son."

As Abraham looked about,
  he spied a ram caught by its horns in the thicket.
So he went and took the ram
  and offered it up as a holocaust in place of his son.

Again the Lord's messenger called to Abraham
      from heaven and said:
"I swear by myself, declares the Lord,
    that because you acted as you did
    in not withholding from me your beloved son,
    I will bless you abundantly
    and make your descendants as countless
    as the stars of the sky and the sands of the seashore;
    your descendants shall take possession
    of the gates of their enemies,
    and in your descendants all the nations of the earth
      shall find blessing —
    all this because you obeyed my command."

RESPONSORIAL PSALM

PSALM 116:10, 15, 16–17, 18–19 (116:9)

R. *I will walk before the Lord, in the land of the living.*

I believed, even when I said,
  "I am greatly afflicted."
Precious in the eyes of the Lord
  is the death of his faithful ones.   R.

O Lord, I am your servant;
  I am your servant, the son of your handmaid;
  you have loosed my bonds.
To you will I offer sacrifice of thanksgiving,
  and I will call upon the name of the Lord.   R.

My vows to the Lord I will pay
  in the presence of all his people,
in the courts of the house of the Lord,
  in your midst, O Jerusalem.   R.

SECOND READING

ROMANS 8:31b–34

GOD DID NOT SPARE HIS OWN SON.

Brothers and sisters:
If God is for us, who can be against us?
He who did not spare his own Son
    but handed him over for us all,
    how will he not also give us everything else
      along with him?

Who will bring a charge against God's chosen ones?
It is God who acquits us, who will condemn?

Christ Jesus it is who died — or, rather, was raised —
who also is at the right hand of God,
who indeed intercedes for us.

VERSE BEFORE
THE GOSPEL

SEE MATTHEW 17:5

From the shining cloud the Father's voice is heard:
This is my beloved Son, listen to him.

GOSPEL

MARK 9:2–10

THIS IS MY BELOVED SON.

Jesus took Peter, James and John
and led them up a high mountain apart by themselves.
And he was transfigured before them,
and his clothes became dazzling white,
such as no fuller on earth could bleach them.

Then Elijah appeared to them along with Moses,
and they were conversing with Jesus.
Then Peter said to Jesus in reply,
"Rabbi, it is good that we are here!
Let us make three tents:
one for you, one for Moses, and one for Elijah."
He hardly knew what to say, they were so terrified.

Then a cloud came, casting a shadow over them;
from the cloud came a voice,
"This is my beloved Son. Listen to him."
Suddenly, looking around, they no longer saw anyone
but Jesus alone with them.

As they were coming down from the mountain,
he charged them not to relate what they had seen
to anyone,
except when the Son of Man had risen from the dead.

So they kept the matter to themselves,
questioning what rising from the dead meant.

27C   SECOND SUNDAY OF LENT

FIRST READING

GENESIS 15:5–12, 17–18

GOD MADE A COVENANT
WITH ABRAHAM, HIS
FAITHFUL SERVANT.

The Lord God took Abram outside and said,
"Look up at the sky and count the stars, if you can.
Just so," he added, "shall your descendants be."
Abram put his faith in the Lord,
who credited it to him as an act of righteousness.

He then said to him,
"I am the LORD who brought you from Ur
of the Chaldeans
to give you this land as a possession."

"O Lord GOD," he asked,
"how am I to know that I shall possess it?"

He answered him,
"Bring me a three-year-old heifer,
a three-year-old she-goat,
a three-year-old ram, a turtledove, and a young pigeon."
Abram brought him all these, split them in two,
and placed each half opposite the other;
but the birds he did not cut up.
Birds of prey swooped down on the carcasses,
but Abram stayed with them.
As the sun was about to set, a trance fell upon Abram,
and a deep, terrifying darkness enveloped him.

When the sun had set and it was dark,
there appeared a smoking fire pot and a flaming torch,
which passed between those pieces.

It was on that occasion that the LORD made a covenant
with Abram,
saying: "To your descendants I give this land,
from the Wadi of Egypt to the Great River,
the Euphrates."

RESPONSORIAL PSALM

PSALM 27:1, 7–8, 8–9, 13–14

R. The Lord is my light and my salvation.

The LORD is my light and my salvation;
whom should I fear?
The LORD is my life's refuge;
of whom should I be afraid?   R.

Hear, O LORD, the sound of my call;
have pity on me, and answer me.
Of you my heart speaks; you my glance seeks.   R.

Your presence, O LORD, I seek.
Hide not your face from me;
do not in anger repel your servant.
You are my helper; cast me not off.   R.

I believe that I shall see the bounty of the LORD
in the land of the living.
Wait for the LORD with courage;
be stouthearted, and wait for the LORD.   R.

LONGER FORM
PHILIPPIANS 3:17—4:1

SHORTER FORM
PHILIPPIANS 3:20—4:1

CHRIST WILL CHANGE
OUR LOWLY BODY TO
CONFORM WITH HIS
GLORIFIED BODY.

Join with others in being imitators of me,
    brothers and sisters,
        and observe those who thus conduct themselves
        according to the model you have in us.
For many, as I have often told you
    and now tell you even in tears,
        conduct themselves as enemies of the cross of Christ.
Their end is destruction.
Their God is their stomach;
    their glory is in their "shame."
Their minds are occupied with earthly things.

But [our citizenship is in heaven,
    and from it we also await a savior, the Lord Jesus Christ.
He will change our lowly body
    to conform with his glorified body
    by the power that enables him also
    to bring all things into subjection to himself.

Therefore, my brothers and sisters,
    whom I love and long for, my joy and crown,
    in this way stand firm in the Lord.]

**VERSE BEFORE
THE GOSPEL**

SEE MATTHEW 17:5

*From the shining cloud the Father's voice is heard:
This is my beloved Son, hear him.*

GOSPEL

LUKE 9:28b–36

WHILE HE WAS PRAYING
HIS FACE CHANGED
IN APPEARANCE AND
HIS CLOTHING BECAME
DAZZLING WHITE.

Jesus took Peter, John, and James
    and went up the mountain to pray.
While he was praying his face changed in appearance
    and his clothing became dazzling white.

And behold, two men were conversing with him,
    Moses and Elijah,
        who appeared in glory and spoke of his exodus
        that he was going to accomplish in Jerusalem.

Peter and his companions had been overcome by sleep,
    but becoming fully awake,
        they saw his glory and the two men standing with him.

As they were about to part from him, Peter said to Jesus,
    "Master, it is good that we are here;
    let us make three tents,
        one for you, one for Moses, and one for Elijah."
But he did not know what he was saying.

While he was still speaking,
  a cloud came and cast a shadow over them,
  and they became frightened when they entered
    the cloud.
Then from the cloud came a voice that said,
  "This is my chosen Son; listen to him."
After the voice had spoken, Jesus was found alone.

They fell silent and did not at that time
  tell anyone what they had seen.

28A   THIRD SUNDAY OF LENT

FIRST READING

EXODUS 17:3–7

GIVE US WATER, SO THAT
WE MAY DRINK.

In those days, in their thirst for water,
  the people grumbled against Moses,
  saying, "Why did you ever make us leave Egypt?
Was it just to have us die here of thirst
  with our children and our livestock?"
So Moses cried out to the LORD,
  "What shall I do with this people?
A little more and they will stone me!"

The LORD answered Moses,
  "Go over there in front of the people,
  along with some of the elders of Israel,
  holding in your hand, as you go,
  the staff with which you struck the river.
I will be standing there in front of you on the rock
    in Horeb.
Strike the rock, and the water will flow from it
  for the people to drink."
This Moses did, in the presence of the elders of Israel.

The place was called Massah and Meribah,
  because the Israelites quarreled there
  and tested the LORD, saying,
  "Is the LORD in our midst or not?"

**RESPONSORIAL
PSALM**

PSALM 95:1–2, 6–7, 8–9 (8)

R. If today you hear his voice, harden not your hearts.

[This psalm is found on page 448 (lectionary number 174).]

SECOND READING

ROMANS 5:1–2, 5–8

THE LOVE OF GOD
HAS BEEN POURED
INTO OUR HEARTS
THROUGH THE HOLY
SPIRIT THAT HAS BEEN
GIVEN TO US.

Brothers and sisters:
Since we have been justified by faith,
    we have peace with God through our Lord Jesus Christ,
    through whom we have gained access by faith
to this grace in which we stand,
    and we boast in hope of the glory of God.

And hope does not disappoint,
    because the love of God has been poured out
        into our hearts
    through the Holy Spirit who has been given to us.
For Christ, while we were still helpless,
    died at the appointed time for the ungodly.
Indeed, only with difficulty does one die for a just person,
    though perhaps for a good person one might even
        find courage to die.
But God proves his love for us
    in that while we were still sinners Christ died for us.

Lord, you are truly the Savior of the world;
give me living water, that I may never thirst again.

GOSPEL

LONGER FORM
JOHN 4:5–42

SHORTER FORM
JOHN 4:5–15, 19b–26, 39a,
40–42

THE WATER THAT I SHALL
GIVE WILL BECOME A
SPRING OF ETERNAL LIFE.

[Jesus came to a town of Samaria called Sychar,
    near the plot of land that Jacob had given
        to his son Joseph.
Jacob's well was there.
Jesus, tired from his journey, sat down there at the well.
It was about noon.

A woman of Samaria came to draw water.
Jesus said to her,
    "Give me a drink."
His disciples had gone into the town to buy food.

The Samaritan woman said to him,
    "How can you, a Jew, ask me, a Samaritan woman,
      for a drink?"
— For Jews use nothing in common with Samaritans. —
Jesus answered and said to her,
    "If you knew the gift of God
    and who is saying to you, 'Give me a drink,'
    you would have asked him
    and he would have given you living water."

The woman said to him,
   "Sir, you do not even have a bucket and the cistern
      is deep;
   where then can you get this living water?
Are you greater than our father Jacob,
   who gave us this cistern and drank from it himself
   with his children and his flocks?"
Jesus answered and said to her,
   "Everyone who drinks this water will be thirsty again;
   but whoever drinks the water I shall give
      will never thirst;
   the water I shall give will become in him
   a spring of water welling up to eternal life."

The woman said to him,
   "Sir, give me this water, so that I may not be thirsty
   or have to keep coming here to draw water."]

Jesus said to her,
   "Go call your husband and come back."
The woman answered and said to him,
   "I do not have a husband."
Jesus answered her,
   "You are right in saying, 'I do not have a husband.'
For you have had five husbands,
   and the one you have now is not your husband.
What you have said is true."

The woman said to him,
   "Sir, [I can see that you are a prophet.
Our ancestors worshiped on this mountain;
   but you people say that the place to worship
      is in Jerusalem."
Jesus said to her,
   "Believe me, woman, the hour is coming
   when you will worship the Father
   neither on this mountain nor in Jerusalem.

"You people worship what you do not understand;
   we worship what we understand,
   because salvation is from the Jews.
But the hour is coming, and is now here,
   when true worshipers will worship the Father
      in Spirit and truth;
   and indeed the Father seeks such people
      to worship him.
God is Spirit, and those who worship him
   must worship in Spirit and truth."

The woman said to him,
  "I know that the Messiah is coming,
    the one called the Christ;
  when he comes, he will tell us everything."
Jesus said to her,
  "I am he, the one speaking with you."]

At that moment his disciples returned,
  and were amazed that he was talking with a woman,
  but still no one said, "What are you looking for?"
  or "Why are you talking with her?"
The woman left her water jar
  and went into the town and said to the people,
  "Come see a man who told me everything I have done.
Could he possibly be the Christ?"
They went out of the town and came to him.
Meanwhile, the disciples urged him, "Rabbi, eat."
But he said to them,
  "I have food to eat of which you do not know."
So the disciples said to one another,
  "Could someone have brought him something to eat?"

Jesus said to them,
  "My food is to do the will of the one who sent me
  and to finish his work.
Do you not say, 'In four months the harvest will be here'?
I tell you, look up and see the fields ripe for the harvest.
The reaper is already receiving payment
  and gathering crops for eternal life,
    so that the sower and reaper can rejoice together.
For here the saying is verified that 'One sows
    and another reaps.'
I sent you to reap what you have not worked for;
  others have done the work,
  and you are sharing the fruits of their work."

[Many of the Samaritans of that town began to believe
    in him]
  because of the word of the woman who testified,
  "He told me everything I have done."
[When the Samaritans came to him,
  they invited him to stay with them;
  and he stayed there two days.
Many more began to believe in him because of his word,
  and they said to the woman,
  "We no longer believe because of your word;
  for we have heard for ourselves,
  and we know that this is truly the savior of the world."]

FIRST READING

LONGER FORM
EXODUS 20:1–17

SHORTER FORM
EXODUS 20:1–3, 7–8, 12–17

THE LAW WAS GIVEN
THROUGH MOSES.

◆

The readings given for Year A,
n. 28, may be used in place
of these.

[In those days, God delivered all these commandments:
"I, the LORD, am your God,
   who brought you out of the land of Egypt,
      that place of slavery.
You shall not have other gods besides me.]
You shall not carve idols for yourselves
   in the shape of anything in the sky above
   or on the earth below or in the waters beneath
      the earth;
   you shall not bow down before them or worship them.

"For I, the LORD, your God, am a jealous God,
   inflicting punishment for their fathers' wickedness
   on the children of those who hate me,
   down to the third and fourth generation;
   but bestowing mercy
      down to the thousandth generation
   on the children of those who love me
      and keep my commandments.

["You shall not take the name of the LORD, your God,
      in vain.
For the LORD will not leave unpunished
   the one who takes his name in vain.

"Remember to keep holy the sabbath day.]
Six days you may labor and do all your work,
   but the seventh day is the sabbath of the LORD,
      your God.
No work may be done then either by you,
   or your son or daughter,
   or your male or female slave, or your beast,
   or by the alien who lives with you.
In six days the LORD made the heavens and the earth,
   the sea and all that is in them;
   but on the seventh day he rested.
That is why the LORD has blessed the sabbath day
   and made it holy.

["Honor your father and your mother,
   that you may have a long life in the land
   which the LORD, your God, is giving you.
You shall not kill.
You shall not commit adultery.
You shall not steal.
You shall not bear false witness against your neighbor.
You shall not covet your neighbor's house.

You shall not covet your neighbor's wife,
nor his male or female slave, nor his ox or ass,
nor anything else that belongs to him."]

RESPONSORIAL PSALM

PSALM 19:8, 9, 10, 11
(JOHN 6:68c)

R. *Lord, you have the words of everlasting life.*

[This psalm is found on page 447 (lectionary number 174).]

SECOND READING

1 CORINTHIANS 1:22–25

WE PROCLAIM CHRIST
CRUCIFIED, A STUMBLING
BLOCK TO MANY, BUT TO
THOSE WHO ARE CALLED,
THE WISDOM OF GOD.

Brothers and sisters:
Jews demand signs and Greeks look for wisdom,
but we proclaim Christ crucified,
a stumbling block to Jews and foolishness to Gentiles,
but to those who are called, Jews and Greeks alike,
Christ the power of God and the wisdom of God.
For the foolishness of God is wiser than human wisdom,
and the weakness of God is stronger
than human strength.

**VERSE BEFORE
THE GOSPEL**

JOHN 3:16

*God so loved the world that he gave his only Son,
so that everyone who believes in him might have eternal life.*

GOSPEL

JOHN 2:13–25

DESTROY THIS TEMPLE,
AND IN THREE DAYS
I WILL RAISE IT UP.

Since the Passover of the Jews was near,
Jesus went up to Jerusalem.
He found in the temple area those who sold oxen,
sheep and doves,
as well as the money changers seated there.
He made a whip out of cords
and drove them all out of the temple area,
with the sheep and oxen,
and spilled the coins of the money changers
and overturned their tables,
and to those who sold doves he said,
"Take these out of here,
and stop making my Father's house a marketplace."

His disciples recalled the words of Scripture,
Zeal for your house will consume me.

At this the Jews answered and said to him,
"What sign can you show us for doing this?"
Jesus answered and said to them,
"Destroy this temple and in three days I will raise it up."

The Jews said,
  "This temple has been under construction
    for forty-six years,
  and you will raise it up in three days?"
But he was speaking about the temple of his body.

Therefore, when he was raised from the dead,
  his disciples remembered that he had said this,
  and they came to believe the Scripture
  and the word Jesus had spoken.

While he was in Jerusalem for the feast of Passover,
  many began to believe in his name
  when they saw the signs he was doing.
But Jesus would not trust himself to them
    because he knew them all,
  and did not need anyone to testify about human nature.
He himself understood it well.

30C   THIRD SUNDAY OF LENT

FIRST READING

EXODUS 3:1–8a, 13–15

"I AM" SENT ME TO YOU.

◆

*The readings given for Year A,
n. 28, may be used in place
of these.*

Moses was tending the flock of his father-in-law Jethro,
  the priest of Midian.
Leading the flock across the desert, he came to Horeb,
  the mountain of God.
There an angel of the LORD appeared to Moses in fire
  flaming out of a bush.
As he looked on, he was surprised to see that the bush,
  though on fire, was not consumed.

So Moses decided,
  "I must go over to look at this remarkable sight,
  and see why the bush is not burned."

When the LORD saw him coming over to look at it
    more closely,
  God called out to him from the bush, "Moses! Moses!"
He answered, "Here I am."
God said, "Come no nearer!
Remove the sandals from your feet,
  for the place where you stand is holy ground.

"I am the God of your fathers," he continued,
  "the God of Abraham, the God of Isaac,
    the God of Jacob."
Moses hid his face, for he was afraid to look at God.

But the LORD said,
"I have witnessed the affliction of my people in Egypt
and have heard their cry of complaint against their
slave drivers,
so I know well what they are suffering.
Therefore I have come down to rescue them
from the hands of the Egyptians
and lead them out of that land into a good and
spacious land,
a land flowing with milk and honey."
Moses said to God, "But when I go to the Israelites
and say to them, 'The God of your fathers
has sent me to you,'
if they ask me, 'What is his name?'
what am I to tell them?"

God replied, "I am who am."
Then he added, "This is what you shall tell the Israelites:
I AM sent me to you."

God spoke further to Moses, "Thus shall you say
to the Israelites:
The LORD, the God of your fathers,
the God of Abraham, the God of Isaac,
the God of Jacob,
has sent me to you.

"This is my name forever;
thus am I to be remembered through all generations."

RESPONSORIAL PSALM

PSALM 103:1–2, 3–4, 6–7, 8, 11 (8a)

R. *The Lord is kind and merciful.*

Bless the LORD, O my soul;
and all my being, bless his holy name.
Bless the LORD, O my soul,
and forget not all his benefits. R.

He pardons all your iniquities,
heals all your ills,
He redeems your life from destruction,
crowns you with kindness and compassion. R.

The LORD secures justice
and the rights of all the oppressed.
He has made known his ways to Moses,
and his deeds to the children of Israel. R.

Merciful and gracious is the LORD,
slow to anger and abounding in kindness.
For as the heavens are high above the earth,
so surpassing is his kindness toward those who fear him. R.

1 CORINTHIANS 10:1–6,
10–12

THE LIFE OF THE PEOPLE
WITH MOSES IN THE
DESERT WAS WRITTEN
DOWN AS A WARNING
TO US.

I do not want you to be unaware, brothers and sisters,
   that our ancestors were all under the cloud
   and all passed through the sea,
   and all of them were baptized into Moses
   in the cloud and in the sea.
All ate the same spiritual food,
   and all drank the same spiritual drink,
   for they drank from a spiritual rock that followed them,
   and the rock was the Christ.

Yet God was not pleased with most of them,
   for they were struck down in the desert.

These things happened as examples for us,
   so that we might not desire evil things, as they did.
Do not grumble as some of them did,
   and suffered death by the destroyer.

These things happened to them as an example,
   and they have been written down as a warning to us,
   upon whom the end of the ages has come.
Therefore, whoever thinks he is standing secure
   should take care not to fall.

VERSE BEFORE
THE GOSPEL

MATTHEW 4:17

Repent, says the Lord;
the kingdom of heaven is at hand.

GOSPEL

LUKE 13:1–9

IF YOU DO NOT REPENT,
YOU WILL ALL PERISH
AS THEY DID.

Some people told Jesus about the Galileans
   whose blood Pilate had mingled with the blood
      of their sacrifices.

Jesus said to them in reply,
   "Do you think that because these Galileans suffered
      in this way
   they were greater sinners than all other Galileans?
By no means!
But I tell you, if you do not repent,
   you will all perish as they did!
Or those eighteen people who were killed
   when the tower at Siloam fell on them —
   do you think they were more guilty
   than everyone else who lived in Jerusalem?
By no means!
But I tell you, if you do not repent,
   you will all perish as they did!"

And he told them this parable:
  "There once was a person who had a fig tree planted
    in his orchard,
  and when he came in search of fruit on it
    but found none,
  he said to the gardener,
  'For three years now I have come in search of fruit
    on this fig tree
  but have found none.
So cut it down.
Why should it exhaust the soil?'

"He said to him in reply,
  'Sir, leave it for this year also,
  and I shall cultivate the ground around it
    and fertilize it;
  it may bear fruit in the future.
If not you can cut it down.'"

31A   FOURTH SUNDAY OF LENT

FIRST READING

1 SAMUEL 16:1b, 6–7, 10–13a

DAVID IS ANOINTED
AS KING OF ISRAEL.

The LORD said to Samuel:
  "Fill your horn with oil, and be on your way.
I am sending you to Jesse of Bethlehem,
  for I have chosen my king from among his sons."

As Jesse and his sons came to the sacrifice,
  Samuel looked at Eliab and thought,
  "Surely the Lord's anointed is here before him."
But the LORD said to Samuel:
  "Do not judge from his appearance
    or from his lofty stature,
  because I have rejected him.
Not as man sees does God see,
  because man sees the appearance
  but the LORD looks into the heart."

In the same way Jesse presented seven sons before Samuel,
  but Samuel said to Jesse,
  "The LORD has not chosen any one of these."
Then Samuel asked Jesse,
  "Are these all the sons you have?"
Jesse replied,
  "There is still the youngest, who is tending the sheep."
Samuel said to Jesse,
  "Send for him;

we will not begin the sacrificial banquet until
    he arrives here."
Jesse sent and had the young man brought to them.
He was ruddy, a youth handsome to behold
    and making a splendid appearance.
The LORD said,
    "There — anoint him, for this is the one!"

Then Samuel, with the horn of oil in hand,
    anointed David in the presence of his brothers;
    and from that day on, the spirit of the LORD rushed
      upon David.

RESPONSORIAL PSALM

PSALM 23: 1–3a, 3b–4, 5, 6 (1)

R. The Lord is my shepherd; there is nothing I shall want.

The LORD is my shepherd; I shall not want.
    In verdant pastures he gives me repose;
beside restful waters he leads me;
    he refreshes my soul.   R.

He guides me in right paths
    for his name's sake.
Even though I walk in the dark valley
    I fear no evil; for you are at my side
with your rod and your staff
    that give me courage.   R.

You spread the table before me
    in the sight of my foes;
you anoint my head with oil;
    my cup overflows.   R.

Only goodness and kindness follow me
    all the days of my life;
and I shall dwell in the house of the LORD
    for years to come.   R.

SECOND READING

EPHESIANS 5:8–14

ARISE FROM THE DEAD, AND CHRIST WILL GIVE YOU LIGHT.

Brothers and sisters:
You were once darkness,
    but now you are light in the Lord.
Live as children of light,
    for light produces every kind of goodness
    and righteousness and truth.

Try to learn what is pleasing to the Lord.
Take no part in the fruitless works of darkness;
    rather expose them, for it is shameful even to mention
    the things done by them in secret;
    but everything exposed by the light becomes visible,
    for everything that becomes visible is light.
Therefore, it says:
    "Awake, O sleeper,

and arise from the dead,
and Christ will give you light."

VERSE BEFORE
THE GOSPEL

JOHN 8:12

I am the light of the world, says the Lord;
whoever follows me will have the light of life.

GOSPEL

LONGER FORM
JOHN 9:1–41

SHORTER FORM
JOHN 9:1, 6–9, 13–17, 34–38

THE MAN WHO WAS BLIND
WENT OFF AND WASHED
HIMSELF AND CAME BACK
ABLE TO SEE.

[As Jesus passed by he saw a man blind from birth.]
His disciples asked him,
     "Rabbi, who sinned, this man or his parents,
     that he was born blind?"

Jesus answered,
     "Neither he nor his parents sinned;
     it is so that the works of God might be made visible
          through him.
We have to do the works of the one who sent me
          while it is day.
Night is coming when no one can work.
While I am in the world, I am the light of the world."
When he had said this, [he spat on the ground
     and made clay with the saliva,
     and smeared the clay on his eyes, and said to him,
     "Go wash in the Pool of Siloam"—which means Sent.
So he went and washed, and came back able to see.

His neighbors and those who had seen him earlier
          as a beggar said,
     "Isn't this the one who used to sit and beg?"
Some said, "It is,"
     but others said, "No, he just looks like him."
He said, "I am."]
So they said to him, "How were your eyes opened?"
He replied,
     "The man called Jesus made clay and anointed my eyes
     and told me, 'Go to Siloam and wash.'
So I went there and washed and was able to see."
And they said to him, "Where is he?"
He said, "I don't know."

[They brought the one who was once blind
          to the Pharisees.
Now Jesus had made clay and opened his eyes
          on a sabbath.
So then the Pharisees also asked him
          how he was able to see.

He said to them,
  "He put clay on my eyes, and I washed,
    and now I can see."
So some of the Pharisees said,
  "This man is not from God,
  because he does not keep the sabbath."
But others said,
  "How can a sinful man do such signs?"
And there was a division among them.
So they said to the blind man again,
  "What do you have to say about him,
  since he opened your eyes?"
He said, "He is a prophet."]

Now the Jews did not believe
    that he had been blind and gained his sight
    until they summoned the parents of the one
      who had gained his sight.
They asked them,
  "Is this your son, who you say was born blind?
How does he now see?"
His parents answered and said,
  "We know that this is our son and that
    he was born blind.
We do not know how he sees now,
  nor do we know who opened his eyes.
Ask him, he is of age;
  he can speak for himself."
His parents said this because they were afraid
  of the Jews, for the Jews had already agreed
    that if anyone acknowledged him as the Christ,
    he would be expelled from the synagogue.
For this reason his parents said,
  "He is of age; question him."

So a second time they called the man who
      had been blind
  and said to him, "Give God the praise!
We know that this man is a sinner."
He replied,
  "If he is a sinner, I do not know.
One thing I do know is that I was blind and now I see."
So they said to him,
  "What did he do to you?
  How did he open your eyes?"
He answered them,
  "I told you already and you did not listen.
Why do you want to hear it again?

Do you want to become his disciples, too?"
They ridiculed him and said,
  "You are that man's disciple;
  we are disciples of Moses!
We know that God spoke to Moses,
  but we do not know where this one is from."

The man answered and said to them,
  "This is what is so amazing,
  that you do not know where he is from,
    yet he opened my eyes.
We know that God does not listen to sinners,
  but if one is devout and does his will, he listens to him.
It is unheard of that anyone ever opened the eyes
    of a person born blind.
If this man were not from God,
  he would not be able to do anything."
[They answered and said to him,
  "You were born totally in sin,
  and are you trying to teach us?"
Then they threw him out.

When Jesus heard that they had thrown him out,
  he found him and said,
    "Do you believe in the Son of Man?"
He answered and said,
  "Who is he, sir, that I may believe in him?"
Jesus said to him,
  "You have seen him,
  the one speaking with you is he."
He said,
  "I do believe, Lord," and he worshiped him.]

Then Jesus said,
  "I came into this world for judgment,
  so that those who do not see might see,
  and those who do see might become blind."
Some of the Pharisees who were with him heard this
  and said to him, "Surely we are not also blind, are we?"
Jesus said to them,
  "If you were blind, you would have no sin;
  but now you are saying, 'We see,' so your sin remains.

FIRST READING

2 CHRONICLES 36:14–16,
19–23

THE WRATH AND THE
MERCY OF THE LORD ARE
REVEALED IN THE EXILE
AND LIBERATION OF HIS
PEOPLE.

◆

*The readings given for Year A,
n. 31, may be used in place
of these.*

In those days, all the princes of Judah, the priests,
    and the people
added infidelity to infidelity,
    practicing all the abominations of the nations
    and polluting the LORD's temple
    which he had consecrated in Jerusalem.

Early and often did the LORD, the God of their fathers,
    send his messengers to them,
    for he had compassion on his people
        and his dwelling place.
But they mocked the messengers of God,
    despised his warnings, and scoffed at his prophets,
    until the anger of the LORD against his people
        was so inflamed
    that there was no remedy.

Their enemies burnt the house of God,
    tore down the walls of Jerusalem,
    set all its palaces afire,
    and destroyed all its precious objects.
Those who escaped the sword were carried captive
        to Babylon,
    where they became servants of the king
        of the Chaldeans and his sons
    until the kingdom of the Persians came to power.
All this was to fulfill the word of the LORD
        spoken by Jeremiah:
    Until the land has retrieved its lost sabbaths,
    during all the time it lies waste it shall have rest
    while seventy years are fulfilled.

In the first year of Cyrus, king of Persia,
    in order to fulfill the word of the LORD
        spoken by Jeremiah,
    the LORD inspired King Cyrus of Persia
    to issue this proclamation throughout his kingdom,
    both by word of mouth and in writing:
    "Thus says Cyrus, king of Persia:
    All the kingdoms of the earth
    the LORD, the God of heaven, has given to me,
    and he has also charged me to build him a house
    in Jerusalem, which is in Judah.
Whoever, therefore, among you belongs to any part
        of his people,
    let him go up, and may his God be with him!"

RESPONSORIAL PSALM

PSALM 137:1–2, 3, 4–5, 6 (6ab)

R. Let my tongue be silenced, if I ever forget you!

By the streams of Babylon
   we sat and wept
   when we remembered Zion.
On the aspens of that land
   we hung up our harps.   R.

For there our captors asked of us
   the lyrics of our songs,
and our despoilers urged us to be joyous:
   "Sing for us the songs of Zion!"   R.

How could we sing a song of the LORD
   in a foreign land?
If I forget you, Jerusalem,
   may my right hand be forgotten!   R.

May my tongue cleave to my palate
   if I remember you not,
if I place not Jerusalem
   ahead of my joy.   R.

SECOND READING

EPHESIANS 2:4–10

THOUGH DEAD IN YOUR TRANSGRESSIONS, BY GRACE YOU HAVE BEEN SAVED.

Brothers and sisters:
God, who is rich in mercy,
   because of the great love he had for us,
   even when we were dead in our transgressions,
   brought us to life with Christ
      — by grace you have been saved —
   raised us up with him,
   and seated us with him in the heavens in Christ Jesus,
   that in the ages to come
   he might show the immeasurable riches of his grace
   in his kindness to us in Christ Jesus.

For by grace you have been saved through faith,
   and this is not from you; it is the gift of God;
   it is not from works, so no one may boast.
For we are his handiwork, created in Christ Jesus
     for the good works
   that God has prepared in advance,
   that we should live in them.

VERSE BEFORE THE GOSPEL

JOHN 3:16

God so loved the world that he gave his only Son,
so everyone who believes in him might have eternal life.

GOSPEL

JOHN 3:14–21

GOD SENT HIS SON SO
THAT THE WORLD MIGHT
BE SAVED THROUGH HIM.

Jesus said to Nicodemus:
"Just as Moses lifted up the serpent in the desert,
    so must the Son of Man be lifted up,
    so that everyone who believes in him may have
        eternal life.

"For God so loved the world that he gave his only Son,
    so that everyone who believes in him might not perish
    but might have eternal life.
For God did not send his Son into the world
        to condemn the world,
    but that the world might be saved through him.
Whoever believes in him will not be condemned,
    but whoever does not believe has already
        been condemned,
    because he has not believed in the name of the only
        Son of God.

"And this is the verdict,
    that the light came into the world,
    but people preferred darkness to light,
    because their works were evil.
For everyone who does wicked things hates the light
    and does not come toward the light,
    so that his works might not be exposed.
But whoever lives the truth comes to the light,
    so that his works may be clearly seen as done in God."

33C   FOURTH SUNDAY OF LENT

FIRST READING

JOSHUA 5:9a, 10–12

THE PEOPLE OF GOD
ENTERED THE PROMISED
LAND AND THERE KEPT
THE PASSOVER.

◆
The readings given for Year A,
n. 31, may be used in place
of these.

The LORD said to Joshua,
    "Today I have removed the reproach of Egypt from you."

While the Israelites were encamped at Gilgal
        on the plains of Jericho,
    they celebrated the Passover
    on the evening of the fourteenth of the month.

On the day after the Passover,
    they ate of the produce of the land
    in the form of unleavened cakes and parched grain.
On that same day after the Passover,
    on which they ate of the produce of the land,
        the manna ceased.
No longer was there manna for the Israelites,
    who that year ate of the yield of the land of Canaan.

R. *Taste and see the goodness of the Lord.*

I will bless the LORD at all times;
  his praise shall be ever in my mouth.
Let my soul glory in the LORD;
  the lowly will hear me and be glad.   R.

Glorify the LORD with me,
  let us together extol his name.
I sought the LORD, and he answered me
  and delivered me from all my fears.   R.

Look to him that you may be radiant with joy,
  and your faces may not blush with shame.
When the poor one called out, the LORD heard,
  and from all his distress he saved him.   R.

SECOND READING

2 CORINTHIANS 5:17–21

GOD RECONCILED US
TO HIMSELF THROUGH
CHRIST.

Brothers and sisters:
Whoever is in Christ is a new creation:
  the old things have passed away;
  behold, new things have come.
And all this is from God,
  who has reconciled us to himself through Christ
  and given us the ministry of reconciliation,
  namely, God was reconciling the world to himself
    in Christ,
  not counting their trespasses against them
  and entrusting to us the message of reconciliation.

So we are ambassadors for Christ,
  as if God were appealing through us.
We implore you on behalf of Christ,
  be reconciled to God.
For our sake he made him to be sin who did not know sin,
  so that we might become the righteousness
    of God in him.

VERSE BEFORE
THE GOSPEL

LUKE 15:18

I will get up and go to my Father and shall say to him:
Father, I have sinned against heaven and against you.

GOSPEL

LUKE 15:1–3, 11–32

YOUR BROTHER WAS
DEAD AND HAS COME
TO LIFE AGAIN.

Tax collectors and sinners were all drawing near
    to listen to Jesus,
  but the Pharisees and scribes began to complain, saying,
  "This man welcomes sinners and eats with them."

So to them Jesus addressed this parable:
"A man had two sons, and the younger son said
    to his father,
  'Father give me the share of your estate that should
    come to me.'
So the father divided the property between them.

"After a few days, the younger son collected
    all his belongings
  and set off to a distant country
  where he squandered his inheritance on a life
    of dissipation.

"When he had freely spent everything,
  a severe famine struck that country,
  and he found himself in dire need.
So he hired himself out to one of the local citizens
  who sent him to his farm to tend the swine.
And he longed to eat his fill of the pods on which
    the swine fed,
  but nobody gave him any.

"Coming to his senses he thought,
  'How many of my father's hired workers
  have more than enough food to eat,
  but here am I, dying from hunger.
I shall get up and go to my father and I shall say to him,
    "Father, I have sinned against heaven and against you.
I no longer deserve to be called your son;
  treat me as you would treat one of your hired workers."'

"So he got up and went back to his father.
While he was still a long way off,
  his father caught sight of him, and was filled
    with compassion.
He ran to his son, embraced him and kissed him.

"His son said to him,
  'Father, I have sinned against heaven and against you;
  I no longer deserve to be called your son.'
But his father ordered his servants,
  'Quickly bring the finest robe and put it on him;
  put a ring on his finger and sandals on his feet.
Take the fattened calf and slaughter it.
Then let us celebrate with a feast,
  because this son of mine was dead, and has come
    to life again;
  he was lost, and has been found.'
Then the celebration began.

"Now the older son had been out in the field
   and, on his way back, as he neared the house,
   he heard the sound of music and dancing.
He called one of the servants and asked what this
      might mean.
The servant said to him,
   'Your brother has returned
   and your father has slaughtered the fattened calf
   because he has him back safe and sound.'

"He became angry,
   and when he refused to enter the house,
   his father came out and pleaded with him.
He said to his father in reply,
   'Look, all these years I served you
   and not once did I disobey your orders;
   yet you never gave me even a young goat
      to feast on with my friends.
But when your son returns
   who swallowed up your property with prostitutes,
   for him you slaughter the fattened calf.'

"He said to him,
   'My son, you are here with me always;
   everything I have is yours.
But now we must celebrate and rejoice,
   because your brother was dead and has come
      to life again;
   he was lost and has been found.'"

34A   FIFTH SUNDAY OF LENT

FIRST READING

EZEKIEL 37:12–14

I WILL PUT MY SPIRIT IN
YOU THAT YOU MAY LIVE.

Thus says the Lord GOD:
O my people, I will open your graves
   and have you rise from them,
   and bring you back to the land of Israel.
Then you shall know that I am the LORD,
   when I open your graves and have you rise from them,
   O my people!

I will put my spirit in you that you may live,
   and I will settle you upon your land;
   thus you shall know that I am the LORD.
I have promised, and I will do it, says the LORD.

R. With the Lord there is mercy and fullness of redemption.

[This psalm is found on page 444 (lectionary number 174).]

SECOND READING

ROMANS 8:8–11

THE SPIRIT OF THE ONE
WHO RAISED JESUS FROM
THE DEAD DWELLS IN YOU.

Brothers and sisters:
Those who are in the flesh cannot please God.
But you are not in the flesh;
    on the contrary, you are in the spirit,
    if only the Spirit of God dwells in you.
Whoever does not have the Spirit of Christ
        does not belong to him.

But if Christ is in you,
    although the body is dead because of sin,
    the spirit is alive because of righteousness.

If the Spirit of the one who raised Jesus from the dead
        dwells in you,
    the one who raised Christ from the dead
    will give life to your mortal bodies also,
    through his Spirit dwelling in you.

**VERSE BEFORE
THE GOSPEL**

JOHN 11:25a, 26

I am the resurrection and the life, says the Lord;
whoever believes in me, will never die.

GOSPEL

LONGER FORM
JOHN 11:1–45

SHORTER FORM
JOHN 11:3–7, 17, 20–27,
33b–45

I AM THE RESURRECTION
AND THE LIFE.

Now a man was ill, Lazarus from Bethany,
    the village of Mary and her sister Martha.
Mary was the one who had anointed the Lord
        with perfumed oil
    and dried his feet with her hair;
    it was her brother Lazarus who was ill.

So [the sisters sent word to Jesus saying,
    "Master, the one you love is ill."
When Jesus heard this he said,
    "This illness is not to end in death,
    but is for the glory of God,
    that the Son of God may be glorified through it."

Now Jesus loved Martha and her sister and Lazarus.
So when he heard that he was ill,
    he remained for two days in the place where he was.
Then after this he said to his disciples,
    "Let us go back to Judea."]

The disciples said to him,
    "Rabbi, the Jews were just trying to stone you,
    and you want to go back there?"
Jesus answered,
    "Are there not twelve hours in a day?
If one walks during the day, he does not stumble,
    because he sees the light of this world.
But if one walks at night, he stumbles,
    because the light is not in him."

He said this, and then told them,
    "Our friend Lazarus is asleep,
    but I am going to awaken him."
So the disciples said to him,
    "Master, if he is asleep, he will be saved."
But Jesus was talking about his death,
    while they thought that he meant ordinary sleep.
So then Jesus said to them clearly,
    "Lazarus has died.
And I am glad for you that I was not there,
    that you may believe.
Let us go to him."
So Thomas, called Didymus, said to his fellow disciples,
    "Let us also go to die with him."

[When Jesus arrived, he found that Lazarus
    had already been in the tomb for four days.]
Now Bethany was near Jerusalem,
        only about two miles away.
And many of the Jews had come to Martha and Mary
    to comfort them about their brother.
[When Martha heard that Jesus was coming,
    she went to meet him;
    but Mary sat at home.
Martha said to Jesus,
    "Lord, if you had been here,
    my brother would not have died.
But even now I know that whatever you ask of God,
    God will give you."
Jesus said to her,
    "Your brother will rise."

Martha said to him,
    "I know he will rise,
    in the resurrection on the last day."
Jesus told her,
    "I am the resurrection and the life;
    whoever believes in me, even if he dies, will live,

and everyone who lives and believes in me
   will never die.
Do you believe this?"
She said to him, "Yes, Lord.
I have come to believe that you are the Christ,
   the Son of God,
  the one who is coming into the world."]

When she had said this,
  she went and called her sister Mary secretly, saying,
  "The teacher is here and is asking for you."
As soon as she heard this,
  she rose quickly and went to him.
For Jesus had not yet come into the village,
  but was still where Martha had met him.
So when the Jews who were with her in the house
   comforting her
  saw Mary get up quickly and go out,
  they followed her,
  presuming that she was going to the tomb
   to weep there.

When Mary came to where Jesus was and saw him,
  she fell at his feet and said to him,
  "Lord, if you had been here,
  my brother would not have died."
When Jesus saw her weeping and the Jews who had come
   with her weeping,
  [he became perturbed and deeply troubled, and said,
  "Where have you laid him?"
They said to him, "Sir, come and see."
And Jesus wept.
So the Jews said, "See how he loved him."
But some of them said,
  "Could not the one who opened the eyes
   of the blind man
  have done something so that this man
   would not have died?"

So Jesus, perturbed again, came to the tomb.
It was a cave, and a stone lay across it.
Jesus said, "Take away the stone."
Martha, the dead man's sister, said to him,
  "Lord, by now there will be a stench;
  he has been dead for four days."
Jesus said to her,
  "Did I not tell you that if you believe
  you will see the glory of God?"

So they took away the stone.
And Jesus raised his eyes and said,
  "Father, I thank you for hearing me.
I know that you always hear me;
  but because of the crowd here I have said this,
  that they may believe that you sent me."

And when he had said this,
  he cried out in a loud voice,
  "Lazarus, come out!"
The dead man came out,
  tied hand and foot with burial bands,
  and his face was wrapped in a cloth.
So Jesus said to them,
  "Untie him and let him go."

Now many of the Jews who had come to Mary
  and seen what he had done began to believe in him.]

35B FIFTH SUNDAY OF LENT

FIRST READING

JEREMIAH 31:31–34

I WILL MAKE A NEW
COVENANT AND
REMEMBER THEIR
SIN NO MORE.

◆

*The readings given for Year A,
n. 34, may be used in place
of these.*

The days are coming, says the LORD,
  when I will make a new covenant with the house
    of Israel
  and the house of Judah.
It will not be like the covenant I made with their fathers
  the day I took them by the hand
  to lead them forth from the land of Egypt;
  for they broke my covenant,
  and I had to show myself their master, says the LORD.

But this is the covenant that I will make
  with the house of Israel after those days, says the LORD.
I will place my law within them and write it
    upon their hearts;
  I will be their God, and they shall be my people.
No longer will they have need to teach their friends
    and relatives
  how to know the LORD.
All, from least to greatest, shall know me, says the LORD,
  for I will forgive their evildoing and remember
    their sin no more.

RESPONSORIAL PSALM

PSALM 51:3–4, 12–13,
14–15 (12a)

R. Create a clean heart in me, O God.

Have mercy on me, O God, in your goodness;
in the greatness of your compassion wipe out my offense.
Thoroughly wash me from my guilt
and of my sin cleanse me.   R.

A clean heart create for me, O God,
and a steadfast spirit renew within me.
Cast me not out from your presence,
and your Holy Spirit take not from me.   R.

Give me back the joy of your salvation,
and a willing spirit sustain in me.
I will teach transgressors your ways,
and sinners shall return to you.   R.

SECOND READING

HEBREWS 5:7–9

CHRIST LEARNED
OBEDIENCE AND BECAME
THE SOURCE OF ETERNAL
SALVATION.

In the days when Christ Jesus was in the flesh,
he offered prayers and supplications
with loud cries and tears
to the one who was able to save him from death,
and he was heard because of his reverence.
Son though he was, he learned obedience
from what he suffered;
and when he was made perfect,
he became the source of eternal salvation
for all who obey him.

VERSE BEFORE THE GOSPEL

JOHN 12:26

Whoever serves me must follow me, says the Lord;
and where I am, there also will my servant be.

GOSPEL

JOHN 12:20–33

IF A GRAIN OF WHEAT
FALLS TO THE GROUND
AND DIES, IT PRODUCES
MUCH FRUIT.

Some Greeks who had come to worship
at the Passover Feast
came to Philip, who was from Bethsaida in Galilee,
and asked him, "Sir, we would like to see Jesus."

Philip went and told Andrew;
then Andrew and Philip went and told Jesus.

Jesus answered them,
"The hour has come for the Son of Man to be glorified.
Amen, amen, I say to you,
unless a grain of wheat falls to the ground and dies,
it remains just a grain of wheat;
but if it dies, it produces much fruit.
Whoever loves his life loses it,
and whoever hates his life in this world
will preserve it for eternal life.

"Whoever serves me must follow me,
  and where I am, there also will my servant be.
The Father will honor whoever serves me.

"I am troubled now. Yet what should I say?
'Father, save me from this hour'?
But it was for this purpose that I came to this hour.
Father, glorify your name."

Then a voice came from heaven,
"I have glorified it and will glorify it again."

The crowd there heard it and said it was thunder;
  but others said, "An angel has spoken to him."
Jesus answered and said,
"This voice did not come for my sake but for yours.
Now is the time of judgment on this world;
  now the ruler of this world will be driven out.
And when I am lifted up from the earth,
  I will draw everyone to myself."
He said this indicating the kind of death he would die.

36C   FIFTH SUNDAY OF LENT

FIRST READING

ISAIAH 43:16–21

SEE, I AM DOING
SOMETHING NEW AND I
GIVE MY PEOPLE DRINK.

◆

The readings given for Year A,
n. 34, may be used in place
of these.

Thus says the LORD,
  who opens a way in the sea
  and a path in the mighty waters,
who leads out chariots and horsemen,
  a powerful army,
till they lie prostrate together, never to rise,
  snuffed out and quenched like a wick.
Remember not the events of the past,
  the things of long ago consider not;
see, I am doing something new!

Now it springs forth, do you not perceive it?
In the desert I make a way,
  in the wasteland, rivers.

Wild beasts honor me,
  jackals and ostriches,
for I put water in the desert
  and rivers in the wasteland
  for my chosen people to drink,
the people whom I formed for myself,
  that they might announce my praise.

RESPONSORIAL

PSALM 126:1–2, 2–3, 4–5,
6 (3)

R. *The Lord has done great things for us;*
   we are filled with joy.

[This psalm is found on page 13 (lectionary number 6).]

SECOND READING

PHILIPPIANS 3:8–14

BECAUSE OF CHRIST,
I CONSIDER EVERYTHING
AS A LOSS, BEING
CONFORMED TO
HIS DEATH.

Brothers and sisters:
I consider everything as a loss
   because of the supreme good of knowing
      Christ Jesus my Lord.
For his sake I have accepted the loss of all things
   and I consider them so much rubbish,
   that I may gain Christ and be found in him,
   not having any righteousness of my own
      based on the law
   but that which comes through faith in Christ,
   the righteousness from God,
   depending on faith to know him and the power
      of his resurrection
   and the sharing of his sufferings by being conformed
      to his death,
   if somehow I may attain the resurrection
      from the dead.

It is not that I have already taken hold of it
   or have already attained perfect maturity,
   but I continue my pursuit in hope that I may possess it,
   since I have indeed been taken possession of
      by Christ Jesus.

Brothers and sisters, I for my part
   do not consider myself to have taken possession.
Just one thing: forgetting what lies behind
   but straining forward to what lies ahead,
   I continue my pursuit toward the goal,
   the prize of God's upward calling, in Christ Jesus.

VERSE BEFORE
THE GOSPEL

JOEL 2:12–13

Even now, says the Lord,
return to me with your whole heart;
for I am gracious and merciful.

GOSPEL

JOHN 8:1–11

LET THE ONE AMONG
YOU WHO IS WITHOUT SIN
BE THE FIRST TO THROW
A STONE AT HER.

Jesus went to the Mount of Olives.
But early in the morning he arrived again
      in the temple area,
   and all the people started coming to him,
   and he sat down and taught them.

Then the scribes and the Pharisees brought a woman
    who had been caught in adultery
    and made her stand in the middle.
They said to him,
    "Teacher, this woman was caught
    in the very act of committing adultery.
Now in the law, Moses commanded us to stone
        such women.
So what do you say?"
They said this to test him,
    so that they could have some charge to bring
        against him.

Jesus bent down and began to write on the ground
        with his finger.
But when they continued asking him,
    he straightened up and said to them,
    "Let the one among you who is without sin
    be the first to throw a stone at her."
Again he bent down and wrote on the ground.

And in response, they went away one by one,
    beginning with the elders.
So he was left alone with the woman before him.

Then Jesus straightened up and said to her,
    "Woman, where are they?
Has no one condemned you?"
She replied, "No one, sir."
Then Jesus said, "Neither do I condemn you.
Go, and from now on do not sin any more."

37A   PALM SUNDAY OF THE LORD'S PASSION
AT THE PROCESSION WITH PALMS

GOSPEL

MATTHEW 21:1–11

BLESSED IS HE WHO
COMES IN THE NAME
OF THE LORD.

When Jesus and the disciples drew near Jerusalem
    and came to Bethphage on the Mount of Olives,
    Jesus sent two disciples, saying to them,
    "Go into the village opposite you,
    and immediately you will find an ass tethered,
    and a colt with her.
Untie them and bring them here to me.
And if anyone should say anything to you, reply,
    'The master has need of them.'
Then he will send them at once."

This happened so that what had been spoken
    through the prophet
  might be fulfilled:
  Say to daughter Zion,
  "Behold, your king comes to you,
  meek and riding on an ass,
  and on a colt, the foal of a beast of burden."

The disciples went and did as Jesus had ordered them.
They brought the ass and the colt and laid their cloaks
    over them,
  and he sat upon them.
The very large crowd spread their cloaks on the road,
  while others cut branches from the trees
  and strewed them on the road.
The crowds preceding him and those following
  kept crying out and saying:
  "Hosanna to the Son of David;
  blessed is the he who comes in the name of the Lord;
  hosanna in the highest."

And when he entered Jerusalem
  the whole city was shaken and asked, "Who is this?"
And the crowds replied,
  "This is Jesus the prophet, from Nazareth in Galilee."

37B   PALM SUNDAY OF THE LORD'S PASSION
AT THE PROCESSION WITH PALMS

GOSPEL

MARK 11:1–10

BLESSED IS HE WHO
COMES IN THE NAME
OF THE LORD.

When Jesus and his disciples drew near to Jerusalem,
  to Bethphage and Bethany at the Mount of Olives,
  he sent two of his disciples and said to them,
  "Go into the village opposite you,
  and immediately on entering it,
  you will find a colt tethered on which no one
    has ever sat.
Untie it and bring it here.
If anyone should say to you,
  'Why are you doing this?' reply,
  'The Master has need of it
  and will send it back here at once.'"

So they went off
  and found a colt tethered at a gate outside
    on the street,
  and they untied it.

Some of the bystanders said to them,
"What are you doing, untying the colt?"
They answered them just as Jesus had told them to,
and they permitted them to do it.

So they brought the colt to Jesus
and put their cloaks over it.
And he sat on it.
Many people spread their cloaks on the road,
and others spread leafy branches
that they had cut from the fields.

Those preceding him as well as those following
kept crying out:
"Hosanna!
Blessed is he who comes in the name of the Lord!
Blessed is the kingdom of our father David
that is to come!
Hosanna in the highest!"

OR:

GOSPEL

JOHN 12:12–16

BLESSED IS HE WHO
COMES IN THE NAME
OF THE LORD.

When the great crowd that had come to the feast heard
that Jesus was coming to Jerusalem,
they took palm branches and went out to meet him,
and cried out:
"Hosanna!
Blessed is he who comes in the name of the Lord,
the king of Israel."

Jesus found an ass and sat upon it, as is written:
Fear no more, O daughter Zion;
see, your king comes, seated upon an ass's colt.

His disciples did not understand this at first,
but when Jesus had been glorified
they remembered that these things were written
about him
and that they had done this for him.

37C PALM SUNDAY OF THE LORD'S PASSION

AT THE PROCESSION WITH PALMS

GOSPEL

LUKE 19:28–40

BLESSED IS HE WHO
COMES IN THE NAME
OF THE LORD.

Jesus proceeded on his journey up to Jerusalem.
As he drew near to Bethphage and Bethany
    at the place called the Mount of Olives,
    he sent two of his disciples.
He said, "Go into the village opposite you,
    and as you enter it you will find a colt tethered
    on which no one has ever sat.
Untie it and bring it here.
And if anyone should ask you,
    'Why are you untying it?'
    you will answer,
    'The Master has need of it.'"

So those who had been sent went off
    and found everything just as he had told them.
And as they were untying the colt, its owners said
        to them,
    "Why are you untying this colt?"
They answered,
    "The Master has need of it."

So they brought it to Jesus,
    threw their cloaks over the colt,
    and helped Jesus to mount.

As he rode along,
    the people were spreading their cloaks on the road;
    and now as he was approaching the slope of
        the Mount of Olives,
    the whole multitude of his disciples
    began to praise God aloud with joy
    for all the mighty deeds they had seen.
They proclaimed:
    "Blessed is the king who comes
    in the name of the Lord.
    Peace in heaven
    and glory in the highest."

Some of the Pharisees in the crowd said to him,
    "Teacher, rebuke your disciples."

He said in reply,
    "I tell you, if they keep silent,
    the stones will cry out!"

FIRST READING

ISAIAH 50:4–7

MY FACE I DID NOT SHIELD
FROM BUFFETS AND
SPITTING, KNOWING THAT
I SHALL NOT BE PUT TO
SHAME.

◆

*The Mass for Palm Sunday is
provided with three readings.
It is strongly recommended that
all three be used, unless pastoral
reasons suggest otherwise.*

*Given, however, the importance
of the account of the Lord's
Passion, the priest, having in mind
the character of each individual
congregation, is authorized to
choose only one of the two
readings prescribed before the
Gospel, or if necessary, he may
read only the account of the
Passion, even in the shorter form.
This permission applies, however,
only to Masses celebrated with a
congregation.*

*The Passion begins directly,
without the greeting or the
acclamation of the people, but
concludes in the usual manner.*

The Lord GOD has given me
   a well-trained tongue,
that I might know how to speak to the weary
   a word that will rouse them.
Morning after morning
   he opens my ear that I may hear;
and I have not rebelled,
   have not turned back.

I gave my back to those who beat me,
   my cheeks to those who plucked my beard;
my face I did not shield
   from buffets and spitting.

The Lord GOD is my help,
   therefore I am not disgraced;
I have set my face like flint,
   knowing that I shall not be put to shame.

RESPONSORIAL PSALM

PSALM 22:8–9, 17–18, 19–20,
23–24 (2a)

R. My God, my God, why have you abandoned me?

[This psalm is found on page 444 (lectionary number 174).]

SECOND READING

PHILIPPIANS 2:6–11

CHRIST HUMBLED HIMSELF.
BECAUSE OF THIS GOD
GREATLY EXALTED HIM.

Christ Jesus, though he was in the form of God,
   did not regard equality with God
   something to be grasped.
Rather, he emptied himself,
   taking the form of a slave,
   coming in human likeness;
   and found human in appearance,
   he humbled himself,
   becoming obedient to the point of death,
   even death on a cross.

Because of this, God greatly exalted him
  and bestowed on him the name
  which is above every name,
  that at the name of Jesus
  every knee should bend,
  of those in heaven and on earth and under the earth,
  and every tongue confess that
  Jesus Christ is Lord,
  to the glory of God the Father.

**VERSE BEFORE
THE GOSPEL**

PHILIPPIANS 2:8–9

*Christ became obedient to the point of death,
even death on a cross.
Because of this, God greatly exalted him
and bestowed on him the name which is above every name.*

GOSPEL A

LONGER FORM
MATTHEW 26:14 — 27:66

SHORTER FORM
MATTHEW 27:11–54

THE PASSION OF OUR
LORD JESUS CHRIST.

One of the Twelve, who was called Judas Iscariot,
  went to the chief priests and said,
  "What are you willing to give me
  if I hand him over to you?"
They paid him thirty pieces of silver,
  and from that time on he looked for an opportunity
  to hand him over.

On the first day of the Feast of Unleavened Bread,
  the disciples approached Jesus and said,
  "Where do you want us to prepare
  for you to eat the Passover?"
He said,
  "Go into the city to a certain man and tell him,
  'The teacher says, "My appointed time draws near;
  in your house I shall celebrate the Passover
    with my disciples."'"
The disciples then did as Jesus had ordered,
  and prepared the Passover.

When it was evening,
  he reclined at table with the Twelve.
And while they were eating, he said,
  "Amen, I say to you, one of you will betray me."
Deeply distressed at this,
  they began to say to him one after another,
  "Surely it is not I, Lord?"
He said in reply,
  "He who has dipped his hand into the dish with me
  is the one who will betray me.

The Son of Man indeed goes, as it is written of him,
    but woe to that man by whom the Son of Man
        is betrayed.
It would be better for that man
        if he had never been born."
Then Judas, his betrayer, said in reply,
    "Surely it is not I, Rabbi?"
He answered, "You have said so."

While they were eating,
    Jesus took bread, said the blessing,
    broke it, and giving it to his disciples said,
    "Take and eat; this is my body."
Then he took a cup, gave thanks, and gave it to them,
        saying,
    "Drink from it, all of you,
    for this is my blood of the covenant,
    which will be shed on behalf of many
    for the forgiveness of sins.
I tell you, from now on I shall not drink this fruit
        of the vine
    until the day when I drink it with you new
    in the kingdom of my Father."
Then, after singing a hymn,
    they went out to the Mount of Olives.

Then Jesus said to them,
    "This night all of you will have your faith in me shaken,
    for it is written:
    I will strike the shepherd,
    and the sheep of the flock will be dispersed;
    but after I have been raised up,
    I shall go before you to Galilee."
Peter said to him in reply,
    "Though all may have their faith in you shaken,
    mine will never be."
Jesus said to him,
    "Amen, I say to you,
    this very night before the cock crows,
    you will deny me three times."
Peter said to him,
    "Even though I should have to die with you,
    I will not deny you."
And all the disciples spoke likewise.

Then Jesus came with them to a place called Gethsemane,
    and he said to his disciples,
    "Sit here while I go over there and pray."

He took along Peter and the two sons of Zebedee,
    and began to feel sorrow and distress.

Then he said to them,
    "My soul is sorrowful even to death.
Remain here and keep watch with me."
He advanced a little and fell prostrate in prayer, saying,
    "My Father, if it is possible,
    let this cup pass from me;
    yet, not as I will, but as you will."
When he returned to his disciples he found them asleep.
He said to Peter,
    "So you could not keep watch with me for one hour?
Watch and pray that you may not undergo the test.
The spirit is willing, but the flesh is weak."
Withdrawing a second time, he prayed again,
    "My Father, if it is not possible that this cup pass
    without my drinking it, your will be done!"
Then he returned once more and found them asleep,
    for they could not keep their eyes open.
He left them and withdrew again and prayed a third time,
    saying the same thing again.
Then he returned to his disciples and said to them,
    "Are you still sleeping and taking your rest?
Behold, the hour is at hand
    when the Son of Man is to be handed over to sinners.
Get up, let us go.
Look, my betrayer is at hand."

While he was still speaking,
    Judas, one of the Twelve, arrived,
    accompanied by a large crowd, with swords and clubs,
    who had come from the chief priests and the elders
    of the people.
His betrayer had arranged a sign with them, saying,
    "The man I shall kiss is the one; arrest him."
Immediately he went over to Jesus and said,
    "Hail, Rabbi!" and he kissed him.
Jesus answered him,
    "Friend, do what you have come for."
Then stepping forward they laid hands on Jesus
    and arrested him.

And behold, one of those who accompanied Jesus
    put his hand to his sword, drew it,
    and struck the high priest's servant, cutting off his ear.
Then Jesus said to him,
    "Put your sword back into its sheath,
    for all who take the sword will perish by the sword.

Do you think that I cannot call upon my Father
    and he will not provide me at this moment
    with more than twelve legions of angels?
But then how would the Scriptures be fulfilled
    which say that it must come to pass in this way?"

At that hour Jesus said to the crowds,
    "Have you come out as against a robber,
    with swords and clubs to seize me?
Day after day I sat teaching in the temple area,
    yet you did not arrest me.
But all this has come to pass
    that the writings of the prophets may be fulfilled."
Then all the disciples left him and fled.

Those who had arrested Jesus led him away
    to Caiaphas the high priest,
    where the scribes and the elders were assembled.

Peter was following him at a distance
    as far as the high priest's courtyard,
    and going inside he sat down with the servants
    to see the outcome.
The chief priests and the entire Sanhedrin
    kept trying to obtain false testimony against Jesus
    in order to put him to death,
    but they found none,
    though many false witnesses came forward.

Finally two came forward who stated,
    "This man said, 'I can destroy the temple of God
    and within three days rebuild it.'"
The high priest rose and addressed him,
    "Have you no answer?
What are these men testifying against you?"
But Jesus was silent.
Then the high priest said to him,
    "I order you to tell us under oath before the living God
    whether you are the Christ, the Son of God."

Jesus said to him in reply,
    "You have said so.
But I tell you:
    From now on you will see *the Son of Man*
    seated at the right hand of the Power'
    and 'coming on the clouds of heaven.'"
Then the high priest tore his robes and said,
    "He has blasphemed!
What further need have we of witnesses?

You have now heard the blasphemy;
     what is your opinion?"
They said in reply,
     "He deserves to die!"
Then they spat in his face and struck him,
     while some slapped him, saying,
     "Prophesy for us, Christ: who is it that struck you?"

Now Peter was sitting outside in the courtyard.
One of the maids came over to him and said,
     "You too were with Jesus the Galilean."
But he denied it in front of everyone, saying,
     "I do not know what you are talking about!"
As he went out to the gate, another girl saw him
     and said to those who were there,
     "This man was with Jesus the Nazarene."
Again he denied it with an oath,
     "I do not know the man!"
A little later the bystanders came over and said to Peter,
     "Surely you too are one of them;
     even your speech gives you away."
At that he began to curse and to swear,
     "I do not know the man."
And immediately a cock crowed.
Then Peter remembered the word that Jesus had spoken:
     "Before the cock crows you will deny me three times."
He went out and began to weep bitterly.

When it was morning,
     all the chief priests and the elders of the people
     took counsel against Jesus to put him to death.
They bound him, led him away,
     and handed him over to Pilate, the governor.

Then Judas, his betrayer, seeing that Jesus
          had been condemned,
     deeply regretted what he had done.
He returned the thirty pieces of silver
     to the chief priests and elders, saying,
     "I have sinned in betraying innocent blood."
They said,
     "What is that to us?
     Look to it yourself."
Flinging the money into the temple,
     he departed and went off and hanged himself.
The chief priests gathered up the money, but said,
     "It is not lawful to deposit this in the temple treasury,
     for it is the price of blood."

After consultation, they used it to buy the potter's field
   as a burial place for foreigners.
That is why that field even today is called
      the Field of Blood.
Then was fulfilled what had been said through Jeremiah
   the prophet,
      And they took the thirty pieces of silver,
      the value of a man with a price on his head,
      a price set by some of the Israelites,
      and they paid it out for the potter's field
      just as the Lord had commanded me.

[Now Jesus stood before the governor,
      who questioned him,
   "Are you the king of the Jews?"
Jesus said, "You say so."
And when he was accused by the chief priests and elders,
   he made no answer.
Then Pilate said to him,
   "Do you not hear how many things they are testifying
      against you?"
But he did not answer him one word,
   so that the governor was greatly amazed.

Now on the occasion of the feast
   the governor was accustomed to release to the crowd
   one prisoner whom they wished.
And at that time they had a notorious prisoner
      called Barabbas.
So when they had assembled, Pilate said to them,
   "Which one do you want me to release to you,
   Barabbas, or Jesus called Christ?"
For he knew that it was out of envy
   that they had handed him over.

While he was still seated on the bench,
   his wife sent him a message,
   "Have nothing to do with that righteous man.
I suffered much in a dream today because of him."

The chief priests and the elders persuaded the crowds
   to ask for Barabbas but to destroy Jesus.
The governor said to them in reply,
   "Which of the two do you want me to release to you?"
They answered, "Barabbas!"
Pilate said to them,
   "Then what shall I do with Jesus called Christ?"
They all said,
   "Let him be crucified!"

But he said,
    "Why? What evil has he done?"
They only shouted the louder,
    "Let him be crucified!"

When Pilate saw that he was not succeeding at all,
    but that a riot was breaking out instead,
    he took water and washed his hands in the sight
      of the crowd,
    saying, "I am innocent of this man's blood.
Look to it yourselves."
And the whole people said in reply,
    "His blood be upon us and upon our children."
Then he released Barabbas to them,
    but after he had Jesus scourged,
    he handed him over to be crucified.

Then the soldiers of the governor took Jesus
      inside the praetorium
    and gathered the whole cohort around him.
They stripped off his clothes
    and threw a scarlet military cloak about him.
Weaving a crown out of thorns, they placed it
      on his head,
    and a reed in his right hand.
And kneeling before him, they mocked him, saying,
    "Hail, King of the Jews!"
They spat upon him and took the reed
    and kept striking him on the head.
And when they had mocked him,
    they stripped him of the cloak,
    dressed him in his own clothes,
    and led him off to crucify him.

As they were going out, they met a Cyrenian
      named Simon;
    this man they pressed into service
    to carry his cross.

And when they came to a place called Golgotha
    — which means Place of the Skull —
    they gave Jesus wine to drink mixed with gall.
But when he had tasted it, he refused to drink.

After they had crucified him,
    they divided his garments by casting lots;
    then they sat down and kept watch over him there.

And they placed over his head the written charge
    against him:
    This is Jesus, the King of the Jews.
Two revolutionaries were crucified with him,
    one on his right and the other on his left.

Those passing by reviled him, shaking their heads
    and saying,
    "You who would destroy the temple and rebuild it
        in three days,
    save yourself, if you are the Son of God,
    and come down from the cross!"
Likewise the chief priests with the scribes and elders
    mocked him and said,
    "He saved others; he cannot save himself.
So he is the king of Israel!
Let him come down from the cross now,
    and we will believe in him.
He trusted in God;
    let him deliver him now if he wants him.
For he said, 'I am the Son of God.'"
The revolutionaries who were crucified with him
    also kept abusing him in the same way.

From noon onward, darkness came over the whole land
    until three in the afternoon.
And about three o'clock Jesus cried out in a loud voice,
    "Eli, Eli, lema sabachthani?"
    which means, "My God, my God,
        why have you forsaken me?"
Some of the bystanders who heard it said,
    "This one is calling for Elijah."
Immediately one of them ran to get a sponge;
    he soaked it in wine, and putting it on a reed,
    gave it to him to drink.
But the rest said,
    "Wait, let us see if Elijah comes to save him."
But Jesus cried out again in a loud voice,
    and gave up his spirit.

♦
*Here all kneel and pause
for a short time.*

And behold, the veil of the sanctuary
    was torn in two from top to bottom.
The earth quaked, rocks were split, tombs were opened,
    and the bodies of many saints who had fallen asleep
        were raised.

And coming forth from their tombs after his resurrection,
   they entered the holy city and appeared to many.

The centurion and the men with him who were
      keeping watch over Jesus
   feared greatly when they saw the earthquake
   and all that was happening, and they said,
   "Truly, this was the Son of God!"]

There were many women there, looking on
      from a distance,
   who had followed Jesus from Galilee,
      ministering to him.
Among them were Mary Magdalene
      and Mary the mother of James and Joseph,
   and the mother of the sons of Zebedee.

When it was evening,
   there came a rich man from Arimathea named Joseph,
   who was himself a disciple of Jesus.
He went to Pilate and asked for the body of Jesus;
   then Pilate ordered it to be handed over.
Taking the body, Joseph wrapped it in clean linen
   and laid it in his new tomb that he had hewn
      in the rock.
Then he rolled a huge stone across the entrance
      to the tomb
   and departed.
But Mary Magdalene and the other Mary
   remained sitting there, facing the tomb.

The next day, the one following the day of preparation,
   the chief priests and the Pharisees
   gathered before Pilate and said,
   "Sir, we remember that this impostor
      while still alive said,
   'After three days I will be raised up.'
Give orders, then, that the grave be secured
      until the third day,
   lest his disciples come and steal him and say
      to the people,
   'He has been raised from the dead.'
This last imposture would be worse than the first."
Pilate said to them,
   "The guard is yours;
   go, secure it as best you can."
So they went and secured the tomb
   by fixing a seal to the stone and setting the guard.

GOSPEL B

LONGER FORM
MARK 14:1 — 15:47

SHORTER FORM
MARK 15:1–39

THE PASSION OF OUR
LORD JESUS CHRIST.

The Passover and the Feast of Unleavened Bread
   were to take place in two days' time.
So the chief priests and the scribes were seeking a way
   to arrest him by treachery and put him to death.
They said, "Not during the festival,
   for fear that there may be a riot among the people."

When he was in Bethany reclining at table
   in the house of Simon the leper,
   a woman came with an alabaster jar of perfumed oil,
   costly genuine spikenard.
She broke the alabaster jar and poured it on his head.
There were some who were indignant.
"Why has there been this waste of perfumed oil?
It could have been sold for more than
    three hundred days' wages
   and the money given to the poor."
They were infuriated with her.

Jesus said, "Let her alone.
Why do you make trouble for her?
She has done a good thing for me.
The poor you will always have with you,
   and whenever you wish you can do good to them,
   but you will not always have me.
She has done what she could.
She has anticipated anointing my body for burial.
Amen, I say to you,
   wherever the gospel is proclaimed to the whole world,
   what she has done will be told in memory of her."

Then Judas Iscariot, one of the Twelve,
   went off to the chief priests to hand him over to them.
When they heard him they were pleased
   and promised to pay him money.
Then he looked for an opportunity to hand him over.

On the first day of the Feast of Unleavened Bread,
   when they sacrificed the Passover lamb,
   his disciples said to him,
   "Where do you want us to go
   and prepare for you to eat the Passover?"
He sent two of his disciples and said to them,
   "Go into the city and a man will meet you,
   carrying a jar of water.
Follow him.
Wherever he enters, say to the master of the house,
   'The Teacher says, "Where is my guest room
   where I may eat the Passover with my disciples?"'"

Then he will show you a large upper room
    furnished and ready.
Make the preparations for us there."
The disciples then went off, entered the city,
    and found it just as he had told them;
    and they prepared the Passover.

When it was evening, he came with the Twelve.
And as they reclined at table and were eating, Jesus said,
    "Amen, I say to you, one of you will betray me,
    one who is eating with me."
They began to be distressed and to say to him, one by one,
    "Surely it is not I?"

He said to them,
    "One of the Twelve, the one who dips with me
        into the dish.
For the Son of Man indeed goes, as it is written of him,
    but woe to that man by whom the Son of Man
        is betrayed.
It would be better for that man if he had never been born."

While they were eating,
    he took bread, said the blessing,
    broke it, and gave it to them, and said,
    "Take it; this is my body."
Then he took a cup, gave thanks, and gave it to them,
    and they all drank from it.
He said to them,
    "This is my blood of the covenant,
    which will be shed for many.
Amen, I say to you,
    I shall not drink again the fruit of the vine
    until the day when I drink it new in the kingdom
        of God."

Then, after singing a hymn,
    they went out to the Mount of Olives.
Then Jesus said to them,
    "All of you will have your faith shaken, for it is written:
    I will strike the shepherd, and the sheep will be dispersed.
But after I have been raised up,
    I shall go before you to Galilee."

Peter said to him,
    "Even though all should have their faith shaken,
    mine will not be."
Then Jesus said to him,
    "Amen, I say to you,

this very night before the cock crows twice
you will deny me three times."
But he vehemently replied,
"Even though I should have to die with you,
I will not deny you."
And they all spoke similarly.

Then they came to a place named Gethsemane,
and he said to his disciples,
"Sit here while I pray."
He took with him Peter, James and John,
and began to be troubled and distressed.
Then he said to them,
"My soul is sorrowful even to death.
Remain here and keep watch."
He advanced a little and fell to the ground and prayed
that if it were possible the hour might pass by him;
he said, "Abba, Father, all things are possible to you.
Take this cup away from me,
but not what I will but what you will."
When he returned he found them asleep.
He said to Peter, "Simon, are you asleep?
Could you not keep watch for one hour?
Watch and pray that you may not undergo the test.
The spirit is willing but the flesh is weak."

Withdrawing again, he prayed, saying the same thing.
Then he returned once more and found them asleep,
for they could not keep their eyes open
and did not know what to answer him.
He returned a third time and said to them,
"Are you still sleeping and taking your rest?
It is enough. The hour has come.
Behold, the Son of Man is to be handed over to sinners.
Get up, let us go.
See, my betrayer is at hand."

Then, while he was still speaking,
Judas, one of the Twelve, arrived,
accompanied by a crowd with swords and clubs
who had come from the chief priests,
the scribes, and the elders.
His betrayer had arranged a signal with them, saying,
"The man I shall kiss is the one;
arrest him and lead him away securely."
He came and immediately went over to him and said,
"Rabbi." And he kissed him.
At this they laid hands on him and arrested him.

One of the bystanders drew his sword,
    struck the high priest's servant, and cut off his ear.

Jesus said to them in reply,
    "Have you come out as against a robber,
    with swords and clubs, to seize me?
Day after day I was with you teaching in the temple area,
    yet you did not arrest me;
    but that the Scriptures may be fulfilled."
And they all left him and fled.
Now a young man followed him
    wearing nothing but a linen cloth about his body.
They seized him,
    but he left the cloth behind and ran off naked.

They led Jesus away to the high priest,
    and all the chief priests and the elders and the scribes
        came together.
Peter followed him at a distance
        into the high priest's courtyard
    and was seated with the guards, warming himself
        at the fire.

The chief priests and the entire Sanhedrin
    kept trying to obtain testimony against Jesus
    in order to put him to death, but they found none.
Many gave false witness against him,
    but their testimony did not agree.
Some took the stand and testified falsely against him,
    alleging, "We heard him say,
    'I will destroy this temple made with hands
    and within three days I will build another
    not made with hands.'"
Even so their testimony did not agree.
The high priest rose before the assembly
        and questioned Jesus,
    saying, "Have you no answer?
What are these men testifying against you?"
But he was silent and answered nothing.
Again the high priest asked him and said to him,
    "Are you the Christ, the son of the Blessed One?"
Then Jesus answered, "I am;
        and *you will see the Son of Man*
            seated at the right hand of the Power
            and coming with the clouds of heaven."

At that the high priest tore his garments and said,
    "What further need have we of witnesses?
You have heard the blasphemy.

What do you think?"
They all condemned him as deserving to die.
Some began to spit on him.
They blindfolded him and struck him and said to him,
    "Prophesy!"
And the guards greeted him with blows.

While Peter was below in the courtyard,
    one of the high priest's maids came along.
Seeing Peter warming himself,
    she looked intently at him and said,
    "You too were with the Nazarene, Jesus."
But he denied it saying,
    "I neither know nor understand
        what you are talking about."
So he went out into the outer court.
Then the cock crowed.
The maid saw him and began again to say
        to the bystanders,
    "This man is one of them."
Once again he denied it.
A little later the bystanders said to Peter once more,
    "Surely you are one of them; for you too are a Galilean."
He began to curse and to swear,
    "I do not know this man about whom you are talking."
And immediately a cock crowed a second time.
Then Peter remembered the word
        that Jesus had said to him,
    "Before the cock crows twice you will deny me
        three times."
He broke down and wept.

[As soon as morning came,
    the chief priests with the elders and the scribes,
    that is, the whole Sanhedrin held a council.
They bound Jesus, led him away, and handed him
        over to Pilate.
Pilate questioned him,
    "Are you the king of the Jews?"
He said to him in reply, "You say so."
The chief priests accused him of many things.
Again Pilate questioned him,
    "Have you no answer?
See how many things they accuse you of."
Jesus gave him no further answer, so that Pilate
        was amazed.

Now on the occasion of the feast he used to release
    to them
  one prisoner whom they requested.
A man called Barabbas was then in prison
  along with the rebels who had committed murder
    in a rebellion.
The crowd came forward and began to ask him
  to do for them as he was accustomed.
Pilate answered,
  "Do you want me to release to you the king
    of the Jews?"
For he knew that it was out of envy
  that the chief priests had handed him over.

But the chief priests stirred up the crowd
  to have him release Barabbas for them instead.
Pilate again said to them in reply,
  "Then what do you want me to do
  with the man you call the king of the Jews?"
They shouted again, "Crucify him."
Pilate said to them, "Why? What evil has he done?"
They only shouted the louder, "Crucify him."
So Pilate, wishing to satisfy the crowd,
  released Barabbas to them and,
    after he had Jesus scourged,
  handed him over to be crucified.

The soldiers led him away inside the palace,
  that is, the praetorium, and assembled
    the whole cohort.
They clothed him in purple and,
  weaving a crown of thorns, placed it on him.
They began to salute him with, "Hail, King of the Jews!"
  and kept striking his head with a reed
    and spitting upon him.
They knelt before him in homage.
And when they had mocked him,
  they stripped him of the purple cloak,
  dressed him in his own clothes,
  and led him out to crucify him.

They pressed into service a passer-by, Simon,
  a Cyrenian, who was coming in from the country,
  the father of Alexander and Rufus,
  to carry his cross.

They brought him to the place of Golgotha
  — which is translated Place of the Skull.

They gave him wine drugged with myrrh,
  but he did not take it.
Then they crucified him and divided his garments
  by casting lots for them to see what each should take.

It was nine o'clock in the morning when they
    crucified him.
The inscription of the charge against him read,
  "The King of the Jews."
With him they crucified two revolutionaries,
  one on his right and one on his left.
Those passing by reviled him,
  shaking their heads and saying,
  "Aha! You who would destroy the temple
  and rebuild it in three days,
  save yourself by coming down from the cross."
Likewise the chief priests, with the scribes,
  mocked him among themselves and said,
  "He saved others; he cannot save himself.
Let the Christ, the King of Israel,
  come down now from the cross
  that we may see and believe."
Those who were crucified with him also kept abusing him.

At noon darkness came over the whole land
  until three in the afternoon.
And at three o'clock Jesus cried out in a loud voice,
  "Eloi, Eloi, lema sabachthani?"
  which is translated,
  "My God, my God, why have you forsaken me?"
Some of the bystanders who heard it said,
  "Look, he is calling Elijah."
One of them ran, soaked a sponge with wine,
    put it on a reed
  and gave it to him to drink saying,
  "Wait, let us see if Elijah comes to take him down."
Jesus gave a loud cry and breathed his last.

◆
*Here all kneel and pause
for a short time.*

The veil of the sanctuary was torn in two
    from top to bottom.
When the centurion who stood facing him
  saw how he breathed his last he said,
  "Truly this man was the Son of God!"]
There were also women looking on from a distance.

Among them were Mary Magdalene,
Mary the mother of the younger James and of Joses,
and Salome.
These women had followed him when he was in Galilee
and ministered to him.
There were also many other women
who had come up with him to Jerusalem.

When it was already evening,
since it was the day of preparation,
the day before the sabbath, Joseph of Arimathea,
a distinguished member of the council,
who was himself awaiting the kingdom of God,
came and courageously went to Pilate
and asked for the body of Jesus.
Pilate was amazed that he was already dead.
He summoned the centurion
and asked him if Jesus had already died.
And when he learned of it from the centurion,
he gave the body to Joseph.
Having bought a linen cloth, he took him down,
wrapped him in the linen cloth,
and laid him in a tomb that had been hewn
out of the rock.
Then he rolled a stone against the entrance to the tomb.
Mary Magdalene and Mary the mother of Joses
watched where he was laid.

GOSPEL C

LONGER FORM
LUKE 22:14 — 23:56

SHORTER FORM
LUKE 23:1–49

THE PASSION OF OUR
LORD JESUS CHRIST.

When the hour came,
Jesus took his place at table with the apostles.
He said to them,
"I have eagerly desired to eat this Passover with you
before I suffer,
for, I tell you, I shall not eat it again
until there is fulfillment in the kingdom of God."

Then he took a cup, gave thanks, and said,
"Take this and share it among yourselves;
for I tell you that from this time on
I shall not drink of the fruit of the vine
until the kingdom of God comes."

Then he took the bread, said the blessing,
broke it, and gave it to them, saying,
"This is my body, which will be given for you;
do this in memory of me."

And likewise the cup after they had eaten, saying,
　　"This cup is the new covenant in my blood,
　　which will be shed for you.

"And yet behold, the hand of the one who is to betray me
　　is with me on the table;
　　for the Son of Man indeed goes as it
　　　　has been determined;
　　but woe to that man by whom he is betrayed."
And they began to debate among themselves
　　who among them would do such a deed.

Then an argument broke out among them
　　about which of them should be regarded as the greatest.
He said to them,
　　"The kings of the Gentiles lord it over them
　　and those in authority over them are addressed as
　　　　'Benefactors';
　　but among you it shall not be so.
Rather, let the greatest among you be as the youngest,
　　and the leader as the servant.
For who is greater:
　　the one seated at table or the one who serves?
Is it not the one seated at table?
I am among you as the one who serves.

"It is you who have stood by me in my trials;
　　and I confer a kingdom on you,
　　just as my Father has conferred one on me,
　　that you may eat and drink at my table in my kingdom;
　　and you will sit on thrones
　　judging the twelve tribes of Israel.

"Simon, Simon, behold Satan has demanded
　　to sift all of you like wheat,
　　but I have prayed that your own faith may not fail;
　　and once you have turned back,
　　you must strengthen your brothers."
He said to him,
　　"Lord, I am prepared to go to prison and to die
　　　　with you."
But he replied,
　　"I tell you, Peter, before the cock crows this day,
　　you will deny three times that you know me."

He said to them,
　　"When I sent you forth without a money bag
　　　　or a sack or sandals,
　　were you in need of anything?"
"No, nothing," they replied.

He said to them,
     "But now one who has a money bag should take it,
     and likewise a sack,
     and one who does not have a sword
     should sell his cloak and buy one.
For I tell you that this Scripture must be fulfilled in me,
     namely, *He was counted among the wicked;*
          and indeed what is written about me is coming
               to fulfillment."

Then they said,
     "Lord, look, there are two swords here."
But he replied, "It is enough!"

Then going out, he went, as was his custom,
          to the Mount of Olives,
     and the disciples followed him.
When he arrived at the place he said to them,
     "Pray that you may not undergo the test."

After withdrawing about a stone's throw from them
          and kneeling,
     he prayed, saying, "Father, if you are willing,
     take this cup away from me;
     still, not my will but yours be done."

And to strengthen him an angel from heaven
          appeared to him.
He was in such agony and he prayed so fervently
     that his sweat became like drops of blood
     falling on the ground.
When he rose from prayer and returned to his disciples,
     he found them sleeping from grief.
He said to them, "Why are you sleeping?
Get up and pray that you may not undergo the test."

While he was still speaking, a crowd approached
     and in front was one of the Twelve, a man named Judas.
He went up to Jesus to kiss him.
Jesus said to him,
     "Judas, are you betraying the Son of Man with a kiss?"

His disciples realized what was about to happen,
          and they asked,
     "Lord, shall we strike with a sword?"
And one of them struck the high priest's servant
     and cut off his right ear.
But Jesus said in reply,
     "Stop, no more of this!"
Then he touched the servant's ear and healed him.

And Jesus said to the chief priests and temple guards
   and elders who had come for him,
    "Have you come out as against a robber,
     with swords and clubs?
Day after day I was with you in the temple area,
   and you did not seize me;
    but this is your hour, the time for the power of darkness."

After arresting him they led him away
   and took him into the house of the high priest;
   Peter was following at a distance.

They lit a fire in the middle of the courtyard
    and sat around it,
   and Peter sat down with them.
When a maid saw him seated in the light,
   she looked intently at him and said,
    "This man too was with him."

But he denied it saying,
   "Woman, I do not know him."
A short while later someone else saw him and said,
   "You too are one of them";
   but Peter answered, "My friend, I am not."
About an hour later, still another insisted,
   "Assuredly, this man too was with him,
   for he also is a Galilean."
But Peter said,
   "My friend, I do not know what you are talking about."
Just as he was saying this, the cock crowed,
   and the Lord turned and looked at Peter;
   and Peter remembered the word of the Lord,
   how he had said to him,
   "Before the cock crows today, you will deny me
    three times."
He went out and began to weep bitterly.

The men who held Jesus in custody were ridiculing
    and beating him.
They blindfolded him and questioned him, saying,
   "Prophesy! Who is it that struck you?"
And they reviled him in saying many other things
    against him.

When day came the council of elders of the people met,
   both chief priests and scribes,
   and they brought him before their Sanhedrin.

They said, "If you are the Christ, tell us,"
    but he replied to them, "If I tell you,
        you will not believe,
    and if I question, you will not respond.
But from this time on the Son of Man will be seated
    at the right hand of the power of God."
They all asked, "Are you then the Son of God?"
He replied to them, "You say that I am."
Then they said, "What further need have we
        for testimony?
We have heard it from his own mouth."

[Then the whole assembly of them arose and brought him
    before Pilate.
They brought charges against him, saying,
    "We found this man misleading our people;
    he opposes the payment of taxes to Caesar
    and maintains that he is the Christ, a king."

Pilate asked him, "Are you the king of the Jews?"
He said to him in reply, "You say so."
Pilate then addressed the chief priests and the crowds,
    "I find this man not guilty."
But they were adamant and said,
    "He is inciting the people with his teaching
        throughout all Judea,
    from Galilee where he began even to here."
On hearing this Pilate asked if the man was a Galilean;
    and upon learning that he was under
        Herod's jurisdiction,
    he sent him to Herod, who was in Jerusalem at that time.

Herod was very glad to see Jesus;
    he had been wanting to see him for a long time,
    for he had heard about him
    and had been hoping to see him perform some sign.
He questioned him at length,
    but he gave him no answer.

The chief priests and scribes, meanwhile,
    stood by accusing him harshly.
Herod and his soldiers treated him contemptuously
        and mocked him,
    and after clothing him in resplendent garb,
    he sent him back to Pilate.
Herod and Pilate became friends that very day,
    even though they had been enemies formerly.
Pilate then summoned the chief priests, the rulers,
    and the people

and said to them, "You brought this man to me
    and accused him of inciting the people to revolt.
I have conducted my investigation in your presence
    and have not found this man guilty
    of the charges you have brought against him,
    nor did Herod, for he sent him back to us.
So no capital crime has been committed by him.
Therefore I shall have him flogged and then release him."

But all together they shouted out,
    "Away with this man!
    Release Barabbas to us."
— Now Barabbas had been imprisoned for a rebellion
    that had taken place in the city and for murder. —
Again Pilate addressed them, still wishing to release Jesus,
    but they continued their shouting,
    "Crucify him! Crucify him!"
Pilate addressed them a third time,
    "What evil has this man done?
    I found him guilty of no capital crime.
Therefore I shall have him flogged and then release him."

With loud shouts, however,
    they persisted in calling for his crucifixion,
    and their voices prevailed.
The verdict of Pilate was that their demand
        should be granted.
So he released the man who had been imprisoned
    for rebellion and murder, for whom they asked,
    and he handed Jesus over to them to deal with
        as they wished.

As they led him away
    they took hold of a certain Simon, a Cyrenian,
    who was coming in from the country;
    and after laying the cross on him,
    they made him carry it behind Jesus.

A large crowd of people followed Jesus,
    including many women who mourned
        and lamented him.
Jesus turned to them and said,
    "Daughters of Jerusalem, do not weep for me;
    weep instead for yourselves and for your children
    for indeed, the days are coming when people will say,
    'Blessed are the barren,
    the wombs that never bore
    and the breasts that never nursed.'

"At that time people will say to the mountains,
    'Fall upon us!'
    and to the hills, 'Cover us!'
    for if these things are done when the wood is green,
    what will happen when it is dry?"

Now two others, both criminals,
    were led away with him to be executed.
When they came to the place called the Skull,
    they crucified him and the criminals there,
    one on his right, the other on his left.

Then Jesus said,
    "Father, forgive them, they know not what they do."
They divided his garments by casting lots.

The people stood by and watched;
    the rulers, meanwhile, sneered at him and said,
    "He saved others, let him save himself
    if he is the chosen one, the Christ of God."

Even the soldiers jeered at him.
As they approached to offer him wine they called out,
    "If you are King of the Jews, save yourself."
Above him there was an inscription that read,
    "This is the King of the Jews."

Now one of the criminals hanging there reviled Jesus,
        saying,
    "Are you not the Christ?
    Save yourself and us."
The other, however, rebuking him, said in reply,
    "Have you no fear of God,
    for you are subject to the same condemnation?
And indeed, we have been condemned justly,
    for the sentence we received corresponds to our crimes,
    but this man has done nothing criminal."
Then he said,
    "Jesus, remember me when you come into
        your kingdom."
He replied to him,
    "Amen, I say to you,
    today you will be with me in Paradise."

It was now about noon and darkness came over
        the whole land
    until three in the afternoon
    because of an eclipse of the sun.
Then the veil of the temple was torn down the middle.

Jesus cried out in a loud voice,
  "Father, into your hands I commend my spirit";
  and when he had said this he breathed his last.

♦
*Here all kneel and pause
for a short time.*

The centurion who witnessed what had happened
    glorified God and said,
  "This man was innocent beyond doubt."
When all the people who had gathered for this spectacle
    saw what had happened,
  they returned home beating their breasts;
  but all his acquaintances stood at a distance,
  including the women who had followed him
    from Galilee
  and saw these events.]

Now there was a virtuous and righteous man
    named Joseph, who,
  though he was a member of the council,
  had not consented to their plan of action.
He came from the Jewish town of Arimathea
  and was awaiting the kingdom of God.
He went to Pilate and asked for the body of Jesus.
After he had taken the body down,
  he wrapped it in a linen cloth
  and laid him in a rock-hewn tomb
  in which no one had yet been buried.

It was the day of preparation,
  and the sabbath was about to begin.
The women who had come from Galilee with him
    followed behind,
  and when they had seen the tomb
  and the way in which his body was laid in it,
    they returned and prepared spices and perfumed oils.
Then they rested on the sabbath according
    to the commandment.

EASTER TRIDUUM

39ABC HOLY THURSDAY
EVENING MASS OF THE LORD'S SUPPER

FIRST READING

EXODUS 12:1–8, 11–14

THE LAW REGARDING
THE PASSOVER MEAL.

The LORD said to Moses and Aaron in the land of Egypt,
"This month shall stand at the head of your calendar;
  you shall reckon it the first month of the year.
Tell the whole community of Israel:
  On the tenth of this month every one of your families
  must procure for itself a lamb, one apiece
    for each household.
If a family is too small for a whole lamb,
  it shall join the nearest household in procuring one
  and shall share in the lamb
  in proportion to the number of persons
    who partake of it.

"The lamb must be a year-old male and without blemish.
You may take it from either the sheep or the goats.
You shall keep it until the fourteenth day of this month,
  and then, with the whole assembly of Israel present,
  it shall be slaughtered during the evening twilight.
They shall take some of its blood
  and apply it to the two doorposts and the lintel
  of every house in which they partake of the lamb.
That same night they shall eat its roasted flesh
  with unleavened bread and bitter herbs.

"This is how you are to eat it:
  with your loins girt, sandals on your feet
    and your staff in hand,
  you shall eat like those who are in flight.
It is the Passover of the LORD.

"For on this same night I will go through Egypt,
  striking down every firstborn of the land,
    both man and beast,
  and executing judgment on all the gods of Egypt —
    I, the LORD!

"But the blood will mark the houses where you are.
Seeing the blood, I will pass over you;
  thus, when I strike the land of Egypt,
  no destructive blow will come upon you.

"This day shall be a memorial feast for you,
    which all your generations shall celebrate
    with pilgrimage to the LORD, as a perpetual institution."

R. Our blessing-cup is a communion with the Blood of Christ.

How shall I make a return to the LORD
    for all the good he has done for me?
The cup of salvation I will take up,
    and I will call upon the name of the LORD.   R.

Precious in the eyes of the LORD
    is the death of his faithful ones.
I am your servant, the son of your handmaid;
    you have loosed my bonds.   R.

To you will I offer sacrifice of thanksgiving,
    and I will call upon the name of the LORD.
My vows to the LORD I will pay
    in the presence of all his people.   R.

SECOND READING

1 CORINTHIANS 11:23–26

FOR AS OFTEN AS YOU EAT
THIS BREAD AND DRINK
THE CUP, YOU PROCLAIM
THE DEATH OF THE LORD.

Brothers and sisters:
I received from the Lord what I also handed on to you,
    that the Lord Jesus, on the night he was handed over,
    took bread, and, after he had given thanks,
    broke it and said, "This is my body that is for you.
Do this in remembrance of me."

In the same way also the cup, after supper, saying,
    "This cup is the new covenant in my blood.
Do this, as often as you drink it, in remembrance of me."
For as often as you eat this bread and drink the cup,
    you proclaim the death of the Lord until he comes.

**VERSE BEFORE
THE GOSPEL**

JOHN 13:34

I give you a new commandment, says the Lord:
Love one another as I have loved you.

GOSPEL

JOHN 13:1–15

JESUS LOVED THEM
TO THE END.

Before the feast of Passover,
    Jesus knew that his hour had come
    to pass from this world to the Father.
He loved his own in the world, and he loved them
    to the end.

The devil had already induced Judas,
    son of Simon the Iscariot, to hand him over.

So, during supper,
  fully aware that the Father had put everything
    into his power
  and that he had come from God and was returning
    to God,
  he rose from supper and took off his outer garments.
He took a towel and tied it around his waist.
Then he poured water into a basin
  and began to wash the disciples' feet
  and dry them with the towel around his waist.

He came to Simon Peter, who said to him,
  "Master, are you going to wash my feet?"
Jesus answered and said to him,
  "What I am doing, you do not understand now,
  but you will understand later."
Peter said to him, "You will never wash my feet."
Jesus answered him,
  "Unless I wash you, you will have no inheritance
    with me."
Simon Peter said to him,
  "Master, then not only my feet, but my hands
    and head as well."
Jesus said to him,
  "Whoever has bathed has no need except to have
    his feet washed,
  for he is clean all over;
  so you are clean, but not all."
For he knew who would betray him;
  for this reason, he said, "Not all of you are clean."

So when he had washed their feet
  and put his garments back on and reclined
    at table again,
  he said to them,
    "Do you realize what I have done for you?
You call me 'teacher' and 'master,' and rightly so,
  for indeed I am.
If I, therefore, the master and teacher,
  have washed your feet,
  you ought to wash one another's feet.
I have given you a model to follow,
  so that as I have done for you, you should also do."

40ABC GOOD FRIDAY OF THE LORD'S PASSION

FIRST READING

ISAIAH 52:13—53:12

HE HIMSELF WAS
WOUNDED FOR OUR SINS.
(FOURTH ORACLE OF THE
SERVANT OF THE LORD).

See, my servant shall prosper,
  he shall be raised high and greatly exalted.
Even as many were amazed at him —
  so marred was his look beyond human semblance
  and his appearance beyond that of the sons of man —
so shall he startle many nations,
  because of him kings shall stand speechless;
for those who have not been told shall see,
  those who have not heard shall ponder it.

Who would believe what we have heard?
  To whom has the arm of the LORD been revealed?
He grew up like a sapling before him,
  like a shoot from the parched earth;
there was in him no stately bearing to make us look
    at him,
  nor appearance that would attract us to him.
He was spurned and avoided by people,
  a man of suffering, accustomed to infirmity,
one of those from whom people hide their faces,
  spurned, and we held him in no esteem.

Yet it was our infirmities that he bore,
  our sufferings that he endured,
while we thought of him as stricken,
  as one smitten by God and afflicted.
But he was pierced for our offenses,
  crushed for our sins;
upon him was the chastisement that makes us whole,
  by his stripes we were healed.

We had all gone astray like sheep,
  each following his own way;
but the LORD laid upon him
  the guilt of us all.

Though he was harshly treated, he submitted
  and opened not his mouth;
like a lamb led to the slaughter
  or a sheep before the shearers,
  he was silent and opened not his mouth.
Oppressed and condemned, he was taken away,
  and who would have thought any more of his destiny?
When he was cut off from the land of the living,
  and smitten for the sin of his people,
a grave was assigned him among the wicked
  and a burial place with evildoers,

though he had done no wrong
    nor spoken any falsehood.
But the LORD was pleased
    to crush him in infirmity.

If he gives his life as an offering for sin,
    he shall see his descendants in a long life,
    and the will of the LORD shall be accomplished
        through him.

Because of his affliction
    he shall see the light
    in fullness of days;
    through his suffering, my servant shall justify many,
    and their guilt he shall bear.

Therefore I will give him his portion among the great,
    and he shall divide the spoils with the mighty,
because he surrendered himself to death
    and was counted among the wicked;
and he shall take away the sins of many,
    and win pardon for their offenses.

RESPONSORIAL PSALM

PSALM 31:2, 6, 12–13, 15–16, 17, 25 (LUKE 23:46)

R. Father, into your hands I commend my spirit.

In you, O LORD, I take refuge;
    let me never be put to shame.
In your justice rescue me.
    Into your hands I commend my spirit;
    you will redeem me, O LORD, O faithful God.   R.

For all my foes I am an object of reproach,
    a laughingstock to my neighbors,
        and a dread to my friends;
    they who see me abroad flee from me.
I am forgotten like the unremembered dead;
    I am like a dish that is broken.   R.

But my trust is in you, O LORD;
    I say, "You are my God.
In your hands is my destiny; rescue me
    from the clutches of my enemies and my persecutors."   R.

Let your face shine upon your servant;
    save me in your kindness.
Take courage and be stouthearted,
    all you who hope in the LORD.   R.

SECOND READING

HEBREWS 4:14–16; 5:7–9

JESUS LEARNED OBEDIENCE
AND BECAME THE SOURCE
OF SALVATION FOR ALL
WHO OBEY HIM.

Brothers and sisters:
Since we have a great high priest who has passed
    through the heavens,
    Jesus, the Son of God,
    let us hold fast to our confession.
For we do not have a high priest
    who is unable to sympathize with our weaknesses,
    but one who has similarly been tested in every way,
    yet without sin.
So let us confidently approach the throne of grace
    to receive mercy and to find grace for timely help.

In the days when Christ was in the flesh,
    he offered prayers and supplications with loud cries
        and tears
    to the one who was able to save him from death,
    and he was heard because of his reverence.
Son though he was, he learned obedience
    from what he suffered;
    and when he was made perfect,
    he became the source of eternal salvation
        for all who obey him.

**VERSE BEFORE
THE GOSPEL**

PHILIPPIANS 2:8–9

*Christ became obedient to the point of death,
even death on a cross.
Because of this, God greatly exalted him
and bestowed on him the name which is above
    every other name.*

GOSPEL

JOHN 18:1—19:42

THE PASSION OF OUR
LORD JESUS CHRIST.

Jesus went out with his disciples across the Kidron valley
    to where there was a garden,
    into which he and his disciples entered.
Judas his betrayer also knew the place,
    because Jesus had often met there with his disciples.
So Judas got a band of soldiers and guards
    from the chief priests and the Pharisees
    and went there with lanterns, torches, and weapons.

Jesus, knowing everything that was going to happen
    to him,
    went out and said to them, "Whom are you looking for?"
They answered him, "Jesus the Nazarene."
He said to them, "I AM."
Judas his betrayer was also with them.
When he said to them, "I AM,"
    they turned away and fell to the ground.

So he again asked them,
  "Whom are you looking for?"
They said, "Jesus the Nazarene."
Jesus answered,
  "I told you that I AM.
So if you are looking for me, let these men go."
This was to fulfill what he had said,
  "I have not lost any of those you gave me."

Then Simon Peter, who had a sword, drew it,
  struck the high priest's slave, and cut off his right ear.
The slave's name was Malchus.
Jesus said to Peter,
  "Put your sword into its scabbard.
Shall I not drink the cup that the Father gave me?"

So the band of soldiers, the tribune, and the Jewish guards
    seized Jesus,
  bound him, and brought him to Annas first.
He was the father-in-law of Caiaphas,
  who was high priest that year.
It was Caiaphas who had counseled the Jews
  that it was better that one man should die
    rather than the people.

Simon Peter and another disciple followed Jesus.
Now the other disciple was known to the high priest,
  and he entered the courtyard of the high priest
    with Jesus.
But Peter stood at the gate outside.
So the other disciple, the acquaintance of the high priest,
  went out and spoke to the gatekeeper
    and brought Peter in.
Then the maid who was the gatekeeper said to Peter,
  "You are not one of this man's disciples, are you?"
He said, "I am not."
Now the slaves and the guards were standing
    around a charcoal fire
  that they had made, because it was cold,
  and were warming themselves.
Peter was also standing there keeping warm.

The high priest questioned Jesus
  about his disciples and about his doctrine.
Jesus answered him,
  "I have spoken publicly to the world.
I have always taught in a synagogue
  or in the temple area where all the Jews gather,
  and in secret I have said nothing. Why ask me?

Ask those who heard me what I said to them.
They know what I said."

When he had said this,
    one of the temple guards standing there struck Jesus
        and said,
    "Is this the way you answer the high priest?"
Jesus answered him,
    "If I have spoken wrongly, testify to the wrong;
    but if I have spoken rightly, why do you strike me?"
Then Annas sent him bound to Caiaphas the high priest.

Now Simon Peter was standing there keeping warm.
And they said to him,
    "You are not one of his disciples, are you?"
He denied it and said,
    "I am not."
One of the slaves of the high priest,
    a relative of the one whose ear Peter had cut off, said,
    "Didn't I see you in the garden with him?"
Again Peter denied it.
And immediately the cock crowed.

Then they brought Jesus from Caiaphas to the praetorium.
It was morning.
And they themselves did not enter the praetorium,
    in order not to be defiled so that they could
        eat the Passover.
So Pilate came out to them and said,
    "What charge do you bring against this man?"
They answered and said to him,
    "If he were not a criminal,
    we would not have handed him over to you."
At this, Pilate said to them,
    "Take him yourselves, and judge him
        according to your law."
The Jews answered him,
    "We do not have the right to execute anyone,"
    in order that the word of Jesus might be fulfilled
    that he said indicating the kind of death he would die.

So Pilate went back into the praetorium
    and summoned Jesus and said to him,
    "Are you the King of the Jews?"
Jesus answered,
    "Do you say this on your own
    or have others told you about me?"
Pilate answered,
    "I am not a Jew, am I?

Your own nation and the chief priests handed you over
   to me.
What have you done?"
Jesus answered,
   "My kingdom does not belong to this world.
If my kingdom did belong to this world,
   my attendants would be fighting
   to keep me from being handed over to the Jews.
But as it is, my kingdom is not here."
So Pilate said to him,
   "Then you are a king?"
Jesus answered,
   "You say I am a king.
For this I was born and for this I came into the world,
   to testify to the truth.
Everyone who belongs to the truth listens to my voice."
Pilate said to him, "What is truth?"

When he had said this,
   he again went out to the Jews and said to them,
   "I find no guilt in him.
But you have a custom that I release one prisoner
   to you at Passover.
Do you want me to release to you the King of the Jews?"
They cried out again,
   "Not this one but Barabbas!"
Now Barabbas was a revolutionary.

Then Pilate took Jesus and had him scourged.
And the soldiers wove a crown out of thorns
   and placed it on his head,
   and clothed him in a purple cloak,
   and they came to him and said,
   "Hail, King of the Jews!"
And they struck him repeatedly.
Once more Pilate went out and said to them,
   "Look, I am bringing him out to you,
   so that you may know that I find no guilt in him."
So Jesus came out,
   wearing the crown of thorns and the purple cloak.
And he said to them, "Behold, the man!"

When the chief priests and the guards saw him
   they cried out,
   "Crucify him, crucify him!"
Pilate said to them,
   "Take him yourselves and crucify him.
I find no guilt in him."

The Jews answered,
   "We have a law, and according to that law
      he ought to die,
   because he made himself the Son of God."

Now when Pilate heard this statement,
   he became even more afraid,
   and went back into the praetorium and said to Jesus,
   "Where are you from?"
Jesus did not answer him.

So Pilate said to him,
   "Do you not speak to me?
Do you not know that I have power to release you
   and I have power to crucify you?"
Jesus answered him,
   "You would have no power over me
   if it had not been given to you from above.
For this reason the one who handed me over to you
   has the greater sin."
Consequently, Pilate tried to release him;
      but the Jews cried out,
   "If you release him, you are not a Friend of Caesar.
Everyone who makes himself a king opposes Caesar."

When Pilate heard these words he brought Jesus out
   and seated him on the judge's bench
   in the place called Stone Pavement,
      in Hebrew, Gabbatha.
It was preparation day for Passover, and it was about noon.
And he said to the Jews,
   "Behold, your king!"
They cried out,
   "Take him away, take him away! Crucify him!"
Pilate said to them,
   "Shall I crucify your king?"
The chief priests answered,
   "We have no king but Caesar."
Then he handed him over to them to be crucified.

So they took Jesus, and, carrying the cross himself,
   he went out to what is called the Place of the Skull,
   in Hebrew, Golgotha.
There they crucified him, and with him two others,
   one on either side, with Jesus in the middle.

Pilate also had an inscription written and put on the cross.
It read,
   "Jesus the Nazarene, the King of the Jews."

Now many of the Jews read this inscription,
  because the place where Jesus was crucified
    was near the city;
  and it was written in Hebrew, Latin, and Greek.

So the chief priests of the Jews said to Pilate,
  "Do not write 'The King of the Jews,'
  but that he said, 'I am the King of the Jews.'"
Pilate answered,
  "What I have written, I have written."

When the soldiers had crucified Jesus,
  they took his clothes and divided them into four shares,
  a share for each soldier.
They also took his tunic, but the tunic was seamless,
  woven in one piece from the top down.
So they said to one another,
  "Let's not tear it, but cast lots for it to see
    whose it will be,"
  in order that the passage of Scripture might be fulfilled
    that says:
  They divided my garments among them,
  and for my vesture they cast lots.
This is what the soldiers did.

Standing by the cross of Jesus were his mother
  and his mother's sister, Mary the wife of Clopas,
  and Mary of Magdala.

When Jesus saw his mother and the disciple there
    whom he loved
  he said to his mother, "Woman, behold, your son."
Then he said to the disciple,
  "Behold, your mother."
And from that hour the disciple took her into his home.

After this, aware that everything was now finished,
  in order that the Scripture might be fulfilled,
  Jesus said, "I thirst."
There was a vessel filled with common wine.
So they put a sponge soaked in wine on a sprig of hyssop
  and put it up to his mouth.
When Jesus had taken the wine, he said,
  "It is finished."
And bowing his head, he handed over the spirit.

◆
Here all kneel and pause
for a short time.

Now since it was preparation day,
    in order that the bodies might not remain
    on the cross on the sabbath,
    for the sabbath day of that week was a solemn one,
    the Jews asked Pilate that their legs be broken
    and that they be taken down.

So the soldiers came and broke the legs of the first
    and then of the other one who was crucified with Jesus.
But when they came to Jesus and saw that he was
      already dead,
    they did not break his legs,
    but one soldier thrust his lance into his side,
    and immediately blood and water flowed out.

An eyewitness has testified, and his testimony is true;
    he knows that he is speaking the truth,
    so that you also may come to believe.

For this happened so that the Scripture passage
      might be fulfilled:
    Not a bone of it will be broken.
And again another passage says:
    They will look upon him whom they have pierced.

After this, Joseph of Arimathea,
    secretly a disciple of Jesus for fear of the Jews,
    asked Pilate if he could remove the body of Jesus.
And Pilate permitted it.
So he came and took his body.

Nicodemus, the one who had first come to him at night,
    also came bringing a mixture of myrrh and aloes
    weighing about one hundred pounds.
They took the body of Jesus
    and bound it with burial cloths along with the spices,
    according to the Jewish burial custom.
Now in the place where he had been crucified
      there was a garden,
    and in the garden a new tomb, in which no one
      had yet been buried.
So they laid Jesus there because of the Jewish
      preparation day;
    for the tomb was close by.

41ABC THE VIGIL IN THE HOLY NIGHT OF EASTER

EASTER SUNDAY: THE RESURRECTION OF THE LORD

FIRST READING

LONGER FORM
GENESIS 1:1—2:2

SHORTER FORM
GENESIS 1:1, 26–31a

GOD LOOKED AT
EVERYTHING HE HAD
MADE, AND HE FOUND
IT VERY GOOD.

◆
Nine readings are assigned to the Easter Vigil: seven from the Old Testament and two from the New. If circumstances demand in individual cases, the number of prescribed readings may be reduced. Three selections from the Old Testament, however, should be read before the epistle and Gospel, although when necessary, two may be read. In any case, the reading from Exodus about the escape through the Red Sea (reading 3) should never be omitted.

[In the beginning, when God created the heavens
    and the earth,]
  the earth was a formless wasteland,
    and darkness covered the abyss,
  while a mighty wind swept over the waters.

Then God said,
  "Let there be light," and there was light.
God saw how good the light was.
God then separated the light from the darkness.
God called the light "day," and the darkness
    he called "night."
Thus evening came, and morning followed—the first day.

Then God said,
  "Let there be a dome in the middle of the waters,
  to separate one body of water from the other."
And so it happened:
  God made the dome,
  and it separated the water above the dome
    from the water below it.
God called the dome "the sky."
Evening came, and morning followed—the second day.

Then God said,
  "Let the water under the sky be gathered
    into a single basin,
  so that the dry land may appear."
And so it happened:
  the water under the sky was gathered into its basin,
  and the dry land appeared.
God called the dry land "the earth,"
  and the basin of the water he called "the sea."
God saw how good it was.
Then God said,
  "Let the earth bring forth vegetation:
  every kind of plant that bears seed
  and every kind of fruit tree on earth
  that bears fruit with its seed in it."
And so it happened:
  the earth brought forth every kind of plant
    that bears seed
  and every kind of fruit tree on earth
  that bears fruit with its seed in it.
God saw how good it was.
Evening came, and morning followed—the third day.

Then God said:
    "Let there be lights in the dome of the sky,
    to separate day from night.
Let them mark the fixed times, the days and the years,
    and serve as luminaries in the dome of the sky,
    to shed light upon the earth."
And so it happened:
    God made the two great lights,
    the greater one to govern the day,
    and the lesser one to govern the night;
    and he made the stars.
God set them in the dome of the sky,
    to shed light upon the earth,
    to govern the day and the night,
    and to separate the light from the darkness.
God saw how good it was.
Evening came, and morning followed — the fourth day.

Then God said,
    "Let the water teem with an abundance
        of living creatures,
    and on the earth let birds fly beneath the dome
        of the sky."
And so it happened:
    God created the great sea monsters
    and all kinds of swimming creatures
        with which the water teems,
    and all kinds of winged birds.
God saw how good it was, and God blessed them, saying,
    "Be fertile, multiply, and fill the water of the seas;
    and let the birds multiply on the earth."
Evening came, and morning followed — the fifth day.

Then God said,
    "Let the earth bring forth all kinds of living creatures:
    cattle, creeping things, and wild animals of all kinds."
And so it happened:
    God made all kinds of wild animals, all kinds of cattle,
    and all kinds of creeping things of the earth.
God saw how good it was.

Then [God said:
    "Let us make man in our image, after our likeness.
Let them have dominion over the fish of the sea,
    the birds of the air, and the cattle,
    and over all the wild animals
    and all the creatures that crawl on the ground."

God created man in his image;
in the image of God he created him;
male and female he created them.

God blessed them, saying:
"Be fertile and multiply;
fill the earth and subdue it.
Have dominion over the fish of the sea,
the birds of the air,
and all the living things that move on the earth."

God also said:
"See, I give you every seed-bearing plant
all over the earth
and every tree that has seed-bearing fruit on it
to be your food;
and to all the animals of the land,
all the birds of the air,
and all the living creatures that crawl on the ground,
I give all the green plants for food."
And so it happened.

God looked at everything he had made,
and he found it very good.]
Evening came, and morning followed — the sixth day.

Thus the heavens and the earth and all their array
were completed.
Since on the seventh day God was finished
with the work he had been doing,
he rested on the seventh day from all the work
he had undertaken.

RESPONSORIAL PSALM

PSALM 104:1–2, 5–6, 10, 12, 13–14, 24, 35 (30)

R. *Lord, send out your Spirit, and renew the face of the earth.*

Bless the LORD, O my soul!
O LORD, my God, you are great indeed!
You are clothed with majesty and glory,
robed in light as with a cloak. R.

You fixed the earth upon its foundation,
not to be moved forever;
with the ocean, as with a garment, you covered it;
above the mountains the waters stood. R.

You send forth springs into the watercourses
that wind among the mountains.
Beside them the birds of heaven dwell;
from among the branches they send forth their song. R.

You water the mountains from your palace;
  the earth is replete with the fruit of your works.
You raise grass for the cattle,
  and vegetation for man's use,
  producing bread from the earth.   R.

How manifold are your works, O LORD!
  In wisdom you have wrought them all—
  the earth is full of your creatures.
Bless the LORD, O my soul!   R.

OR:

PSALM 33:4–5, 6–7, 12–13, 20–22 (5b)

R. The earth is full of the goodness of the Lord.

Upright is the word of the LORD,
  and all his works are trustworthy.
He loves justice and right;
  of the kindness of the LORD the earth is full.   R.

By the word of the LORD the heavens were made;
  by the breath of his mouth all their host.
He gathers the waters of the sea as in a flask;
  in cellars he confines the deep.   R.

Blessed the nation whose God is the LORD,
  the people he has chosen for his own inheritance.
From heaven the LORD looks down;
  he sees all mankind.   R.

Our soul waits for the LORD,
  who is our help and our shield.
May your kindness, O LORD, be upon us
  who have put our hope in you.   R.

SECOND READING

LONGER FORM
GENESIS 22:1–18

SHORTER FORM
GENESIS 22:1–2, 9a, 10–13, 15–18

THE SACRIFICE OF ABRAHAM, OUR FATHER IN FAITH.

[God put Abraham to the test.
He called to him, "Abraham!"
"Here I am," he replied.
Then God said:
  "Take your son Isaac, your only one, whom you love,
  and go to the land of Moriah.
There you shall offer him up as a holocaust
  on a height that I will point out to you."]

Early the next morning Abraham saddled his donkey,
  took with him his son Isaac and two of his servants
    as well,
  and with the wood that he had cut for the holocaust,
  set out for the place of which God had told him.

On the third day Abraham got sight of the place
    from afar.
Then he said to his servants:
  "Both of you stay here with the donkey,
  while the boy and I go on over yonder.
We will worship and then come back to you."

Thereupon Abraham took the wood for the holocaust
and laid it on his son Isaac's shoulders,
while he himself carried the fire and the knife.

As the two walked on together,
Isaac spoke to his father Abraham:
"Father!" Isaac said.
"Yes, son," he replied.
Isaac continued, "Here are the fire and the wood,
but where is the sheep for the holocaust?"
"Son," Abraham answered,
"God himself will provide the sheep for the holocaust."
Then the two continued going forward.

[When they came to the place of which God
had told him,
Abraham built an altar there and arranged the wood
on it.]
Next he tied up his son Isaac,
and put him on top of the wood on the altar.

[Then he reached out and took the knife
to slaughter his son.
But the Lord's messenger called to him from heaven,
"Abraham, Abraham!"
"Here I am," he answered.
"Do not lay your hand on the boy," said the messenger.
"Do not do the least thing to him.
I know now how devoted you are to God,
since you did not withhold from me your own
beloved son."
As Abraham looked about,
he spied a ram caught by its horns in the thicket.
So he went and took the ram
and offered it up as a holocaust in place of his son.]
Abraham named the site Yahweh-yireh;
hence people now say,
"On the mountain the Lord will see."

[Again the Lord's messenger called to Abraham
from heaven and said:
"I swear by myself, declares the Lord,
that because you acted as you did
in not withholding from me your beloved son,
I will bless you abundantly
and make your descendants as countless
as the stars of the sky and the sands of the seashore;
your descendants shall take possession
of the gates of their enemies,

and in your descendants all the nations of the earth
    shall find blessing—
all this because you obeyed my command."]

RESPONSORIAL PSALM

PSALM 16:5, 8, 9–10, 11 (1)

R. You are my inheritance, O Lord.

O Lord, my allotted portion and my cup,
    you it is who hold fast my lot.
I set the Lord ever before me;
    with him at my right hand I shall not be disturbed.   R.

Therefore my heart is glad and my soul rejoices,
    my body, too, abides in confidence;
because you will not abandon my soul
      to the netherworld,
    nor will you suffer your faithful one
      to undergo corruption.   R.

You will show me the path to life,
    fullness of joys in your presence,
    the delights at your right hand forever.   R.

THIRD READING

EXODUS 14:15—15:1

THE ISRAELITES MARCHED
ON DRY LAND THROUGH
THE MIDST OF THE SEA.

The Lord said to Moses, "Why are you crying out to me?
Tell the Israelites to go forward.
And you, lift up your staff and, with hand outstretched
    over the sea,
  split the sea in two,
  that the Israelites may pass through it on dry land.
But I will make the Egyptians so obstinate
  that they will go in after them.
Then I will receive glory through Pharaoh
    and all his army,
  his chariots and charioteers.
The Egyptians shall know that I am the Lord,
  when I receive glory through Pharaoh
  and his chariots and charioteers."

The angel of God, who had been leading Israel's camp,
  now moved and went around behind them.
The column of cloud also, leaving the front,
  took up its place behind them,
  so that it came between the camp of the Egyptians
  and that of Israel.
But the cloud now became dark,
    and thus the night passed
  without the rival camps coming any closer together
  all night long.

Then Moses stretched out his hand over the sea,
   and the LORD swept the sea
   with a strong east wind throughout the night
   and so turned it into dry land.
When the water was thus divided,
   the Israelites marched into the midst of the sea
     on dry land,
   with the water like a wall to their right and to their left.

The Egyptians followed in pursuit;
   all Pharaoh's horses and chariots and charioteers
     went after them
   right into the midst of the sea.
In the night watch just before dawn
   the LORD cast through the column of the fiery cloud
   upon the Egyptian force a glance that threw it
     into a panic;
   and he so clogged their chariot wheels
   that they could hardly drive.
With that the Egyptians sounded the retreat before Israel,
   because the LORD was fighting for them
     against the Egyptians.

Then the LORD told Moses,
   "Stretch out your hand over the sea,
   that the water may flow back upon the Egyptians,
   upon their chariots and their charioteers."
So Moses stretched out his hand over the sea,
   and at dawn the sea flowed back to its normal depth.
The Egyptians were fleeing head on toward the sea,
   when the LORD hurled them into its midst.
As the water flowed back,
   it covered the chariots and the charioteers
     of Pharaoh's whole army
   which had followed the Israelites into the sea.
Not a single one of them escaped.

But the Israelites had marched on dry land
   through the midst of the sea,
   with the water like a wall to their right and to their left.
Thus the LORD saved Israel on that day
   from the power of the Egyptians.
When Israel saw the Egyptians lying dead on the seashore
   and beheld the great power that the LORD
   had shown against the Egyptians,
   they feared the LORD and believed in him
     and in his servant Moses.

Then Moses and the Israelites sang this song to the LORD:
I will sing to the LORD, for he is gloriously triumphant;
horse and chariot he has cast into the sea.

RESPONSORIAL PSALM

EXODUS 15:1–2, 3–4, 5–6, 17–18 (1b)

R. *Let us sing to the Lord; he has covered himself in glory.*

I will sing to the LORD, for he is gloriously triumphant;
horse and chariot he has cast into the sea.
My strength and my courage is the LORD,
and he has been my savior.
He is my God, I praise him;
the God of my father, I extol him.   R.

The LORD is a warrior,
LORD is his name!
Pharaoh's chariots and army he hurled into the sea;
the elite of his officers were submerged in the Red Sea.   R.

The flood waters covered them,
they sank into the depths like a stone.
Your right hand, O LORD, magnificent in power,
your right hand, O LORD, has shattered the enemy.   R.

You brought in the people you redeemed
and planted them on the mountain
of your inheritance —
the place where you made your seat, O LORD,
the sanctuary, LORD, which your hands established.
The LORD shall reign forever and ever.   R.

FOURTH READING

ISAIAH 54:5–14

WITH ENDURING LOVE, THE LORD YOUR REDEEMER TAKES PITY ON YOU.

The One who has become your husband is your Maker;
his name is the LORD of hosts;
your redeemer is the Holy One of Israel,
called God of all the earth.
The LORD calls you back,
like a wife forsaken and grieved in spirit,
a wife married in youth and then cast off,
says your God.

For a brief moment I abandoned you,
but with great tenderness I will take you back.
In an outburst of wrath, for a moment
I hid my face from you;
but with enduring love I take pity on you,
says the LORD, your redeemer.

This is for me like the days of Noah,
when I swore that the waters of Noah
should never again deluge the earth;
so I have sworn not to be angry with you,
or to rebuke you.

Though the mountains leave their place
and the hills be shaken,
my love shall never leave you
nor my covenant of peace be shaken,
says the LORD, who has mercy on you.

O afflicted one, storm-battered and unconsoled,
I lay your pavements in carnelians,
and your foundations in sapphires;
I will make your battlements of rubies,
your gates of carbuncles,
and all your walls of precious stones.

All your children shall be taught by the LORD,
and great shall be the peace of your children.
In justice shall you be established,
far from the fear of oppression,
where destruction cannot come near you.

RESPONSORIAL PSALM

PSALM 30:2, 4, 5–6, 11–12, 13 (2a)

R. I will praise you, Lord, for you have rescued me.

I will extol you, O LORD, for you drew me clear
and did not let my enemies rejoice over me.
O LORD, you brought me up from the netherworld;
you preserved me from among those going down
into the pit.   R.

Sing praise to the LORD, you his faithful ones,
and give thanks to his holy name.
For his anger lasts but a moment;
a lifetime, his good will.
At nightfall, weeping enters in,
but with the dawn, rejoicing.   R.

Hear, O LORD, and have pity on me;
O LORD, be my helper.
You changed my mourning into dancing;
O LORD, my God, forever will I give you thanks.   R.

FIFTH READING

ISAIAH 55:1–11

COME TO ME THAT YOU MAY HAVE LIFE. I WILL RENEW WITH YOU AN EVERLASTING COVENANT.

[This reading is found on page 52 (lectionary number 21).]

R. *You will draw water joyfully from the springs of salvation.*

God indeed is my savior;
  I am confident and unafraid.
My strength and my courage is the LORD,
  and he has been my savior.
With joy you will draw water
  at the fountain of salvation.   R.

Give thanks to the LORD, acclaim his name;
  among the nations make known his deeds,
  proclaim how exalted is his name.   R.

Sing praise to the LORD for his glorious achievement;
  let this be known throughout all the earth.
Shout with exultation, O city of Zion,
  for great in your midst
  is the Holy One of Israel!   R.

SIXTH READING

BARUCH 3:9–15, 32—4:4

WALK TOWARD THE
SPLENDOR OF THE LORD.

Hear, O Israel, the commandments of life:
  listen, and know prudence!
How is it, Israel,
  that you are in the land of your foes,
  grown old in a foreign land,
defiled with the dead,
  accounted with those destined for the netherworld?
You have forsaken the fountain of wisdom!
Had you walked in the way of God,
  you would have dwelt in enduring peace.

Learn where prudence is,
  where strength, where understanding;
that you may know also
  where are length of days, and life,
  where light of the eyes, and peace.
Who has found the place of wisdom,
  who has entered into her treasures?

The One who knows all things knows her;
  he has probed her by his knowledge —
the One who established the earth for all time,
  and filled it with four-footed beasts;
  he who dismisses the light, and it departs,
  calls it, and it obeys him trembling;
before whom the stars at their posts
  shine and rejoice;
when he calls them, they answer, "Here we are!"
  shining with joy for their Maker.

Such is our God;
  no other is to be compared to him:

He has traced out the whole way of understanding,
    and has given her to Jacob, his servant,
    to Israel, his beloved son.

Since then she has appeared on earth,
    and moved among people.
She is the book of the precepts of God,
    the law that endures forever;
all who cling to her will live,
    but those will die who forsake her.

Turn, O Jacob, and receive her:
    walk by her light toward splendor.
Give not your glory to another,
    your privileges to an alien race.
Blessed are we, O Israel;
    for what pleases God is known to us!

RESPONSORIAL PSALM

PSALM 19:8, 9, 10, 11
(JOHN 6:68c)

R. Lord, you have the words of everlasting life.

The law of the LORD is perfect,
    refreshing the soul;
the decree of the LORD is trustworthy,
    giving wisdom to the simple.   R.

The precepts of the LORD are right,
    rejoicing the heart;
the command of the LORD is clear,
    enlightening the eye.   R.

The fear of the LORD is pure,
    enduring forever;
the ordinances of the LORD are true,
    all of them just.   R.

They are more precious than gold,
    than a heap of purest gold;
sweeter also than syrup
    or honey from the comb.   R.

SEVENTH READING

EZEKIEL 36:16–17a, 18–28

I SHALL SPRINKLE CLEAN
WATER UPON YOU AND
I SHALL GIVE YOU A NEW
HEART.

The word of the LORD came to me, saying:
    Son of man, when the house of Israel lived in their land,
    they defiled it by their conduct and deeds.
Therefore I poured out my fury upon them
    because of the blood that they poured out
        on the ground,
    and because they defiled it with idols.
I scattered them among the nations,
    dispersing them over foreign lands;
    according to their conduct and deeds I judged them.

But when they came among the nations
    wherever they came,
  they served to profane my holy name,
  because it was said of them:
    "These are the people of the LORD,
  yet they had to leave their land."

So I have relented because of my holy name
  which the house of Israel profaned
  among the nations where they came.
Therefore say to the house of Israel:
Thus says the Lord GOD:
  Not for your sakes do I act, house of Israel,
  but for the sake of my holy name,
  which you profaned among the nations
    to which you came.

I will prove the holiness of my great name,
    profaned among the nations,
  in whose midst you have profaned it.
Thus the nations shall know that I am the LORD,
    says the Lord GOD,
  when in their sight I prove my holiness through you.

For I will take you away from among the nations,
  gather you from all the foreign lands,
  and bring you back to your own land.

I will sprinkle clean water upon you
    to cleanse you from all your impurities,
  and from all your idols I will cleanse you.
I will give you a new heart and place a new spirit
    within you,
  taking from your bodies your stony hearts
  and giving you natural hearts.
I will put my spirit within you and make you live
    by my statutes,
  careful to observe my decrees.
You shall live in the land I gave your fathers;
  you shall be my people, and I will be your God.

RESPONSORIAL PSALM

PSALM 42:3, 5; 43:3, 4 (42:2)

◆
A *When baptism is celebrated*

R. *Like a deer that longs for running streams,*
    my soul longs for you, my God.

Athirst is my soul for God, the living God.
    When shall I go and behold the face of God?   R.

I went with the throng
    and led them in procession to the house of God,
amid loud cries of joy and thanksgiving,
    with the multitude keeping festival.   R.

Send forth your light and your fidelity;
    they shall lead me on
and bring me to your holy mountain,
    to your dwelling-place.   R.

Then will I go in to the altar of God,
    the God of my gladness and joy;
then will I give you thanks upon the harp,
    O God, my God!   R.

ISAIAH 12:2–3, 4bcd, 5–6 (3)

◆
B *When baptism is not celebrated*

R. *You will draw water joyfully from the springs*
    of salvation.

God indeed is my savior;
    I am confident and unafraid.
My strength and my courage is the Lord,
    and he has been my savior.
With joy you will draw water
    at the fountain of salvation.   R.

Give thanks to the Lord, *acclaim his name;*
    among the nations make known his deeds,
    proclaim how exalted is his name.   R.

Sing praise to the Lord *for his glorious achievement;*
    let this be known throughout all the earth.
Shout with exultation, O city of Zion,
    for great in your midst
    is the Holy One of Israel!   R.

PSALM 51:12–13, 14–15,
18–19 (12a)

◆
C *When baptism is not celebrated*

R. *Create a clean heart in me, O God.*

A clean heart create for me, O God,
    and a steadfast spirit renew within me.
Cast me not out from your presence,
    and your Holy Spirit take not from me.   R.

Give me back the joy of your salvation,
    and a willing spirit sustain in me.
I will teach transgressors your ways,
    and sinners shall return to you.   R.

For you are not pleased with sacrifices;
*   should I offer a holocaust, you would not accept it.*
My sacrifice, O God, is a contrite spirit;
*   a heart contrite and humbled, O God,*
*   you will not spurn.   R.*

EPISTLE

ROMANS 6:3–11

CHRIST, RAISED FROM THE
DEAD, DIES NO MORE.

Brothers and sisters:
Are you unaware that we who were baptized
        into Christ Jesus
    were baptized into his death?
We were indeed buried with him through baptism
        into death,
    so that, just as Christ was raised from the dead
    by the glory of the Father,
    we too might live in newness of life.

For if we have grown into union with him
        through a death like his,
    we shall also be united with him in the resurrection.
We know that our old self was crucified with him,
    so that our sinful body might be done away with,
    that we might no longer be in slavery to sin.
For a dead person has been absolved from sin.
If, then, we have died with Christ,
    we believe that we shall also live with him.

We know that Christ, raised from the dead, dies no more;
    death no longer has power over him.
As to his death, he died to sin once and for all;
    as to his life, he lives for God.
Consequently, you too must think of yourselves
        as being dead to sin
    and living for God in Christ Jesus.

**RESPONSORIAL
PSALM**

PSALM 118:1–2, 16–17, 22–23

R. Alleluia, alleluia, alleluia.

[This psalm is found on page 445 (lectionary number 174).]

GOSPEL: YEAR A

MATTHEW 28:1–10

HE HAS BEEN RAISED
FROM THE DEAD AND
IS GOING BEFORE YOU
TO GALILEE.

After the sabbath, as the first day of the week
        was dawning,
    Mary Magdalene and the other Mary
        came to see the tomb.
And behold, there was a great earthquake;
    for an angel of the Lord descended from heaven,
    approached, rolled back the stone, and sat upon it.

His appearance was like lightning
and his clothing was white as snow.
The guards were shaken with fear of him
and became like dead men.

Then the angel said to the women in reply,
"Do not be afraid!
I know that you are seeking Jesus the crucified.
He is not here, for he has been raised just as he said.
Come and see the place where he lay.
Then go quickly and tell his disciples,
'He has been raised from the dead,
and he is going before you to Galilee;
there you will see him.'
Behold, I have told you."

Then they went away quickly from the tomb,
fearful yet overjoyed,
and ran to announce this to his disciples.

And behold, Jesus met them on their way
and greeted them.
They approached, embraced his feet, and did him homage.
Then Jesus said to them, "Do not be afraid.
Go tell my brothers to go to Galilee,
and there they will see me."

GOSPEL: YEAR B

MARK 16:1–7

JESUS OF NAZARETH,
THE CRUCIFIED, HAS
BEEN RAISED.

When the sabbath was over,
Mary Magdalene, Mary, the mother of James,
and Salome
bought spices so that they might go and anoint him.
Very early when the sun had risen,
on the first day of the week, they came to the tomb.
They were saying to one another,
"Who will roll back the stone for us
from the entrance to the tomb?"
When they looked up,
they saw that the stone had been rolled back;
it was very large.

On entering the tomb they saw a young man
sitting on the right side, clothed in a white robe,
and they were utterly amazed.
He said to them, "Do not be amazed!
You seek Jesus of Nazareth, the crucified.
He has been raised; he is not here.
Behold the place where they laid him.

"But go and tell his disciples and Peter,
   'He is going before you to Galilee;
   there you will see him, as he told you.'"

GOSPEL: YEAR C

LUKE 24:1–12

WHY DO YOU SEEK THE
LIVING ONE AMONG
THE DEAD?

At daybreak on the first day of the week
   the women who had come from Galilee with Jesus
   took the spices they had prepared
   and went to the tomb.
They found the stone rolled away from the tomb;
   but when they entered,
   they did not find the body of the Lord Jesus.

While they were puzzling over this, behold,
   two men in dazzling garments appeared to them.
They were terrified and bowed their faces to the ground.
They said to them,
   "Why do you seek the living one among the dead?
He is not here, but he has been raised.
Remember what he said to you
    while he was still in Galilee,
   that the Son of Man must be handed over to sinners
   and be crucified, and rise on the third day."
And they remembered his words.

Then they returned from the tomb
   and announced all these things to the eleven
   and to all the others.
The women were Mary Magdalene, Joanna,
   and Mary the mother of James;
   the others who accompanied them also told this
    to the apostles,
   but their story seemed like nonsense
   and they did not believe them.

But Peter got up and ran to the tomb,
   bent down, and saw the burial cloths alone;
   then he went home amazed at what had happened.

SEASON OF EASTER

42ABC EASTER SUNDAY
THE RESURRECTION OF THE LORD | THE MASS OF EASTER DAY

FIRST READING

ACTS 10:34a, 37–43

WE ATE AND DRANK WITH
HIM AFTER HE ROSE FROM
THE DEAD.

Peter proceeded to speak and said:
"You know what has happened all over Judea,
  beginning in Galilee after the baptism
  that John preached,
  how God anointed Jesus of Nazareth
  with the Holy Spirit and power.
He went about doing good
  and healing all those oppressed by the devil,
  for God was with him.

"We are witnesses of all that he did
  both in the country of the Jews and in Jerusalem.
They put him to death by hanging him on a tree.
This man God raised on the third day
  and granted that he be visible,
  not to all the people, but to us,
  the witnesses chosen by God in advance,
  who ate and drank with him after he rose
    from the dead.

"He commissioned us to preach to the people
  and testify that he is the one appointed by God
  as judge of the living and the dead.
To him all the prophets bear witness,
  that everyone who believes in him
  will receive forgiveness of sins through his name."

**RESPONSORIAL
PSALM**

PSALM 118:1–2, 16–17,
22–23 (24)

R. *This is the day the Lord has made; let us rejoice and be glad.*
  or:
R. *Alleluia.*

[This psalm is found on page 445 (lectionary number 174).]

SECOND READING

COLOSSIANS 3:1–4

SEEK WHAT IS ABOVE,
WHERE CHRIST IS.

Brothers and sisters:
If then you were raised with Christ, seek what is above,
  where Christ is seated at the right hand of God.
Think of what is above, not of what is on earth.
For you have died, and your life is hidden
    with Christ in God.

When Christ your life appears,
   then you too will appear with him in glory.

OR:

SECOND READING

1 CORINTHIANS 5:6b–8

CLEAR OUT THE OLD
YEAST, SO THAT YOU MAY
BECOME A FRESH BATCH
OF DOUGH.

Brothers and sisters:
Do you not know that a little yeast leavens all the dough?
Clear out the old yeast,
   so that you may become a fresh batch of dough,
   inasmuch as you are unleavened.
For our paschal lamb, Christ, has been sacrificed.
Therefore, let us celebrate the feast,
   not with the old yeast, the yeast of malice
      and wickedness,
   but with the unleavened bread of sincerity and truth.

SEQUENCE

VICTIMAE PASCHALI
LAUDES

Christians, to the Paschal Victim
   Offer your thankful praises!

A Lamb the sheep redeems;
   Christ, who only is sinless,
   Reconciles sinners to the Father.

Death and life have contended in that combat stupendous:
   The Prince of life, who died, reigns immortal.

Speak, Mary, declaring
   What you saw, wayfaring.

"The tomb of Christ, who is living,
   The glory of Jesus' resurrection;

"Bright angels attesting,
   The shroud and napkin resting.

"Yes, Christ my hope is arisen;
   to Galilee he goes before you."

Christ indeed from death is risen, our new life obtaining.
   Have mercy, victor King, ever reigning!
   Amen. Alleluia.

ALLELUIA

SEE 1 CORINTHIANS 5:7b–8a

R. Alleluia, alleluia.

Christ, our paschal lamb, has been sacrificed;
let us then feast with joy in the Lord.   R.

GOSPEL

JOHN 20:1–9

HE HAD TO RISE
FROM THE DEAD.

♦

*The Gospel from the Easter Vigil
(see n. 41) may also be read in
place of this Gospel at any time
of the day.*

*At an afternoon or evening Mass,
another Gospel may be read: Luke
24, 13–35 — Stay with us since
it is almost evening (see n. 46).*

On the first day of the week,
    Mary of Magdala came to the tomb
        early in the morning,
    while it was still dark,
    and saw the stone removed from the tomb.
So she ran and went to Simon Peter
    and to the other disciple whom Jesus loved,
        and told them,
    "They have taken the Lord from the tomb,
    and we don't know where they put him."

So Peter and the other disciple went out and came
        to the tomb.
They both ran, but the other disciple ran faster than Peter
    and arrived at the tomb first;
    he bent down and saw the burial cloths there,
        but did not go in.

When Simon Peter arrived after him,
    he went into the tomb and saw the burial cloths there,
    and the cloth that had covered his head,
    not with the burial cloths but rolled up
        in a separate place.
Then the other disciple also went in,
    the one who had arrived at the tomb first,
    and he saw and believed.
For they did not yet understand the Scripture
    that he had to rise from the dead.

43A   SECOND SUNDAY OF EASTER

FIRST READING

ACTS 2:42–47

ALL WHO BELIEVED WERE
TOGETHER AND HAD
ALL THINGS IN COMMON.

They devoted themselves
    to the teaching of the apostles
        and to the communal life,
    to the breaking of bread and to the prayers.

Awe came upon everyone,
    and many wonders and signs were done
        through the apostles.

All who believed were together and had all things
        in common;
    they would sell their property and possessions
    and divide them among all according to
        each one's need.

Every day they devoted themselves
   to meeting together in the temple area
   and to breaking bread in their homes.
They ate their meals with exultation
   and sincerity of heart,
   praising God and enjoying favor with all the people.
And every day the Lord added to their number
   those who were being saved.

RESPONSORIAL PSALM

PSALM 118:2–4, 13–15, 22–24 (1)

R. Give thanks to the Lord, for he is good,
   his love is everlasting.
   or:
R. Alleluia.

Let the house of Israel say,
   "His mercy endures forever."
Let the house of Aaron say,
   "His mercy endures forever."
Let those who fear the LORD say,
   "His mercy endures forever." R.

I was hard pressed and was falling,
   but the LORD helped me.
My strength and my courage is the LORD,
   and he has been my savior.
The joyful shout of victory
   in the tents of the just. R.

The stone which the builders rejected
   has become the cornerstone.
By the LORD has this been done;
   it is wonderful in our eyes.
This is the day the LORD has made;
   let us be glad and rejoice in it. R.

SECOND READING

1 PETER 1:3–9

GOD HAS GIVEN US NEW BIRTH TO A LIVING HOPE THROUGH THE RESURRECTION OF JESUS CHRIST FROM THE DEAD.

Blessed be the God and Father of our Lord Jesus Christ,
   who in his great mercy gave us a new birth
     to a living hope
   through the resurrection of Jesus Christ from the dead,
   to an inheritance that is imperishable, undefiled,
     and unfading,
   kept in heaven for you
   who by the power of God are safeguarded through faith,
   to a salvation that is ready to be revealed
     in the final time.

In this you rejoice, although now for a little while
   you may have to suffer through various trials,
   so that the genuineness of your faith,
     more precious than gold that is perishable even though
     tested by fire,

may prove to be for praise, glory, and honor
at the revelation of Jesus Christ.

Although you have not seen him you love him;
even though you do not see him now yet believe in him,
you rejoice with an indescribable and glorious joy,
as you attain the goal of your faith, the salvation
of your souls.

ALLELUIA

JOHN 20:29

R. Alleluia, alleluia.

*You believe in me, Thomas, because you
have seen me, says the Lord;
blessed are they who have not seen me,
but still believe! R.*

GOSPEL

JOHN 20:19–31

EIGHT DAYS LATER
JESUS CAME AND STOOD
IN THEIR MIDST.

On the evening of that first day of the week,
when the doors were locked, where the disciples were,
for fear of the Jews,
Jesus came and stood in their midst
and said to them, "Peace be with you."
When he had said this, he showed them his hands
and his side.
The disciples rejoiced when they saw the Lord.

Jesus said to them again, "Peace be with you.
As the Father has sent me, so I send you."

And when he had said this, he breathed on them
and said to them,
"Receive the Holy Spirit.
Whose sins you forgive are forgiven them,
and whose sins you retain are retained."

Thomas, called Didymus, one of the Twelve,
was not with them when Jesus came.
So the other disciples said to him,
"We have seen the Lord."
But he said to them,
"Unless I see the mark of the nails in his hands
and put my finger into the nailmarks
and put my hand into his side, I will not believe."

Now a week later his disciples were again inside
and Thomas was with them.
Jesus came, although the doors were locked,
and stood in their midst and said, "Peace be with you."

Then he said to Thomas,
"Put your finger here and see my hands,
and bring your hand and put it into my side,
and do not be unbelieving, but believe."
Thomas answered and said to him,
"My Lord and my God!"

Jesus said to him, "Have you come to believe because
you have seen me?
Blessed are those who have not seen and have believed."

Now, Jesus did many other signs in the presence
of his disciples
that are not written in this book.
But these are written that you may come to believe
that Jesus is the Christ, the Son of God,
and that through this belief you may have life
in his name.

44B   SECOND SUNDAY OF EASTER

FIRST READING

ACTS 4:32–35

THEY WERE OF ONE
HEART AND MIND.

The community of believers was of one heart and mind,
and no one claimed that any of his possessions
was his own,
but they had everything in common.

With great power the apostles bore witness
to the resurrection of the Lord Jesus,
and great favor was accorded them all.

There was no needy person among them,
for those who owned property or houses
would sell them,
bring the proceeds of the sale,
and put them at the feet of the apostles,
and they were distributed to each according to need.

**RESPONSORIAL
PSALM**

PSALM 118:2–4, 13–15,
22–24 (1)

R. Give thanks to the Lord, for he is good, his love is everlasting.
    or:
R. Alleluia.

[This psalm is found on page 157 (lectionary number 43).]

1 JOHN 5:1–6

WHOEVER IS BEGOTTEN
BY GOD CONQUERS
THE WORLD.

Beloved:
Everyone who believes that Jesus is the Christ
    is begotten by God,
    and everyone who loves the Father
    loves also the one begotten by him.

In this way we know that we love the children of God
    when we love God and obey his commandments.
For the love of God is this,
    that we keep his commandments.
And his commandments are not burdensome,
    for whoever is begotten by God conquers the world.

And the victory that conquers the world is our faith.
Who indeed is the victor over the world
    but the one who believes that Jesus is the Son of God?

This is the one who came through water and blood,
    Jesus Christ,
    not by water alone, but by water and blood.
The Spirit is the one that testifies,
    and the Spirit is truth.

ALLELUIA

JOHN 20:29

R. Alleluia, alleluia.

You believe in me, Thomas, because you have seen me, says the Lord;
blessed are those who have not seen me, but still believe!   R.

GOSPEL

JOHN 20:19–31

EIGHT DAYS LATER JESUS
CAME AND STOOD IN
THEIR MIDST.

[This reading is found on page 158
(lectionary number 43).]

45C   SECOND SUNDAY OF EASTER

FIRST READING

ACTS 5:12–16

MORE THAN EVER,
BELIEVERS IN THE LORD,
GREAT NUMBERS OF
MEN AND WOMEN, WERE
ADDED TO THEM.

Many signs and wonders were done among the people
    at the hands of the apostles.
They were all together in Solomon's portico.
None of the others dared to join them, but the people
    esteemed them.

Yet more than ever, believers in the Lord,
    great numbers of men and women, were added to them.

Thus they even carried the sick out into the streets
and laid them on cots and mats
so that when Peter came by,
at least his shadow might fall on one or another of them.

A large number of people from the towns
in the vicinity of Jerusalem also gathered,
bringing the sick and those disturbed by unclean spirits,
and they were all cured.

RESPONSORIAL PSALM

PSALM 118:2–4, 13–15, 22–24 (1)

R. *Give thanks to the Lord for he is good, his love is everlasting.*
or:
R. *Alleluia.*

[This psalm is found on page 157 (lectionary number 43).]

SECOND READING

REVELATION 1:9–11a, 12–13, 17–19

I WAS DEAD, BUT NOW I AM ALIVE FOR EVER AND EVER.

I, John, your brother, who share with you
the distress, the kingdom, and the endurance
we have in Jesus,
found myself on the island called Patmos
because I proclaimed God's word and gave testimony
to Jesus.
I was caught up in spirit on the Lord's day
and heard behind me a voice as loud as a trumpet,
which said,
"Write on a scroll what you see."

Then I turned to see whose voice it was that spoke to me,
and when I turned, I saw seven gold lampstands
and in the midst of the lampstands one like
a son of man,
wearing an ankle-length robe, with a gold sash
around his chest.

When I caught sight of him, I fell down at his feet
as though dead.
He touched me with his right hand and said,
"Do not be afraid.
I am the first and the last, the one who lives.
Once I was dead, but now I am alive forever and ever.
I hold the keys to death and the netherworld.
Write down, therefore, what you have seen,
and what is happening, and what will
happen afterwards."

R. Alleluia, alleluia.

You believe in me, Thomas, because you have seen me, says the Lord:
Blessed are they who have not seen me, but still believe!   R.

GOSPEL

JOHN 20:19–31

EIGHT DAYS LATER JESUS
CAME AND STOOD IN
THEIR MIDST.

[This reading is found on page 158
(lectionary number 43).]

46A   THIRD SUNDAY OF EASTER

FIRST READING

ACTS 2:14, 22–33

IT WAS IMPOSSIBLE
FOR JESUS TO BE HELD
BY DEATH.

Then Peter stood up with the Eleven,
 raised his voice, and proclaimed:
"You who are Jews, indeed all of you staying in Jerusalem.
Let this be known to you, and listen to my words.
You who are Israelites, hear these words.
Jesus the Nazarene was a man commended to you by God
  with mighty deeds, wonders, and signs,
   which God worked through him in your midst,
    as you yourselves know.
This man, delivered up by the set plan
   and foreknowledge of God,
    you killed, using lawless men to crucify him.

"But God raised him up, releasing him
   from the throes of death,
   because it was impossible for him to be held by it.
For David says of him:
  I saw the Lord ever before me,
  with him at my right hand I shall not be disturbed.
  Therefore my heart has been glad and my tongue has exulted;
  my flesh, too, will dwell in hope,
  because you will not abandon my soul to the netherworld,
  nor will you suffer your holy one to see corruption.
  You have made known to me the paths of life;
  you will fill me with joy in your presence.

"My brothers, one can confidently say to you
   about the patriarch David that he died and was buried,
   and his tomb is in our midst to this day.
But since he was a prophet and knew that God had sworn
   an oath to him
   that he would set one of his descendants
    upon his throne,

he foresaw and spoke of the resurrection of the Christ,
   that neither was he abandoned to the netherworld
   nor did his flesh see corruption.

"God raised this Jesus;
   of this we are all witnesses.
Exalted at the right hand of God,
   he received the promise of the Holy Spirit
      from the Father
   and poured him forth, as you see and hear."

RESPONSORIAL
PSALM

PSALM 16:1–2, 5, 7–8, 9–10,
11 (11a)

R. Lord, you will show us the path of life.
   or:
R. Alleluia.

Keep me, O God, for in you I take refuge;
   *I say to the L*ORD, *"My L*ORD *are you."*
*O L*ORD, *my allotted portion and my cup,*
   you it is who hold fast my lot.   R.

*I bless the L*ORD *who counsels me;*
   even in the night my heart exhorts me.
*I set the L*ORD *ever before me;*
   with him at my right hand, I shall not be disturbed.   R.

Therefore my heart is glad and my soul rejoices;
   my body, too, abides in confidence,
because you will not abandon my soul to the netherworld,
   nor will you suffer your faithful one to undergo corruption.   R.

You will show me the path to life,
   abounding joy in your presence,
   the delights at your right hand forever.   R.

SECOND READING

1 PETER 1:17–21

YOU WERE SAVED WITH
THE PRECIOUS BLOOD
OF CHRIST, AS WITH
THAT OF A SPOTLESS,
UNBLEMISHED LAMB.

Beloved:
If you invoke as Father him who judges impartially
   according to each one's works,
      conduct yourselves with reverence during the time
         of your sojourning,
   realizing that you were ransomed
      from your futile conduct,
   handed on by your ancestors,
   not with perishable things like silver or gold
   but with the precious blood of Christ
   as of a spotless unblemished lamb.

He was known before the foundation of the world
   but revealed in the final time for you,
   who through him believe in God
   who raised him from the dead and gave him glory,
   so that your faith and hope are in God.

R. *Alleluia, alleluia.*

Lord Jesus, open the Scriptures to us;
make our hearts burn while you speak to us. R.

That very day, the first day of the week,
   two of Jesus' disciples were going
   to a village seven miles from Jerusalem called Emmaus,
   and they were conversing about all the things
      that had occurred.
And it happened that while they were conversing
      and debating,
   Jesus himself drew near and walked with them,
   but their eyes were prevented from recognizing him.

He asked them,
   "What are you discussing as you walk along?"
They stopped, looking downcast.
One of them, named Cleopas, said to him in reply,
   "Are you the only visitor to Jerusalem
   who does not know of the things
   that have taken place there in these days?"

And he replied to them, "What sort of things?"
They said to him,
   "The things that happened to Jesus the Nazarene,
   who was a prophet mighty in deed and word
   before God and all the people,
   how our chief priests and rulers both handed him over
   to a sentence of death and crucified him.
But we were hoping that he would be the one
      to redeem Israel;
   and besides all this,
   it is now the third day since this took place.
Some women from our group, however,
      have astounded us:
   they were at the tomb early in the morning
   and did not find his body;
   they came back and reported
   that they had indeed seen a vision of angels
   who announced that he was alive.

"Then some of those with us went to the tomb
   and found things just as the women had described,
   but him they did not see."

And he said to them, "Oh, how foolish you are!
How slow of heart to believe all that the prophets spoke!

Was it not necessary that the Christ should suffer
    these things
  and enter into his glory?"

Then beginning with Moses and all the prophets,
  he interpreted to them what referred to him
    in all the Scriptures.
As they approached the village to which they were going,
  he gave the impression that he was going on farther.
But they urged him, "Stay with us,
  for it is nearly evening and the day is almost over."
So he went in to stay with them.

And it happened that, while he was with them at table,
  he took bread, said the blessing,
    broke it, and gave it to them.
With that their eyes were opened
    and they recognized him,
  but he vanished from their sight.

Then they said to each other,
  "Were not our hearts burning within us
  while he spoke to us on the way
    and opened the Scriptures to us?"

So they set out at once and returned to Jerusalem
  where they found gathered together
  the eleven and those with them who were saying,
  "The Lord has truly been raised
    and has appeared to Simon!"

Then the two recounted
  what had taken place on the way
  and how he was made known to them
    in the breaking of bread.

47B   THIRD SUNDAY OF EASTER

FIRST READING

ACTS 3:13–15, 17–19

THE AUTHOR OF LIFE
YOU PUT TO DEATH, BUT
GOD RAISED HIM FROM
THE DEAD.

Peter said to the people:
"The God of Abraham,
    the God of Isaac, and the God of Jacob,
    the God of our fathers, has glorified his servant Jesus,
    whom you handed over and denied in Pilate's presence
    when he had decided to release him.

"You denied the Holy and Righteous One
    and asked that a murderer be released to you.

The author of life you put to death,
    but God raised him from the dead;
        of this we are witnesses.

"Now I know, brothers,
    that you acted out of ignorance, just as your leaders did;
    but God has thus brought to fulfillment
    what he had announced beforehand
    through the mouth of all the prophets,
    that his Christ would suffer.

"Repent, therefore, and be converted,
    that your sins may be wiped away."

RESPONSORIAL PSALM

PSALM 4:2, 4, 7–8, 9 (7a)

R. Lord, let your face shine on us.
    or:
R. Alleluia.

When I call, answer me, O my just God,
    you who relieve me when I am in distress;
    have pity on me, and hear my prayer!   R.

Know that the LORD does wonders for his faithful one;
    the LORD will hear me when I call upon him.   R.

O LORD, let the light of your countenance shine upon us!
    You put gladness into my heart.   R.

As soon as I lie down, I fall peacefully asleep,
    for you alone, O LORD,
    bring security to my dwelling.   R.

SECOND READING

1 JOHN 2:1–5a

JESUS CHRIST IS
EXPIATION NOT FOR OUR
SINS ONLY BUT FOR THOSE
OF THE WHOLE WORLD.

My children, I am writing this to you
    so that you may not commit sin.
But if anyone does sin, we have an Advocate
        with the Father,
    Jesus Christ the righteous one.
He is expiation for our sins,
    and not for our sins only but for those
        of the whole world.

The way we may be sure that we know him
    is to keep his commandments.
Those who say, "I know him,"
        but do not keep his commandments
    are liars, and the truth is not in them.
But whoever keeps his word,
    the love of God is truly perfected in him.

ALLELUIA

SEE LUKE 24:32

GOSPEL

LUKE 24:35–48

THUS IT WAS WRITTEN
THAT THE CHRIST WOULD
SUFFER AND RISE FROM THE
DEAD ON THE THIRD DAY.

R. Alleluia, alleluia.

Lord Jesus, open the Scriptures to us;
make our hearts burn while you speak to us.   R.

The two disciples recounted what had taken place
   on the way,
    and how Jesus was made known to them
    in the breaking of bread.

While they were still speaking about this,
   he stood in their midst and said to them,
   "Peace be with you."
But they were startled and terrified
   and thought that they were seeing a ghost.
Then he said to them, "Why are you troubled?
And why do questions arise in your hearts?
Look at my hands and my feet, that it is I myself.
Touch me and see, because a ghost does not
    have flesh and bones
   as you can see I have."

And as he said this,
   he showed them his hands and his feet.
While they were still incredulous for joy
    and were amazed,
   he asked them, "Have you anything here to eat?"
They gave him a piece of baked fish;
   he took it and ate it in front of them.

He said to them,
   "These are my words that I spoke to you
    while I was still with you,
   that everything written about me in the law of Moses
   and in the prophets and psalms must be fulfilled."
Then he opened their minds to understand the Scriptures.
And he said to them,
   "Thus it is written that the Christ would suffer
   and rise from the dead on the third day
   and that repentance, for the forgiveness of sins,
   would be preached in his name
   to all the nations, beginning from Jerusalem.
You are witnesses of these things."

FIRST READING

ACTS 5:27–32, 40b–41

WE ARE WITNESSES OF
THESE WORDS AS IS THE
HOLY SPIRIT.

When the captain and the court officers had brought
    the apostles in
and made them stand before the Sanhedrin,
    the high priest questioned them,
    "We gave you strict orders, did we not,
    to stop teaching in that name?
Yet you have filled Jerusalem with your teaching
    and want to bring this man's blood upon us."

But Peter and the apostles said in reply,
    "We must obey God rather than men.
The God of our ancestors raised Jesus,
    though you had him killed by hanging him on a tree.
God exalted him at his right hand as leader and savior
    to grant Israel repentance and forgiveness of sins.
We are witnesses of these things,
    as is the Holy Spirit whom God has given to those
        who obey him."

The Sanhedrin ordered the apostles
    to stop speaking in the name of Jesus,
    and dismissed them.
So they left the presence of the Sanhedrin,
    rejoicing that they had been found worthy
    to suffer dishonor for the sake of the name.

**RESPONSORIAL
PSALM**

PSALM 30:2, 4, 5–6, 11–12,
13 (2a)

R. I will praise you, Lord, for you have rescued me.
    or:
R. Alleluia.

[This psalm is found on page 146 (lectionary number 41).]

SECOND READING

REVELATION 5:11–14

WORTHY IS THE LAMB
THAT WAS SLAIN TO
RECEIVE POWER AND
RICHES.

I, John, looked and heard the voices of many angels
    who surrounded the throne
    and the living creatures and the elders.
They were countless in number, and they cried out
    in a loud voice:
    "Worthy is the Lamb that was slain
        to receive power and riches, wisdom and strength,
        honor and glory and blessing."

Then I heard every creature in heaven and on earth
    and under the earth and in the sea,
    everything in the universe, cry out:

"To the one who sits on the throne and to the Lamb
    be blessing and honor, glory and might,
    forever and ever."
The four living creatures answered, "Amen,"
    and the elders fell down and worshiped.

ALLELUIA

R. Alleluia, alleluia.

Christ is risen, creator of all;
he has shown pity on all people.   R.

GOSPEL

LONGER FORM
JOHN 21:1–19

SHORTER FORM
JOHN 21:1–14

JESUS CAME AND TOOK
THE BREAD AND GAVE IT
TO THEM, AND IN LIKE
MANNER, THE FISH.

[At that time, Jesus revealed himself again
    to his disciples at the Sea of Tiberias.
He revealed himself in this way.
Together were Simon Peter, Thomas called Didymus,
    Nathanael from Cana in Galilee,
    Zebedee's sons, and two others of his disciples.
Simon Peter said to them, "I am going fishing."
They said to him, "We also will come with you."
So they went out and got into the boat,
    but that night they caught nothing.

When it was already dawn, Jesus was standing
    on the shore;
    but the disciples did not realize that it was Jesus.
Jesus said to them, "Children, have you caught
    anything to eat?"
They answered him, "No."
So he said to them, "Cast the net over the right side
    of the boat
    and you will find something."
So they cast it, and were not able to pull it in
    because of the number of fish.

So the disciple whom Jesus loved said to Peter,
    "It is the Lord."
When Simon Peter heard that it was the Lord,
    he tucked in his garment, for he was lightly clad,
    and jumped into the sea.
The other disciples came in the boat,
    for they were not far from shore, only about
    a hundred yards,
    dragging the net with the fish.

When they climbed out on shore,
    they saw a charcoal fire with fish on it and bread.

Jesus said to them, "Bring some of the fish
    you just caught."
So Simon Peter went over and dragged the net ashore
    full of one hundred fifty-three large fish.
Even though there were so many, the net was not torn.
Jesus said to them, "Come, have breakfast."
And none of the disciples dared to ask him,
    "Who are you?"
  because they realized it was the Lord.
Jesus came over and took the bread and gave it to them,
    and in like manner the fish.
This was now the third time Jesus was revealed
    to his disciples
  after being raised from the dead.]

When they had finished breakfast, Jesus said
    to Simon Peter,
  "Simon, son of John, do you love me more than these?"
Simon Peter answered him,
    "Yes, Lord, you know that I love you."
Jesus said to him, "Feed my lambs."

He then said to Simon Peter a second time,
  "Simon, son of John, do you love me?"
Simon Peter answered him,
    "Yes, Lord, you know that I love you."
Jesus said to him, "Tend my sheep."

Jesus said to him the third time,
  "Simon, son of John, do you love me?"
Peter was distressed that Jesus had said to him a third time,
  "Do you love me?" and he said to him,
  "Lord, you know everything; you know that I love you."
Jesus said to him, "Feed my sheep.

"Amen, amen, I say to you, when you were younger,
  you used to dress yourself and go where you wanted;
  but when you grow old, you will stretch out your hands,
  and someone else will dress you
  and lead you where you do not want to go."
He said this signifying by what kind of death
    he would glorify God.
And when he had said this, he said to him, "Follow me."

FIRST READING

ACTS 2:1, 4a, 36–41

GOD HAS MADE JESUS
BOTH LORD AND CHRIST.

Then Peter stood up with the Eleven,
  raised his voice, and proclaimed:
"Let the whole house of Israel know for certain
  that God has made both Lord and Christ,
  this Jesus whom you crucified."

Now when they heard this, they were cut to the heart,
  and they asked Peter and the other apostles,
  "What are we to do, my brothers?"
Peter said to them,
  "Repent and be baptized, every one of you,
  in the name of Jesus Christ for the forgiveness
    of your sins;
  and you will receive the gift of the Holy Spirit.
For the promise is made to you and to your children
  and to all those far off,
  whomever the Lord our God will call."

He testified with many other arguments,
  and was exhorting them,
  "Save yourselves from this corrupt generation."
Those who accepted his message were baptized,
  and about three thousand persons were added that day.

**RESPONSORIAL
PSALM**

PSALM 23:1–3a, 3b–4, 5, 6 (1)

R. *The Lord is my shepherd; there is nothing I shall want.*
  or:
R. *Alleluia.*

[This psalm is found on page 80 (lectionary number 31).]

SECOND READING

1 PETER 2:20b–25

YOU HAVE RETURNED
TO THE SHEPHERD AND
GUARDIAN OF YOUR
SOULS.

Beloved:
If you are patient when you suffer for doing what is good,
  this is a grace before God.
For to this you have been called,
  because Christ also suffered for you,
  leaving you an example that you should follow
    in his footsteps.
He committed no sin, and no deceit was found in his mouth.

When he was insulted, he returned no insult;
  when he suffered, he did not threaten;
  instead, he handed himself over to the one
    who judges justly.

He himself bore our sins in his body upon the cross,
    so that, free from sin, we might live for righteousness.
By his wounds you have been healed.

For you had gone astray like sheep,
    but you have now returned to the shepherd
        and guardian of your souls.

ALLELUIA

JOHN 10:14

R. Alleluia, alleluia.

I am the good shepherd, says the Lord;
I know my sheep, and mine know me.   *R.*

GOSPEL

JOHN 10:1–10

I AM THE GATE FOR
THE SHEEP.

Jesus said:
"Amen, amen, I say to you,
    whoever does not enter a sheepfold through the gate
    but climbs over elsewhere is a thief and a robber.
But whoever enters through the gate is the shepherd
    of the sheep.
The gatekeeper opens it for him, and the sheep
    hear his voice,
    as the shepherd calls his own sheep by name
    and leads them out.
When he has driven out all his own,
    he walks ahead of them, and the sheep follow him,
    because they recognize his voice.
But they will not follow a stranger;
    they will run away from him,
    because they do not recognize the voice of strangers."
Although Jesus used this figure of speech,
    the Pharisees did not realize what he was trying
    to tell them.

So Jesus said again, "Amen, amen, I say to you,
    I am the gate for the sheep.
All who came before me are thieves and robbers,
    but the sheep did not listen to them.
I am the gate.
Whoever enters through me will be saved,
    and will come in and go out and find pasture.
A thief comes only to steal and slaughter and destroy;
    I came so that they might have life
    and have it more abundantly."

FIRST READING

ACTS 4:8–12

THERE IS NO SALVATION
THROUGH ANYONE ELSE.

Peter, filled with the Holy Spirit, said:
"Leaders of the people and elders:
  If we are being examined today
  about a good deed done to a cripple,
  namely, by what means he was saved,
  then all of you and all the people of Israel should know
  that it was in the name of Jesus Christ the Nazarene
  whom you crucified, whom God raised from the dead;
  in his name this man stands before you healed.

"He is *the stone rejected by you, the builders,*
  which has become the cornerstone.
There is no salvation through anyone else,
  nor is there any other name under heaven
  given to the human race by which we are to be saved."

**RESPONSORIAL
PSALM**

PSALM 118:1, 8–9, 21–23, 26,
28, 29 (22)

R. *The stone rejected by the builders has become the cornerstone.*
  or:
R. *Alleluia.*

Give thanks to the LORD, for he is good,
  for his mercy endures forever.
It is better to take refuge in the LORD
  than to trust in man.
It is better to take refuge in the LORD
  than to trust in princes.   R.

I will give thanks to you, for you have answered me
  and have been my savior.
The stone which the builders rejected
  has become the cornerstone.
By the LORD has this been done;
  it is wonderful in our eyes.   R.

Blessed is he who comes in the name of the LORD;
  we bless you from the house of the LORD.
I will give thanks to you, for you have answered me
  and have been my savior.
Give thanks to the LORD, for he is good;
  for his kindness endures forever.   R.

SECOND READING

1 JOHN 3:1–2

WE SHALL SEE GOD AS HE
REALLY IS.

Beloved:
See what love the Father has bestowed on us
  that we may be called the children of God.
Yet so we are.
The reason the world does not know us
  is that it did not know him.

Beloved, we are God's children now;
    what we shall be has not yet been revealed.
We do know that when it is revealed we shall be like him,
    for we shall see him as he is.

ALLELUIA

JOHN 10:14

R. Alleluia, alleluia.

I am the good shepherd, says the Lord;
I know my sheep, and mine know me.   R.

GOSPEL

JOHN 10:11–18

THE GOOD SHEPHERD
LAYS DOWN HIS LIFE
FOR THE SHEEP.

Jesus said:
"I am the good shepherd.
A good shepherd lays down his life for the sheep.
A hired man, who is not a shepherd
    and whose sheep are not his own,
        sees a wolf coming and leaves the sheep and runs away,
        and the wolf catches and scatters them.
This is because he works for pay and has no concern
        for the sheep.

"I am the good shepherd,
    and I know mine and mine know me,
        just as the Father knows me and I know the Father;
    and I will lay down my life for the sheep.
I have other sheep that do not belong to this fold.
These also I must lead, and they will hear my voice,
    and there will be one flock, one shepherd.

"This is why the Father loves me,
    because I lay down my life in order to take it up again.
No one takes it from me, but I lay it down on my own.
I have power to lay it down, and power to take it up again.
This command I have received from my Father."

51C   FOURTH SUNDAY OF EASTER

FIRST READING

ACTS 13:14, 43–52

WE NOW TURN TO
THE GENTILES.

Paul and Barnabas continued on from Perga
    and reached Antioch in Pisidia.
On the sabbath they entered the synagogue
    and took their seats.

Many Jews and worshipers who were converts to Judaism
    followed Paul and Barnabas, who spoke to them
    and urged them to remain faithful to the grace of God.

On the following sabbath almost the whole city gathered
to hear the word of the Lord.
When the Jews saw the crowds, they were filled
with jealousy
and with violent abuse contradicted what Paul said.

Both Paul and Barnabas spoke out boldly and said,
"It was necessary that the word of God be spoken
to you first,
but since you reject it
and condemn yourselves as unworthy of eternal life,
we now turn to the Gentiles.
For so the Lord has commanded us,
I have made you a light to the Gentiles,
that you may be an instrument of salvation
to the ends of the earth."

The Gentiles were delighted when they heard this
and glorified the word of the Lord.
All who were destined for eternal life came to believe,
and the word of the Lord continued to spread
through the whole region.
The Jews, however, incited the women of prominence
who were worshipers
and the leading men of the city,
stirred up a persecution against Paul and Barnabas,
and expelled them from their territory.
So they shook the dust from their feet in protest
against them,
and went to Iconium.
The disciples were filled with joy and the Holy Spirit.

RESPONSORIAL PSALM

PSALM 100:1–2, 3, 5 (3c)

R. We are his people, the sheep of his flock.
or:
R. Alleluia.

Sing joyfully to the LORD, all you lands;
serve the LORD with gladness;
come before him with joyful song.   R.

Know that the LORD is God;
he made us, his we are,
his people, the flock he tends.   R.

The LORD is good:
His kindness endures forever,
and his faithfulness, to all generations.   R.

SECOND READING

REVELATION 7:9, 14b–17

THE LAMB WILL SHEPHERD
THEM AND LEAD THEM TO
SPRINGS OF LIFE-GIVING
WATER.

I, John, had a vision of a great multitude,
    which no one could count,
      from every nation, race, people, and tongue.
They stood before the throne and before the Lamb,
    wearing white robes and holding palm branches
      in their hands.
Then one of the elders said to me,
    "These are the ones who have survived the time
      of great distress;
    they have washed their robes
    and made them white in the blood of the Lamb.

"For this reason they stand before God's throne
    and worship him day and night in his temple.
The one who sits on the throne will shelter them.
They will not hunger or thirst anymore,
    nor will the sun or any heat strike them.
For the Lamb who is in the center of the throne
    will shepherd them
    and lead them to springs of life-giving water,
      and God will wipe away every tear from their eyes."

ALLELUIA

JOHN 10:14

R. Alleluia, alleluia.

I am the good shepherd, says the Lord;
I know my sheep, and mine know me.   R.

GOSPEL

JOHN 10:27–30

I GIVE MY SHEEP
ETERNAL LIFE.

Jesus said:
"My sheep hear my voice;
    I know them, and they follow me.
I give them eternal life, and they shall never perish.
No one can take them out of my hand.
My Father, who has given them to me, is greater than all,
    and no one can take them out of the Father's hand.
The Father and I are one."

52A   FIFTH SUNDAY OF EASTER

FIRST READING

ACTS 6:1–7

THEY CHOSE SEVEN MEN
FILLED WITH THE SPIRIT.

As the number of disciples continued to grow,
    the Hellenists complained against the Hebrews
    because their widows
    were being neglected in the daily distribution.

So the Twelve called together the community
 of the disciples and said,
 "It is not right for us to neglect the word of God
  to serve at table.
Brothers, select from among you seven reputable men,
 filled with the Spirit and wisdom,
 whom we shall appoint to this task,
 whereas we shall devote ourselves to prayer
 and to the ministry of the word."

The proposal was acceptable to the whole community,
 so they chose Stephen, a man filled with faith
  and the Holy Spirit,
 also Philip, Prochorus, Nicanor, Timon, Parmenas,
 and Nicholas of Antioch, a convert to Judaism.
They presented these men to the apostles
 who prayed and laid hands on them.

The word of God continued to spread,
 and the number of the disciples in Jerusalem
  increased greatly;
 even a large group of priests were becoming obedient
  to the faith.

RESPONSORIAL PSALM

PSALM 33:1–2, 4–5,
18–19 (22)

R. Lord, let your mercy be on us, as we place our trust in you.
 or:
R. Alleluia.

Exult, you just, in the LORD;
 praise from the upright is fitting.
Give thanks to the LORD on the harp;
 with the ten-stringed lyre chant his praises. R.

Upright is the word of the LORD,
 and all his works are trustworthy.
He loves justice and right;
 of the kindness of the LORD the earth is full. R.

See, the eyes of the LORD are upon those who fear him,
 upon those who hope for his kindness,
to deliver them from death
 and preserve them in spite of famine. R.

SECOND READING

1 PETER 2:4–9

YOU ARE A CHOSEN RACE,
A ROYAL PRIESTHOOD.

Beloved:
Come to him, a living stone, rejected by human beings
 but chosen and precious in the sight of God,
 and, like living stones,
 let yourselves be built into a spiritual house
 to be a holy priesthood to offer spiritual sacrifices
 acceptable to God through Jesus Christ.

For it says in Scripture:
Behold, I am laying a stone in Zion,
a cornerstone, chosen and precious,
and whoever believes in it shall not be put to shame.
Therefore, its value is for you who have faith,
   but for those without faith:
The stone that the builders rejected
has become the cornerstone,
a stone that will make people stumble,
and a rock that will make them fall.
They stumble by disobeying the word, as is their destiny.

You are *a chosen race, a royal priesthood,*
a holy nation, a people of his own,
so that you may announce the praises of him
who called you out of darkness into his wonderful light.

ALLELUIA

JOHN 14:6

R. Alleluia, alleluia.

I am the way, the truth and the life, says the Lord;
no one comes to the Father, except through me.   R.

GOSPEL

JOHN 14:1–12

I AM THE WAY AND THE
TRUTH AND THE LIFE.

Jesus said to his disciples:
   "Do not let your hearts be troubled.
You have faith in God; have faith also in me.
In my Father's house there are many dwelling places.
If there were not,
   would I have told you that I am going
   to prepare a place for you?
And if I go and prepare a place for you,
   I will come back again and take you to myself,
   so that where I am you also may be.
Where I am going you know the way."

Thomas said to him,
   "Master, we do not know where you are going;
   how can we know the way?"

Jesus said to him,
   "I am the way and the truth and the life.
No one comes to the Father except through me.
If you know me, then you will also know my Father.
From now on you do know him and have seen him."

Philip said to him,
   "Master, show us the Father, and that will be
      enough for us."

Jesus said to him, "Have I been with you for so long a time
  and you still do not know me, Philip?
Whoever has seen me has seen the Father.
How can you say, 'Show us the Father'?
Do you not believe that I am in the Father
  and the Father is in me?
The words that I speak to you I do not speak on my own.
The Father who dwells in me is doing his works.
Believe me that I am in the Father and the Father
    is in me,
  or else, believe because of the works themselves.
Amen, amen, I say to you,
  whoever believes in me will do the works that I do,
  and will do greater ones than these,
  because I am going to the Father."

53B   FIFTH SUNDAY OF EASTER

FIRST READING

ACTS 9:26–31

BARNABAS REPORTED TO
THE APOSTLES HOW SAUL
HAD SEEN THE LORD ON
THE WAY.

When Saul arrived in Jerusalem he tried to join
    the disciples,
  but they were all afraid of him,
  not believing that he was a disciple.
Then Barnabas took charge of him and brought him
    to the apostles,
  and he reported to them how he had seen the Lord,
  and that he had spoken to him,
  and how in Damascus he had spoken out boldly
    in the name of Jesus.
He moved about freely with them in Jerusalem,
  and spoke out boldly in the name of the Lord.
He also spoke and debated with the Hellenists,
  but they tried to kill him.
And when the brothers learned of this,
  they took him down to Caesarea
  and sent him on his way to Tarsus.

The church throughout all Judea, Galilee and Samaria
    was at peace.
It was being built up and walked in the fear of the Lord,
  and with the consolation of the Holy Spirit
    it grew in numbers.

R. I will praise you, Lord, in the assembly of your people.
    or:
R. Alleluia.

I will fulfill my vows before those who fear the LORD.
    The lowly shall eat their fill;
they who seek the LORD shall praise him:
    "May your hearts live forever!"   R.

All the ends of the earth
    shall remember and turn to the LORD;
all the families of the nations
    shall bow down before him.   R.

To him alone shall bow down
    all who sleep in the earth;
before him shall bend
    all who go down into the dust.   R.

And to him my soul shall live;
    my descendants shall serve him.
Let the coming generation be told of the LORD
    that they may proclaim to a people yet to be born
    the justice he has shown.   R.

SECOND READING

1 JOHN 3:18–24

THIS IS HIS COMMANDMENT:
THAT WE MAY BELIEVE
AND LOVE.

Children, let us love not in word or speech
    but in deed and truth.
Now this is how we shall know that we belong
        to the truth
    and reassure our hearts before him
    in whatever our hearts condemn,
    for God is greater than our hearts
        and knows everything.

Beloved, if our hearts do not condemn us,
    we have confidence in God
    and receive from him whatever we ask,
    because we keep his commandments and do
        what pleases him.

And his commandment is this:
    we should believe in the name of his Son, Jesus Christ,
    and love one another just as he commanded us.
Those who keep his commandments remain in him,
        and he in them,
    and the way we know that he remains in us
    is from the Spirit he gave us.

ALLELUIA

JOHN 15:4a, 5b

R. Alleluia, alleluia.

Remain in me as I remain in you, says the Lord.
Whoever remains in me will bear much fruit.   R.

Jesus said to his disciples:
"I am the true vine, and my Father is the vine grower.
He takes away every branch in me that does not bear fruit,
    and every one that does he prunes so that it bears
        more fruit.
You are already pruned because of the word
    that I spoke to you.

"Remain in me, as I remain in you.
Just as a branch cannot bear fruit on its own
    unless it remains on the vine,
    so neither can you unless you remain in me.
I am the vine, you are the branches.
Whoever remains in me and I in him will bear much fruit,
    because without me you can do nothing.

"Anyone who does not remain in me
    will be thrown out like a branch and wither;
    people will gather them and throw them into a fire
    and they will be burned.

"If you remain in me and my words remain in you,
    ask for whatever you want and it will be done for you.
By this is my Father glorified,
    that you bear much fruit and become my disciples."

54C   FIFTH SUNDAY OF EASTER

FIRST READING

ACTS 14:21–27

THEY CALLED THE
CHURCH TOGETHER AND
REPORTED WHAT GOD
HAD DONE WITH THEM.

After Paul and Barnabas had proclaimed the good news
        to that city
    and made a considerable number of disciples,
    they returned to Lystra and to Iconium and to Antioch.
They strengthened the spirits of the disciples
    and exhorted them to persevere in the faith, saying,
    "It is necessary for us to undergo many hardships
    to enter the kingdom of God."
They appointed elders for them in each church and,
    with prayer and fasting, commended them to the Lord
    in whom they had put their faith.

Then they traveled through Pisidia
        and reached Pamphylia.
After proclaiming the word at Perga they went down
        to Attalia.
From there they sailed to Antioch,
    where they had been commended to the grace of God
    for the work they had now accomplished.

And when they arrived, they called the church together
    and reported what God had done with them
    and how he had opened the door of faith
        to the Gentiles.

RESPONSORIAL PSALM

PSALM 145:8–9, 10–11, 12–13
(SEE 1)

R. I will praise your name for ever, my king and my God.
    or:
R. Alleluia.

The LORD is gracious and merciful,
    slow to anger and of great kindness.
The LORD is good to all
    and compassionate toward all his works. R.

Let all your works give you thanks, O LORD,
    and let your faithful ones bless you.
Let them discourse of the glory of your kingdom
    and speak of your might. R.

Let them make known your might to the children of Adam,
    and the glorious splendor of your kingdom.
Your kingdom is a kingdom for all ages,
    and your dominion endures through all generations. R.

SECOND READING

REVELATION 21:1–5a

GOD WILL WIPE EVERY
TEAR FROM THEIR EYES.

Then I, John, saw a new heaven and a new earth.
The former heaven and the former earth had passed away,
    and the sea was no more.

I also saw the holy city, a new Jerusalem,
    coming down out of heaven from God,
    prepared as a bride adorned for her husband.

I heard a loud voice from the throne saying,
    "Behold, God's dwelling is with the human race.
He will dwell with them and they will be his people
    and God himself will always be with them as their God.
He will wipe every tear from their eyes,
    and there shall be no more death or mourning,
        wailing or pain,
    for the old order has passed away."

The One who sat on the throne said,
    "Behold, I make all things new."

ALLELUIA

JOHN 13:34

R. Alleluia, alleluia.

I give you a new commandment, says the Lord:
love one another as I have loved you. R.

JOHN 13:31–33a, 34–35

I GIVE YOU A NEW
COMMANDMENT:
LOVE ONE ANOTHER.

When Judas had left them, Jesus said,
  "Now is the Son of Man glorified,
    and God is glorified in him.
If God is glorified in him,
  God will also glorify him in himself,
  and God will glorify him at once.

"My children, I will be with you only a little while longer.
I give you a new commandment: love one another.
As I have loved you, so you also should love one another.
This is how all will know that you are my disciples,
  if you have love for one another."

55A   SIXTH SUNDAY OF EASTER

FIRST READING

ACTS 8:5–8, 14–17

PETER AND JOHN LAID
HANDS ON THEM,
AND THEY RECEIVED
THE HOLY SPIRIT.

◆

*When the Ascension of the Lord is
celebrated the following Sunday,
the Second Reading and Gospel
from the Seventh Sunday of Easter
(see n. 59) may be read on the
Sixth Sunday of Easter.*

Philip went down to the city of Samaria
  and proclaimed the Christ to them.
With one accord, the crowds paid attention
    to what was said by Philip
  when they heard it and saw the signs he was doing.
For unclean spirits, crying out in a loud voice,
  came out of many possessed people,
  and many paralyzed or crippled people were cured.
There was great joy in that city.

Now when the apostles in Jerusalem
  heard that Samaria had accepted the word of God,
  they sent them Peter and John,
  who went down and prayed for them,
  that they might receive the Holy Spirit,
  for it had not yet fallen upon any of them;
  they had only been baptized in the name
    of the Lord Jesus.
Then they laid hands on them
  and they received the Holy Spirit.

**RESPONSORIAL
PSALM**

PSALM 66:1–3, 4–5, 6–7,
16, 20 (1)

R. *Let all the earth cry out to God with joy.*
    or:
R. *Alleluia.*

[This psalm is found on page 446 (lectionary number 174).]

SECOND READING

1 PETER 3:15–18

PUT TO DEATH IN THE
FLESH, CHRIST WAS RAISED
TO LIFE IN THE SPIRIT.

Beloved:
Sanctify Christ as Lord in your hearts.
Always be ready to give an explanation
    to anyone who asks you for a reason for your hope,
    but do it with gentleness and reverence,
    keeping your conscience clear,
    so that, when you are maligned,
    those who defame your good conduct in Christ
    may themselves be put to shame.
For it is better to suffer for doing good,
    if that be the will of God, than for doing evil.

For Christ also suffered for sins once,
    the righteous for the sake of the unrighteous,
    that he might lead you to God.
Put to death in the flesh,
    he was brought to life in the Spirit.

R. Alleluia, alleluia.

Whoever loves me will keep my word, says the Lord,
and my Father will love him and we will come to him.   R.

GOSPEL

JOHN 14:15–21

I WILL ASK THE FATHER
AND HE WILL GIVE YOU
ANOTHER ADVOCATE.

Jesus said to his disciples:
"If you love me, you will keep my commandments.
And I will ask the Father,
    and he will give you another Advocate
        to be with you always,
    the Spirit of truth, whom the world cannot accept,
    because it neither sees nor knows him.
But you know him, because he remains with you,
    and will be in you.

"I will not leave you orphans; I will come to you.
In a little while the world will no longer see me,
    but you will see me, because I live and you will live.
On that day you will realize that I am in my Father
    and you are in me and I in you.

"Whoever has my commandments and observes them
    is the one who loves me.
And whoever loves me will be loved by my Father,
    and I will love him and reveal myself to him."

56B SIXTH SUNDAY OF EASTER

FIRST READING

ACTS 10:25–26, 34–35, 44–48

THE GIFT OF THE HOLY
SPIRIT WAS POURED OUT
ON THE GENTILES ALSO.

◆

*When the Ascension of the Lord is
celebrated the following Sunday,
the Second Reading and Gospel
from the Seventh Sunday of Easter
(see n. 60) may be read on the
Sixth Sunday of Easter.*

When Peter entered, Cornelius met him
   and, falling at his feet, paid him homage.
Peter, however, raised him up, saying,
   "Get up. I myself am also a human being."

Then Peter proceeded to speak and said,
"In truth, I see that God shows no partiality.
Rather, in every nation whoever fears him
     and acts uprightly
   is acceptable to him."

While Peter was still speaking these things,
   the Holy Spirit fell upon all who were listening
     to the word.
The circumcised believers who had accompanied Peter
   were astounded that the gift of the Holy Spirit
    should have been poured out on the Gentiles also,
   for they could hear them speaking in tongues
    and glorifying God.

Then Peter responded,
"Can anyone withhold the water for baptizing
    these people,
   who have received the Holy Spirit even as we have?"
He ordered them to be baptized in the name
    of Jesus Christ.

RESPONSORIAL PSALM

PSALM 98:1, 2–3, 3–4
(SEE 2b)

R. The Lord has revealed to the nations his saving power.
   or:
R. Alleluia.

Sing to the LORD a new song,
   for he has done wondrous deeds;
His right hand has won victory for him,
   his holy arm.   R.

The LORD has made his salvation known:
   in the sight of the nations he has revealed his justice.
He has remembered his kindness and his faithfulness
   toward the house of Israel.   R.

All the ends of the earth have seen
   the salvation by our God.
Sing joyfully to the LORD, all you lands;
   break into song; sing praise.   R.

SECOND READING

1 JOHN 4:7–10

GOD IS LOVE.

Beloved, let us love one another,
  because love is of God;
    everyone who loves is begotten by God and knows God.
Whoever is without love does not know God,
    for God is love.

In this way the love of God was revealed to us:
  God sent his only Son into the world
  so that we might have life through him.
In this is love:
  not that we have loved God, but that he loved us
  and sent his Son as expiation for our sins.

ALLELUIA

JOHN 14:23

R. Alleluia, alleluia.

Whoever loves me will keep my word, says the Lord,
and my Father will love him and we will come to him.   R.

GOSPEL

JOHN 15:9–17

NO ONE HAS GREATER
LOVE THAN THIS: TO LAY
DOWN ONE'S LIFE FOR
ONE'S FRIENDS.

Jesus said to his disciples:
"As the Father loves me, so I also love you.
Remain in my love.
If you keep my commandments, you will remain
    in my love,
  just as I have kept my Father's commandments
  and remain in his love.

"I have told you this so that my joy may be in you
  and your joy might be complete.
This is my commandment: love one another as I love you.
No one has greater love than this,
  to lay down one's life for one's friends.

"You are my friends if you do what I command you.
I no longer call you slaves,
  because a slave does not know what his master is doing.
I have called you friends,
  because I have told you everything I have heard
    from my Father.

"It was not you who chose me, but I who chose you
  and appointed you to go and bear fruit that will remain,
  so that whatever you ask the Father in my name
    he may give you.
This I command you: love one another."

FIRST READING

ACTS 15:1–2, 22–29

IT IS THE DECISION OF THE
HOLY SPIRIT AND OF US
NOT TO PLACE ON YOU
ANY BURDEN BEYOND
THESE NECESSITIES.

◆

*When the Ascension of the Lord is
celebrated the following Sunday,
the Second Reading and Gospel
from the Seventh Sunday of Easter
(see n. 61) may be read on the
Sixth Sunday of Easter.*

Some who had come down from Judea were instructing
    the brothers,
  "Unless you are circumcised according to
    the Mosaic practice,
  you cannot be saved."
Because there arose no little dissension and debate
  by Paul and Barnabas with them,
    it was decided that Paul, Barnabas and some
      of the others
    should go up to Jerusalem to the apostles and elders
    about this question.

The apostles and elders, in agreement with
      the whole church,
    decided to choose representatives
    and to send them to Antioch with Paul and Barnabas.
The ones chosen were Judas, who was called Barsabbas,
    and Silas, leaders among the brothers.
This is the letter delivered by them:

"The apostles and the elders, your brothers,
    to the brothers in Antioch, Syria and Cilicia
    of Gentile origin: greetings.
Since we have heard that some of our number
    who went out without any mandate from us
    have upset you with their teachings
    and disturbed your peace of mind,
    we have with one accord decided
      to choose representatives
    and to send them to you along with our beloved
      Barnabas and Paul,
    who have dedicated their lives to the name of
      our Lord Jesus Christ.

"So we are sending Judas and Silas
    who will also convey this same message
      by word of mouth:
    'It is the decision of the Holy Spirit and of us
    not to place on you any burden beyond these necessities,
    namely, to abstain from meat sacrificed to idols,
    from blood, from meats of strangled animals,
    and from unlawful marriage.
If you keep free of these,
    you will be doing what is right. Farewell.'"

R. O God, let all the nations praise you!
    or:
R. Alleluia.

[This psalm is found on page 45 (lectionary number 18).]

SECOND READING

REVELATION 21:10–14,
22–23

THE ANGEL SHOWED ME
THE HOLY CITY COMING
DOWN OUT OF HEAVEN.

The angel took me in spirit to a great, high mountain
    and showed me the holy city Jerusalem
    coming down out of heaven from God.
It gleamed with the splendor of God.
Its radiance was like that of a precious stone,
    like jasper, clear as crystal.

It had a massive, high wall,
    with twelve gates where twelve angels were stationed
    and on which names were inscribed,
    the names of the twelve tribes of the Israelites.
There were three gates facing east,
    three north, three south, and three west.
The wall of the city had twelve courses of stones
        as its foundation,
    on which were inscribed the twelve names
    of the twelve apostles of the Lamb.

I saw no temple in the city
    for its temple is the Lord God almighty and the Lamb.
The city had no need of sun or moon to shine on it,
    for the glory of God gave it light,
    and its lamp was the Lamb.

ALLELUIA

JOHN 14:23

R. Alleluia, alleluia.

*Whoever loves me will keep my word, says the Lord,
and my Father will love him and we will come to him.   R.*

GOSPEL

JOHN 14:23–29

THE HOLY SPIRIT WILL
TEACH YOU EVERYTHING
AND REMIND YOU OF ALL
THAT I TOLD YOU.

Jesus said to his disciples:
    "Whoever loves me will keep my word,
    and my Father will love him,
    and we will come to him and make our dwelling
        with him.
Whoever does not love me does not keep my words;
    yet the word you hear is not mine
    but that of the Father who sent me.

"I have told you this while I am with you.
The Advocate, the Holy Spirit,
    whom the Father will send in my name,

will teach you everything
and remind you of all that I told you.

"Peace I leave with you; my peace I give to you.
Not as the world gives do I give it to you.
Do not let your hearts be troubled or afraid.

"You heard me tell you,
'I am going away and I will come back to you.'
If you loved me,
you would rejoice that I am going to the Father;
for the Father is greater than I.
And now I have told you this before it happens,
so that when it happens you may believe."

58A   THE ASCENSION OF THE LORD

FIRST READING

ACTS 1:1–11

AS THE APOSTLES WERE
LOOKING ON, JESUS WAS
LIFTED UP.

In the first book, Theophilus,
I dealt with all that Jesus did and taught
until the day he was taken up,
after giving instructions through the Holy Spirit
to the apostles whom he had chosen.
He presented himself alive to them
by many proofs after he had suffered,
appearing to them during forty days
and speaking about the kingdom of God.

While meeting with the them,
he enjoined them not to depart from Jerusalem,
but to wait for "the promise of the Father
about which you have heard me speak;
for John baptized with water,
but in a few days you will be baptized
with the Holy Spirit."

When they had gathered together they asked him,
"Lord, are you at this time going to restore
the kingdom to Israel?"
He answered them,
"It is not for you to know the times or seasons
that the Father has established by his own authority.
But you will receive power when the Holy Spirit
comes upon you,
and you will be my witnesses in Jerusalem,
throughout Judea and Samaria,
and to the ends of the earth."

When he had said this, as they were looking on,
    he was lifted up, and a cloud took him from their sight.
While they were looking intently at the sky
        as he was going,
    suddenly two men dressed in white garments
        stood beside them.

They said, "Men of Galilee,
    why are you standing there looking at the sky?
This Jesus who has been taken up from you into heaven
    will return in the same way as you have seen him
        going into heaven."

**RESPONSORIAL
PSALM**

PSALM 47:2–3, 6–7, 8–9 (6)

R. *God mounts his throne to shouts of joy:*
    a blare of trumpets for the Lord.
    or:
R. *Alleluia.*

[This psalm is found on page 446 (lectionary number 174).]

SECOND READING

EPHESIANS 1:17–23

GOD SEATED JESUS AT HIS
RIGHT HAND IN THE
HEAVENS.

Brothers and sisters:
May the God of our Lord Jesus Christ, the Father of glory,
    give you a spirit of wisdom and revelation
    resulting in knowledge of him.

May the eyes of your hearts be enlightened,
    that you may know what is the hope that belongs
        to his call,
    what are the riches of glory
    in his inheritance among the holy ones,
    and what is the surpassing greatness of his power
    for us who believe,
    in accord with the exercise of his great might,
    which he worked in Christ,
    raising him from the dead
    and seating him at his right hand in the heavens,
    far above every principality, authority, power
        and dominion,
    and every name that is named
    not only in this age but also in the one to come.

And he put all things beneath his feet
    and gave him as head over all things to the church,
    which is his body,
    the fullness of the one who fills all things in every way.

R. Alleluia, alleluia.

Go and teach all nations, says the Lord;
I am with you always, until the end of the world.   R.

GOSPEL

MATTHEW 28:16–20

ALL POWER IN HEAVEN
AND ON EARTH HAS
BEEN GIVEN TO ME.

The eleven disciples went to Galilee,
 to the mountain to which Jesus had ordered them.
When they saw him, they worshiped, but they doubted.

Then Jesus approached and said to them,
 "All power in heaven and on earth
  has been given to me.
Go, therefore, and make disciples of all nations,
 baptizing them in the name of the Father,
 and of the Son, and of the Holy Spirit,
 teaching them to observe all that I have
  commanded you.

"And behold, I am with you always,
 until the end of the age."

58B   THE ASCENSION OF THE LORD

FIRST READING

ACTS 1:1–11

AS THE APOSTLES WERE
LOOKING ON, JESUS WAS
LIFTED UP.

[This reading is found on page 189
(lectionary number 58A).]

**RESPONSORIAL
PSALM**

PSALM 47:2–3, 6–7, 8–9 (6)

R. God mounts his throne to shouts of joy:
 a blare of trumpets for the Lord.
 or:
R. Alleluia.

[This psalm is found on page 446 (lectionary number 174).]

LONGER FORM
EPHESIANS 4:1–13

SHORTER FORM
EPHESIANS 4:1–7, 11–13

TO THE EXTENT OF THE
FULL STATURE OF CHRIST.

◆

*The Second Reading from Year A
may be used.*

[Brothers and sisters,
I, a prisoner for the Lord,
   urge you to live in a manner worthy of the call
      you have received,
   with all humility and gentleness, with patience,
   bearing with one another through love,
   striving to preserve the unity of the spirit
   through the bond of peace:
   one body and one Spirit,
   as you were also called to the one hope of your call;
   one Lord, one faith, one baptism;
   one God and Father of all,
   who is over all and through all and in all.

But grace was given to each of us
   according to the measure of Christ's gift.]
Therefore, it says:
   He ascended on high and took prisoners captive;
   he gave gifts to men.

What does "he ascended" mean except that
   he also descended
into the lower regions of the earth?
The one who descended is also the one who ascended
   far above all the heavens,
   that he might fill all things.

[And he gave some as apostles, others as prophets,
   others as evangelists, others as pastors and teachers,
   to equip the holy ones for the work of ministry,
   for building up the body of Christ,
   until we all attain to the unity of faith
   and knowledge of the Son of God,
      to mature to manhood,
   to the extent of the full stature of Christ.]

ALLELUIA

MATTHEW 28:19a, 20b

R. Alleluia, alleluia.

Go and teach all nations, says the Lord;
I am with you always, until the end of the world.   *R.*

GOSPEL

MARK 16:15–20

THE LORD JESUS WAS
TAKEN UP INTO HEAVEN
AND TOOK HIS SEAT AT
THE RIGHT HAND OF GOD.

Jesus said to his disciples:
"Go into the whole world
   and proclaim the gospel to every creature.
Whoever believes and is baptized will be saved;
   whoever does not believe will be condemned.

These signs will accompany those who believe:
in my name they will drive out demons,
they will speak new languages.
They will pick up serpents with their hands,
and if they drink any deadly thing,
it will not harm them.
They will lay hands on the sick, and they will recover."

So then the Lord Jesus, after he spoke to them,
was taken up into heaven
and took his seat at the right hand of God.
But they went forth and preached everywhere,
while the Lord worked with them
and confirmed the word through accompanying signs.

58C   THE ASCENSION OF THE LORD

FIRST READING

ACTS 1:1–11

AS THE APOSTLES WERE
LOOKING ON, JESUS WAS
TAKEN UP.

[This reading is found on page 189
(lectionary number 58A).]

**RESPONSORIAL
PSALM**

PSALM 47:2–3, 6–7, 8–9 (6)

R. *God mounts his throne to shouts of joy:*
   a blare of trumpets for the Lord.
   or:
R. *Alleluia.*

[*This psalm is found on page 446 (lectionary number 174).*]

SECOND READING

HEBREWS 9:24–28; 10:19–23

CHRIST HAS ENTERED
INTO HEAVEN ITSELF.

♦

*The Second Reading from Year A
may be used.*

Christ did not enter into a sanctuary made by hands,
a copy of the true one, but heaven itself,
that he might now appear before God on our behalf.
Not that he might offer himself repeatedly,
as the high priest enters each year into the sanctuary
with blood that is not his own;
if that were so, he would have had to suffer repeatedly
from the foundation of the world.
But now once for all he has appeared at the end
of the ages
to take away sin by his sacrifice.

Just as it is appointed that men and women die once,
and after this the judgment, so also Christ,
offered once to take away the sins of many,
will appear a second time, not to take away sin
but to bring salvation to those who eagerly await him.

Therefore, brothers and sisters,
since through the blood of Jesus
we have confidence of entrance into the sanctuary
by the new and living way he opened for us
through the veil, that is, his flesh,
and since we have "a great priest over the house
of God,"
let us approach with a sincere heart
and in absolute trust,
with our hearts sprinkled clean from an evil conscience
and our bodies washed in pure water.
Let us hold unwaveringly to our confession
that gives us hope,
for he who made the promise is trustworthy.

ALLELUIA

MATTHEW 28:19a, 20b

R. Alleluia, alleluia.

Go and teach all nations, says the Lord;
I am with you always, until the end of the world. R.

GOSPEL

LUKE 24:46–53

AS HE BLESSED THEM,
HE WAS TAKEN UP
TO HEAVEN.

Jesus said to his disciples:
"Thus it is written that the Christ would suffer
and rise from the dead on the third day
and that repentance, for the forgiveness of sins,
would be preached in his name
to all the nations, beginning from Jerusalem.
You are witnesses of these things.
And behold I am sending the promise of my Father
upon you;
but stay in the city
until you are clothed with power from on high."

Then he led them out as far as Bethany,
raised his hands, and blessed them.
As he blessed them he parted from them
and was taken up to heaven.
They did him homage
and then returned to Jerusalem with great joy,
and they were continually in the temple praising God.

FIRST READING

ACTS 1:12–14

ALL THESE DEVOTED THEMSELVES WITH ONE ACCORD TO PRAYER.

After Jesus had been taken up to heaven the apostles
    returned to Jerusalem
        from the mount called Olivet, which is near Jerusalem,
    a sabbath day's journey away.

When they entered the city
    they went to the upper room where they were staying,
    Peter and John and James and Andrew,
        Philip and Thomas, Bartholomew and Matthew,
    James son of Alphaeus, Simon the Zealot,
    and Judas son of James.

All these devoted themselves with one accord to prayer,
    together with some women,
        and Mary the mother of Jesus, and his brothers.

RESPONSORIAL PSALM

PSALM 27:1, 4, 7–8 (13)

R. I believe that I shall see the good things of the Lord
    in the land of the living.
    or:
R. Alleluia.

The LORD is my light and my salvation;
    whom should I fear?
The LORD is my life's refuge;
    of whom should I be afraid?   R.

One thing I ask of the LORD; this I seek:
    to dwell in the house of the LORD
all the days of my life,
    that I may gaze on the loveliness of the LORD
    and contemplate his temple.   R.

Hear, O Lord, the sound of my call;
    have pity on me, and answer me.
Of you my heart speaks; you my glance seeks.   R.

SECOND READING

1 PETER 4:13–16

IF YOU ARE INSULTED FOR THE NAME OF CHRIST, BLESSED ARE YOU.

Beloved:
Rejoice to the extent that you share in the sufferings
        of Christ,
    so that when his glory is revealed
    you may also rejoice exultantly.
If you are insulted for the name of Christ, blessed are you,
    for the Spirit of glory and of God rests upon you.

But let no one among you be made to suffer
    as a murderer, a thief, an evildoer, or as an intriguer.
But whoever is made to suffer as a Christian should not
        be ashamed
    but glorify God because of the name.

R. Alleluia, alleluia.

I will not leave you orphans, says the Lord.
I will come back to you, and your heart will rejoice.   R.

Jesus raised his eyes to heaven and said,
"Father, the hour has come.
Give glory to your son, so that your son may glorify you,
    just as you gave him authority over all people,
    so that your son may give eternal life
        to all you gave him.
Now this is eternal life,
    that they should know you, the only true God,
    and the one whom you sent, Jesus Christ.

"I glorified you on earth
    by accomplishing the work that you gave me to do.
Now glorify me, Father, with you,
    with the glory that I had with you
        before the world began.

"I revealed your name to those whom you gave me
        out of the world.
They belonged to you, and you gave them to me,
    and they have kept your word.
Now they know that everything you gave me is from you,
    because the words you gave to me I have given to them,
    and they accepted them and truly understood
        that I came from you,
    and they have believed that you sent me.

"I pray for them.
I do not pray for the world but for the ones
        you have given me,
    because they are yours, and everything of mine is yours
    and everything of yours is mine,
    and I have been glorified in them.
And now I will no longer be in the world,
    but they are in the world, while I am coming to you."

FIRST READING

ACTS 1:15–17, 20a, 20c–26

IT IS NECESSARY THAT
ONE OF THE MEN WHO
ACCOMPANIED US BECOME
WITH US A WITNESS TO
THE RESURRECTION.

Peter stood up in the midst of the brothers
  — there was a group of about one hundred
    and twenty persons
in the one place.
He said, "My brothers,
  the Scripture had to be fulfilled
  which the Holy Spirit spoke beforehand
  through the mouth of David, concerning Judas,
  who was the guide for those who arrested Jesus.
He was numbered among us
  and was allotted a share in this ministry.

"For it is written in the Book of Psalms:
  May another take his office.

"Therefore, it is necessary that one of the men
  who accompanied us the whole time
  the Lord Jesus came and went among us,
  beginning from the baptism of John
  until the day on which he was taken up from us,
  become with us a witness to his resurrection."

So they proposed two, Judas called Barsabbas,
  who was also known as Justus, and Matthias.
Then they prayed,
  "You, Lord, who know the hearts of all,
  show which one of these two you have chosen
  to take the place in this apostolic ministry
  from which Judas turned away to go to his own place."
Then they gave lots to them, and the lot fell
    upon Matthias,
  and he was counted with the eleven apostles.

**RESPONSORIAL
PSALM**

PSALM 103:1–2, 11–12,
19–20 (19a)

R. *The Lord has set his throne in heaven.*
    or:
R. *Alleluia.*

Bless the LORD, O my soul;
  and all my being, bless his holy name.
Bless the LORD, O my soul,
  and forget not all his benefits.   R.

For as the heavens are high above the earth,
  so surpassing is his kindness toward those who fear him.
As far as the east is from the west,
  so far has he put our transgressions from us.   R.

The Lord has established his throne in heaven,
  and his kingdom rules over all.
Bless the Lord, all you his angels,
  you mighty in strength, who do his bidding.   R.

SECOND READING

1 JOHN 4:11–16

WHOEVER REMAINS IN
LOVE, REMAINS IN GOD,
AND GOD IN HIM.

Beloved, if God so loved us,
  we also must love one another.

No one has ever seen God.
Yet, if we love one another, God remains in us,
  and his love is brought to perfection in us.
This is how we know that we remain in him and he in us,
  that he has given us of his Spirit.
Moreover, we have seen and testify
  that the Father sent his Son as savior of the world.

Whoever acknowledges that Jesus is the Son of God,
  God remains in him and he in God.
We have come to know and to believe in the love
    God has for us.
God is love, and whoever remains in love
  remains in God and God in him.

ALLELUIA

SEE JOHN 14:18

R. Alleluia, alleluia.

I will not leave you orphans, says the Lord.
I will come back to you, and your hearts will rejoice.   R.

GOSPEL

JOHN 17:11b–19

THAT THEY MAY BE ONE
JUST AS WE ARE ONE!

Lifting up his eyes to heaven, Jesus prayed saying:
"Holy Father, keep them in your name
    that you have given me,
  so that they may be one just as we are one.
When I was with them I protected them in your name
    that you gave me,
  and I guarded them, and none of them was lost
  except the son of destruction,
  in order that the Scripture might be fulfilled.

"But now I am coming to you.
I speak this in the world
  so that they may share my joy completely.
I gave them your word, and the world hated them,
  because they do not belong to the world
  any more than I belong to the world.
I do not ask that you take them out of the world
  but that you keep them from the evil one.

"They do not belong to the world
  any more than I belong to the world.
Consecrate them in the truth. Your word is truth.
As you sent me into the world,
  so I sent them into the world.
And I consecrate myself for them,
  so that they also may be consecrated in truth."

61C   SEVENTH SUNDAY OF EASTER

FIRST READING

ACTS 7:55–60

I SEE THE SON OF MAN
STANDING AT THE RIGHT
HAND OF GOD.

Stephen, filled with the Holy Spirit,
  looked up intently to heaven and saw the glory of God
  and Jesus standing at the right hand of God,
  and Stephen said, "Behold, I see the heavens opened
  and the Son of Man standing at the right hand of God."

But they cried out in a loud voice,
  covered their ears, and rushed upon him together.
They threw him out of the city, and began to stone him.
The witnesses laid down their cloaks
  at the feet of a young man named Saul.

As they were stoning Stephen, he called out,
  "Lord Jesus, receive my spirit."
Then he fell to his knees and cried out in a loud voice,
  "Lord, do not hold this sin against them";
  and when he said this, he fell asleep.

**RESPONSORIAL
PSALM**

PSALM 97:1–2, 6–7, 9 (1a, 9a)

R. *The Lord is king, the most high over all the earth.*
  or:
R. *Alleluia.*

The Lord is king; let the earth rejoice;
  let the many islands be glad.
Justice and judgment are the foundation of his throne. R.

The heavens proclaim his justice,
  and all peoples see his glory.
All gods are prostrate before him. R.

You, O Lord, are the Most High over all the earth,
  exalted far above all gods. R.

SECOND READING

REVELATION 22:12–14,
16–17, 20

COME, LORD JESUS!

I, John, heard a voice saying to me:
  "Behold, I am coming soon.
I bring with me the recompense I will give to each
  according to his deeds.

I am the Alpha and the Omega, the first and the last,
  the beginning and the end."

Blessed are they who wash their robes
  so as to have the right to the tree of life
  and enter the city through its gates.

"I, Jesus, sent my angel to give you this testimony
    for the churches.
I am the root and offspring of David,
  the bright morning star."

The Spirit and the bride say, "Come."
Let the hearer say, "Come."
Let the one who thirsts come forward,
  and the one who wants it receive the gift
    of life-giving water.

The one who gives this testimony says,
    "Yes, I am coming soon."
Amen! Come, Lord Jesus!

ALLELUIA

SEE JOHN 14:18

R. Alleluia, alleluia.

I will not leave you orphans, says the Lord.
I will come back to you, and your hearts will rejoice.   R.

GOSPEL

JOHN 17:20–26

THAT THEY MAY BE BROUGHT
TO PERFECTION AS ONE!

Lifting up his eyes to heaven, Jesus prayed saying:
"Holy Father, I pray not only for them,
  but also for those who will believe in me through
    their word,
  so that they may all be one,
  as you, Father, are in me and I in you,
  that they also may be in us,
  that the world may believe that you sent me.
And I have given them the glory you gave me,
  so that they may be one, as we are one,
  I in them and you in me,
  that they may be brought to perfection as one,
  that the world may know that you sent me,
  and that you loved them even as you loved me.

"Father, they are your gift to me.
I wish that where I am they also may be with me,
  that they may see my glory that you gave me,
  because you loved me before the foundation
    of the world.

"Righteous Father, the world also does not know you,
    but I know you, and they know that you sent me.
I made known to them your name
    and I will make it known,
    that the love with which you loved me
    may be in them and I in them."

62ABC PENTECOST SUNDAY
AT THE VIGIL MASS

FIRST READING

GENESIS 11:1–9

IT WAS CALLED BABEL
BECAUSE THERE THE LORD
CONFUSED THE SPEECH OF
ALL THE WORLD.

◆

*These readings are used at
Saturday Evening Mass celebrated
either before or after Evening
Prayer I of Pentecost Sunday.*

The whole world spoke the same language,
    using the same words.
While the people were migrating in the east,
    they came upon a valley in the land of Shinar
        and settled there.
They said to one another,
    "Come, let us mold bricks and harden them with fire."
They used bricks for stone, and bitumen for mortar.

Then they said, "Come, let us build ourselves a city
    and a tower with its top in the sky,
    and so make a name for ourselves;
    otherwise we shall be scattered all over the earth."

The LORD came down to see the city and the tower
    that the people had built.
Then the LORD said: "If now, while they are one people,
    all speaking the same language,
    they have started to do this,
    nothing will later stop them from doing
        whatever they presume to do.
Let us then go down there and confuse their language,
    so that one will not understand what another says."

Thus the LORD scattered them from there
        all over the earth,
    and they stopped building the city.
That is why it was called Babel,
    because there the LORD confused the speech
        of all the world.
It was from that place that he scattered them
    all over the earth.

OR:

EXODUS 19:3–8a, 16–20b

THE LORD CAME DOWN
UPON MOUNT SINAI
BEFORE ALL THE PEOPLE.

Moses went up the mountain to God.
Then the LORD called to him and said,
"Thus shall you say to the house of Jacob;
    tell the Israelites:
    You have seen for yourselves how I treated the Egyptians
    and how I bore you up on eagle wings
    and brought you here to myself.

"Therefore, if you hearken to my voice and keep
        my covenant,
    you shall be my special possession,
    dearer to me than all other people,
    though all the earth is mine.
You shall be to me a kingdom of priests, a holy nation.
That is what you must tell the Israelites."

So Moses went and summoned the elders of the people.
When he set before them
    all that the LORD had ordered him to tell them,
    the people all answered together,
    "Everything the LORD has said, we will do."

On the morning of the third day
    there were peals of thunder and lightning,
    and a heavy cloud over the mountain,
    and a very loud trumpet blast,
    so that all the people in the camp trembled.
But Moses led the people out of the camp to meet God,
    and they stationed themselves at the foot
        of the mountain.
Mount Sinai was all wrapped in smoke,
    for the LORD came down upon it in fire.
The smoke rose from it as though from a furnace,
    and the whole mountain trembled violently.
The trumpet blast grew louder and louder,
        while Moses was speaking,
    and God answering him with thunder.

When the LORD came down to the top of Mount Sinai,
    he summoned Moses to the top of the mountain.

OR:

EZEKIEL 37:1–14

DRY BONES OF ISRAEL, I
WILL BRING SPIRIT INTO
YOU, THAT YOU MAY
COME TO LIFE.

The hand of the LORD came upon me,
    and he led me out in the spirit of the LORD
    and set me in the center of the plain,
    which was now filled with bones.
He made me walk among the bones in every direction
    so that I saw how many they were on the surface
        of the plain.

How dry they were!
He asked me:
    Son of man, can these bones come to life?
I answered, "Lord God, you alone know that."

Then he said to me:
    Prophesy over these bones, and say to them:
    Dry bones, hear the word of the Lord!
Thus says the Lord God to these bones:
    See! I will bring spirit into you, that you
        may come to life.
I will put sinews upon you, make flesh grow over you,
    cover you with skin, and put spirit in you
    so that you may come to life and know
        that I am the Lord.

I, Ezekiel, prophesied as I had been told,
    and even as I was prophesying I heard a noise;
    it was a rattling as the bones came together,
        bone joining bone.
I saw the sinews and the flesh come upon them,
    and the skin cover them, but there was no spirit
        in them.

Then the Lord said to me:
    Prophesy to the spirit, prophesy, son of man,
    and say to the spirit: Thus says the Lord God:
    From the four winds come, O spirit,
    and breathe into these slain that they may come to life.
I prophesied as he told me, and the spirit came into them;
    they came alive and stood upright, a vast army.

Then he said to me:
    Son of man, these bones are the whole house of Israel.
They have been saying,
    "Our bones are dried up,
    our hope is lost, and we are cut off."
Therefore, prophesy and say to them:
    Thus says the Lord God:
    O my people, I will open your graves
    and have you rise from them,
    and bring you back to the land of Israel.

Then you shall know that I am the Lord,
    when I open your graves and have you rise from them,
    O my people!
I will put my spirit in you that you may live,
    and I will settle you upon your land;
    thus you shall know that I am the Lord.
I have promised, and I will do it, says the Lord.

OR:

JOEL 3:1–5

I WILL POUR OUT MY SPIRIT
UPON THE SERVANTS AND
HANDMAIDS.

Thus says the Lord:
I will pour out my spirit upon all flesh.
Your sons and daughters shall prophesy,
    your old men shall dream dreams,
    your young men shall see visions;
even upon the servants and the handmaids,
    in those days, I will pour out my spirit.
And I will work wonders in the heavens and on the earth,
    blood, fire, and columns of smoke;
the sun will be turned to darkness,
    and the moon to blood,
at the coming of the day of the LORD,
    the great and terrible day.

Then everyone shall be rescued
    who calls on the name of the LORD;
for on Mount Zion there shall be a remnant,
    as the LORD has said,
and in Jerusalem survivors
    whom the LORD shall call.

**RESPONSORIAL
PSALM**

PSALM 104:1–2, 24, 35,
27–28, 29, 30 (SEE 30)

R. *Lord, send out your Spirit, and renew the face of the earth.*
    or:
R. *Alleluia.*

Bless the LORD, O my soul!
    O LORD, my God, you are great indeed!
You are clothed with majesty and glory,
    robed in light as with a cloak. R.

How manifold are your works, O LORD!
    In wisdom you have wrought them all—
    the earth is full of your creatures;
bless the LORD, O my soul! Alleluia. R.

Creatures all look to you
    to give them food in due time.
When you give it to them, they gather it;
    when you open your hand, they are filled with good things. R.

If you take away their breath, they perish
    and return to their dust.
When you send forth your spirit, they are created,
    and you renew the face of the earth. R.

SECOND READING

ROMANS 8:22–27

THE SPIRIT INTERCEDES
WITH INEXPRESSIBLE
GROANINGS.

Brothers and sisters:
We know that all creation is groaning in labor pains
    even until now;
    and not only that, but we ourselves,
    who have the firstfruits of the Spirit,
    we also groan within ourselves
    as we wait for adoption, the redemption of our bodies.

For in hope we were saved.
Now hope that sees is not hope.
For who hopes for what one sees?
But if we hope for what we do not see,
    we wait with endurance.

In the same way, the Spirit too comes to the aid
    of our weakness;
    for we do not know how to pray as we ought,
    but the Spirit himself intercedes
    with inexpressible groanings.
And the one who searches hearts
    knows what is the intention of the Spirit,
    because he intercedes for the holy ones
    according to God's will.

ALLELUIA

R. Alleluia, alleluia.

Come, Holy Spirit, fill the hearts of the faithful
and kindle in them the fire of your love.   R.

GOSPEL

JOHN 7:37–39

RIVERS OF LIVING WATER
WILL FLOW.

On the last and greatest day of the feast,
    Jesus stood up and exclaimed,
    "Let anyone who thirsts come to me and drink.
As Scripture says:
    *Rivers of living water will flow from within him
        who believes in me.*"

He said this in reference to the Spirit
    that those who came to believe in him were to receive.
There was, of course, no Spirit yet,
    because Jesus had not yet been glorified.

63A   PENTECOST SUNDAY
MASS DURING THE DAY

FIRST READING

ACTS 2:1–11

THEY WERE ALL FILLED
WITH THE HOLY SPIRIT,
AND BEGAN TO SPEAK.

When the time for Pentecost was fulfilled,
    they were all in one place together.
And suddenly there came from the sky
    a noise like a strong driving wind,
    and it filled the entire house in which they were.
Then there appeared to them tongues as of fire,
    which parted and came to rest on each one of them.

And they were all filled with the Holy Spirit
 and began to speak in different tongues,
 as the Spirit enabled them to proclaim.

Now there were devout Jews from every nation
 under heaven
 staying in Jerusalem.
At this sound, they gathered in a large crowd,
 but they were confused
 because each one heard them speaking
 in his own language.
They were astounded, and in amazement they asked,
 "Are not all these people who are speaking Galileans?
Then how does each of us hear them
 in his native language?
We are Parthians, Medes, and Elamites,
 inhabitants of Mesopotamia, Judea and Cappadocia,
 Pontus and Asia, Phrygia and Pamphylia,
 Egypt and the districts of Libya near Cyrene,
 as well as travelers from Rome,
 both Jews and converts to Judaism, Cretans and Arabs,
 yet we hear them speaking in our own tongues
 of the mighty acts of God."

RESPONSORIAL PSALM

PSALM 104:1, 24, 29–30, 31, 34 (SEE 30)

R. Lord, send out your Spirit, and renew the face of the earth.
 or:
R. Alleluia.

[This psalm is found on page 446 (lectionary number 174).]

SECOND READING

1 CORINTHIANS 12:3b–7, 12–13

IN ONE SPIRIT WE WERE ALL BAPTIZED INTO ONE BODY.

Brothers and sisters:
No one can say, "Jesus is Lord," except by the Holy Spirit.
There are different kinds of spiritual gifts
 but the same Spirit;
 there are different forms of service but the same Lord;
 there are different workings but the same God
 who produces all of them in everyone.
To each individual the manifestation of the Spirit
 is given for some benefit.

As a body is one though it has many parts,
 and all the parts of the body, though many,
 are one body,
 so also Christ.
For in one Spirit we were all baptized into one body,
 whether Jews or Greeks, slaves or free persons,
 and we were all given to drink of one Spirit.

Come, Holy Spirit, come!
And from your celestial home
Shed a ray of light divine!

Come, Father of the poor!
Come, source of all our store!
Come, within our bosoms shine.

You, of comforters the best;
You, the soul's most welcome guest;
Sweet refreshment here below;

In our labor, rest most sweet;
Grateful coolness in the heat;
Solace in the midst of woe.

O most blessed Light divine,
Shine within these hearts of yours,
And our inmost being fill!

Where you are not, we have naught,
Nothing good in deed or thought,
Nothing free from taint of ill.

Heal our wounds, our strength renew;
On our dryness pour your dew;
Wash the stains of guilt away:

Bend the stubborn heart and will;
Melt the frozen, warm the chill;
Guide the steps that go astray.

On the faithful, who adore
And confess you, evermore
In your sevenfold gift descend;

Give them virtue's sure reward;
Give them your salvation, Lord;
Give them joys that never end. Amen.
Alleluia.

ALLELUIA

R. Alleluia, alleluia.

Come, Holy Spirit, fill the hearts of your faithful
and kindle in them the fire of your love.   R.

GOSPEL

JOHN 20:19–23

AS THE FATHER SENT ME,
SO I SEND YOU: RECEIVE
THE HOLY SPIRIT.

On the evening of that first day of the week,
 when the doors were locked, where the disciples were,
 for fear of the Jews,
 Jesus came and stood in their midst
 and said to them, "Peace be with you."
When he had said this, he showed them his hands
 and his side.
The disciples rejoiced when they saw the Lord.

Jesus said to them again, "Peace be with you.
As the Father has sent me, so I send you."

And when he had said this, he breathed on them
and said to them,
"Receive the Holy Spirit.
Whose sins you forgive are forgiven them,
and whose sins you retain are retained."

63B PENTECOST SUNDAY
MASS DURING THE DAY

FIRST READING

ACTS 2:1–11

THEY WERE ALL FILLED
WITH THE HOLY SPIRIT,
AND BEGAN TO SPEAK.

[This reading is found on page 205
(lectionary number 63A).]

**RESPONSORIAL
PSALM**

PSALM 104:1, 24, 29–30, 31,
34 (SEE 30)

R. *Lord, send out your Spirit, and renew the face of the earth.*
or:
R. *Alleluia.*

[This psalm is found on page 446 (lectionary number 174).]

SECOND READING

GALATIANS 5:16–25

THE FRUIT OF THE SPIRIT.

◆

*The Second Reading from Year A
and/or the Gospel from Year A
may be used.*

Brothers and sisters, live by the Spirit
and you will certainly not gratify the desire of the flesh.
For the flesh has desires against the Spirit,
and the Spirit against the flesh;
these are opposed to each other,
so that you may not do what you want.

But if you are guided by the Spirit,
you are not under the law.
Now the works of the flesh are obvious:
immorality, impurity, lust, idolatry,
sorcery, hatreds, rivalry, jealousy,
outbursts of fury, acts of selfishness,
dissensions, factions, occasions of envy,
drinking bouts, orgies and the like.

I warn you, as I warned you before,
that those who do such things will not inherit
the kingdom of God.

In contrast, the fruit of the Spirit is love, joy, peace,
patience, kindness, generosity,
faithfulness, gentleness, self-control.
Against such there is no law.

Now those who belong to Christ Jesus have crucified
their flesh
with its passions and desires.
If we live in the Spirit, let us also follow the Spirit.

SEQUENCE

VENI, SANCTE SPIRITUS

[This sequence is found on page 207 (lectionary number 63A).]

ALLELUIA

R. Alleluia, alleluia.

*Come, Holy Spirit, fill the hearts of your faithful
and kindle in them the fire of your love.   R.*

GOSPEL

JOHN 15:26–27; 16:12–15

THE SPIRIT OF TRUTH
WILL GUIDE YOU TO ALL
THE TRUTH.

Jesus said to his disciples:
"When the Advocate comes whom I will send you
from the Father,
the Spirit of truth that proceeds from the Father,
he will testify to me.
And you also testify,
because you have been with me from the beginning.

"I have much more to tell you, but you cannot bear it now.
But when he comes, the Spirit of truth,
he will guide you to all truth.
He will not speak on his own,
but he will speak what he hears,
and will declare to you the things that are coming.
He will glorify me,
because he will take from what is mine
and declare it to you.

"Everything that the Father has is mine;
for this reason I told you that he will take
from what is mine
and declare it to you."

63C   PENTECOST SUNDAY

MASS DURING THE DAY

FIRST READING

ACTS 2:1–11

THEY WERE FILLED WITH
THE HOLY SPIRIT, AND
BEGAN TO SPEAK.

[This reading is found on page 205
(lectionary number 63A).]

R. *Lord, send out your Spirit, and renew the face of the earth.*
   or:
R. *Alleluia.*

[This psalm is found on page 446 (lectionary number 174).]

SECOND READING

ROMANS 8:8–17

THOSE WHO ARE LED BY
THE SPIRIT OF GOD ARE
CHILDREN OF GOD.

♦

*The Second Reading from Year A
and/or The Gospel from Year A
may be used.*

Brothers and sisters:
Those who are in the flesh cannot please God.
But you are not in the flesh;
   on the contrary, you are in the spirit,
   if only the Spirit of God dwells in you.
Whoever does not have the Spirit of Christ does not
      belong to him.

But if Christ is in you,
   although the body is dead because of sin,
   the spirit is alive because of righteousness.
If the Spirit of the one who raised Jesus from the dead
      dwells in you,
   the one who raised Christ from the dead
   will give life to your mortal bodies also,
   through his Spirit that dwells in you.

Consequently, brothers and sisters,
   we are not debtors to the flesh,
   to live according to the flesh.
For if you live according to the flesh, you will die,
   but if by the Spirit you put to death
      the deeds of the body,
      you will live.

For those who are led by the Spirit of God are sons of God.
For you did not receive a spirit of slavery to fall back
      into fear,
   but you received a spirit of adoption,
   through whom we cry, "Abba, Father!"
The Spirit himself bears witness with our spirit
   that we are children of God,
   and if children, then heirs,
   heirs of God and joint heirs with Christ,
   if only we suffer with him
   so that we may also be glorified with him.

SEQUENCE

VENI, SANCTE SPIRITUS

[This sequence is found on page 207 (lectionary number 63A).]

ALLELUIA

R. *Alleluia, alleluia.*

Come, Holy Spirit, fill the hearts of your faithful
and kindle in them the fire of your love.   *R.*

GOSPEL

JOHN 14:15–16, 23b–26

THE HOLY SPIRIT WILL
TEACH YOU EVERYTHING.

◆

If it is customary or obligatory
for the faithful to attend Mass on
the Monday or even the Tuesday
after Pentecost, the readings from
the Mass of Pentecost Sunday may
be repeated or the readings of
the Ritual Mass for Confirmation,
nos. 764 – 768, may be used in
its place.

Jesus said to his disciples:
"If you love me, you will keep my commandments.
And I will ask the Father,
    and he will give you another Advocate
        to be with you always.

"Whoever loves me will keep my word,
    and my Father will love him,
    and we will come to him and make our dwelling
        with him.
Those who do not love me do not keep my words;
    yet the word you hear is not mine
    but that of the Father who sent me.

"I have told you this while I am with you.
The Advocate, the Holy Spirit whom the Father
        will send in my name,
    will teach you everything
    and remind you of all that I told you."

ORDINARY TIME

64A   SECOND SUNDAY IN ORDINARY TIME

ISAIAH 49:3, 5–6

I WILL MAKE YOU
A LIGHT TO THE NATIONS,
THAT MY SALVATION
MAY REACH TO THE ENDS
OF THE EARTH.

◆

*The First Sunday of Ordinary Time
is the Feast of the Baptism of the
Lord (see n. 21).*

The LORD said to me: You are my servant,
  Israel, through whom I show my glory.
Now the LORD has spoken
  who formed me as his servant from the womb,
  that Jacob may be brought back to him
  and Israel gathered to him;
  and I am made glorious in the sight of the LORD,
  and my God is now my strength!

It is too little, the LORD says, for you to be my servant,
  to raise up the tribes of Jacob,
  and restore the survivors of Israel;
I will make you a light to the nations,
  that my salvation may reach to the ends of the earth.

**RESPONSORIAL
PSALM**

PSALM 40:2, 4, 7–8, 8–9, 10
(8a, 9a)

R. Here am I, Lord; I come to do your will.

*I have waited, waited for the LORD,
  and he stooped toward me and heard my cry.
And he put a new song into my mouth,
  a hymn to our God.   R.*

*Sacrifice or offering you wished not,
  but ears open to obedience you gave me.
Holocausts or sin-offerings you sought not;
  then said I, "Behold I come."   R.*

*"In the written scroll it is prescribed for me,
  to do your will, O my God, is my delight,
and your law is within my heart!"   R.*

*I announced your justice in the vast assembly;
  I did not restrain my lips, as you, O LORD, know.   R.*

SECOND READING

1 CORINTHIANS 1:1–3

GRACE TO YOU AND
PEACE FROM GOD OUR
FATHER AND THE LORD
JESUS CHRIST.

Paul, called to be an apostle of Christ Jesus
    by the will of God,
  and Sosthenes our brother,
  to the church of God that is in Corinth,
  to you who have been sanctified in Christ Jesus,
  called to be holy,
  with all those everywhere who call upon the name
    of our Lord
Jesus Christ, their Lord and ours.

212   ORDINARY TIME: SECOND SUNDAY A

Grace to you and peace from God our Father
and the Lord Jesus Christ.

ALLELUIA

JOHN 1:14a, 12a

R. Alleluia, alleluia.

The Word of God became flesh and dwelt among us.
To those who accepted him,
he gave power to become children of God.   R.

GOSPEL

JOHN 1:29–34

BEHOLD, THE LAMB OF
GOD, WHO TAKES AWAY
THE SIN OF THE WORLD.

John the Baptist saw Jesus coming toward him and said,
    "Behold, the Lamb of God, who takes away the sin
        of the world.
He is the one of whom I said,
    'A man is coming after me who ranks ahead of me
    because he existed before me.'
I did not know him,
    but the reason why I came baptizing with water
    was that he might be made known to Israel."

John testified further, saying,
    "I saw the Spirit come down like a dove from heaven
    and remain upon him.
I did not know him,
    but the one who sent me to baptize with water told me,
    'On whomever you see the Spirit come down
        and remain,
    he is the one who will baptize with the Holy Spirit.'
Now I have seen and testified that he is the Son of God."

65B   SECOND SUNDAY IN ORDINARY TIME

FIRST READING

1 SAMUEL 3:3b–10, 19

SPEAK, LORD, FOR YOUR
SERVANT IS LISTENING.

Samuel was sleeping in the temple of the LORD
    where the ark of God was.
The LORD called to Samuel, who answered, "Here I am."
Samuel ran to Eli and said, "Here I am. You called me."
"I did not call you," Eli said. "Go back to sleep."
So he went back to sleep.

Again the LORD called Samuel, who rose and went to Eli.
"Here I am," he said. "You called me."
But Eli answered, "I did not call you, my son.
    Go back to sleep."
At that time Samuel was not familiar with the LORD,
    because the LORD had not revealed anything to him
    as yet.

The LORD called Samuel again, for the third time.
Getting up and going to Eli, he said, "Here I am.
    You called me."
Then Eli understood that the LORD was calling the youth.
So he said to Samuel,
    "Go to sleep, and if you are called, reply,
    'Speak, LORD, for your servant is listening.'"
When Samuel went to sleep in his place,
    the LORD came and revealed his presence,
    calling out as before, "Samuel, Samuel!"
Samuel answered, "Speak, for your servant is listening."

Samuel grew up, and the LORD was with him,
    not permitting any word of his to be without effect.

RESPONSORIAL PSALM

PSALM 40:2, 4, 7–8, 8–9, 10
(8a, 9a)

R. Here am I, Lord; I come to do your will.

[This psalm is found on page 212 (lectionary number 64).]

SECOND READING

1 CORINTHIANS 6:13c–15a,
17–20

YOUR BODIES ARE
MEMBERS OF CHRIST.

Brothers and sisters:
The body is not for immorality, but for the Lord,
    and the Lord is for the body;
    God raised the Lord and will also raise us by his power.

Do you not know that your bodies are members of Christ?
But whoever is joined to the Lord becomes one Spirit
        with him.
Avoid immorality.
Every other sin a person commits is outside the body,
    but the immoral person sins against his own body.

Do you not know that your body
    is a temple of the Holy Spirit within you,
    whom you have from God, and that you are
        not your own?
For you have been purchased at a price.
Therefore glorify God in your body.

ALLELUIA

JOHN 1:41, 17b

R. Alleluia, alleluia.

We have found the Messiah:
Jesus Christ, who brings us truth and grace. R.

JOHN 1:35–42

THEY SAW WHERE HE
WAS STAYING AND THEY
STAYED WITH HIM.

John was standing with two of his disciples,
　　and as he watched Jesus walk by, he said,
　　"Behold, the Lamb of God."
The two disciples heard what he said and followed Jesus.

Jesus turned and saw them following him
　　　and said to them,
　　"What are you looking for?"
They said to him, "Rabbi"
　　　— which translated means Teacher —
　　"where are you staying?"
He said to them, "Come, and you will see."
So they went and saw where Jesus was staying,
　　and they stayed with him that day.
It was about four in the afternoon.

Andrew, the brother of Simon Peter,
　　was one of the two who heard John and followed Jesus.
He first found his own brother Simon and told him,
　　"We have found the Messiah" —
　　　which is translated Christ.
Then he brought him to Jesus.
Jesus looked at him and said,
　　"You are Simon the son of John;
　　　you will be called Cephas" — which is translated Peter.

66C　SECOND SUNDAY IN ORDINARY TIME

FIRST READING

ISAIAH 62:1–5

THE BRIDEGROOM
REJOICES IN HIS BRIDE.

[This reading is found on page 27
(lectionary number 13).]

**RESPONSORIAL
PSALM**

PSALM 96:1–2, 2–3, 7–8,
9–10 (3)

R. Proclaim his marvelous deeds to all the nations.

Sing to the LORD a new song;
　　sing to the LORD, all you lands.
Sing to the LORD; bless his name.　R.

Announce his salvation, day after day.
　　Tell his glory among the nations;
among all peoples, his wondrous deeds.　R.

Give to the LORD, you families of nations,
　　give to the LORD glory and praise;
give to the LORD the glory due his name!　R.

Worship the LORD in holy attire.
Tremble before him, all the earth;
say among the nations: The LORD is king.
He governs the peoples with equity. R.

SECOND READING

1 CORINTHIANS 12:4–11

ONE AND THE SAME SPIRIT
DISTRIBUTING THEM
INDIVIDUALLY TO EACH
PERSON AS HE WISHES.

Brothers and sisters:
There are different kinds of spiritual gifts
   but the same Spirit;
  there are different forms of service but the same Lord;
  there are different workings but the same God
  who produces all of them in everyone.

To each individual the manifestation of the Spirit
  is given for some benefit.
To one is given through the Spirit the expression
   of wisdom;
  to another, the expression of knowledge according
   to the same Spirit;
  to another, faith by the same Spirit;
  to another, gifts of healing by the one Spirit;
  to another, mighty deeds;
  to another, prophecy;
  to another, discernment of spirits;
  to another, varieties of tongues;
  to another, interpretation of tongues.

But one and the same Spirit produces all of these,
  distributing them individually to each person
   as he wishes.

ALLELUIA

SEE 2 THESSALONIANS 2:14

R. Alleluia, alleluia.

God has called us through the Gospel
to possess the glory of our Lord Jesus Christ. R.

GOSPEL

JOHN 2:1–11

JESUS DID THIS AS THE
BEGINNING OF HIS SIGNS
AT CANA IN GALILEE.

There was a wedding at Cana in Galilee,
  and the mother of Jesus was there.
Jesus and his disciples were also invited to the wedding.

When the wine ran short,
  the mother of Jesus said to him,
  "They have no wine."
And Jesus said to her,
  "Woman, how does your concern affect me?
My hour has not yet come."
His mother said to the servers,
  "Do whatever he tells you."

Now there were six stone water jars there for Jewish
    ceremonial washings,
  each holding twenty to thirty gallons.
Jesus told them,
  "Fill the jars with water."
So they filled them to the brim.
Then he told them,
  "Draw some out now and take it to the headwaiter."
So they took it.

And when the headwaiter tasted the water that had
    become wine,
  without knowing where it came from
  —although the servers who had drawn the
    water knew—
  the headwaiter called the bridegroom and said to him,
  "Everyone serves good wine first,
  and then when people have drunk freely,
    an inferior one;
  but you have kept the good wine until now."

Jesus did this as the beginning of his signs at Cana
    in Galilee
  and so revealed his glory,
  and his disciples began to believe in him.

67A   THIRD SUNDAY IN ORDINARY TIME

FIRST READING

ISAIAH 8:23—9:3

IN GALILEE OF THE
GENTILES, THE PEOPLE
HAVE SEEN A GREAT
LIGHT.

First the Lord degraded the land of Zebulun
    and the land of Naphtali;
  but in the end he has glorified the seaward road,
  the land west of the Jordan,
  the District of the Gentiles.

Anguish has taken wing, dispelled is darkness:
  for there is no gloom where but now there was distress.

The people who walked in darkness
  have seen a great light;
  upon those who dwelt in the land of gloom
    a light has shone.
You have brought them abundant joy
  and great rejoicing,
  as they rejoice before you as at the harvest,
  as people make merry when dividing spoils.

For the yoke that burdened them,
    the pole on their shoulder,
    and the rod of their taskmaster
    you have smashed, as on the day of Midian.

RESPONSORIAL PSALM

PSALM 27:1, 4, 13–14 (1a)

R. The Lord is my light and my salvation.

[This psalm is found on page 447 (lectionary number 174).]

SECOND READING

1 CORINTHIANS 1:10–13, 17

THAT ALL OF YOU MAY AGREE IN WHAT YOU SAY, AND THAT THERE BE NO DIVISIONS AMONG YOU.

I urge you, brothers and sisters, in the name
    of our Lord Jesus Christ,
    that all of you agree in what you say,
    and that there be no divisions among you,
    but that you be united in the same mind
        and in the same purpose.

For it has been reported to me about you,
    my brothers and sisters,
    by Chloe's people, that there are rivalries among you.
I mean that each of you is saying,
    "I belong to Paul," or "I belong to Apollos,"
    or "I belong to Cephas," or "I belong to Christ."

Is Christ divided?
Was Paul crucified for you?
Or were you baptized in the name of Paul?

For Christ did not send me to baptize
    but to preach the gospel,
    and not with the wisdom of human eloquence,
    so that the cross of Christ might not be emptied
        of its meaning.

ALLELUIA

SEE MATTHEW 4:23

R. Alleluia, alleluia.

*Jesus proclaimed the Gospel of the kingdom
and cured every disease among the people.   R.*

LONGER FORM
MATTHEW 4:12–23

SHORTER FORM
MATTHEW 4:12–17

JESUS WENT TO
CAPERNAUM, SO THAT
WHAT HAD BEEN SAID
THROUGH ISAIAH MIGHT
BE FULFILLED.

[When Jesus heard that John had been arrested,
  he withdrew to Galilee.
He left Nazareth and went to live in Capernaum
    by the sea,
  in the region of Zebulun and Naphtali,
  that what had been said through Isaiah the prophet
  might be fulfilled:
  Land of Zebulun and land of Naphtali,
  the way to the sea, beyond the Jordan,
  Galilee of the Gentiles,
  the people who sit in darkness have seen a great light,
  on those dwelling in a land overshadowed by death
  light has arisen.
From that time on, Jesus began to preach and say,
  "Repent, for the kingdom of heaven is at hand."]

As he was walking by the Sea of Galilee,
  he saw two brothers,
  Simon who is called Peter, and his brother Andrew,
  casting a net into the sea; they were fishermen.
He said to them,
  "Come after me, and I will make you fishers of men."
At once they left their nets and followed him.
He walked along from there and saw two other brothers,
  James, the son of Zebedee, and his brother John.
They were in a boat, with their father Zebedee,
  mending their nets.
He called them, and immediately they left their boat
    and their father
    and followed him.

He went around all of Galilee,
teaching in their synagogues, proclaiming the gospel
    of the kingdom,
  and curing every disease and illness among the people.

68B   THIRD SUNDAY IN ORDINARY TIME

The word of the LORD came to Jonah, saying:
  "Set out for the great city of Nineveh,
  and announce to it the message that I will tell you."
So Jonah made ready and went to Nineveh,
  according to the LORD's bidding.

Now Nineveh was an enormously large city;
  it took three days to go through it.

Jonah began his journey through the city,
    and had gone but a single day's walk announcing,
    "Forty days more and Nineveh shall be destroyed, "
    when the people of Nineveh believed God;
    they proclaimed a fast
    and all of them, great and small, put on sackcloth.

When God saw by their actions how they turned
        from their evil way,
    he repented of the evil that he had threatened
        to do to them;
    he did not carry it out.

RESPONSORIAL PSALM

PSALM 25:4–5, 6–7, 8–9 (4a)

R. Teach me your ways, O Lord.

[This psalm is found on page 60 (lectionary number 23).]

SECOND READING

1 CORINTHIANS 7:29–31

THE WORLD
IN ITS PRESENT FORM
IS PASSING AWAY.

I tell you, brothers and sisters, the time is running out.
From now on, let those having wives act as not
        having them,
    those weeping as not weeping,
    those rejoicing as not rejoicing,
    those buying as not owning,
    those using the world as not using it fully.
For the world in its present form is passing away.

ALLELUIA

MARK 1:15

R. Alleluia, alleluia.

The kingdom of God is at hand.
Repent and believe in the Gospel.   R.

GOSPEL

MARK 1:14–20

REPENT AND BELIEVE IN
THE GOSPEL.

After John had been arrested,
    Jesus came to Galilee proclaiming the gospel of God:
    "This is the time of fulfillment.
The kingdom of God is at hand.
Repent, and believe in the gospel."

As he passed by the Sea of Galilee,
    he saw Simon and his brother Andrew casting their nets
        into the sea;
    they were fishermen.
Jesus said to them,
    "Come after me, and I will make you fishers of men."
Then they abandoned their nets and followed him.

He walked along a little farther
  and saw James, the son of Zebedee,
    and his brother John.
They too were in a boat mending their nets.
Then he called them.
So they left their father Zebedee in the boat
  along with the hired men and followed him.

69C   THIRD SUNDAY IN ORDINARY TIME

FIRST READING

NEHEMIAH 8:2–4a, 5–6, 8–10

THEY READ FROM
THE BOOK OF THE LAW
AND THEY UNDERSTOOD
WHAT WAS READ.

Ezra the priest brought the law before the assembly,
  which consisted of men, women,
    and those children old enough to understand.
Standing at one end of the open place that was before
    the Water Gate,
  he read out of the book from daybreak till midday,
  in the presence of the men, the women,
  and those children old enough to understand;
  and all the people listened attentively to the book
    of the law.
Ezra the scribe stood on a wooden platform
  that had been made for the occasion.

He opened the scroll
  so that all the people might see it
  — for he was standing higher up
    than any of the people —
  and, as he opened it, all the people rose.
Ezra blessed the LORD, the great God,
  and all the people, their hands raised high, answered,
    "Amen, amen!"
Then they bowed down and prostrated themselves
    before the LORD,
  their faces to the ground.

Ezra read plainly from the book of the law of God,
  interpreting it so that all could understand
    what was read.
Then Nehemiah, that is, His Excellency,
    and Ezra the priest-scribe
  and the Levites who were instructing the people
  said to all the people:
  "Today is holy to the LORD your God.
Do not be sad, and do not weep" —
  for all the people were weeping as they heard
    the words of the law.

He said further: "Go, eat rich foods and drink sweet drinks,
    and allot portions to those who had nothing prepared;
    for today is holy to our Lord.
Do not be saddened this day,
    for rejoicing in the Lord must be your strength!"

RESPONSORIAL PSALM

PSALM 19:8, 9, 10, 15
(SEE JOHN 6:63c)

R. Your words, Lord, are Spirit and life.

The law of the Lord is perfect,
    refreshing the soul;
the decree of the Lord is trustworthy,
    giving wisdom to the simple. R.

The precepts of the Lord are right,
    rejoicing the heart;
the command of the Lord is clear,
    enlightening the eye. R.

The fear of the Lord is pure,
    enduring forever;
the ordinances of the Lord are true,
    all of them just. R.

Let the words of my mouth and the thought of my heart
    find favor before you,
O Lord, my rock and my redeemer. R.

SECOND READING

LONGER FORM
1 CORINTHIANS 12:12–30

SHORTER FORM
1 CORINTHIANS 12:12–14, 27

YOU ARE CHRIST'S BODY
AND INDIVIDUALLY PARTS
OF IT.

[Brothers and sisters:
As a body is one though it has many parts,
    and all the parts of the body, though many,
        are one body,
    so also Christ.

For in one Spirit we were all baptized into one body,
    whether Jews or Greeks, slaves or free persons,
    and we were all given to drink of one Spirit.

Now the body is not a single part, but many.]
If a foot should say,
    "Because I am not a hand I do not belong to the body,"
    it does not for this reason belong any less to the body.
Or if an ear should say,
    "Because I am not an eye I do not belong to the body,"
    it does not for this reason belong any less to the body.
If the whole body were an eye,
    where would the hearing be?
If the whole body were hearing,
    where would the sense of smell be?

But as it is, God placed the parts,
    each one of them, in the body as he intended.

If they were all one part, where would the body be?
But as it is, there are many parts, yet one body.
The eye cannot say to the hand, "I do not need you,"
   nor again the head to the feet, "I do not need you."
Indeed, the parts of the body that seem to be weaker
  are all the more necessary,
  and those parts of the body that we consider
   less honorable
  we surround with greater honor,
  and our less presentable parts are treated
   with greater propriety,
  whereas our more presentable parts do not need this.

But God has so constructed the body
  as to give greater honor to a part that is without it,
  so that there may be no division in the body,
  but that the parts may have the same concern
   for one another.
If one part suffers, all the parts suffer with it;
  if one part is honored, all the parts share its joy.

Now [you are Christ's body, and individually parts of it.]
Some people God has designated in the church
  to be, first, apostles; second, prophets; third, teachers;
  then, mighty deeds;
  then gifts of healing, assistance, administration,
  and varieties of tongues.

Are all apostles? Are all prophets? Are all teachers?
Do all work mighty deeds? Do all have gifts of healing?
Do all speak in tongues? Do all interpret?

ALLELUIA

SEE LUKE 4:18

R. Alleluia, alleluia.

*The Lord sent me to bring glad tidings to the poor,
and to proclaim liberty to captives. R.*

GOSPEL

LUKE 1:1–4; 4:14–21

TODAY THIS SCRIPTURE
PASSAGE IS FULFILLED.

Since many have undertaken to compile a narrative
  of the events
  that have been fulfilled among us,
  just as those who were eyewitnesses from the beginning
  and ministers of the word have handed them down
   to us,
  I too have decided,
  after investigating everything accurately anew,
  to write it down in an orderly sequence for you,
  most excellent Theophilus,

so that you may realize the certainty of the teachings
you have received.

Jesus returned to Galilee in the power of the Spirit,
and news of him spread throughout the whole region.
He taught in their synagogues and was praised by all.

He came to Nazareth, where he had grown up,
and went according to his custom
into the synagogue on the sabbath day.

He stood up to read and was handed a scroll
of the prophet Isaiah.
He unrolled the scroll and found the passage
where it was written:
The Spirit of the LORD is upon me,
because he has anointed me
to bring glad tidings to the poor.
He has sent me to proclaim liberty to captives
and recovery of sight to the blind,
to let the oppressed go free,
and to proclaim a year acceptable to the Lord.

Rolling up the scroll, he handed it back to the attendant
and sat down,
and the eyes of all in the synagogue looked intently
at him.

He said to them,
"Today this Scripture passage is fulfilled in your hearing."

70A FOURTH SUNDAY IN ORDINARY TIME

FIRST READING

ZEPHANIAH 2:3; 3:12–13

I WILL LEAVE IN YOUR
MIDST A PEOPLE HUMBLE
AND LOWLY.

Seek the LORD, all you humble of the earth,
who have observed his law;
seek justice, seek humility;
perhaps you may be sheltered
on the day of the LORD's anger.

But I will leave as a remnant in your midst
a people humble and lowly,
who shall take refuge in the name of the LORD:
the remnant of Israel.
They shall do no wrong
and speak no lies;
nor shall there be found in their mouths
a deceitful tongue;

they shall pasture and couch their flocks
with none to disturb them.

RESPONSORIAL
PSALM

PSALM 146:6–7, 8–9, 9–10
(MATTHEW 5:3)

R. Blessed the poor in spirit; the kingdom of heaven is theirs!
    or:
R. Alleluia.

[This psalm is found on page 15 (lectionary number 7).]

SECOND READING

1 CORINTHIANS 1:26–31

GOD CHOSE THE WEAK
OF THE WORLD.

Consider your own calling, brothers and sisters.
Not many of you were wise by human standards,
    not many were powerful,
    not many were of noble birth.
Rather, God chose the foolish of the world
        to shame the wise,
    and God chose the weak of the world
        to shame the strong,
    and God chose the lowly and despised of the world,
    those who count for nothing,
    to reduce to nothing those who are something,
    so that no human being might boast before God.

It is due to him that you are in Christ Jesus,
    who became for us wisdom from God,
    as well as righteousness, sanctification, and redemption,
    so that, as it is written,
    "Whoever boasts, should boast in the Lord."

ALLELUIA

MATTHEW 5:12a

R. Alleluia, alleluia.

Rejoice and be glad;
your reward will be great in heaven.   R.

GOSPEL

MATTHEW 5:1–12a

BLESSED ARE THE POOR
IN SPIRIT.

When Jesus saw the crowds, he went up the mountain,
    and after he had sat down, his disciples came to him.
He began to teach them, saying:
"Blessed are the poor in spirit,
    for theirs is the kingdom of heaven.
Blessed are they who mourn,
    for they will be comforted.

"Blessed are the meek,
    for they will inherit the land.
Blessed are they who hunger and thirst for righteousness,
    for they will be satisfied.

"Blessed are the merciful,
   for they will be shown mercy.
Blessed are the clean of heart,
   for they will see God.

"Blessed are the peacemakers,
   for they will be called children of God.
Blessed are they who are persecuted for the sake
     of righteousness,
   for theirs is the kingdom of heaven.

"Blessed are you when they insult you and persecute you
   and utter every kind of evil against you falsely
     because of me.
Rejoice and be glad,
   for your reward will be great in heaven."

71B FOURTH SUNDAY IN ORDINARY TIME

FIRST READING

DEUTERONOMY 18:15–20

I WILL RAISE UP A PROPHET
AND I WILL PUT MY WORDS
INTO HIS MOUTH.

Moses spoke to all the people, saying:
"A prophet like me will the Lord, your God,
   raise up for you
from among your own kin;
   to him you shall listen.
This is exactly what you requested of the Lord,
   your God, at Horeb
  on the day of the assembly, when you said,
'Let us not again hear the voice of the Lord, our God,
  nor see this great fire any more, lest we die.'

"And the Lord said to me, 'This was well said.
I will raise up for them a prophet like you
   from among their kin,
  and will put my words into his mouth;
  he shall tell them all that I command him.

"'Whoever will not listen to my words which he speaks
   in my name,
  I myself will make him answer for it.
But if a prophet presumes to speak in my name
   an oracle that I have not commanded him to speak,
   or speaks in the name of other gods, he shall die.'"

PSALM 95:1–2, 6–7, 7–9 (8)

R. *If today you hear his voice, harden not your hearts.*

[This psalm is found on page 448 (lectionary number 174).]

SECOND READING

1 CORINTHIANS 7:32–35

A VIRGIN IS ANXIOUS ABOUT THE THINGS OF THE LORD, THAT SHE MAY BE HOLY.

Brothers and sisters:
I should like you to be free of anxieties.
An unmarried man is anxious about the things
   of the Lord,
   how he may please the Lord.
But a married man is anxious about the things
   of the world,
   how he may please his wife, and he is divided.

An unmarried woman or a virgin is anxious about
   the things of the Lord,
   so that she may be holy in both body and spirit.
A married woman, on the other hand,
   is anxious about the things of the world,
   how she may please her husband.

I am telling you this for your own benefit,
   not to impose a restraint upon you,
   but for the sake of propriety
   and adherence to the Lord without distraction.

ALLELUIA

MATTHEW 4:16

R. *Alleluia, alleluia.*

The people who sit in darkness have seen a great light;
on those dwelling in a land overshadowed by death,
light has arisen. R.

GOSPEL

MARK 1:21–28

HE TAUGHT THEM AS ONE HAVING AUTHORITY.

Then they came to Capernaum,
   and on the sabbath Jesus entered the synagogue
   and taught.
The people were astonished at his teaching,
   for he taught them as one having authority and not
   as the scribes.
In their synagogue was a man with an unclean spirit;
   he cried out, "What have you to do with us,
   Jesus of Nazareth?
Have you come to destroy us?
I know who you are — the Holy One of God!"

Jesus rebuked him and said,
   "Quiet! Come out of him!"

The unclean spirit convulsed him and with a loud cry
    came out of him.
All were amazed and asked one another,
   "What is this?
A new teaching with authority.
He commands even the unclean spirits
    and they obey him."
His fame spread everywhere throughout the whole
    region of Galilee.

72C   FOURTH SUNDAY IN ORDINARY TIME

FIRST READING

JEREMIAH 1:4–5, 17–19

A PROPHET TO THE
NATIONS I APPOINTED
YOU.

The word of the LORD came to me, saying:
Before I formed you in the womb I knew you,
   before you were born I dedicated you,
   a prophet to the nations I appointed you.

But do you gird your loins;
   stand up and tell them
   all that I command you.
Be not crushed on their account,
   as though I would leave you crushed before them;
for it is I this day
   who have made you a fortified city,
a pillar of iron, a wall of brass,
   against the whole land:
against Judah's kings and princes,
   against its priests and people.
They will fight against you but not prevail over you,
   for I am with you to deliver you, says the LORD.

**RESPONSORIAL
PSALM**

PSALM 71:1–2, 3–4, 5–6,
15–17 (SEE 15ab)

R. I will sing of your salvation.

In you, O LORD, I take refuge;
   let me never be put to shame.
In your justice rescue me, and deliver me;
   incline your ear to me, and save me.   R.

Be my rock of refuge,
   a stronghold to give me safety,
for you are my rock and my fortress.
   O my God, rescue me from the hand of the wicked.   R.

For you are my hope, O LORD;
   my trust, O God, from my youth.
On you I depend from birth;
   from my mother's womb you are my strength.   R.

My mouth shall declare your justice,
*   day by day your salvation.*
O God, you have taught me from my youth,
*   and till the present I proclaim your wondrous deeds.   R.*

SECOND READING

LONGER FORM
1 CORINTHIANS 12:31—
13:13

SHORTER FORM
1 CORINTHIANS 13:4–13

SO FAITH, HOPE, LOVE
REMAIN, THESE THREE;
BUT THE GREATEST OF
THESE IS LOVE.

[Brothers and sisters:]
Strive eagerly for the greatest spiritual gifts.
But I shall show you a still more excellent way.

If I speak in human and angelic tongues,
    but do not have love,
    I am a resounding gong or a clashing cymbal.
And if I have the gift of prophecy,
    and comprehend all mysteries and all knowledge;
    if I have all faith so as to move mountains,
    but do not have love, I am nothing.
If I give away everything I own,
    and if I hand my body over so that I may boast,
    but do not have love, I gain nothing.

[Love is patient, love is kind.
It is not jealous, it is not pompous,
    it is not inflated, it is not rude,
    it does not seek its own interests,
    it is not quick-tempered, it does not brood over injury,
    it does not rejoice over wrongdoing
    but rejoices with the truth.
It bears all things, believes all things,
    hopes all things, endures all things.

Love never fails.
If there are prophecies, they will be brought to nothing;
    if tongues, they will cease;
    if knowledge, it will be brought to nothing.

For we know partially and we prophesy partially,
    but when the perfect comes, the partial will pass away.
When I was a child, I used to talk as a child,
    think as a child, reason as a child;
    when I became a man, I put aside childish things.
At present we see indistinctly, as in a mirror,
    but then face to face.
At present I know partially;
    then I shall know fully, as I am fully known.

So faith, hope, love remain, these three;
    but the greatest of these is love.]

R. Alleluia, alleluia.

The Lord sent me to bring glad tidings to the poor,
to proclaim liberty to captives.   R.

GOSPEL

LUKE 4:21–30

LIKE ELIJA AND ELISHA,
JESUS WAS NOT SENT
ONLY TO THE JEWS.

Jesus began speaking in the synagogue, saying:
    "Today this Scripture passage is fulfilled in your hearing."
And all spoke highly of him
    and were amazed at the gracious words that came
        from his mouth.
They also asked, "Isn't this the son of Joseph?"

He said to them, "Surely you will quote me this proverb,
    'Physician, cure yourself,' and say,
    'Do here in your native place
    the things that we heard were done in Capernaum.'"

And he said, "Amen, I say to you,
    no prophet is accepted in his own native place.
Indeed, I tell you,
    there were many widows in Israel in the days of Elijah
    when the sky was closed for three and a half years
    and a severe famine spread over the entire land.
It was to none of these that Elijah was sent,
    but only to a widow in Zarephath in the land of Sidon.
Again, there were many lepers in Israel
    during the time of Elisha the prophet;
    yet not one of them was cleansed,
        but only Naaman the Syrian."

When the people in the synagogue heard this,
    they were all filled with fury.
They rose up, drove him out of the town,
    and led him to the brow of the hill
    on which their town had been built,
    to hurl him down headlong.
But Jesus passed through the midst of them
    and went away.

73A   FIFTH SUNDAY IN ORDINARY TIME

FIRST READING

ISAIAH 58:7–10

YOUR LIGHT SHALL BREAK
FORTH LIKE THE DAWN.

Thus says the LORD:
Share your bread with the hungry,
    shelter the oppressed and the homeless;
clothe the naked when you see them,
    and do not turn your back on your own.

Then your light shall break forth like the dawn,
    and your wound shall quickly be healed;
your vindication shall go before you,
    and the glory of the LORD shall be your rear guard.
Then you shall call, and the LORD will answer;
    you shall cry for help, and he will say: Here I am!

If you remove from your midst oppression,
    false accusation and malicious speech;
if you bestow your bread on the hungry
    and satisfy the afflicted;
then light shall rise for you in the darkness,
    and the gloom shall become for you like midday.

**RESPONSORIAL
PSALM**

PSALM 112:4–5, 6–7, 8–9 (4a)

R. The just man is a light in darkness to the upright.
    or:
R. Alleluia.

Light shines through the darkness for the upright;
    he is gracious and merciful and just.
Well for the man who is gracious and lends,
    who conducts his affairs with justice.   R.

He shall never be moved;
    the just one shall be in everlasting remembrance.
An evil report he shall not fear;
    his heart is firm, trusting in the LORD.   R.

His heart is steadfast; he shall not fear.
    Lavishly he gives to the poor;
his justice shall endure forever;
    his horn shall be exalted in glory.   R.

SECOND READING

1 CORINTHIANS 2:1–5

I HAVE ANNOUNCED
TO YOU THE MYSTERY
OF CHRIST CRUCIFIED.

When I came to you, brothers and sisters,
    proclaiming the mystery of God,
    I did not come with sublimity of words or of wisdom.
For I resolved to know nothing while I was with you
    except Jesus Christ, and him crucified.

I came to you in weakness and fear and much trembling,
    and my message and my proclamation
    were not with persuasive words of wisdom,
    but with a demonstration of Spirit and power,
    so that your faith might rest not on human wisdom
    but on the power of God.

ALLELUIA

JOHN 8:12

R. *Alleluia, alleluia.*

I am the light of the world, says the Lord;
whoever follows me will have the light of life. *R.*

GOSPEL

MATTHEW 5:13–16

YOU ARE THE LIGHT
OF THE WORLD.

Jesus said to his disciples:
"You are the salt of the earth.
But if salt loses its taste, with what can it be seasoned?
It is no longer good for anything
    but to be thrown out and trampled underfoot.

"You are the light of the world.
A city set on a mountain cannot be hidden.
Nor do they light a lamp and then put it under
    a bushel basket;
    it is set on a lampstand,
    where it gives light to all in the house.
Just so, your light must shine before others,
    that they may see your good deeds
    and glorify your heavenly Father."

74B   FIFTH SUNDAY IN ORDINARY TIME

FIRST READING

JOB 7:1–4, 6–7

I AM FILLED WITH
RESTLESSNESS UNTIL
THE DAWN.

Job spoke, saying:
Is not man's life on earth a drudgery?
    Are not his days those of hirelings?
He is a slave who longs for the shade,
    a hireling who waits for his wages.
So I have been assigned months of misery,
    and troubled nights have been allotted to me.

If in bed I say, "When shall I arise?"
    then the night drags on;
    I am filled with restlessness until the dawn.

My days are swifter than a weaver's shuttle;
    they come to an end without hope.
Remember that my life is like the wind;
    I shall not see happiness again.

**RESPONSORIAL
PSALM**

PSALM 147:1–2, 3–4, 5–6
(SEE 3a)

R. *Praise the Lord, who heals the brokenhearted.*
    or:
R. *Alleluia.*

Praise the LORD, for he is good;
*   sing praise to our God, for he is gracious;*
*   it is fitting to praise him.*
The LORD rebuilds Jerusalem;
*   the dispersed of Israel he gathers.   R.*

He heals the brokenhearted
*   and binds up their wounds.*
He tells the number of the stars;
*   he calls each by name.   R.*

Great is our Lord and mighty in power;
*   to his wisdom there is no limit.*
The LORD sustains the lowly;
*   the wicked he casts to the ground.   R.*

SECOND READING

1 CORINTHIANS 9:16–19, 22–23

WOE TO ME IF I DO NOT PREACH THE GOSPEL.

Brothers and sisters:
If I preach the gospel, this is no reason for me to boast,
    for an obligation has been imposed on me,
    and woe to me if I do not preach it!
If I do so willingly, I have a recompense,
    but if unwillingly, then I have been entrusted
        with a stewardship.
What then is my recompense?
That, when I preach,
    I offer the gospel free of charge
    so as not to make full use of my right in the gospel.

Although I am free in regard to all,
    I have made myself a slave to all
    so as to win over as many as possible.

To the weak I became weak, to win over the weak.
I have become all things to all, to save at least some.
All this I do for the sake of the gospel,
    so that I too may have a share in it.

ALLELUIA

MATTHEW 8:17

R. Alleluia, alleluia.

Christ took away our infirmities
and bore our diseases.   R.

GOSPEL

MARK 1:29–39

JESUS CURED MANY WHO WERE SICK WITH VARIOUS DISEASES.

On leaving the synagogue
    Jesus entered the house of Simon and Andrew
        with James and John.
Simon's mother-in-law lay sick with a fever.
They immediately told him about her.
He approached, grasped her hand, and helped her up.
Then the fever left her and she waited on them.

When it was evening, after sunset,
    they brought to him all who were ill or possessed
        by demons.
The whole town was gathered at the door.
He cured many who were sick with various diseases,
    and he drove out many demons,
        not permitting them to speak because they knew him.

Rising very early before dawn, he left
    and went off to a deserted place, where he prayed.
Simon and those who were with him pursued him
    and on finding him said, "Everyone is looking for you."

He told them, "Let us go on to the nearby villages
    that I may preach there also.
For this purpose have I come."
So he went into their synagogues,
    preaching and driving out demons
        throughout the whole of Galilee.

75C FIFTH SUNDAY IN ORDINARY TIME

FIRST READING

ISAIAH 6:1–2a, 3–8

HERE I AM! SEND ME.

In the year King Uzziah died,
    I saw the Lord seated on a high and lofty throne,
    with the train of his garment filling the temple.
Seraphim were stationed above.

They cried one to the other,
    "Holy, holy, holy is the LORD of hosts!
All the earth is filled with his glory!"
At the sound of that cry, the frame of the door shook
    and the house was filled with smoke.

Then I said, "Woe is me, I am doomed!
For I am a man of unclean lips,
    living among a people of unclean lips;
        yet my eyes have seen the King, the LORD of hosts!"
Then one of the seraphim flew to me,
    holding an ember that he had taken with tongs
        from the altar.

He touched my mouth with it, and said,
    "See, now that this has touched your lips,
    your wickedness is removed, your sin purged."

Then I heard the voice of the Lord saying,
    "Whom shall I send? Who will go for us?"
"Here I am," I said; "send me!"

PSALM 138:1–2, 2–3, 4–5,
7–8 (1c)

R. *In the sight of the angels I will sing your praises, Lord.*

I will give thanks to you, O Lᴏʀᴅ, with all my heart,
  for you have heard the words of my mouth;
  in the presence of the angels I will sing your praise;
I will worship at your holy temple
  and give thanks to your name.   R.

Because of your kindness and your truth;
  for you have made great above all things
  your name and your promise.
When I called, you answered me;
  you built up strength within me.   R.

All the kings of the earth shall give thanks to you, O Lᴏʀᴅ,
  when they hear the words of your mouth;
and they shall sing of the ways of the Lᴏʀᴅ:
  "Great is the glory of the Lᴏʀᴅ."   R.

Your right hand saves me.
  The Lᴏʀᴅ will complete what he has done for me;
your kindness, O Lᴏʀᴅ, endures forever;
  forsake not the work of your hands.   R.

SECOND READING

LONGER FORM
1 CORINTHIANS 15:1–11

SHORTER FORM
1 CORINTHIANS 15:3–8, 11

SO WE PREACHED AND SO
YOU BELIEVE.

I am reminding you, [brothers and sisters,]
  of the gospel I preached to you,
  which you indeed received and in which you also stand.
Through it you are also being saved,
  if you hold fast to the word I preached to you,
  unless you believed in vain.

For [I handed on to you as of first importance what
    I also received:
  that Christ died for our sins
    in accordance with the Scriptures;
  that he was buried;
  that he was raised on the third day
    in accordance with the Scriptures;
  that he appeared to Cephas, then to the Twelve.

After that, Christ appeared to more
    than five hundred brothers at once,
  most of whom are still living,
    though some have fallen asleep.
After that he appeared to James,
  then to all the apostles.

Last of all, as to one born abnormally,
  he appeared to me.]
For I am the least of the apostles,
  not fit to be called an apostle,
  because I persecuted the church of God.
But by the grace of God I am what I am,
  and his grace to me has not been ineffective.

Indeed, I have toiled harder than all of them;
   not I, however, but the grace of God that is with me.

[Therefore, whether it be I or they,
   so we preach and so you believed.]

ALLELUIA

MATTHEW 4:19

R. Alleluia, alleluia.

Come after me
and I will make you fishers of men. R.

GOSPEL

LUKE 5:1–11

THEY LEFT EVERYTHING
AND FOLLOWED JESUS.

While the crowd was pressing in on Jesus and listening
   to the word of God,
  he was standing by the Lake of Gennesaret.
He saw two boats there alongside the lake;
  the fishermen had disembarked and were washing
   their nets.

Getting into one of the boats, the one belonging
   to Simon,
  he asked him to put out a short distance from the shore.
Then he sat down and taught the crowds from the boat.
After he had finished speaking, he said to Simon,
   "Put out into deep water and lower your nets
    for a catch."
Simon said in reply,
   "Master, we have worked hard all night
    and have caught nothing,
  but at your command I will lower the nets."
When they had done this, they caught a great number
   of fish
  and their nets were tearing.
They signaled to their partners in the other boat
  to come to help them.
They came and filled both boats
  so that the boats were in danger of sinking.

When Simon Peter saw this, he fell at the knees
   of Jesus and said,
  "Depart from me, Lord, for I am a sinful man."

For astonishment at the catch of fish they had made
   seized him
  and all those with him,
   and likewise James and John, the sons of Zebedee,
  who were partners of Simon.
Jesus said to Simon, "Do not be afraid;
  from now on you will be catching men."

When they brought their boats to the shore,
they left everything and followed him.

76A   SIXTH SUNDAY IN ORDINARY TIME

FIRST READING

SIRACH 15:15–20

NO ONE DOES HE
COMMAND TO ACT
UNJUSTLY.

If you choose you can keep the commandments,
    they will save you;
    if you trust in God, you too shall live;
he has set before you fire and water
    to whichever you choose, stretch forth your hand.
Before man are life and death, good and evil,
    whichever he chooses shall be given him.

Immense is the wisdom of the Lord;
    he is mighty in power, and all-seeing.
The eyes of God are on those who fear him;
    he understands man's every deed.
No one does he command to act unjustly,
    to none does he give license to sin.

**RESPONSORIAL
PSALM**

PSALM 119:1–2, 4–5, 17–18,
33–34 (1b)

R. Blessed are they who follow the law of the Lord!

Blessed are they whose way is blameless,
    who walk in the law of the LORD.
Blessed are they who observe his decrees,
    who seek him with all their heart.   R.

You have commanded that your precepts
    be diligently kept.
Oh, that I might be firm in the ways
    of keeping your statutes!   R.

Be good to your servant, that I may live
    and keep your words.
Open my eyes, that I may consider
    the wonders of your law.   R.

Instruct me, O LORD, in the way of your statutes,
    that I may exactly observe them.
Give me discernment, that I may observe your law
    and keep it with all my heart.   R.

SECOND READING

1 CORINTHIANS 2:6–10

GOD PREDESTINED
WISDOM BEFORE THE AGES
FOR OUR GLORY.

Brothers and sisters:
We speak a wisdom to those who are mature,
    not a wisdom of this age,
    nor of the rulers of this age who are passing away.
Rather, we speak God's wisdom, mysterious, hidden,
    which God predetermined before the ages for our glory,
    and which none of the rulers of this age knew;

for, if they had known it,
they would not have crucified the Lord of glory.

But as it is written:
What eye has not seen, and ear has not heard,
and what has not entered the human heart,
what God has prepared for those who love him,
this God has revealed to us through the Spirit.

For the Spirit scrutinizes everything,
even the depths of God.

ALLELUIA

SEE MATTHEW 11:25

R. *Alleluia, alleluia.*

Blessed are you, Father, Lord of heaven and earth;
you have revealed to little ones the mysteries of the kingdom.   R.

GOSPEL

LONGER FORM
MATTHEW 5:17–37

SHORTER FORM
MATTHEW 5:20–22a, 27–28,
33–34a, 37

SO IT WAS SAID TO YOUR
ANCESTORS; BUT I SAY
THIS TO YOU.

[Jesus said to his disciples:]
"Do not think that I have come to abolish the law
or the prophets.
I have come not to abolish but to fulfill.
Amen, I say to you, until heaven and earth pass away,
not the smallest letter or the smallest part of a letter
will pass from the law,
until all things have taken place.

"Therefore, whoever breaks one of the least
of these commandments
and teaches others to do so
will be called least in the kingdom of heaven.
But whoever obeys and teaches these commandments
will be called greatest in the kingdom of heaven.
[I tell you, unless your righteousness surpasses
that of the scribes and Pharisees,
you will not enter the kingdom of heaven.

"You have heard that it was said to your ancestors,
You shall not kill; and whoever kills
will be liable to judgment.
But I say to you,
whoever is angry with his brother
will be liable to judgment;]
and whoever says to his brother, 'Raqa,'
will be answerable to the Sanhedrin;
and whoever says, 'You fool,'
will be liable to fiery Gehenna.

"Therefore, if you bring your gift to the altar,
and there recall that your brother

has anything against you,
leave your gift there at the altar,
go first and be reconciled with your brother,
and then come and offer your gift.

"Settle with your opponent quickly while on the way
    to court.
Otherwise your opponent will hand you over to the judge,
    and the judge will hand you over to the guard,
    and you will be thrown into prison.
Amen, I say to you,
    you will not be released until you have paid
        the last penny.

["You have heard that it was said,
    You shall not commit adultery.
But I say to you,
    everyone who looks at a woman with lust
    has already committed adultery with her in his heart.]

"If your right eye causes you to sin,
    tear it out and throw it away.
It is better for you to lose one of your members
    than to have your whole body thrown into Gehenna.

"And if your right hand causes you to sin,
    cut it off and throw it away.
It is better for you to lose one of your members
    than to have your whole body go into Gehenna.

"It was also said,
    Whoever divorces his wife must give her a bill of divorce.
But I say to you,
    whoever divorces his wife
        — unless the marriage is unlawful —
    causes her to commit adultery,
    and whoever marries a divorced woman
        commits adultery.

["Again you have heard that it was said to your ancestors,
    Do not take a false oath,
    but make good to the LORD *all that you vow.*
But I say to you, do not swear at all;]
    not by heaven, for it is God's throne;
    nor by the earth, for it is his footstool;
    nor by Jerusalem, for it is the city of the great King.
Do not swear by your head,
    for you cannot make a single hair white or black.
[Let your 'Yes' mean 'Yes,' and your 'No' mean 'No.'
Anything more is from the evil one."]

FIRST READING

LEVITICUS 13:1–2, 44–46

THE LEPER WILL DWELL
APART, MAKING AN ABODE
OUTSIDE THE CAMP.

The Lord said to Moses and Aaron,
"If someone has on his skin a scab or pustule or blotch
    which appears to be the sore of leprosy,
    he shall be brought to Aaron, the priest,
    or to one of the priests among his descendants.
If the man is leprous and unclean,
    the priest shall declare him unclean
    by reason of the sore on his head.

"The one who bears the sore of leprosy
    shall keep his garments rent and his head bare,
    and shall muffle his beard;
    he shall cry out, 'Unclean, unclean!'
As long as the sore is on him he shall declare
        himself unclean,
    since he is in fact unclean.
He shall dwell apart, making his abode outside the camp."

**RESPONSORIAL
PSALM**

PSALM 32:1–2, 5, 11 (7)

*R. I turn to you, Lord, in time of trouble,
        and you fill me with the joy of salvation.*

*Blessed is he whose fault is taken away,
    whose sin is covered.
Blessed the man to whom the LORD imputes not guilt,
    in whose spirit there is no guile.   R.*

*Then I acknowledged my sin to you,
    my guilt I covered not.
I said, "I confess my faults to the LORD,"
    and you took away the guilt of my sin.   R.*

*Be glad in the LORD and rejoice, you just;
    exult, all you upright of heart.   R.*

SECOND READING

1 CORINTHIANS 10:31—11:1

BE IMITATORS OF ME,
AS I AM OF CHRIST.

Brothers and sisters,
whether you eat or drink, or whatever you do,
    do everything for the glory of God.

Avoid giving offense, whether to the Jews or Greeks
        or the church of God,
    just as I try to please everyone in every way,
    not seeking my own benefit but that of the many,
    that they may be saved.

Be imitators of me, as I am of Christ.

R. Alleluia, alleluia.

A great prophet has arisen in our midst,
God has visited his people.   R.

GOSPEL

MARK 1:40–45

THE LEPROSY LEFT HIM,
AND HE WAS MADE CLEAN.

A leper came to Jesus and kneeling down begged him
        and said,
    "If you wish, you can make me clean."
Moved with pity, he stretched out his hand,
    touched him, and said to him,
    "I do will it. Be made clean."
The leprosy left him immediately, and he was made clean.

Then, warning him sternly, he dismissed him at once.
He said to him, "See that you tell no one anything,
    but go, show yourself to the priest
    and offer for your cleansing what Moses prescribed;
    that will be proof for them."

The man went away and began to publicize
        the whole matter.
He spread the report abroad
    so that it was impossible for Jesus to enter a town openly.
He remained outside in deserted places,
    and people kept coming to him from everywhere.

78C   SIXTH SUNDAY IN ORDINARY TIME

FIRST READING

JEREMIAH 17:5–8

CURSED IS THE ONE
WHO TRUSTS IN HUMAN
BEINGS; BLESSED IS
THE ONE WHO TRUSTS
IN THE LORD.

Thus says the LORD:
Cursed is the one who trusts in human beings,
    who seeks his strength in flesh,
    whose heart turns away from the LORD.
He is like a barren bush in the desert
    that enjoys no change of season,
but stands in a lava waste,
    a salt and empty earth.

Blessed is the one who trusts in the LORD,
    whose hope is the LORD.
He is like a tree planted beside the waters
    that stretches out its roots to the stream:
It fears not the heat when it comes;
    its leaves stay green;
in the year of drought it shows no distress,
    but still bears fruit.

R. *Blessed are they who hope in the Lord.*

Blessed the man who follows not
the counsel of the wicked,
nor walks in the way of sinners,
nor sits in the company of the insolent,
but delights in the law of the LORD
and meditates on his law day and night. R.

He is like a tree
planted near running water,
that yields its fruit in due season,
and whose leaves never fade.
Whatever he does, prospers. R.

Not so the wicked, not so;
they are like chaff which the wind drives away.
For the LORD *watches over the way of the just,*
but the way of the wicked vanishes. R.

SECOND READING

1 CORINTHIANS 15:12,
16–20

IF CHRIST HAS NOT BEEN
RAISED, YOUR FAITH IS
IN VAIN.

Brothers and sisters:
If Christ is preached as raised from the dead,
   how can some among you say there is no resurrection
      of the dead?

If the dead are not raised, neither has Christ been raised,
   and if Christ has not been raised, your faith is vain;
      you are still in your sins.
Then those who have fallen asleep in Christ
      have perished.

If for this life only we have hoped in Christ,
   we are the most pitiable people of all.
But now Christ has been raised from the dead,
   the firstfruits of those who have fallen asleep.

ALLELUIA

LUKE 6:23ab

R. *Alleluia, alleluia.*

Rejoice and be glad;
your reward will be great in heaven. R.

GOSPEL

LUKE 6:17, 20–26

BLESSED ARE THE POOR.
WOE TO YOU WHO ARE
RICH.

Jesus came down with the twelve
   and stood on a stretch of level ground
   with a great crowd of his disciples
   and a large number of the people
   from all Judea and Jerusalem
   and the coastal region of Tyre and Sidon.

And raising his eyes toward his disciples he said:
"Blessed are you who are poor,
   for the kingdom of God is yours.

Blessed are you who are now hungry,
    for you will be satisfied.
Blessed are you who are now weeping,
    for you will laugh.
Blessed are you when people hate you,
    and when they exclude and insult you,
    and denounce your name as evil
    on account of the Son of Man.

"Rejoice and leap for joy on that day!
Behold, your reward will be great in heaven.
For their ancestors treated the prophets in the same way.

"But woe to you who are rich,
    for you have received your consolation.
Woe to you who are filled now,
    for you will be hungry.
Woe to you who laugh now,
    for you will grieve and weep.
Woe to you when all speak well of you,
    for their ancestors treated the false prophets
        in this way."

79A   SEVENTH SUNDAY IN ORDINARY TIME

FIRST READING

LEVITICUS 19:1–2, 17–18

YOU SHALL LOVE YOUR
NEIGHBOR AS YOURSELF.

The LORD said to Moses,
"Speak to the whole Israelite community and tell them:
    Be holy, for I, the LORD, your God, am holy.

"You shall not bear hatred for your brother or sister
    in your heart.
Though you may have to reprove your fellow citizen,
    do not incur sin because of him.
Take no revenge and cherish no grudge against any
    of your people.
You shall love your neighbor as yourself.
I am the LORD."

**RESPONSORIAL
PSALM**

PSALM 103:1–2, 3–4, 8, 10,
12–13 (8a)

R. The Lord is kind and merciful.

[This psalm is found on page 449 (lectionary number 174).]

SECOND READING

1 CORINTHIANS 3:16–23

ALL THINGS BELONG TO
YOU, AND YOU TO CHRIST,
AND CHRIST TO GOD.

Brothers and sisters:
Do you not know that you are the temple of God,
    and that the Spirit of God dwells in you?
If anyone destroys God's temple, God will destroy
        that person;
    for the temple of God, which you are, is holy.

Let no one deceive himself.
If any one among you considers himself wise in this age,
    let him become a fool, so as to become wise.
For the wisdom of this world is foolishness
        in the eyes of God,
    for it is written:
    God catches the wise in their own ruses,
and again:
    The Lord knows the thoughts of the wise,
    that they are vain.

So let no one boast about human beings,
        for everything belongs to you,
    Paul or Apollos or Cephas,
    or the world or life or death,
    or the present or the future:
    all belong to you, and you to Christ, and Christ to God.

R. Alleluia, alleluia.

Whoever keeps the word of Christ,
the love of God is truly perfected in him.   R.

Jesus said to his disciples:
"You have heard that it was said,
    An eye for an eye and a tooth for a tooth.
But I say to you, offer no resistance to one who is evil.
When someone strikes you on your right cheek,
    turn the other one as well.
If anyone wants to go to law with you over your tunic,
    hand over your cloak as well.
Should anyone press you into service for one mile,
    go for two miles.
Give to the one who asks of you,
    and do not turn your back on one who wants to borrow.

"You have heard that it was said,
    You shall love your neighbor and hate your enemy.
But I say to you, love your enemies
    and pray for those who persecute you,

that you may be children of your heavenly Father,
for he makes his sun rise on the bad and the good,
and causes rain to fall on the just and the unjust.

"For if you love those who love you, what recompense
    will you have?
Do not the tax collectors do the same?
And if you greet your brothers only,
    what is unusual about that?
Do not the pagans do the same?
So be perfect, just as your heavenly Father is perfect."

80B   SEVENTH SUNDAY IN ORDINARY TIME

FIRST READING

ISAIAH 43:18–19, 21–22,
24b–25

IT IS I WHO WIPE OUT,
FOR MY OWN SAKE,
YOUR OFFENSES.

Thus says the LORD:
Remember not the events of the past,
    the things of long ago consider not;
see, I am doing something new!
    Now it springs forth, do you not perceive it?
In the desert I make a way,
    in the wasteland, rivers.

The people I formed for myself,
    that they might announce my praise.

Yet you did not call upon me, O Jacob,
    for you grew weary of me, O Israel.
You burdened me with your sins,
    and wearied me with your crimes.

It is I, I, who wipe out,
    for my own sake, your offenses;
    your sins I remember no more.

**RESPONSORIAL
PSALM**

PSALM 41:2–3, 4–5,
13–14 (5b)

R. Lord, heal my soul, for I have sinned against you.

Blessed is the one who has regard for the lowly and the poor;
    in the day of misfortune the LORD will deliver him.
The LORD will keep and preserve him;
    and make him blessed on earth,
    and not give him over to the will of his enemies.   R.

The LORD will help him on his sickbed,
    he will take away all his ailment when he is ill.
Once I said, "O LORD, have pity on me;
    heal me, though I have sinned against you."   R.

But because of my integrity you sustain me
    and let me stand before you forever.
Blessed be the LORD, the God of Israel,
    from all eternity. Amen. Amen.   R.

Brothers and sisters:
As God is faithful,
    our word to you is not "yes" and "no."
For the Son of God, Jesus Christ,
    who was proclaimed to you by us, Silvanus
        and Timothy and me,
    was not "yes" and "no," but "yes" has been in him.

For however many are the promises of God,
        their Yes is in him;
    therefore, the Amen from us also goes through him
        to God for glory.
But the one who gives us security with you in Christ
    and who anointed us is God;
    he has also put his seal upon us
    and given the Spirit in our hearts as a first installment.

ALLELUIA

SEE LUKE 4:18

R. Alleluia, alleluia.

The Lord sent me to bring glad tidings to the poor,
and to proclaim liberty to captives.   R.

GOSPEL

MARK 2:1–12

THE SON OF MAN HAS
AUTHORITY ON EARTH
TO FORGIVE SINS.

When Jesus returned to Capernaum after some days,
    it became known that he was at home.
Many gathered together so that there was no longer
        room for them,
    not even around the door,
    and he preached the word to them.

They came bringing to him a paralytic carried
        by four men.
Unable to get near Jesus because of the crowd,
    they opened up the roof above him.
After they had broken through,
    they let down the mat on which the paralytic was lying.

When Jesus saw their faith, he said to the paralytic,
    "Child, your sins are forgiven."
Now some of the scribes were sitting there
        asking themselves,
    "Why does this man speak that way? He is blaspheming.
Who but God alone can forgive sins?"

Jesus immediately knew in his mind
    what they were thinking to themselves,
    so he said, "Why are you thinking such things
        in your hearts?

Which is easier, to say to the paralytic,
  'Your sins are forgiven,'
  or to say, 'Rise, pick up your mat and walk?'

"But that you may know
  that the Son of Man has authority to forgive sins
    on earth"
  — he said to the paralytic,
  "I say to you, rise, pick up your mat, and go home."

He rose, picked up his mat at once,
  and went away in the sight of everyone.
They were all astounded
  and glorified God, saying,
    "We have never seen anything like this."

81C   SEVENTH SUNDAY IN ORDINARY TIME

FIRST READING

1 SAMUEL 26:2, 7–9, 12–13, 22–23

THOUGH THE LORD DELIVERED YOU INTO MY GRASP, I WOULD NOT HARM YOU.

In those days, Saul went down to the desert of Ziph
  with three thousand picked men of Israel,
  to search for David in the desert of Ziph.

So David and Abishai went among Saul's soldiers by night
  and found Saul lying asleep within the barricade,
  with his spear thrust into the ground at his head
  and Abner and his men sleeping around him.
Abishai whispered to David:
  "God has delivered your enemy into your grasp this day.
Let me nail him to the ground with one thrust
    of the spear;
  I will not need a second thrust!"
But David said to Abishai, "Do not harm him,
  for who can lay hands on the LORD's anointed
    and remain unpunished?"

So David took the spear and the water jug from their
    place at Saul's head,
  and they got away without anyone's seeing
    or knowing or awakening.
All remained asleep,
  because the LORD had put them into a deep slumber.

Going across to an opposite slope,
  David stood on a remote hilltop
  at a great distance from Abner, son of Ner,
    and the troops.
He said: "Here is the king's spear.

Let an attendant come over to get it.
The LORD will reward each man for his justice
    and faithfulness.
Today, though the LORD delivered you into my grasp,
    I would not harm the LORD's anointed."

RESPONSORIAL PSALM

PSALM 103:1–2, 3–4, 8, 10, 12–13 (8a)

R. The Lord is kind and merciful.

[This psalm is found on page 449 (lectionary number 174).]

SECOND READING

1 CORINTHIANS 15:45–49

JUST AS WE HAVE BORNE THE IMAGE OF THE EARTHLY ONE, WE SHALL ALSO BEAR THE IMAGE OF THE HEAVENLY ONE.

Brothers and sisters:
It is written, *The first man, Adam, became a living being,*
    the last Adam a life-giving spirit.
But the spiritual was not first;
    rather the natural and then the spiritual.

The first man was from the earth, earthly;
    the second man, from heaven.
As was the earthly one, so also are the earthly,
    and as is the heavenly one, so also are the heavenly.

Just as we have borne the image of the earthly one,
    we shall also bear the image of the heavenly one.

ALLELUIA

JOHN 13:34

R. Alleluia, alleluia.

I give you a new commandment, says the Lord:
Love one another as I have loved you.   R.

GOSPEL

LUKE 6:27–38

BE MERCIFUL, JUST AS YOUR FATHER IS MERCIFUL.

Jesus said to his disciples:
"To you who hear I say,
    love your enemies, do good to those who hate you,
    bless those who curse you, pray for those who
        mistreat you.
To the person who strikes you on one cheek,
    offer the other one as well,
    and from the person who takes your cloak,
    do not withhold even your tunic.
Give to everyone who asks of you,
    and from the one who takes what is yours
        do not demand it back.
Do to others as you would have them do to you.

"For if you love those who love you,
    what credit is that to you?
Even sinners love those who love them.
And if you do good to those who do good to you,
    what credit is that to you?
Even sinners do the same.
If you lend money to those from whom
        you expect repayment,
    what credit is that to you?
Even sinners lend to sinners,
    and get back the same amount.
But rather, love your enemies and do good to them,
    and lend expecting nothing back;
    then your reward will be great
    and you will be children of the Most High,
        for he himself is kind to the ungrateful and the wicked.
Be merciful, just as your Father is merciful.

"Stop judging and you will not be judged.
Stop condemning and you will not be condemned.
Forgive and you will be forgiven.
Give and gifts will be given to you;
    a good measure, packed together, shaken down,
        and overflowing,
    will be poured into your lap.
For the measure with which you measure
    will in return be measured out to you."

82A EIGHTH SUNDAY IN ORDINARY TIME

FIRST READING

ISAIAH 49:14–15

I WILL NEVER FORGET YOU.

Zion said, "The Lord has forsaken me;
    my Lord has forgotten me."
Can a mother forget her infant,
    be without tenderness for the child of her womb?
Even should she forget,
    I will never forget you.

RESPONSORIAL PSALM

PSALM 62:2–3, 6–7, 8–9 (6a)

R. *Rest in God alone, my soul.*

Only in God is my soul at rest;
    from him comes my salvation.
He only is my rock and my salvation,
    my stronghold; I shall not be disturbed at all. R.

Only in God be at rest, my soul,
    for from him comes my hope.
He only is my rock and my salvation,
    my stronghold; I shall not be disturbed.   R.

With God is my safety and my glory,
    he is the rock of my strength; my refuge is in God.
Trust in him at all times, O my people!
    Pour out your hearts before him.   R.

SECOND READING

1 CORINTHIANS 4:1–5

THE LORD WILL MANIFEST
THE MOTIVES OF OUR
HEARTS.

Brothers and sisters:
Thus should one regard us: as servants of Christ
    and stewards of the mysteries of God.
Now it is of course required of stewards
    that they be found trustworthy.

It does not concern me in the least
    that I be judged by you or any human tribunal;
    I do not even pass judgment on myself;
    I am not conscious of anything against me,
    but I do not thereby stand acquitted;
    the one who judges me is the Lord.

Therefore do not make any judgment
    before the appointed time,
    until the Lord comes,
    for he will bring to light what is hidden in darkness
    and will manifest the motives of our hearts,
    and then everyone will receive praise from God.

ALLELUIA

HEBREWS 4:12

R. Alleluia, alleluia.

The word of God is living and effective;
discerning reflections and thoughts of the heart.   R.

GOSPEL

MATTHEW 6:24–34

DO NOT WORRY
ABOUT TOMORROW.

Jesus said to his disciples:
"No one can serve two masters.
He will either hate one and love the other,
    or be devoted to one and despise the other.
You cannot serve God and mammon.

"Therefore I tell you, do not worry about your life,
    what you will eat or drink,
    or about your body, what you will wear.
Is not life more than food and the body more
        than clothing?

Look at the birds in the sky;
    they do not sow or reap, they gather nothing into barns,
    yet your heavenly Father feeds them.
Are not you more important than they?
Can any of you by worrying add a single moment
    to your life-span?

"Why are you anxious about clothes?
Learn from the way the wild flowers grow.
They do not work or spin.
But I tell you that not even Solomon in all his splendor
    was clothed like one of them.
If God so clothes the grass of the field,
    which grows today and is thrown into
      the oven tomorrow,
    will he not much more provide for you,
      O you of little faith?

"So do not worry and say, 'What are we to eat?'
    or 'What are we to drink?'or 'What are we to wear?'
All these things the pagans seek.
Your heavenly Father knows that you need them all.
But seek first the kingdom of God and his righteousness,
    and all these things will be given you besides.

"Do not worry about tomorrow;
    tomorrow will take care of itself.
Sufficient for a day is its own evil."

83B   EIGHTH SUNDAY IN ORDINARY TIME

FIRST READING

HOSEA 2:16b, 17b, 21–22

I WILL ESPOUSE YOU
TO ME FOREVER.

Thus says the LORD:
I will lead her into the desert
    and speak to her heart.
She shall respond there as in the days of her youth,
    when she came up from the land of Egypt.

I will espouse you to me forever:
    I will espouse you in right and in justice,
    in love and in mercy;
I will espouse you in fidelity,
    and you shall know the LORD.

R. The Lord is kind and merciful.

[This psalm is found on page 449 (lectionary number 174).]

SECOND READING

2 CORINTHIANS 3:1b–6

YOU ARE A LETTER
OF CHRIST MINISTERED
BY US.

Brothers and sisters:
Do we need, as some do,
    letters of recommendation to you or from you?
You are our letter, written on our hearts,
    known and read by all,
        shown to be a letter of Christ ministered by us,
        written not in ink but by the Spirit of the living God,
        not on tablets of stone but on tablets that are hearts
            of flesh.

Such confidence we have through Christ toward God.
Not that of ourselves we are qualified
    to take credit for anything as coming from us;
    rather, our qualification comes from God,
    who has indeed qualified us as ministers
        of a new covenant,
    not of letter but of spirit;
        for the letter brings death, but the Spirit gives life.

ALLELUIA

JAMES 1:18

R. Alleluia, alleluia.

*The Father willed to give us birth by the word of truth
that we may be a kind of firstfruits of his creatures.   R.*

GOSPEL

MARK 2:18–22

THE BRIDEGROOM
IS STILL WITH THEM.

The disciples of John and of the Pharisees
        were accustomed to fast.
People came to him and objected,
    "Why do the disciples of John
        and the disciples of the Pharisees fast,
    but your disciples do not fast?"

Jesus answered them,
    "Can the wedding guests fast while the bridegroom
        is with them?
As long as they have the bridegroom with them
        they cannot fast.
But the days will come when the bridegroom
        is taken away from them,
        and then they will fast on that day.

"No one sews a piece of unshrunken cloth on an old cloak.
If he does, its fullness pulls away,
    the new from the old, and the tear gets worse.
Likewise, no one pours new wine into old wineskins.
Otherwise, the wine will burst the skins,
    and both the wine and the skins are ruined.
Rather, new wine is poured into fresh wineskins."

84C   EIGHTH SUNDAY IN ORDINARY TIME

FIRST READING

SIRACH 27:4–7

PRAISE NO ONE BEFORE
HE SPEAKS.

When a sieve is shaken, the husks appear;
    so do one's faults when one speaks.
As the test of what the potter molds is in the furnace,
    so in tribulation is the test of the just.

The fruit of a tree shows the care it has had;
    so too does one's speech disclose the bent of one's mind.
Praise no one before he speaks,
    for it is then that people are tested.

**RESPONSORIAL
PSALM**

PSALM 92:2–3, 13–14, 15–16
(SEE 2a)

R. Lord, it is good to give thanks to you.

It is good to give thanks to the LORD,
    to sing praise to your name, Most High,
To proclaim your kindness at dawn
    and your faithfulness throughout the night.   R.

The just one shall flourish like the palm tree,
    like a cedar of Lebanon shall he grow.
They that are planted in the house of the LORD
    shall flourish in the courts of our God.   R.

They shall bear fruit even in old age;
    vigorous and sturdy shall they be,
declaring how just is the LORD,
    my rock, in whom there is no wrong.   R.

SECOND READING

1 CORINTHIANS 15:54–58

GOD GIVES US VICTORY
THROUGH OUR LORD
JESUS CHRIST.

Brothers and sisters:
When this which is corruptible clothes itself
        with incorruptibility
    and this which is mortal clothes itself
        with immortality,
    then the word that is written shall come about:
    Death is swallowed up in victory.
    Where, O death, is your victory?
    Where, O death, is your sting?

The sting of death is sin,
  and the power of sin is the law.
But thanks be to God who gives us the victory
  through our Lord Jesus Christ.

Therefore, my beloved brothers and sisters,
  be firm, steadfast, always fully devoted to the work
    of the Lord,
  knowing that in the Lord your labor is not in vain.

ALLELUIA

PHILIPPIANS 2:15d, 16a

R. *Alleluia, alleluia.*

*Shine like lights in the world
as you hold on to the word of life.*   R.

GOSPEL

LUKE 6:39–45

FROM THE FULLNESS OF
THE HEART THE MOUTH
SPEAKS.

Jesus told his disciples a parable,
"Can a blind person guide a blind person?
Will not both fall into a pit?
No disciple is superior to the teacher;
  but when fully trained,
    every disciple will be like his teacher.

"Why do you notice the splinter in your brother's eye,
  but do not perceive the wooden beam in your own?
How can you say to your brother,
  'Brother, let me remove that splinter in your eye,'
  when you do not even notice the wooden beam
    in your own eye?
You hypocrite! Remove the wooden beam
    from your eye first;
  then you will see clearly
  to remove the splinter in your brother's eye.

"A good tree does not bear rotten fruit,
  nor does a rotten tree bear good fruit.
For every tree is known by its own fruit.
For people do not pick figs from thornbushes,
  nor do they gather grapes from brambles.

"A good person out of the store of goodness in his heart
    produces good,
  but an evil person out of a store of evil produces evil;
  for from the fullness of the heart the mouth speaks."

FIRST READING

DEUTERONOMY 11:18,
26–28, 32

I SET BEFORE YOU HERE
THIS DAY A BLESSING AND
A CURSE.

Moses told the people,
"Take these words of mine into your heart and soul.
Bind them at your wrist as a sign,
    and let them be a pendant on your forehead.

"I set before you here, this day, a blessing and a curse:
    a blessing for obeying the commandments of the Lord,
        your God,
    which I enjoin on you today;
    a curse if you do not obey the commandments
        of the Lord, your God,
    but turn aside from the way I ordain for you today,
    to follow other gods, whom you have not known.
Be careful to observe all the statutes and decrees
    that I set before you today."

**RESPONSORIAL
PSALM**

PSALM 31:2–3, 3–4, 17,
25 (3b)

R. Lord, be my rock of safety.

In you, O Lord, I take refuge;
    let me never be put to shame.
In your justice rescue me,
    incline your ear to me,
    make haste to deliver me! R.

Be my rock of refuge,
    a stronghold to give me safety.
You are my rock and my fortress;
    for your name's sake you will lead and guide me. R.

Let your face shine upon your servant;
    save me in your kindness.
Take courage and be stouthearted,
    all you who hope in the Lord. R.

SECOND READING

ROMANS 3:21–25, 28

A PERSON IS JUSTIFIED
BY FAITH APART FROM
WORKS OF THE LAW.

Brothers and sisters,
Now the righteousness of God has been manifested
    apart from the law,
    though testified to by the law and the prophets,
    the righteousness of God through faith in Jesus Christ
    for all who believe.

For there is no distinction;
    all have sinned and are deprived of the glory of God.
They are justified freely by his grace
    through the redemption in Christ Jesus,
    whom God set forth as an expiation,
    through faith, by his blood.

For we consider that a person is justified by faith
  apart from works of the law.

ALLELUIA

JOHN 15:5

R. Alleluia, alleluia.

I am the vine, you are the branches, says the Lord;
whoever remains in me and I in him will bear much fruit. R.

GOSPEL

MATTHEW 7:21–27

THE HOUSE BUILT ON
ROCK, AND THE HOUSE
BUILT ON SAND.

Jesus said to his disciples:
"Not everyone who says to me, 'Lord, Lord,'
  will enter the kingdom of heaven,
    but only the one who does the will of my Father
      in heaven.
Many will say to me on that day,
  'Lord, Lord, did we not prophesy in your name?
Did we not drive out demons in your name?
Did we not do mighty deeds in your name?'
Then I will declare to them solemnly,
  'I never knew you. Depart from me, you evildoers.'

"Everyone who listens to these words of mine
    and acts on them
  will be like a wise man who built his house on rock.
The rain fell, the floods came,
  and the winds blew and buffeted the house.
But it did not collapse; it had been set solidly on rock.
And everyone who listens to these words of mine
  but does not act on them
  will be like a fool who built his house on sand.
The rain fell, the floods came,
  and the winds blew and buffeted the house.
And it collapsed and was completely ruined."

86B   NINTH SUNDAY IN ORDINARY TIME

FIRST READING

DEUTERONOMY 5:12–15

REMEMBER THAT YOU
TOO WERE ONCE A SLAVE
IN EGYPT.

Thus says the Lord:
"Take care to keep holy the sabbath day
  as the LORD, your God, commanded you.
Six days you may labor and do all your work;
  but the seventh day is the sabbath of the LORD,
    your God.
No work may be done then, whether by you,
  or your son or daughter,
  or your male or female slave,
  or your ox or ass or any of your beasts,

or the alien who lives with you.
Your male and female slave should rest as you do.

"For remember that you too were once a slave in Egypt,
and the LORD, your God, brought you from there
with his strong hand and outstretched arm.
That is why the LORD, your God, has commanded you
to observe the sabbath day."

RESPONSORIAL PSALM

PSALM 81:3–4, 5–6, 6–8,
10–11 (2a)

R. Sing with joy to God our help.

Take up a melody, and sound the timbrel,
the pleasant harp and the lyre.
Blow the trumpet at the new moon,
at the full moon, on our solemn feast.   R.

For it is a statute in Israel,
an ordinance of the God of Jacob,
Who made it a decree for Joseph
when he came forth from the land of Egypt.   R.

An unfamiliar speech I hear:
"I relieved his shoulder of the burden;
his hands were freed from the basket.
In distress you called, and I rescued you."   R.

"There shall be no strange god among you
nor shall you worship any alien god.
I, the LORD, am your God
who led you forth from the land of Egypt."   R.

SECOND READING

2 CORINTHIANS 4:6–11

THE LIFE OF JESUS IS
MANIFESTED IN OUR BODY.

Brothers and sisters:
God who said, *Let light shine out of darkness*,
has shone in our hearts to bring to light
the knowledge of the glory of God on the face
of Jesus Christ.

But we hold this treasure in earthen vessels,
that the surpassing power may be of God
and not from us.
We are afflicted in every way, but not constrained;
perplexed, but not driven to despair;
persecuted, but not abandoned;
struck down, but not destroyed;
always carrying about in the body the dying of Jesus,
so that the life of Jesus may also be manifested
in our body.

For we who live are constantly being given up to death
for the sake of Jesus,
so that the life of Jesus may be manifested
in our mortal flesh.

ALLELUIA

SEE JOHN 17:17b, 17a

R. Alleluia, alleluia.

Your word, O Lord, is truth;
consecrate us in the truth. R.

GOSPEL

LONGER FORM
MARK 2:23—3:6

SHORTER FORM
MARK 2:23–28

THE SON OF MAN IS LORD
EVEN OF THE SABBATH.

[As Jesus was passing through a field of grain
   on the sabbath,
   his disciples began to make a path while picking
   the heads of grain.
At this the Pharisees said to him,
   "Look, why are they doing what is unlawful
   on the sabbath?"

He said to them, "Have you never read what David did
   when he was in need and he and his companions
   were hungry?
How he went into the house of God when Abiathar
   was high priest
   and ate the bread of offering
   that only the priests could lawfully eat,
   and shared it with his companions?"

Then he said to them,
   "The sabbath was made for man, not man
   for the sabbath.
That is why the Son of Man is lord even of the sabbath."]

Again he entered the synagogue.
There was a man there who had a withered hand.
They watched him closely
   to see if he would cure him on the sabbath
   so that they might accuse him.
He said to the man with the withered hand,
   "Come up here before us."
Then he said to them,
   "Is it lawful to do good on the sabbath rather than
   to do evil,
   to save life rather than to destroy it?"
But they remained silent.

Looking around at them with anger
   and grieved at their hardness of heart,
   he said to the man, "Stretch out your hand."
He stretched it out and his hand was restored.

The Pharisees went out
   and immediately took counsel with the Herodians
   against him
   to put him to death.

FIRST READING

1 KINGS 8:41–43

WHEN FOREIGNERS COME, LISTEN TO THEM.

In those days, Solomon prayed in the temple, saying,
"To the foreigner, who is not of your people Israel,
  but comes from a distant land to honor you
  — since they will learn of your great name
  and your mighty hand and your outstretched arm —
  when he comes and prays toward this temple,
  listen from your heavenly dwelling.

"Do all that foreigner asks of you,
  that all the peoples of the earth may know your name,
  may fear you as do your people Israel,
  and may acknowledge that this temple
    which I have built
  is dedicated to your honor."

RESPONSORIAL PSALM

PSALM 117:1, 2
(MARK 16:15)

R. Go out to all the world and tell the good news.
  or:
R. Alleluia.

Praise the Lord, all you nations;
  glorify him, all you peoples!   R.

For steadfast is his kindness toward us,
  and the fidelity of the Lord endures forever.   R.

SECOND READING

GALATIANS 1:1–2, 6–10

IF I WERE TRYING TO PLEASE PEOPLE, I WOULD NOT BE A SLAVE OF CHRIST.

Paul, an apostle not from human beings nor through
    a human being
  but through Jesus Christ and God the Father
  who raised him from the dead,
  and all the brothers who are with me,
  to the churches of Galatia.

I am amazed that you are so quickly forsaking
  the one who called you by the grace of Christ
  for a different gospel — not that there is another.
But there are some who are disturbing you
  and wish to pervert the gospel of Christ.

But even if we or an angel from heaven
  should preach to you a gospel
  other than the one that we preached to you,
  let that one be accursed!
As we have said before, and now I say again,
  if anyone preaches to you a gospel
  other than what you have received,
    let that one be accursed!

Am I now currying favor with humans or with God?
Or am I seeking to please people?
If I were still trying to please people,
    I would not be a slave of Christ.

R. Alleluia, alleluia.

God so loved the world that he gave his only Son,
so that everyone who believes in him might have eternal life.   R.

When Jesus had finished all his words to the people,
    he entered Capernaum.
A centurion there had a slave who was ill
    and about to die,
    and he was valuable to him.
When he heard about Jesus, he sent elders of the Jews
    to him,
    asking him to come and save the life of his slave.

They approached Jesus and strongly urged him
    to come, saying,
    "He deserves to have you do this for him,
    for he loves our nation and built the synagogue for us."

And Jesus went with them,
    but when he was only a short distance from the house,
    the centurion sent friends to tell him,
    "Lord, do not trouble yourself,
    for I am not worthy to have you enter under my roof.
Therefore, I did not consider myself worthy
    to come to you;
    but say the word and let my servant be healed.
For I too am a person subject to authority,
    with soldiers subject to me.
And I say to one, 'Go,' and he goes;
    and to another, 'Come here,' and he comes;
    and to my slave, 'Do this,' and he does it."

When Jesus heard this he was amazed at him
    and, turning, said to the crowd following him,
    "I tell you, not even in Israel have I found such faith."

When the messengers returned to the house,
    they found the slave in good health.

FIRST READING

HOSEA 6:3–6

IT IS LOVE THAT I DESIRE,
NOT SACRIFICE.

In their affliction, people will say:
"Let us know, let us strive to know the Lord;
    as certain as the dawn is his coming,
    and his judgment shines forth like the light of day!
He will come to us like the rain,
    like spring rain that waters the earth."

What can I do with you, Ephraim?
    What can I do with you, Judah?
Your piety is like a morning cloud,
    like the dew that early passes away.
For this reason I smote them through the prophets,
    I slew them by the words of my mouth;
for it is love that I desire, not sacrifice,
    and knowledge of God rather than holocausts.

**RESPONSORIAL
PSALM**

PSALM 50:1, 8, 12–13,
14–15 (23b)

R. To the upright I will show the saving power of God.

God the LORD has spoken and summoned the earth,
    from the rising of the sun to its setting.
"Not for your sacrifices do I rebuke you,
    for your holocausts are before me always."   R.

"If I were hungry, I would not tell you,
    for mine are the world and its fullness.
Do I eat the flesh of strong bulls,
    or is the blood of goats my drink?"   R.

"Offer to God praise as your sacrifice
    and fulfill your vows to the Most High;
then call upon me in time of distress;
    I will rescue you, and you shall glorify me."   R.

SECOND READING

ROMANS 4:18–25

ABRAHAM WAS
STRENGTHENED BY FAITH
AND GAVE GLORY TO GOD.

Brothers and sisters:
Abraham believed, hoping against hope,
    that he would become *the father of many nations*,
    according to what was said,
        Thus shall your descendants be.
He did not weaken in faith when he considered
    his own body as already dead
        — for he was almost a hundred years old —
    and the dead womb of Sarah.
He did not doubt God's promise in unbelief;
    rather, he was strengthened by faith
        and gave glory to God
    and was fully convinced that what he had promised
    he was also able to do.

That is why *it was credited to him as righteousness*.
But it was not for him alone that it was written
    that *it was credited to him*;
    it was also for us, to whom it will be credited,
    who believe in the one who raised Jesus our Lord
        from the dead,
    who was handed over for our transgressions
    and was raised for our justification.

ALLELUIA

SEE LUKE 4:18

R. Alleluia, alleluia.

The Lord sent me to bring glad tidings to the poor,
and to proclaim liberty to captives.   R.

GOSPEL

MATTHEW 9:9–13

I DID NOT COME TO CALL
THE RIGHTEOUS BUT
SINNERS.

As Jesus passed on from there,
    he saw a man named Matthew sitting
        at the customs post.
He said to him, "Follow me."
And he got up and followed him.
While he was at table in his house,
    many tax collectors and sinners came
    and sat with Jesus and his disciples.
The Pharisees saw this and said to his disciples,
    "Why does your teacher eat with tax collectors
        and sinners?"

He heard this and said,
    "Those who are well do not need a physician,
        but the sick do.
Go and learn the meaning of the words,
    'I desire mercy, not sacrifice.'
I did not come to call the righteous but sinners."

89B   TENTH SUNDAY IN ORDINARY TIME

FIRST READING

GENESIS 3:9–15

I WILL PUT ENMITY
BETWEEN YOUR OFFSPRING
AND HER OFFSPRING.

After the man, Adam, had eaten of the tree,
    the Lord God called to the man and asked him,
        "Where are you?"
He answered, "I heard you in the garden;
    but I was afraid, because I was naked,
    so I hid myself."

Then he asked, "Who told you that you were naked?
You have eaten, then,
    from the tree of which I had forbidden you to eat!"

The man replied,
   "The woman whom you put here with me —
   she gave me fruit from the tree, and so I ate it."

The Lord God then asked the woman,
"Why did you do such a thing?"
The woman answered,
      "The serpent tricked me into it, so I ate it."

Then the Lord God said to the serpent:
"Because you have done this, you shall be banned
   from all the animals
   and from all the wild creatures;
on your belly shall you crawl,
   and dirt shall you eat
   all the days of your life.
I will put enmity between you and the woman,
   and between your offspring and hers;
he will strike at your head,
   while you strike at his heel."

RESPONSORIAL PSALM

PSALM 130:1–2, 3–4, 5–6, 7–8 (7bc)

R. With the Lord there is mercy, and fullness of redemption.

[This psalm is found on page 444 (lectionary number 174).]

SECOND READING

2 CORINTHIANS 4:13—5:1

WE TOO BELIEVE AND THEREFORE WE SPEAK.

Bothers and sisters:
Since we have the same spirit of faith,
   according to what is written, *I believed, therefore I spoke,*
   we too believe and therefore we speak,
   knowing that the one who raised the Lord Jesus
   will raise us also with Jesus
   and place us with you in his presence.
Everything indeed is for you,
   so that the grace bestowed in abundance on more
      and more people
   may cause the thanksgiving to overflow
      for the glory of God.

Therefore, we are not discouraged;
   rather, although our outer self is wasting away,
   our inner self is being renewed day by day.
For this momentary light affliction
   is producing for us an eternal weight of glory
      beyond all comparison,
   as we look not to what is seen but to what is unseen;
   for what is seen is transitory, but what is unseen
      is eternal.

For we know that if our earthly dwelling, a tent,
    should be destroyed,
  we have a building from God,
    a dwelling not made with hands, eternal in heaven.

ALLELUIA

JOHN 12:31b–32

R. Alleluia, alleluia.

Now the ruler of this world will be driven out, says the Lord;
and when I am lifted up from the earth,
  I will draw everyone to myself. R.

GOSPEL

MARK 3:20–35

IT IS THE END OF SATAN.

Jesus came home with his disciples.
Again the crowd gathered,
  making it impossible for them even to eat.
When his relatives heard of this they set out to seize him,
  for they said, "He is out of his mind."

The scribes who had come from Jerusalem said,
  "He is possessed by Beelzebul,"
  and "By the prince of demons he drives out demons."

Summoning them, he began to speak to them in parables,
  "How can Satan drive out Satan?
If a kingdom is divided against itself,
  that kingdom cannot stand.
And if a house is divided against itself,
  that house will not be able to stand.
And if Satan has risen up against himself
  and is divided, he cannot stand;
  that is the end of him.
But no one can enter a strong man's house
    to plunder his property
  unless he first ties up the strong man.
Then he can plunder the house.

"Amen, I say to you,
  all sins and all blasphemies that people utter
    will be forgiven them.
But whoever blasphemes against the Holy Spirit
  will never have forgiveness,
  but is guilty of an everlasting sin."
For they had said, "He has an unclean spirit."

His mother and his brothers arrived.
Standing outside they sent word to him and called him.
A crowd seated around him told him,
  "Your mother and your brothers and your sisters
  are outside asking for you."

But he said to them in reply,
　"Who are my mother and my brothers?"

And looking around at those seated in the circle he said,
　"Here are my mother and my brothers.
For whoever does the will of God
　is my brother and sister and mother."

90C　TENTH SUNDAY IN ORDINARY TIME

FIRST READING

1 KINGS 17:17–24

SEE! YOUR SON IS ALIVE.

Elijah went to Zarephath of Sidon to the house
　of a widow.
The son of the mistress of the house fell sick,
　and his sickness grew more severe until he
　　stopped breathing.

So she said to Elijah,
　"Why have you done this to me, O man of God?
Have you come to me to call attention to my guilt
　and to kill my son?"

Elijah said to her, "Give me your son."
Taking him from her lap, he carried the son
　　to the upper room
　where he was staying, and put him on his bed.
Elijah called out to the LORD:
　"O LORD, my God,
　will you afflict even the widow with whom
　　I am staying
　by killing her son?"
Then he stretched himself out upon the child three times
　and called out to the LORD:
　"O LORD, my God,
　let the life breath return to the body of this child."

The LORD heard the prayer of Elijah;
　the life breath returned to the child's body
　　and he revived.

Taking the child, Elijah brought him down into the house
　from the upper room and gave him to his mother.
Elijah said to her, "See! Your son is alive."

The woman replied to Elijah,
　"Now indeed I know that you are a man of God.
The word of the LORD comes truly from your mouth."

RESPONSORIAL PSALM

PSALM 30:2, 4, 5–6, 11, 12, 13 (2a)

R. I will praise you, Lord, for you have rescued me.

[This psalm is found on page 146 (lectionary number 41).]

SECOND READING

GALATIANS 1:11–19

GOD REVEALED HIS SON TO ME, SO THAT I MIGHT PROCLAIM HIM TO THE GENTILES.

I want you to know, brothers and sisters,
    that the gospel preached by me is not of human origin.
For I did not receive it from a human being,
        nor was I taught it,
    but it came through a revelation of Jesus Christ.

For you heard of my former way of life in Judaism,
    how I persecuted the church of God beyond measure
    and tried to destroy it, and progressed in Judaism
    beyond many of my contemporaries among my race,
    since I was even more a zealot for my
        ancestral traditions.

But when God, who from my mother's womb
        had set me apart
    and called me through his grace,
    was pleased to reveal his Son to me,
    so that I might proclaim him to the Gentiles,
    I did not immediately consult flesh and blood,
    nor did I go up to Jerusalem
    to those who were apostles before me;
    rather, I went into Arabia and then returned
        to Damascus.

Then after three years I went up to Jerusalem
    to confer with Cephas and remained with him
        for fifteen days.
But I did not see any other of the apostles,
    only James the brother of the Lord.

ALLELUIA

LUKE 7:16

R. Alleluia, alleluia.

*A great prophet has risen in our midst,
God has visited his people.   R.*

GOSPEL

LUKE 7:11–17

YOUNG MAN, I TELL YOU, ARISE!

Jesus journeyed to a city called Nain,
    and his disciples and a large crowd accompanied him.
As he drew near to the gate of the city,
    a man who had died was being carried out,
    the only son of his mother, and she was a widow.
A large crowd from the city was with her.

When the Lord saw her,
    he was moved with pity for her and said to her,
    "Do not weep."

He stepped forward and touched the coffin;
    at this the bearers halted,
    and he said, "Young man, I tell you, arise!"
The dead man sat up and began to speak,
    and Jesus gave him to his mother.

Fear seized them all, and they glorified God, exclaiming,
    "A great prophet has arisen in our midst,"
    and "God has visited his people."
This report about him spread through the whole of Judea
    and in all the surrounding region.

91A   ELEVENTH SUNDAY IN ORDINARY TIME

FIRST READING

EXODUS 19:2–6a

YOU SHALL BE TO ME
A KINGDOM OF PRIESTS,
A HOLY NATION.

In those days, the Israelites came to the desert of Sinai
    and pitched camp.
While Israel was encamped here in front of the mountain,
    Moses went up the mountain to God.
Then the Lord called to him and said,
    "Thus shall you say to the house of Jacob;
    tell the Israelites:
    You have seen for yourselves how I treated the Egyptians
    and how I bore you up on eagle wings
    and brought you here to myself.
Therefore, if you hearken to my voice and keep
      my covenant,
    you shall be my special possession,
    dearer to me than all other people,
    though all the earth is mine.
You shall be to me a kingdom of priests, a holy nation."

**RESPONSORIAL
PSALM**

PSALM 100:1–2, 3, 5 (3c)

R. We are his people, the sheep of his flock.

[This psalm is found on page 175 (lectionary number 51).]

SECOND READING

ROMANS 5:6–11

IF WE WERE RECONCILED
TO GOD THROUGH THE
DEATH OF HIS SON, HOW
MUCH MORE WILL WE BE
SAVED BY HIS LIFE.

Brothers and sisters:
Christ, while we were still helpless,
    yet died at the appointed time for the ungodly.
Indeed, only with difficulty does one die for a just person,
    though perhaps for a good person
    one might even find courage to die.
But God proves his love for us
    in that while we were still sinners Christ died for us.
How much more then, since we are now justified
        by his blood,
    will we be saved through him from the wrath.

Indeed, if, while we were enemies,
    we were reconciled to God through the death
        of his Son,
    how much more, once reconciled,
    will we be saved by his life.
Not only that,
    but we also boast of God through our Lord Jesus Christ,
    through whom we have now received reconciliation.

R. Alleluia, alleluia.

The kingdom of God is at hand.
Repent and believe in the Gospel.   R.

At the sight of the crowds, Jesus' heart was moved
        with pity for them
    because they were troubled and abandoned,
    like sheep without a shepherd.
Then he said to his disciples,
    "The harvest is abundant but the laborers are few;
    so ask the master of the harvest
    to send out laborers for his harvest."

Then he summoned his twelve disciples
    and gave them authority over unclean spirits
    to drive them out and to cure every disease
        and every illness.
The names of the twelve apostles are these:
    first, Simon called Peter, and his brother Andrew;
    James, the son of Zebedee, and his brother John;
    Philip and Bartholomew, Thomas and Matthew
        the tax collector;
    James, the son of Alphaeus, and Thaddeus;
    Simon from Cana, and Judas Iscariot who betrayed him.

Jesus sent out these twelve after instructing them thus,
  "Do not go into pagan territory or enter
    a Samaritan town.
Go rather to the lost sheep of the house of Israel.
As you go, make this proclamation:
  'The kingdom of heaven is at hand.'
Cure the sick, raise the dead, cleanse lepers,
    drive out demons.
Without cost you have received;
    without cost you are to give."

92B   ELEVENTH SUNDAY IN ORDINARY TIME

FIRST READING

EZEKIEL 17:22–24

I HAVE LIFTED HIGH
THE LOWLY TREE.

Thus says the Lord God:
I, too, will take from the crest of the cedar,
  from its topmost branches tear off a tender shoot,
and plant it on a high and lofty mountain;
  on the mountain heights of Israel I will plant it.
It shall put forth branches and bear fruit,
  and become a majestic cedar.
Birds of every kind shall dwell beneath it,
  every winged thing in the shade of its boughs.

And all the trees of the field shall know
  that I, the Lord,
bring low the high tree,
  lift high the lowly tree,
wither up the green tree,
  and make the withered tree bloom.
As I, the Lord, have spoken, so will I do.

**RESPONSORIAL
PSALM**

PSALM 92:2–3, 13–14, 15–16
(SEE 2a)

R. Lord, it is good to give thanks to you.

[This psalm is found on page 253 (lectionary number 84).]

SECOND READING

2 CORINTHIANS 5:6–10

WHETHER WE ARE AT
HOME OR AWAY, WE ASPIRE
TO PLEASE THE LORD.

Brothers and sisters:
We are always courageous,
  although we know that while we are at home
    in the body
  we are away from the Lord,
  for we walk by faith, not by sight.
Yet we are courageous,
  and we would rather leave the body and go home
    to the Lord.

Therefore, we aspire to please him,
   whether we are at home or away.
For we must all appear before the judgment seat of Christ,
    so that each may receive recompense,
    according to what he did in the body,
      whether good or evil.

ALLELUIA

R. Alleluia, alleluia.

The seed is the word of God, Christ is the sower.
All who come to him will live for ever.   R.

GOSPEL

MARK 4:26–34

IT IS THE SMALLEST OF
ALL SEEDS, AND BECOMES
THE LARGEST OF PLANTS.

Jesus said to the crowds:
"This is how it is with the kingdom of God;
   it is as if a man were to scatter seed on the land
   and would sleep and rise night and day
   and through it all the seed would sprout and grow,
   he knows not how.
Of its own accord the land yields fruit,
   first the blade, then the ear, then the full grain
    in the ear.
And when the grain is ripe, he wields the sickle at once,
   for the harvest has come."

He said,
"To what shall we compare the kingdom of God,
   or what parable can we use for it?
It is like a mustard seed that, when it is sown
    in the ground,
   is the smallest of all the seeds on the earth.
But once it is sown, it springs up and becomes
    the largest of plants
   and puts forth large branches,
   so that the birds of the sky can dwell in its shade."

With many such parables
   he spoke the word to them as they were able
    to understand it.
Without parables he did not speak to them,
   but to his own disciples he explained everything
    in private.

FIRST READING

2 SAMUEL 12:7–10, 13

THE LORD HAS FORGIVEN
YOUR SIN; YOU SHALL
NOT DIE.

Nathan said to David:
"Thus says the LORD God of Israel:
  'I anointed you king of Israel.
I rescued you from the hand of Saul.
I gave you your lord's house and your lord's wives
      for your own.
I gave you the house of Israel and of Judah.
And if this were not enough, I could count up for you
      still more.

"'Why have you spurned the LORD and done evil
      in his sight?
You have cut down Uriah the Hittite with the sword;
   you took his wife as your own,
   and him you killed with the sword of the Ammonites.

"'Now, therefore, the sword shall never depart
      from your house,
   because you have despised me
   and have taken the wife of Uriah to be your wife.'"

Then David said to Nathan,
   "I have sinned against the LORD."
Nathan answered David:
   "The LORD on his part has forgiven your sin:
   you shall not die."

RESPONSORIAL PSALM

PSALM 32:1–2, 5, 7, 11
(SEE 5c)

R. Lord, forgive the wrong I have done.

Blessed is the one whose fault is taken away,
   whose sin is covered.
Blessed the man to whom the LORD imputes not guilt,
   in whose spirit there is no guile. R.

I acknowledged my sin to you,
   my guilt I covered not.
I said, "I confess my faults to the LORD,"
   and you took away the guilt of my sin. R.

You are my shelter; from distress you will preserve me;
   with glad cries of freedom you will ring me round. R.

Be glad in the LORD and rejoice, you just;
   exult, all you upright of heart. R.

Brothers and sisters:
We who know that a person is not justified by works
    of the law
    but through faith in Jesus Christ,
    even we have believed in Christ Jesus
    that we may be justified by faith in Christ
    and not by works of the law,
    because by works of the law no one will be justified.
For through the law I died to the law,
    that I might live for God.

I have been crucified with Christ;
    yet I live, no longer I, but Christ lives in me;
    insofar as I now live in the flesh,
    I live by faith in the Son of God
    who has loved me and given himself up for me.
I do not nullify the grace of God;
    for if justification comes through the law,
    then Christ died for nothing.

R. Alleluia, alleluia.

God loved us and sent his Son
as expiation for our sins.   R.

GOSPEL

LONGER FORM
LUKE 7:36—8:3

SHORTER FORM
LUKE 7:36–50

HER MANY SINS HAVE BEEN
FORGIVEN, BECAUSE SHE
HAS SHOWN GREAT LOVE.

[A Pharisee invited Jesus to dine with him,
    and he entered the Pharisee's house
        and reclined at table.

Now there was a sinful woman in the city
    who learned that he was at table in the house
        of the Pharisee.
Bringing an alabaster flask of ointment,
    she stood behind him at his feet weeping
    and began to bathe his feet with her tears.
Then she wiped them with her hair,
    kissed them, and anointed them with the ointment.

When the Pharisee who had invited him saw this
    he said to himself,
    "If this man were a prophet,
    he would know who and what sort of woman this is
        who is touching him,
    that she is a sinner."

Jesus said to him in reply,
    "Simon, I have something to say to you."
"Tell me, teacher," he said.

"Two people were in debt to a certain creditor;
   one owed five hundred days' wages and the other
      owed fifty.
Since they were unable to repay the debt,
   he forgave it for both.
Which of them will love him more?"
Simon said in reply,
   "The one, I suppose, whose larger debt was forgiven."
He said to him, "You have judged rightly."

Then he turned to the woman and said to Simon,
   "Do you see this woman?
When I entered your house, you did not give me water
      for my feet,
   but she has bathed them with her tears
   and wiped them with her hair.
You did not give me a kiss,
   but she has not ceased kissing my feet since the time
      I entered.
You did not anoint my head with oil,
   but she anointed my feet with ointment.

"So I tell you, her many sins have been forgiven
   because she has shown great love.
But the one to whom little is forgiven, loves little."
He said to her, "Your sins are forgiven."

The others at table said to themselves,
   "Who is this who even forgives sins?"
But he said to the woman,
   "Your faith has saved you; go in peace."]

Afterward he journeyed from one town and village
      to another,
   preaching and proclaiming the good news
      of the kingdom of God.
Accompanying him were the Twelve
   and some women who had been cured of evil spirits
      and infirmities,
   Mary, called Magdalene, from whom seven demons
      had gone out,
   Joanna, the wife of Herod's steward Chuza,
   Susanna, and many others who provided for them
      out of their resources.

FIRST READING

JEREMIAH 20:10–13

HE HAS RESCUED THE LIFE
OF THE POOR FROM THE
POWER OF THE WICKED.

Jeremiah said:
"I hear the whisperings of many:
  'Terror on every side!
  Denounce! let us denounce him!'
All those who were my friends
  are on the watch for any misstep of mine.
'Perhaps he will be trapped; then we can prevail,
  and take our vengeance on him.'

"But the LORD is with me, like a mighty champion:
  my persecutors will stumble, they will not triumph.
In their failure they will be put to utter shame,
  to lasting, unforgettable confusion.

"O LORD of hosts, you who test the just,
  who probe mind and heart,
let me witness the vengeance you take on them,
  for to you I have entrusted my cause.

"Sing to the LORD,
  praise the LORD,
for he has rescued the life of the poor
  from the power of the wicked!"

**RESPONSORIAL
PSALM**

PSALM 69:8–10, 14, 17,
33–35 (14c)

R. Lord, in your great love, answer me.

For your sake I bear insult,
  and shame covers my face.
I have become an outcast to my brothers,
  a stranger to my mother's children,
because zeal for your house consumes me,
  and the insults of those who blaspheme you fall upon me.   R.

I pray to you, O Lord,
  for the time of your favor, O God!
In your great kindness answer me
  with your constant help.
Answer me, O Lord, for bounteous is your kindness;
  in your great mercy turn toward me.   R.

"See, you lowly ones, and be glad;
  you who seek God, may your hearts revive!
For the Lord hears the poor,
  and his own who are in bonds he spurns not.
Let the heavens and the earth praise him,
  the seas and whatever moves in them!"   R.

Brothers and sisters:
Through one man sin entered the world,
  and through sin, death,
  and thus death came to all men,
    inasmuch as all sinned —
  for up to the time of the law, sin was in the world,
  though sin is not accounted when there is no law.

But death reigned from Adam to Moses,
  even over those who did not sin
  after the pattern of the trespass of Adam,
  who is the type of the one who was to come.

But the gift is not like the transgression.
For if by the transgression of the one the many died,
  how much more did the grace of God
  and the gracious gift of the one man Jesus Christ
  overflow for the many.

R. Alleluia, alleluia.

The Spirit of truth will testify to me, says the Lord;
and you also will testify.   R.

Jesus said to the Twelve:
"Fear no one.
Nothing is concealed that will not be revealed,
  nor secret that will not be known.
What I say to you in the darkness, speak in the light;
  what you hear whispered, proclaim on the housetops.

"And do not be afraid of those who kill the body
    but cannot kill the soul;
  rather, be afraid of the one who can destroy
  both soul and body in Gehenna.
Are not two sparrows sold for a small coin?
Yet not one of them falls to the ground
    without your Father's knowledge.
Even all the hairs of your head are counted.
So do not be afraid; you are worth more
    than many sparrows.

"Everyone who acknowledges me before others
  I will acknowledge before my heavenly Father.
But whoever denies me before others,
  I will deny before my heavenly Father."

FIRST READING

JOB 38:1, 8–11

HERE SHALL YOUR PROUD
WAVES BE STILLED!

The LORD addressed Job out of the storm and said:
Who shut within doors the sea,
   when it burst forth from the womb;
when I made the clouds its garment
   and thick darkness its swaddling bands?
When I set limits for it
   and fastened the bar of its door,
and said: Thus far shall you come but no farther,
   and here shall your proud waves be stilled!

**RESPONSORIAL
PSALM**

PSALM 107:23–24, 25–26,
28–29, 30–31 (1b)

R. Give thanks to the Lord, his love is everlasting.
   or:
R. Alleluia.

They who sailed the sea in ships,
   trading on the deep waters,
these saw the works of the LORD
   and his wonders in the abyss.   R.

His command raised up a storm wind
   which tossed its waves on high.
They mounted up to heaven; they sank to the depths;
   their hearts melted away in their plight.   R.

They cried to the LORD in their distress;
   from their straits he rescued them.
He hushed the storm to a gentle breeze,
   and the billows of the sea were stilled.   R.

They rejoiced that they were calmed,
   and he brought them to their desired haven.
Let them give thanks to the LORD for his kindness
   and his wondrous deeds to the children of men.   R.

SECOND READING

2 CORINTHIANS 5:14–17

BEHOLD, NEW THINGS
HAVE COME.

Brothers and sisters:
The love of Christ impels us,
   once we have come to the conviction
     that one died for all;
   therefore, all have died.
He indeed died for all,
   so that those who live might no longer live
     for themselves
   but for him who for their sake died and was raised.

Consequently, from now on we regard no one
     according to the flesh;
   even if we once knew Christ according to the flesh,
   yet now we know him so no longer.

So whoever is in Christ is a new creation:
the old things have passed away;
behold, new things have come.

ALLELUIA

LUKE 7:16

R. Alleluia, alleluia.

A great prophet has risen in our midst
God has visited his people. R.

GOSPEL

MARK 4:35–41

WHO IS THIS WHOM EVEN
WIND AND SEA OBEY?

On that day, as evening drew on, Jesus said to his disciples:
"Let us cross to the other side."
Leaving the crowd, they took Jesus with them in the boat
just as he was.
And other boats were with him.

A violent squall came up and waves were breaking
over the boat,
so that it was already filling up.
Jesus was in the stern, asleep on a cushion.
They woke him and said to him,
"Teacher, do you not care that we are perishing?"
He woke up,
rebuked the wind, and said to the sea, "Quiet! Be still!"
The wind ceased and there was great calm.

Then he asked them, "Why are you terrified?
Do you not yet have faith?"
They were filled with great awe and said to one another,
"Who then is this whom even wind and sea obey?"

96C   TWELFTH SUNDAY IN ORDINARY TIME

FIRST READING

ZECHARIAH 12:10–11; 13:1

THEY SHALL LOOK
ON HIM WHOM THEY
HAVE PIERCED.

Thus says the Lord:
I will pour out on the house of David
and on the inhabitants of Jerusalem
a spirit of grace and petition;
and they shall look on him whom they have pierced,
and they shall mourn for him as one mourns
for an only son,
and they shall grieve over him as one grieves
over a firstborn.

On that day the mourning in Jerusalem shall be as great
as the mourning of Hadadrimmon in the plain
of Megiddo.

On that day there shall be open to the house of David
and to the inhabitants of Jerusalem,
a fountain to purify from sin and uncleanness.

**RESPONSORIAL
PSALM**

PSALM 63:2, 3–4, 5–6,
8–9 (2b)

R. My soul is thirsting for you, O Lord my God.

[This psalm is found on page 448 (lectionary number 174).]

SECOND READING

GALATIANS 3:26–29

ALL OF YOU WHO WERE
BAPTIZED HAVE CLOTHED
YOURSELVES WITH CHRIST.

Brothers and sisters:
Through faith you are all children of God in Christ Jesus.
For all of you who were baptized into Christ
have clothed yourselves with Christ.

There is neither Jew nor Greek,
there is neither slave nor free person,
there is not male and female;
for you are all one in Christ Jesus.

And if you belong to Christ,
then you are Abraham's descendant,
heirs according to the promise.

ALLELUIA

JOHN 10:27

R. Alleluia, alleluia.

*My sheep hear my voice, says the Lord;
I know them, and they follow me.   R.*

GOSPEL

LUKE 9:18–24

THE SON OF MAN MUST
SUFFER GREATLY.

Once when Jesus was praying in solitude,
and the disciples were with him,
he asked them, "Who do the crowds say that I am?"

They said in reply, "John the Baptist;
others, Elijah;
still others, 'One of the ancient prophets has arisen.'"
Then he said to them, "But who do you say that I am?"
Peter said in reply, "The Christ of God."

He rebuked them
and directed them not to tell this to anyone.
He said, "The Son of Man must suffer greatly
and be rejected by the elders, the chief priests,
and the scribes,
and be killed and on the third day be raised."

Then he said to all,
   "If anyone wishes to come after me,
     he must deny himself
  and take up his cross daily and follow me.
For whoever wishes to save his life will lose it,
   but whoever loses his life for my sake will save it."

97A   THIRTEENTH SUNDAY IN ORDINARY TIME

FIRST READING

2 KINGS 4:8–11, 14–16a

ELISHA IS A HOLY MAN
OF GOD, LET HIM REMAIN.

One day Elisha came to Shunem,
   where there was a woman of influence,
     who urged him to dine with her.
Afterward, whenever he passed by,
   he used to stop there to dine.
So she said to her husband,
   "I know that Elisha is a holy man of God.
Since he visits us often, let us arrange a little room
     on the roof
   and furnish it for him with a bed, table, chair, and lamp,
   so that when he comes to us he can stay there."
Sometime later Elisha arrived and stayed
   in the room overnight.

Later Elisha asked, "Can something be done for her?"
His servant Gehazi answered, "Yes!
   She has no son, and her husband is getting on in years."
Elisha said, "Call her."
When the woman had been called and stood at the door,
   Elisha promised, "This time next year
   you will be fondling a baby son."

**RESPONSORIAL
PSALM**

PSALM 89:2–3, 16–17,
18–19 (2a)

R. *For ever I will sing the goodness of the Lord.*

The promises of the Lord I will sing forever,
   through all generations my mouth shall proclaim your faithfulness.
For you have said, "My kindness is established forever;"
   in heaven you have confirmed your faithfulness. R.

Blessed the people who know the joyful shout;
   in the light of your countenance, O Lord, they walk.
At your name they rejoice all the day,
   and through your justice they are exalted. R.

You are the splendor of their strength,
   and by your favor our horn is exalted.
For to the Lord belongs our shield,
   and the Holy One of Israel, our king. R.

SECOND READING

ROMANS 6:3–4, 8–11

BURIED WITH CHRIST IN
BAPTISM, WE SHALL WALK
IN THE NEWNESS OF LIFE.

Brothers and sisters:
Are you unaware that we who were baptized into
      Christ Jesus
   were baptized into his death?
We were indeed buried with him through baptism
      into death,
   so that, just as Christ was raised from the dead
   by the glory of the Father,
   we too might live in newness of life.

If, then, we have died with Christ,
   we believe that we shall also live with him.
We know that Christ, raised from the dead, dies no more;
   death no longer has power over him.
As to his death, he died to sin once and for all;
   as to his life, he lives for God.
Consequently, you too must think of yourselves
      as dead to sin
   and living for God in Christ Jesus.

ALLELUIA

1 PETER 2:9

R. Alleluia, alleluia.

You are a chosen race, a royal priesthood, a holy nation;
announce the praises of him who called you
   out of darkness into his wonderful light.   R.

GOSPEL

MATTHEW 10:37–42

WHOEVER DOES NOT
TAKE UP HIS CROSS
IS NOT WORTHY OF ME.
WHOEVER RECEIVES
YOU, RECEIVES ME.

Jesus said to his apostles:
"Whoever loves father or mother more than me
      is not worthy of me,
   and whoever loves son or daughter more than me
      is not worthy of me;
   and whoever does not take up his cross
   and follow after me is not worthy of me.
Whoever finds his life will lose it,
   and whoever loses his life for my sake will find it.

"Whoever receives you receives me,
   and whoever receives me receives the one who sent me.
Whoever receives a prophet because he is a prophet
   will receive a prophet's reward,
   and whoever receives a righteous man
   because he is a righteous man
   will receive a righteous man's reward.
And whoever gives only a cup of cold water
   to one of these little ones to drink
   because the little one is a disciple —
   amen, I say to you, he will surely not lose his reward."

FIRST READING

WISDOM 1:13–15; 2:23–24

BY THE ENVY OF THE
DEVIL, DEATH ENTERED
THE WORLD.

God did not make death,
  nor does he rejoice in the destruction of the living.
For he fashioned all things that they might have being;
  and the creatures of the world are wholesome,
  and there is not a destructive drug among them
  nor any domain of the netherworld on earth,
  for justice is undying.

For God formed man to be imperishable;
  the image of his own nature he made him.
But by the envy of the devil, death entered the world,
  and they who belong to his company experience it.

**RESPONSORIAL
PSALM**

PSALM 30:2, 4, 5–6, 11, 12,
13 (2a)

R. *I will praise you, Lord, for you have rescued me.*

[This psalm is found on page 146 (lectionary number 41).]

SECOND READING

2 CORINTHIANS 8:7, 9,
13–15

YOUR ABUNDANCE
SHOULD SUPPLY THE
NEEDS OF THE POOR.

Brothers and sisters:
As you excel in every respect, in faith, discourse,
  knowledge, all earnestness, and in the love
    we have for you,
  may you excel in this gracious act also.

For you know the gracious act of our Lord Jesus Christ,
  that though he was rich, for your sake he became poor,
  so that by his poverty you might become rich.

Not that others should have relief while you are burdened,
  but that as a matter of equality
  your abundance at the present time should supply
    their needs,
  so that their abundance may also supply your needs,
  that there may be equality.

As it is written:
  Whoever had much did not have more,
  and whoever had little did not have less.

ALLELUIA

SEE 2 TIMOTHY 1:10

R. *Alleluia, alleluia.*

Our Savior Jesus Christ destroyed death
and brought life to light through the Gospel.   R.

GOSPEL

LONGER FORM
MARK 5:21–43

SHORTER FORM
MARK 5:21–24, 35b–43

LITTLE GIRL, I SAY
TO YOU, ARISE!

[When Jesus had crossed again in the boat
   to the other side,
    a large crowd gathered around him, and he stayed
     close to the sea.
One of the synagogue officials, named Jairus,
   came forward.
Seeing him he fell at his feet and pleaded earnestly
    with him, saying,
  "My daughter is at the point of death.
Please, come lay your hands on her
   that she may get well and live."
He went off with him,
   and a large crowd followed him and pressed upon him.]

There was a woman afflicted with hemorrhages
   for twelve years.
She had suffered greatly at the hands of many doctors
   and had spent all that she had.
Yet she was not helped but only grew worse.
She had heard about Jesus and came up behind him
   in the crowd
   and touched his cloak.
She said, "If I but touch his clothes, I shall be cured."
Immediately her flow of blood dried up.
She felt in her body that she was healed of her affliction.

Jesus, aware at once that power had gone out from him,
   turned around in the crowd and asked,
  "Who has touched my clothes?"
But his disciples said to Jesus,
  "You see how the crowd is pressing upon you,
  and yet you ask, 'Who touched me?'"
And he looked around to see who had done it.

The woman, realizing what had happened to her,
   approached in fear and trembling.
She fell down before Jesus and told him the whole truth.
He said to her, "Daughter, your faith has saved you.
Go in peace and be cured of your affliction."

[While he was still speaking,
   people from the synagogue official's house arrived
    and said,
  "Your daughter has died; why trouble the teacher
    any longer?"
Disregarding the message that was reported,
   Jesus said to the synagogue official,
  "Do not be afraid; just have faith."

He did not allow anyone to accompany him inside
  except Peter, James, and John, the brother of James.
When they arrived at the house of the synagogue official,
  he caught sight of a commotion,
  people weeping and wailing loudly.
So he went in and said to them,
  "Why this commotion and weeping?
The child is not dead but asleep."
And they ridiculed him.

Then he put them all out.
He took along the child's father and mother
  and those who were with him
  and entered the room where the child was.
He took the child by the hand and said to her,
  "Talitha koum,"
  which means, "Little girl, I say to you, arise!"
The girl, a child of twelve, arose immediately
  and walked around.
At that they were utterly astounded.

He gave strict orders that no one should know this
  and said that she should be given something to eat.]

99C   THIRTEENTH SUNDAY IN ORDINARY TIME

READING

1 KINGS 19:16b, 19–21

THEN ELISHA LEFT AND
FOLLOWED ELIJAH AS HIS
ATTENDANT.

The LORD said to Elijah:
  "You shall anoint Elisha, son of Shaphat
    of Abelmeholah,
  as prophet to succeed you."

Elijah set out and came upon Elisha, son of Shaphat,
  as he was plowing with twelve yoke of oxen;
  he was following the twelfth.

Elijah went over to him and threw his cloak over him.
Elisha left the oxen, ran after Elijah, and said,
  "Please, let me kiss my father and mother goodbye,
  and I will follow you."

Elijah answered, "Go back!
Have I done anything to you?"
Elisha left him, and taking the yoke of oxen,
    slaughtered them;
  he used the plowing equipment for fuel
    to boil their flesh,
  and gave it to his people to eat.
Then Elisha left and followed Elijah as his attendant.

R. You are my inheritance, O Lord.

[This psalm is found on page 163 (lectionary number 46).]

SECOND READING

GALATIANS 5:1, 13–18

YOU WERE CALLED
FOR FREEDOM.

Brothers and sisters:
For freedom Christ set us free;
    so stand firm and do not submit again to the yoke
      of slavery.

For you were called for freedom, brothers and sisters.
But do not use this freedom
    as an opportunity for the flesh;
    rather, serve one another through love.
For the whole law is fulfilled in one statement,
    namely, "You shall love your neighbor as yourself."
But if you go on biting and devouring one another,
    beware that you are not consumed by one another.

I say, then: live by the Spirit
    and you will certainly not gratify the desire of the flesh.
For the flesh has desires against the Spirit,
    and the Spirit against the flesh;
    these are opposed to each other,
    so that you may not do what you want.
But if you are guided by the Spirit,
    you are not under the law.

ALLELUIA

1 SAMUEL 3:9; JOHN 6:68c

R. Alleluia, alleluia.

Speak, Lord, your servant is listening;
you have the words of everlasting life.   R.

GOSPEL

LUKE 9:51–62

HE RESOLUTELY
DETERMINED TO JOURNEY
TO JERUSALEM. I WILL
FOLLOW YOU WHEREVER
YOU GO.

When the days for Jesus' being taken up were fulfilled,
    he resolutely determined to journey to Jerusalem,
    and he sent messengers ahead of him.

On the way they entered a Samaritan village
    to prepare for his reception there,
    but they would not welcome him
    because the destination of his journey was Jerusalem.

When the disciples James and John saw this they asked,
    "Lord, do you want us to call down fire from heaven
    to consume them?"
Jesus turned and rebuked them, and they journeyed
    to another village.

As they were proceeding on their journey someone
    said to him,
  "I will follow you wherever you go."
Jesus answered him,
    "Foxes have dens and birds of the sky have nests,
    but the Son of Man has nowhere to rest his head."

And to another he said, "Follow me."
But he replied, "Lord, let me go first and bury my father."
But he answered him, "Let the dead bury their dead.
But you, go and proclaim the kingdom of God."

And another said, "I will follow you, Lord,
  but first let me say farewell to my family at home."
To him Jesus said, "No one who sets a hand to the plow
    and looks to what was left behind is fit
      for the kingdom of God."

100A   FOURTEENTH SUNDAY IN ORDINARY TIME

FIRST READING

ZECHARIAH 9:9–10

SEE, YOUR KING COMES
TO YOU HUMBLY.

Thus says the LORD:
Rejoice heartily, O daughter Zion,
    shout for joy, O daughter Jerusalem!
See, your king shall come to you;
    a just savior is he,
meek, and riding on an ass,
    on a colt, the foal of an ass.

He shall banish the chariot from Ephraim,
    and the horse from Jerusalem;
the warrior's bow shall be banished,
    and he shall proclaim peace to the nations.
His dominion shall be from sea to sea,
    and from the River to the ends of the earth.

**RESPONSORIAL
PSALM**

PSALM 145:1–2, 8–9, 10–11,
13–14 (SEE 1)

R. I will praise your name for ever, my king and my God.
    or:
R. Alleluia.

[This psalm is found on page 449 (lectionary number 174).]

SECOND READING ·

ROMANS 8:9, 11–13

IF BY THE SPIRIT YOU PUT
TO DEATH THE DEEDS OF
THE BODY, YOU WILL LIVE.

Brothers and sisters:
You are not in the flesh;
   on the contrary, you are in the spirit,
   if only the Spirit of God dwells in you.
Whoever does not have the Spirit of Christ does not
    belong to him.

If the Spirit of the one who raised Jesus from the dead
    dwells in you,
   the one who raised Christ from the dead
   will give life to your mortal bodies also,
   through his Spirit that dwells in you.

Consequently, brothers and sisters,
   we are not debtors to the flesh,
   to live according to the flesh.
For if you live according to the flesh, you will die,
   but if by the Spirit you put to death the deeds
    of the body,
   you will live.

R. Alleluia, alleluia.

Blessed are you, Father, Lord of heaven and earth;
you have revealed to little ones the mysteries of the kingdom. R.

At that time Jesus exclaimed:
"I give praise to you, Father, Lord of heaven and earth,
   for although you have hidden these things
   from the wise and the learned
   you have revealed them to little ones.
Yes, Father, such has been your gracious will.

"All things have been handed over to me by my Father.
No one knows the Son except the Father,
   and no one knows the Father except the Son
   and anyone to whom the Son wishes to reveal him.

"Come to me, all you who labor and are burdened,
   and I will give you rest.
Take my yoke upon you and learn from me,
   for I am meek and humble of heart;
   and you will find rest for yourselves.
For my yoke is easy, and my burden light."

FIRST READING

EZEKIEL 2:2–5

THEY ARE A REBELLIOUS
HOUSE BUT SHALL KNOW
THAT A PROPHET HAS
BEEN AMONG THEM.

As the Lord spoke to me, the spirit entered into me
    and set me on my feet,
        and I heard the one who was speaking say to me:
    Son of man, I am sending you to the Israelites,
    rebels who have rebelled against me;
        they and their ancestors have revolted against me
            to this very day.
Hard of face and obstinate of heart
    are they to whom I am sending you.
But you shall say to them: Thus says the Lord God!
And whether they heed or resist
        —for they are a rebellious house—
        they shall know that a prophet has been among them.

**RESPONSORIAL
PSALM**

PSALM 123:1–2, 2, 3–4 (2cd)

R. Our eyes are fixed on the Lord, pleading for his mercy.

To you I lift up my eyes
    who are enthroned in heaven—
as the eyes of servants
    are on the hands of their masters.   R.

As the eyes of a maid
    are on the hands of her mistress,
so are our eyes on the Lord, our God,
    till he have pity on us.   R.

Have pity on us, O Lord, have pity on us,
    for we are more than sated with contempt;
our souls are more than sated
    with the mockery of the arrogant,
    with the contempt of the proud.   R.

SECOND READING

2 CORINTHIANS 12:7–10

I WILL BOAST IN MY
WEAKNESSES, IN ORDER
THAT THE POWER OF
CHRIST MAY DWELL IN ME.

Brothers and sisters:
That I, Paul, might not become too elated,
    because of the abundance of the revelations,
    a thorn in the flesh was given to me, an angel of Satan,
    to beat me, to keep me from being too elated.

Three times I begged the Lord about this,
        that it might leave me,
    but he said to me, "My grace is sufficient for you,
    for power is made perfect in weakness."
I will rather boast most gladly of my weaknesses,
    in order that the power of Christ may dwell with me.

Therefore, I am content with weaknesses, insults,
    hardships, persecutions, and constraints,
        for the sake of Christ;
        for when I am weak, then I am strong.

R. Alleluia, alleluia.

The Spirit of the Lord is upon me
for he sent me to bring glad tidings to the poor.   *R.*

GOSPEL

MARK 6:1–6

A PROPHET IS NOT
WITHOUT HONOR EXCEPT
IN HIS NATIVE PLACE.

Jesus departed from there and came to his native place,
 accompanied by his disciples.
When the sabbath came he began to teach
 in the synagogue,
 and many who heard him were astonished.
They said, "Where did this man get all this?
What kind of wisdom has been given him?
What mighty deeds are wrought by his hands!
Is he not the carpenter, the son of Mary,
 and the brother of James and Joses and Judas
  and Simon?
And are not his sisters here with us?"
And they took offense at him.

Jesus said to them,
 "A prophet is not without honor except
 in his native place
 and among his own kin and in his own house."

So he was not able to perform any mighty deed there,
 apart from curing a few sick people by laying
  his hands on them.
He was amazed at their lack of faith.

102C   FOURTEENTH SUNDAY IN ORDINARY TIME

FIRST READING

ISAIAH 66:10–14c

BEHOLD, I WILL SPREAD
PROSPERITY OVER HER
LIKE A RIVER.

Thus says the LORD:
Rejoice with Jerusalem and be glad because of her,
 all you who love her;
exult, exult with her,
 all you who were mourning over her!
Oh, that you may suck fully
 of the milk of her comfort,
that you may nurse with delight
 at her abundant breasts!

For thus says the LORD:
Lo, I will spread prosperity over Jerusalem like a river,
 and the wealth of the nations
  like an overflowing torrent.

As nurslings, you shall be carried in her arms,
and fondled in her lap;
as a mother comforts her child,
so will I comfort you;
in Jerusalem you shall find your comfort.

When you see this, your heart shall rejoice
and your bodies flourish like the grass;
the Lord's power shall be known to his servants.

RESPONSORIAL PSALM

PSALM 66:1–3, 4–5, 6–7, 16, 20 (1)

R. Let all the earth cry out to God with joy.

[This psalm is found on page 446 (lectionary number 174).]

SECOND READING

GALATIANS 6:14–18

I BEAR THE MARKS
OF JESUS ON MY BODY.

Brothers and sisters:
May I never boast except in the cross of our
Lord Jesus Christ,
through which the world has been crucified to me,
and I to the world.
For neither does circumcision mean anything,
nor does uncircumcision,
but only a new creation.
Peace and mercy be to all who follow this rule
and to the Israel of God.
From now on, let no one make troubles for me;
for I bear the marks of Jesus on my body.

The grace of our Lord Jesus Christ be with your spirit,
brothers and sisters. Amen.

ALLELUIA

COLOSSIANS 3:15a, 16a

R. Alleluia, alleluia.

Let the peace of Christ control your hearts;
let the word of Christ dwell in you richly.   R.

GOSPEL

LONGER FORM
LUKE 10:1–12, 17–20

SHORTER FORM
LUKE 10:1–9

YOUR PEACE WILL REST
ON THAT PERSON.

[At that time the Lord appointed seventy-two others
whom he sent ahead of him in pairs
to every town and place he intended to visit.

He said to them,
"The harvest is abundant but the laborers are few;
so ask the master of the harvest
to send out laborers for his harvest.
Go on your way;
behold, I am sending you like lambs among wolves.

Carry no money bag, no sack, no sandals;
   and greet no one along the way.

"Into whatever house you enter, first say,
   'Peace to this household.'
If a peaceful person lives there,
   your peace will rest on him;
   but if not, it will return to you.
Stay in the same house and eat and drink what is
      offered to you,
   for the laborer deserves his payment.
Do not move about from one house to another.

"Whatever town you enter and they welcome you,
   eat what is set before you,
   cure the sick in it and say to them,
   'The kingdom of God is at hand for you.']

"Whatever town you enter and they do not receive you,
   go out into the streets and say,
   'The dust of your town that clings to our feet,
   even that we shake off against you.'
Yet know this: the kingdom of God is at hand.
I tell you,
   it will be more tolerable for Sodom on that day
      than for that town."

The seventy-two returned rejoicing, and said,
   "Lord, even the demons are subject to us because
      of your name."
Jesus said, "I have observed Satan fall like lightning
      from the sky.
Behold, I have given you the power to
   'tread upon serpents' and scorpions
   and upon the full force of the enemy
   and nothing will harm you.
Nevertheless, do not rejoice because the spirits
      are subject to you,
   but rejoice because your names are written in heaven."

103A   FIFTEENTH SUNDAY IN ORDINARY TIME

FIRST READING

ISAIAH 55:10–11

THE RAIN MAKES
THE EARTH FRUITFUL.

Thus says the LORD:
Just as from the heavens
   the rain and snow come down
and do not return there
   till they have watered the earth,
   making it fertile and fruitful,

giving seed to the one who sows
    and bread to the one who eats,
so shall my word be
    that goes forth from my mouth;
my word shall not return to me void,
    but shall do my will,
      achieving the end for which I sent it.

RESPONSORIAL PSALM

PSALM 65:10, 11, 12–13, 14
(LUKE 8:8)

R. The seed that falls on good ground will yield a fruitful harvest.

You have visited the land and watered it;
*   greatly have you enriched it.*
God's watercourses are filled;
*   you have prepared the grain. R.*

Thus have you prepared the land: drenching its furrows,
*   breaking up its clods,*
Softening it with showers,
*   blessing its yield. R.*

You have crowned the year with your bounty,
*   and your paths overflow with a rich harvest;*
the untilled meadows overflow with it,
*   and rejoicing clothes the hills. R.*

The fields are garmented with flocks
*   and the valleys blanketed with grain.*
They shout and sing for joy. R.

SECOND READING

ROMANS 8:18–23

CREATION AWAITS THE
REVELATION OF THE
CHILDREN OF GOD.

Brothers and sisters:
I consider that the sufferings of this present time
    are as nothing
    compared with the glory to be revealed for us.
For creation awaits with eager expectation
    the revelation of the children of God;
    for creation was made subject to futility,
    not of its own accord but because of the one
      who subjected it,
    in hope that creation itself
    would be set free from slavery to corruption
    and share in the glorious freedom of the children
      of God.

We know that all creation is groaning in labor pains
    even until now;
    and not only that, but we ourselves,
    who have the firstfruits of the Spirit,
    we also groan within ourselves
    as we wait for adoption, the redemption of our bodies.

ALLELUIA

R. *Alleluia, alleluia.*

The seed is the word of God, Christ is the sower.
All who come to him will have life forever. R.

GOSPEL

LONGER FORM
MATTHEW 13:1–23

SHORTER FORM
MATTHEW 13:1–9

A SOWER WENT OUT
TO SOW.

[On that day, Jesus went out of the house and sat down
    by the sea.
Such large crowds gathered around him
    that he got into a boat and sat down,
    and the whole crowd stood along the shore.

And he spoke to them at length in parables, saying:
    "A sower went out to sow.
And as he sowed, some seed fell on the path,
    and birds came and ate it up.
Some fell on rocky ground, where it had little soil.
It sprang up at once because the soil was not deep,
    and when the sun rose it was scorched,
    and it withered for lack of roots.
Some seed fell among thorns, and the thorns grew up
    and choked it.
But some seed fell on rich soil, and produced fruit,
    a hundred or sixty or thirtyfold.
Whoever has ears ought to hear."]

The disciples approached him and said,
    "Why do you speak to them in parables?"
He said to them in reply,
    "Because knowledge of the mysteries of the kingdom
        of heaven
    has been granted to you, but to them it has not
        been granted.
To anyone who has, more will be given
    and he will grow rich;
    from anyone who has not, even what he has
        will be taken away.

"This is why I speak to them in parables, because
    they look but do not see and hear but do not listen
        or understand.
Isaiah's prophecy is fulfilled in them, which says:
    You shall indeed hear but not understand,
    you shall indeed look but never see.
    Gross is the heart of this people,
    they will hardly hear with their ears,
    they have closed their eyes,
    lest they see with their eyes
    and hear with their ears

and understand with their hearts and be converted,
and I heal them.

"But blessed are your eyes, because they see,
and your ears, because they hear.
Amen, I say to you, many prophets and righteous people
longed to see what you see but did not see it,
and to hear what you hear but did not hear it.

"Hear then the parable of the sower.
The seed sown on the path is the one
who hears the word of the kingdom without
understanding it,
and the evil one comes and steals away
what was sown in his heart.
The seed sown on rocky ground
is the one who hears the word and receives it
at once with joy.
But he has no root and lasts only for a time.
When some tribulation or persecution comes
because of the word,
he immediately falls away.
The seed sown among thorns is the one
who hears the word,
but then worldly anxiety and the lure of riches
choke the word
and it bears no fruit.

"But the seed sown on rich soil
is the one who hears the word and understands it,
who indeed bears fruit and yields a hundred or sixty
or thirtyfold."

104B   FIFTEENTH SUNDAY IN ORDINARY TIME

FIRST READING

AMOS 7:12–15

GO, PROPHESY TO
MY PEOPLE.

Amaziah, priest of Bethel, said to Amos,
"Off with you, visionary, flee to the land of Judah!
There earn your bread by prophesying,
but never again prophesy in Bethel;
for it is the king's sanctuary and a royal temple."

Amos answered Amaziah, "I was no prophet,
nor have I belonged to a company of prophets;
I was a shepherd and a dresser of sycamores.
The LORD took me from following the flock,
and said to me,
Go, prophesy to my people Israel."

PSALM 85:9–10, 11–12,
13–14 (8)

R. *Lord, let us see your kindness, and grant us your salvation.*

[This psalm is found on page 441 (lectionary number 174).]

SECOND READING

LONGER FORM
EPHESIANS 1:3–14

SHORTER FORM
EPHESIANS 1:3–10

GOD CHOSE US IN CHRIST,
BEFORE THE FOUNDATION
OF THE WORLD.

[Blessed be the God and Father of our Lord Jesus Christ,
    who has blessed us in Christ
    with every spiritual blessing in the heavens,
    as he chose us in him, before the foundation
        of the world,
    to be holy and without blemish before him.

In love he destined us for adoption to himself
        through Jesus Christ,
    in accord with the favor of his will,
    for the praise of the glory of his grace
    that he granted us in the beloved.

In him we have redemption by his blood,
    the forgiveness of transgressions,
    in accord with the riches of his grace
        that he lavished upon us.
In all wisdom and insight, he has made known to us
    the mystery of his will in accord with his favor
    that he set forth in him as a plan for the fullness
        of times,
    to sum up all things in Christ, in heaven and on earth.]

In him we were also chosen,
    destined in accord with the purpose of the One
    who accomplishes all things
        according to the intention of his will,
    so that we might exist for the praise of his glory,
    we who first hoped in Christ.

In him you also, who have heard the word of truth,
    the gospel of your salvation, and have believed in him,
    were sealed with the promised holy Spirit,
    which is the first installment of our inheritance
    toward redemption as God's possession, to the praise
        of his glory.

ALLELUIA

SEE EPHESIANS 1:17–18

R. *Alleluia, alleluia.*

*May the Father of our Lord Jesus Christ
    enlighten the eyes of our hearts,
that we may know what is the hope that
    belongs to our call.* R.

Jesus summoned the Twelve and began to send them out
    two by two
  and gave them authority over unclean spirits.
He instructed them to take nothing for the journey
    but a walking stick—
  no food, no sack, no money in their belts.
They were, however, to wear sandals
  but not a second tunic.

He said to them,
  "Wherever you enter a house, stay there until you leave.
Whatever place does not welcome you or listen to you,
  leave there and shake the dust off your feet
  in testimony against them."
So they went off and preached repentance.
The Twelve drove out many demons,
  and they anointed with oil many who were sick
    and cured them.

105C   FIFTEENTH SUNDAY IN ORDINARY TIME

FIRST READING

DEUTERONOMY 30:10–14

THE WORD IS VERY NEAR
TO YOU: YOU HAVE ONLY
TO CARRY IT OUT.

Moses said to the people:
  "If only you would heed the voice of the LORD,
    your God,
  and keep his commandments and statutes
  that are written in this book of the law,
  when you return to the LORD, your God,
  with all your heart and all your soul.

"For this command that I enjoin on you today
  is not too mysterious and remote for you.
It is not up in the sky, that you should say,
  'Who will go up in the sky to get it for us
  and tell us of it, that we may carry it out?'

"Nor is it across the sea, that you should say,
  'Who will cross the sea to get it for us
  and tell us of it, that we may carry it out?'

"No, it is something very near to you,
  already in your mouths and in your hearts;
  you have only to carry it out."

RESPONSORIAL PSALM

1.

PSALM 69:14, 17, 30–31, 33–34, 36, 37 (SEE 33)

R. Turn to the Lord in your need, and you will live.

I pray to you, O LORD,
    for the time of your favor, O God!
In your great kindness answer me
    with your constant help.
Answer me, O LORD, for bounteous is your kindness;
    in your great mercy turn toward me.   R.

I am afflicted and in pain;
    let your saving help, O God, protect me.
I will praise the name of God in song,
    and I will glorify him with thanksgiving.   R.

"See, you lowly ones, and be glad;
    you who seek God, may your hearts revive!
For the LORD hears the poor,
    and his own who are in bonds he spurns not."   R.

For God will save Zion
    and rebuild the cities of Judah.
The descendants of his servants shall inherit it,
    and those who love his name shall inhabit it.

OR:

2.

PSALM 19:8, 9, 10, 11 (9a)

R. Your words, Lord, are Spirit and life.

[This psalm is found on page 447 (lectionary number 174).]

SECOND READING

COLOSSIANS 1:15–20

ALL THINGS WERE CREATED THROUGH HIM AND FOR HIM.

Christ Jesus is the image of the invisible God,
    the firstborn of all creation.
For in him were created all things in heaven
      and on earth,
    the visible and the invisible,
      whether thrones or dominions or principalities
        or powers;
    all things were created through him and for him.

He is before all things,
    and in him all things hold together.
He is the head of the body, the church.
He is the beginning, the firstborn from the dead,
    that in all things he himself might be preeminent.

For in him all the fullness was pleased to dwell,
    and through him to reconcile all things for him,
    making peace by the blood of his cross
      through him, whether those on earth or those
        in heaven.

R. Alleluia, alleluia.

Your words, Lord, are Spirit and life;
you have the words of everlasting life. R.

There was a scholar of the law who stood up to test
    him and said,
    "Teacher, what must I do to inherit eternal life?"

Jesus said to him, "What is written in the law?
How do you read it?"
He said in reply,
    You shall love the LORD, *your God,*
    with all your heart,
    with all your being,
    with all your strength,
    and with all your mind,
    and your neighbor as yourself.

He replied to him, "You have answered correctly;
    do this and you will live."
But because he wished to justify himself, he said to Jesus,
    "And who is my neighbor?"

Jesus replied,
    "A man fell victim to robbers
    as he went down from Jerusalem to Jericho.
They stripped and beat him and went off
    leaving him half-dead.
A priest happened to be going down that road,
    but when he saw him, he passed by on the opposite side.
Likewise a Levite came to the place,
    and when he saw him, he passed by
        on the opposite side.

"But a Samaritan traveler who came upon him
    was moved with compassion at the sight.
He approached the victim,
    poured oil and wine over his wounds and
        bandaged them.
Then he lifted him up on his own animal,
    took him to an inn, and cared for him.

"The next day he took out two silver coins
    and gave them to the innkeeper with the instruction,
    'Take care of him.
If you spend more than what I have given you,
    I shall repay you on my way back.'

"Which of these three, in your opinion,
    was neighbor to the robbers' victim?"
He answered, "The one who treated him with mercy."
Jesus said to him, "Go and do likewise."

106A   SIXTEENTH SUNDAY IN ORDINARY TIME

FIRST READING

WISDOM 12:13, 16–19

YOU GIVE REPENTANCE
FOR SINS.

There is no god besides you who have the care of all,
    that you need show you have not unjustly condemned.
For your might is the source of justice;
    your mastery over all things makes you lenient to all.
For you show your might when the perfection
        of your power is disbelieved;
    and in those who know you, you rebuke temerity.
But though you are master of might, you judge
        with clemency,
    and with much lenience you govern us;
    for power, whenever you will, attends you.

And you taught your people, by these deeds,
    that those who are just must be kind;
and you gave your children good ground for hope
    that you would permit repentance for their sins.

**RESPONSORIAL
PSALM**

PSALM 86:5–6, 9–10,
15–16 (5a)

R. Lord, you are good and forgiving.

You, O Lord, are good and forgiving,
    abounding in kindness to all who call upon you.
Hearken, O Lord, to my prayer
    and attend to the sound of my pleading.   R.

All the nations you have made shall come
    and worship you, O Lord,
    and glorify your name.
For you are great, and you do wondrous deeds;
    you alone are God.   R.

You, O Lord, are a God merciful and gracious,
    slow to anger, abounding in kindness and fidelity.
Turn toward me, and have pity on me;
    give your strength to your servant.   R.

SECOND READING

ROMANS 8:26–27

THE SPIRIT INTERCEDES
WITH INEXPRESSIBLE
GROANINGS.

Brothers and sisters:
The Spirit comes to the aid of our weakness;
    for we do not know how to pray as we ought,
    but the Spirit himself intercedes with
        inexpressible groanings.

And the one who searches hearts
    knows what is the intention of the Spirit,
    because he intercedes for the holy ones
    according to God's will.

ALLELUIA

SEE MATTHEW 11:25

R. Alleluia, alleluia.

Blessed are you, Father, Lord of heaven and earth;
you have revealed to little ones the mysteries of the kingdom.   R.

GOSPEL

LONGER FORM
MATTHEW 13:24–43

SHORTER FORM
MATTHEW 13:24–30

LET THEM GROW
TOGETHER UNTIL
HARVEST.

[Jesus proposed another parable to the crowds, saying:
"The kingdom of heaven may be likened to a man
    who sowed good seed in his field.
While everyone was asleep his enemy came
    and sowed weeds all through the wheat,
      and then went off.

"When the crop grew and bore fruit, the weeds
    appeared as well.
The slaves of the householder came to him and said,
    'Master, did you not sow good seed in your field?
Where have the weeds come from?'
He answered, 'An enemy has done this.'
His slaves said to him,
    'Do you want us to go and pull them up?'
He replied, 'No, if you pull up the weeds
    you might uproot the wheat along with them.
Let them grow together until harvest;
    then at harvest time I will say to the harvesters,
    "First collect the weeds and tie them in bundles
      for burning;
    but gather the wheat into my barn."'"]

He proposed another parable to them.
"The kingdom of heaven is like a mustard seed
    that a person took and sowed in a field.
It is the smallest of all the seeds,
    yet when full-grown it is the largest of plants.
It becomes a large bush,
    and the 'birds of the sky come and dwell
      in its branches.'"

He spoke to them another parable.
"The kingdom of heaven is like yeast
    that a woman took and mixed with three measures
      of wheat flour
    until the whole batch was leavened."

All these things Jesus spoke to the crowds in parables.
He spoke to them only in parables,
   to fulfill what had been said through the prophet:
   I will open my mouth in parables,
   I will announce what has lain hidden from the foundation
   of the world.

Then, dismissing the crowds, he went into the house.
His disciples approached him and said,
   "Explain to us the parable of the weeds in the field."
He said in reply, "He who sows good seed
      is the Son of Man,
   the field is the world, the good seed the children
      of the kingdom.
The weeds are the children of the evil one,
   and the enemy who sows them is the devil.
The harvest is the end of the age, and the harvesters
      are angels.

"Just as weeds are collected and burned up with fire,
   so will it be at the end of the age.
The Son of Man will send his angels,
   and they will collect out of his kingdom
   all who cause others to sin and all evildoers.
They will throw them into the fiery furnace,
   where there will be wailing and grinding of teeth.
Then the righteous will shine like the sun
   in the kingdom of their Father.
Whoever has ears ought to hear."

107B   SIXTEENTH SUNDAY IN ORDINARY TIME

FIRST READING

JEREMIAH 23:1–6

I WILL GATHER THE
REMNANT OF MY FLOCK
AND APPOINT SHEPHERDS
FOR THEM.

Woe to the shepherds
   who mislead and scatter the flock of my pasture,
   says the LORD.
Therefore, thus says the LORD, the God of Israel,
   against the shepherds who shepherd my people:
You have scattered my sheep and driven them away.
You have not cared for them,
   but I will take care to punish your evil deeds.

I myself will gather the remnant of my flock
   from all the lands to which I have driven them
   and bring them back to their meadow;
   there they shall increase and multiply.

I will appoint shepherds for them who will shepherd them
    so that they need no longer fear and tremble;
    and none shall be missing, says the LORD.

Behold, the days are coming, says the LORD,
    when I will raise up a righteous shoot to David;
as king he shall reign and govern wisely,
    he shall do what is just and right in the land.
In his days Judah shall be saved,
    Israel shall dwell in security.
This is the name they give him:
    "The LORD our justice."

RESPONSORIAL PSALM

PSALM 23:1–3, 3–4, 5, 6 (1)

R. *The Lord is my shepherd; there is nothing I shall want.*

[This psalm is found on page 80 (lectionary number 31).]

SECOND READING

EPHESIANS 2:13–18

CHRIST IS OUR PEACE
WHO MADE BOTH ONE.

Brothers and sisters:
In Christ Jesus you who once were far off
    have become near by the blood of Christ.
For he is our peace, he who made both one
    and broke down the dividing wall of enmity,
        through his flesh,
    abolishing the law with its commandments
        and legal claims,
    that he might create in himself one new person
        in place of the two,
    thus establishing peace,
    and might reconcile both with God,
    in one body, through the cross,
    putting that enmity to death by it.

He came and preached peace to you who were far off
    and peace to those who were near,
    for through him we both have access in one Spirit
        to the Father.

ALLELUIA

JOHN 10:27

R. *Alleluia, alleluia.*

My sheep hear my voice, says the Lord;
I know them, and they follow me.   R.

The apostles gathered together with Jesus
   and reported all they had done and taught.

He said to them,
"Come away by yourselves to a deserted place
   and rest a while."
People were coming and going in great numbers,
   and they had no opportunity even to eat.
So they went off in the boat by themselves
   to a deserted place.
People saw them leaving and many came to know
   about it.
They hastened there on foot from all the towns
   and arrived at the place before them.

When he disembarked and saw the vast crowd,
   his heart was moved with pity for them,
   for they were like sheep without a shepherd;
   and he began to teach them many things.

108C   SIXTEENTH SUNDAY IN ORDINARY TIME

FIRST READING

GENESIS 18:1–10a

LORD, DO NOT GO ON
PAST YOUR SERVANT.

The LORD appeared to Abraham by the terebinth
   of Mamre,
   as he sat in the entrance of his tent,
   while the day was growing hot.
Looking up, Abraham saw three men standing nearby.
When he saw them, he ran from the entrance of the tent
   to greet them;
   and bowing to the ground, he said:
   "Sir, if I may ask you this favor,
   please do not go on past your servant.
Let some water be brought, that you may bathe your feet,
   and then rest yourselves under the tree.
Now that you have come this close to your servant,
   let me bring you a little food, that you may
     refresh yourselves;
   and afterward you may go on your way."
The men replied, "Very well, do as you have said."

Abraham hastened into the tent and told Sarah,
   "Quick, three measures of fine flour! Knead it
     and make rolls."
He ran to the herd, picked out a tender, choice steer,
   and gave it to a servant, who quickly prepared it.
Then Abraham got some curds and milk,
   as well as the steer that had been prepared,

and set these before the three men;
and he waited on them under the tree while they ate.

They asked Abraham, "Where is your wife Sarah?"
He replied, "There in the tent."
One of them said, "I will surely return to you about
    this time next year,
    and Sarah will then have a son."

RESPONSORIAL
PSALM

PSALM 15:2–3, 3–4, 5 (1a)

R. He who does justice will live in the presence of the Lord.

One who walks blamelessly and does justice;
    who thinks the truth in his heart
    and slanders not with his tongue.   R.

Who harms not his fellow man,
    nor takes up a reproach against his neighbor;
by whom the reprobate is despised,
    while he honors those who fear the LORD.   R.

Who lends not his money at usury
    and accepts no bribe against the innocent.
One who does these things
    shall never be disturbed.   R.

SECOND READING

COLOSSIANS 1:24–28

THE MYSTERY HIDDEN
FROM AGES HAS NOW
BEEN MANIFESTED
TO HIS HOLY ONES.

Brothers and sisters:
Now I rejoice in my sufferings for your sake,
    and in my flesh I am filling up
    what is lacking in the afflictions of Christ
    on behalf of his body, which is the church,
    of which I am a minister
    in accordance with God's stewardship given to me
    to bring to completion for you the word of God,
    the mystery hidden from ages and from
        generations past.

But now it has been manifested to his holy ones,
    to whom God chose to make known the riches
        of the glory
    of this mystery among the Gentiles;
    it is Christ in you, the hope for glory.
It is he whom we proclaim,
    admonishing everyone and teaching everyone
        with all wisdom,
    that we may present everyone perfect in Christ.

R. Alleluia, alleluia.

*Blessed are they who have kept the word with a generous heart
and yield a harvest through perseverance.   R.*

GOSPEL

LUKE 10:38–42

MARTHA WELCOMED HIM.
MARY HAS CHOSEN THE
BETTER PART.

Jesus entered a village
   where a woman whose name was Martha
     welcomed him.
She had a sister named Mary
   who sat beside the Lord at his feet listening
     to him speak.

Martha, burdened with much serving, came to him
     and said,
   "Lord, do you not care
   that my sister has left me by myself to do the serving?
Tell her to help me."

The Lord said to her in reply,
   "Martha, Martha, you are anxious and worried
     about many things.
There is need of only one thing.
Mary has chosen the better part
   and it will not be taken from her."

109A   SEVENTEENTH SUNDAY IN ORDINARY TIME

FIRST READING

1 KINGS 3:5, 7–12

YOU HAVE ASKED
FOR WISDOM.

The Lord appeared to Solomon in a dream at night.
God said, "Ask something of me and I will give it to you."
Solomon answered:
"O Lord, my God, you have made me, your servant, king
   to succeed my father David;
     but I am a mere youth, not knowing at all how to act.
I serve you in the midst of the people whom you
     have chosen,
     a people so vast that it cannot be numbered or counted.

"Give your servant, therefore, an understanding heart
   to judge your people and to distinguish right
     from wrong.
For who is able to govern this vast people of yours?"

The Lord was pleased that Solomon made this request.
So God said to him:
   "Because you have asked for this —
   not for a long life for yourself,
   nor for riches,

nor for the life of your enemies,
but for understanding so that you may know
what is right—
I do as you requested.
I give you a heart so wise and understanding
that there has never been anyone like you up to now,
and after you there will come no one to equal you."

RESPONSORIAL PSALM

PSALM 119:57, 72, 76–77,
127–128, 129–130 (97a)

R. Lord, I love your commands.

I have said, O Lord, that my part
is to keep your words.
The law of your mouth is to me more precious
than thousands of gold and silver pieces.   R.

Let your kindness comfort me
according to your promise to your servants.
Let your compassion come to me that I may live,
for your law is my delight.   R.

For I love your command
more than gold, however fine.
For in all your precepts I go forward;
every false way I hate.   R.

Wonderful are your decrees;
therefore I observe them.
The revelation of your words sheds light,
giving understanding to the simple.   R.

SECOND READING

ROMANS 8:28–30

GOD PREDESTINED US
TO BE CONFORMED TO
THE IMAGE OF HIS SON.

Brothers and sisters:
We know that all things work for good for those
who love God,
who are called according to his purpose.
For those he foreknew he also predestined
to be conformed to the image of his Son,
so that he might be the firstborn
among many brothers and sisters.
And those he predestined he also called;
and those he called he also justified;
and those he justified he also glorified.

ALLELUIA

SEE MATTHEW 11:25

R. Alleluia, alleluia.

Blessed are you, Father, Lord of heaven and earth;
for you have revealed to little ones the mysteries
of the kingdom.   R.

GOSPEL

LONGER FORM
MATTHEW 13:44–52

SHORTER FORM
MATTHEW 13:44–46

HE SELLS ALL THAT HE
HAS AND BUYS THE FIELD.

[Jesus said to his disciples:
"The kingdom of heaven is like a treasure buried
    in a field,
    which a person finds and hides again,
    and out of joy goes and sells all that he has
        and buys that field.

"Again, the kingdom of heaven is like a merchant
    searching for fine pearls.
When he finds a pearl of great price,
    he goes and sells all that he has and buys it.]

"Again, the kingdom of heaven is like a net thrown
        into the sea,
    which collects fish of every kind.
When it is full they haul it ashore
    and sit down to put what is good into buckets.
What is bad they throw away.

"Thus it will be at the end of the age.
The angels will go out and separate the wicked
        from the righteous
    and throw them into the fiery furnace,
    where there will be wailing and grinding of teeth.

"Do you understand all these things?"
They answered, "Yes."
And he replied,
"Then every scribe who has been instructed
        in the kingdom of heaven
    is like the head of a household
    who brings from his storeroom both the new
        and the old."

110B   SEVENTEENTH SUNDAY IN ORDINARY TIME

A man came from Baal-shalishah bringing to Elisha,
        the man of God,
    twenty barley loaves made from the firstfruits,
    and fresh grain in the ear.
Elisha said, "Give it to the people to eat."

But his servant objected,
    "How can I set this before a hundred people?"
Elisha insisted, "Give it to the people to eat."
"For thus says the LORD,
    'They shall eat and there shall be some left over.'"

And when they had eaten, there was some left over,
as the LORD had said.

**RESPONSORIAL
PSALM**

PSALM 145:10–11, 15–16,
17–18 (SEE 16)

R. The hand of the Lord feeds us; he answers all our needs.

*Let all your works give you thanks, O Lord,
    and let your faithful ones bless you.
Let them discourse of the glory of your kingdom
    and speak of your might.   R.*

*The eyes of all look hopefully to you,
    and you give them their food in due season;
you open your hand
    and satisfy the desire of every living thing.   R.*

*The Lord is just in all his ways
    and holy in all his works.
The Lord is near to all who call upon him,
    to all who call upon him in truth.   R.*

SECOND READING

EPHESIANS 4:1–6

ONE BODY, ONE LORD,
ONE FAITH, ONE BAPTISM.

Brothers and sisters:
I, a prisoner for the Lord,
    urge you to live in a manner worthy of the call
        you have received,
    with all humility and gentleness, with patience,
    bearing with one another through love,
    striving to preserve the unity of the spirit
        through the bond of peace:
    one body and one Spirit,
    as you were also called to the one hope of your call;
    one Lord, one faith, one baptism;
    one God and Father of all,
    who is over all and through all and in all.

ALLELUIA

LUKE 7:16

R. Alleluia, alleluia.

*A great prophet has risen in our midst
God has visited his people.   R.*

GOSPEL

JOHN 6:1–15

HE DISTRIBUTED AS MUCH
AS THEY WANTED TO THOSE
WHO WERE RECLINING.

Jesus went across the Sea of Galilee.
A large crowd followed him,
    because they saw the signs he was performing
        on the sick.
Jesus went up on the mountain,
    and there he sat down with his disciples.
The Jewish feast of Passover was near.

When Jesus raised his eyes
and saw that a large crowd was coming to him,
he said to Philip,
"Where can we buy enough food for them to eat?"
He said this to test him,
because he himself knew what he was going to do.

Philip answered him,
"Two hundred days' wages worth of food
would not be enough
for each of them to have a little."

One of his disciples,
Andrew, the brother of Simon Peter, said to him,
"There is a boy here who has five barley loaves
and two fish;
but what good are these for so many?"
Jesus said, "Have the people recline."
Now there was a great deal of grass in that place.
So the men reclined, about five thousand in number.

Then Jesus took the loaves, gave thanks,
and distributed them to those who were reclining,
and also as much of the fish as they wanted.

When they had had their fill, he said to his disciples,
"Gather the fragments left over,
so that nothing will be wasted."
So they collected them,
and filled twelve wicker baskets with fragments
from the five barley loaves
that had been more than they could eat.

When the people saw the sign he had done, they said,
"This is truly the Prophet, the one who is to come
into the world."
Since Jesus knew that they were going to come
and carry him off
to make him king,
he withdrew again to the mountain alone.

111C   SEVENTEENTH SUNDAY IN ORDINARY TIME

FIRST READING

GENESIS 18:20–32

LET NOT MY LORD GROW
ANGRY IF I SPEAK.

In those days, the LORD said:
"The outcry against Sodom and Gomorrah is so great,
and their sin so grave,

that I must go down and see whether or not
their actions fully correspond to the cry against them
that comes to me.
I mean to find out."

While Abraham's visitors walked on farther
toward Sodom,
the LORD remained standing before Abraham.
Then Abraham drew nearer and said:
"Will you sweep away the innocent with the guilty?
Suppose there were fifty innocent people in the city;
would you wipe out the place, rather than spare it
for the sake of the fifty innocent people within it?
Far be it from you to do such a thing,
to make the innocent die with the guilty
so that the innocent and the guilty would be
treated alike!
Should not the judge of all the world act with justice?"
The LORD replied,
"If I find fifty innocent people in the city of Sodom,
I will spare the whole place for their sake."

Abraham spoke up again:
"See how I am presuming to speak to my Lord,
though I am but dust and ashes!
What if there are five less than fifty innocent people?
Will you destroy the whole city because of those five?"
He answered, "I will not destroy it, if I find
forty-five there."

But Abraham persisted, saying,
"What if only forty are found there?"
He replied, "I will forbear doing it for the sake of the forty."
Then Abraham said,
"Let not my Lord grow impatient if I go on.
What if only thirty are found there?"
He replied,
"I will forbear doing it if I can find but thirty there."

Still Abraham went on,
"Since I have thus dared to speak to my Lord,
what if there are no more than twenty?"
The LORD answered,
"I will not destroy it, for the sake of the twenty."
But he still persisted:
"Please, let not my Lord grow angry if I speak up
this last time.

What if there are at least ten there?"
He replied, "For the sake of those ten,
   I will not destroy it."

RESPONSORIAL PSALM

PSALM 138:1–2, 2–3, 6–7, 7–8 (3a)

R. *Lord, on the day I called for help, you answered me.*

I will give thanks to you, O Lord, with all my heart,
   for you have heard the words of my mouth;
     in the presence of the angels I will sing your praise;
I will worship at your holy temple
   and give thanks to your name.   R.

Because of your kindness and your truth;
   for you have made great above all things
   your name and your promise.
When I called you answered me;
   you built up strength within me.   R.

The Lord is exalted, yet the lowly he sees,
   and the proud he knows from afar.
Though I walk amid distress, you preserve me;
   against the anger of my enemies you raise your hand.   R.

Your right hand saves me.
The Lord will complete what he has done for me;
   your kindness, O Lord, endures forever;
   forsake not the work of your hands.   R.

SECOND READING

COLOSSIANS 2:12–14

GOD HAS BROUGHT YOU TO LIFE ALONG WITH CHRIST, HAVING FORGIVEN US ALL OUR TRANSGRESSIONS.

Brothers and sisters:
You were buried with him in baptism,
   in which you were also raised with him
   through faith in the power of God,
   who raised him from the dead.

And even when you were dead
   in transgressions and the uncircumcision of your flesh,
   he brought you to life along with him,
   having forgiven us all our transgressions;
   obliterating the bond against us, with its legal claims,
   which was opposed to us,
   he also removed it from our midst,
     nailing it to the cross.

ALLELUIA

ROMANS 8:15bc

R. *Alleluia, alleluia.*

You have received a spirit of adoption,
through which we cry, Abba, Father.   R.

Jesus was praying in a certain place,
and when he had finished,
one of his disciples said to him,
"Lord, teach us to pray just as John taught his disciples."
He said to them, "When you pray, say:
Father, hallowed be your name,
your kingdom come.
Give us each day our daily bread
and forgive us our sins
for we ourselves forgive everyone in debt to us,
and do not subject us to the final test."

And he said to them, "Suppose one of you has a friend
to whom he goes at midnight and says,
'Friend, lend me three loaves of bread,
for a friend of mine has arrived at my house
from a journey
and I have nothing to offer him,'
and he says in reply from within,
'Do not bother me; the door has already been locked
and my children and I are already in bed.
I cannot get up to give you anything.'

"I tell you,
if he does not get up to give the visitor the loaves
because of their friendship,
he will get up to give him whatever he needs
because of his persistence.

"And I tell you, ask and you will receive;
seek and you will find;
knock and the door will be opened to you.
For everyone who asks, receives;
and the one who seeks, finds;
and to the one who knocks, the door will be opened.

"What father among you would hand his son a snake
when he asks for a fish?
Or hand him a scorpion when he asks for an egg?

"If you then, who are wicked,
know how to give good gifts to your children,
how much more will the Father in heaven
give the Holy Spirit to those who ask him?"

FIRST READING

ISAIAH 55:1–3

HASTEN AND EAT.

Thus says the Lord:
All you who are thirsty,
  come to the water!
You who have no money,
  come, receive grain and eat;
Come, without paying and without cost,
  drink wine and milk!

Why spend your money for what is not bread;
  your wages for what fails to satisfy?
Heed me, and you shall eat well,
  you shall delight in rich fare.
Come to me heedfully,
  listen, that you may have life.
I will renew with you the everlasting covenant,
  the benefits assured to David.

RESPONSORIAL PSALM

PSALM 145:8–9, 15–16, 17–18
(SEE 16)

R. *The hand of the Lord feeds us; he answers all our needs.*

The Lord is gracious and merciful,
  slow to anger and of great kindness.
The Lord is good to all
  and compassionate toward all his works. R.

The eyes of all look hopefully to you,
  and you give them their food in due season;
you open your hand
  and satisfy the desire of every living thing. R.

The Lord is just in all his ways
  and holy in all his works.
The Lord is near to all who call upon him,
  to all who call upon him in truth. R.

SECOND READING

ROMANS 8:35, 37–39

NO CREATURE WILL BE
ABLE TO SEPARATE US
FROM THE LOVE OF GOD
IN CHRIST JESUS.

Brothers and sisters:
What will separate us from the love of Christ?
Will anguish, or distress, or persecution, or famine,
  or nakedness, or peril, or the sword?
No, in all these things we conquer overwhelmingly
  through him who loved us.

For I am convinced that neither death, nor life,
  nor angels, nor principalities,
  nor present things, nor future things,
  nor powers, nor height, nor depth,
  nor any other creature will be able to separate us
  from the love of God in Christ Jesus our Lord.

R. *Alleluia, alleluia.*

One does not live on bread alone,
but on every word that comes forth from the mouth of God. R.

When Jesus heard of the death of John the Baptist,
he withdrew in a boat to a deserted place by himself.
The crowds heard of this and followed him on foot
from their towns.
When he disembarked and saw the vast crowd,
his heart was moved with pity for them,
and he cured their sick.

When it was evening, the disciples approached him
and said,
"This is a deserted place and it is already late;
dismiss the crowds so that they can go to the villages
and buy food for themselves."
Jesus said to them, "There is no need for them to go away;
give them some food yourselves."
But they said to him,
"Five loaves and two fish are all we have here."
Then he said, "Bring them here to me,"
and he ordered the crowds to sit down on the grass.

Taking the five loaves and the two fish, and looking up
to heaven,
he said the blessing, broke the loaves,
and gave them to the disciples,
who in turn gave them to the crowds.

They all ate and were satisfied,
and they picked up the fragments left over —
twelve wicker baskets full.
Those who ate were about five thousand men,
not counting women and children.

113B   EIGHTEENTH SUNDAY IN ORDINARY TIME

The whole Israelite community grumbled
against Moses and Aaron.
The Israelites said to them,
"Would that we had died at the LORD's hand
in the land of Egypt,
as we sat by our fleshpots and ate our fill of bread!

But you had to lead us into this desert
   to make the whole community die of famine!"

Then the Lord said to Moses,
"I will now rain down bread from heaven for you.
Each day the people are to go out and gather their
      daily portion;
   thus will I test them,
   to see whether they follow my instructions or not.

"I have heard the grumbling of the Israelites.
Tell them: In the evening twilight you shall eat flesh,
   and in the morning you shall have your fill of bread,
   so that you may know that I, the Lord, am your God."

In the evening quail came up and covered the camp.
In the morning a dew lay all about the camp,
   and when the dew evaporated, there on the surface
      of the desert
   were fine flakes like hoarfrost on the ground.
On seeing it, the Israelites asked one another,
      "What is this?"
   for they did not know what it was.
But Moses told them,
      "This is the bread that the Lord has given you to eat."

RESPONSORIAL
PSALM

PSALM 78:3–4, 23–24, 25,
54 (24b)

R. The Lord gave them bread from heaven.

What we have heard and know,
   and what our fathers have declared to us,
we will declare to the generation to come
   the glorious deeds of the Lord and his strength
   and the wonders that he wrought.   R.

He commanded the skies above
   and opened the doors of heaven;
he rained manna upon them for food
   and gave them heavenly bread.   R.

Man ate the bread of angels,
   food he sent them in abundance.
And he brought them to his holy land,
   to the mountains his right hand had won.   R.

SECOND READING

EPHESIANS 4:17, 20–24

PUT ON THE NEW SELF
THAT HAS BEEN CREATED
IN GOD'S WAY.

Brothers and sisters:
I declare and testify in the Lord
   that you must no longer live as the Gentiles do,
   in the futility of their minds;
   that is not how you learned Christ,
   assuming that you have heard of him
      and were taught in him,

as truth is in Jesus,
that you should put away the old self of your former
way of life,
corrupted through deceitful desires,
and be renewed in the spirit of your minds,
and put on the new self,
created in God's way in righteousness and holiness
of truth.

ALLELUIA

MATTHEW 4:4b

R. Alleluia, alleluia.

One does not live on bread alone, but by every
word that comes forth from the mouth of God. R.

GOSPEL

JOHN 6:24–35

WHOEVER COMES TO ME
WILL NEVER HUNGER, AND
WHOEVER BELIEVES IN ME
WILL NEVER THIRST.

When the crowd saw that neither Jesus
nor his disciples were there,
they themselves got into boats
and came to Capernaum looking for Jesus.

And when they found him across the sea they said to him,
"Rabbi, when did you get here?"
Jesus answered them and said,
"Amen, amen, I say to you,
you are looking for me not because you saw signs
but because you ate the loaves and were filled.
Do not work for food that perishes
but for the food that endures for eternal life,
which the Son of Man will give you.
For on him the Father, God, has set his seal."
So they said to him,
"What can we do to accomplish the works of God?"

Jesus answered and said to them,
"This is the work of God, that you believe
in the one he sent."
So they said to him,
"What sign can you do, that we may see
and believe in you?
What can you do?
Our ancestors ate manna in the desert, as it is written:
He gave them bread from heaven to eat."

So Jesus said to them,
"Amen, amen, I say to you,
it was not Moses who gave the bread from heaven;
my Father gives you the true bread from heaven.

For the bread of God is that which comes down
    from heaven
and gives life to the world."

So they said to him,
    "Sir, give us this bread always."
Jesus said to them,
    "I am the bread of life;
    whoever comes to me will never hunger,
    and whoever believes in me will never thirst."

114C   EIGHTEENTH SUNDAY IN ORDINARY TIME

FIRST READING

ECCLESIASTES 1:2; 2:21–23

WHAT PROFIT COMES TO
A MAN FROM ALL HIS TOIL?

Vanity of vanities, says Qoheleth,
    vanity of vanities! All things are vanity!

Here is one who has labored with wisdom and
    knowledge and skill,
    and yet to another who has not labored over it,
    he must leave property.
This also is vanity and a great misfortune.

For what profit comes to man from all the toil
    and anxiety of heart
with which he has labored under the sun?
All his days sorrow and grief are their occupation;
    even at night his mind is not at rest.
This also is vanity.

**RESPONSORIAL
PSALM**

PSALM 90:3–4, 5–6, 12–13,
14, 17 (1)

R. If today you hear his voice, harden not your hearts.

You turn man back to dust,
    saying, "Return, O children of men."
For a thousand years in your sight
    are as yesterday, now that it is past,
    or as a watch of the night.   R.

You make an end of them in their sleep;
    the next morning they are like the changing grass,
which at dawn springs up anew,
    but by evening wilts and fades.   R.

Teach us to number our days aright,
    that we may gain wisdom of heart.
Return, O LORD! How long?
    Have pity on your servants!   R.

Fill us at daybreak with your kindness,
    that we may shout for joy and gladness all our days.
And may the gracious care of the LORD our God be ours;
    prosper the work of our hands for us!
    Prosper the work of our hands!   R.

COLOSSIANS 3:1–5, 9–11

SEEK WHAT IS ABOVE,
WHERE CHRIST IS.

Brothers and sisters:
If you were raised with Christ, seek what is above,
    where Christ is seated at the right hand of God.

Think of what is above, not of what is on earth.
For you have died,
    and your life is hidden with Christ in God.
When Christ your life appears,
    then you too will appear with him in glory.

Put to death, then, the parts of you that are earthly:
    immorality, impurity, passion, evil desire,
    and the greed that is idolatry.

Stop lying to one another,
    since you have taken off the old self with its practices
    and have put on the new self,
    which is being renewed, for knowledge,
    in the image of its creator.

Here there is not Greek and Jew,
    circumcision and uncircumcision,
    barbarian, Scythian, slave, free;
    but Christ is all and in all.

ALLELUIA

MATTHEW 5:3

R. Alleluia, alleluia.

Blessed are the poor in spirit,
for theirs is the kingdom of heaven. R.

GOSPEL

LUKE 12:13–21

THE THINGS YOU HAVE
PREPARED, TO WHOM
WILL THEY BELONG?

Someone in the crowd said to Jesus,
    "Teacher, tell my brother to share the inheritance
      with me."
He replied to him,
    "Friend, who appointed me as your judge
      and arbitrator?"

Then he said to the crowd,
    "Take care to guard against all greed,
    for though one may be rich,
    one's life does not consist of possessions."

Then he told them a parable.
"There was a rich man whose land produced
    a bountiful harvest.
He asked himself, 'What shall I do,
    for I do not have space to store my harvest?'
And he said, 'This is what I shall do:
    I shall tear down my barns and build larger ones.

There I shall store all my grain and other goods
and I shall say to myself, "Now as for you,
you have so many good things stored up for many years,
rest, eat, drink, be merry!"'

"But God said to him,
'You fool, this night your life will be demanded of you;
and the things you have prepared, to whom
will they belong?'
Thus will it be for all who store up treasure for themselves
but are not rich in what matters to God."

115A NINETEENTH SUNDAY IN ORDINARY TIME

FIRST READING

1 KINGS 19:9a, 11–13a

GO OUTSIDE AND STAND
ON THE MOUNTAIN
BEFORE THE LORD.

At the mountain of God, Horeb,
Elijah came to a cave where he took shelter.
Then the LORD said to him,
"Go outside and stand on the mountain
before the LORD;
the LORD will be passing by."

A strong and heavy wind was rending the mountains
and crushing rocks before the LORD —
but the LORD was not in the wind.
After the wind there was an earthquake —
but the LORD was not in the earthquake.
After the earthquake there was fire —
but the LORD was not in the fire.
After the fire there was a tiny whispering sound.

When he heard this,
Elijah hid his face in his cloak
and went and stood at the entrance of the cave.

**RESPONSORIAL
PSALM**

PSALM 85:9, 10, 11–12,
13–14 (8)

R. Lord, let us see your kindness, and grant us your salvation.

[This psalm is found on page 441 (lectionary number 174).]

SECOND READING

ROMANS 9:1–5

I COULD WISH THAT I WERE
ACCURSED FOR THE SAKE
OF MY OWN PEOPLE.

Brothers and sisters:
I speak the truth in Christ, I do not lie;
my conscience joins with the Holy Spirit
in bearing me witness
that I have great sorrow and constant anguish
in my heart.

For I could wish that I myself were accursed and cut off
    from Christ
  for the sake of my own people,
  my kindred according to the flesh.
They are Israelites;
  theirs the adoption, the glory, the covenants,
  the giving of the law, the worship, and the promises;
  theirs the patriarchs, and from them,
  according to the flesh, is the Christ,
  who is over all, God blessed forever. Amen.

ALLELUIA

SEE PSALM 130:5

R. Alleluia, alleluia.

I wait for the Lord;
my soul waits for his word.   R.

GOSPEL

MATTHEW 14:22–33

COMMAND ME TO COME
TO YOU ON THE WATER.

After he had fed the people, Jesus made the disciples
    get into a boat
  and precede him to the other side,
  while he dismissed the crowds.
After doing so, he went up on the mountain by himself
    to pray.

When it was evening he was there alone.
Meanwhile the boat, already a few miles offshore,
  was being tossed about by the waves, for the wind
    was against it.

During the fourth watch of the night,
  he came toward them walking on the sea.
When the disciples saw him walking on the sea
    they were terrified.
"It is a ghost," they said, and they cried out in fear.
At once Jesus spoke to them, "Take courage, it is I;
    do not be afraid."

Peter said to him in reply,
  "Lord, if it is you, command me to come to you
    on the water."
He said, "Come."
Peter got out of the boat and began to walk
  on the water toward Jesus.
But when he saw how strong the wind was
    he became frightened;
  and, beginning to sink, he cried out, "Lord, save me!"

Immediately Jesus stretched out his hand
and caught Peter,
and said to him, "O you of little faith,
why did you doubt?"
After they got into the boat, the wind died down.
Those who were in the boat did him homage, saying,
"Truly, you are the Son of God."

116B   NINETEENTH SUNDAY IN ORDINARY TIME

FIRST READING

1 KINGS 19:4–8

STRENGTHENED BY THAT
FOOD, HE WALKED TO
THE MOUNTAIN OF GOD.

Elijah went a day's journey into the desert,
until he came to a broom tree and sat beneath it.
He prayed for death saying:
"This is enough, O LORD!
Take my life, for I am no better than my fathers."

He lay down and fell asleep under the broom tree,
but then an angel touched him and ordered him
to get up and eat.
Elijah looked and there at his head was a hearth cake
and a jug of water.

After he ate and drank, he lay down again,
but the angel of the LORD came back a second time,
touched him, and ordered,
"Get up and eat, else the journey will be too long
for you!"

He got up, ate, and drank;
then strengthened by that food,
he walked forty days and forty nights
to the mountain of God, Horeb.

**RESPONSORIAL
PSALM**

PSALM 34:2–3, 4–5, 6–7,
8–9 (9a)

R. Taste and see the goodness of the Lord.

[This psalm is found on page 448 (lectionary number 174).]

SECOND READING

EPHESIANS 4:30—5:2

WALK IN LOVE,
JUST LIKE CHRIST.

Brothers and sisters:
Do not grieve the Holy Spirit of God,
with which you were sealed for the day of redemption.
All bitterness, fury, anger, shouting, and reviling
must be removed from you, along with all malice.
And be kind to one another, compassionate,
forgiving one another as God has forgiven you in Christ.

So be imitators of God, as beloved children,
  and live in love,
    as Christ loved us and handed himself over for us
    as a sacrificial offering to God for a fragrant aroma.

ALLELUIA

JOHN 6:51

R. Alleluia, alleluia.

*I am the living bread that came down from heaven, says the Lord;
whoever eats this bread will live forever. R.*

GOSPEL

JOHN 6:41–51

I AM THE LIVING BREAD
THAT CAME DOWN FROM
HEAVEN.

The Jews murmured about Jesus because he said,
  "I am the bread that came down from heaven,"
  and they said,
  "Is this not Jesus, the son of Joseph?
Do we not know his father and mother?
Then how can he say,
  'I have come down from heaven'?"

Jesus answered and said to them,
  "Stop murmuring among yourselves.
No one can come to me unless the Father who sent me
    draw him,
  and I will raise him on the last day.
It is written in the prophets:
  They shall all be taught by God.
Everyone who listens to my Father and learns from him
    comes to me.
Not that anyone has seen the Father
  except the one who is from God;
  he has seen the Father.
Amen, amen, I say to you,
  whoever believes has eternal life.

"I am the bread of life.
Your ancestors ate the manna in the desert, but they died;
  this is the bread that comes down from heaven
    so that one may eat it and not die.
I am the living bread that came down from heaven;
  whoever eats this bread will live forever;
    and the bread that I will give is my flesh for the life
      of the world."

FIRST READING

WISDOM 18:6–9

JUST AS YOU PUNISHED
OUR ADVERSARIES,
YOU GLORIFIED US WHOM
YOU HAD SUMMONED.

The night of the passover was known beforehand
    to our fathers,
that, with sure knowledge of the oaths in which they
    put their faith,
they might have courage.

Your people awaited the salvation of the just
    and the destruction of their foes.
For when you punished our adversaries,
    in this you glorified us whom you had summoned.

For in secret the holy children of the good
    were offering sacrifice
and putting into effect with one accord
    the divine institution.

RESPONSORIAL PSALM

PSALM 33:1, 12, 18–19,
20–22 (12b)

R. Blessed the people the Lord has chosen to be his own.

Exult, you just, in the LORD;
    praise from the upright is fitting.
Blessed the nation whose God is the LORD,
    the people he has chosen for his own inheritance.   R.

See, the eyes of the LORD are upon those who fear him,
    upon those who hope for his kindness,
to deliver them from death
    and preserve them in spite of famine.   R.

Our soul waits for the LORD,
    who is our help and our shield.
May your kindness, O LORD, be upon us
    who have put our hope in you.   R.

SECOND READING

LONGER FORM
HEBREWS 11:1–2, 8–19

SHORTER FORM
HEBREWS 11:1–2, 8–12

ABRAHAM LOOKED
FORWARD TO THE CITY
WHOSE ARCHITECT
AND MAKER IS GOD.

[Brothers and sisters:
Faith is the realization of what is hoped for
    and evidence of things not seen.
Because of it the ancients were well attested.

By faith Abraham obeyed when he was called
    to go out to a place
that he was to receive as an inheritance;
he went out, not knowing where he was to go.
By faith he sojourned in the promised land
    as in a foreign country,
dwelling in tents with Isaac and Jacob,
    heirs of the same promise;
for he was looking forward to the city with foundations,
whose architect and maker is God.

By faith he received power to generate,
    even though he was past the normal age
    — and Sarah herself was sterile —
    for he thought that the one who had made
        the promise was trustworthy.
So it was that there came forth from one man,
    himself as good as dead,
    descendants as numerous as the stars in the sky
    and as countless as the sands on the seashore.]

All these died in faith.
They did not receive what had been promised
    but saw it and greeted it from afar
    and acknowledged themselves to be strangers
        and aliens on earth,
    for those who speak thus show that they are seeking
        a homeland.
If they had been thinking of the land from which
        they had come,
    they would have had opportunity to return.
But now they desire a better homeland, a heavenly one.
Therefore, God is not ashamed to be called their God,
    for he has prepared a city for them.

By faith Abraham, when put to the test, offered up Isaac,
    and he who had received the promises was ready
        to offer his only son,
    of whom it was said,
    "Through Isaac descendants shall bear your name."
He reasoned that God was able to raise
        even from the dead,
    and he received Isaac back as a symbol.

R. Alleluia, alleluia.

Stay awake and be ready!
For you do not know on what day your Lord will come.   R.

GOSPEL

LONGER FORM
LUKE 12:32–48

SHORTER FORM
LUKE 12:35–40

YOU ALSO MUST
BE PREPARED.

[Jesus said to his disciples:]
    "Do not be afraid any longer, little flock,
    for your Father is pleased to give you the kingdom.
Sell your belongings and give alms.
Provide money bags for yourselves that do not wear out,
    an inexhaustible treasure in heaven
    that no thief can reach nor moth destroy.
For where your treasure is, there also will your heart be.

["Gird your loins and light your lamps
    and be like servants who await their master's return
        from a wedding,
    ready to open immediately when he comes and knocks.
Blessed are those servants
    whom the master finds vigilant on his arrival.
Amen, I say to you, he will gird himself,
    have them recline at table, and proceed to wait
        on them.
And should he come in the second or third watch
    and find them prepared in this way,
    blessed are those servants.

"Be sure of this:
    if the master of the house had known the hour
    when the thief was coming,
    he would not have let his house be broken into.

"You also must be prepared, for at an hour
        you do not expect,
    the Son of Man will come."]

Then Peter said,
    "Lord, is this parable meant for us or for everyone?"
And the Lord replied,
    "Who, then, is the faithful and prudent steward
    whom the master will put in charge of his servants
    to distribute the food allowance at the proper time?
Blessed is that servant whom his master on arrival
        finds doing so.
Truly, I say to you, the master will put the servant
    in charge of all his property.
But if that servant says to himself,
    'My master is delayed in coming,'
    and begins to beat the menservants and
        the maidservants,
    to eat and drink and get drunk,
    then that servant's master will come
    on an unexpected day and at an unknown hour
    and will punish the servant severely
    and assign him a place with the unfaithful.

"That servant who knew his master's will
    but did not make preparations nor act in accord
        with his will
    shall be beaten severely;
    and the servant who was ignorant of his master's will
    but acted in a way deserving of a severe beating
    shall be beaten only lightly.

"Much will be required of the person entrusted with much, and still more will be demanded of the person entrusted with more."

118A   TWENTIETH SUNDAY IN ORDINARY TIME

FIRST READING

ISAIAH 56:1, 6–7

I WILL BRING FOREIGNERS
TO MY HOLY MOUNTAIN.

Thus says the LORD:
Observe what is right, do what is just;
    for my salvation is about to come,
      my justice, about to be revealed.

The foreigners who join themselves to the LORD,
    ministering to him,
loving the name of the LORD,
    and becoming his servants —
all who keep the sabbath free from profanation
    and hold to my covenant,
them I will bring to my holy mountain
    and make joyful in my house of prayer;
their burnt offerings and sacrifices
    will be acceptable on my altar,
for my house shall be called
    a house of prayer for all peoples.

**RESPONSORIAL
PSALM**

PSALM 67:2–3, 5, 6, 8 (4)

R. O God, let all the nations praise you!

[This psalm is found on page 45 (lectionary number 18).]

SECOND READING

ROMANS 11:13–15, 29–32

THE GIFTS AND THE CALL
OF GOD FOR ISRAEL ARE
IRREVOCABLE.

Brothers and sisters:
I am speaking to you Gentiles.
Inasmuch as I am the apostle to the Gentiles,
    I glory in my ministry in order to make my race jealous
    and thus save some of them.
For if their rejection is the reconciliation of the world,
    what will their acceptance be but life from the dead?

For the gifts and the call of God are irrevocable.
Just as you once disobeyed God
    but have now received mercy because
      of their disobedience,
    so they have now disobeyed in order that,
    by virtue of the mercy shown to you,
    they too may now receive mercy.
For God delivered all to disobedience,
    that he might have mercy upon all.

R. Alleluia, alleluia.

*Jesus proclaimed the Gospel of the kingdom
and cured every disease among the people.   R.*

GOSPEL

MATTHEW 15:21–28

O WOMAN, GREAT IS
YOUR FAITH!

At that time, Jesus withdrew to the region
      of Tyre and Sidon.
And behold, a Canaanite woman of that district came
      and called out,
   "Have pity on me, Lord, Son of David!
My daughter is tormented by a demon."
But Jesus did not say a word in answer to her.

Jesus' disciples came and asked him,
   "Send her away, for she keeps calling out after us."
He said in reply,
   "I was sent only to the lost sheep of the house of Israel."

But the woman came and did Jesus homage, saying,
      "Lord, help me."
He said in reply,
   "It is not right to take the food of the children
   and throw it to the dogs."
She said, "Please, Lord, for even the dogs eat the scraps
   that fall from the table of their masters."

Then Jesus said to her in reply,
   "O woman, great is your faith!
Let it be done for you as you wish."
And the woman's daughter was healed from that hour.

119B   TWENTIETH SUNDAY IN ORDINARY TIME

FIRST READING

PROVERBS 9:1–6

COME, EAT OF MY FOOD
AND DRINK OF THE WINE
I HAVE MIXED.

Wisdom has built her house,
   she has set up her seven columns;
she has dressed her meat, mixed her wine,
   yes, she has spread her table.
She has sent out her maidens; she calls
   from the heights out over the city:
"Let whoever is simple turn in here";
   to the one who lacks understanding, she says,
"Come, eat of my food,
   and drink of the wine I have mixed!
Forsake foolishness that you may live;
   advance in the way of understanding."

PSALM 34:2–3, 10–11, 12–13,
14–15 (9a)

R. *Taste and see the goodness of the Lord.*

[This psalm is found on page 87 (lectionary number 33).]

SECOND READING

EPHESIANS 5:15–20

UNDERSTAND WHAT IS
THE WILL OF THE LORD.

Brothers and sisters:
Watch carefully how you live,
   not as foolish persons but as wise,
   making the most of the opportunity,
   because the days are evil.
Therefore, do not continue in ignorance,
   but try to understand what is the will of the Lord.

And do not get drunk on wine, in which lies debauchery,
   but be filled with the Spirit,
   addressing one another in psalms and hymns
    and spiritual songs,
   singing and playing to the Lord in your hearts,
   giving thanks always and for everything
   in the name of our Lord Jesus Christ to God the Father.

ALLELUIA

JOHN 6:56

R. *Alleluia, alleluia.*

*Whoever eats my flesh and drinks my blood
remains in me and I in him, says the Lord.*   R.

GOSPEL

JOHN 6:51–58

MY FLESH IS TRUE FOOD
AND MY BLOOD IS TRUE
DRINK.

Jesus said to the crowds:
   "I am the living bread that came down from heaven;
   whoever eats this bread will live forever;
   and the bread that I will give
   is my flesh for the life of the world."

The Jews quarreled among themselves, saying,
   "How can this man give us his flesh to eat?"

Jesus said to them,
   "Amen, amen, I say to you,
   unless you eat the flesh of the Son of Man
    and drink his blood,
   you do not have life within you.
Whoever eats my flesh and drinks my blood
   has eternal life,
   and I will raise him on the last day.
For my flesh is true food,
   and my blood is true drink.
Whoever eats my flesh and drinks my blood
   remains in me and I in him.

"Just as the living Father sent me
  and I have life because of the Father,
  so also the one who feeds on me
  will have life because of me.
This is the bread that came down from heaven.
Unlike your ancestors who ate and still died,
  whoever eats this bread will live forever."

120C   TWENTIETH SUNDAY IN ORDINARY TIME

FIRST READING

JEREMIAH 38:4–6, 8–10

A MAN OF STRIFE AND
CONTENTION TO ALL
THE LAND.

In those days, the princes said to the king:
"Jeremiah ought to be put to death;
  he is demoralizing the soldiers who are left in this city,
  and all the people, by speaking such things to them;
  he is not interested in the welfare of our people,
  but in their ruin."

King Zedekiah answered: "He is in your power";
  for the king could do nothing with them.

And so they took Jeremiah
  and threw him into the cistern of Prince Malchiah,
  which was in the quarters of the guard,
  letting him down with ropes.
There was no water in the cistern, only mud,
  and Jeremiah sank into the mud.

Ebed-melech, a court official,
  went there from the palace and said to him:
"My lord king,
  these men have been at fault
  in all they have done to the prophet Jeremiah,
  casting him into the cistern.
He will die of famine on the spot,
  for there is no more food in the city."
Then the king ordered Ebed-melech the Cushite
  to take three men along with him,
  and draw the prophet Jeremiah out of the cistern
    before he should die.

**RESPONSORIAL
PSALM**

PSALM 40:2, 3, 4, 18 (14b)

R. Lord, come to my aid!

*I have waited, waited for the Lord,
  and he stooped toward me.   R.*

The Lord heard my cry.
He drew me out of the pit of destruction,
    out of the mud of the swamp;
he set my feet upon a crag;
    he made firm my steps.   R.

And he put a new song into my mouth,
    a hymn to our God.
Many shall look on in awe
    and trust in the Lord.   R.

Though I am afflicted and poor,
    yet the Lord thinks of me.
You are my help and my deliverer;
    O my God, hold not back!   R.

SECOND READING

HEBREWS 12:1–4

LET US PERSEVERE
IN RUNNING THE RACE
THAT LIES BEFORE US.

Brothers and sisters:
Since we are surrounded by so great a cloud of witnesses,
    let us rid ourselves of every burden and sin
        that clings to us
    and persevere in running the race that lies before us
    while keeping our eyes fixed on Jesus,
    the leader and perfecter of faith.
For the sake of the joy that lay before him
    he endured the cross, despising its shame,
    and has taken his seat at the right of the throne of God.

Consider how he endured such opposition from sinners,
    in order that you may not grow weary and lose heart.
In your struggle against sin
    you have not yet resisted to the point of shedding blood.

ALLELUIA

JOHN 10:27

R. Alleluia, alleluia.

My sheep hear my voice, says the Lord;
I know them, and they follow me.   R.

GOSPEL

LUKE 12:49–53

I HAVE COME NOT TO
ESTABLISH PEACE, BUT
RATHER DIVISION.

Jesus said to his disciples:
    "I have come to set the earth on fire,
    and how I wish it were already blazing!
There is a baptism with which I must be baptized,
    and how great is my anguish until it is accomplished!

"Do you think that I have come to establish peace
        on the earth?
No, I tell you, but rather division.
From now on a household of five will be divided,
    three against two and two against three;
    a father will be divided against his son

and a son against his father,
a mother against her daughter
and a daughter against her mother,
a mother-in-law against her daughter-in-law
and a daughter-in-law against her mother-in-law."

121A   TWENTY-FIRST SUNDAY IN ORDINARY TIME

FIRST READING

ISAIAH 22:19–23

I WILL PLACE THE KEY
OF THE HOUSE OF DAVID
UPON HIS SHOULDER.

Thus says the Lord to Shebna, master of the palace:
"I will thrust you from your office
    and pull you down from your station.
On that day I will summon my servant
    Eliakim, son of Hilkiah;
I will clothe him with your robe,
    and gird him with your sash,
    and give over to him your authority.
He shall be a father to the inhabitants of Jerusalem,
    and to the house of Judah.

"I will place the key of the House of David
        on Eliakim's shoulder;
    when he opens, no one shall shut
    when he shuts, no one shall open.
I will fix him like a peg in a sure spot,
    to be a place of honor for his family."

**RESPONSORIAL
PSALM**

PSALM 138:1–2, 2–3, 6,
8 (8bc)

R. Lord, your love is eternal; do not forsake the work of your hands.

*I will give thanks to you, O Lord, with all my heart,
    for you have heard the words of my mouth;
in the presence of the angels I will sing your praise;
    I will worship at your holy temple.   R.*

*I will give thanks to your name,
    because of your kindness and your truth:
When I called, you answered me;
    you built up strength within me.   R.*

*The Lord is exalted, yet the lowly he sees,
    and the proud he knows from afar.
Your kindness, O Lord, endures forever;
    forsake not the work of your hands.   R.*

SECOND READING

ROMANS 11:33–36

FROM GOD AND THROUGH
HIM AND FOR HIM ARE
ALL THINGS.

Oh, the depth of the riches and wisdom and
        knowledge of God!
How inscrutable are his judgments and
        how unsearchable his ways!

For who has known the mind of the Lord
or who has been his counselor?
Or who has given the Lord anything
that he may be repaid?
For from him and through him and for him are all things.
To him be glory forever. Amen.

ALLELUIA

MATTHEW 16:18

R. Alleluia, alleluia.

You are Peter and upon this rock I will build my Church,
and the gates of the netherworld shall not prevail against it.   R.

GOSPEL

MATTHEW 16:13–20

YOU ARE PETER, AND TO
YOU I WILL GIVE THE KEYS
OF THE KINGDOM OF
HEAVEN.

Jesus went into the region of Caesarea Philippi
    and he asked his disciples,
    "Who do people say that the Son of Man is?"
They replied, "Some say John the Baptist, others Elijah,
    still others Jeremiah or one of the prophets."

He said to them, "But who do you say that I am?"
Simon Peter said in reply,
    "You are the Christ, the Son of the living God."

Jesus said to him in reply,
    "Blessed are you, Simon son of Jonah.
For flesh and blood has not revealed this to you,
    but my heavenly Father.
And so I say to you, you are Peter,
    and upon this rock I will build my church,
    and the gates of the netherworld shall not prevail
        against it.
I will give you the keys to the kingdom of heaven.
Whatever you bind on earth shall be bound in heaven;
    and whatever you loose on earth shall be loosed
        in heaven."
Then he strictly ordered his disciples
    to tell no one that he was the Christ.

122B   TWENTY-FIRST SUNDAY IN ORDINARY TIME

FIRST READING

JOSHUA 24:1–2a, 15–17, 18b

WE WILL SERVE THE LORD,
FOR HE IS OUR GOD.

Joshua gathered together all the tribes of Israel
    at Shechem,
    summoning their elders, their leaders,
    their judges, and their officers.
When they stood in ranks before God,
    Joshua addressed all the people:

"If it does not please you to serve the Lord,
decide today whom you will serve,
the gods your fathers served beyond the River
or the gods of the Amorites in whose country
you are now dwelling.
As for me and my household, we will serve the Lord."

But the people answered,
"Far be it from us to forsake the Lord
for the service of other gods.
For it was the Lord, our God,
who brought us and our fathers up out of the land
of Egypt,
out of a state of slavery.
He performed those great miracles before our very eyes
and protected us along our entire journey
and among the peoples through whom we passed.
Therefore we also will serve the Lord, for he is our God."

RESPONSORIAL
PSALM

PSALM 34:2–3, 16–17, 18–19,
20–21, 22–23 (9a)

R. Taste and see the goodness of the Lord.

I will bless the Lord at all times;
    his praise shall be ever in my mouth.
Let my soul glory in the Lord;
    the lowly will hear me and be glad.   R.

The Lord has eyes for the just,
    and ears for their cry.
The Lord confronts the evildoers,
    to destroy remembrance of them from the earth.   R.

When the just cry out, the Lord hears them,
    and from all their distress he rescues them.
The Lord is close to the brokenhearted;
    and those who are crushed in spirit he saves.   R.

Many are the troubles of the just one,
    but out of them all the Lord delivers him;
he watches over all his bones;
    not one of them shall be broken.   R.

SECOND READING

LONGER FORM
EPHESIANS 5:21–32

SHORTER FORM
EPHESIANS 5:2A, 25–32

THIS IS A GREAT MYSTERY,
REGARDING CHRIST AND
THE CHURCH.

[Brothers and sisters:]
Be subordinate to one another out of reverence for Christ.
Wives should be subordinate to their husbands
    as to the Lord.
For the husband is head of his wife
    just as Christ is head of the church,
    he himself the savior of the body.
As the church is subordinate to Christ,
    so wives should be subordinate to their husbands
    in everything.

[Husbands, love your wives,
   even as Christ loved the church
   and handed himself over for her to sanctify her,
   cleansing her by the bath of water with the word,
   that he might present to himself the church in splendor,
   without spot or wrinkle or any such thing,
   that she might be holy and without blemish.

So also husbands should love their wives
   as their own bodies.
He who loves his wife loves himself.
For no one hates his own flesh
   but rather nourishes and cherishes it,
   even as Christ does the church,
   because we are members of his body.
For this reason a man shall leave his father and his mother
   and be joined to his wife,
   and the two shall become one flesh.

This is a great mystery,
   but I speak in reference to Christ and the church.]

ALLELUIA

JOHN 6:63c, 68c

R. Alleluia, alleluia.

Your words, Lord, are Spirit and life;
you have the words of everlasting life.   R.

GOSPEL

JOHN 6:60–69

TO WHOM SHALL WE GO?
YOU HAVE THE WORDS OF
ETERNAL LIFE.

Many of Jesus'disciples who were listening said,
"This saying is hard; who can accept it?"

Since Jesus knew that his disciples were murmuring
      about this,
   he said to them, "Does this shock you?
What if you were to see the Son of Man ascending
   to where he was before?
It is the spirit that gives life,
   while the flesh is of no avail.
The words I have spoken to you are Spirit and life.
But there are some of you who do not believe."
Jesus knew from the beginning the ones
      who would not believe
   and the one who would betray him.

And he said,
"For this reason I have told you that no one
      can come to me
   unless it is granted him by my Father."

As a result of this,
    many of his disciples returned to their former way of life
    and no longer accompanied him.
Jesus then said to the Twelve, "Do you also want to leave?"

Simon Peter answered him, "Master, to whom shall we go?
You have the words of eternal life.
We have come to believe
    and are convinced that you are the Holy One of God."

123C   TWENTY-FIRST SUNDAY IN ORDINARY TIME

FIRST READING

ISAIAH 66:18–21

THEY SHALL BRING ALL
YOUR BROTHERS AND
SISTERS FROM ALL THE
NATIONS.

Thus says the LORD:
I know their works and their thoughts,
and I come to gather nations of every language;
    they shall come and see my glory.

I will set a sign among them;
    from them I will send fugitives to the nations:
    to Tarshish, Put and Lud, Mosoch, Tubal and Javan,
    to the distant coastlands
    that have never heard of my fame, or seen my glory;
    and they shall proclaim my glory among the nations.

They shall bring all your brothers and sisters
        from all the nations
    as an offering to the LORD,
    on horses and in chariots, in carts, upon mules
        and dromedaries,
    to Jerusalem, my holy mountain, says the LORD,
    just as the Israelites bring their offering
    to the house of the LORD in clean vessels.

Some of these I will take as priests and Levites,
    says the LORD.

**RESPONSORIAL
PSALM**

PSALM 117:1, 2 (MARK 16:15)

R. Go out to all the world and tell the Good News.
or
R. Alleluia.

[This psalm is found on page 259 (lectionary number 87).]

Brothers and sisters,
You have forgotten the exhortation addressed to you
       as children:
"My son, do not disdain the discipline of the Lord
    or lose heart when reproved by him;
    for whom the Lord loves, he disciplines;
    he scourges every son he acknowledges."

Endure your trials as "discipline";
    God treats you as sons.
For what "son" is there whom his father
       does not discipline?

At the time,
    all discipline seems a cause not for joy but for pain,
    yet later it brings the peaceful fruit of righteousness
    to those who are trained by it.

So strengthen your drooping hands and your weak knees.
Make straight paths for your feet,
    that what is lame may not be disjointed but healed.

R. Alleluia, alleluia.

I am the way, the truth and the life, says the Lord;
no one comes to the Father, except through me.   R.

GOSPEL

LUKE 13:22–30

THEY WILL COME FROM
EAST AND WEST AND
RECLINE AT TABLE IN
THE KINGDOM OF GOD.

Jesus passed through towns and villages,
    teaching as he went and making his way to Jerusalem.
Someone asked him,
"Lord, will only a few people be saved?"

He answered them,
"Strive to enter through the narrow gate,
    for many, I tell you, will attempt to enter
    but will not be strong enough.

"After the master of the house has arisen
       and locked the door,
    then will you stand outside knocking and saying,
    'Lord, open the door for us.'
He will say to you in reply,
    'I do not know where you are from.'

"And you will say,
    'We ate and drank in your company and you taught
       in our streets.'

Then he will say to you,
  'I do not know where you are from.
Depart from me, all you evildoers!'

"And there will be wailing and grinding of teeth
  when you see Abraham, Isaac, and Jacob
  and all the prophets in the kingdom of God
  and you yourselves cast out.
And people will come from the east and the west
  and from the north and the south
  and will recline at table in the kingdom of God.

"For behold, some are last who will be first,
  and some are first who will be last."

124A TWENTY-SECOND SUNDAY IN ORDINARY TIME

FIRST READING

JEREMIAH 20:7–9

THE WORD OF THE
LORD HAS BROUGHT
ME DERISION.

You duped me, O LORD, and I let myself be duped;
  you were too strong for me, and you triumphed.
All the day I am an object of laughter;
  everyone mocks me.

Whenever I speak, I must cry out,
  violence and outrage is my message;
the word of the LORD has brought me
  derision and reproach all the day.

I say to myself, I will not mention him,
  I will speak in his name no more.
But then it becomes like fire burning in my heart,
  imprisoned in my bones;
I grow weary holding it in, I cannot endure it.

**RESPONSORIAL
PSALM**

PSALM 63:2, 3–4, 5–6, 8–9
(2b)

R. My soul is thirsting for you, O Lord my God.

[This psalm is found on page 448 (lectionary number 174).]

SECOND READING

ROMANS 12:1–2

OFFER YOUR BODIES
AS A LIVING SACRIFICE.

I urge you, brothers and sisters, by the mercies of God,
  to offer your bodies as a living sacrifice,
  holy and pleasing to God, your spiritual worship.
Do not conform yourselves to this age
  but be transformed by the renewal of your mind,
  that you may discern what is the will of God,
  what is good and pleasing and perfect.

ALLELUIA

SEE EPHESIANS 1:17–18

R. *Alleluia, alleluia.*

May the Father of our Lord Jesus Christ
enlighten the eyes of our hearts,
that we may know what is the hope
that belongs to our call. R.

GOSPEL

MATTHEW 16:21–27

WHOEVER WISHES TO
COME AFTER ME MUST
DENY HIMSELF.

Jesus began to show his disciples
    that he must go to Jerusalem and suffer greatly
    from the elders, the chief priests, and the scribes,
    and be killed and on the third day be raised.

Then Peter took Jesus aside and began to rebuke him,
    "God forbid, Lord! No such thing shall ever happen
        to you."
He turned and said to Peter,
    "Get behind me, Satan! You are an obstacle to me.
You are thinking not as God does,
        but as human beings do."

Then Jesus said to his disciples,
    "Whoever wishes to come after me must deny himself,
    take up his cross, and follow me.
For whoever wishes to save his life will lose it,
    but whoever loses his life for my sake will find it.
What profit would there be for one to gain
        the whole world
    and forfeit his life?
Or what can one give in exchange for his life?

"For the Son of Man will come with his angels
        in his Father's glory,
    and then he will repay all according to his conduct."

125B   TWENTY-SECOND SUNDAY IN ORDINARY TIME

FIRST READING

DEUTERONOMY 4:1–2, 6–8

YOU SHALL NOT ADD TO
WHAT I COMMAND YOU.
KEEP THE COMMANDS
OF THE LORD.

Moses said to the people:
"Now, Israel, hear the statutes and decrees
    which I am teaching you to observe,
        that you may live, and may enter in and take possession
        of the land
    which the LORD, the God of your fathers, is giving you.
In your observance of the commandments of the LORD,
        your God,
    which I enjoin upon you,
        you shall not add to what I command you
            nor subtract from it.

"Observe them carefully,
    for thus will you give evidence
    of your wisdom and intelligence to the nations,
    who will hear of all these statutes and say,
    'This great nation is truly a wise and intelligent people.'
For what great nation is there
    that has gods so close to it as the LORD, our God,
        is to us
    whenever we call upon him?
Or what great nation has statutes and decrees
    that are as just as this whole law
    which I am setting before you today?"

RESPONSORIAL PSALM

PSALM 15:2–3, 3–4, 4–5 (1a)

R. The one who does justice will live in the presence of the Lord.

[This psalm is found on page 303 (lectionary number 108).]

SECOND READING

JAMES 1:17–18, 21B–22, 27

BE DOERS OF THE WORD.

Dearest brothers and sisters:
All good giving and every perfect gift is from above,
    coming down from the Father of lights,
        with whom there is no alteration or shadow caused
          by change.
He willed to give us birth by the word of truth
    that we may be a kind of firstfruits of his creatures.

Humbly welcome the word that has been planted in you
    and is able to save your souls.
Be doers of the word and not hearers only,
        deluding yourselves.
Religion that is pure and undefiled before God
        and the Father is this:
    to care for orphans and widows in their affliction
    and to keep oneself unstained by the world.

ALLELUIA

JAMES 1:18

R. Alleluia, alleluia.

The Father willed to give us birth by the word of truth
that we may be a kind of firstfruits of his creatures.   R.

GOSPEL

MARK 7:1–8, 14–15, 21–23

YOU DISREGARD GOD'S COMMANDMENT BUT CLING TO HUMAN TRADITION.

When the Pharisees with some scribes who had come
      from Jerusalem
    gathered around Jesus,
    they observed that some of his disciples ate their meals
    with unclean, that is, unwashed, hands.

(For the Pharisees and, in fact, all Jews,
  do not eat without carefully washing their hands,
  keeping the tradition of the elders.
And on coming from the marketplace
  they do not eat without purifying themselves.
And there are many other things that they
    have traditionally observed,
  the purification of cups and jugs and kettles and beds.)
So the Pharisees and scribes questioned him,
"Why do your disciples not follow the tradition
    of the elders
  but instead eat a meal with unclean hands?"

He responded,
"Well did Isaiah prophesy about you hypocrites,
    as it is written:
  This people honors me with their lips,
  but their hearts are far from me;
  in vain do they worship me,
  teaching as doctrines human precepts.
You disregard God's commandment but cling
    to human tradition."

He summoned the crowd again and said to them,
"Hear me, all of you, and understand.
Nothing that enters one from outside can defile
    that person;
  but the things that come out from within
    are what defile.

"From within people, from their hearts,
  come evil thoughts, unchastity, theft, murder,
  adultery, greed, malice, deceit,
  licentiousness, envy, blasphemy, arrogance, folly.
All these evils come from within and they defile."

126C   TWENTY-SECOND SUNDAY IN ORDINARY TIME

FIRST READING

SIRACH 3:17–18, 20, 28–29

HUMBLE YOURSELF AND
YOU WILL FIND FAVOR
WITH GOD.

My child, conduct your affairs with humility,
  and you will be loved more than a giver of gifts.
Humble yourself the more, the greater you are,
  and you will find favor with God.
What is too sublime for you, seek not,
  into things beyond your strength search not.

The mind of a sage appreciates proverbs,
  and an attentive ear is the joy of the wise.

Water quenches a flaming fire,
and alms atone for sins.

RESPONSORIAL PSALM

PSALM 68:4–5, 6–7, 10–11
(SEE 11b)

R. *God, in your goodness, you have made a home for the poor.*

The just rejoice and exult before God;
they are glad and rejoice.
Sing to God, chant praise to his name;
whose name is the LORD. R.

The father of orphans and the defender of widows
is God in his holy dwelling.
God gives a home to the forsaken;
he leads forth prisoners to prosperity. R.

A bountiful rain you showered down, O God, upon your inheritance;
you restored the land when it languished;
your flock settled in it;
in your goodness, O God, you provided it for the needy. R.

SECOND READING

HEBREWS 12:18–19, 22–24a

YOU HAVE APPROACHED
MOUNT ZION AND THE
CITY OF THE LIVING GOD.

Brothers and sisters:
You have not approached that which could be touched
and a blazing fire and gloomy darkness
and storm and a trumpet blast
and a voice speaking words such that those who heard
begged that no message be further addressed to them.

No, you have approached Mount Zion
and the city of the living God, the heavenly Jerusalem,
and countless angels in festal gathering,
and the assembly of the firstborn enrolled in heaven,
and God the judge of all,
and the spirits of the just made perfect,
and Jesus, the mediator of a new covenant,
and the sprinkled blood that speaks more eloquently
than that of Abel.

ALLELUIA

MATTHEW 11:29ab

R. *Alleluia, alleluia.*

Take my yoke upon you, says the Lord,
and learn from me, for I am meek and humble of heart. R.

GOSPEL

LUKE 14:1, 7–14

EVERYONE WHO EXALTS
HIMSELF WILL BE HUMBLED,
EVERYONE WHO HUMBLES
HIMSELF WILL BE EXALTED.

On a sabbath Jesus went to dine
at the home of one of the leading Pharisees,
and the people there were observing him carefully.

He told a parable to those who had been invited,
noticing how they were choosing the places of honor
at the table.

"When you are invited by someone to a wedding banquet,
  do not recline at table in the place of honor.
A more distinguished guest than you may have been
      invited by him,
  and the host who invited both of you may approach
      you and say,
  'Give your place to this man,'
  and then you would proceed with embarrassment
  to take the lowest place.

"Rather, when you are invited,
  go and take the lowest place
  so that when the host comes to you he may say,
  'My friend, move up to a higher position.'
Then you will enjoy the esteem of your companions
      at the table.
For every one who exalts himself will be humbled,
  but the one who humbles himself will be exalted."

Then he said to the host who invited him,
  "When you hold a lunch or a dinner,
  do not invite your friends or your brothers
  or your relatives or your wealthy neighbors,
  in case they may invite you back and you
      have repayment.
Rather, when you hold a banquet,
  invite the poor, the crippled, the lame, the blind;
  blessed indeed will you be because of their inability
      to repay you.
For you will be repaid at the resurrection
      of the righteous."

127A TWENTY-THIRD SUNDAY IN ORDINARY TIME

FIRST READING

EZEKIEL 33:7–9

IF YOU DO NOT SPEAK OUT
TO DISSUADE THE WICKED
FROM HIS WAY, I WILL
HOLD YOU RESPONSIBLE
FOR HIS DEATH.

Thus says the LORD:
You, son of man, I have appointed watchman
      for the house of Israel;
  when you hear me say anything, you shall warn
      them for me.

If I tell the wicked, "O wicked one, you shall surely die,"
  and you do not speak out to dissuade the wicked
      from his way,
  the wicked shall die for his guilt,
  but I will hold you responsible for his death.

But if you warn the wicked,
    trying to turn him from his way,
    and he refuses to turn from his way,
    he shall die for his guilt,
    but you shall save yourself.

RESPONSORIAL PSALM

PSALM 95:1–2, 6–7, 8–9 (8)

R. If today you hear his voice, harden not your hearts.

[This psalm is found on page 448 (lectionary number 174).]

SECOND READING

ROMANS 13:8–10

LOVE IS THE FULFILLMENT OF THE LAW.

Brothers and sisters:
Owe nothing to anyone, except to love one another;
    for the one who loves another has fulfilled the law.

The commandments, "You shall not commit adultery;
    you shall not kill; you shall not steal;
        you shall not covet,"
    and whatever other commandment there may be,
    are summed up in this saying, namely,
    "You shall love your neighbor as yourself."

Love does no evil to the neighbor;
    hence, love is the fulfillment of the law.

ALLELUIA

2 CORINTHIANS 5:19

R. Alleluia, alleluia.

*God was reconciling the world to himself in Christ
and entrusting to us the message of reconciliation.*   *R.*

GOSPEL

MATTHEW 18:15–20

IF YOUR BROTHER OR SISTER LISTENS TO YOU, YOU HAVE WON THEM OVER.

Jesus said to his disciples:
"If your brother sins against you,
    go and tell him his fault between you and him alone.
If he listens to you, you have won over your brother.
If he does not listen,
    take one or two others along with you,
    so that 'every fact may be established
    on the testimony of two or three witnesses.'
If he refuses to listen to them, tell the church.
If he refuses to listen even to the church,
    then treat him as you would a Gentile or a tax collector.

"Amen, I say to you,
    whatever you bind on earth shall be bound in heaven,
    and whatever you loose on earth shall be loosed
        in heaven.

Again, amen, I say to you,
   if two of you agree on earth
   about anything for which they are to pray,
   it shall be granted to them by my heavenly Father.
For where two or three are gathered together in my name,
   there am I in the midst of them."

128B   TWENTY-THIRD SUNDAY IN ORDINARY TIME

FIRST READING

ISAIAH 35:4–7a

THE EARS OF THOSE WHO
ARE DEAF WILL BE
CLEARED; AND THE
TONGUE OF THOSE WHO
ARE MUTE WILL SING.

Thus says the LORD:
Say to those whose hearts are frightened:
   Be strong, fear not!
Here is your God,
   he comes with vindication;
with divine recompense
   he comes to save you.

Then will the eyes of the blind be opened,
   the ears of the deaf be cleared;
then will the lame leap like a stag,
   then the tongue of the mute will sing.

Streams will burst forth in the desert,
   and rivers in the steppe.
The burning sands will become pools,
   and the thirsty ground, springs of water.

**RESPONSORIAL
PSALM**

PSALM 146:7, 8–9, 9–10 (1B)

R. *Praise the Lord, my soul!*
   or:
R. *Alleluia.*

[This psalm is found on page 15 (lectionary number 7).]

SECOND READING

JAMES 2:1–5

DID NOT GOD CHOOSE
THE POOR TO BE HEIRS
OF THE KINGDOM?

My brothers and sisters, show no partiality
   as you adhere to the faith in our glorious
      Lord Jesus Christ.
For if a man with gold rings and fine clothes
   comes into your assembly,
   and a poor person in shabby clothes also comes in,
   and you pay attention to the one wearing
      the fine clothes
   and say, "Sit here, please,"
   while you say to the poor one, "Stand there,"
      or "Sit at my feet,"

have you not made distinctions among yourselves
and become judges with evil designs?

Listen, my beloved brothers and sisters.
Did not God choose those who are poor in the world
    to be rich in faith and heirs of the kingdom
    that he promised to those who love him?

ALLELUIA

SEE MATTHEW 4:23

R. Alleluia, alleluia.

*Jesus proclaimed the Gospel of the kingdom
and cured every disease among the people.* R.

GOSPEL

MARK 7:31–37

HE MAKES THE DEAF HEAR
AND THE MUTE SPEAK.

Again Jesus left the district of Tyre
    and went by way of Sidon to the Sea of Galilee,
    into the district of the Decapolis.

And people brought to him a deaf man who had
        a speech impediment
    and begged him to lay his hand on him.
He took him off by himself away from the crowd.
He put his finger into the man's ears
    and, spitting, touched his tongue;
    then he looked up to heaven and groaned,
        and said to him,
    "*Ephphatha!*" — that is, "Be opened!"
And immediately the man's ears were opened,
    his speech impediment was removed,
    and he spoke plainly.

He ordered them not to tell anyone.
But the more he ordered them not to,
    the more they proclaimed it.
They were exceedingly astonished and they said,
    "He has done all things well.
He makes the deaf hear and the mute speak."

129C   TWENTY-THIRD SUNDAY IN ORDINARY TIME

FIRST READING

WISDOM 9:13–18b

WHO CAN CONCEIVE
WHAT THE LORD INTENDS?

Who can know God's counsel,
    or who can conceive what the LORD intends?
For the deliberations of mortals are timid,
    and unsure are our plans.

For the corruptible body burdens the soul
    and the earthen shelter weighs down the mind
        that has many concerns.

And scarce do we guess the things on earth,
    and what is within our grasp we find with difficulty;
    but when things are in heaven, who can search
        them out?
Or who ever knew your counsel, except you
        had given wisdom
and sent your holy spirit from on high?
And thus were the paths of those on earth made straight.

RESPONSORIAL PSALM

PSALM 90:3–4, 5–6, 12–13, 14–17 (1)

R. In every age, O Lord, you have been our refuge.

[This psalm is found on page 316 (lectionary number 114).]

SECOND READING

PHILEMON 9–10, 12–17

RECEIVE HIM NO LONGER AS A SLAVE BUT AS A BELOVED BROTHER.

I, Paul, an old man,
    and now also a prisoner for Christ Jesus,
    urge you on behalf of my child Onesimus,
    whose father I have become in my imprisonment;
    I am sending him, that is, my own heart, back to you.

I should have liked to retain him for myself,
    so that he might serve me on your behalf
    in my imprisonment for the gospel,
    but I did not want to do anything without your consent,
    so that the good you do might not be forced
        but voluntary.

Perhaps this is why he was away from you for a while,
    that you might have him back forever,
    no longer as a slave
    but more than a slave, a brother,
    beloved especially to me, but even more so to you,
    as a man and in the Lord.

So if you regard me as a partner, welcome him
        as you would me.

ALLELUIA

PSALM 119:135

R. Alleluia, alleluia.

*Let your face shine upon your servant;
and teach me your laws.   R.*

GOSPEL

LUKE 14:25–33

ANYONE OF YOU WHO
DOES NOT RENOUNCE ALL
POSSESSIONS CANNOT BE
MY DISCIPLE.

Great crowds were traveling with Jesus,
    and he turned and addressed them,
    "If anyone comes to me without hating his father
        and mother,
    wife and children, brothers and sisters,
    and even his own life,
        he cannot be my disciple.
Whoever does not carry his own cross and come after me
    cannot be my disciple.

"Which of you wishing to construct a tower
    does not first sit down and calculate the cost
    to see if there is enough for its completion?
Otherwise, after laying the foundation
    and finding himself unable to finish the work
    the onlookers should laugh at him and say,
    'This one began to build but did not have
        the resources to finish.'

"Or what king marching into battle would not
        first sit down
    and decide whether with ten thousand troops
    he can successfully oppose another king
    advancing upon him with twenty thousand troops?
But if not, while he is still far away,
    he will send a delegation to ask for peace terms.

"In the same way,
    anyone of you who does not renounce all his possessions
    cannot be my disciple."

130A TWENTY-FOURTH SUNDAY IN ORDINARY TIME

FIRST READING

SIRACH 27:30 — 28:7

FORGIVE YOUR
NEIGHBOR'S INJUSTICE;
THEN WHEN YOU PRAY,
YOUR OWN SINS WILL BE
FORGIVEN.

Wrath and anger are hateful things,
    yet the sinner hugs them tight.
The vengeful will suffer the LORD's vengeance,
    for he remembers their sins in detail.
Forgive your neighbor's injustice;
    then when you pray, your own sins will be forgiven.

Could anyone nourish anger against another
    and expect healing from the LORD?
Could anyone refuse mercy to another like himself,
    can he seek pardon for his own sins?
If one who is but flesh cherishes wrath,
    who will forgive his sins?

Remember your last days, set enmity aside;
   remember death and decay, and cease from sin!
Think of the commandments, hate not your neighbor;
   remember the Most High's covenant,
     and overlook faults.

RESPONSORIAL PSALM

PSALM 103:1–2, 3–4, 9–10, 11–12 (8)

*R. The Lord is kind and merciful, slow to anger,
   and rich in compassion.*

*Bless the Lord, O my soul;
   and all my being, bless his holy name.
Bless the Lord, O my soul,
   and forget not all his benefits. R.*

*He pardons all your iniquities,
   heals all your ills.
redeems your life from destruction,
   he crowns you with kindness and compassion. R.*

*He will not always chide,
   nor does he keep his wrath forever.
Not according to our sins does he deal with us,
   nor does he requite us according to our crimes. R.*

*For as the heavens are high above the earth,
   so surpassing is his kindness toward those who fear him.
As far as the east is from the west,
   so far has he put our transgressions from us. R.*

SECOND READING

ROMANS 14:7–9

WHETHER WE LIVE OR DIE, WE ARE THE LORD'S.

Brothers and sisters:
None of us lives for oneself, and no one dies for oneself.
For if we live, we live for the Lord,
   and if we die, we die for the Lord;
   so then, whether we live or die, we are the Lord's.
For this is why Christ died and came to life,
   that he might be Lord of both the dead and the living.

ALLELUIA

JOHN 13:34

R. Alleluia, alleluia.

*I give you a new commandment, says the Lord;
love one another as I have loved you. R.*

GOSPEL

MATTHEW 18:21–35

I SAY TO YOU, FORGIVE NOT SEVEN TIMES, BUT SEVENTY-SEVEN TIMES.

Peter approached Jesus and asked him,
"Lord, if my brother sins against me,
   how often must I forgive?
As many as seven times?"

Jesus answered, "I say to you, not seven times
   but seventy-seven times.

That is why the kingdom of heaven may be likened
    to a king
  who decided to settle accounts with his servants.
When he began the accounting,
    a debtor was brought before him who owed him
      a huge amount.
Since he had no way of paying it back,
    his master ordered him to be sold,
      along with his wife, his children, and all his property,
    in payment of the debt.
At that, the servant fell down, did him homage, and said,
    'Be patient with me, and I will pay you back in full.'
Moved with compassion the master of that servant
    let him go and forgave him the loan.

"When that servant had left, he found one of his
    fellow servants
  who owed him a much smaller amount.
He seized him and started to choke him, demanding,
    'Pay back what you owe.'
Falling to his knees, his fellow servant begged him,
    'Be patient with me, and I will pay you back.'
But he refused.
Instead, he had the fellow servant put in prison
    until he paid back the debt.

"Now when his fellow servants saw what had happened,
    they were deeply disturbed, and went to their master
    and reported the whole affair.
His master summoned him and said to him,
    'You wicked servant!
I forgave you your entire debt because you begged me to.
Should you not have had pity on your fellow servant,
    as I had pity on you?'
Then in anger his master handed him over
    to the torturers
  until he should pay back the whole debt.

"So will my heavenly Father do to you,
    unless each of you forgives your brother
      from your heart."

FIRST READING

ISAIAH 50:5–9a

I GAVE MY BACK TO THOSE
WHO BEAT ME.

The Lord GOD opens my ear that I may hear;
and I have not rebelled,
    have not turned back.
I gave my back to those who beat me,
    my cheeks to those who plucked my beard;
my face I did not shield
    from buffets and spitting.

The Lord GOD is my help,
    therefore I am not disgraced;
I have set my face like flint,
    knowing that I shall not be put to shame.
He is near who upholds my right;
    if anyone wishes to oppose me,
    let us appear together.

Who disputes my right?
    Let that man confront me.
See, the Lord GOD is my help;
    who will prove me wrong?

**RESPONSORIAL
PSALM**

PSALM 116:1–2, 3–4, 5–6,
8–9 (9)

R. I will walk before the Lord, in the land of the living.
    or:
R. Alleluia.

I love the Lord because he has heard
    my voice in supplication,
because he has inclined his ear to me
    the day I called.   R.

The cords of death encompassed me;
    the snares of the netherworld seized upon me;
    I fell into distress and sorrow,
and I called upon the name of the Lord,
    "O Lord, save my life!"   R.

Gracious is the Lord and just;
    yes, our God is merciful.
The Lord keeps the little ones;
    I was brought low, and he saved me.   R.

For he has freed my soul from death,
    my eyes from tears, my feet from stumbling.
I shall walk before the Lord
    in the land of the living.   R.

SECOND READING

JAMES 2:14–18

FAITH, IF IT DOES NOT
HAVE WORKS, IS DEAD.

What good is it, my brothers and sisters,
    if someone says he has faith but does not have works?
Can that faith save him?

If a brother or sister has nothing to wear
    and has no food for the day,
    and one of you says to them,
    "Go in peace, keep warm, and eat well,"
    but you do not give them the necessities of the body,
    what good is it?
So also faith of itself,
    if it does not have works, is dead.

Indeed someone might say,
    "You have faith and I have works."
Demonstrate your faith to me without works,
    and I will demonstrate my faith to you from my works.

ALLELUIA

GALATIANS 6:14

R. Alleluia, alleluia.

*May I never boast except in the cross of our Lord
through which the world has been crucified to me and I to the world.*   R.

GOSPEL

MARK 8:27–35

YOU ARE THE CHRIST . . .
THE SON OF MAN MUST
SUFFER GREATLY.

Jesus and his disciples set out
    for the villages of Caesarea Philippi.
Along the way he asked his disciples,
    "Who do people say that I am?"
They said in reply,
    "John the Baptist, others Elijah,
    still others one of the prophets."

And he asked them,
    "But who do you say that I am?"
Peter said to him in reply,
    "You are the Christ."
Then he warned them not to tell anyone about him.

He began to teach them
    that the Son of Man must suffer greatly
    and be rejected by the elders, the chief priests,
        and the scribes,
    and be killed, and rise after three days.
He spoke this openly.

Then Peter took him aside and began to rebuke him.
At this he turned around and, looking at his disciples,
    rebuked Peter and said, "Get behind me, Satan.
You are thinking not as God does,
    but as human beings do."

He summoned the crowd with his disciples
and said to them,
"Whoever wishes to come after me must deny himself,
take up his cross, and follow me.
For whoever wishes to save his life will lose it,
but whoever loses his life for my sake
and that of the gospel will save it."

132C   TWENTY-FOURTH SUNDAY IN ORDINARY TIME

FIRST READING

EXODUS 32:7–11, 13–14

THE LORD RELENTED IN
THE PUNISHMENT HE HAD
THREATENED TO INFLICT
ON HIS PEOPLE.

The LORD said to Moses,
"Go down at once to your people,
whom you brought out of the land of Egypt,
for they have become depraved.
They have soon turned aside from the way I pointed
out to them,
making for themselves a molten calf and worshiping it,
sacrificing to it and crying out,
'This is your God, O Israel,
who brought you out of the land of Egypt!'

"I see how stiff-necked this people is," continued
the LORD to Moses.
"Let me alone, then,
that my wrath may blaze up against them
to consume them.
Then I will make of you a great nation."

But Moses implored the LORD, his God, saying,
"Why, O LORD, should your wrath blaze up against
your own people,
whom you brought out of the land of Egypt
with such great power and with so strong a hand?
Remember your servants Abraham, Isaac, and Israel,
and how you swore to them by your own self, saying,
'I will make your descendants as numerous as
the stars in the sky;
and all this land that I promised,
I will give your descendants as their perpetual heritage.'"

So the LORD relented in the punishment
he had threatened to inflict on his people.

RESPONSORIAL PSALM

PSALM 51:3–4, 12–13, 17, 19
(LUKE 15:18)

R. I will rise and go to my father.

Have mercy on me, O God, in your goodness;
*   in the greatness of your compassion wipe out my offense.*
Thoroughly wash me from my guilt
*   and of my sin cleanse me.   R.*

A clean heart create for me, O God,
*   and a steadfast spirit renew within me.*
Cast me not out from your presence,
*   and your holy spirit take not from me.   R.*

O LORD, open my lips,
*   and my mouth shall proclaim your praise.*
My sacrifice, O God, is a contrite spirit;
*   a heart contrite and humbled, O God, you will not spurn.   R.*

SECOND READING

1 TIMOTHY 1:12–17

CHRIST CAME TO SAVE SINNERS.

Beloved:
I am grateful to him who has strengthened me,
    Christ Jesus our Lord,
    because he considered me trustworthy
    in appointing me to the ministry.
I was once a blasphemer and a persecutor and arrogant,
    but I have been mercifully treated
    because I acted out of ignorance in my unbelief.

Indeed, the grace of our Lord has been abundant,
    along with the faith and love that are in Christ Jesus.

This saying is trustworthy and deserves full acceptance:
    Christ Jesus came into the world to save sinners.
Of these I am the foremost.

But for that reason I was mercifully treated,
    so that in me, as the foremost,
    Christ Jesus might display all his patience as an example
    for those who would come to believe in him
        for everlasting life.

To the king of ages, incorruptible, invisible, the only God,
    honor and glory forever and ever. Amen.

ALLELUIA

2 CORINTHIANS 5:19

R. Alleluia, alleluia.

God was reconciling the world to himself in Christ
and entrusting to us the message of reconciliation.   R.

GOSPEL

LONGER FORM
LUKE 15:1–32

SHORTER FORM
LUKE 15:1–10

THERE WILL BE GREAT JOY
IN HEAVEN OVER ONE
SINNER WHO REPENTS.

[Tax collectors and sinners were all drawing near
    to listen to Jesus,
  but the Pharisees and scribes began to complain, saying,
  "This man welcomes sinners and eats with them."

So to them he addressed this parable.
"What man among you having a hundred sheep
    and losing one of them
  would not leave the ninety-nine in the desert
  and go after the lost one until he finds it?
And when he does find it,
  he sets it on his shoulders with great joy
  and, upon his arrival home,
  he calls together his friends and neighbors
    and says to them,
  'Rejoice with me because I have found my lost sheep.'
I tell you, in just the same way
  there will be more joy in heaven over one sinner
    who repents
  than over ninety-nine righteous people
  who have no need of repentance.

"Or what woman having ten coins and losing one
  would not light a lamp and sweep the house,
  searching carefully until she finds it?
And when she does find it,
  she calls together her friends and neighbors
  and says to them,
  'Rejoice with me because I have found the coin
    that I lost.'

"In just the same way, I tell you,
  there will be rejoicing among the angels of God
  over one sinner who repents."]

Then he said,
  "A man had two sons, and the younger son
    said to his father,
  'Father give me the share of your estate that should
    come to me.'
So the father divided the property between them.

"After a few days, the younger son collected all
    his belongings
  and set off to a distant country
  where he squandered his inheritance on a life
    of dissipation.
When he had freely spent everything,
  a severe famine struck that country,
  and he found himself in dire need.

So he hired himself out to one of the local citizens
  who sent him to his farm to tend the swine.
And he longed to eat his fill of the pods on which
    the swine fed,
  but nobody gave him any.

"Coming to his senses he thought,
  'How many of my father's hired workers
  have more than enough food to eat,
  but here am I, dying from hunger.
I shall get up and go to my father and I shall say to him,
  "Father, I have sinned against heaven and against you.
I no longer deserve to be called your son;
  treat me as you would treat one of your hired workers."'

"So he got up and went back to his father.
While he was still a long way off,
  his father caught sight of him,
  and was filled with compassion.
He ran to his son, embraced him and kissed him.
His son said to him,
  'Father, I have sinned against heaven and against you;
  I no longer deserve to be called your son.'

"But his father ordered his servants,
  'Quickly bring the finest robe and put it on him;
  put a ring on his finger and sandals on his feet.
Take the fattened calf and slaughter it.
Then let us celebrate with a feast,
  because this son of mine was dead, and has come
    to life again;
  he was lost, and has been found.'
Then the celebration began.

"Now the older son had been out in the field
  and, on his way back, as he neared the house,
  he heard the sound of music and dancing.
He called one of the servants and asked what
    this might mean.
The servant said to him,
  'Your brother has returned
  and your father has slaughtered the fattened calf
  because he has him back safe and sound.'
He became angry,
  and when he refused to enter the house,
  his father came out and pleaded with him.
He said to his father in reply,
  'Look, all these years I served you
  and not once did I disobey your orders;

yet you never gave me even a young goat to feast
    on with my friends.
But when your son returns,
    who swallowed up your property with prostitutes,
    for him you slaughter the fattened calf.'

"He said to him,
    'My son, you are here with me always;
    everything I have is yours.
But now we must celebrate and rejoice,
    because your brother was dead and has come
        to life again;
    he was lost and has been found.'"

133A   TWENTY-FIFTH SUNDAY IN ORDINARY TIME

FIRST READING

ISAIAH 55:6–9

MY THOUGHTS ARE NOT
YOUR THOUGHTS.

Seek the LORD while he may be found,
    call him while he is near.
Let the scoundrel forsake his way,
    and the wicked his thoughts;
let him turn to the LORD for mercy;
    to our God, who is generous in forgiving.

For my thoughts are not your thoughts,
    nor are your ways my ways, says the LORD.
As high as the heavens are above the earth,
    so high are my ways above your ways
    and my thoughts above your thoughts.

**RESPONSORIAL
PSALM**

PSALM 145:2–3, 8–9,
17–18 (18a)

R. *The Lord is near to all who call upon him.*

Every day will I bless you,
    and I will praise your name forever and ever.
Great is the Lord and highly to be praised;
    his greatness is unsearchable. R.

The Lord is gracious and merciful,
    slow to anger and of great kindness.
The Lord is good to all
    and compassionate toward all his works. R.

The Lord is just in all his ways
    and holy in all his works.
The Lord is near to all who call upon him,
    to all who call upon him in truth. R.

Brothers and sisters:
Christ will be magnified in my body, whether by life
    or by death.
For to me life is Christ, and death is gain.
If I go on living in the flesh,
    that means fruitful labor for me.
And I do not know which I shall choose.
I am caught between the two.
I long to depart this life and be with Christ,
    for that is far better.
Yet that I remain in the flesh
    is more necessary for your benefit.

Only, conduct yourselves in a way worthy of the gospel
    of Christ.

ALLELUIA

SEE ACTS 16:14b

R. Alleluia, alleluia.

Open our hearts, O Lord,
to listen to the words of your Son.   R.

GOSPEL

MATTHEW 20:1–16a

ARE YOU ENVIOUS
BECAUSE I AM GENEROUS?

Jesus told his disciples this parable:
    "The kingdom of heaven is like a landowner
    who went out at dawn to hire laborers for his vineyard.
After agreeing with them for the usual daily wage,
    he sent them into his vineyard.
Going out about nine o'clock,
    the landowner saw others standing idle
        in the marketplace,
    and he said to them, 'You too go into my vineyard,
    and I will give you what is just.'
So they went off.

"And he went out again around noon,
    and around three o'clock, and did likewise.
Going out about five o'clock,
    the landowner found others standing around,
        and said to them,
    'Why do you stand here idle all day?'
They answered, 'Because no one has hired us.'
He said to them, 'You too go into my vineyard.'

"When it was evening the owner of the vineyard
    said to his foreman,
    'Summon the laborers and give them their pay,
    beginning with the last and ending with the first.'

When those who had started about five o'clock came,
    each received the usual daily wage.
So when the first came, they thought that they
      would receive more,
    but each of them also got the usual wage.
And on receiving it they grumbled against the landowner,
      saying,
    'These last ones worked only one hour,
    and you have made them equal to us,
    who bore the day's burden and the heat.'
He said to one of them in reply,
    'My friend, I am not cheating you.
Did you not agree with me for the usual daily wage?
Take what is yours and go.
What if I wish to give this last one the same as you?
Or am I not free to do as I wish with my own money?
Are you envious because I am generous?'

"Thus, the last will be first, and the first will be last."

134B   TWENTY-FIFTH SUNDAY IN ORDINARY TIME

FIRST READING

WISDOM 2:12, 17–20

LET US CONDEMN HIM
TO A SHAMEFUL DEATH.

The wicked say:
Let us beset the just one, because he is obnoxious to us;
    he sets himself against our doings,
      reproaches us for transgressions of the law
      and charges us with violations of our training.

Let us see whether his words be true;
    let us find out what will happen to him.
For if the just one be the son of God, God will defend him
    and deliver him from the hand of his foes.

With revilement and torture let us put the just one
      to the test
    that we may have proof of his gentleness
    and try his patience.
Let us condemn him to a shameful death;
    for according to his own words, God will take care
      of him.

**RESPONSORIAL
PSALM**

PSALM 54:3–4, 5, 6–8 (6b)

R. The Lord upholds my life.

O God, by your name save me,
    and by your might defend my cause.
O God, hear my prayer;
    hearken to the words of my mouth.   R.

For the haughty men have risen up against me,
the ruthless seek my life;
they set not God before their eyes.   R.

Behold, God is my helper;
the Lord sustains my life.
Freely will I offer you sacrifice;
I will praise your name, O Lord, for its goodness.   R.

SECOND READING

JAMES 3:16—4:3

THE FRUIT OF
RIGHTEOUSNESS IS SOWN
IN PEACE FOR THOSE WHO
CULTIVATE PEACE.

Beloved:
Where jealousy and selfish ambition exist,
    there is disorder and every foul practice.
But the wisdom from above is first of all pure,
        then peaceable, gentle, compliant,
        full of mercy and good fruits,
        without inconstancy or insincerity.
And the fruit of righteousness is sown in peace
        for those who cultivate peace.

Where do the wars
        and where do the conflicts among you come from?
Is it not from your passions
        that make war within your members?
You covet but do not possess.
You kill and envy but you cannot obtain;
        you fight and wage war.

You do not possess because you do not ask.
You ask but do not receive,
        because you ask wrongly, to spend it on your passions.

ALLELUIA

SEE 2 THESSALONIANS 2:14

R. Alleluia, alleluia.

God has called us through the Gospel
to possess the glory of our Lord Jesus Christ.   R.

GOSPEL

MARK 9:30–37

THE SON OF MAN IS TO BE
HANDED OVER. WHOEVER
WISHES TO BE FIRST WILL
BE THE SERVANT OF ALL.

Jesus and his disciples left from there and began a journey
        through Galilee,
    but he did not wish anyone to know about it.
He was teaching his disciples and telling them,
    "The Son of Man is to be handed over to men
    and they will kill him,
    and three days after his death the Son of Man will rise."
But they did not understand the saying,
    and they were afraid to question him.

They came to Capernaum and, once inside the house,
   he began to ask them,
   "What were you arguing about on the way?"
But they remained silent.
They had been discussing among themselves on the way
   who was the greatest.

Then he sat down, called the Twelve, and said to them,
   "If anyone wishes to be first,
   he shall be the last of all and the servant of all."

Taking a child, he placed it in the their midst,
   and putting his arms around it, he said to them,
   "Whoever receives one child such as this in my name,
     receives me;
   and whoever receives me,
   receives not me but the One who sent me."

135C   TWENTY-FIFTH SUNDAY IN ORDINARY TIME

FIRST READING

AMOS 8:4–7

AGAINST THOSE WHO BUY
THE POOR FOR MONEY.

Hear this, you who trample upon the needy
   and destroy the poor of the land!
"When will the new moon be over," you ask,
   "that we may sell our grain,
   and the sabbath, that we may display the wheat?
We will diminish the ephah,
   add to the shekel,
   and fix our scales for cheating!
We will buy the lowly for silver,
   and the poor for a pair of sandals;
   even the refuse of the wheat we will sell!"

The Lord has sworn by the pride of Jacob:
   Never will I forget a thing they have done!

RESPONSORIAL PSALM

PSALM 113:1–2, 4–6, 7–8
(SEE 1a, 7b)

R. *Praise the Lord who lifts up the poor.*
   or:
R. *Alleluia.*

Praise, you servants of the Lord,
   praise the name of the Lord.
Blessed be the name of the Lord
   both now and forever. R.

High above all nations is the Lord;
   above the heavens is his glory.
Who is like the Lord, our God, who is enthroned on high
   and looks upon the heavens and the earth below? R.

He raises up the lowly from the dust;
  from the dunghill he lifts up the poor
to seat them with princes,
  with the princes of his own people.   R.

SECOND READING

1 TIMOTHY 2:1–8

LET PRAYERS BE OFFERED
FOR EVERYONE TO GOD
WHO WILLS EVERYONE
TO BE SAVED.

Beloved:
First of all, I ask that supplications, prayers,
    petitions, and thanksgivings be offered for everyone,
    for kings and for all in authority,
    that we may lead a quiet and tranquil life
    in all devotion and dignity.
This is good and pleasing to God our savior,
    who wills everyone to be saved
    and to come to knowledge of the truth.

For there is one God.
There is also one mediator between God and men,
    the man Christ Jesus,
    who gave himself as ransom for all.
This was the testimony at the proper time.

For this I was appointed preacher and apostle
    — I am speaking the truth, I am not lying —
    teacher of the Gentiles in faith and truth.

It is my wish, then, that in every place the men
    should pray,
    lifting up holy hands, without anger or argument.

ALLELUIA

SEE 2 CORINTHIANS 8:9

R. Alleluia, alleluia.

Though our Lord Jesus Christ was rich, he became poor,
so that by his poverty you might become rich.   R.

GOSPEL

LONGER FORM
LUKE 16:1–13

SHORTER FORM
LUKE 16:10–13

YOU CANNOT SERVE BOTH
GOD AND MAMMON.

[Jesus said to his disciples,]
    "A rich man had a steward
    who was reported to him for squandering his property.

"He summoned him and said,
    'What is this I hear about you?
Prepare a full account of your stewardship,
    because you can no longer be my steward.'

"The steward said to himself, 'What shall I do,
    now that my master is taking the position of steward
        away from me?
I am not strong enough to dig and I am ashamed to beg.

I know what I shall do so that,
    when I am removed from the stewardship,
    they may welcome me into their homes.'

"He called in his master's debtors one by one.
To the first he said,
    'How much do you owe my master?'
He replied, 'One hundred measures of olive oil.'
He said to him, 'Here is your promissory note.
Sit down and quickly write one for fifty.'
Then to another the steward said, 'And you,
        how much do you owe?'
He replied, 'One hundred kors of wheat.'
The steward said to him, 'Here is your promissory note;
    write one for eighty.'

"And the master commended that dishonest steward
        for acting prudently.
For the children of this world
    are more prudent in dealing with their own generation
    than are the children of light.

"I tell you, make friends for yourselves with
        dishonest wealth,
    so that when it fails, you will be welcomed into
        eternal dwellings.
[The person who is trustworthy in very small matters
    is also trustworthy in great ones;
        and the person who is dishonest in very small matters
    is also dishonest in great ones.
If, therefore, you are not trustworthy with
        dishonest wealth,
    who will trust you with true wealth?
If you are not trustworthy with what belongs to another,
    who will give you what is yours?

"No servant can serve two masters.
He will either hate one and love the other,
    or be devoted to one and despise the other.
You cannot serve both God and mammon."]

FIRST READING

EZEKIEL 18:25–28

BY TURNING FROM
WICKEDNESS, A WICKED
PERSON SHALL PRESERVE
HIS LIFE.

Thus says the LORD:
You say, "The LORD's way is not fair!"
Hear now, house of Israel:
  Is it my way that is unfair, or rather, are not your
    ways unfair?

When someone virtuous turns away from virtue
    to commit iniquity, and dies,
  it is because of the iniquity he committed that
    he must die.

But if he turns from the wickedness he has committed,
  he does what is right and just,
  he shall preserve his life;
  since he has turned away from all the sins
    that he has committed,
  he shall surely live, he shall not die.

RESPONSORIAL PSALM

PSALM 25:4–5, 6–7,
8–9, (6a)

R. Remember your mercies, O Lord.

[This psalm is found on page 60 (lectionary number 23).]

SECOND READING

LONGER FORM
PHILIPPIANS 2:1–11

SHORTER FORM
PHILIPPIANS 2:1–5

HAVE IN YOU THE SAME
ATTITUDE THAT IS ALSO
IN CHRIST JESUS.

[Brothers and sisters:
If there is any encouragement in Christ,
  any solace in love,
  any participation in the Spirit,
  any compassion and mercy,
  complete my joy by being of the same mind,
    with the same love,
  united in heart, thinking one thing.
Do nothing out of selfishness or out of vainglory;
  rather, humbly regard others as more important
    than yourselves,
  each looking out not for his own interests,
  but also for those of others.

Have in you the same attitude
  that is also in Christ Jesus,]
  Who, though he was in the form of God,
  did not regard equality with God
  something to be grasped.
Rather, he emptied himself,
  taking the form of a slave,
  coming in human likeness;

and found human in appearance,
he humbled himself,
becoming obedient to the point of death,
even death on a cross.

Because of this, God greatly exalted him
and bestowed on him the name
which is above every name,
that at the name of Jesus
every knee should bend,
of those in heaven and on earth and under the earth,
and every tongue confess that
Jesus Christ is Lord,
to the glory of God the Father.

ALLELUIA

JOHN 10:27

R. Alleluia, alleluia.

My sheep hear my voice, says the Lord;
I know them, and they follow me.   R.

GOSPEL

MATTHEW 21:28–32

HE CHANGED HIS MIND
AND WENT. TAX
COLLECTORS AND
PROSTITUTES ARE
ENTERING THE KINGDOM
OF HEAVEN BEFORE YOU.

Jesus said to the chief priests and elders of the people:
"What is your opinion?
A man had two sons.
He came to the first and said,
    'Son, go out and work in the vineyard today.'
He said in reply, 'I will not,'
    but afterwards changed his mind and went.
The man came to the other son and gave the same order.
He said in reply, 'Yes, sir,' but did not go.
Which of the two did his father's will?"
They answered, "The first."

Jesus said to them, "Amen, I say to you,
    tax collectors and prostitutes
    are entering the kingdom of God before you.
When John came to you in the way of righteousness,
    you did not believe him;
    but tax collectors and prostitutes did.
Yet even when you saw that,
    you did not later change your minds and believe him."

FIRST READING

NUMBERS 11:25-29

ARE YOU JEALOUS FOR MY
SAKE? WOULD THAT ALL
THE PEOPLE OF THE LORD
WERE PROPHETS!

The LORD came down in the cloud and spoke to Moses.
Taking some of the spirit that was on Moses,
   the Lord bestowed it on the seventy elders;
   and as the spirit came to rest on them, they prophesied.

Now two men, one named Eldad and the other Medad,
   were not in the gathering but had been left in the camp.
They too had been on the list, but had not gone out
     to the tent;
   yet the spirit came to rest on them also,
   and they prophesied in the camp.

So, when a young man quickly told Moses,
   "Eldad and Medad are prophesying in the camp,"
   Joshua, son of Nun, who from his youth had been
     Moses' aide, said,
   "Moses, my lord, stop them."

But Moses answered him,
   "Are you jealous for my sake?
Would that all the people of the LORD were prophets!
Would that the LORD might bestow his spirit on them all!"

**RESPONSORIAL
PSALM**

PSALM 19:8, 10, 12-13,
14 (9a)

R. The precepts of the Lord give joy to the heart.

[This psalm is found on page 447 (lectionary number 174).]

SECOND READING

JAMES 5:1-6

YOUR WEALTH HAS
ROTTED AWAY.

Come now, you rich, weep and wail over your
     impending miseries.
Your wealth has rotted away, your clothes
     have become moth-eaten,
   your gold and silver have corroded,
   and that corrosion will be a testimony against you;
   it will devour your flesh like a fire.

You have stored up treasure for the last days.
Behold, the wages you withheld from the workers
   who harvested your fields are crying aloud;
   and the cries of the harvesters
   have reached the ears of the Lord of hosts.

You have lived on earth in luxury and pleasure;
   you have fattened your hearts for the day of slaughter.

You have condemned;
   you have murdered the righteous one;
   he offers you no resistance.

ALLELUIA

SEE JOHN 17:17b, 17a

R. Alleluia, alleluia.

Your word, O Lord, is truth;
consecrate us in the truth.   R.

GOSPEL

MARK 9:38–43, 45, 47–48

WHOEVER IS NOT
AGAINST US IS FOR US. IF
YOUR HAND CAUSES YOU
TO SIN, CUT IT OFF.

At that time, John said to Jesus,
"Teacher, we saw someone driving out demons
      in your name,
   and we tried to prevent him because he does not
      follow us."
Jesus replied, "Do not prevent him.
There is no one who performs a mighty deed in my name
   who can at the same time speak ill of me.

"For whoever is not against us is for us.
Anyone who gives you a cup of water to drink
   because you belong to Christ,
   amen, I say to you, will surely not lose his reward.

"Whoever causes one of these little ones who believe
      in me to sin,
   it would be better for him if a great millstone
   were put around his neck
   and he were thrown into the sea.

"If your hand causes you to sin, cut it off.
It is better for you to enter into life maimed
   than with two hands to go into Gehenna,
   into the unquenchable fire.
And if your foot causes you to sin, cut if off.
It is better for you to enter into life crippled
   than with two feet to be thrown into Gehenna.
And if your eye causes you to sin, pluck it out.
Better for you to enter into the kingdom of God
      with one eye
   than with two eyes to be thrown into Gehenna,
   where 'their worm does not die, and the fire
      is not quenched.'"

FIRST READING

AMOS 6:1a, 4–7

THEIR WANTON REVELRY
SHALL BE DONE AWAY
WITH.

Thus says the LORD the God of hosts:
Woe to the complacent in Zion!

Lying upon beds of ivory,
   stretched comfortably on their couches,
they eat lambs taken from the flock,
   and calves from the stall!
Improvising to the music of the harp,
   like David, they devise their own accompaniment.
They drink wine from bowls
   and anoint themselves with the best oils;
      yet they are not made ill by the collapse of Joseph!

Therefore, now they shall be the first to go into exile,
   and their wanton revelry shall be done away with.

**RESPONSORIAL
PSALM**

PSALM 146:7, 8–9,
9–10 (1b)

R. Praise the Lord, my soul!
   or:
R. Alleluia.

[This psalm is found on page 15 (lectionary number 7).]

SECOND READING

1 TIMOTHY 6:11–16

KEEP THIS COMMANDMENT
UNTIL THE APPEARANCE
OF THE LORD JESUS CHRIST.

But you, man of God, pursue righteousness,
   devotion, faith, love, patience, and gentleness.
Compete well for the faith.
Lay hold of eternal life, to which you were called
   when you made the noble confession in the presence
      of many witnesses.

I charge you before God, who gives life to all things,
   and before Christ Jesus,
   who gave testimony under Pontius Pilate
      for the noble confession,
   to keep the commandment without stain or reproach
   until the appearance of our Lord Jesus Christ
   that the blessed and only ruler
   will make manifest at the proper time,
   the King of kings and Lord of lords,
   who alone has immortality, who dwells
      in unapproachable light,
   and whom no human being has seen or can see.
To him be honor and eternal power. Amen.

R. Alleluia, alleluia.

*Though our Lord Jesus Christ was rich, he became poor,
so that by his poverty you might become rich.   R.*

GOSPEL

LUKE 16:19–31

YOU RECEIVED WHAT WAS
GOOD, LAZARUS WHAT
WAS BAD; NOW HE IS
COMFORTED, WHEREAS
YOU ARE TORMENTED.

Jesus said to the Pharisees:
"There was a rich man who dressed in purple
     garments and fine linen
  and dined sumptuously each day.
And lying at his door was a poor man named Lazarus,
     covered with sores,
  who would gladly have eaten his fill of the scraps
  that fell from the rich man's table.
Dogs even used to come and lick his sores.

"When the poor man died,
  he was carried away by angels to the bosom of Abraham.
The rich man also died and was buried,
  and from the netherworld, where he was in torment,
  he raised his eyes and saw Abraham far off
  and Lazarus at his side.
And he cried out, 'Father Abraham, have pity on me.
Send Lazarus to dip the tip of his finger in water
     and cool my tongue,
  for I am suffering torment in these flames.'

"Abraham replied,
  'My child, remember that you received
  what was good during your lifetime
  while Lazarus likewise received what was bad;
  but now he is comforted here, whereas you
     are tormented.
Moreover, between us and you a great chasm
     is established
  to prevent anyone from crossing who might wish to go
  from our side to yours or from your side to ours.'

"He said, 'Then I beg you, father,
  send him to my father's house, for I have five brothers,
  so that he may warn them,
  lest they too come to this place of torment.'

"But Abraham replied, 'They have Moses
     and the prophets.
Let them listen to them.'
He said, 'Oh no, father Abraham,
  but if someone from the dead goes to them,
     they will repent.'

Then Abraham said, 'If they will not listen to Moses
and the prophets,
neither will they be persuaded if someone should rise
from the dead.'"

139A   TWENTY-SEVENTH SUNDAY IN ORDINARY TIME

FIRST READING

ISAIAH 5:1–7

THE VINEYARD OF THE
LORD OF HOSTS IS THE
HOUSE OF ISRAEL.

Let me now sing of my friend,
   my friend's song concerning his vineyard.
My friend had a vineyard
   on a fertile hillside;
he spaded it, cleared it of stones,
   and planted the choicest vines;
within it he built a watchtower,
   and hewed out a wine press.
Then he looked for the crop of grapes,
   but what it yielded was wild grapes.

Now, inhabitants of Jerusalem and people of Judah,
   judge between me and my vineyard:
What more was there to do for my vineyard
   that I had not done?
Why, when I looked for the crop of grapes,
   did it bring forth wild grapes?

Now, I will let you know
   what I mean to do with my vineyard:
take away its hedge, give it to grazing,
   break through its wall, let it be trampled!
Yes, I will make it a ruin:
   it shall not be pruned or hoed,
   but overgrown with thorns and briers;
I will command the clouds
   not to send rain upon it.
The vineyard of the LORD of hosts is the house of Israel,
   and the people of Judah are his cherished plant;
he looked for judgment, but see, bloodshed!
   for justice, but hark, the outcry!

**RESPONSORIAL
PSALM**

PSALM 80:9, 12, 13–14,
15–16, 19–20 (ISAIAH 5:7a)

R. *The vineyard of the Lord is the house of Israel.*

A vine from Egypt you transplanted;
   you drove away the nations and planted it.
It put forth its foliage to the Sea,
   its shoots as far as the River.   R.

Why have you broken down its walls,
  so that every passer-by plucks its fruit,
the boar from the forest lays it waste,
  and the beasts of the field feed upon it? R.

Once again, O Lord of hosts,
  look down from heaven, and see;
take care of this vine,
  and protect what your right hand has planted
the son of man whom you yourself made strong. R.

Then we will no more withdraw from you;
  give us new life, and we will call upon your name.
O Lord, God of hosts, restore us;
  if your face shine upon us, then we shall be saved. R.

SECOND READING

PHILIPPIANS 4:6–9

DO THESE THINGS, AND
THE GOD OF PEACE WILL
BE WITH YOU.

Brothers and sisters:
Have no anxiety at all, but in everything,
  by prayer and petition, with thanksgiving,
    make your requests known to God.
Then the peace of God that surpasses all understanding
  will guard your hearts and minds in Christ Jesus.

Finally, brothers and sisters,
  whatever is true, whatever is honorable,
  whatever is just, whatever is pure,
  whatever is lovely, whatever is gracious,
  if there is any excellence
  and if there is anything worthy of praise,
    think about these things.
Keep on doing what you have learned and received
  and heard and seen in me.
Then the God of peace will be with you.

ALLELUIA

SEE JOHN 15:16

R. Alleluia, alleluia.

I have chosen you from the world, says the Lord,
to go and bear fruit that will remain. R.

GOSPEL

MATTHEW 21:33–43

HE WILL LEASE HIS
VINEYARD TO OTHER
TENANTS.

Jesus said to the chief priests and the elders of the people:
"Hear another parable.
There was a landowner who planted a vineyard,
  put a hedge around it, dug a wine press in it,
    and built a tower.
Then he leased it to tenants and went on a journey.

"When vintage time drew near,
  he sent his servants to the tenants to obtain his produce.

But the tenants seized the servants and one they beat,
  another they killed, and a third they stoned.
Again he sent other servants, more numerous
    than the first ones,
  but they treated them in the same way.

"Finally, he sent his son to them, thinking,
  'They will respect my son.'
But when the tenants saw the son, they said
    to one another,
  'This is the heir.
Come, let us kill him and acquire his inheritance.'
They seized him, threw him out of the vineyard,
    and killed him.

"What will the owner of the vineyard do to those tenants
    when he comes?"
They answered him,
  "He will put those wretched men to a wretched death
  and lease his vineyard to other tenants
  who will give him the produce at the proper times."

Jesus said to them, "Did you never read in the Scriptures:
  The stone that the builders rejected
  has become the cornerstone;
  by the Lord has this been done,
  and it is wonderful in our eyes?
Therefore, I say to you,
  the kingdom of God will be taken away from you
  and given to a people that will produce its fruit."

140B   TWENTY-SEVENTH SUNDAY IN ORDINARY TIME

FIRST READING

GENESIS 2:18–24

THE TWO OF THEM
BECOME ONE FLESH.

The LORD God said: "It is not good for the man
    to be alone.
I will make a suitable partner for him."
So the LORD God formed out of the ground
    various wild animals and various birds of the air,
    and he brought them to the man to see what
      he would call them;
    whatever the man called each of them
      would be its name.
The man gave names to all the cattle,
    all the birds of the air, and all wild animals;
    but none proved to be the suitable partner for the man.

So the LORD God cast a deep sleep on the man,
  and while he was asleep,
    he took out one of his ribs and closed up its place
      with flesh.
The LORD God then built up into a woman the rib
  that he had taken from the man.

When he brought her to the man, the man said:
"This one, at last, is bone of my bones
  and flesh of my flesh;
    this one shall be called 'woman,'
      for out of 'her man' this one has been taken."
That is why a man leaves his father and mother
  and clings to his wife,
    and the two of them become one flesh.

**RESPONSORIAL
PSALM**

PSALM 128:1–2, 3, 4–5, 6
(SEE 5)

R. May the Lord bless us all the days of our lives.

Blessed are you who fear the LORD,
  who walk in his ways!
For you shall eat the fruit of your handiwork;
  blessed shall you be, and favored.   R.

Your wife shall be like a fruitful vine
  in the recesses of your home;
your children like olive plants
  around your table.   R.

Behold, thus is the man blessed
  who fears the LORD.
The LORD bless you from Zion:
  may you see the prosperity of Jerusalem
  all the days of your life.   R.

May you see your children's children.
  Peace be upon Israel!   R.

SECOND READING

HEBREWS 2:9–11

HE WHO CONSECRATES
AND THOSE WHO ARE
BEING CONSECRATED
ALL HAVE ONE ORIGIN.

Brothers and sisters:
He for a little while was made lower than the angels,
  that by the grace of God he might taste death
    for everyone.

For it was fitting that he,
  for whom and through whom all things exist,
    in bringing many children to glory,
      should make the leader to their salvation perfect
        through suffering.

He who consecrates and those who are being consecrated
  all have one origin.
Therefore, he is not ashamed to call them "brothers."

R. Alleluia, alleluia.

*If we love one another, God remains in us
and his love is brought to perfection in us.   R.*

GOSPEL

LONGER FORM
MARK 10:2–16

SHORTER FORM
MARK 10:2–12

THEREFORE WHAT GOD
HAS JOINED TOGETHER,
LET NO HUMAN BEING
SEPARATE.

[The Pharisees approached Jesus and asked,
　"Is it lawful for a husband to divorce his wife?"
They were testing him.
He said to them in reply, "What did Moses
　　command you?"
They replied,
　"Moses permitted a husband to write a bill of divorce
　and dismiss her."

But Jesus told them,
　"Because of the hardness of your hearts
　he wrote you this commandment.
But from the beginning of creation, *God made them
　　male and female.*
*For this reason a man shall leave his father and mother
　and be joined to his wife,*
　and the two shall become one flesh.
So they are no longer two but one flesh.
Therefore what God has joined together,
　no human being must separate."

In the house the disciples again questioned Jesus
　　about this.
He said to them,
　"Whoever divorces his wife and marries another
　commits adultery against her;
　and if she divorces her husband and marries another,
　she commits adultery."]

And people were bringing children to him that he might
　　touch them,
　but the disciples rebuked them.
When Jesus saw this he became indignant and said
　　to them,
　"Let the children come to me;
　do not prevent them, for the kingdom of God belongs
　　to such as these.
Amen, I say to you,
　whoever does not accept the kingdom of God
　　like a child
　will not enter it."

Then he embraced them and blessed them,
　placing his hands on them.

FIRST READING

HABAKKUK 1:2–3; 2:2–4

THE JUST ONE, BECAUSE
OF HIS FAITH, SHALL LIVE.

How long, O Lord? I cry for help
  but you do not listen!
I cry out to you, "Violence!"
  but you do not intervene.
Why do you let me see ruin;
  why must I look at misery?
Destruction and violence are before me;
  there is strife, and clamorous discord.

Then the Lord answered me and said:
  Write down the vision clearly upon the tablets,
  so that one can read it readily.
For the vision still has its time,
  presses on to fulfillment, and will not disappoint;
if it delays, wait for it,
  it will surely come, it will not be late.
The rash one has no integrity;
  but the just one, because of his faith, shall live.

**RESPONSORIAL
PSALM**

PSALM 95:1–2, 6–7, 8–9 (8)

R. If today you hear his voice, harden not your hearts.

[This psalm is found on page 448 (lectionary number 174).]

SECOND READING

2 TIMOTHY 1:6–8, 13–14

DO NOT BE ASHAMED OF
YOUR TESTIMONY TO OUR
LORD.

Beloved:
I remind you, to stir into flame
  the gift of God that you have through the imposition
    of my hands.
For God did not give us a spirit of cowardice
  but rather of power and love and self-control.
So do not be ashamed of your testimony to our Lord,
  nor of me, a prisoner for his sake;
  but bear your share of hardship for the gospel
  with the strength that comes from God.

Take as your norm the sound words that you heard
    from me,
  in the faith and love that are in Christ Jesus.
Guard this rich trust with the help of the Holy Spirit
  that dwells within us.

R. Alleluia, alleluia.

The word of the Lord remains for ever.
This is the word that has been proclaimed to you.   R.

GOSPEL

LUKE 17:5–10

IF YOU HAVE FAITH!

The apostles said to the Lord, "Increase our faith."
The Lord replied,
   "If you have faith the size of a mustard seed,
   you would say to this mulberry tree,
   'Be uprooted and planted in the sea,'
      and it would obey you.

"Who among you would say to your servant
   who has just come in from plowing or tending sheep
      in the field,
      'Come here immediately and take your place at table'?
Would he not rather say to him,
   'Prepare something for me to eat.
Put on your apron and wait on me while I eat and drink.
You may eat and drink when I am finished'?
Is he grateful to that servant because he did what
      was commanded?
So should it be with you.
When you have done all you have been commanded,
   say, 'We are unprofitable servants;
   we have done what we were obliged to do.'"

142A   TWENTY-EIGHTH SUNDAY IN ORDINARY TIME

FIRST READING

ISAIAH 25:6–10a

THE LORD WILL PREPARE
A FEAST AND WIPE AWAY
THE TEARS FROM EVERY
FACE.

On this mountain the LORD of hosts
   will provide for all peoples
a feast of rich food and choice wines,
   juicy, rich food and pure, choice wines.

On this mountain he will destroy
   the veil that veils all peoples,
the web that is woven over all nations;
   he will destroy death forever.
The Lord GOD will wipe away
   the tears from every face;
the reproach of his people he will remove
   from the whole earth; for the LORD has spoken.

On that day it will be said:
"Behold our God, to whom we looked to save us!
  This is the LORD for whom we looked;
  let us rejoice and be glad that he has saved us!"
For the hand of the LORD will rest on this mountain.

RESPONSORIAL PSALM

PSALM 23:1–3a, 3b–4, 5, 6 (6cd)

R. I shall live in the house of the Lord all the days of my life.

[This psalm is found on page 80 (lectionary number 31).]

SECOND READING

PHILIPPIANS 4:12–14, 19–20

I CAN DO ALL THINGS IN HIM WHO STRENGTHENS ME.

Brothers and sisters:
I know how to live in humble circumstances;
  I know also how to live with abundance.
In every circumstance and in all things
  I have learned the secret of being well fed
    and of going hungry,
  of living in abundance and of being in need.

I can do all things in him who strengthens me.
Still, it was kind of you to share in my distress.

My God will fully supply whatever you need,
  in accord with his glorious riches in Christ Jesus.
To our God and Father, glory forever and ever. Amen.

ALLELUIA

SEE EPHESIANS 1:17–18

R. Alleluia, alleluia.

*May the Father of Our Lord Jesus Christ
enlighten the eyes of our hearts,
so that we may know what is the hope
that belongs to our call.   R.*

GOSPEL

LONGER FORM
MATTHEW 22:1–14

SHORTER FORM
MATTHEW 22:1–10

INVITE TO THE WEDDING FEAST WHOMEVER YOU FIND.

[Jesus again in reply spoke to the chief priests and elders
    of the people
  in parables, saying,
"The kingdom of heaven may be likened to a king
  who gave a wedding feast for his son.
He dispatched his servants
  to summon the invited guests to the feast,
  but they refused to come.
A second time he sent other servants, saying,
  'Tell those invited:
    "Behold, I have prepared my banquet,
  my calves and fattened cattle are killed,
  and everything is ready; come to the feast."'

Some ignored the invitation and went away,
   one to his farm, another to his business.
The rest laid hold of his servants,
   mistreated them, and killed them.
The king was enraged and sent his troops,
   destroyed those murderers, and burned their city.

"Then he said to his servants, 'The feast is ready,
   but those who were invited were not worthy to come.
Go out, therefore, into the main roads
   and invite to the feast whomever you find.'
The servants went out into the streets
   and gathered all they found, bad and good alike,
   and the hall was filled with guests.]

"But when the king came in to meet the guests,
   he saw a man there not dressed in a wedding garment.
The king said to him, 'My friend, how is it
   that you came in here without a wedding garment?'
But he was reduced to silence.
Then the king said to his attendants,
   'Bind his hands and feet,
   and cast him into the darkness outside,
   where there will be wailing and grinding of teeth.'
Many are invited, but few are chosen."

143B   TWENTY-EIGHTH SUNDAY IN ORDINARY TIME

FIRST READING

WISDOM 7:7–11

I DEEMED RICHES
NOTHING IN COMPARISON
TO WISDOM.

I prayed, and prudence was given me;
   I pleaded, and the spirit of wisdom came to me.

I preferred her to scepter and throne,
and deemed riches nothing in comparison with her,
   nor did I liken any priceless gem to her;
because all gold, in view of her, is a little sand,
   and before her, silver is to be accounted mire.

Beyond health and comeliness I loved her,
and I chose to have her rather than the light,
   because the splendor of her never yields to sleep.
Yet all good things together came to me in her company,
   and countless riches at her hands.

R. Fill us with your love, O Lord, and we will sing for joy!

Teach us to number our days aright,
*   that we may gain wisdom of heart.*
Return, O Lord! How long?
*   Have pity on your servants!   R.*

Fill us at daybreak with your kindness,
*   that we may shout for joy and gladness all our days.*
Make us glad, for the days when you afflicted us,
*   for the years when we saw evil.   R.*

Let your work be seen by your servants
*   and your glory by their children;*
and may the gracious care of the Lord our God be ours;
*   prosper the work of our hands for us!*
*   Prosper the work of our hands!   R.*

SECOND READING

HEBREWS 4:12–13

THE WORD OF GOD
DISCERNS REFLECTIONS
AND THOUGHTS OF THE
HEART.

Brothers and sisters:
Indeed the word of God is living and effective,
    sharper than any two-edged sword,
    penetrating even between soul and spirit,
        joints and marrow,
    and able to discern reflections and thoughts
        of the heart.

No creature is concealed from him,
    but everything is naked and exposed to the eyes of him
    to whom we must render an account.

ALLELUIA

MATTHEW 5:3

R. Alleluia, alleluia.

Blessed are the poor in spirit,
for theirs is the kingdom of heaven.   R.

GOSPEL

LONGER FORM
MARK 10:17–30

SHORTER FORM
MARK 10:17–27

SELL WHAT YOU HAVE,
AND FOLLOW ME.

[As Jesus was setting out on a journey, a man ran up,
    knelt down before him, and asked him,
    "Good teacher, what must I do to inherit eternal life?"

Jesus answered him, "Why do you call me good?
No one is good but God alone.
You know the commandments: *You shall not kill;*
    you shall not commit adultery;
    you shall not steal;
    you shall not bear false witness;
    you shall not defraud;
    honor your father and your mother."

He replied and said to him,
    "Teacher, all of these I have observed from my youth."

Jesus, looking at him, loved him and said to him,
"You are lacking in one thing.
Go, sell what you have, and give to the poor
and you will have treasure in heaven; then come,
follow me."

At that statement his face fell,
and he went away sad, for he had many possessions.

Jesus looked around and said to his disciples,
"How hard it is for those who have wealth
to enter the kingdom of God!"
The disciples were amazed at his words.
So Jesus again said to them in reply,
"Children, how hard it is to enter the kingdom of God!
It is easier for a camel to pass through the eye of a needle
than for one who is rich to enter the kingdom of God."

They were exceedingly astonished and said among
themselves,
"Then who can be saved?"
Jesus looked at them and said,
"For human beings it is impossible, but not for God.
All things are possible for God."]

Peter began to say to him,
"We have given up everything and followed you."
Jesus said, "Amen, I say to you,
there is no one who has given up house
or brothers or sisters
or mother or father or children or lands
for my sake and for the sake of the gospel
who will not receive a hundred times more now
in this present age:
houses and brothers and sisters
and mothers and children and lands,
with persecutions, and eternal life in the age to come."

144C   TWENTY-EIGHTH SUNDAY IN ORDINARY TIME

FIRST READING

2 KINGS 5:14–17

NAAMAN RETURNED
TO THE MAN OF GOD
AND ACKNOWLEDGED
THE LORD.

Naaman went down and plunged into the Jordan
seven times
at the word of Elisha, the man of God.
His flesh became again like the flesh of a little child,
and he was clean of his leprosy.

Naaman returned with his whole retinue
    to the man of God.
On his arrival he stood before Elisha and said,
    "Now I know that there is no God in all the earth,
    except in Israel.
Please accept a gift from your servant."

Elisha replied, "As the LORD lives whom I serve,
    I will not take it,"
and despite Naaman's urging, he still refused.

Naaman said: "If you will not accept,
    please let me, your servant, have two mule-loads
        of earth,
    for I will no longer offer holocaust or sacrifice
    to any other god except to the LORD."

**RESPONSORIAL
PSALM**

PSALM 98:1, 2–3, 3–4 (SEE 2b)

R. The Lord has revealed to the nations his saving power.

[This psalm is found on page 185 (lectionary number 56).]

SECOND READING

2 TIMOTHY 2:8–13

IF WE PERSEVERE WE SHALL
ALSO REIGN WITH CHRIST.

Beloved:
Remember Jesus Christ, raised from the dead,
    a descendant of David:
    such is my gospel, for which I am suffering,
    even to the point of chains, like a criminal.
But the word of God is not chained.

Therefore, I bear with everything for the sake of
        those who are chosen,
    so that they too may obtain the salvation that is
        in Christ Jesus,
    together with eternal glory.

This saying is trustworthy:
If we have died with him
    we shall also live with him;
if we persevere
    we shall also reign with him.
But if we deny him
    he will deny us.
If we are unfaithful
    he remains faithful,
    for he cannot deny himself.

R. Alleluia, alleluia.

In all circumstances, give thanks,
for this is the will of God for you in Christ Jesus.   R.

GOSPEL

LUKE 17:11–19

NONE BUT THIS
FOREIGNER HAS
RETURNED TO GIVE
THANKS TO GOD.

As Jesus continued his journey to Jerusalem,
    he traveled through Samaria and Galilee.

As he was entering a village, ten lepers met him.
They stood at a distance from him and raised their
        voices, saying,
    "Jesus, Master! Have pity on us!"

And when he saw them, he said,
    "Go show yourselves to the priests."
As they were going they were cleansed.
And one of them, realizing he had been healed,
    returned, glorifying God in a loud voice;
        and he fell at the feet of Jesus and thanked him.
He was a Samaritan.

Jesus said in reply,
    "Ten were cleansed, were they not?
Where are the other nine?
Has none but this foreigner returned to give thanks
        to God?"

Then he said to him, "Stand up and go;
    your faith has saved you."

145A   TWENTY-NINTH SUNDAY IN ORDINARY TIME

FIRST READING

ISAIAH 45:1, 4–6

I HAVE GRASPED THE
RIGHT HAND OF CYRUS
TO SUBDUE THE NATIONS
BEFORE HIM.

Thus says the LORD to his anointed, Cyrus,
    whose right hand I grasp,
subduing nations before him,
    and making kings run in his service,
opening doors before him
    and leaving the gates unbarred:

For the sake of Jacob, my servant,
    of Israel, my chosen one,
I have called you by your name,
    giving you a title, though you knew me not.
I am the LORD and there is no other,
    there is no God besides me.

It is I who arm you, though you know me not,
    so that toward the rising and the setting of the sun
    people may know that there is none besides me.
I am the Lord, there is no other.

RESPONSORIAL PSALM

PSALM 96:1, 3, 4–5, 7–8,
9–10 (7b)

R. *Give the Lord glory and honor.*

Sing to the Lord a new song;
    sing to the Lord, all you lands.
Tell his glory among the nations;
    among all peoples, his wondrous deeds.   R.

For great is the Lord and highly to be praised;
    awesome is he, beyond all gods.
For all the gods of the nations are things of nought,
    but the Lord made the heavens.   R.

Give to the Lord, you families of nations,
    give to the Lord glory and praise;
give to the Lord the glory due his name!
    Bring gifts, and enter his courts.   R.

Worship the Lord, in holy attire;
    tremble before him, all the earth;
say among the nations: The Lord is king,
    he governs the peoples with equity.   R.

SECOND READING

1 THESSALONIANS 1:1–5b

CALLING TO MIND FAITH,
LOVE AND HOPE.

Paul, Silvanus, and Timothy to the church
    of the Thessalonians
in God the Father and the Lord Jesus Christ:
grace to you and peace.

We give thanks to God always for all of you,
    remembering you in our prayers,
    unceasingly calling to mind your work of faith
        and labor of love
    and endurance in hope of our Lord Jesus Christ,
    before our God and Father,
    knowing, brothers and sisters loved by God,
    how you were chosen.
For our gospel did not come to you in word alone,
    but also in power and in the Holy Spirit
        and with much conviction.

ALLELUIA

PHILIPPIANS 2:15d, 16a

R. *Alleluia, alleluia.*

Shine like lights in the world
as you hold on to the word of life.   R.

GOSPEL

MATTHEW 22:15–21

REPAY TO CAESAR WHAT
BELONGS TO CAESAR AND
TO GOD WHAT BELONGS
TO GOD.

The Pharisees went off
   and plotted how they might entrap Jesus in speech.
They sent their disciples to him, with the Herodians,
   saying,
   "Teacher, we know that you are a truthful man
   and that you teach the way of God in accordance
      with the truth.
And you are not concerned with anyone's opinion,
   for you do not regard a person's status.
Tell us, then, what is your opinion:
   Is it lawful to pay the census tax to Caesar or not?"

Knowing their malice, Jesus said,
   "Why are you testing me, you hypocrites?
Show me the coin that pays the census tax."
Then they handed him the Roman coin.
He said to them, "Whose image is this
   and whose inscription?"
They replied, "Caesar's."
At that he said to them,
   "Then repay to Caesar what belongs to Caesar
   and to God what belongs to God."

146B   TWENTY-NINTH SUNDAY IN ORDINARY TIME

FIRST READING

ISAIAH 53:10–11

IF HE GIVES HIS LIFE AS
AN OFFERING FOR SIN, HE
SHALL SEE HIS DESCENDANTS
IN A LONG LIFE.

The LORD was pleased
   to crush him in infirmity.

If he gives his life as an offering for sin,
   he shall see his descendants in a long life,
   and the will of the LORD shall be accomplished
      through him.

Because of his affliction
   he shall see the light in fullness of days;
through his suffering, my servant shall justify many,
   and their guilt he shall bear.

R. Lord, let your mercy be on us, as we place our trust in you.

[This psalm is found on page 64 (lectionary number 25).]

SECOND READING

HEBREWS 4:14–16

LET US CONFIDENTLY
APPROACH THE THRONE
OF GRACE.

Brothers and sisters:
Since we have a great high priest who has passed
    through the heavens,
  Jesus, the Son of God,
  let us hold fast to our confession.
For we do not have a high priest
  who is unable to sympathize with our weaknesses,
  but one who has similarly been tested in every way,
  yet without sin.

So let us confidently approach the throne of grace
  to receive mercy and to find grace for timely help.

ALLELUIA

MARK 10:45

R. Alleluia, alleluia.

The Son of Man came to serve
and to give his life as a ransom for many. R.

GOSPEL

LONGER FORM
MARK 10:35–45

SHORTER FORM
MARK 10:42–45

THE SON OF MAN CAME
TO GIVE HIS LIFE AS
A RANSOM FOR MANY.

James and John, the sons of Zebedee, came to Jesus
    and said to him,
"Teacher, we want you to do for us whatever we ask
    of you."
He replied, "What do you wish me to do for you?"
They answered him, "Grant that in your glory
  we may sit one at your right and the other at your left."

Jesus said to them, "You do not know what you are asking.
Can you drink the cup that I drink
  or be baptized with the baptism with which
    I am baptized?"
They said to him, "We can."

Jesus said to them, "The cup that I drink, you will drink,
  and with the baptism with which I am baptized,
    you will be baptized;
  but to sit at my right or at my left is not mine to give
  but is for those for whom it has been prepared."
When the ten heard this, they became indignant
    at James and John.

[Jesus summoned them and said to them,
  "You know that those who are recognized as rulers
      over the Gentiles
  lord it over them,
  and their great ones make their authority
      over them felt.
But it shall not be so among you.

Rather, whoever wishes to be great among you
　　will be your servant;
　　whoever wishes to be first among you will
　　　　be the slave of all.
For the Son of Man did not come to be served
　　but to serve and to give his life as a ransom for many."]

147C TWENTY-NINTH SUNDAY IN ORDINARY TIME

FIRST READING

EXODUS 17:8–13

AS LONG AS MOSES KEPT
HIS HANDS RAISED UP,
ISRAEL HAD THE BETTER
OF THE FIGHT.

In those days, Amalek came and waged war against Israel.
Moses, therefore, said to Joshua,
　　"Pick out certain men,
　　and tomorrow go out and engage Amalek in battle.
I will be standing on top of the hill
　　with the staff of God in my hand."

So Joshua did as Moses told him:
　　he engaged Amalek in battle
　　after Moses had climbed to the top of the hill
　　　　with Aaron and Hur.

As long as Moses kept his hands raised up,
　　Israel had the better of the fight,
　　but when he let his hands rest,
　　Amalek had the better of the fight.
Moses' hands, however, grew tired;
　　so they put a rock in place for him to sit on.
Meanwhile Aaron and Hur supported his hands,
　　one on one side and one on the other,
　　so that his hands remained steady till sunset.

And Joshua mowed down Amalek and his people
　　with the edge of the sword.

RESPONSORIAL PSALM

PSALM 121:1–2, 3–4, 5–6, 7–8
(SEE 2)

R. *Our help is from the Lord, who made heaven and earth.*

I lift up my eyes toward the mountains;
　　whence shall help come to me?
My help is from the LORD,
　　who made heaven and earth. R.

May he not suffer your foot to slip;
　　may he slumber not who guards you:
indeed he neither slumbers nor sleeps,
　　the guardian of Israel. R.

The LORD is your guardian; the LORD is your shade;
　　he is beside you at your right hand.
The sun shall not harm you by day,
　　nor the moon by night. R.

The LORD will guard you from all evil;
he will guard your life.
The LORD will guard your coming and your going,
both now and forever.   R.

SECOND READING

2 TIMOTHY 3:14—4:2

ONE WHO BELONGS TO
GOD MAY BE COMPETENT,
EQUIPPED FOR EVERY
GOOD WORK.

Beloved:
Remain faithful to what you have learned and believed,
    because you know from whom you learned it,
    and that from infancy you have known
        the sacred Scriptures,
    which are capable of giving you wisdom for salvation
    through faith in Christ Jesus.

All Scripture is inspired by God
    and is useful for teaching, for refutation, for correction,
    and for training in righteousness,
    so that one who belongs to God may be competent,
    equipped for every good work.

I charge you in the presence of God and of Christ Jesus,
    who will judge the living and the dead,
    and by his appearing and his kingly power:
    proclaim the word;
    be persistent whether it is convenient or inconvenient;
    convince, reprimand, encourage through all patience
        and teaching.

ALLELUIA

HEBREWS 4:12

R. Alleluia, alleluia.

The word of God is living and effective,
discerning reflections and thoughts of the heart.   R.

GOSPEL

LUKE 18:1–8

GOD WILL SECURE THE
RIGHTS OF HIS CHOSEN
ONES WHO CALL OUT
TO HIM.

Jesus told his disciples a parable
    about the necessity for them to pray always without
        becoming weary.

He said, "There was a judge in a certain town
    who neither feared God nor respected any
        human being.
And a widow in that town used to come to him and say,
    'Render a just decision for me against my adversary.'

"For a long time the judge was unwilling, but eventually
        he thought,
    'While it is true that I neither fear God nor respect
        any human being,
    because this widow keeps bothering me

I shall deliver a just decision for her
    lest she finally come and strike me.'"

The Lord said, "Pay attention to what the dishonest
        judge says.
Will not God then secure the rights of his chosen ones
    who call out to him day and night?
Will he be slow to answer them?
I tell you, he will see to it that justice is done
        for them speedily.
But when the Son of Man comes, will he find faith
        on earth?"

148A   THIRTIETH SUNDAY IN ORDINARY TIME

FIRST READING

EXODUS 22:20–26

IF YOU WRONG THE
WIDOW AND THE ORPHAN,
MY WRATH WILL FLARE UP
AGAINST YOU.

Thus says the Lord:
"You shall not molest or oppress an alien,
    for you were once aliens yourselves in the land of Egypt.
You shall not wrong any widow or orphan.
If ever you wrong them and they cry out to me,
    I will surely hear their cry.
My wrath will flare up, and I will kill you with the sword;
    then your own wives will be widows,
        and your children orphans.

"If you lend money to one of your poor neighbors
        among my people,
    you shall not act like an extortioner toward him
    by demanding interest from him.
If you take your neighbor's cloak as a pledge,
    you shall return it to him before sunset;
        for this cloak of his is the only covering he has
        for his body.
What else has he to sleep in?
If he cries out to me, I will hear him;
        for I am compassionate."

**RESPONSORIAL
PSALM**

PSALM 18:2–3, 3–4, 47, 51 (2)

R. I love you, Lord, my strength.

I love you, O LORD, my strength,
    O LORD, my rock, my fortress, my deliverer. R.

My God, my rock of refuge,
    my shield, the horn of my salvation, my stronghold!
Praised be the LORD, I exclaim,
    and I am safe from my enemies. R.

The Lord lives and blessed be my rock!
  Extolled be God my savior.
You who gave great victories to your king
  and showed kindness to your anointed.   R.

SECOND READING

1 THESSALONIANS 1:5c–10

YOU TURNED FROM IDOLS
TO SERVE THE LIVING AND
TRUE GOD AND TO AWAIT
HIS SON FROM HEAVEN.

Brothers and sisters:
You know what sort of people we were among you
    for your sake.
And you became imitators of us and of the Lord,
    receiving the word in great affliction,
        with joy from the Holy Spirit,
    so that you became a model for all the believers
    in Macedonia and in Achaia.
For from you the word of the Lord has sounded forth
    not only in Macedonia and in Achaia,
        but in every place your faith in God has gone forth,
    so that we have no need to say anything.
For they themselves openly declare about us
    what sort of reception we had among you,
    and how you turned to God from idols
    to serve the living and true God
    and to await his Son from heaven,
    whom he raised from the dead,
    Jesus, who delivers us from the coming wrath.

ALLELUIA

JOHN 14:23

R. Alleluia, alleluia.

Whoever loves me will keep my word, says the Lord,
and my Father will love him and we will come to him.   R.

GOSPEL

MATTHEW 22:34–40

YOU SHALL LOVE THE
LORD YOUR GOD AND
YOUR NEIGHBOR AS
YOURSELF.

When the Pharisees heard that Jesus had silenced
    the Sadducees,
    they gathered together, and one of them,
    a scholar of the law, tested him by asking,
    "Teacher, which commandment in the law
    is the greatest?"

He said to him,
"You shall love the Lord, your God,
    with all your heart,
    with all your soul,
    and with all your mind.
This is the greatest and the first commandment.

"The second is like it:
    You shall love your neighbor as yourself.

The whole law and the prophets depend
on these two commandments."

149B   THIRTIETH SUNDAY IN ORDINARY TIME

FIRST READING

JEREMIAH 31:7–9

THE BLIND AND THE LAME
I WILL BRING BACK; I WILL
CONSOLE THEM.

Thus says the LORD:
Shout with joy for Jacob,
    exult at the head of the nations;
    proclaim your praise and say:
The LORD has delivered his people,
    the remnant of Israel.

Behold, I will bring them back
    from the land of the north;
I will gather them from the ends of the world,
    with the blind and the lame in their midst,
the mothers and those with child;
    they shall return as an immense throng.

They departed in tears,
    but I will console them and guide them;
I will lead them to brooks of water,
    on a level road, so that none shall stumble.
For I am a father to Israel,
    Ephraim is my first-born.

**RESPONSORIAL
PSALM**

PSALM 126:1–2, 2–3, 4–5,
6 (3)

R. The Lord has done great things for us; we are filled with joy.

[This psalm is found on page 13 (lectionary number 6).]

SECOND READING

HEBREWS 5:1–6

YOU ARE A PRIEST
FOREVER ACCORDING
TO THE ORDER OF
MELCHIZEDEK.

Brothers and sisters:
Every high priest is taken from among men
    and made their representative before God,
    to offer gifts and sacrifices for sins.
He is able to deal patiently with the ignorant and erring,
    for he himself is beset by weakness
    and so, for this reason, must make sin offerings
        for himself
    as well as for the people.
No one takes this honor upon himself
    but only when called by God,
        just as Aaron was.

In the same way,
   it was not Christ who glorified himself in becoming
      high priest,
   but rather the one who said to him:
   You are my son:
   this day I have begotten you;
   just as he says in another place:
   You are a priest forever
      according to the order of Melchizedek.

ALLELUIA

SEE 2 TIMOTHY 1:10

R. Alleluia, alleluia.

Our Savior Jesus Christ destroyed death
and brought life to light through the Gospel.   R.

GOSPEL

MARK 10:46–52

MASTER, I WANT TO SEE.

As Jesus was leaving Jericho with his disciples
      and a sizable crowd,
   Bartimaeus, a blind man, the son of Timaeus,
   sat by the roadside begging.
On hearing that it was Jesus of Nazareth,
   he began to cry out and say,
   "Jesus, son of David, have pity on me."

And many rebuked him, telling him to be silent.
But he kept calling out all the more,
   "Son of David, have pity on me."
Jesus stopped and said, "Call him."
So they called the blind man, saying to him,
   "Take courage; get up, Jesus is calling you."
He threw aside his cloak, sprang up, and came to Jesus.

Jesus said to him in reply,
   "What do you want me to do for you?"
The blind man replied to him, "Master, I want to see."
Jesus told him, "Go your way; your faith has saved you."
Immediately he received his sight
   and followed him on the way.

FIRST READING

SIRACH 35:12–14, 16–18

THE PRAYER OF THE LOWLY
PIERCES THE CLOUDS.

The Lord is a God of justice,
   who knows no favorites.
Though not unduly partial toward the weak,
   yet he hears the cry of the oppressed.
The Lord is not deaf to the wail of the orphan,
   nor to the widow when she pours out her complaint.

The one who serves God willingly is heard;
   his petition reaches the heavens.
The prayer of the lowly pierces the clouds;
   it does not rest till it reaches its goal,
nor will it withdraw till the Most High responds,
   judges justly and affirms the right,
and the Lord will not delay.

RESPONSORIAL PSALM

PSALM 34:2–3, 17–18, 19,
23 (7a)

R. *The Lord hears the cry of the poor.*

I will bless the Lord at all times;
   his praise shall be ever in my mouth.
Let my soul glory in the Lord;
   the lowly will hear me and be glad.   R.

The Lord confronts the evildoers,
   to destroy remembrance of them from the earth.
When the just cry out, the Lord hears them,
   and from all their distress he rescues them.   R.

The Lord is close to the brokenhearted;
   and those who are crushed in spirit he saves.
The Lord redeems the lives of his servants;
   no one incurs guilt who takes refuge in him.   R.

SECOND READING

2 TIMOTHY 4:6–8, 16–18

FROM NOW ON, THE CROWN
OF RIGHTEOUSNESS
AWAITS ME.

Beloved:
I am already being poured out like a libation,
   and the time of my departure is at hand.
I have competed well; I have finished the race;
   I have kept the faith.

From now on the crown of righteousness awaits me,
   which the Lord, the just judge,
     will award to me on that day, and not only to me,
     but to all who have longed for his appearance.
At my first defense no one appeared on my behalf,
   but everyone deserted me.
May it not be held against them!

But the Lord stood by me and gave me strength,
  so that through me the proclamation might
    be completed
  and all the Gentiles might hear it.
And I was rescued from the lion's mouth.

The Lord will rescue me from every evil threat
  and will bring me safe to his heavenly kingdom.
To him be glory forever and ever. Amen.

ALLELUIA

2 CORINTHIANS 5:19

R. Alleluia, alleluia.

God was reconciling the world to himself in Christ,
and entrusting to us the message of salvation. R.

GOSPEL

LUKE 18:9–14

THE TAX COLLECTOR,
NOT THE PHARISEE,
WENT HOME JUSTIFIED.

Jesus addressed this parable
  to those who were convinced of their own
    righteousness
  and despised everyone else.

"Two people went up to the temple area to pray;
  one was a Pharisee and the other was a tax collector.
The Pharisee took up his position and spoke this prayer
    to himself,
  'O God, I thank you that I am not like the rest
  of humanity —
  greedy, dishonest, adulterous — or even like this
    tax collector.
I fast twice a week, and I pay tithes on my whole income.'

"But the tax collector stood off at a distance
  and would not even raise his eyes to heaven
  but beat his breast and prayed,
  'O God, be merciful to me a sinner.'

"I tell you, the latter went home justified, not the former;
  for whoever exalts himself will be humbled,
  and the one who humbles himself will be exalted."

FIRST READING

MALACHI 1:14b—2:2b, 8–10

YOU HAVE TURNED ASIDE
FROM THE WAY, AND HAVE
CAUSED MANY TO FALTER
BY YOUR INSTRUCTION.

A great King am I, says the LORD of hosts,
    and my name will be feared among the nations.

And now, O priests, this commandment is for you:
    If you do not listen,
if you do not lay it to heart,
    to give glory to my name, says the LORD of hosts,
I will send a curse upon you
    and of your blessing I will make a curse.

You have turned aside from the way,
    and have caused many to falter by your instruction;
you have made void the covenant of Levi,
    says the LORD of hosts.
I, therefore, have made you contemptible
    and base before all the people,
since you do not keep my ways,
    but show partiality in your decisions.

Have we not all the one father?
    Has not the one God created us?
Why then do we break faith with one another,
    violating the covenant of our fathers?

RESPONSORIAL PSALM

PSALM 131:1, 2, 3

R. In you, Lord, I have found my peace.

O LORD, my heart is not proud,
    nor are my eyes haughty;
I busy not myself with great things,
    nor with things too sublime for me.   R.

Nay rather, I have stilled and quieted
    my soul like a weaned child.
Like a weaned child on its mother's lap,
    so is my soul within me.   R.

O Israel, hope in the LORD,
    both now and forever.   R.

SECOND READING

1 THESSALONIANS 2:7b–9, 13

WE WERE DETERMINED
TO SHARE WITH YOU
NOT ONLY THE GOSPEL
OF GOD, BUT OUR VERY
SELVES AS WELL.

Brothers and sisters:
We were gentle among you, as a nursing mother cares
        for her children.
With such affection for you, we were determined
        to share with you
    not only the gospel of God, but our very selves as well,
    so dearly beloved had you become to us.
You recall, brothers and sisters, our toil and drudgery.

Working night and day in order not to burden any of you,
   we proclaimed to you the gospel of God.

And for this reason we too give thanks to God
      unceasingly,
   that, in receiving the word of God from hearing us,
   you received not a human word but, as it truly is,
      the word of God,
   which is now at work in you who believe.

ALLELUIA

MATTHEW 23:9b, 10b

R. Alleluia, alleluia.

*You have but one Father in heaven
and one master, the Christ.   R.*

GOSPEL

MATTHEW 23:1–12

THEY PREACH BUT THEY
DO NOT PRACTICE.

Jesus spoke to the crowds and to his disciples, saying,
"The scribes and the Pharisees
   have taken their seat on the chair of Moses.
Therefore, do and observe all things whatsoever
      they tell you,
   but do not follow their example.
For they preach but they do not practice.
They tie up heavy burdens hard to carry
   and lay them on people's shoulders,
   but they will not lift a finger to move them.
All their works are performed to be seen.
They widen their phylacteries and lengthen their tassels.
They love places of honor at banquets, seats of honor
      in synagogues,
   greetings in marketplaces, and the salutation 'Rabbi.'

"As for you, do not be called 'Rabbi.'
You have but one teacher, and you are all brothers.
Call no one on earth your father;
   you have but one Father in heaven.
Do not be called 'Master';
   you have but one master, the Christ.
The greatest among you must be your servant.
Whoever exalts himself will be humbled;
   but whoever humbles himself will be exalted."

FIRST READING

DEUTERONOMY 6:2–6

HEAR O ISRAEL! YOU
SHALL LOVE THE LORD
YOUR GOD WITH ALL
YOUR HEART.

Moses spoke to the people, saying:
"Fear the LORD, your God,
  and keep, throughout the days of your lives,
  all his statutes and commandments
      which I enjoin on you,
  and thus have long life.

"Hear then, Israel, and be careful to observe them,
  that you may grow and prosper the more,
  in keeping with the promise of the LORD,
      the God of your fathers,
  to give you a land flowing with milk and honey.

"Hear, O Israel! The LORD is our God, the LORD alone!
Therefore, you shall love the LORD, your God,
  with all your heart,
  and with all your soul,
  and with all your strength.
Take to heart these words which I enjoin on you today."

**RESPONSORIAL
PSALM**

PSALM 18:2–3, 3–4, 47, 51 (2)

R. I love you, Lord, my strength.

[This psalm is found on page 386 (lectionary number 148).]

SECOND READING

HEBREWS 7:23–28

BECAUSE HE REMAINS
FOREVER, HE HAS A
PRIESTHOOD THAT DOES
NOT PASS AWAY.

Brothers and sisters:
The levitical priests were many
  because they were prevented by death
      from remaining in office,
  but Jesus, because he remains forever,
  has a priesthood that does not pass away.
Therefore, he is always able to save those
      who approach God through him,
  since he lives forever to make intercession for them.

It was fitting that we should have such a high priest:
  holy, innocent, undefiled, separated from sinners,
  higher than the heavens.
He has no need, as did the high priests,
  to offer sacrifice day after day,
      first for his own sins and then for those of the people;
  he did that once for all when he offered himself.

For the law appoints men subject to weakness
    to be high priests,
  but the word of the oath, which was taken after the law,
  appoints a son,
  who has been made perfect forever.

ALLELUIA

JOHN 14:23

R. Alleluia, alleluia.

Whoever loves me will keep my word,
says the Lord; and my Father will love him
and we will come to him. R.

GOSPEL

MARK 12:28b–34

LOVE THE LORD YOUR GOD.
LOVE YOUR NEIGHBOR.

One of the scribes came to Jesus and asked him,
  "Which is the first of all the commandments?"

Jesus replied, "The first is this:
  Hear, O Israel!
  The Lord our God is Lord alone!
  You shall love the Lord your God with all your heart,
  with all your soul,
  with all your mind,
  and with all your strength.
The second is this:
  You shall love your neighbor as yourself.
There is no other commandment greater than these."

The scribe said to him, "Well said, teacher.
You are right in saying,
  'He is One and there is no other than he.'
And 'to love him with all your heart,
  with all your understanding,
  with all your strength,
  and to love your neighbor as yourself'
  is worth more than all burnt offerings and sacrifices."

And when Jesus saw that he answered with understanding,
  he said to him,
  "You are not far from the kingdom of God."
And no one dared to ask him any more questions.

FIRST READING

WISDOM 11:22—12:2

YOU HAVE MERCY ON ALL
BECAUSE YOU LOVE ALL
THINGS THAT ARE.

Before the LORD the whole universe is as a grain
    from a balance
or a drop of morning dew come down upon the earth.
But you have mercy on all, because you can do all things;
    and you overlook people's sins that they may repent.

For you love all things that are
    and loathe nothing that you have made;
    for what you hated, you would not have fashioned.
And how could a thing remain, unless you willed it;
    or be preserved, had it not been called forth by you?

But you spare all things, because they are yours,
    O LORD and lover of souls,
    for your imperishable spirit is in all things!
Therefore you rebuke offenders little by little,
    warn them and remind them of the sins
        they are committing,
    that they may abandon their wickedness
        and believe in you, O LORD!

**RESPONSORIAL
PSALM**

PSALM 145:1–2, 8–9, 10–11,
13, 14 (SEE 1)

R. I will praise your name for ever, my king and my God.

[This psalm is found on page 449 (lectionary number 174).]

SECOND READING

2 THESSALONIANS 1:11—2:2

MAY THE NAME OF CHRIST
BE GLORIFIED IN YOU AND
YOU IN HIM.

Brothers and sisters:
We always pray for you,
    that our God may make you worthy of his calling
    and powerfully bring to fulfillment every good purpose
    and every effort of faith,
    that the name of our Lord Jesus may be glorified in you,
    and you in him,
    in accord with the grace of our God and Lord
        Jesus Christ.

We ask you, brothers and sisters,
    with regard to the coming of our Lord Jesus Christ
    and our assembling with him,
    not to be shaken out of your minds suddenly,
        or to be alarmed
    either by a "spirit," or by an oral statement,
    or by a letter allegedly from us
    to the effect that the day of the Lord is at hand.

R. Alleluia, alleluia.

God so loved the world that he gave his only Son,
so that everyone who believes in him might have eternal life.   R.

GOSPEL

LUKE 19:1–10

THE SON OF MAN HAS
COME TO SEEK AND TO
SAVE WHAT WAS LOST.

At that time, Jesus came to Jericho and intended
    to pass through the town.
Now a man there named Zacchaeus,
    who was a chief tax collector and also a wealthy man,
    was seeking to see who Jesus was;
    but he could not see him because of the crowd,
    for he was short in stature.

So he ran ahead and climbed a sycamore tree in order
        to see Jesus,
    who was about to pass that way.
When he reached the place, Jesus looked up and said,
    "Zacchaeus, come down quickly,
    for today I must stay at your house."

And he came down quickly and received him with joy.
When they all saw this, they began to grumble, saying,
    "He has gone to stay at the house of a sinner."

But Zacchaeus stood there and said to the Lord,
    "Behold, half of my possessions, Lord, I shall give
        to the poor,
    and if I have extorted anything from anyone
    I shall repay it four times over."

And Jesus said to him,
    "Today salvation has come to this house
    because this man too is a descendant of Abraham.
For the Son of Man has come to seek
    and to save what was lost."

154A   THIRTY-SECOND SUNDAY IN ORDINARY TIME

FIRST READING

WISDOM 6:12–16

WISDOM IS FOUND BY
THOSE WHO SEEK HER.

Resplendent and unfading is wisdom,
    and she is readily perceived by those who love her,
    and found by those who seek her.
She hastens to make herself known in anticipation
        of their desire;
    whoever watches for her at dawn shall not
        be disappointed,
    for he shall find her sitting by his gate.

For taking thought of wisdom is the perfection
     of prudence,
   and whoever for her sake keeps vigil
   shall quickly be free from care;
   because she makes her own rounds, seeking those
     worthy of her,
   and graciously appears to them in the ways,
   and meets them with all solicitude.

RESPONSORIAL
PSALM

PSALM 63:2, 3–4, 5–6,
7–8 (2b)

R. My soul is thirsting for you, O Lord my God.

O God, you are my God whom I seek;
   for you my flesh pines and my soul thirsts
   like the earth, parched, lifeless and without water.   R.

Thus have I gazed toward you in the sanctuary
   to see your power and your glory,
for your kindness is a greater good than life;
   my lips shall glorify you.   R.

Thus will I bless you while I live;
   lifting up my hands, I will call upon your name.
As with the riches of a banquet shall my soul be satisfied,
   and with exultant lips my mouth shall praise you.   R.

I will remember you upon my couch,
   and through the night-watches I will meditate on you:
You are my help,
   and in the shadow of your wings I shout for joy.   R.

SECOND READING

LONGER FORM
1 THESSALONIANS 4:13–18

SHORTER FORM
1 THESSALONIANS 4:13–14

GOD, THROUGH JESUS,
WILL BRING WITH HIM
THOSE WHO HAVE FALLEN
ASLEEP.

[We do not want you to be unaware, brothers and sisters,
   about those who have fallen asleep,
   so that you may not grieve like the rest,
     who have no hope.
For if we believe that Jesus died and rose,
   so too will God, through Jesus,
   bring with him those who have fallen asleep.]
Indeed, we tell you this, on the word of the Lord,
   that we who are alive,
   who are left until the coming of the Lord,
   will surely not precede those who have fallen asleep.

For the Lord himself, with a word of command,
   with the voice of an archangel and with the trumpet
     of God,
   will come down from heaven,
   and the dead in Christ will rise first.
Then we who are alive, who are left,
   will be caught up together with them in the clouds
   to meet the Lord in the air.

Thus we shall always be with the Lord.
Therefore, console one another with these words.

ALLELUIA

MATTHEW 24:42a, 44

R. *Alleluia, alleluia.*

Stay awake and be ready!
For you do not know on what day your Lord will come. R.

GOSPEL

MATTHEW 25:1–13

BEHOLD, THE BRIDEGROOM!
COME OUT TO MEET HIM!

Jesus told his disciples this parable:
"The kingdom of heaven will be like ten virgins
    who took their lamps and went out to meet
        the bridegroom.
Five of them were foolish and five were wise.
The foolish ones, when taking their lamps,
    brought no oil with them,
    but the wise brought flasks of oil with their lamps.
Since the bridegroom was long delayed,
    they all became drowsy and fell asleep.

"At midnight, there was a cry,
    'Behold, the bridegroom! Come out to meet him!'
Then all those virgins got up and trimmed their lamps.
The foolish ones said to the wise,
    'Give us some of your oil,
    for our lamps are going out.'
But the wise ones replied,
    'No, for there may not be enough for us and you.
Go instead to the merchants and buy some for yourselves.'
While they went off to buy it,
    the bridegroom came
    and those who were ready went into the wedding
        feast with him.
Then the door was locked.

"Afterwards the other virgins came and said,
    'Lord, Lord, open the door for us!'
But he said in reply,
    'Amen, I say to you, I do not know you.'
Therefore, stay awake,
    for you know neither the day nor the hour."

FIRST READING

1 KINGS 17:10–16

THE WIDOW MADE A
LITTLE CAKE FROM HER
FLOUR AND GAVE IT
TO ELIJAH.

In those days, Elijah the prophet went to Zarephath.
As he arrived at the entrance of the city,
   a widow was gathering sticks there; he called out to her,
   "Please bring me a small cupful of water to drink."
She left to get it, and he called out after her,
   "Please bring along a bit of bread."

She answered, "As the LORD, your God, lives,
   I have nothing baked; there is only a handful of flour
     in my jar
   and a little oil in my jug.
Just now I was collecting a couple of sticks,
   to go in and prepare something for myself and my son;
   when we have eaten it, we shall die."

Elijah said to her, "Do not be afraid.
Go and do as you propose.
But first make me a little cake and bring it to me.
Then you can prepare something for yourself
     and your son.
For the LORD, the God of Israel, says,
   'The jar of flour shall not go empty,
   nor the jug of oil run dry,
   until the day when the LORD sends rain
     upon the earth.'"

She left and did as Elijah had said.
She was able to eat for a year, and he and her son as well;
   the jar of flour did not go empty,
   nor the jug of oil run dry,
   as the LORD had foretold through Elijah.

**RESPONSORIAL
PSALM**

PSALM 146:7, 8–9, 9–10 (1b)

R. *Praise the Lord, my soul!*
  or:
R. *Alleluia.*

[This psalm is found on page 15 (lectionary number 7).]

SECOND READING

HEBREWS 9:24–28

CHRIST WAS OFFERED
ONCE TO TAKE AWAY
THE SINS OF MANY.

Christ did not enter into a sanctuary made by hands,
   a copy of the true one, but heaven itself,
   that he might now appear before God on our behalf.

Not that he might offer himself repeatedly,
   as the high priest enters each year into the sanctuary
   with blood that is not his own;

if that were so, he would have had to suffer repeatedly
from the foundation of the world.

But now once for all he has appeared at the end
        of the ages
    to take away sin by his sacrifice.
Just as it is appointed that human beings die once,
        and after this the judgment, so also Christ,
        offered once to take away the sins of many,
        will appear a second time, not to take away sin
        but to bring salvation to those who eagerly await him.

ALLELUIA

MATTHEW 5:3

R. Alleluia, alleluia.

Blessed are the poor in spirit,
for theirs is the kingdom of heaven.   R.

GOSPEL

LONGER FORM
MARK 12:38–44

SHORTER FORM
MARK 12:41–44

THIS POOR WIDOW PUT
IN MORE THAN ALL THE
OTHERS.

In the course of his teaching Jesus said to the crowds,
    "Beware of the scribes, who like to go around
        in long robes
    and accept greetings in the marketplaces,
    seats of honor in synagogues,
    and places of honor at banquets.
They devour the houses of widows and, as a pretext
    recite lengthy prayers.
They will receive a very severe condemnation."

[He sat down opposite the treasury
    and observed how the crowd put money
        into the treasury.
Many rich people put in large sums.
A poor widow also came and put in two small coins
        worth a few cents.
Calling his disciples to himself, he said to them,
"Amen, I say to you, this poor widow put in more
    than all the other contributors to the treasury.
For they have all contributed from their surplus wealth,
    but she, from her poverty, has contributed all she had,
    her whole livelihood."]

FIRST READING

2 MACCABEES 7:1–2, 9–14

THE KING OF THE WORLD
WILL RAISE US UP TO LIVE
AGAIN FOREVER.

It happened that seven brothers with their mother
  were arrested
  and tortured with whips and scourges by the king,
  to force them to eat pork in violation of God's law.
One of the brothers, speaking for the others, said:
  "What do you expect to achieve by questioning us?
We are ready to die rather than transgress the laws of
  our ancestors."

At the point of death he said:
  "You accursed fiend, you are depriving us of this
    present life,
  but the King of the world will raise us up to live
    again forever.
It is for his laws that we are dying."

After him the third suffered their cruel sport.
He put out his tongue at once when told to do so,
  and bravely held out his hands, as he spoke these
    noble words:
  "It was from Heaven that I received these;
  for the sake of his laws I disdain them;
  from him I hope to receive them again."
Even the king and his attendants marveled at the young
    man's courage,
  because he regarded his sufferings as nothing.

After he had died,
  they tortured and maltreated the fourth brother
    in the same way.
When he was near death, he said,
  "It is my choice to die at the hands of men
  with the hope God gives of being raised up by him;
  but for you, there will be no resurrection to life."

**RESPONSORIAL
PSALM**

PSALM 17:1, 5–6, 8, 15 (15b)

R. *Lord, when your glory appears, my joy will be full.*

Hear, O LORD, *a just suit;*
  attend to my outcry;
  hearken to my prayer from lips without deceit. R.

My steps have been steadfast in your paths,
  my feet have not faltered.
I call upon you, for you will answer me, O God;
  incline your ear to me; hear my word. R.

Keep me as the apple of your eye,
 hide me in the shadow of your wings.
But I in justice shall behold your face;
 on waking I shall be content in your presence.   R.

SECOND READING

2 THESSALONIANS 2:16—3:5

MAY THE LORD ENCOURAGE
YOUR HEARTS AND
STRENGTHEN THEM
IN EVERY GOOD DEED
AND WORD.

Brothers and sisters:
May our Lord Jesus Christ himself and God our Father,
 who has loved us and given us everlasting
  encouragement
 and good hope through his grace,
 encourage your hearts and strengthen them
  in every good deed and word.

Finally, brothers and sisters, pray for us,
 so that the word of the Lord may speed forward
  and be glorified,
 as it did among you,
 and that we may be delivered from perverse
  and wicked people,
 for not all have faith.

But the Lord is faithful;
 he will strengthen you and guard you from the evil one.
We are confident of you in the Lord that what we
  instruct you,
 you are doing and will continue to do.
May the Lord direct your hearts to the love of God
 and to the endurance of Christ.

ALLELUIA

REVELATION 1:5a, 6b

R. Alleluia, alleluia.

Jesus Christ is the first born of the dead;
to him be glory and power, forever and ever.   R.

GOSPEL

LONGER FORM
LUKE 20:27–38

SHORTER FORM
LUKE 20:27, 34–38

HE IS NOT GOD OF THE
DEAD, BUT OF THE LIVING.

[Some Sadducees, those who deny that there is
  a resurrection,
 came forward] and put this question to Jesus, saying,
 "Teacher, Moses wrote for us,
 If someone's brother dies leaving a wife but no child,
 his brother must take the wife
 and raise up descendants for his brother.
Now there were seven brothers;
 the first married a woman but died childless.

"Then the second and the third married her,
 and likewise all the seven died childless.
Finally the woman also died.

Now at the resurrection whose wife will that woman be?
For all seven had been married to her."

[Jesus said to them,
    "The children of this age marry and remarry;
    but those who are deemed worthy to attain to
        the coming age
    and to the resurrection of the dead
    neither marry nor are given in marriage.
They can no longer die,
    for they are like angels;
    and they are the children of God
    because they are the ones who will rise.

"That the dead will rise
    even Moses made known in the passage about the bush,
    when he called out 'Lord,'
    the God of Abraham, the God of Isaac, and the God
        of Jacob;
    and he is not God of the dead, but of the living,
    for to him all are alive."]

157A   THIRTY-THIRD SUNDAY IN ORDINARY TIME

FIRST READING

PROVERBS 31:10–13, 19–20,
30–31

SHE WORKS WITH LOVING
HANDS.

When one finds a worthy wife,
    her value is far beyond pearls.
Her husband, entrusting his heart to her,
    has an unfailing prize.
She brings him good, and not evil,
    all the days of her life.
She obtains wool and flax
    and works with loving hands.

She puts her hands to the distaff,
    and her fingers ply the spindle.
She reaches out her hands to the poor,
    and extends her arms to the needy.

Charm is deceptive and beauty fleeting;
    the woman who fears the LORD is to be praised.
Give her a reward for her labors,
    and let her works praise her at the city gates.

PSALM 128:1–2, 3, 4–5
(SEE 1a)

R. Blessed are those who fear the Lord.

[This psalm is found on page 371 (lectionary number 140).]

SECOND READING

1 THESSALONIANS 5:1–6

LET THE DAY OF THE LORD
NOT OVERTAKE YOU LIKE
A THIEF.

Concerning times and seasons, brothers and sisters,
　　you have no need for anything to be written to you.
For you yourselves know very well that the day
　　　　of the Lord will come
　　like a thief at night.
When people are saying, "Peace and security,"
　　then sudden disaster comes upon them,
　　like labor pains upon a pregnant woman,
　　and they will not escape.

But you, brothers and sisters, are not in darkness,
　　for that day to overtake you like a thief.
For all of you are children of the light
　　and children of the day.
We are not of the night or of darkness.
Therefore, let us not sleep as the rest do,
　　but let us stay alert and sober.

ALLELUIA

JOHN 15:4a, 5b

R. Alleluia, alleluia.

Remain in me as I remain in you, says the Lord.
Whoever remains in me bears much fruit.　R.

GOSPEL

LONGER FORM
MATTHEW 25:14–30

SHORTER FORM
MATTHEW 25:14–15, 19–21

SINCE YOU WERE
FAITHFUL IN SMALL
MATTERS, COME, SHARE
YOUR MASTER'S JOY.

[Jesus told his disciples this parable:
"A man going on a journey
　　called in his servants and entrusted his possessions
　　　　to them.
To one he gave five talents; to another, two;
　　　　to a third, one —
　　to each according to his ability.
Then he went away.]

"Immediately the one who received five talents
　　went and traded with them,
　　and made another five.
Likewise, the one who received two made another two.
But the man who received one went off and dug a hole
　　in the ground
　　and buried his master's money.

["After a long time
   the master of those servants came back
   and settled accounts with them.
The one who had received five talents came forward
   bringing the additional five.
He said, 'Master, you gave me five talents.
See, I have made five more.'
His master said to him, 'Well done, my good
    and faithful servant.
Since you were faithful in small matters,
   I will give you great responsibilities.
Come, share your master's joy.']

"Then the one who had received two talents also came
    forward and said,
   'Master, you gave me two talents.
See, I have made two more.'
His master said to him,
    'Well done, my good and faithful servant.
Since you were faithful in small matters,
   I will give you great responsibilities.
Come, share your master's joy.'

"Then the one who had received the one talent came
    forward and said,
   'Master, I knew you were a demanding person,
   harvesting where you did not plant
   and gathering where you did not scatter;
   so out of fear I went off and buried your talent
    in the ground.
Here it is back.'

"His master said to him in reply,
    'You wicked, lazy servant!
So you knew that I harvest where I did not plant
   and gather where I did not scatter?
Should you not then have put my money in the bank
   so that I could have got it back with interest
    on my return?
Now then! Take the talent from him and give it
    to the one with ten.
For to everyone who has,
   more will be given and he will grow rich;
   but from the one who has not,
   even what he has will be taken away.
And throw this useless servant into the darkness outside,
   where there will be wailing and grinding of teeth.'"

FIRST READING

DANIEL 12:1–3

AT THAT TIME YOUR
PEOPLE SHALL ESCAPE.

In those days, I Daniel,
  heard this word of the Lord:
"At that time there shall arise
  Michael, the great prince,
  guardian of your people;
it shall be a time unsurpassed in distress
  since nations began until that time.
At that time your people shall escape,
  everyone who is found written in the book.

"Many of those who sleep in the dust of the earth
    shall awake;
  some shall live forever,
  others shall be an everlasting horror and disgrace.

"But the wise shall shine brightly
  like the splendor of the firmament,
and those who lead the many to justice
  shall be like the stars forever."

**RESPONSORIAL
PSALM**

PSALM 16:5, 8, 9–10, 11 (1)

R. You are my inheritance, O Lord!

[This psalm is found on page 143 (lectionary number 41).]

SECOND READING

HEBREWS 10:11–14, 18

BY ONE OFFERING HE HAS
MADE PERFECT FOREVER
THOSE WHO ARE BEING
CONSECRATED.

Brothers and sisters:
Every priest stands daily at his ministry,
  offering frequently those same sacrifices
  that can never take away sins.

But this one offered one sacrifice for sins,
  and took his seat forever at the right hand of God;
  now he waits until his enemies are made his footstool.
For by one offering
  he has made perfect forever those who are
    being consecrated.

Where there is forgiveness of these,
  there is no longer offering for sin.

ALLELUIA

LUKE 21:36

R. Alleluia, alleluia.

*Be vigilant at all times
and pray that you have the strength to stand before the Son of Man.   R.*

Jesus said to his disciples:
"In those days after that tribulation
    the sun will be darkened,
    and the moon will not give its light,
    and the stars will be falling from the sky,
    and the powers in the heavens will be shaken.

"And then they will see 'the Son of Man coming
      in the clouds'
    with great power and glory,
    and then he will send out the angels
    and gather his elect from the four winds,
    from the end of the earth to the end of the sky.

"Learn a lesson from the fig tree.
When its branch becomes tender and sprouts leaves,
    you know that summer is near.
In the same way, when you see these things happening,
    know that he is near, at the gates.

Amen, I say to you,
    this generation will not pass away
    until all these things have taken place.
Heaven and earth will pass away,
    but my words will not pass away.

"But of that day or hour, no one knows,
    neither the angels in heaven, nor the Son,
      but only the Father."

159C THIRTY-THIRD SUNDAY IN ORDINARY TIME

FIRST READING

MALACHI 3:19–20a

THE SUN OF JUSTICE WILL
SHINE ON YOU.

Lo, the day is coming, blazing like an oven,
    when all the proud and all evildoers will be stubble,
and the day that is coming will set them on fire,
    leaving them neither root nor branch,
    says the LORD of hosts.

But for you who fear my name, there will arise
    the sun of justice with its healing rays.

**RESPONSORIAL
PSALM**

PSALM 98:5–6, 7–8, 9 (SEE 9)

R. *The Lord comes to rule the earth with justice.*

Sing praise to the LORD with the harp,
    with the harp and melodious song.
With trumpets and the sound of the horn
    sing joyfully before the King, the LORD.   R.

Let the sea and what fills it resound,
the world and those who dwell in it;
let the rivers clap their hands,
the mountains shout with them for joy.   R.

*Before the L*ORD, *for he comes,*
for he comes to rule the earth,
He will rule the world with justice
and the peoples with equity.   R.

SECOND READING

2 THESSALONIANS 3:7–12

IF ANYONE IS UNWILLING
TO WORK, NEITHER
SHOULD THAT ONE EAT.

Brothers and sisters:
You know how one must imitate us.
For we did not act in a disorderly way among you,
    nor did we eat food received free from anyone.
On the contrary, in toil and drudgery, night and day
    we worked, so as not to burden any of you.

Not that we do not have the right.
Rather, we wanted to present ourselves as a model for you,
    so that you might imitate us.
In fact, when we were with you,
    we instructed you that if anyone was unwilling to work,
    neither should that one eat.

We hear that some are conducting themselves
    among you in a disorderly way,
    by not keeping busy but minding the business of others.
Such people we instruct and urge in the Lord Jesus Christ
    to work quietly
    and to eat their own food.

ALLELUIA

LUKE 21:28

R. Alleluia, alleluia.

Stand erect and raise your heads
because your redemption is at hand.   R.

GOSPEL

LUKE 21:5–19

BY YOUR PERSEVERANCE
YOU WILL SECURE YOUR
LIVES.

While some people were speaking about
    how the temple was adorned with costly stones and
        votive offerings,
    Jesus said, "All that you see here —
    the days will come when there will not be left
    a stone upon another stone that will not be
        thrown down."

Then they asked him,
"Teacher, when will this happen?
And what sign will there be when all these things are
    about to happen?"

He answered,
"See that you not be deceived,
   for many will come in my name, saying,
   'I am he,' and 'The time has come.'
Do not follow them!

"When you hear of wars and insurrections,
   do not be terrified; for such things must happen first,
   but it will not immediately be the end."

Then he said to them,
"Nation will rise against nation, and kingdom
      against kingdom.
There will be powerful earthquakes, famines, and plagues
   from place to place;
   and awesome sights and mighty signs will come
      from the sky.

"Before all this happens, however,
   they will seize and persecute you,
   they will hand you over to the synagogues and
      to prisons,
   and they will have you led before kings and governors
   because of my name.

"It will lead to your giving testimony.
Remember, you are not to prepare your defense
      beforehand,
   for I myself shall give you a wisdom in speaking
   that all your adversaries will be powerless to resist
      or refute.

"You will even be handed over by parents, brothers,
      relatives, and friends,
   and they will put some of you to death.
You will be hated by all because of my name,
   but not a hair on your head will be destroyed.
By your perseverance you will secure your lives."

160A   LAST SUNDAY IN ORDINARY TIME

OUR LORD JESUS CHRIST THE KING

THIRTY-FOURTH SUNDAY IN ORDINARY TIME

FIRST READING

EZEKIEL 34:11–12, 15–17

AS FOR YOU, MY FLOCK,
I WILL JUDGE BETWEEN
ONE SHEEP AND ANOTHER.

Thus says the Lord GOD:
I myself will look after and tend my sheep.
As a shepherd tends his flock
 when he finds himself among his scattered sheep,
  so will I tend my sheep.
I will rescue them from every place
  where they were scattered
  when it was cloudy and dark.

I myself will pasture my sheep;
 I myself will give them rest, says the Lord GOD.
The lost I will seek out,
 the strayed I will bring back,
 the injured I will bind up,
 the sick I will heal,
  but the sleek and the strong I will destroy,
  shepherding them rightly.

As for you, my sheep, says the Lord GOD,
 I will judge between one sheep and another,
 between rams and goats.

**RESPONSORIAL
PSALM**

PSALM 23:1–2, 2–3, 5–6 (1)

R. The Lord is my shepherd; there is nothing I shall want.

The LORD is my shepherd; I shall not want.
 In verdant pastures he gives me repose.   R.

Beside restful waters he leads me;
 he refreshes my soul.
He guides me in right paths
 for his name's sake.   R.

You spread the table before me
 in the sight of my foes;
you anoint my head with oil;
 my cup overflows.   R.

Only goodness and kindness follow me
 all the days of my life;
and I shall dwell in the house of the LORD
 for years to come.   R.

SECOND READING

1 CORINTHIANS 15:20–26, 28

CHRIST WILL HAND OVER
THE KINGDOM TO HIS GOD
AND FATHER SO THAT
GOD MAY BE ALL IN ALL.

Brothers and sisters:
Christ has been raised from the dead,
   the firstfruits of those who have fallen asleep.
For since death came through man,
   the resurrection of the dead came also through man.
For just as in Adam all die,
    so too in Christ shall all be brought to life,
    but each one in proper order:
    Christ the firstfruits;
    then, at his coming, those who belong to Christ;
    then comes the end,
    when he hands over the kingdom to his God
      and Father,
    when he has destroyed every sovereignty
    and every authority and power.
For he must reign until he has put all his enemies
     under his feet.
The last enemy to be destroyed is death.

When everything is subjected to him,
   then the Son himself will also be subjected
   to the one who subjected everything to him,
   so that God may be all in all.

R. Alleluia, alleluia.

Blessed is he who comes in the name of the Lord!
Blessed is the kingdom of our father David that is to come! R.

GOSPEL

MATTHEW 25:31–46

THE SON OF MAN WILL
SIT UPON HIS GLORIOUS
THRONE AND HE WILL
SEPARATE THEM ONE
FROM ANOTHER.

Jesus said to his disciples:
"When the Son of Man comes in his glory,
   and all the angels with him,
   he will sit upon his glorious throne,
   and all the nations will be assembled before him.
And he will separate them one from another,
   as a shepherd separates the sheep from the goats.
He will place the sheep on his right and the goats
    on his left.

"Then the king will say to those on his right,
   'Come, you who are blessed by my Father.
Inherit the kingdom prepared for you
    from the foundation of the world.
For I was hungry and you gave me food,
   I was thirsty and you gave me drink,
   a stranger and you welcomed me,
   naked and you clothed me,

ill and you cared for me,
in prison and you visited me.'

"Then the righteous will answer him and say,
'Lord, when did we see you hungry and feed you,
or thirsty and give you drink?
When did we see you a stranger and welcome you,
or naked and clothe you?
When did we see you ill or in prison, and visit you?'
And the king will say to them in reply,
'Amen, I say to you, whatever you did
for one of the least brothers of mine, you did for me.'

"Then he will say to those on his left,
'Depart from me, you accursed,
into the eternal fire prepared for the devil
and his angels.
For I was hungry and you gave me no food,
I was thirsty and you gave me no drink,
a stranger and you gave me no welcome,
naked and you gave me no clothing,
ill and in prison, and you did not care for me.'

"Then they will answer and say,
'Lord, when did we see you hungry or thirsty
or a stranger or naked or ill or in prison,
and not minister to your needs?'
He will answer them, 'Amen, I say to you,
what you did not do for one of these least ones,
you did not do for me.'
And these will go off to eternal punishment,
but the righteous to eternal life."

161B   LAST SUNDAY IN ORDINARY TIME
OUR LORD JESUS CHRIST THE KING
THIRTY-FOURTH SUNDAY IN ORDINARY TIME

FIRST READING

DANIEL 7:13–14

HIS DOMINION IS AN
EVERLASTING DOMINION.

As the visions during the night continued, I saw
one like a Son of man coming,
on the clouds of heaven;
when he reached the Ancient One
and was presented before him,
the one like a Son of man received dominion, glory,
and kingship;
all peoples, nations, and languages serve him.

His dominion is an everlasting dominion
   that shall not be taken away,
     his kingship shall not be destroyed.

RESPONSORIAL PSALM

PSALM 93:1, 1–2, 5 (1a)

R. The Lord is king; he is robed in majesty.

The Lord is king, in splendor robed;
   robed is the Lord and girt about with strength. R.

And he has made the world firm,
   not to be moved.
Your throne stands firm from of old;
   from everlasting you are, O Lord. R.

Your decrees are worthy of trust indeed;
   holiness befits your house,
   O Lord, for length of days. R.

SECOND READING

REVELATION 1:5–8

THE RULER OF THE KINGS OF THE EARTH HAS MADE US INTO A KINGDOM, PRIESTS FOR HIS GOD AND FATHER.

Jesus Christ is the faithful witness,
   the firstborn of the dead and ruler of the kings
     of the earth.
To him who loves us and has freed us from our sins
     by his blood,
   who has made us into a kingdom, priests for his God
     and Father,
   to him be glory and power forever and ever. Amen.

Behold, he is coming amid the clouds,
   and every eye will see him,
     even those who pierced him.
All the peoples of the earth will lament him.
   Yes. Amen.

"I am the Alpha and the Omega," says the Lord God,
   "the one who is and who was and who is to come,
     the almighty."

ALLELUIA

MARK 11:9, 10

R. Alleluia, alleluia.

Blessed is he who comes in the name of the Lord!
Blessed is the kingdom of our father David that is to come! R.

GOSPEL

JOHN 18:33B–37

YOU SAY I AM A KING.

Pilate said to Jesus,
"Are you the King of the Jews?"
Jesus answered, "Do you say this on your own
   or have others told you about me?"
Pilate answered, "I am not a Jew, am I?

Your own nation and the chief priests handed you over
    to me.
What have you done?"

Jesus answered,
    "My kingdom does not belong to this world.
If my kingdom did belong to this world,
    my attendants would be fighting
    to keep me from being handed over to the Jews.
But as it is, my kingdom is not here."

So Pilate said to him, "Then you are a king?"
Jesus answered, "You say I am a king.
For this I was born and for this I came into the world,
    to testify to the truth.
Everyone who belongs to the truth listens to my voice."

162C   LAST SUNDAY IN ORDINARY TIME

OUR LORD JESUS CHRIST THE KING

THIRTY-FOURTH SUNDAY IN ORDINARY TIME

FIRST READING

2 SAMUEL 5:1–3

In those days, all the tribes of Israel came to David in
    Hebron and said:
    "Here we are, your bone and your flesh.
In days past, when Saul was our king,
    it was you who led the Israelites out and brought
      them back.
And the LORD said to you,
    'You shall shepherd my people Israel
    and shall be commander of Israel.'"

When all the elders of Israel came to David in Hebron,
    King David made an agreement with them there
      before the LORD,
    and they anointed him king of Israel.

RESPONSORIAL PSALM

PSALM 122:1–2, 3–4, 4–5
(SEE 1)

R. Let us go rejoicing to the house of the Lord.

I rejoiced because they said to me,
    "We will go up to the house of the LORD."
And now we have set foot
    within your gates, O Jerusalem.   R.

Jerusalem, built as a city
    with compact unity.
To it the tribes go up,
    the tribes of the LORD.   R.

According to the decree for Israel,
  *to give thanks to the name of the L*ORD.
In it are set up judgment seats,
  seats for the house of David. R.

SECOND READING

COLOSSIANS 1:12–20

HE TRANSFERRED US TO
THE KINGDOM OF HIS
BELOVED SON.

Brothers and sisters:
Let us give thanks to the Father,
  who has made you fit to share
  in the inheritance of the holy ones in light.

He delivered us from the power of darkness
  and transferred us to the kingdom of his beloved Son,
  in whom we have redemption, the forgiveness of sins.

He is the image of the invisible God,
  the firstborn of all creation.
For in him were created all things in heaven
    and on earth,
  the visible and the invisible,
  whether thrones or dominions or principalities
    or powers;
  all things were created through him and for him.
He is before all things,
  and in him all things hold together.

He is the head of the body, the church.
He is the beginning, the firstborn from the dead,
  that in all things he himself might be preeminent.
For in him all the fullness was pleased to dwell,
  and through him to reconcile all things for him,
  making peace by the blood of his cross
  through him, whether those on earth or those
    in heaven.

ALLELUIA

MARK 11:9, 10

R. Alleluia, alleluia.

Blessed is he who comes in the name of the Lord!
Blessed is the kingdom of our father David that is to come! R.

GOSPEL

LUKE 23:35–43

LORD, REMEMBER ME
WHEN YOU COME INTO
YOUR KINGDOM.

The rulers sneered at Jesus and said,
  "He saved others, let him save himself
  if he is the chosen one, the Christ of God."
Even the soldiers jeered at him.
As they approached to offer him wine they called out,
  "If you are King of the Jews, save yourself."
Above him there was an inscription that read,
  "This is the King of the Jews."

Now one of the criminals hanging there reviled Jesus,
    saying,
  "Are you not the Christ?
Save yourself and us."

The other, however, rebuking him, said in reply,
  "Have you no fear of God,
    for you are subject to the same condemnation?
And indeed, we have been condemned justly,
    for the sentence we received corresponds to our crimes,
    but this man has done nothing criminal."
Then he said,
  "Jesus, remember me when you come into
    your kingdom."

He replied to him,
  "Amen, I say to you,
    today you will be with me in Paradise."

ALLELUIA VERSES FOR SUNDAYS IN ORDINARY TIME

◆

These texts may be used in place of the texts proposed for each day.

Lectionary Number 163

1.
1 SAMUEL 3:9; JOHN 6:68c

*Speak, Lord, your servant is listening;
you have the words of everlasting life.*

2.
SEE MATTHEW 11:25

*Blessed are you, Father, Lord of heaven and earth;
you have revealed to little ones the mysteries
    of the kingdom.*

3.
SEE LUKE 19:38; 2:14

*Blessed is the king who comes in the name of the Lord:
glory to God in the highest and peace to God's people
    on earth.*

4.
JOHN 1:14a, 12b

*The Word of God became flesh and made his dwelling
    among us.
To those who accepted him,
he gave power to become children of God.*

5.
SEE JOHN 6:63c, 68c

*Your words, Lord, are Spirit and life;
you have the words of everlasting life.*

6.
JOHN 8:12

*I am the light of the world, says the Lord;
whoever follows me will have the light of life.*

7.
JOHN 10:27

*My sheep hear my voice, says the Lord;
I know them, and they follow me.*

8.
JOHN 14:6

*I am the way, the truth, and the life, says the Lord;
no one comes to the Father, except through me.*

9.
JOHN 14:23

*Whoever loves me will keep my word, says the Lord,
and my Father will love him and we will come to him.*

10.
JOHN 15:15b

*I call you my friends, says the Lord,
for I have made known to you all that the Father
    has told me.*

11.
SEE JOHN 17:17b, 17a

*Your word, O Lord, is truth;
consecrate us in the truth.*

12.
SEE ACTS 16:14b

*Open our hearts, O Lord,
to listen to the words of your Son.*

13.
SEE EPHESIANS 1:17–18

*May the Father of our Lord Jesus Christ
enlighten the eyes of our hearts,
that we may know what is the hope that
belongs to our call.*

◆

Last Sundays in Ordinary Time

14.
MATTHEW 24:42a, 44

*Be watchful and ready:
you know not when the Son of Man is coming.*

15.
LUKE 21:36

Be watchful, pray constantly,
that you may be worthy to stand before
the Son of Man.

16.
REVELATIONS 2:10c

Be faithful until death, says the Lord,
and I will give you the crown of life.

◆

The following texts for weekdays
in Ordinary Time may also
be used in place of the texts
proposed for each Sunday.

Lectionary Number 509

1.
1 SAMUEL 3:9; JOHN 6:68c

Speak, Lord, your servant is listening;
you have the words of everlasting life.

2.
SEE PSALM 19:9

Your words, O Lord, give joy to my heart,
your teaching is light to my eyes.

3.
PSALM 25:4b, 5a

Teach me your paths, my God,
and lead me in your truth.

4.
SEE PSALM 27:11

Teach me your way, O Lord,
and lead me on a straight road.

5.
PSALM 95:7d–8a

If today you hear God's voice,
harden not your hearts.

6.
PSALM 111:7b–8a

Your laws are all made firm, O Lord,
established for evermore.

7.
PSALM 119:18

Unveil my eyes, O Lord,
and I will see the marvels of your law.

8.
PSALM 119:27

Instruct me in the way of your rules,
and I will reflect on all your wonders.

9.
PSALM 119:34

Teach me the meaning of your law, O Lord,
and I will guard it with all my heart.

10.
PSALM 119:36a, 29b

Turn my heart to do your will;
teach me your law, O God.

11.
PSALM 119:88

In your mercy, give me life, O Lord,
and I will do your commands.

12.
PSALM 119:105

Your word is a lamp for my feet
and a light on my path.

13.
PSALM 119:135

Let your face shine on your servant,
and teach me your laws.

14.
SEE PSALM 130:5

I wait for the Lord;
my soul waits for his word.

15.
PSALM 145:13cd

The Lord is faithful in all his words
and holy in all his deeds.

16.
PSALM 147:12a, 15a

Praise the Lord, Jerusalem;
God's word speeds forth to the earth.

17.
MATTHEW 4:4b

One does not live on bread alone,
but on every word that comes forth
from the mouth of God.

18.
SEE MATTHEW 11:25

Blessed are you, Father, Lord of heaven and earth;
you have revealed to little ones the mysteries
of the kingdom.

19.
SEE LUKE 8:15

Blessed are they who have kept the word
with a generous heart
and yield a harvest through perseverance.

20.
SEE JOHN 6:63c, 68c

Your words, Lord, are Spirit and life:
you have the words of everlasting life.

21.
JOHN 8:12

I am the light of the world, says the Lord;
whoever follows me will have the light of life.

22.
JOHN 10:27

My sheep hear my voice, says the Lord;
I know them, and they follow me.

23.
JOHN 14:6

I am the way, the truth, and the life, says the Lord;
no one comes to the Father, except through me.

24.
JOHN 14:23

Whoever loves me will keep my word, says the Lord,
and my Father will love him and we will come to him.

25.
JOHN 15:15b

I call you my friends, says the Lord,
for I have made known to you all that the Father
has told me.

26.
SEE JOHN 17:17b, 17a

Your word, O Lord, is truth;
make us holy in the truth.

27.
SEE ACTS 16:14b

Open our hearts, O Lord,
to listen to the words of your Son.

28.
2 CORINTHIANS 5:19

God was in Christ, to reconcile the world to himself;
and the good news of reconciliation he has entrusted
to us.

29.
SEE EPHESIANS 1:17–18

*May the Father of our Lord Jesus Christ
enlighten the eyes of our hearts,
that we may know what is the hope
that belongs to our call.*

30.
PHILIPPIANS 2:15d, 16a

*Shine like lights in the world
as you hold on to the word of life.*

31.
SEE COLOSSIANS 3:16a, 17c

*Give thanks to God our Father through Jesus Christ
    our Lord,
and may the fullness of his message live within you.*

32.
SEE 1 THESSALONIANS 2:13

*Receive this message not as human words,
but as truly the word of God.*

33.
SEE 2 THESSALONIANS 2:14

*God has called us through the Gospel,
to possess the glory of our Lord Jesus Christ.*

34.
SEE 2 TIMOTHY 1:10

*Our Savior Jesus Christ has done away with death
and brought us life through the Gospel.*

35.
HEBREWS 4:12

*The word of God is living and effective,
discerning reflections and thoughts of the heart.*

36.
JAMES 1:18

*The Father willed to give us birth by the word of truth
that we may be a kind of firstfruits of his creatures.*

37.
JAMES 1:21bc

*Receive and submit to the word planted in you;
it is able to save your souls.*

38.
1 PETER 1:25

*The word of the Lord remains for ever.
This is the word that has been proclaimed to you.*

39.
1 JOHN 2:5

*Whoever keeps the word of Christ,
the love of God is truly perfected in him.*

◆
The Last Weeks in Ordinary Time

1.
MATTHEW 24:42a, 44

*Be watchful and ready:
you know not when the Son of Man is coming.*

2.
LUKE 21:28

*Lift up your heads and see;
your redemption is near at hand.*

3.
LUKE 21:36

*Be watchful, pray constantly,
that you may be worthy to stand before
    the Son of Man.*

4.
REVELATION 2:10c

*Be faithful until death, says the Lord,
and I will give you the crown of life.*

SOLEMNITIES OF THE LORD DURING ORDINARY TIME

164A THE MOST HOLY TRINITY
SUNDAY AFTER PENTECOST

FIRST READING

EXODUS 34:4b–6, 8–9

THE LORD, THE LORD,
A MERCIFUL AND
GRACIOUS GOD.

Early in the morning Moses went up Mount Sinai
    as the Lord had commanded him,
    taking along the two stone tablets.

Having come down in a cloud, the Lord stood
        with Moses there
    and proclaimed his name, "Lord."
Thus the Lord passed before him and cried out,
    "The Lord, the Lord, a merciful and gracious God,
    slow to anger and rich in kindness and fidelity."

Moses at once bowed down to the ground in worship.
Then he said, "If I find favor with you, O Lord,
    do come along in our company.
This is indeed a stiff-necked people;
        yet pardon our wickedness and sins,
    and receive us as your own."

RESPONSORIAL PSALM

DANIEL 3:52, 53, 54, 55,
56 (52b)

R. Glory and praise for ever!

Blessed are you, O Lord, the God of our fathers,
    praiseworthy and exalted above all forever;
And blessed is your holy and glorious name,
    praiseworthy and exalted above all for all ages. R.

Blessed are you in the temple of your holy glory,
    praiseworthy and glorious above all forever. R.

Blessed are you on the throne of your kingdom,
    praiseworthy and exalted above all forever. R.

Blessed are you who look into the depths
    from your throne upon the cherubim,
    praiseworthy and exalted above all forever. R.

SECOND READING

2 CORINTHIANS 13:11–13

THE GRACE OF JESUS
CHRIST AND THE LOVE OF
GOD AND THE FELLOWSHIP
OF THE HOLY SPIRIT.

Brothers and sisters, rejoice. Mend your ways,
    encourage one another,
    agree with one another, live in peace,
    and the God of love and peace will be with you.
Greet one another with a holy kiss.
All the holy ones greet you.

The grace of the Lord Jesus Christ
and the love of God
and the fellowship of the Holy Spirit be with all of you.

R. Alleluia, alleluia.

Glory to the Father, the Son, and the Holy Spirit;
to God who is, who was, and who is to come.   R.

God so loved the world that he gave his only Son,
so that everyone who believes in him might not perish
but might have eternal life.

For God did not send his Son into the world
to condemn the world,
but that the world might be saved through him.
Whoever believes in him will not be condemned,
but whoever does not believe has already
been condemned,
because he has not believed in the name of the only
Son of God.

165B   THE MOST HOLY TRINITY
SUNDAY AFTER PENTECOST

READING

DEUTERONOMY 4:32–34,
39–40

THE LORD IS GOD IN THE
HEAVENS ABOVE AND ON
EARTH BELOW AND THERE
IS NO OTHER.

Moses said to the people:
"Ask now of the days of old, before your time,
ever since God created man upon the earth;
ask from one end of the sky to the other:
Did anything so great ever happen before?
Was it ever heard of?

"Did a people ever hear the voice of God
speaking from the midst of fire, as you did, and live?
Or did any god venture to go and take a nation for himself
from the midst of another nation,
by testings, by signs and wonders, by war,
with strong hand and outstretched arm,
and by great terrors,
all of which the LORD, your God,
did for you in Egypt before your very eyes?

"This is why you must now know,
and fix in your heart, that the LORD is God
in the heavens above and on earth below,
and that there is no other.

You must keep his statutes and commandments
    that I enjoin on you today,
  that you and your children after you may prosper,
  and that you may have long life on the land
  which the Lord, your God, is giving you forever."

RESPONSORIAL PSALM

PSALM 33:4–5, 6, 9, 18–19, 20, 22 (12b)

R. Blessed the people the Lord has chosen to be his own.

Upright is the word of the Lord,
  and all his works are trustworthy.
He loves justice and right;
  of the kindness of the Lord the earth is full.   R.

By the word of the Lord the heavens were made;
  by the breath of his mouth all their host.
For he spoke, and it was made;
  he commanded, and it stood forth.   R.

See, the eyes of the Lord are upon those who fear him,
  upon those who hope for his kindness,
to deliver them from death
  and preserve them in spite of famine.   R.

Our soul waits for the Lord,
  who is our help and our shield.
May your kindness, O Lord, be upon us
  who have put our hope in you.   R.

SECOND READING

ROMANS 8:14–17

YOU RECEIVED A SPIRIT OF ADOPTION, THROUGH WHOM WE CRY, "ABBA, FATHER!"

Brothers and sisters:
For those who are led by the Spirit of God are sons of God.
For you did not receive a spirit of slavery to fall back
    into fear,
  but you received a Spirit of adoption,
  through whom we cry, "Abba, Father!"
The Spirit himself bears witness with our spirit
  that we are children of God,
  and if children, then heirs,
  heirs of God and joint heirs with Christ,
  if only we suffer with him
  so that we may also be glorified with him.

ALLELUIA

REVELATION 1:8

R. Alleluia, alleluia.

Glory to the Father, the Son, and the Holy Spirit;
to God who is, who was, and who is to come.   R.

GOSPEL

MATTHEW 28:16–20

BAPTIZING THEM IN THE
NAME OF THE FATHER,
AND OF THE SON, AND
OF THE HOLY SPIRIT.

[This reading is found on page 191
(lectionary number 58).]

166C   THE MOST HOLY TRINITY
SUNDAY AFTER PENTECOST

FIRST READING

PROVERBS 8:22–31

BEFORE THE EARTH WAS
MADE, WISDOM WAS
CONCEIVED.

Thus says the wisdom of God:
"The LORD possessed me, the beginning of his ways,
   the forerunner of his prodigies of long ago;
from of old I was poured forth,
   at the first, before the earth.
When there were no depths I was brought forth,
   when there were no fountains or springs of water;
before the mountains were settled into place,
   before the hills, I was brought forth;
while as yet the earth and fields were not made,
   nor the first clods of the world.

"When the LORD established the heavens I was there,
   when he marked out the vault over the face
     of the deep;
when he made firm the skies above,
   when he fixed fast the foundations of the earth;
when he set for the sea its limit,
   so that the waters should not transgress his command;
then was I beside him as his craftsman,
   and I was his delight day by day,
playing before him all the while,
   playing on the surface of his earth;
   and I found delight in the human race."

**RESPONSORIAL
PSALM**

PSALM 8:4–5, 6–7, 8–9 (2a)

R. O Lord, our God, how wonderful your name in all the earth!

*When I behold your heavens, the work of your fingers,
   the moon and the stars which you set in place—
what is man that you should be mindful of him,
   or the son of man that you should care for him?   R.*

*You have made him little less than the angels,
   and crowned him with glory and honor.
You have given him rule over the works of your hands,
   putting all things under his feet.   R.*

All sheep and oxen,
yes, and the beasts of the field,
the birds of the air, the fishes of the sea,
and whatever swims the paths of the seas.   R.

SECOND READING

ROMANS 5:1–5

TO GOD, THROUGH
CHRIST, IN LOVE POURED
OUT THROUGH THE HOLY
SPIRIT.

Brothers and sisters:
Therefore, since we have been justified by faith,
we have peace with God through our Lord Jesus Christ,
through whom we have gained access by faith
to this grace in which we stand,
and we boast in hope of the glory of God.

Not only that, but we even boast of our afflictions,
knowing that affliction produces endurance,
and endurance, proven character,
and proven character, hope,
and hope does not disappoint,
because the love of God has been poured out
into our hearts
through the Holy Spirit that has been given to us.

ALLELUIA

SEE REVELATION 1:8

R. Alleluia, alleluia.

Glory to the Father, the Son, and the Holy Spirit;
to God who is, who was, and who is to come.   R.

GOSPEL

JOHN 16:12–15

EVERYTHING THAT THE
FATHER HAS IS MINE; THE
SPIRIT WILL TAKE FROM
WHAT IS MINE AND
DECLARE IT TO YOU.

Jesus said to his disciples:
"I have much more to tell you, but you cannot
bear it now.
But when he comes, the Spirit of truth,
he will guide you to all truth.
He will not speak on his own,
but he will speak what he hears,
and will declare to you the things that are coming.
He will glorify me,
because he will take from what is mine and declare
it to you.
Everything that the Father has is mine;
for this reason I told you that he will take from what
is mine
and declare it to you."

167A THE MOST HOLY BODY AND BLOOD OF CHRIST

SUNDAY AFTER TRINITY SUNDAY

FIRST READING

DEUTERONOMY 8:2–3,
14B–16a

HE GAVE YOU A FOOD
UNKNOWN TO YOU AND
YOUR FATHERS.

Moses said to the people:
"Remember how for forty years now the LORD, your God,
   has directed all your journeying in the desert,
   so as to test you by affliction
   and find out whether or not it was your intention
   to keep his commandments.

"He therefore let you be afflicted with hunger,
   and then fed you with manna,
   a food unknown to you and your fathers,
   in order to show you that not by bread alone
     does one live,
   but by every word that comes forth from the mouth
     of the LORD.

"Do not forget the LORD, your God,
   who brought you out of the land of Egypt,
   that place of slavery;
   who guided you through the vast and terrible desert
   with its saraph serpents and scorpions,
   its parched and waterless ground;
   who brought forth water for you from the flinty rock
   and fed you in the desert with manna,
   a food unknown to your fathers."

**RESPONSORIAL
PSALM**

PSALM 147:12–13, 14–15,
19–20 (12)

R. Praise the Lord, Jerusalem.
   or:
R. Alleluia.

[This psalm is found on page 46 (lectionary number 19).]

SECOND READING

1 CORINTHIANS 10:16–17

THE BREAD IS ONE, AND
WE, THOUGH MANY, ARE
ONE BODY.

Brothers and sisters:
The cup of blessing that we bless,
   is it not a participation in the blood of Christ?
The bread that we break,
   is it not a participation in the body of Christ?

Because the loaf of bread is one,
   we, though many, are one body,
   for we all partake of the one loaf.

♦

The sequence Laud, O Zion
(Lauda Sion), *or the shorter form
beginning with the verse* Lo! the
angel's food is given, *may be sung
optionally before the Alleluia.*

Laud, O Zion, your salvation,
Laud with hymns of exultation,
   Christ, your king and shepherd true:

Bring him all the praise you know,
He is more than you bestow.
   Never can you reach his due.

Special theme for glad thanksgiving
Is the quick'ning and the living
   Bread today before you set:

From his hands of old partaken,
As we know, by faith unshaken,
   Where the Twelve at supper met.

Full and clear ring out your chanting,
Joy nor sweetest grace be wanting,
   From your heart let praises burst:

For today the feast is holden,
When the institution olden
   Of that supper was rehearsed.

Here the new law's new oblation,
By the new king's revelation,
   Ends the form of ancient rite:

Now the new the old effaces,
Truth away the shadow chases,
   Light dispels the gloom of night.

What he did at supper seated,
Christ ordained to be repeated,
   His memorial ne'er to cease:

And his rule for guidance taking,
Bread and wine we hallow, making
   Thus our sacrifice of peace.

This the truth each Christian learns,
Bread into his flesh he turns,
   To his precious blood the wine:

Sight has fail'd, nor thought conceives,
But a dauntless faith believes,
   Resting on a pow'r divine.

Here beneath these signs are hidden
Priceless things to sense forbidden;
   Sign, not things are all we see:

Blood is poured and flesh is broken,
Yet in either wondrous token
   Christ entire we know to be.

Whoso of this food partakes,
Does not rend the Lord nor breaks;
   Christ is whole to all that tastes:

Thousands are, as one, receivers,
One, as thousands of believers,
   Eats of him who cannot waste.

Bad and good the feast are sharing,
Of what divers dooms preparing,
   Endless death, or endless life.

Life to these, to those damnation,
See how like participation
*   Is with unlike issues rife.*

When the sacrament is broken,
Doubt not, but believe 'tis spoken,
*   That each sever'd outward token*
*   doth the very whole contain.*

Nought the precious gift divides,
Breaking but the sign betides
*   Jesus still the same abides,*
*   still unbroken does remain.*

Lo! the angel's food is given
To the pilgrim who has striven;
*   see the children's bread from heaven,*
*   which on dogs may not be spent.*

Truth the ancient types fulfilling,
Isaac bound, a victim willing,
*   Paschal lamb, its lifeblood spilling,*
*   manna to the fathers sent.*

Very bread, good shepherd, tend us,
Jesu, of your love befriend us,
*   You refresh us, you defend us,*
*   Your eternal goodness send us*
In the land of life to see.

You who all things can and know,
Who on earth such food bestow,
*   Grant us with your saints, though lowest,*
*   Where the heav'nly feast you show,*
Fellow heirs and guests to be. Amen. Alleluia.

◆
The shorter form of the sequence begins here.

ALLELUIA

JOHN 6:51

R. *Alleluia, alleluia.*

I am the living bread that came down from heaven, says the Lord;
whoever eats this bread will live forever.   R.

GOSPEL

JOHN 6:51–58

MY FLESH IS TRUE FOOD, AND MY BLOOD IS TRUE DRINK.

[This reading is found on page 327 (lectionary number 119).]

FIRST READING

EXODUS 24:3–8

THIS IS THE BLOOD
OF THE COVENANT THAT
THE LORD HAS MADE
WITH YOU.

When Moses came to the people
    and related all the words and ordinances of the LORD,
    they all answered with one voice,
    "We will do everything that the LORD has told us."

Moses then wrote down all the words of the LORD and,
    rising early the next day,
    he erected at the foot of the mountain an altar
    and twelve pillars for the twelve tribes of Israel.
Then, having sent certain young men of the Israelites
    to offer holocausts and sacrifice young bulls
    as peace offerings to the LORD,
    Moses took half of the blood and put it in large bowls;
    the other half he splashed on the altar.

Taking the book of the covenant, he read it aloud
        to the people,
    who answered, "All that the LORD has said,
        we will heed and do."

Then he took the blood and sprinkled it on the people,
        saying,
    "This is the blood of the covenant
    that the LORD has made with you
    in accordance with all these words of his."

**RESPONSORIAL
PSALM**

PSALM 116:12–13, 15–16,
17–18 (13)

R. *I will take the cup of salvation, and call on the name of the Lord.*
    or:
R. *Alleluia.*

[This psalm is found on page 127 (lectionary number 39).]

SECOND READING

HEBREWS 9:11–15

THE BLOOD OF CHRIST
WILL CLEANSE OUR
CONSCIENCES.

Brothers and sisters:
When Christ came as high priest
    of the good things that have come to be,
    passing through the greater and more perfect tabernacle
    not made by hands, that is, not belonging
        to this creation,
    he entered once for all into the sanctuary,
    not with the blood of goats and calves
    but with his own blood, thus obtaining
        eternal redemption.

For if the blood of goats and bulls
   and the sprinkling of a heifer's ashes
   can sanctify those who are defiled
   so that their flesh is cleansed,
   how much more will the blood of Christ,
   who through the eternal Spirit offered himself
      unblemished to God,
   cleanse our consciences from dead works
   to worship the living God.

For this reason he is mediator of a new covenant:
   since a death has taken place for deliverance
   from transgressions under the first covenant,
   those who are called may receive the promised
      eternal inheritance.

SEQUENCE

LAUDA SION

[This sequence is found on page 428 (lectionary number 167).]

ALLELUIA

JOHN 6:51

R. Alleluia, alleluia.

*I am the living bread that came down from heaven, says the Lord;
whoever eats this bread will live forever.   R.*

GOSPEL

MARK 14:12–16, 22–26

THIS IS MY BODY. THIS
IS MY BLOOD.

On the first day of the Feast of Unleavened Bread,
   when they sacrificed the Passover lamb,
   Jesus' disciples said to him,
   "Where do you want us to go
   and prepare for you to eat the Passover?"

He sent two of his disciples and said to them,
   "Go into the city and a man will meet you,
   carrying a jar of water.
Follow him.
Wherever he enters, say to the master of the house,
   'The Teacher says, "Where is my guest room
   where I may eat the Passover with my disciples?"'
Then he will show you a large upper room furnished
      and ready.
Make the preparations for us there."

The disciples then went off, entered the city,
   and found it just as he had told them;
   and they prepared the Passover.

While they were eating,
he took bread, said the blessing,
broke it, gave it to them, and said,
"Take it; this is my body."

Then he took a cup, gave thanks, and gave it to them,
and they all drank from it.
He said to them,
"This is my blood of the covenant,
which will be shed for many.
Amen, I say to you,
I shall not drink again the fruit of the vine
until the day when I drink it new in the kingdom
of God."

Then, after singing a hymn,
they went out to the Mount of Olives.

169C   THE MOST HOLY BODY AND BLOOD OF CHRIST
SUNDAY AFTER TRINITY SUNDAY

FIRST READING

GENESIS 14:18–20

MELCHIZEDEK BROUGHT
OUT BREAD AND WINE.

In those days, Melchizedek, king of Salem,
brought out bread and wine,
and being a priest of God Most High,
he blessed Abram with these words:
"Blessed be Abram by God Most High,
the creator of heaven and earth;
and blessed be God Most High,
who delivered your foes into your hand."
Then Abram gave him a tenth of everything.

**RESPONSORIAL
PSALM**

PSALM 110:1, 2, 3, 4 (4b)

R. You are a priest for ever, in the line of Melchizedek.

The LORD said to my lord: "Sit at my right hand
till I make your enemies your footstool."   R.

The scepter of your power the LORD will stretch forth from Zion:
"Rule in the midst of your enemies."   R.

"Yours is princely power in the day of your birth, in holy splendor;
before the daystar, like the dew, I have begotten you."   R.

The LORD has sworn, and he will not repent:
"You are a priest forever, according to the order of Melchizedek."   R.

SECOND READING

1 CORINTHIANS 11:23–26

FOR AS OFTEN AS YOU
EAT AND DRINK, YOU
PROCLAIM THE DEATH
OF THE LORD.

[This reading is found on page 127
(lectionary number 39).]

SEQUENCE

LAUDA SION

[This sequence is found on page 428 (lectionary number 167).]

ALLELUIA

JOHN 6:51

R. Alleluia, alleluia.

I am the living bread that came down from heaven, says the Lord;
whoever eats this bread will live forever.   R.

GOSPEL

LUKE 9:11b–17

THEY ALL ATE AND
WERE SATISFIED.

Jesus spoke to the crowds about the kingdom of God,
    and he healed those who needed to be cured.

As the day was drawing to a close,
    the Twelve approached him and said,
    "Dismiss the crowd
    so that they can go to the surrounding villages
        and farms
    and find lodging and provisions;
    for we are in a deserted place here."

He said to them, "Give them some food yourselves."
They replied, "Five loaves and two fish are all we have,
    unless we ourselves go and buy food for all these people."
Now the men there numbered about five thousand.

Then he said to his disciples,
    "Have them sit down in groups of about fifty."
They did so and made them all sit down.
Then taking the five loaves and the two fish,
    and looking up to heaven,
        he said the blessing over them, broke them,
        and gave them to the disciples to set before the crowd.

They all ate and were satisfied.
And when the leftover fragments were picked up,
    they filled twelve wicker baskets.

FIRST READING

DEUTERONOMY 7:6–11

THE LORD SET HIS HEART
ON YOU AND CHOSE YOU.

Moses said to the people:
"You are a people sacred to the LORD, your God;
  he has chosen you from all the nations on the face
    of the earth
  to be a people peculiarly his own.

"It was not because you are the largest of all nations
  that the LORD set his heart on you and chose you,
  for you are really the smallest of all nations.
It was because the LORD loved you
  and because of his fidelity to the oath he had sworn
    your fathers,
  that he brought you out with his strong hand
  from the place of slavery,
  and ransomed you from the hand of Pharaoh,
    king of Egypt.

"Understand, then, that the LORD, your God,
    is God indeed,
  the faithful God who keeps his merciful covenant
  down to the thousandth generation
  toward those who love him and keep
    his commandments,
  but who repays with destruction a person
    who hates him;
  he does not dally with such a one,
  but makes them personally pay for it.

"You shall therefore carefully observe the commandments,
  the statutes and the decrees that I enjoin on you today."

**RESPONSORIAL
PSALM**

PSALM 103:1–2, 3–4, 6–7, 8,
10 (SEE 17)

R. The Lord's kindness is everlasting to those who fear him.

Bless the LORD, O my soul;
  all my being, bless his holy name.
Bless the LORD, O my soul;
  and forget not all his benefits.   R.

He pardons all your iniquities,
  heals all your ills.
He redeems your life from destruction,
  crowns you with kindness and compassion.   R.

Merciful and gracious is the Lord,
  slow to anger and abounding in kindness.
Not according to our sins does he deal with us,
  nor does he requite us according to our crimes.   R.

1 JOHN 4:7–16

GOD LOVED US.

Beloved, let us love one another,
    because love is of God;
    everyone who loves is begotten by God
        and knows God.
Whoever is without love does not know God,
    for God is love.

In this way the love of God was revealed to us:
    God sent his only Son into the world
    so that we might have life through him.
In this is love:
    not that we have loved God, but that he loved us
    and sent his Son as expiation for our sins.

Beloved, if God so loved us,
    we also must love one another.
No one has ever seen God.
Yet, if we love one another, God remains in us,
    and his love is brought to perfection in us.

This is how we know that we remain in him
        and he in us,
    that he has given us of his Spirit.
Moreover, we have seen and testify
    that the Father sent his Son as savior of the world.
Whoever acknowledges that Jesus is the Son of God,
    God remains in him and he in God.
We have come to know and to believe in the love
        God has for us.

God is love, and whoever remains in love
    remains in God and God in him.

ALLELUIA

MATTHEW 11:29ab

R. *Alleluia, alleluia.*

Take my yoke upon you, says the Lord;
and learn from me, for I am meek and humble of heart.   R.

GOSPEL

MATTHEW 11:25–30

I AM MEEK AND HUMBLE
OF HEART.

[This reading is found on page 286
(lectionary number 100).]

171B THE MOST SACRED HEART OF JESUS

FRIDAY AFTER THE SECOND SUNDAY AFTER PENTECOST

FIRST READING

HOSEA 11:1, 3–4, 8C–9

MY HEART IS OVERWHELMED.

Thus says the LORD:
When Israel was a child I loved him,
   out of Egypt I called my son.
Yet it was I who taught Ephraim to walk,
   who took them in my arms;
I drew them with human cords,
   with bands of love;
I fostered them like one
   who raises an infant to his cheeks;
Yet, though I stooped to feed my child,
   they did not know that I was their healer.

My heart is overwhelmed,
   my pity is stirred.
I will not give vent to my blazing anger,
   I will not destroy Ephraim again;
For I am God and not a man,
    the Holy One present among you;
    I will not let the flames consume you.

RESPONSORIAL PSALM

ISAIAH 12:2–3, 4, 5–6 (3)

R. *You will draw water joyfully from the springs of salvation.*

God indeed is my savior;
   I am confident and unafraid.
My strength and my courage is the LORD,
   and he has been my savior.
With joy you will draw water
   at the fountain of salvation. R.

Give thanks to the LORD, acclaim his name;
   among the nations make known his deeds,
   proclaim how exalted is his name. R.

Sing praise to the LORD for his glorious achievement;
   let this be known throughout all the earth.
Shout with exultation, O city of Zion,
   for great in your midst
   is the Holy One of Israel! R.

SECOND READING

EPHESIANS 3:8–12, 14–19

TO KNOW THE LOVE OF
CHRIST WHICH SURPASSES
KNOWLEDGE.

Brothers and sisters:
To me, the very least of all the holy ones,
    this grace was given,
    to preach to the Gentiles the inscrutable riches
     of Christ,
    and to bring to light for all what is the plan
     of the mystery

hidden from ages past in God who created all things,
so that the manifold wisdom of God
might now be made known through the church
to the principalities and authorities in the heavens.

This was according to the eternal purpose
that he accomplished in Christ Jesus our Lord,
in whom we have boldness of speech
and confidence of access through faith in him.

For this reason I kneel before the Father,
from whom every family in heaven and on earth
is named,
that he may grant you in accord with the riches
of his glory
to be strengthened with power through his Spirit
in the inner self,
and that Christ may dwell in your hearts through faith;
that you, rooted and grounded in love,
may have strength to comprehend
with all the holy ones
what is the breadth and length and height and depth,
and to know the love of Christ
which surpasses knowledge,
so that you may be filled with all the fullness of God.

ALLELUIA

MATTHEW 11:29ab

R. Alleluia, alleluia.

*Take my yoke upon you, says the Lord;
and learn from me, for I am meek and humble of heart.   R.*

OR:

1 JOHN 4:10b

R. Alleluia, alleluia.

*God first loved us
and sent his Son as expiation for our sins.   R.*

GOSPEL

JOHN 19:31–37

ONE SOLDIER THRUST HIS
LANCE INTO HIS SIDE,
AND IMMEDIATELY BLOOD
AND WATER FLOWED OUT.

Since it was preparation day,
in order that the bodies might not remain
on the cross on the sabbath,
for the sabbath day of that week was a solemn one,
the Jews asked Pilate that their legs be broken
and they be taken down.

So the soldiers came and broke the legs of the first
and then of the other one who was crucified with Jesus.
But when they came to Jesus and saw
that he was already dead,
they did not break his legs,
but one soldier thrust his lance into his side,
and immediately blood and water flowed out.

An eyewitness has testified, and his testimony is true;
he knows that he is speaking the truth,
so that you also may come to believe.

For this happened so that the Scripture passage
might be fulfilled:
Not a bone of it will be broken.
And again another passage says:
They will look upon him whom they have pierced.

172C   THE MOST SACRED HEART OF JESUS
FRIDAY AFTER THE SECOND SUNDAY AFTER PENTECOST

FIRST READING

EZEKIEL 34:11–16

I MYSELF WILL PASTURE
MY SHEEP AND I MYSELF
WILL GIVE THEM REST.

Thus says the Lord God:
I myself will look after and tend my sheep.
As a shepherd tends his flock
when he finds himself among his scattered sheep,
so will I tend my sheep.
I will rescue them from every place where
they were scattered
when it was cloudy and dark.

I will lead them out from among the peoples
and gather them from the foreign lands;
I will bring them back to their own country
and pasture them upon the mountains of Israel
in the land's ravines and all its inhabited places.

In good pastures will I pasture them,
and on the mountain heights of Israel
shall be their grazing ground.
There they shall lie down on good grazing ground,
and in rich pastures shall they be pastured
on the mountains of Israel.

I myself will pasture my sheep;
I myself will give them rest, says the Lord God.

The lost I will seek out,
the strayed I will bring back,

the injured I will bind up,
the sick I will heal,
but the sleek and the strong I will destroy,
shepherding them rightly.

RESPONSORIAL PSALM

PSALM 23:1–3a, 3b–4, 5, 6 (1)

R. *The Lord is my shepherd; there is nothing I shall want.*

[This psalm is found on page 80 (lectionary number 31).]

SECOND READING

ROMANS 5:5b–11

GOD PROVES HIS LOVE
FOR US.

Brothers and sisters:
The love of God has been poured out into our hearts
    through the Holy Spirit that has been given to us.

For Christ, while we were still helpless,
    died at the appointed time for the ungodly.
Indeed, only with difficulty does one die for a just person,
    though perhaps for a good person
    one might even find courage to die.
But God proves his love for us
    in that while we were still sinners Christ died for us.
How much more then, since we are now justified
        by his blood,
    will we be saved through him from the wrath.

Indeed, if, while we were enemies,
    we were reconciled to God through the death
        of his Son,
    how much more, once reconciled,
    will we be saved by his life.

Not only that,
    but we also boast of God through our Lord Jesus Christ,
    through whom we have now received reconciliation.

ALLELUIA

MATTHEW 11:29ab

R. *Alleluia, alleluia.*

Take my yoke upon you, says the Lord,
and learn from me, for I am meek and humble of heart.   R.

OR:

JOHN 10:14

R. *Alleluia, alleluia.*

I am the good shepherd, says the Lord,
I know my sheep, and mine know me.   R.

Jesus addressed this parable to the Pharisees and scribes:
"What man among you having a hundred sheep
    and losing one of them
  would not leave the ninety-nine in the desert
  and go after the lost one until he finds it?
And when he does find it,
  he sets it on his shoulders with great joy
  and, upon his arrival home,
  he calls together his friends and neighbors
    and says to them,
  'Rejoice with me because I have found my lost sheep.'

"I tell you, in just the same way
  there will be more joy in heaven over one sinner
    who repents
  than over ninety-nine righteous people
  who have no need of repentance."

COMMON TEXTS FOR SUNG RESPONSORIAL PSALMS

RESPONSES

LECTIONARY NUMBER 173

♦

The psalm as a rule is drawn from the Lectionary because the individual psalm texts are directly connected with the individual readings: the choice of psalm depends therefore on the readings.

Nevertheless, in order that the people may be able to join in the responsorial psalm more readily, some texts of responses and psalms have been chosen, according to the different seasons of the year and classes of saints, for optional use, whenever the psalm is sung, in place of the text corresponding to the reading (see General Instruction of the Roman Missal, n. 36).

SEASON OF ADVENT	*Come, O Lord, and set us free.*
SEASON OF CHRISTMAS	*Lord, today we have seen your glory.*
SEASON OF LENT	*Remember, O Lord, your faithfulness and love.*
SEASON OF EASTER	*Alleluia (two or three times).*

ORDINARY TIME

A) PSALM OF PRAISE

Praise the Lord for he is good.
  or:
We praise you, O Lord, for all your works
    are wonderful.
  or:
Sing to the Lord a new song.

B) PSALM OF PETITION:

The Lord is near to all who call on him.
  or:
Hear us, Lord, and save us.
  or:
The Lord is kind and merciful.

PSALMS

LECTIONARY NUMBER 174

SEASON OF ADVENT

1.
PSALM 25:4–5, 8–9, 10, 14 (1)

R. *To you, O Lord, I lift my soul.*

Your ways, O Lord, make known to me;
  teach me your paths.
Guide me in your truth and teach me,
  for you are God my savior.   R.

Good and upright is the Lord,
  thus he shows sinners the way.
He guides the humble to justice and
  teaches the humble his way.   R.

All the paths of the Lord are kindness
    and constancy
    toward those who keep his covenant
    and his decrees.
The friendship of the Lord is with those
    who fear him,
    and his covenant for their instruction.   R.

2.
PSALM 85:9–10, 11–12, 13–14
(8A)

R. *Lord, show us your mercy and love.*

I will hear what God proclaims;
  the Lord — for he proclaims peace.

Near indeed is his salvation to those
  who fear him,
    glory dwelling in our land.   R.

Kindness and truth shall meet;
  justice and peace shall kiss.
Truth shall spring out of the earth,
  and justice shall look down from heaven. R.

The Lord himself will give his benefits;
  our land shall yield its increase.
Justice shall walk before him,
  and prepare the way of his steps.   R.

SEASON OF CHRISTMAS

3.
PSALM 98:1, 2–3ab, 3cd–4,
5–6 (3cd)

R. All the ends of the earth have seen
    the saving power of God.

Sing to the Lord a new song,
  for he has done wondrous deeds:
His right hand has won victory for him,
  his holy arm.   R.

The Lord has made his salvation known:
  in the sight of the nations he has revealed
    his justice.
He has remembered his kindness and
  his faithfulness
    toward the house of Israel.   R.

All the ends of the earth have seen
  the salvation by our God.
Sing joyfully to the Lord, all you lands;
  break into song; sing praise.   R.

Sing praise to the Lord with the harp,
  with the harp and melodious song.
With trumpets and the sound of the horn,
  sing joyfully before the King, the Lord.   R.

EPIPHANY

4.
PSALM 72:1–2, 7–8, 10–11,
12–13 (SEE 11)

R. Lord, every nation on earth will adore you.

O God, with your judgment endow the king,
  and with your justice the king's son;
he shall govern your people with justice
  and your afflicted ones with judgment.   R.

Justice shall flower in his days,
  and profound peace, till the moon be no more.
May he rule from sea to sea,
  and from the River to the ends of the earth.   R.

The kings of Tarshish and the Islands
  shall offer gifts;
    the kings of Arabia and Seba shall bring tribute.
All kings shall pay him homage,
  all nations shall serve him.   R.

For he shall rescue the poor when he cries out,
 and the afflicted when he has no one
  to help him.
He shall have pity for the lowly and the poor;
 the lives of the poor he shall save.   R.

SEASON OF LENT

5.

PSALM 51:3–4, 5–6, 12–13,
14, 17 (SEE 3a)

R. Be merciful, O Lord, for we have sinned.

Have mercy on me, God, in your goodness;
 in the greatness of your compassion
  wipe out my offense.
Thoroughly wash me from my guilt;
 and of my sin cleanse me.   R.

For I acknowledge my offense,
 and my sin is before me always.
"Against you only have I sinned,
 and done what is evil in your sight."   R.

A clean heart create for me, O God;
 and a steadfast spirit renew within me.
Cast me not out from your presence,
 and your holy spirit take not from me.   R.

Give me back the joy of your salvation,
 and a willing spirit sustain in me.
O Lord, open my lips,
 and my mouth shall proclaim your praise.   R.

6.

PSALM 91:1–2, 10–11, 12–13,
14, 16 (SEE 15b)

R. Be with me, Lord, when I am in trouble.

You who dwell in the shelter of the Most High,
 who abide in the shadow of the Almighty,
say to the LORD, "My refuge and my fortress,
 my God, in whom I trust."   R.

No evil shall befall you,
 nor affliction come near your tent.
For God commands the angels
 to guard you in all your ways.   R.

Upon their hands they shall bear you up,
 lest you dash your foot against a stone.
You shall tread upon the asp and the viper;
 you shall trample down the lion
  and the dragon.   R.

Because he clings to me, I will deliver him;
 I will set him on high because he
  acknowledges my name.
He shall call upon me, and I will answer him;
 I will be with him in distress;
 I will deliver him and glorify him. R.

7.
PSALM 130:1–2, 3–4, 4–6,
7–8 (7bc)

R. With the Lord there is mercy,
    and fullness of redemption.

Out of the depths I cry to you, O LORD;
    Lord, hear my voice!
Let your ears be attentive
    to my voice in supplication.   R.

If you, LORD, mark our iniquities,
    Lord, who can stand?
But with you is forgiveness
    and so you may be revered.   R.

I trust in the LORD;
    my soul trusts in his word.
My soul waits for the LORD
    more than sentinels wait for the dawn.   R.

For with the LORD is kindness
    and with him is plenteous redemption;
and he will redeem Israel
    from all their iniquities.   R.

HOLY WEEK

8.
PSALM 22:8–9, 17–18, 19–20,
23–24 (2a)

R. My God, my God, why have you
    abandoned me?

All who see me scoff at me;
    they mock me with parted lips,
they wag their heads:
    "He relied on the LORD; let him deliver him,
    let him rescue him, if he loves him."   R.

Many dogs surround me,
    a pack of evildoers closes in upon me.
They have pierced my hands and my feet;
    I can count all my bones.   R.

They divide my garments among them,
    and for my vesture they cast lots.
But you, O LORD, be not far from me;
    O my help, hasten to aid me.   R.

I will proclaim your name to my brethren;
    in the midst of the assembly I will praise you:
"You who fear the Lord, praise him;
    all you descendants of Jacob give glory to him;
    revere him, all you descendants of Israel!"   R.

EASTER VIGIL

9A.
PSALM 136:1–3, 4–6, 7–9,
24–26

R. God's love is everlasting.

Give thanks to the LORD, for he is good,
    for his mercy endures forever;
give thanks to the God of gods,
    for his mercy endures forever;
give thanks to the LORD of lords,
    for his mercy endures forever.   R.

Who alone does great wonders,
for his mercy endures forever;
who made the heavens in wisdom,
for his mercy endures forever;
who spread out the earth upon the waters,
for his mercy endures forever.   R.

Who made the great lights,
for his mercy endures forever;
the sun to rule over the day,
for his mercy endures forever;
the moon and the stars to rule over the night,
for his mercy endures forever.   R.

Who freed us from our foes,
for his mercy endures forever;
who gives food to all flesh,
for his mercy endures forever;
give thanks to the God of heaven,
for his mercy endures forever.   R.

9B.
PSALM 136:1, 3, 16, 21–23,
24–26

R. God's love is everlasting.

Give thanks to the LORD, for he is good,
for his mercy endures forever;
give thanks to the LORD of lords,
for his mercy endures forever;
who led his people through the wilderness,
for his mercy endures forever.   R.

Who made their land a heritage,
for his mercy endures forever;
the heritage of Israel, his servant,
for his mercy endures forever;
who remembered us in our abjection,
for his mercy endures forever.   R.

Who freed us from our foes,
for his mercy endures forever;
who gives food to all flesh,
for his mercy endures forever;
give thanks to the God of heaven,
for his mercy endures forever.   R.

SEASON OF EASTER

10.
PSALM 118:1–2, 16–17,
22–23 (24)

R. This is the day the Lord has made;
let us rejoice and be glad.

Give thanks to the LORD, for he is good,
for his mercy endures forever.
Let the house of Israel say,
"His mercy endures forever."   R.

The right hand of the LORD is exalted;
the right hand of the LORD has struck
with power.
I shall not die, but live,
and declare the works of the LORD.   R.

The stone which the builders rejected
has become the cornerstone.
By the Lᴏʀᴅ has this been done;
it is wonderful in our eyes.   R.

11.
PSALM 66:1–3, 4–5, 6–7, 16,
20 (1)

R. Let all the earth cry out to God with joy,
alleluia.

Shout joyfully to God, all the earth;
sing praise to the glory of his name;
proclaim his glorious praise.
Say to God, "How tremendous are
your deeds!"   R.

"Let all on earth worship and sing praise to you,
sing praise to your name!"
Come and see the works of God,
his tremendous deeds among the children
of Adam.   R.

He changed the sea into dry land;
through the river they passed on foot;
therefore let us rejoice in him,
he rules by his might forever. R.

Hear now, all you who fear God,
while I declare what he has been done for me.
Blessed be God, who refused me not
my prayer or his kindness!   R.

ASCENSION

12.
PSALM 47:2–3, 6–7, 8–9 (6a)

R. God mounts his throne to shouts of joy.

All you peoples, clap your hands,
shout to God with cries or gladness,
for the Lᴏʀᴅ, the Most High, the awesome,
is the great king over all the earth.   R.

God mounts his throne amid shouts of joy;
the Lᴏʀᴅ, amid trumpet blasts.
Sing praise to God, sing praise;
sing praise to our king, sing praise.   R.

For king of all the earth is God;
sing hymns of praise.
God reigns over the nations,
God sits upon his holy throne.   R.

PENTECOST

13.
PSALM 104:1, 24, 29–30, 31,
34 (SEE 30)

R. Lord, send out your Spirit, and renew the face
of the earth.

Bless the Lᴏʀᴅ, O my soul!
O Lᴏʀᴅ, my God, you are great indeed!
How manifold are your works, O Lᴏʀᴅ!
The earth is full of your creatures.   R.

If you take away their breath, they perish,
and return to their dust.
When you send forth your spirit,
they are created,
and you renew the face of the earth.   R.

May the glory of the LORD endure forever;
may the LORD be glad in his works!
Pleasing to him be my theme;
I will be glad in the LORD. R.

ORDINARY TIME

14.
PSALM 19:8, 9, 10, 11
(JOHN 6:68c)
(SEE JOHN 6:63c)

R. Lord, you have the words of everlasting life.
or:
R. Your words, Lord, are Spirit and life.

The law of the LORD is perfect,
refreshing the soul.
The decree of the LORD is trustworthy,
giving wisdom to the simple.   R.

The precepts of the LORD are right,
rejoicing the heart.
The command of the LORD is clear,
enlightening the eye.   R.

The fear of the LORD is pure,
enduring forever.
The ordinances of the LORD are true,
all of them just.   R.

They are more precious than gold,
than a heap of purest gold;
sweeter also than syrup
or honey from the comb.   R.

15.
PSALM 27:1, 4, 13–14 (1a)

R. The Lord is my light and my salvation.

The LORD is my light and my salvation;
whom should I fear?
The LORD is my life's refuge;
of whom should I be afraid?   R.

One thing I ask of the LORD;
this I seek:
to dwell in the house of the LORD
all the days of my life,
that I may gaze on the loveliness of the LORD,
and contemplate his temple.   R.

I believe that I shall see the bounty of the LORD
in the land of the living.
Wait for the LORD, with courage;
be stouthearted, and wait for the LORD!   R.

16.
PSALM 34:2–3, 4–5, 6–7, 8–9
(2)(9a)

R. *I will bless the Lord at all times.*
   or:
R. *Taste and see the goodness of the Lord.*

I will bless the LORD at all times;
   his praise shall be ever in my mouth.
Let my soul glory in the LORD;
   the lowly will hear me and be glad.   R.

Glorify the LORD with me;
   let us extol his name.
I sought the LORD, and he answered me,
   and delivered me from all my fears.   R.

Look to him that you may be radiant with joy,
   and your faces may not blush with shame.
When the poor one called out, the LORD heard
   and from all his distress he saved him.   R.

The angel of the LORD encamps
   around those who fear him, and delivers them.
Taste and see how good the LORD is;
   blessed the man who takes refuge in him. R.

17.

PSALM 63:2, 3–4, 5–6,
8–9 (2b)

R. *My soul is thirsting for you, O Lord my God.*

O God, you are my God, whom I seek;
   for you my flesh pines and my soul thirsts
like the earth, parched, lifeless
   and without water.   R.

Thus have I gazed toward you in the sanctuary
   to see your power and your glory,
for your kindness is a greater good than life;
   my lips shall glorify you.   R.

Thus I will bless you as I live;
   lifting up my hands, I will call upon your name.
As with the riches of the banquet
   shall my soul be satisfied,
   and with exultant lips my mouth
   shall praise you.   R.

You are my help,
   and in the shadow of your wings
   I shout for joy.
My soul clings fast to you;
   your right hand upholds me.   R.

18.
PSALM 95: 1–2. 6–7, 8–9 (8)

R. *If today you hear his voice, harden not*
      your hearts.

Come, let us sing joyfully to the LORD;
   let us acclaim the Rock of our salvation.
Let us come into his presence with thanksgiving;
   let us joyfully sing psalms to him.   R.

Come, let us bow down and worship;
  let us kneel before the LORD who made us.
For he is our God,
  and we are the people he shepherds,
    the flock he guides. R.

Oh, that today you would hear his voice:
  "Harden not your hearts as at Meribah,
as in the day of Massah in the desert."
  Where your fathers tempted me;
they tested me though they had seen
  my works. R.

19.
PSALM 100:2, 3, 5 (3c)

R. We are his people, the sheep of his flock.

Sing joyfully to the LORD, all you lands;
  serve the LORD with gladness;
come before him with joyful song. R.

Know that the LORD is God,
  he made us, his we are;
his people, the flock he tends. R.

The LORD is good:
  his kindness endures forever,
and his faithfulness, to all generations. R.

20.
PSALM 103:1–2, 3–4, 8, 10,
12–13 (8a)

R. The Lord is kind and merciful.

Bless the LORD, O my soul;
  all my being, bless his holy name.
Bless the LORD, O my soul;
  forget not all his benefits. R.

He pardons all your iniquities,
  heals all your ills.
He redeems your life from destruction,
  crowns you with kindness and compassion. R.

Merciful and gracious is the LORD,
  slow to anger, and abounding in kindness.
Not according to our sins does he deal with us,
  nor does he requite us according to
    our crimes. R.

As far as the east is from the west,
  so far has he put our transgressions from us.
As a father has compassion on his children,
  so the LORD has compassion on those
    who fear him. R.

21.
PSALM 145:1–2, 8–9, 10–11,
13–14 (SEE 1)

R. I will praise your name for ever,
    my king and my God.

I will extol you, O my God and king;
  and I will bless your name forever and ever.

Every day I will bless you;
   and I will praise your name forever
      and ever.   R.

The L<small>ORD</small> is gracious and merciful,
   slow to anger and of great kindness.
The L<small>ORD</small> is good to all,
   and compassionate toward all his works.   R.

Let all your works give you thanks, O L<small>ORD</small>,
   and let your faithful ones bless you.
Let them discourse of the glory of your kingdom
   and speak of your might.   R.

The L<small>ORD</small> is faithful in all his words
   and holy in all his works.
The L<small>ORD</small> lifts up all who are falling
   and raises up all who are bowed down.   R.

LAST WEEKS IN ORDINARY TIME

22.
PSALM 122:1–2, 3–4, 4–5, 6–7,
8–9 (SEE 1)

R. Let us go rejoicing to the house of the Lord.

I rejoiced because they said to me
   "We will go up the house of the L<small>ORD</small>,"
And now we have set foot
   within your gates, O Jerusalem.   R.

Jerusalem, built as a city
   with compact unity.
To it the tribes go up,
   the tribes of the L<small>ORD</small>.   R.

According to the decree for Israel,
   to give thanks to the name of the L<small>ORD</small>.
In it are set up judgment seats,
   seats for the house of David.   R.

Pray for the peace of Jerusalem!
   May those who love you prosper!
May peace be within your walls,
   prosperity in your buildings.   R.

Because of my relatives and friends
   I will say, "Peace be within you!"
Because of the house of the L<small>ORD</small>, our God,
   I will pray for your good.   R.

FIRST READING

ISAIAH 61:1–3ab, 6a, 8b–9

THE LORD HAS ANOINTED ME; HE HAS SENT ME TO BRING GLAD TIDINGS TO THE POOR AND TO GIVE THEM OIL OF GLADNESS.

The spirit of the Lord GOD is upon me,
    because the LORD has anointed me;
he has sent me to bring glad tidings to the poor,
    to heal the brokenhearted,
to proclaim liberty to the captives
    and release to the prisoners,
to announce a year of favor from the LORD
    and a day of vindication by our God,
    to comfort all who mourn;
to place on those who mourn in Zion
    a diadem instead of ashes,
to give them oil of gladness in place of mourning,
    a glorious mantle instead of a listless spirit.

You yourselves shall be named priests of the LORD,
    ministers of our God you shall be called.

I will give them their recompense faithfully,
    a lasting covenant I will make with them.
Their descendants shall be renowned among the nations,
    and their offspring among the peoples;
all who see them shall acknowledge them
    as a race the LORD has blessed.

RESPONSORIAL PSALM

PSALM 89:1, 2–3, 3–4, 5–6 (2a)

R. For ever I will sing the goodness of the Lord.

I have found David, my servant;
    with my holy oil I have anointed him,
that my hand may be always with him,
    and that my arm may make his strong.   R.

My faithfulness and my kindness shall be with him,
    and through my name shall his horn be exalted.
"He shall cry to me, 'You are my father,
    my God, the Rock my savior.'"   R.

SECOND READING

REVELATION 1:5–8

HE HAS MADE US INTO A KINGDOM, PRIESTS FOR HIS GOD AND FATHER.

Jesus Christ is the faithful witness,
    the firstborn of the dead and ruler of the kings
        of the earth.
To him who loves us and has freed us from our sins
    by his blood,
        who has made us into a kingdom, priests for his God
        and Father,
        to him be glory and power forever and ever. Amen.

Behold, he is coming amid the clouds,
    and every eye will see him,
    even those who pierced him.
All the peoples of the earth will lament him.
Yes. Amen.

"I am the Alpha and the Omega," says the Lord God,
    "the one who is and who was
    and who is to come, the almighty."

**VERSE BEFORE
THE GOSPEL**

ISAIAH 61:1 (CITED IN
LUKE 4:18)

*The Spirit of the Lord is upon me
for he sent me to bring glad tidings to the poor.*

GOSPEL

LUKE 4:16–21

THE SPIRIT OF THE LORD
IS UPON ME, BECAUSE HE
HAS ANOINTED ME.

Jesus came to Nazareth, where he had grown up,
    and went according to his custom
    into the synagogue on the sabbath day.

He stood up to read and was handed a scroll
    of the prophet Isaiah.
He unrolled the scroll and found the passage
    where it was written:
    *The Spirit of the Lord is upon me,
    because he has anointed me
    to bring glad tidings to the poor.
    He has sent me to proclaim liberty to captives
    and recovery of sight to the blind,
    to let the oppressed go free,
    and to proclaim a year acceptable to the Lord.*

Rolling up the scroll, he handed it back to the
    attendant and sat down,
    and the eyes of all in the synagogue looked intently
    at him.
    He said to them,
    "Today this Scripture passage is fulfilled
    in your hearing."

EASTER MONDAY

FIRST READING

ACTS 2:14, 22–33

GOD RAISED THIS JESUS;
OF THIS WE ARE ALL
WITNESSES.

On the day of Pentecost, Peter stood up with the Eleven,
  raised his voice, and proclaimed:
"You who are Jews, indeed all of you staying in Jerusalem.
Let this be known to you, and listen to my words.
You who are Israelites, hear these words.
Jesus the Nazarene was a man commended to you by God
    with mighty deeds, wonders, and signs,
    which God worked through him in your midst,
      as you yourselves know.
This man, delivered up by the set plan and
    foreknowledge of God,
    you killed, using lawless men to crucify him.

"But God raised him up, releasing him from the throes
    of death,
  because it was impossible for him to be held by it.
For David says of him:
  I saw the Lord ever before me,
  with him at my right hand I shall not be disturbed.
  Therefore my heart has been glad and my tongue
    has exulted;
  my flesh, too, will dwell in hope,
  because you will not abandon my soul to the netherworld,
  nor will you suffer your holy one to see corruption.
  You have made known to me the paths of life;
  you will fill me with joy in your presence.

"My brothers, one can confidently say to you
    about the patriarch David that he died and was buried,
    and his tomb is in our midst to this day.
But since he was a prophet and knew that God
    had sworn an oath to him
    that he would set one of his descendants
      upon his throne,
  he foresaw and spoke of the resurrection of the Christ,
    that neither was he abandoned to the netherworld
    nor did his flesh see corruption.

"God raised this Jesus;
  of this we are all witnesses.
Exalted at the right hand of God,
    he received the promise of the Holy Spirit
      from the Father
    and poured it forth, as you both see and hear."

R. *You are my inheritance, O Lord.*
    or:
R. *Alleluia.*

[This psalm is found on page 163 (lectionary number 46).]

ALLELUIA

PSALM 118:24

R. *Alleluia, alleluia.*

This is the day the Lord has made;
let us rejoice in it and be glad.   R.

GOSPEL

MATTHEW 28:8–15

GO TELL MY BROTHERS
TO GO TO GALILEE, AND
THERE THEY WILL SEE ME.

The women went away quickly from the tomb,
    fearful yet overjoyed,
        and ran to announce the news to his disciples.
And behold, Jesus met them on their way
        and greeted them.
They approached, embraced his feet,
        and did him homage.
Then Jesus said to them, "Do not be afraid.
Go tell my brothers to go to Galilee,
    and there they will see me."

While they were going, some of the guard
        went into the city
    and told the chief priests all that had happened.
They assembled with the elders and took counsel;
    then they gave a large sum of money to the soldiers,
    telling them, "You are to say,
    'His disciples came by night and stole him
        while we were asleep.'
And if this gets to the ears of the governor,
    we will satisfy him and keep you out of trouble."
The soldiers took the money and did as they
        were instructed.
And this story has circulated among the Jews
        to the present day.

262   OCTAVE OF EASTER

EASTER TUESDAY

FIRST READING

ACTS 2:36–41

REPENT AND BE BAPTIZED,
EVERY ONE OF YOU,
IN THE NAME OF JESUS.

On the day of Pentecost, Peter said to the Jews,
    "Let the whole house of Israel know for certain
    that God has made him both Lord and Christ,
    this Jesus whom you crucified."

Now when they heard this, they were cut to the heart,
and they asked Peter and the other apostles,
"What are we to do, my brothers?"
Peter said to them,
"Repent and be baptized, every one of you,
in the name of Jesus Christ, for the forgiveness
of your sins;
and you will receive the gift of the Holy Spirit.
For the promise is made to you and to your children
and to all those far off,
whomever the Lord our God will call."

He testified with many other arguments,
and was exhorting them,
"Save yourselves from this corrupt generation."
Those who accepted his message were baptized,
and about three thousand persons were added that day.

RESPONSORIAL PSALM

PSALM 33:4–5, 18–19, 20, 22 (5b)

R. The earth is full of the goodness of the Lord.
  or:
R. Alleluia.

Upright is the word of the LORD,
  and all his works are trustworthy.
He loves justice and right;
  of the kindness of the LORD the earth is full.   R.

See, the eyes of the LORD are upon those who fear him,
  upon those who hope for his kindness,
to deliver them from death,
  and preserve them in spite of famine.   R.

Our soul waits for the LORD,
  who is our help and our shield.
May your kindness, O LORD, be upon us;
  who have put our hope in you.   R.

ALLELUIA

PSALM 118:24

R. Alleluia, alleluia.

This is the day the Lord has made;
let us rejoice in it and be glad.   R.

GOSPEL

JOHN 20:11–18

"I HAVE SEEN THE LORD, "
SHE SAID AND THEN
REPORTED WHAT HE
HAD TOLD HER.

Mary stayed outside the tomb weeping.
And as she wept, she bent over into the tomb
and saw two angels in white sitting there,
one at the head and one at the feet
where the body of Jesus had been.
And they said to her, "Woman, why are you weeping?"

She said to them, "They have taken my Lord,
    and I don't know where they laid him."
When she had said this, she turned around
        and saw Jesus there,
    but did not know it was Jesus.

Jesus said to her, "Woman, why are you weeping?
Whom are you looking for?"
She thought it was the gardener and said to him,
    "Sir, if you carried him away,
    tell me where you laid him,
    and I will take him."

Jesus said to her, "Mary!"
She turned and said to him in Hebrew, "Rabbouni,"
    which means Teacher.

Jesus said to her, "Stop holding on to me,
    for I have not yet ascended to the Father.
But go to my brothers and tell them,
    'I am going to my Father and your Father,
    to my God and your God.'"

Mary of Magdala went and announced to the disciples,
    "I have seen the Lord,"
and then reported what he had told her.

263   OCTAVE OF EASTER

EASTER WEDNESDAY

FIRST READING

ACTS 3:1–10

WHAT I DO HAVE, I GIVE
YOU: IN THE NAME OF
JESUS, RISE AND WALK.

Peter and John were going up to the temple area
    for the three o'clock hour of prayer.
And a man crippled from birth was carried
    and placed at the gate of the temple called
        "the Beautiful Gate"
    every day to beg for alms from the people
        who entered the temple.

When he saw Peter and John about to go into the temple,
    he asked for alms.
But Peter looked intently at him, as did John,
    and said, "Look at us."

He paid attention to them, expecting to receive
        something from them.
Peter said, "I have neither silver nor gold,
    but what I do have I give you:
        in the name of Jesus Christ the Nazarene,
        rise and walk."

Then Peter took him by the right hand
    and raised him up,
    and immediately his feet and ankles grew strong.
He leaped up, stood, and walked around,
    and went into the temple with them,
    walking and jumping and praising God.

When all the people saw him walking and praising God,
    they recognized him as the one
    who used to sit begging at the Beautiful Gate
        of the temple,
    and they were filled with amazement and astonishment
    at what had happened to him.

RESPONSORIAL PSALM

PSALM 105:1–2, 3–4, 6–7, 8–9 (3b)

R. Let all who seek the Lord rejoice.
    or:
R. Alleluia.

[This psalm is found on page 39 (lectionary number 17).]

ALLELUIA

PSALM 118:24

R. Alleluia, alleluia.

This is the day the Lord has made;
let us rejoice in it and be glad.   R.

GOSPEL

LUKE 24:13–35

THE LORD WAS MADE KNOWN TO THEM IN THE BREAKING OF BREAD.

That very day, the first day of the week,
    two of Jesus' disciples were going
    to a village seven miles from Jerusalem called Emmaus
    and they were conversing about all the things
        that had occurred.
And it happened that while they were conversing
        and debating,
    Jesus himself drew near and walked with them,
    but their eyes were prevented from recognizing him.

He asked them,
    "What are you discussing as you walk along?"
They stopped, looking downcast.
One of them, named Cleopas, said to him in reply,
    "Are you the only visitor to Jerusalem
    who does not know of the things
    that have taken place there in these days?"

And he replied to them, "What sort of things?"
They said to him,
    "The things that happened to Jesus the Nazarene,
    who was a prophet mighty in deed and word

before God and all the people,
how our chief priests and rulers both handed him over
to a sentence of death and crucified him.
But we were hoping that he would be the one
to redeem Israel;
and besides all this,
it is now the third day since this took place.
Some women from our group, however,
have astounded us:
they were at the tomb early in the morning
and did not find his body;
they came back and reported
that they had indeed seen a vision of angels
who announced that he was alive.
Then some of those with us went to the tomb
and found things just as the women had described,
but him they did not see."

And he said to them, "Oh, how foolish you are!
How slow of heart to believe all that the prophets spoke!
Was it not necessary that the Christ should suffer
these things
and enter into his glory?"

Then beginning with Moses and all the prophets,
he interpreted to them what referred to him
in all the Scriptures.
As they approached the village to which they were going,
he gave the impression that he was going on farther.
But they urged him, "Stay with us,
for it is nearly evening and the day is almost over."
So he went in to stay with them.

And it happened that, while he was with them at table,
he took bread, said the blessing,
broke it, and gave it to them.
With that their eyes were opened
and they recognized him,
but he vanished from their sight.

Then they said to each other,
"Were not our hearts burning within us
while he spoke to us on the way and opened
the Scriptures to us?"

So they set out at once and returned to Jerusalem
where they found gathered together
the eleven and those with them, who were saying,
"The Lord has truly been raised and has appeared
to Simon!"

Then the two recounted to them
what had taken place on the way
and how he was made known to them
in the breaking of bread.

264 OCTAVE OF EASTER

EASTER THURSDAY

FIRST READING

ACTS 3:11–26

THE AUTHOR OF LIFE
YOU PUT DEATH, BUT
GOD RAISED HIM FROM
THE DEAD.

As the crippled man who had been cured
    clung to Peter and John,
    all the people hurried in amazement toward them
    in the portico called "Solomon's Portico."

When Peter saw this, he addressed the people,
"You Israelites, why are you amazed at this,
    and why do you look so intently at us
    as if we had made him walk by our own power or piety?
The God of Abraham, the God of Isaac, and the God
        of Jacob,
    the God of our fathers, has glorified his servant Jesus
    whom you handed over and denied in Pilate's presence,
    when he had decided to release him.

"You denied the Holy and Righteous One
    and asked that a murderer be released to you.
The author of life you put to death,
    but God raised him from the dead;
        of this we are witnesses.

"And by faith in his name,
    this man, whom you see and know,
        his name has made strong,
    and the faith that comes through it
    has given him perfect health,
    in the presence of all of you.

"Now I know, brothers,
    that you acted out of ignorance, just as your leaders did;
    but God has thus brought to fulfillment
    what he had announced beforehand
    through the mouth of all the prophets,
    that his Christ would suffer.

"Repent, therefore, and be converted, that your sins
        may be wiped away,
    and that the Lord may grant you times of refreshment

and send you the Christ already appointed for you,
Jesus, whom heaven must receive until the times
of universal restoration
of which God spoke through the mouth
of his holy prophets from of old.

"For Moses said:
A prophet like me will the Lord, your God, raise up for you
from among your own kinsmen;
to him you shall listen in all that he may say to you.
Everyone who does not listen to that prophet
will be cut off from the people.

"Moreover, all the prophets who spoke,
from Samuel and those afterwards,
also announced these days.
You are the children of the prophets
and of the covenant that God made with your ancestors
when he said to Abraham,
In your offspring all the families of the earth shall be blessed.
For you first, God raised up his servant and sent him
to bless you
by turning each of you from your evil ways."

RESPONSORIAL PSALM

PSALM 8:2, 5, 6–7, 8–9 (2ab)

R. *O Lord, our God, how wonderful your name in all the earth!*
    or:
R. *Alleluia.*

O LORD, *our Lord,*
    how glorious is your name over all the earth!
What is man that you should be mindful of him,
    or the son of man that you should care for him?   R.

You have made him little less than the angels,
    and crowned him with glory and honor.
You have given him rule over the works of your hands,
    putting all things under his feet.   R.

All sheep and oxen,
    yes, and the beasts of the field,
the birds of the air, the fishes of the sea,
    and whatever swims the paths of the seas.   R.

ALLELUIA

PSALM 118:24

R. *Alleluia, alleluia.*

This is the day the Lord has made;
let us rejoice in it and be glad.   R.

GOSPEL

LUKE 24:35–48

THUS IT IS WRITTEN THAT
THE CHRIST WOULD SUFFER
AND RISE FROM THE DEAD
ON THE THIRD DAY.

The two disciples of Jesus recounted
 what had taken place on the way to Emmaus,
 and how he was made known to them
  in the breaking of bread.

While they were still speaking about this,
 he stood in their midst and said to them,
 "Peace be with you."
But they were startled and terrified
 and thought that they were seeing a ghost.
Then he said to them, "Why are you troubled?
And why do questions arise in your hearts?
Look at my hands and my feet, that it is I myself.
Touch me and see, because a ghost does not have
  flesh and bones
 as you can see I have."

And as he said this,
 he showed them his hands and his feet.
While they were still incredulous for joy
  and were amazed,
 he asked them, "Have you anything here to eat?"
They gave him a piece of baked fish;
 he took it and ate it in front of them.

He said to them,
 "These are my words that I spoke to you
  while I was still with you,
 that everything written about me in the law of Moses
 and in the prophets and psalms must be fulfilled."
Then he opened their minds to understand the Scriptures.
And he said to them,
 "Thus it is written that the Christ would suffer
 and rise from the dead on the third day
 and that repentance, for the forgiveness of sins,
 would be preached in his name
 to all the nations, beginning from Jerusalem.
You are witnesses of these things."

265 OCTAVE OF EASTER

EASTER FRIDAY

While Peter and John were still speaking to the people,
 the priests, the captain of the temple guard,
 and the Sadducees confronted them,
 disturbed that they were teaching the people
 and proclaiming in Jesus the resurrection of the dead.

They laid hands on them
and put them in custody until the next day,
since it was already evening.
But many of those who heard the word came to believe
and the number of men grew to about five thousand.

On the next day, their leaders, elders, and scribes
were assembled in Jerusalem, with Annas
the high priest,
Caiaphas, John, Alexander,
and all who were of the high-priestly class.
They brought them into their presence
and questioned them,
"By what power or by what name have you done this?"
Then Peter, filled with the Holy Spirit, answered them,
"Leaders of the people and elders:
If we are being examined today
about a good deed done to a cripple,
namely, by what means he was saved,
then all of you and all the people of Israel should know
that it was in the name of Jesus Christ the Nazarene
whom you crucified, whom God raised from the dead;
in his name this man stands before you healed.

"He is *the stone rejected by you, the builders,*
which has become the cornerstone.
There is no salvation through anyone else,
nor is there any other name under heaven
given to the human race by which we are to be saved."

RESPONSORIAL
PSALM

PSALM 118:1–2, 4, 22–24,
25–27 (22)

R. *The stone rejected by the builders has become the cornerstone.*
    or:
R. *Alleluia.*

Give thanks to the Lord, for he is good,
    for his mercy endures forever.
Let the house of Israel say:
    "His mercy endures forever."
Let those who fear the Lord say,
    "His mercy endures forever."   R.

The stone which the builders rejected
    has become the cornerstone.
By the Lord has this been done;
    it is wonderful in our eyes.
This is the day the Lord has made;
    let us be glad and rejoice in it.   R.

O Lord, grant salvation!
    O Lord, grant prosperity!
Blessed is he who comes in the name of the Lord;
    we bless you from the house of the Lord.
The Lord is God and he has given us light.   R.

GOSPEL

JOHN 21:1–14

JESUS CAME AND TOOK
THE BREAD AND GAVE
IT TO THEM, AND IN LIKE
MANNER THE FISH.

R. Alleluia, alleluia.

This is the day the Lord has made;
let us rejoice in it and be glad.   R.

Jesus revealed himself again to his disciples
    at the Sea of Tiberias.
He revealed himself in this way.
Together were Simon Peter, Thomas called Didymus,
    Nathanael from Cana in Galilee,
    Zebedee's sons, and two others of his disciples.
Simon Peter said to them, "I am going fishing."
They said to him, "We also will come with you."
So they went out and got into the boat,
    but that night they caught nothing.

When it was already dawn, Jesus was standing
    on the shore;
    but the disciples did not realize that it was Jesus.
Jesus said to them,
    "Children, have you caught anything to eat?"
They answered him, "No."
So he said to them,
    "Cast the net over the right side of the boat
    and you will find something."
So they cast it, and were not able to pull it in
    because of the number of fish.

So the disciple whom Jesus loved said to Peter,
    "It is the Lord."
When Simon Peter heard that it was the Lord,
    he tucked in his garment, for he was lightly clad,
    and jumped into the sea.
The other disciples came in the boat,
    for they were not far from shore,
        only about a hundred yards,
    dragging the net with the fish.

When they climbed out on shore,
    they saw a charcoal fire with fish on it and bread.
Jesus said to them,
    "Bring some of the fish you just caught."
So Simon Peter went over and dragged the net ashore
    full of one hundred fifty-three large fish.
Even though there were so many, the net was not torn.

Jesus said to them, "Come, have breakfast."
And none of the disciples dared to ask him,
    "Who are you?"
    because they realized it was the Lord.
Jesus came over and took the bread and gave it to them,
    and in like manner the fish.
This was now the third time Jesus was revealed
        to his disciples
    after being raised from the dead.

266   OCTAVE OF EASTER

EASTER SATURDAY

FIRST READING

ACTS 4:13–21

IT IS IMPOSSIBLE FOR US
NOT TO SPEAK ABOUT WHAT
WE HAVE SEEN AND HEARD.

Observing the boldness of Peter and John
    and perceiving them to be uneducated, ordinary men,
    the Jews were amazed,
    and they recognized them as the companions of Jesus.
Then when they saw the man who had been cured
        standing there with them,
    they could say nothing in reply.
So they ordered them to leave the Sanhedrin,
    and conferred with one another, saying,
    "What are we to do with these men?
Everyone living in Jerusalem knows
        that a remarkable sign
    was done through them, and we cannot deny it.
But so that it may not be spread any further
        among the people,
    let us give them a stern warning
    never again to speak to anyone in this name."

So they called them back
    and ordered them not to speak or teach at all
        in the name of Jesus.
Peter and John, however, said to them in reply,
    "Whether it is right in the sight of God
    for us to obey you rather than God, you be the judges.
It is impossible for us not to speak about what we have
        seen and heard."
After threatening them further,
    the Jews released them,
    finding no way to punish them,
    on account of the people who were all praising God
    for what had happened.

R. *I praise you, Lord, for you have answered me.*
  or:
R. *Alleluia.*

Give thanks to the Lord, for he is good,
  for his mercy endures forever.
My strength and my courage is the Lord,
  and he has been my savior.
The joyful shout of victory
  in the tents of the just. R.

"The right hand of the Lord is exalted;
  The right hand of the Lord has struck with power."
I shall not die, but live,
  and declare the works of the Lord.
Though the Lord has chastised me,
  yet he has not delivered me to death. R.

Open to me the gates of justice;
  I will enter them and give thanks to the Lord.
This is the gate of the Lord;
  the just shall enter it.
I will give thanks to you, for you have answered me
  and have been my savior. R.

ALLELUIA

PSALM 118:24

R. *Alleluia, alleluia.*

This is the day the Lord has made;
let us rejoice in it and be glad. R.

GOSPEL

MARK 16:9–15

GO INTO THE WHOLE
WORLD AND PROCLAIM
THE GOSPEL.

When Jesus had risen, early on the first day of the week,
  he appeared first to Mary Magdalene,
    out of whom he had driven seven demons.
She went and told his companions who were mourning
    and weeping.
When they heard that he was alive
  and had been seen by her, they did not believe.

After this he appeared in another form
  to two of them walking along on their way
    to the country.
They returned and told the others;
  but they did not believe them either.

But later, as the eleven were at table,
    Jesus appeared to them
  and rebuked them for their unbelief and hardness
    of heart
  because they had not believed those
  who saw him after he had been raised.
He said to them, "Go into the whole world
  and proclaim the gospel to every creature."

SOLEMNITIES AND FEASTS
OF THE LORD
AND SAINTS

FIRST READING

MALACHI 3:1–4

THERE WILL COME TO THE
TEMPLE THE LORD WHOM
YOU SEEK.

Thus says the Lord GOD:
Lo, I am sending my messenger
    to prepare the way before me;
and suddenly there will come to the temple
    the LORD whom you seek,
and the messenger of the covenant whom you desire.
    Yes, he is coming, says the LORD of hosts.

But who will endure the day of his coming?
    And who can stand when he appears?
For he is like the refiner's fire,
    or like the fuller's lye.
He will sit refining and purifying silver,
    and he will purify the sons of Levi,
refining them like gold or like silver
    that they may offer due sacrifice to the LORD.
Then the sacrifice of Judah and Jerusalem
    will please the LORD,
        as in the days of old, as in years gone by.

RESPONSORIAL PSALM

PSALM 24:7, 8, 9, 10 (10b)

R. Who is this king of glory? It is the Lord!

Lift up, O gates, your lintels;
    reach up, you ancient portals,
    that the king of glory may come in!   R.

Who is this king of glory?
    The LORD, strong and mighty,
    the LORD, mighty in battle.   R.

Lift up, O gates, your lintels;
    reach up, you ancient portals,
    that the king of glory may come in!   R.

Who is this king of glory?
    The LORD of hosts; he is the king of glory.   R.

SECOND READING

HEBREWS 2:14–18

HE HAD TO BECOME LIKE
HIS BROTHERS AND
SISTERS IN EVERY WAY.

Since the children share in blood and flesh,
    Jesus likewise shared in them,
        that through death he might destroy the one
    who has the power of death, that is, the devil,
    and free those who through fear of death
    had been subject to slavery all their life.

Surely he did not help angels
    but rather the descendants of Abraham;

therefore, he had to become like his brothers
and sisters in every way,
that he might be a merciful and faithful high priest
before God
to expiate the sins of the people.

Because he himself was tested through what he suffered,
he is able to help those who are being tested.

ALLELUIA

LUKE 2:32

R. Alleluia, alleluia.

A light of revelation to the Gentiles
and glory for your people Israel.   R.

GOSPEL

LONGER FORM
LUKE 2:22–40

SHORTER FORM
LUKE 2:22–32

MY EYES HAVE SEEN
YOUR SALVATION.

[When the days were completed for their purification
according to the law of Moses,
Mary and Joseph took Jesus up to Jerusalem
to present him to the Lord,
just as it is written in the law of the Lord,
*Every male that opens the womb shall be consecrated
to the Lord,*
and to offer the sacrifice of
a pair of turtledoves or two young pigeons,
in accordance with the dictate in the law of the Lord.

Now there was a man in Jerusalem whose name
was Simeon.
This man was righteous and devout,
awaiting the consolation of Israel,
and the Holy Spirit was upon him.
It had been revealed to him by the Holy Spirit
that he should not see death
before he had seen the Christ of the Lord.

He came in the Spirit into the temple;
and when the parents brought in the child Jesus
to perform the custom of the law in regard to him,
he took him into his arms and blessed God, saying:
"Now, Master, you may let your servant go
in peace, according to your word,
for my eyes have seen your salvation,
which you prepared in sight of all the peoples,
a light for revelation to the Gentiles,
and glory for your people Israel."]

The child's father and mother were amazed
at what was said about him;
and Simeon blessed them and said to Mary his mother,

"Behold, this child is destined
for the fall and rise of many in Israel,
and to be a sign that will be contradicted
— and you yourself a sword will pierce —
so that the thoughts of many hearts may be revealed."

There was also a prophetess, Anna,
the daughter of Phanuel, of the tribe of Asher.
She was advanced in years,
having lived seven years with her husband
after her marriage,
and then as a widow until she was eighty-four.
She never left the temple,
but worshiped night and day with fasting and prayer.

And coming forward at that very time,
she gave thanks to God and spoke about the child
to all who were awaiting the redemption of Jerusalem.

When they had fulfilled all the prescriptions
of the law of the Lord,
they returned to Galilee, to their own town
of Nazareth.
The child grew and became strong, filled with wisdom;
and the favor of God was upon him.

543   SAINT JOSEPH, HUSBAND OF THE BLESSED VIRGIN MARY

MARCH 19 | FEAST

FIRST READING

2 SAMUEL 7:4–5a, 12–14a, 16

THE LORD GOD WILL GIVE HIM THE THRONE OF DAVID HIS FATHER.

The Lord spoke to Nathan and said:
"Go, tell my servant David,
'When your time comes and you rest
with your ancestors,
I will raise up your heir after you,
sprung from your loins,
and I will make his kingdom firm.

"'It is he who shall build a house for my name.
And I will make his royal throne firm forever.
I will be a father to him,
and he shall be a son to me.
Your house and your kingdom shall endure forever
before me;
your throne shall stand firm forever.'"

R. *The son of David will live for ever.*

The promises of the Lord *I will sing forever,*
    through all generations my mouth will proclaim your faithfulness,
for you have said, "My kindness is established for ever;"
    In heaven you have confirmed your faithfulness.   R.

"I have made a covenant with my chosen one;
    I have sworn to David my servant:
forever will I confirm your posterity
    and establish your throne for all generations."   R.

"He shall say of me, 'You are my father,
    my God, the Rock my savior!'
Forever I will maintain my kindness toward him,
    my covenant with him stands firm."   R.

SECOND READING

ROMANS 4:13, 16–18, 22

ABRAHAM BELIEVED,
HOPING AGAINST HOPE.

Brothers and sisters:
It was not through the law
    that the promise was made to Abraham
        and his descendants
    that he would inherit the world,
    but through the righteousness that comes from faith.

For this reason, it depends on faith,
    so that it may be a gift,
    and the promise may be guaranteed to all
        his descendants,
not to those who only adhere to the law
    but to those who follow the faith of Abraham,
    who is the father of all of us, as it is written,
    I have made you father of many nations.

He is our father in the sight of God,
    in whom he believed, who gives life to the dead
    and calls into being what does not exist.

He believed, hoping against hope,
    that he would become *the father of many nations,*
    according to what was said,
        Thus shall your descendants be.

That is why *it was credited to him as righteousness.*

**VERSE BEFORE
THE GOSPEL
OR ALLELUIA**

PSALM 84:5

R. *[Alleluia, alleluia.]*

Blessed are those who dwell in your house, O Lord,
they never cease to praise you. R.

Jacob was the father of Joseph, the husband of Mary.
Of her was born Jesus who is called the Christ.

Now this is how the birth of Jesus Christ came about.
When his mother Mary was betrothed to Joseph,
  but before they lived together,
  she was found with child through the Holy Spirit.

Joseph her husband, since he was a righteous man,
  yet unwilling to expose her to shame,
  decided to divorce her quietly.

Such was his intention when, behold,
the angel of the Lord appeared to him in a dream
    and said,
  "Joseph, son of David,
  do not be afraid to take Mary your wife into your home.
For it is through the Holy Spirit
  that this child has been conceived in her.
She will bear a son and you are to name him Jesus,
  because he will save his people from their sins."

When Joseph awoke,
  he did as the angel of the Lord had commanded him
  and took his wife into his home.

OR:

LUKE 2:41–51a

YOUR FATHER AND I HAVE
BEEN LOOKING FOR YOU
WITH GREAT ANXIETY.

Each year Jesus' parents went to Jerusalem for the feast
    of Passover,
  and when he was twelve years old,
  they went up according to festival custom.

After they had completed its days, as they were returning,
  the boy Jesus remained behind in Jerusalem,
  but his parents did not know it.
Thinking that he was in the caravan,
  they journeyed for a day
  and looked for him among their relatives
    and acquaintances,
  but not finding him,
  they returned to Jerusalem to look for him.

After three days they found him in the temple,
  sitting in the midst of the teachers,
  listening to them and asking them questions,
  and all who heard him were astounded
  at his understanding and his answers.

When his parents saw him,
  they were astonished,
  and his mother said to him,
    "Son, why have you done this to us?
Your father and I have been looking for you
    with great anxiety."
And he said to them,
  "Why were you looking for me?
Did you not know that I must be in my Father's house?"
But they did not understand what he said to them.
He went down with them and came to Nazareth,
  and was obedient to them.

545 THE ANNUNCIATION OF THE LORD

MARCH 25 | SOLEMNITY

FIRST READING

ISAIAH 7:10–14; 8:10

BEHOLD, THE VIRGIN
SHALL CONCEIVE.

The LORD spoke to Ahaz, saying:
  Ask for a sign from the LORD, your God;
  let it be deep as the netherworld, or high as the sky!

But Ahaz answered,
  "I will not ask! I will not tempt the LORD!"

Then Isaiah said:
  Listen, O house of David!
Is it not enough for you to weary people,
  must you also weary my God?
Therefore the Lord himself will give you this sign:
  the virgin shall conceive, and bear a son,
  and shall name him Emmanuel,
  which means "God is with us!"

RESPONSORIAL PSALM

PSALM 40:7–8, 8–9, 10, 11
(8a, 9a)

R. Here am I, Lord; I come to do your will.

Sacrifice or offering you wished not,
  but ears open to obedience you gave me.
Holocausts and sin-offerings you sought not;
  then said I, "Behold, I come." R.

"In the written scroll it is prescribed for me.
To do your will, O God, is my delight,
  and your law is within my heart!" R.

I announced your justice in the vast assembly;
  I did not restrain my lips, as you, O LORD, know. R.

Your justice I kept not hid within my heart;
  your faithfulness and your salvation I have spoken of;
I have made no secret of your kindness and your truth
  in the vast assembly. R.

SECOND READING

HEBREWS 10:4–10

AS IS WRITTEN OF ME IN
THE SCROLL, BEHOLD,
I COME TO DO YOUR WILL,
O GOD.

Brothers and sisters:
It is impossible that the blood of bulls and goats
    takes away sins.
For this reason, when Christ came into the world,
    he said:
  "Sacrifice and offering you did not desire,
  but a body you prepared for me;
  in holocausts and sin offerings you took no delight.
Then I said, 'As is written of me in the scroll,
  behold, I come to do your will, O God.'"

First Christ says, "Sacrifices and offerings,
  holocausts and sin offerings,
  you neither desired nor delighted in."
These are offered according to the law.
Then he says, "Behold, I come to do your will."
He takes away the first to establish the second.

By this "will," we have been consecrated
through the offering of the body of Jesus Christ
    once for all.

R. [Alleluia, alleluia.]

*The Word became flesh and made his dwelling among us
and we saw his glory.* *R.*

The angel Gabriel was sent from God
  to a town of Galilee called Nazareth,
  to a virgin betrothed to a man named Joseph,
  of the house of David,
  and the virgin's name was Mary.

And coming to her, he said,
  "Hail, full of grace! The Lord is with you."
But she was greatly troubled at what was said
  and pondered what sort of greeting this might be.

Then the angel said to her,
  "Do not be afraid, Mary,
  for you have found favor with God.
Behold, you will conceive in your womb and bear a son,
  and you shall name him Jesus.
He will be great and will be called Son of the Most High,
  and the Lord God will give him the throne of David
    his father,
  and he will rule over the house of Jacob forever,
  and of his kingdom there will be no end."

But Mary said to the angel,
    "How can this be,
    since I have no relations with a man?"
And the angel said to her in reply,
    "The Holy Spirit will come upon you,
    and the power of the Most High will overshadow you.
Therefore the child to be born
    will be called holy, the Son of God.
And behold, Elizabeth, your relative,
    has also conceived a son in her old age,
    and this is the sixth month for her
      who was called barren;
    for nothing will be impossible for God."

Mary said, "Behold, I am the handmaid of the Lord.
May it be done to me according to your word."
Then the angel departed from her.

586   THE NATIVITY OF SAINT JOHN THE BAPTIST

JUNE 23 | AT THE VIGIL MASS

FIRST READING

JEREMIAH 1:4–10

BEFORE I FORMED YOU IN
THE WOMB I KNEW YOU.

In the days of King Josiah, the word of the LORD
    came to me, saying:
Before I formed you in the womb I knew you,
    before you were born I dedicated you,
    a prophet to the nations I appointed you.

"Ah, Lord GOD!" I said,
    "I know not how to speak; I am too young."
But the LORD answered me,
    Say not, "I am too young."
To whomever I send you, you shall go;
    whatever I command you, you shall speak.
Have no fear before them,
    because I am with you to deliver you, says the LORD.

Then the LORD extended his hand and touched
    my mouth, saying,
See, I place my words in your mouth!
This day I set you
    over nations and over kingdoms,
    to root up and to tear down,
    to destroy and to demolish,
    to build and to plant.

RESPONSORIAL PSALM

PSALM 71:1–2, 3–4, 5–6, 15, 17 (6b)

R. Since my mother's womb, you have been my strength.

[This psalm is found on page 228 (lectionary number 72).]

SECOND READING

1 PETER 1:8–12

THE PROPHETS WHO PROPHESIED ABOUT THE GRACE THAT WAS TO BE YOURS SEARCHED AND INVESTIGATED IT.

Beloved:
Although you have not seen Jesus Christ you love him;
    even though you do not see him now
        yet believe in him,
    you rejoice with an indescribable and glorious joy,
    as you attain the goal of your faith, the salvation
        of your souls.

Concerning this salvation,
    prophets who prophesied about the grace that was
        to be yours
    searched and investigated it,
    investigating the time and circumstances
    that the Spirit of Christ within them indicated
    when he testified in advance
    to the sufferings destined for Christ
    and the glories to follow them.

It was revealed to them that they were serving
    not themselves but you
    with regard to the things that have now been
        announced to you
    by those who preached the good news to you
    through the Holy Spirit sent from heaven,
    things into which angels longed to look.

ALLELUIA

SEE JOHN 1:7; LUKE 1:17

R. Alleluia, alleluia.

He came to testify to the light,
to prepare a people fit for the Lord.   R.

GOSPEL

LUKE 1:5–17

YOUR WIFE ELIZABETH WILL BEAR YOU A SON, AND YOU SHALL NAME HIM JOHN.

In the days of Herod, King of Judea,
    there was a priest named Zechariah
    of the priestly division of Abijah;
    his wife was from the daughters of Aaron,
    and her name was Elizabeth.
Both were righteous in the eyes of God,
    observing all the commandments
    and ordinances of the Lord blamelessly.
But they had no child, because Elizabeth was barren
    and both were advanced in years.

Once when he was serving
as priest in his division's turn before God,
according to the practice of the priestly service,
he was chosen by lot
to enter the sanctuary of the Lord to burn incense.
Then, when the whole assembly of the people
was praying outside
at the hour of the incense offering,
the angel of the Lord appeared to him,
standing at the right of the altar of incense.
Zechariah was troubled by what he saw,
and fear came upon him.

But the angel said to him, "Do not be afraid, Zechariah,
because your prayer has been heard.
Your wife Elizabeth will bear you a son,
and you shall name him John.

"And you will have joy and gladness,
and many will rejoice at his birth,
for he will be great in the sight of the Lord.
John will drink neither wine nor strong drink.
He will be filled with the Holy Spirit
even from his mother's womb,
and he will turn many of the children of Israel
to the Lord their God.

"He will go before him in the spirit and power of Elijah
to turn their hearts toward their children
and the disobedient to the understanding
of the righteous,
to prepare a people fit for the Lord."

587   THE NATIVITY OF SAINT JOHN THE BAPTIST

JUNE 24, SOLEMNITY | MASS DURING THE DAY

FIRST READING

ISAIAH 49:1–6

I WILL MAKE YOU A LIGHT
TO THE NATIONS.

Hear me, O coastlands
listen, O distant peoples.
The LORD called me from birth,
from my mother's womb he gave me my name.

He made of me a sharp-edged sword
and concealed me in the shadow of his arm.
He made me a polished arrow,
in his quiver he hid me.

You are my servant, he said to me,
Israel, through whom I show my glory.

Though I thought I had toiled in vain,
    and for nothing, uselessly, spent my strength,
yet my reward is with the LORD,
    my recompense is with my God.

For now the LORD has spoken
    who formed me as his servant from the womb,
that Jacob may be brought back to him
    and Israel gathered to him;
and I am made glorious in the sight of the Lord,
    and my God is now my strength!

It is too little, he says, for you to be my servant,
    to raise up the tribes of Jacob,
    and restore the survivors of Israel;
I will make you a light to the nations,
    that my salvation may reach to the ends of the earth.

RESPONSORIAL
PSALM

PSALM 139:1–3, 13–14,
14–15 (14a)

R. I praise you for I am wonderfully made.

O LORD you have probed me and you know me;
    you know when I sit and when I stand;
    you understand my thoughts from afar.
My journeys and my rest you scrutinize,
    with all my ways you are familiar.   R.

Truly you have formed my inmost being;
    you knit me in my mother's womb.
I give you thanks that I am fearfully, wonderfully made;
    wonderful are your works.   R.

My soul also you knew full well;
    nor was my frame unknown to you
when I was made in secret,
    when I was fashioned in the depths of the earth.   R.

SECOND READING

ACTS 13:22–26

JOHN HERALDED HIS
COMING BY PROCLAIMING
A BAPTISM OF REPENTANCE.

In those days, Paul said:
"God raised up David as their king;
    of him he testified,
    'I have found David, son of Jesse,
        a man after my own heart;
        he will carry out my every wish.'

"From this man's descendants God, according
        to his promise,
    has brought to Israel a savior, Jesus.
John heralded his coming by proclaiming a baptism
        of repentance
    to all the people of Israel;
    and as John was completing his course, he would say,
    'What do you suppose that I am? I am not he.

Behold, one is coming after me;
    I am not worthy to unfasten the sandals of his feet.'

"My brothers, children of the family of Abraham,
    and those others among you who are God-fearing,
    to us this word of salvation has been sent."

ALLELUIA

SEE LUKE 1:76

R. Alleluia, alleluia.

You, child, will be called prophet of the Most High,
for you will go before the Lord to prepare his way. R.

GOSPEL

LUKE 1:57–66, 80

JOHN IS HIS NAME.

When the time arrived for Elizabeth to have her child
    she gave birth to a son.
Her neighbors and relatives heard
    that the Lord had shown his great mercy toward her,
    and they rejoiced with her.

When they came on the eighth day to circumcise
    the child,
    they were going to call him Zechariah after his father,
    but his mother said in reply,
    "No. He will be called John."
But they answered her,
    "There is no one among your relatives
      who has this name."
So they made signs, asking his father what he wished him
    to be called.

He asked for a tablet and wrote, "John is his name,"
    and all were amazed.
Immediately his mouth was opened, his tongue freed,
    and he spoke blessing God.

Then fear came upon all their neighbors,
    and all these matters were discussed
    throughout the hill country of Judea.
All who heard these things took them to heart, saying,
    "What, then, will this child be?"
For surely the hand of the Lord was with him.

The child grew and became strong in spirit,
    and he was in the desert until the day
    of his manifestation to Israel.

FIRST READING

ACTS 3:1–10

WHAT I DO HAVE I GIVE
YOU: IN THE NAME OF
JESUS, RISE AND WALK.

♦

*For a votive Mass of Saint Peter
the readings are taken from the
Feast of the Chair of Saint Peter
the Apostle, February 22, n. 535.*

*For a votive Mass of Saint Paul
the readings are taken from the
Feast of the Conversion of Saint
Paul the Apostle, n. 519.*

Peter and John were going up to the temple area
	for the three o'clock hour of prayer.
And a man crippled from birth was carried
	and placed at the gate of the temple called
		"the Beautiful Gate"
	every day to beg for alms from the people
		who entered the temple.

When he saw Peter and John about to go into the temple,
	he asked for alms.
But Peter looked intently at him, as did John,
	and said, "Look at us."

He paid attention to them, expecting to receive
		something from them.
Peter said, "I have neither silver nor gold,
	but what I do have I give you:
		in the name of Jesus Christ the Nazarene,
			rise and walk."
Then Peter took him by the right hand and raised him up,
	and immediately his feet and ankles grew strong.
He leaped up, stood, and walked around,
	and went into the temple with them,
	walking and jumping and praising God.

When all the people saw the man walking
		and praising God,
	they recognized him as the one who used to sit begging
	at the Beautiful Gate of the temple,
	and they were filled with amazement and astonishment
	at what had happened to him.

RESPONSORIAL PSALM

PSALM 19:2–3, 4–5 (5a)

R. *Their message goes out through all the earth.*

*The heavens declare the glory of God,
	and the firmament proclaims his handiwork.
Day pours out the word to day,
	and night to night imparts knowledge.* R.

*Not a word nor a discourse
	whose voice is not heard;
through all the earth their voice resounds,
	and to the ends of the world, their message.* R.

I want you to know, brothers and sisters,
   that the gospel preached by me is not of human origin.
For I did not receive it from a human being,
     nor was I taught it,
   but it came through a revelation of Jesus Christ.

For you heard of my former way of life in Judaism,
   how I persecuted the church of God beyond measure
   and tried to destroy it, and progressed in Judaism
   beyond many of my contemporaries among my race,
   since I was even more a zealot for my ancestral
     traditions.

But when God, who from my mother's womb
     had set me apart
   and called me through his grace,
   was pleased to reveal his Son to me,
   so that I might proclaim him to the Gentiles,
   I did not immediately consult flesh and blood,
   nor did I go up to Jerusalem
   to those who were apostles before me;
   rather, I went into Arabia and then returned
     to Damascus.

Then after three years I went up to Jerusalem
   to confer with Cephas and remained with him
     for fifteen days.
But I did not see any other of the apostles,
   only James the brother of the Lord.
— As to what I am writing to you, behold,
   before God, I am not lying.

R. *Alleluia, alleluia.*

Lord, you know everything;
you know that I love you.   R.

Jesus revealed himself to his disciples and,
   when they had finished breakfast, said to Simon Peter,
   "Simon, son of John, do you love me more than these?"
He answered him, "Yes, Lord, you know that I love you."
Jesus said to him, "Feed my lambs."

He then said to him a second time,
   "Simon, son of John, do you love me?"
He answered him, "Yes, Lord, you know that I love you."
He said to him, "Tend my sheep."

He said to him the third time,
  "Simon, son of John, do you love me?"
Peter was distressed that Jesus had said to him
    a third time,
  "Do you love me?" and he said to him,
  "Lord, you know everything; you know that I love you."
Jesus said to him, "Feed my sheep.

"Amen, amen, I say to you, when you were younger,
  you used to dress yourself and go where you wanted;
  but when you grow old, you will stretch out your hands,
  and someone else will dress you
  and lead you where you do not want to go."

He said this signifying by what kind of death
  he would glorify God.
And when he had said this, he said to him, "Follow me."

591   SAINTS PETER AND PAUL, APOSTLES
JUNE 29, SOLEMNITY | MASS DURING THE DAY

FIRST READING

ACTS 12:1–11

NOW I KNOW FOR CERTAIN
THAT THE LORD RESCUED
ME FROM THE HAND OF
HEROD.

In those days, King Herod laid hands upon some
    members of the church to harm them.
He had James, the brother of John, killed by the sword,
  and when he saw that this was pleasing to the Jews
  He proceeded to arrest Peter also.
— It was the feast of Unleavened Bread.

He had him taken into custody and put in prison
  under the guard of four squads of four soldiers each.
He intended to bring him before the people
    after Passover.
Peter thus was being kept in prison,
  but prayer by the church was fervently being made
  to God on his behalf.

On the very night before Herod was to bring him to trial,
  Peter, secured by double chains,
  was sleeping between two soldiers,
  while outside the door guards kept watch on the prison.
Suddenly the angel of the Lord stood by him
  and a light shone in the cell.
He tapped Peter on the side and awakened him, saying,
  "Get up quickly."
The chains fell from his wrists.

The angel said to him,
  "Put on your belt and your sandals."

He did so.
Then he said to him, "Put on your cloak and follow me."
So he followed him out,
    not realizing that what was happening
        through the angel was real;
    he thought he was seeing a vision.

They passed the first guard, then the second,
    and came to the iron gate leading out to the city,
    which opened for them by itself.
They emerged and made their way down an alley,
    and suddenly the angel left him.

RESPONSORIAL PSALM

PSALM 34:2–3, 4–5, 6–7, 8–9 (5b)

R. The angel of the Lord will rescue those who fear him.

[This psalm is found on page 448 (lectionary number 174).]

SECOND READING

2 TIMOTHY 4:6–8, 17–18

FROM NOW ON THE CROWN OF RIGHTEOUSNESS AWAITS ME.

I, Paul, am already being poured out like a libation,
    and the time of my departure is at hand.
I have competed well; I have finished the race;
    I have kept the faith.
From now on the crown of righteousness awaits me,
    which the Lord, the just judge,
        will award to me on that day, and not only to me,
    but to all who have longed for his appearance.

The Lord stood by me and gave me strength,
    so that through me the proclamation might
        be completed
    and all the Gentiles might hear it.
And I was rescued from the lion's mouth.
The Lord will rescue me from every evil threat
    and will bring me safe to his heavenly kingdom.
To him be glory forever and ever. Amen.

ALLELUIA

MATTHEW 16:18

R. Alleluia, alleluia.

*You are Peter and upon this rock I will build my church,
and the gates of the netherworld shall not prevail against it.   R.*

MATTHEW 16:13–19

YOU ARE PETER, AND I
WILL GIVE YOU THE KEYS
TO THE KINGDOM OF
HEAVEN.

When Jesus went into the region of Caesarea Philippi
   he asked his disciples,
   "Who do people say that the Son of Man is?"

They replied, "Some say John the Baptist, others Elijah,
   still others Jeremiah or one of the prophets."
He said to them, "But who do you say that I am?"
Simon Peter said in reply,
   "You are the Christ, the Son of the living God."

Jesus said to him in reply,
   "Blessed are you, Simon son of Jonah.
For flesh and blood has not revealed this to you,
   but my heavenly Father.
And so I say to you, you are Peter,
   and upon this rock I will build my church,
   and the gates of the netherworld shall not prevail
     against it.

"I will give you the keys to the kingdom of heaven.
Whatever you bind on earth shall be bound in heaven;
   and whatever you loose on earth shall be loosed
     in heaven."

614   THE TRANSFIGURATION OF THE LORD
AUGUST 6 | FEAST

FIRST READING

DANIEL 7:9–10, 13–14

HIS CLOTHING WAS
SNOW BRIGHT.

As I watched:
Thrones were set up
   and the Ancient One took his throne.
His clothing was snow bright,
   and the hair on his head as white as wool;
his throne was flames of fire,
   with wheels of burning fire.
A surging stream of fire
   flowed out from where he sat;
thousands upon thousands were ministering to him,
   and myriads upon myriads attended him.
The court was convened and the books were opened.

As the visions during the night continued, I saw
   one like a Son of man coming,
   on the clouds of heaven;
when he reached the Ancient One
   and was presented before him,
the one like a Son of man received dominion, glory,
    and kingship;
   all peoples, nations, and languages serve him.

His dominion is an everlasting dominion
    that shall not be taken away,
    his kingship shall not be destroyed.

RESPONSORIAL PSALM

PSALM 97:1–2, 5–6, 9 (1a, 9a)

R. The Lord is king, the most high over all the earth.

The LORD is king; let the earth rejoice;
    let the many islands be glad.
Clouds and darkness are round about him;
    justice and judgment are the foundation of his throne. R.

The mountains melt like wax before the LORD,
    before the LORD of all the earth.
The heavens proclaim his justice;
    all peoples see his glory. R.

Because you, O Lord, are the Most High over all the earth,
    exalted far above all gods. R.

SECOND READING

2 PETER 1:16–19

WE OURSELVES HEARD
THIS VOICE COME FROM
HEAVEN.

Beloved:
We did not follow cleverly devised myths
    when we made known to you
        the power and coming of our Lord Jesus Christ,
        but we had been eyewitnesses of his majesty.
For he received honor and glory from God the Father
    when that unique declaration came to him
        from the majestic glory,
    "This is my Son, my beloved, with whom
        I am well pleased."

We ourselves heard this voice come from heaven
    while we were with him on the holy mountain.
Moreover, we possess the prophetic message
    that is altogether reliable.
You will do well to be attentive to it,
    as to a lamp shining in a dark place,
        until day dawns and the morning star rises
        in your hearts.

ALLELUIA

MATTHEW 17:5c

R. Alleluia, alleluia.

This is my beloved Son with whom I am well pleased;
listen to him. R.

Jesus took Peter, James, and his brother, John,
 and led them up a high mountain by themselves.
And he was transfigured before them;
 his face shone like the sun
 and his clothes became white as light.
And behold, Moses and Elijah appeared to them,
 conversing with him.

Then Peter said to Jesus in reply,
 "Lord, it is good that we are here.
If you wish, I will make three tents here,
 one for you, one for Moses, and one for Elijah."

While he was still speaking, behold,
 a bright cloud cast a shadow over them,
 then from the cloud came a voice that said,
 "This is my beloved Son, with whom I am well pleased;
 listen to him."

When the disciples heard this, they fell prostrate
 and were very much afraid.
But Jesus came and touched them, saying,
 "Rise, and do not be afraid."
And when the disciples raised their eyes,
 they saw no one else but Jesus alone.

As they were coming down from the mountain,
 Jesus charged them,
 "Do not tell the vision to anyone
 until the Son of Man has been raised from the dead."

Jesus took Peter, James, and John
 and led them up a high mountain apart by themselves.
And he was transfigured before them,
 and his clothes became dazzling white,
 such as no fuller on earth could bleach them.

Then Elijah appeared to them along with Moses,
 and they were conversing with Jesus.
Then Peter said to Jesus in reply,
 "Rabbi, it is good that we are here!
Let us make three tents:
 one for you, one for Moses, and one for Elijah."
He hardly knew what to say, they were so terrified.

Then a cloud came, casting a shadow over them;
 from the cloud came a voice,
 "This is my beloved Son. Listen to him."

Suddenly, looking around, they no longer saw anyone
    but Jesus alone with them.

As they were coming down from the mountain,
    he charged them not to relate what they had seen
        to anyone,
    except when the Son of Man had risen from the dead.
So they kept the matter to themselves,
    questioning what rising from the dead meant.

GOSPEL C

LUKE 9:28b–36

WHILE JESUS WAS PRAYING
HIS FACE CHANGED IN
APPEARANCE.

Jesus took Peter, John, and James
    and went up a mountain to pray.
While he was praying his face changed in appearance
    and his clothing became dazzling white.

And behold, two men were conversing with him,
        Moses and Elijah,
    who appeared in glory and spoke of his exodus
    that he was going to accomplish in Jerusalem.

Peter and his companions had been overcome by sleep,
    but becoming fully awake,
    they saw his glory and the two men standing with him.

As they were about to part from him, Peter said to Jesus,
    "Master, it is good that we are here;
    let us make three tents,
    one for you, one for Moses, and one for Elijah."
But he did not know what he was saying.

While he was still speaking,
    a cloud came and cast a shadow over them,
    and they became frightened when they entered
        the cloud.
Then from the cloud came a voice that said,
    "This is my chosen Son; listen to him."
After the voice had spoken, Jesus was found alone.
They fell silent and did not at that time
    tell anyone what they had seen.

FIRST READING

1 CHRONICLES 15:3–4,
15–16; 16:1–2

THEY BROUGHT IN THE
ARK OF GOD AND SET
IT WITHIN THE TENT
WHICH DAVID HAD
PITCHED FOR IT.

David assembled all Israel in Jerusalem to bring the ark
    of the LORD
  to the place that he had prepared for it.
David also called together the sons of Aaron
    and the Levites.

The Levites bore the ark of God on their shoulders
        with poles, as Moses had ordained
    according to the word of the LORD.

David commanded the chiefs of the Levites
    to appoint their kinsmen as chanters,
    to play on musical instruments, harps, lyres,
        and cymbals,
    to make a loud sound of rejoicing.

They brought in the ark of God and set it within the tent
    which David had pitched for it.
Then they offered up burnt offerings
    and peace offerings to God.
When David had finished offering up the burnt offerings
    and peace offerings,
    he blessed the people in the name of the LORD.

**RESPONSORIAL
PSALM**

PSALM 132:6–7, 9–10,
13–14 (8)

R. Lord, go up to the place of your rest,
    you and the ark of your holiness.

Behold, we heard of it in Ephrathah;
    we found it in the fields of Jaar.
Let us enter into his dwelling,
    let us worship at his footstool.   R.

May your priests be clothed with justice;
    let your faithful ones shout merrily for joy.
For the sake of David your servant,
    reject not the plea of your anointed.   R.

For the LORD has chosen Zion;
    he prefers her for his dwelling.
"Zion is my resting place forever;
    in her will I dwell, for I prefer her."   R.

SECOND READING

1 CORINTHIANS 15:54b–57

GOD GAVE US THE VICTORY
THROUGH JESUS CHRIST.

Brothers and sisters:
When that which is mortal clothes itself
    with immortality,
        then the word that is written shall come about:

Death is swallowed up in victory.
Where, O death, is your victory?
Where, O death, is your sting?

The sting of death is sin,
and the power of sin is the law.
But thanks be to God who gives us the victory
through our Lord Jesus Christ.

R. Alleluia, alleluia.

Blessed are they who hear the word of God
and observe it.   R.

GOSPEL

LUKE 11:27–28

BLESSED IS THE WOMB
THAT CARRIED YOU!

While Jesus was speaking,
a woman from the crowd called out and said to him,
"Blessed is the womb that carried you
and the breasts at which you nursed."

He replied,
"Rather, blessed are those
who hear the word of God and observe it."

622   THE ASSUMPTION OF THE BLESSED VIRGIN MARY
AUGUST 15, SOLEMNITY | MASS DURING THE DAY

FIRST READING

REVELATION 11:19a;
12:1–6a, 10ab

A WOMAN CLOTHED WITH
THE SUN, WITH THE MOON
BENEATH HER FEET.

God's temple in heaven was opened,
and the ark of his covenant could be seen
in the temple.

A great sign appeared in the sky, a woman clothed
with the sun,
with the moon beneath her feet,
and on her head a crown of twelve stars.
She was with child and wailed aloud in pain
as she labored to give birth.

Then another sign appeared in the sky;
it was a huge red dragon, with seven heads
and ten horns,
and on its heads were seven diadems.
Its tail swept away a third of the stars in the sky
and hurled them down to the earth.
Then the dragon stood before the woman
about to give birth,
to devour her child when she gave birth.

She gave birth to a son, a male child,
   destined to rule all the nations with an iron rod.
Her child was caught up to God and his throne.
The woman herself fled into the desert
   where she had a place prepared by God.

Then I heard a loud voice in heaven say:
   "Now have salvation and power come,
   and the kingdom of our God
   and the authority of his Anointed One."

RESPONSORIAL PSALM

PSALM 45:10, 11, 12, 16
(10bc)

R. The queen stands at your right hand, arrayed in gold.

The queen takes her place at your right hand
   in gold of Ophir.   R.

Hear, O daughter, and see; turn your ear,
   forget your people and your father's house.   R.

So shall the king desire your beauty;
   for he is your lord.   R.

They are borne in with gladness and joy;
   they enter the palace of the king.   R.

SECOND READING

1 CORINTHIANS 15:20–27

CHRIST, THE FIRSTFRUITS;
THEN THOSE WHO BELONG
TO HIM.

Brothers and sisters:
Christ has been raised from the dead,
   the firstfruits of those who have fallen asleep.
For since death came through man,
   the resurrection of the dead came also through man.
For just as in Adam all die,
   so too in Christ shall all be brought to life,
   but each one in proper order:
   Christ the firstfruits;
   then, at his coming, those who belong to Christ;
   then comes the end,
   when he hands over the kingdom to his God
     and Father,
   when he has destroyed every sovereignty
   and every authority and power.

For he must reign until he has put all his enemies
   under his feet.
The last enemy to be destroyed is death,
   for "he subjected everything under his feet."

R. *Alleluia, alleluia.*

Mary is taken up to heaven;
a chorus of angels exults.   R.

GOSPEL

LUKE 1:39–56

THE MIGHTY ONE HAS
DONE GREAT THINGS FOR
ME: HE HAS RAISED UP
THE LOWLY.

Mary set out
  and traveled to the hill country in haste
  to a town of Judah,
  where she entered the house of Zechariah
  and greeted Elizabeth.

When Elizabeth heard Mary's greeting,
  the infant leaped in her womb,
  and Elizabeth, filled with the Holy Spirit,
  cried out in a loud voice and said,
  "Blessed are you among women,
  and blessed is the fruit of your womb.
And how does this happen to me,
  that the mother of my Lord should come to me?
For at the moment the sound of your greeting
    reached my ears,
  the infant in my womb leaped for joy.
Blessed are you who believed
  that what was spoken to you by the Lord
  would be fulfilled."

And Mary said:
  "My soul proclaims the greatness of the Lord;
  my spirit rejoices in God my Savior
  for he has looked upon his lowly servant.
  From this day all generations will call me blessed:
  the Almighty has done great things for me,
  and holy is his Name.
  He has mercy on those who fear him
  in every generation.

"He has shown the strength of his arm,
  and has scattered the proud in their conceit.
  He has cast down the mighty from their thrones,
  and has lifted up the lowly.
  He has filled the hungry with good things,
  and the rich he has sent away empty.
  He has come to the help of his servant Israel
  for he has remembered his promise of mercy,
  the promise he made to our fathers,
  to Abraham and his children for ever."

Mary remained with her about three months
  and then returned to her home.

FIRST READING

NUMBERS 21:4b–9

WHENEVER ANYONE
WHO HAD BEEN BITTEN
BY A SERPENT LOOKED
AT THE BRONZE SERPENT,
HE LIVED.

With their patience worn out by the journey,
  the people complained against God and Moses,
  "Why have you brought us up from Egypt
    to die in this desert,
  where there is no food or water?
We are disgusted with this wretched food!"

In punishment the LORD sent among the people
    saraph serpents,
  which bit the people so that many of them died.
Then the people came to Moses and said,
  "We have sinned in complaining against the LORD
    and you.
Pray the LORD to take the serpents from us."

So Moses prayed for the people,
  and the LORD said to Moses,
  "Make a saraph and mount it on a pole,
  and if any who have been bitten look at it,
    they will live."
Moses accordingly made a bronze serpent
    and mounted it on a pole,
  and whenever anyone who had been bitten
    by a serpent
  looked at the bronze serpent, he lived.

RESPONSORIAL PSALM

PSALM 78:1–2, 34–35, 36–37,
38 (SEE 7b)

R. Do not forget the works of the Lord!

Hearken, my people, to my teaching;
  incline your ears to the words of my mouth.
I will open my mouth in a parable,
  I will utter mysteries from of old.   R.

While he slew them they sought him
  and inquired after God again,
remembering that God was their rock
  and the Most High God, their redeemer.   R.

But they flattered him with their mouths
  and lied to him with their tongues,
though their hearts were not steadfast toward him,
  nor were they faithful to his covenant.   R.

Yet he, being merciful, forgave their sin
  and destroyed them not;
often he turned back his anger
  and let none of his wrath be roused.   R.

PHILIPPIANS 2:6–11

HE HUMBLED HIMSELF;
BECAUSE OF THIS GOD
GREATLY EXALTED HIM.

Brothers and sisters:
Christ Jesus, though he was in the form of God,
    did not regard equality with God
    something to be grasped.
Rather, he emptied himself,
    taking the form of a slave,
    coming in human likeness;
    and found human in appearance,
    he humbled himself,
    becoming obedient to the point of death,
    even death on a cross.

Because of this, God greatly exalted him
    and bestowed on him the name
    which is above every name,
    that at the name of Jesus
    every knee should bend,
    of those in heaven and on earth and under the earth,
    and every tongue confess that
    Jesus Christ is Lord,
    to the glory of God the Father.

ALLELUIA

R. *Alleluia, alleluia.*

We adore you, O Christ, and we bless you,
because by your Cross you have redeemed the world. R.

GOSPEL

JOHN 3:13–17

SO THE SON OF MAN MUST
BE LIFTED UP.

Jesus said to Nicodemus:
"No one has gone up to heaven
    except the one who has come down from heaven,
        the Son of Man.
And just as Moses lifted up the serpent in the desert,
    so must the Son of Man be lifted up,
    so that everyone who believes in him
        may have eternal life."

For God so loved the world that he gave his only Son,
    so he who believes in him might not perish
    but might have eternal life.
For God did not send his Son into the world
        to condemn the world,
    but that the world might be saved through him.

FIRST READING

REVELATION 7:2–4, 9–14

I HAD A VISION OF A
GREAT MULTITUDE,
WHICH NO ONE COULD
COUNT, FROM EVERY
NATION, RACE, PEOPLE
AND TONGUE.

I, John, saw another angel come up from the East,
    holding the seal of the living God.
He cried out in a loud voice to the four angels
    who were given power to damage the land and the sea,
    "Do not damage the land or the sea or the trees
    until we put the seal on the foreheads of the servants
        of our God."
I heard the number of those who had been marked
        with the seal,
    one hundred and forty-four thousand marked
    from every tribe of the Israelites.

After this I had a vision of a great multitude,
    which no one could count,
    from every nation, race, people, and tongue.
They stood before the throne and before the Lamb,
    wearing white robes and holding palm branches
        in their hands.
They cried out in a loud voice:
    "Salvation comes from our God,
    who is seated on the throne,
    and from the Lamb."

All the angels stood around the throne
    and around the elders and the four living creatures.
They prostrated themselves before the throne,
    worshiped God, and exclaimed:
    "Amen. Blessing and glory, wisdom and thanksgiving,
    honor, power, and might
    be to our God forever and ever. Amen."

Then one of the elders spoke up and said to me,
    "Who are these wearing white robes,
        and where did they come from?"
I said to him, "My lord, you are the one who knows."
He said to me,
    "These are the ones who have survived the time
        of great distress;
    they have washed their robes
    and made them white in the blood of the Lamb."

RESPONSORIAL PSALM

PSALM 24:1–2, 3–4, 5–6
(SEE 6)

R. Lord, this is the people that longs to see your face.

[This psalm is found on page 21 (lectionary number 10).]

SECOND READING

1 JOHN 3:1–3

WE SHALL SEE GOD
AS HE IS.

Beloved:
See what love the Father has bestowed on us
   that we may be called the children of God.
Yet so we are.
The reason the world does not know us
   is that it did not know him.

Beloved, we are God's children now;
   what we shall be has not yet been revealed.
We do know that when it is revealed we shall
    be like him,
   for we shall see him as he is.

Everyone who has this hope based on him
   makes himself pure, as he is pure.

ALLELUIA

MATTHEW 11:28

R. Alleluia, alleluia.

*Come to me, all you who labor and are burdened
and I will give you rest, says the Lord.   R.*

GOSPEL

MATTHEW 5:1–12a

REJOICE AND BE GLAD,
FOR YOUR REWARD WILL
BE GREAT IN HEAVEN.

When Jesus saw the crowds, he went up the mountain,
   and after he had sat down, his disciples came to him.
He began to teach them, saying:
"Blessed are the poor in spirit,
   for theirs is the kingdom of heaven.
Blessed are they who mourn,
   for they will be comforted.

"Blessed are the meek,
   for they will inherit the land.
Blessed are they who hunger and thirst for righteousness,
   for they will be satisfied.

"Blessed are the merciful,
   for they will be shown mercy.
Blessed are the clean of heart,
   for they will see God.

"Blessed are the peacemakers,
  for they will be called children of God.
Blessed are they who are persecuted for the sake
    of righteousness,
  for theirs is the kingdom of heaven.

"Blessed are you when they insult you and persecute you
  and utter every kind of evil against you falsely
    because of me.
Rejoice and be glad,
  for your reward will be great in heaven."

668   THE COMMEMORATION
OF ALL THE FAITHFUL DEPARTED

NOVEMBER 2 | ALL SOULS

FIRST READING

1.
WISDOM 3:1–9

AS SACRIFICIAL
OFFERINGS HE TOOK
THEM TO HIMSELF.

◆

*The following readings or those
given in the Masses for the Dead,
nos. 1011–1015, may be used.*

The souls of the just are in the hand of God,
  and no torment shall touch them.
They seemed, in the view of the foolish, to be dead;
  and their passing away was thought an affliction
  and their going forth from us, utter destruction.
But they are in peace.

For if in the sight of others, indeed they be punished,
  yet is their hope full of immortality;
chastised a little, they shall be greatly blessed,
  because God tried them
  and found them worthy of himself.
As gold in the furnace, he proved them,
  and as sacrificial offerings he took them to himself.

In the time of their visitation they shall shine,
  and shall dart about as sparks through stubble;
they shall judge nations and rule over peoples,
  and the Lord shall be their King forever.

Those who trust in him shall understand truth,
  and the faithful shall abide with him in love.

2.
WISDOM 4:7–15

AN UNSULLIED LIFE, THE
ATTAINMENT OF OLD AGE.

The just man, though he die early,
  shall be at rest.
For the age that is honorable comes not
  with the passing of time,
  nor can it be measured in terms of years.
Rather, understanding is the hoary crown for men,
  and an unsullied life, the attainment of old age.

He who pleased God was loved;
   he who lived among sinners was transported—
snatched away, lest wickedness pervert his mind
   or deceit beguile his soul;
for the witchery of paltry things obscures what is right
   and the whirl of desire transforms the innocent mind.
Having become perfect in a short while,
   he reached the fullness of a long career;
   for his soul was pleasing to the LORD,
   therefore he sped him out of the midst of wickedness.
But the people saw and did not understand,
   nor did they take this into account.
Because grace and mercy are with his holy ones,
   and his care is with his elect.

3.
ISAIAH 25:6–9

THE LORD WILL DESTROY
DEATH FOREVER.

On this mountain the LORD of hosts
   will provide for all peoples.
On this mountain he will destroy
   the veil that veils all peoples,
the web that is woven over all nations;
   he will destroy death forever.
The Lord GOD will wipe away
   the tears from all faces;
the reproach of his people he will remove
   from the whole earth; for the LORD has spoken.

On that day it will said:
"Behold our God, to whom we looked to save us!
   This is the LORD for whom we looked;
   let us rejoice and be glad that he has saved us!"

RESPONSORIAL
PSALM

1.
PSALM 23:1–3a, 3b–4, 5, 6
(1)(4ab)

R. *The Lord is my shepherd; there is nothing I shall want.*
   or:
R. *Though I walk in the valley of darkness,*
   I fear no evil, for you are with me.

The LORD is my shepherd; I shall not want.
   In verdant pastures he gives me repose;
beside restful waters he leads me;
   he refreshes my soul.   R.

He guides me in right paths
   for his name's sake.
Even though I walk in the dark valley
   I fear no evil; for you are at my side
with your rod and your staff
   that give me courage.   R.

You spread the table before me
in the sight of my foes;
you anoint my head with oil;
my cup overflows.   R.

Only goodness and kindness follow me
all the days of my life;
and I shall dwell in the house of the Lord
for years to come.   R.

2.
PSALM 25:6 AND 7b, 17–18,
20–21 (1)(3a)

R. *To you, O Lord, I lift my soul.*
or:
R. *No one who waits for you, O Lord,*
will ever be put to shame.

Remember that your compassion, O Lord;
and your love are from of old.
In your kindness remember me,
because of your goodness, O Lord.   R.

Relieve the troubles of my heart,
and bring me out of my distress.
Put an end to my affliction and my suffering;
and take away all my sins.   R.

Preserve my life and rescue me;
let me not be put to shame, for I take refuge in you,
Let integrity and uprightness preserve me,
because I wait for you, O Lord.   R.

3.
PSALM 27:1, 4, 7, 8b, 9a,
13–14 (1a)(13)

R. *The Lord is my light and my salvation.*
or:
R. *I believe that I shall see the good things of the Lord*
in the land of the living.

The Lord is my light and my salvation;
whom should I fear?
The Lord is my life's refuge;
of whom should I afraid?   R.

One thing I ask of the Lord;
this I seek:
To dwell in the house of the Lord
all the days of my life,
that I may gaze on the loveliness of the Lord
and contemplate his temple.   R.

Hear, O Lord, the sound of my call;
have pity on me and answer me.
Your presence, O Lord, I seek!
Hide not your face from me.   R.

I believe I shall see the bounty of the Lord
in the land of the living.
Wait for the Lord with courage;
be stouthearted and wait for the Lord!   R.

1.
ROMANS 5:5–11

JUSTIFIED BY HIS BLOOD,
WE WILL BE SAVED
THROUGH CHRIST FROM
THE WRATH.

Brothers and sisters:
Hope does not disappoint,
    because the love of God has been poured out
        into our hearts
    through the Holy Spirit that has been given to us.

For Christ, while we were still helpless,
    died at the appointed time for the ungodly.
Indeed, only with difficulty does one die for a just person,
    though perhaps for a good person
    one might even find courage to die.
But God proves his love for us
    in that while we were still sinners Christ died for us.
How much more then, since we are now justified
      by his blood,
    will we be saved through him from the wrath.

Indeed, if, while we were enemies,
    we were reconciled to God through the death
      of his Son,
    how much more, once reconciled,
    will we be saved by his life.

Not only that,
    but we also boast of God through our Lord Jesus Christ,
    through whom we have now received reconciliation.

2.
ROMANS 5:17–21

WHERE SIN INCREASED,
GRACE OVERFLOWED ALL
THE MORE.

Brothers and sisters:
If, by the transgression of the one,
    death came to reign through that one,
    how much more will those who receive
      the abundance of grace
    and of the gift of justification
    come to reign in life through the one Jesus Christ.

In conclusion, just as through one transgression
    condemnation came upon all,
    so, through one righteous act,
    acquittal and life came to all.
For just as through the disobedience of the one man
    the many were made sinners,
    so through the obedience of the one
    the many will be made righteous.

The law entered in so that transgression might increase
    but, where sin increased, grace overflowed
      all the more, so that,
    as sin reigned in death,

grace also might reign through justification
    for eternal life
through Jesus Christ our Lord.

3.

ROMANS 6:3–9

LET US WALK IN NEWNESS
OF LIFE.

Brothers and sisters:
Are you unaware that we who were baptized
    into Christ Jesus
were baptized into his death?
We were indeed buried with him through baptism
    into death,
    so that, just as Christ was raised from the dead
    by the glory of the Father,
    we too might live in newness of life.

For if we have grown into union with him
    through a death like his,
    we shall also be united with him in the resurrection.
We know that our old self was crucified with him,
    so that our sinful body might be done away with,
    that we might no longer be in slavery to sin.
For a dead person has been absolved from sin.
If, then, we have died with Christ,
    we believe that we shall also live with him.
We know that Christ, raised from the dead, dies no more;
    death no longer has power over him.

4.

ROMANS 8:14–23

WE WAIT FOR THE
REDEMPTION OF OUR
BODIES.

Brothers and sisters:
Those who are led by the Spirit of God
    are sons of God.
For you did not receive a spirit of slavery to fall back
    into fear,
    but you received a Spirit of adoption,
    through whom we cry, "Abba, Father!"
The Spirit himself bears witness with our spirit
    that we are children of God,
    and if children, then heirs,
    heirs of God and joint heirs with Christ,
    if only we suffer with him
    so that we may also be glorified with him.

I consider that the sufferings of this present time
    are as nothing
    compared with the glory to be revealed for us.
For creation awaits with eager expectation
    the revelation of the children of God;
    for creation was made subject to futility,

not of its own accord but because of the one
    who subjected it,
in hope that creation itself
would be set free from slavery to corruption
and share in the glorious freedom of the children
    of God.

We know that all creation is groaning in labor pains
    even until now;
and not only that, but we ourselves,
who have the firstfruits of the Spirit,
we also groan within ourselves
as we wait for adoption, the redemption of our bodies.

5.
ROMANS 8:31b–35, 37–39

WHAT WILL SEPARATE US
FROM THE LOVE OF GOD ?

Brothers and sisters:
If God is for us, who can be against us?
He did not spare his own Son
    but handed him over for us all,
    will he not also give us everything else along with him?

Who will bring a charge against God's chosen ones?
It is God who acquits us.
Who will condemn?

It is Christ Jesus who died, rather, was raised,
    who also is at the right hand of God,
    who indeed intercedes for us.

What will separate us from the love of Christ?
Will anguish, or distress or persecution, or famine,
    or nakedness, or peril, or the sword?

No, in all these things, we conquer overwhelmingly
    through him who loved us.
For I am convinced that neither death, nor life,
    nor angels, nor principalities,
    nor present things, nor future things,
    nor powers, nor height, nor depth,
    nor any other creature will be able to separate us
    from the love of God in Christ Jesus our Lord.

6.
ROMANS 14:7–9, 10c–12

WHETHER WE LIVE OR DIE,
WE ARE THE LORD'S.

Brothers and sisters:
None of us lives for oneself,
    and no one dies for oneself.
For if we live, we live for the Lord,
    and if we die, we die for the Lord;
    so then, whether we live or die, we are the Lord's.

For this is why Christ died and came to life,
that he might be Lord of both the dead and the living.

Why then do you judge your brother?
Or you, why do you look down on your brother?
For we shall all stand before the judgment seat of God;
for it is written:
As I live, says the Lord, every knee
shall bend before me,
and every tongue shall give praise to God.
So then each of us shall give an account of himself
to God.

7.
1 CORINTHIANS 15:20–28

IN CHRIST ALL SHALL BE
BROUGHT TO LIFE.

Brothers and sisters:
Christ has been raised from the dead,
the firstfruits of those who have fallen asleep.
For since death came through a human being,
the resurrection of the dead came also
through a human being.
For just as in Adam all die,
so too in Christ shall all be brought to life,
but each one in proper order:
Christ the firstfruits;
then, at his coming, those who belong to Christ;
then comes the end,
when he hands over the kingdom to his God
and Father.

For he must reign until he has put all his enemies
under his feet.
The last enemy to be destroyed is death,
for he subjected everything under his feet.
But when it says that everything has been subjected,
it is clear that it excludes the one who subjected
everything to him.
When everything is subjected to him,
then the Son himself will also be subjected
to the one who subjected everything to him,
so that God may be all in all.

8.
1 CORINTHIANS 15:51–57

DEATH IS SWALLOWED UP
IN VICTORY.

Brothers and sisters:
Behold, I tell you a mystery.
We shall not all fall asleep, but we will all be changed,
in an instant, in the blink of an eye, at the last trumpet.

For the trumpet will sound,
   the dead will be raised incorruptible,
   and we shall be changed.
For that which is corruptible must clothe itself
    with incorruptibility,
   and that which is mortal must clothe itself
    with immortality.
And when this which is corruptible
  clothes itself with incorruptibility
  and this which is mortal clothes itself
    with immortality,
  then the word that is written shall come about:
  Death is swallowed up in victory.
  Where, O death, is your victory?
  Where, O death, is your sting?

The sting of death is sin,
  and the power of sin is the law.
But thanks be to God who gives us the victory
  through our Lord Jesus Christ.

9.
2 CORINTHIANS 4:14—5:1

WHAT IS SEEN IS
TRANSITORY; WHAT IS
UNSEEN IS ETERNAL.

Brothers and sisters:
We know that the One who raised the Lord Jesus
  will raise us also with Jesus
  and place us with you in his presence.
Everything indeed is for you,
  so that the grace bestowed in abundance on more
    and more people
  may cause the thanksgiving to overflow for the glory
    of God.

Therefore, we are not discouraged;
  rather, although our outer self is wasting away,
  our inner self is being renewed day by day.
For this momentary light affliction
  is producing for us an eternal weight of glory
    beyond all comparison,
  as we look not to what is seen but to what is unseen;
  for what is seen is transitory, but what is unseen
    is eternal.

For we know that if our earthly dwelling, a tent,
  should be destroyed,
  we have a building from God,
  a dwelling not made with hands, eternal in heaven.

WE HAVE AN ETERNAL
DWELLING IN HEAVEN.

Brothers and sisters:
We know that if our earthly dwelling, a tent,
   should be destroyed,
   we have a building from God,
   a dwelling not made with hands,
   eternal in heaven.

We are always courageous,
   although we know that while we are at home
     in the body
   we are away from the Lord,
   for we walk by faith, not by sight.
Yet we are courageous,
   and we would rather leave the body and go home
     to the Lord.

Therefore, we aspire to please him,
   whether we are at home or away.
For we must all appear before the judgment seat of Christ,
   so that each may receive recompense,
   according to what was done in the body,
     whether good or evil.

11.
PHILIPPIANS 3:20–21

THE LORD JESUS WILL
CHANGE OUR LOWLY BODY
TO CONFORM WITH HIS
GLORIFIED BODY.

Brothers and sisters:
Our citizenship is in heaven,
   and from it we also await a savior, the Lord Jesus Christ.
He will change our lowly body
   to conform with his glorified body
   by the power that enables him also
   to bring all things into subjection to himself.

12.
1 THESSALONIANS 4:13–18

WE SHALL ALWAYS BE
WITH THE LORD.

We do not want you to be unaware, brothers and sisters,
   about those who have fallen asleep,
   so that you may not grieve like the rest,
     who have no hope.
For if we believe that Jesus died and rose,
   so too will God, through Jesus,
   bring with him those who have fallen asleep.
Indeed, we tell you this, on the word of the Lord,
   that we who are alive,
   who are left until the coming of the Lord,
   will surely not precede those who have fallen asleep.

For the Lord himself, with a word of command,
   with the voice of an archangel and with the trumpet
     of God,

will come down from heaven,
and the dead in Christ will rise first.
Then we who are alive, who are left,
will be caught up together with them in the clouds
to meet the Lord in the air.
Thus we shall always be with the Lord.
Therefore, console one another with these words.

13.
2 TIMOTHY 2:8–13

IF WE HAVE DIED WITH
CHRIST, WE SHALL ALSO
LIVE WITH HIM.

Beloved:
Remember Jesus Christ, raised from the dead,
a descendant of David:
such is my gospel, for which I am suffering,
even to the point of chains, like a criminal.
But the word of God is not chained.
Therefore, I bear with everything for the sake
of those who are chosen,
so that they too may obtain the salvation that is
in Christ Jesus,
together with eternal glory.

This saying is trustworthy:
If we have died with him
we shall also live with him;
if we persevere
we shall also reign with him.
But if we deny him
he will deny us.
If we are unfaithful
he remains faithful,
for he cannot deny himself.

ALLELUIA VERSE AND VERSE BEFORE THE GOSPEL

MATTHEW 25:34

Come, you who are blessed by my Father;
inherit the kingdom prepared for you
from the foundation of the world.

OR:

SEE JOHN 3:16

God so loved the world that he gave his only Son
so that everyone who sees the Son and believes in him
may have eternal life, says the Lord.

OR:

SEE JOHN 6:40

This is the will of my Father, says the Lord,
that everyone who sees the Son and believes in him
may have eternal life.

OR:

JOHN 6:51

I am the living bread that came down from heaven, says the Lord;
whoever eats this bread will live forever.

OR:

JOHN 11:25a, 26

I am the resurrection and the life, says the Lord;
whoever believes in me, even if he dies, will live forever.

GOSPEL

1.
MATTHEW 5:1–12a

REJOICE AND BE GLAD,
FOR YOUR REWARD WILL
BE GREAT IN HEAVEN.

When Jesus saw the crowds, he went up the mountain,
   and after he had sat down, his disciples came to him.
He began to teach them, saying:
"Blessed are the poor in spirit,
   for theirs is the kingdom of heaven.
Blessed are they who mourn,
   for they will be comforted.

"Blessed are the meek,
   for they will inherit the land.
Blessed are they who hunger and thirst for righteousness,
   for they will be satisfied.

"Blessed are the merciful,
   for they will be shown mercy.
Blessed are the clean of heart,
   for they will see God.

"Blessed are the peacemakers,
   for they will be called children of God.
Blessed are they who are persecuted for the sake
    of righteousness,
   for theirs is the kingdom of heaven.

"Blessed are you when they insult you and persecute you
   and utter every kind of evil against you falsely
    because of me.
Rejoice and be glad,
   for your reward will be great in heaven."

2.
MATTHEW 11:25–30

COME TO ME . . . AND
I WILL GIVE YOU REST.

At that time Jesus exclaimed:
"I give praise to you, Father, Lord of heaven and earth,
   for although you have hidden these things
   from the wise and the learned
   you have revealed them to little ones.
Yes, Father, such has been your gracious will.
All things have been handed over to me by my Father.
No one knows the Son except the Father,
   and no one knows the Father except the Son
   and anyone to whom the Son wishes to reveal him."

Come to me, all you who labor and are burdened,
    and I will give you rest.
Take my yoke upon you and learn from me,
    for I am meek and humble of heart;
    and you will find rest for yourselves.

"For my yoke is easy, and my burden light."

3.
MATTHEW 25:31–46

COME, YOU WHO ARE
BLESSED BY MY FATHER.

Jesus said to his disciples:
"When the Son of Man comes in his glory,
    and all the angels with him,
    he will sit upon his glorious throne,
    and all the nations will be assembled before him.
And he will separate them one from another,
    as a shepherd separates the sheep from the goats.
He will place the sheep on his right and the goats
    on his left.

"Then the king will say to those on his right,
    'Come, you who are blessed by my Father.
Inherit the kingdom prepared for you from the foundation
    of the world.
For I was hungry and you gave me food,
    I was thirsty and you gave me drink,
    a stranger and you welcomed me,
    naked and you clothed me,
    ill and you cared for me,
    in prison and you visited me.'

"Then the righteous will answer him and say,
    'Lord, when did we see you hungry and feed you,
    or thirsty and give you drink?
When did we see you a stranger and welcome you,
    or naked and clothe you?
When did we see you ill or in prison, and visit you?'
And the king will say to them in reply,
    'Amen, I say to you, whatever you did
    for one of these least brothers of mine, you did for me.'

"Then he will say to those on his left,
    'Depart from me, you accursed,
    into the eternal fire prepared for the devil
    and his angels.
For I was hungry and you gave me no food,
    I was thirsty and you gave me no drink,
    a stranger and you gave me no welcome,
    naked and you gave me no clothing,
    ill and in prison, and you did not care for me.'

"Then they will answer and say,
    'Lord, when did we see you hungry or thirsty
    or a stranger or naked or ill or in prison,
    and not minister to your needs?'
He will answer them, 'Amen, I say to you,
    what you did not do for one of the least of these,
    you did not do for me.'
And these will go off to eternal punishment,
    but the righteous to eternal life."

4.
LUKE 7:11–17

YOUNG MAN, I TELL YOU,
ARISE!

Jesus journeyed to a city called Nain,
    and his disciples and a large crowd accompanied him.
As he drew near to the gate of the city,
    a man who had died was being carried out,
    the only son of his mother, and she was a widow.
A large crowd from the city was with her.

When the Lord saw her,
    he was moved with pity for her and said to her,
    "Do not weep."

He stepped forward and touched the coffin;
    at this the bearers halted,
    and he said, "Young man, I tell you, arise!"
The dead man sat up and began to speak,
    and Jesus gave him to his mother.

Fear seized them all, and they glorified God, exclaiming,
    "A great prophet has arisen in our midst,"
    and "God has visited his people."
This report about him spread through the whole of Judea
    and in all the surrounding region.

5.
LUKE 23:44–46, 50, 52–53;
24:1–6a

FATHER, INTO YOUR HANDS
I COMMEND MY SPIRIT.

It was about noon and darkness came over the whole land
    until three in the afternoon
    because of an eclipse of the sun.
Then the veil of the temple was torn down the middle.
Jesus cried out in a loud voice,
"Father, into your hands I commend my spirit";
    and when he had said this he breathed his last.

Now there was a virtuous and righteous man
        named Joseph who,
    though he was a member of the council,
    went to Pilate and asked for the body of Jesus.
After he had taken the body down,
    he wrapped it in a linen cloth

and laid him in a rock-hewn tomb
in which no one had yet been buried.

At daybreak on the first day of the week
they took the spices they had prepared
and went to the tomb.
They found the stone rolled away from the tomb;
but when they entered,
they did not find the body of the Lord Jesus.
While they were puzzling over this, behold,
two men in dazzling garments appeared to them.
They were terrified and bowed their faces to the ground.

They said to them,
"Why do you seek the living one among the dead?
He is not here, but he has been raised."

6.
LUKE 24:13–16, 28–35

WAS IT NOT NECESSARY
THAT THE CHRIST SHOULD
SUFFER THESE THINGS AND
ENTER INTO HIS GLORY?

That very day, the first day of the week,
two of Jesus' disciples were going
to a village seven miles from Jerusalem called Emmaus,
and they were conversing about all the things
that had occurred.
And it happened that while they were conversing
and debating,
Jesus himself drew near and walked with them,
but their eyes were prevented from recognizing him.

As they approached the village to which they were going,
he gave the impression that he was going on farther.
But they urged him, "Stay with us,
for it is nearly evening and the day is almost over."
So he went in to stay with them.

And it happened that, while he was with them at table,
he took bread, said the blessing,
broke it, and gave it to them.
With that their eyes were opened
and they recognized him,
but he vanished from their sight.

Then they said to each other,
"Were not our hearts burning within us
while he spoke to us on the way and opened
the Scriptures to us?"
So they set out at once and returned to Jerusalem
where they found gathered together
the eleven and those with them, who were saying,
"The Lord has truly been raised and has appeared
to Simon!"

Then the two recounted to them
   what had taken place on the way
   and how he was made known to them
      in the breaking of bread.

7.
JOHN 5:24–29

WHOEVER HEARS MY WORD
AND BELIEVES HAS PASSED
FROM DEATH TO LIFE.

Jesus answered the Jews and said to them:
"Amen, amen, I say to you, whoever hears my word
   and believes in the one who sent me
   has eternal life and will not come to condemnation,
   but has passed from death to life.
Amen, amen, I say to you, the hour is coming
      and is now here
   when the dead will hear the voice of the Son of God,
   and those who hear will live.

"For just as the Father has life in himself,
   so also he gave to his Son the possession of life
      in himself.
And he gave him power to exercise judgment,
   because he is the Son of Man.

"Do not be amazed at this,
   because the hour is coming in which all who are
      in the tombs
   will hear his voice and will come out,
   those who have done good deeds
   to the resurrection of life,
   but those who have done wicked deeds
   to the resurrection of condemnation."

8.
JOHN 6:37–40

EVERYONE WHO BELIEVES
IN THE SON WILL HAVE
ETERNAL LIFE AND
I SHALL RAISE HIM UP
ON THE LAST DAY.

Jesus said to the crowds:
"Everything that the Father gives me will come to me,
   and I will not reject anyone who comes to me,
   because I came down from heaven not to do
      my own will
   but the will of the one who sent me.
And this is the will of the one who sent me,
   that I should not lose anything of what he gave me,
   but that I should raise it on the last day.
For this is the will of my Father,
   that everyone who sees the Son and believes in him
   may have eternal life,
   and I shall raise him up on the last day."

9.
JOHN 6:51–59

WHOEVER EATS THIS
BREAD HAS ETERNAL LIFE
AND I WILL RAISE HIM ON
THE LAST DAY.

Jesus said to the crowds:
"I am the living bread that came down from heaven;
    whoever eats this bread will live forever;
    and the bread that I will give is my flesh
    for the life of the world."

The Jews quarreled among themselves, saying,
"How can this man give us his flesh to eat?"
Jesus said to them,
"Amen, amen, I say to you,
    unless you eat the flesh of the Son of Man
        and drink his blood,
    you do not have life within you.
He who eats my flesh and drinks my blood
    has eternal life,
    and I will raise him on the last day.
For my flesh is true food,
    and my blood is true drink.
He who eats my flesh and drinks my blood
    remains in me and I in him.

"Just as the living Father sent me
    and I have life because of the Father,
    so also he who feeds on me
    will have life because of me.
This is the bread that came down from heaven.

"Unlike your ancestors who ate and still died,
    he who eats this bread will live forever."

10.
JOHN 11:17–27

I AM THE RESURRECTION
AND THE LIFE.

When Jesus arrived in Bethany, he found that Lazarus
    had already been in the tomb for four days.
Now Bethany was near Jerusalem, only about
        two miles away.

Many of the Jews had come to Martha and Mary
    to comfort them about their brother.
When Martha heard that Jesus was coming,
    she went to meet him;
    but Mary sat at home.

Martha said to Jesus,
    "Lord, if you had been here,
    my brother would not have died.
But even now I know that whatever you ask of God,
    God will give you."

Jesus said to her,
  "Your brother will rise."
Martha said to him,
  "I know he will rise,
  in the resurrection on the last day."

Jesus told her,
  "I am the resurrection and the life;
  he who believes in me, even if he dies, will live,
  and he who lives and believes in me will never die.
Do you believe this?"
She said to him, "Yes, Lord.
I have come to believe that you are the Christ,
    the Son of God,
  the one who is coming into the world."

11.
JOHN 11:32–45

LAZARUS, COME OUT!

When Mary, the sister of Lazarus, came to where Jesus was
    and saw him,
  she fell at his feet and said to him,
  "Lord, if you had been here,
  my brother would not have died."

When Jesus saw her weeping and the Jews
  who had come with her weeping,
  he became perturbed and deeply troubled, and said,
  "Where have you laid him?"
They said to him, "Sir, come and see."
And Jesus wept.

So the Jews said, "See how he loved him."
But some of them said,
  "Could not the one who opened the eyes
    of the blind man
  have done something so that this man would
    not have died?"

So Jesus, perturbed again, came to the tomb.
It was a cave, and a stone lay across it.
Jesus said, "Take away the stone."
Martha, the dead man's sister, said to him,
  "Lord, by now there will be a stench;
  he has been dead for four days."

Jesus said to her,
  "Did I not tell you that if you believe
  you will see the glory of God?"

So they took away the stone.
And Jesus raised his eyes and said,

"Father, I thank you for hearing me.
I know that you always hear me;
  but because of the crowd here I have said this,
  that they may believe that you sent me."

And when he had said this,
  he cried out in a loud voice,
  "Lazarus, come out!"
The dead man came out,
  tied hand and foot with burial bands,
  and his face was wrapped in a cloth.

So Jesus said to the crowd,
  "Untie him and let him go."

Now many of Jews who had come to Mary
  and seen what he had done began to believe in him.

Jesus said to his disciples:
  "Do not let your hearts be troubled.
You have faith in God; have faith also in me.

"In my Father's house there are many dwelling places.
If there were not,
  would I have told you that I am going to prepare
    a place for you?
And if I go and prepare a place for you,
  I will come back again and take you to myself,
  so that where I am you also may be.
Where I am going you know the way."

Thomas said to him,
"Master, we do not know where you are going;
  how can we know the way?"
Jesus said to him,
    "I am the way and the truth and the life.
No one comes to the Father except through me."

FIRST READING

EZEKIEL 47:1–2, 8–9, 12

I SAW WATER FLOWING
FROM THE TEMPLE, AND
ALL WHO WERE TOUCHED
BY IT WERE SAVED.

The angel brought me
    back to the entrance of the temple,
    and I saw water flowing out
    from beneath the threshold of the temple
        toward the east,
    for the facade of the temple was toward the east;
    the water flowed down from the southern side
        of the temple,
    south of the altar.

He led me outside by the north gate,
    and around to the outer gate facing the east,
    where I saw water trickling from the southern side.

He said to me,
    "This water flows into the eastern district
        down upon the Arabah,
    and empties into the sea, the salt waters,
        which it makes fresh.
Wherever the river flows,
    every sort of living creature that can multiply shall live,
    and there shall be abundant fish,
    for wherever this water comes the sea shall be
        made fresh.

"Along both banks of the river,
        fruit trees of every kind shall grow;
    their leaves shall not fade, nor their fruit fail.
Every month they shall bear fresh fruit,
    for they shall be watered by the flow from the sanctuary.
Their fruit shall serve for food, and their leaves
        for medicine."

**RESPONSORIAL
PSALM**

PSALM 46:3, 4, 5–6, 8, 11 (5)

R. The waters of the river gladden the city of God,
    the holy dwelling of the Most High.

God is our refuge and our strength,
    an ever-present help in distress.
Therefore we fear not, though the earth be shaken
    and mountains plunge into the depths of the sea.   R.

There is a stream whose runlets gladden the city of God,
    the holy dwelling of the Most High.
God is in its midst; it shall not be disturbed;
    God will help it at the break of dawn.   R.

The LORD of hosts is with us;
  our stronghold is the God of Jacob.
Come! behold the deeds of the LORD,
  the astounding things he has wrought on earth. R.

SECOND READING

1 CORINTHIANS 3:9c–11, 16–17

YOU ARE GOD'S TEMPLE.

Brothers and sisters:
You are God's building.
According to the grace of God given to me,
  like a wise master builder I laid a foundation,
  and another is building upon it.
But each one must be careful how he builds upon it,
  for no one can lay a foundation other than
    the one that is there,
  namely, Jesus Christ.

Do you not know that you are the temple of God,
  and that the Spirit of God dwells in you?
If anyone destroys God's temple,
  God will destroy that person;
  for the temple of God, which you are, is holy.

ALLELUIA

2 CHRONICLES 7:16

R. Alleluia, alleluia.

I have chosen and consecrated this house, says the Lord,
that my name may be there forever. R.

GOSPEL

JOHN 2:13–22

JESUS WAS SPEAKING ABOUT THE TEMPLE OF HIS BODY.

Since the Passover of the Jews was near,
  Jesus went up to Jerusalem.
He found in the temple area those who sold oxen,
    sheep, and doves,
  as well as the money changers seated there.

He made a whip out of cords
  and drove them all out of the temple area,
    with the sheep and oxen,
  and spilled the coins of the money changers
  and overturned their tables,
  and to those who sold doves he said,
  "Take these out of here,
  and stop making my Father's house a marketplace."

His disciples recalled the words of Scripture,
  Zeal for your house will consume me.

At this the Jews answered and said to him,
  "What sign can you show us for doing this?"

Jesus answered and said to them,
 "Destroy this temple and in three days I will raise it up."

The Jews said,
 "This temple has been under construction
   for forty-six years,
 and you will raise it up in three days?"
But he was speaking about the temple of his body.
Therefore, when he was raised from the dead,
   his disciples remembered that he had said this,
   and they came to believe the Scripture
   and the word Jesus had spoken.

689   THE IMMACULATE CONCEPTION OF THE BLESSED VIRGIN MARY

DECEMBER 8 | SOLEMNITY

FIRST READING

GENESIS 3:9–15, 20

I WILL PUT ENMITY
BETWEEN YOUR
OFFSPRING AND HERS.

After the man, Adam, had eaten of the tree,
   the Lord God called to the man and asked him,
     "Where are you?"
He answered, "I heard you in the garden;
   but I was afraid, because I was naked,
   so I hid myself."

Then he asked, "Who told you that you were naked?
You have eaten, then,
   from the tree of which I had forbidden you to eat!"
The man replied,
   "The woman whom you put here with me —
   she gave me fruit from the tree, and so I ate it."
The Lord God then asked the woman,
   "Why did you do such a thing?"
The woman answered,
   "The serpent tricked me into it, so I ate it."

Then the Lord God said to the serpent:
   "Because you have done this, you shall be banned
   from all the animals
   and from all the wild creatures;
   on your belly shall you crawl,
   and dirt shall you eat
   all the days of your life.
   I will put enmity between you and the woman,
   and between your offspring and hers;
   he will strike at your head,
   while you strike at his heel."

The man called his wife Eve,
    because she became the mother of all the living.

RESPONSORIAL PSALM

PSALM 98:1, 2–3, 3–4 (1a)

R. Sing to the Lord a new song, for he has done marvelous deeds.

Sing to the Lord a new song,
    for he has done wondrous deeds;
his right hand has won victory for him,
    his holy arm. R.

The Lord has made his salvation known:
    in the sight of the nations he has revealed his justice.
He has remembered his kindness and his faithfulness
    toward the house of Israel. R.

All the ends of the earth have seen
    the salvation by our God.
Sing joyfully to the Lord, all you lands;
    break into song; sing praise. R.

SECOND READING

EPHESIANS 1:3–6, 11–12

HE CHOSE US IN CHRIST BEFORE THE FOUNDATION OF THE WORLD.

Brothers and sisters:
Blessed be the God and Father of our Lord Jesus Christ,
    who has blessed us in Christ
        with every spiritual blessing in the heavens,
        as he chose us in him, before the foundation
            of the world,
        to be holy and without blemish before him.

In love he destined us for adoption to himself
        through Jesus Christ,
    in accord with the favor of his will,
    for the praise of the glory of his grace
    that he granted us in the beloved.

In him we were also chosen,
    destined in accord with the purpose of the One
    who accomplishes all things according to the
        intention of his will,
    so that we might exist for the praise of his glory,
    we who first hoped in Christ.

ALLELUIA

SEE LUKE 1:28

R. Alleluia, alleluia.

Hail, Mary, full of grace, the Lord is with you;
blessed are you among women. R.

The angel Gabriel was sent from God
   to a town of Galilee called Nazareth,
   to a virgin betrothed to a man named Joseph,
   of the house of David,
   and the virgin's name was Mary.
And coming to her, he said,
   "Hail, full of grace! The Lord is with you."

But she was greatly troubled at what was said
   and pondered what sort of greeting this might be.
Then the angel said to her,
   "Do not be afraid, Mary,
   for you have found favor with God.
Behold, you will conceive in your womb and bear a son,
   and you shall name him Jesus.
He will be great and will be called Son of the Most High,
   and the Lord God will give him the throne of David
     his father,
   and he will rule over the house of Jacob forever,
   and of his kingdom there will be no end."

But Mary said to the angel,
   "How can this be,
   since I have no relations with a man?"

And the angel said to her in reply,
   "The Holy Spirit will come upon you,
   and the power of the Most High will overshadow you.
Therefore the child to be born
   will be called holy, the Son of God.
And behold, Elizabeth, your relative,
   has also conceived a son in her old age,
   and this is the sixth month for her
     who was called barren;
   for nothing will be impossible for God."

Mary said, "Behold, I am the handmaid of the Lord.
May it be done to me according to your word."
Then the angel departed from her.

APPENDICES AND TABLES

APPENDIX I: SEQUENCES

THROUGHOUT THE EASTER OCTAVE

Victimæ paschali laudes

Victimæ paschali laudes
immolent Christiani.

Agnus redemit oves:
Christus innocens Patri
reconciliavit peccatores.

Mors et vita duello
conflixere mirando:
duæ vitæ mortuus regnat vivus.

Dic nobis, Maria,
quid vidisti in via?

Sepulcrum Christi viventis,
et gloriam vidi resurgentis

Angelicos testes,
sudarium et vestes.

Surrexit Christus spes mea:
præcedet suos in Galilæam.

Scimus Christum surrexisse
a mortuis vere:
tu nobis, victor Rex, miserere.

ON PENTECOST SUNDAY

Veni, Sancte Spiritus

Veni, Sancte Spiritus,
et emitte cælitus
lucis tuæ radium.

Veni, pater pauperum,
veni, dator munerum,
veni, lumen cordium.

Consolator optime,
dulcis hospes animæ,
dulce refrigerium.

In labore requies,
in æstu temperies,
in fletu solacium.

O lux beatissima,
reple cordis intima
tuorum fidelium.

Sine tuo numine,
nihil est in homine,
nihil est innoxium.

Lava quod est sordidum,
riga quod est aridum,
sana quod est saucium.

Flecte quod est rigidum,
fove quod est frigidum,
rege quod est devium.

Da tuis fidelibus,
in te confidentibus,
sacrum septenarium.

Da virtutis meritum,
da salutis exitum,
da perenne gaudium.

♦
These sequences are for optional use, with the exception of Easter Sunday and Pentecost Sunday, when the text proper to those days is obligatory (see General Instruction of the Roman Missal, *n. 40). The Latin text is given here for use in those particular circumstances where it may be pastorally suitable, and especially when they are sung according to the plain chant melodies found in the* Graduale Romanum.

ON THE SOLEMNITY OF THE MOST HOLY BODY AND BLOOD OF CHRIST

◆

This sequence may be sung in its entirety, or in the shorter form beginning with the verse *Ecce panis (Lo! the angel's food is given).

Lauda, Sion, Salvatorem

Lauda, Sion, Salvatorem,
lauda ducem et pastorem
in hymnis et canticis.

Quantum potes, tantum aude:
quia maior omni laude,
nec laudare sufficis.

Laudis thema specialis,
panis vivus et vitalis
hodie proponitur.

Quem in sacra mensa cenæ,
turba fratrum duodenæ
datum non ambigitur.

Sit laus plena, sit sonora,
sit iucunda, sit decora
mentis iubilatio.

Dies enim sollemnis agitur,
in qua mensæ prima recolitur
huius institutio.

In hac mensa novi Regis,
novum Pascha novæ legis
Phase vetus terminat.

Vetustatem novitas,
umbram fugat veritas,
noctem lux eliminat.

Quod in cena Christus gessit,
faciendum hoc expressit
in sui memoriam.

Docti sacris institutis,
panem, vinum in salutis
consecramus hostiam.

Dogma datur Christianis,
quod in carnem transit panis,
et vinum in sanguinem.

Quod non capis, quod non vides,
animosa firmat fides,
præter rerum ordinem.

Sub diversis speciebus,
signis tantum, et non rebus,
latent res eximiæ.

Caro cibus, sanguis potus:
manet tamen Christus totus,
sub utraque specie.

A sumente non concisus,
non confractus, non divisus:
integer accipitur.

Sumit unus, sumunt mille:
quantum isti, tantum ille:
nec sumptus consumitur.

Sumunt boni, sumunt mali:
sorte tamen inæquali,
vitæ vel interitus.

Mors est malis, vita bonis:
vide paris sumptionis
quam sit dispar exitus.

Fracto demum sacramento,
ne vacilles, sed memento
tantum esse sub fragmento,
quantum toto tegitur.

Nulla rei fit scissura:
signi tantum fit fractura,
qua nec status nec statura
signati minuitur.

*Ecce panis angelorum,
factus cibus viatorum:
vere panis filiorum,
non mittendus canibus.

In figuris praesignatur,
cum Isaac immolatur,
agnus Paschæ deputatur,
datur manna patribus.

Bone Pastor, panis vere,
Iesu, nostri miserere:
tu nos pasce, nos tuere,
tu nos bona fac videre
in terra viventium.

Tu, qui cuncta scis et vales,
qui nos pascis hic mortales:
tuos ibi commensales,
coheredes et sodales
fac sanctorum civium.

◆

The long and short readings of the same pericope are indicated by an asterisk. The bold numbers after the scripture citations refer to the "Lectionary Number" assigned in the Lectionary for Mass, volumes 1 and 2. The final letter(s) or Roman numeral refers to the cycle of readings.

GENESIS

1:1—2:2*	**41**	ABC
1-19	**329**	I
20—2:4a	**330**	I
2:4b-9, 15-17	**331**	I
7-9; 3:1-7	**22**	A
18-25	**332**	I
18-24	**140**	B
3:1-8	**333**	I
9-24	**334**	I
9-15	**89**	B
4:1-15, 25	**335**	I
6:5-8; 7:1-5, 10	**336**	I
8:6-13, 20-22	**337**	I
9:1-13	**338**	I
8-15	**23**	B
11:1-9	**62** ABC; **339**	I
12:1-9	**371**	I
1-4a	**25**	A
13:2, 5-18	**372**	I
14:18-20	**169**	C
15:1-12, 17-18	**373**	I
1-6; 21:1-3	**17**	B
5-12, 17-18	**27**	C
16:1-12, 15-16	**374**	I
17:1, 9-10, 15-22	**375**	I
3-9	**254**	I, II
18:1-15	**376**	I
1-10a	**108**	C
16-33	**377**	I
20-32	**111**	C
19:15-29	**378**	I
21:5, 8-20	**379**	I
22:1-19	**380**	I
1-18	**41**	ABC
1-2, 9a, 10-13, 15-18	**26**	B
23:1-4, 19; 24:1-8, 62-67	**381**	I
27:1-5, 15-29	**382**	I
28:10-22a	**383**	I
32:22-32	**384**	I
37:3-4, 12-13a, 17b-28	**234**	I, II
41:55-57; 42:5-7a, 17-24a	**385**	I
44:18-21, 23b-29; 45:1-5	**386**	I
46:1-7, 28-30	**387**	I
49:2, 8-10	**193**	I, II
29-32; 50:15-26a	**388**	I

EXODUS

1:8-14, 22	**389**	I
2:1-15a	**390**	I
3:1-8a, 13-15	**30**	C
1-6, 9-12	**391**	I
13-20	**392**	I
11:10—12:14	**393**	I
12:1-8, 11-14	**39**	ABC
37-42	**394**	I
14:5-18	**395**	I
15-15:1	**41**	ABC
21—15:1	**396**	I
16:1-5, 9-15	**397**	I
2-4, 12-15	**113**	B
17:1-7	**236**	I, II
3-7	**28**	A
8-13	**147**	C
19:1-2, 9-11, 16-20b	**398**	I
2-6a	**91**	A
3-8a, 16-20b	**62**	ABC
20:1-17	**29** B; **399**	I
22:20-26	**148**	A
24:3-8	**168** B; **400**	I
32:7-14	**247**	I, II
7-11, 13-14	**132**	C
15-24, 30-34	**401**	I
33:7-11; 34:5b-9, 28	**402**	I
34:4b-6, 8-9	**164**	A
29-35	**403**	I
40:16-21, 34-38	**404**	I

LEVITICUS

13:1-2, 44-46	**77**	B
19:1-2, 11-18	**224**	I, II
1-2, 17-18	**79**	A
23:1, 4-11, 15-16, 27, 34b-37	**405**	I
25:1, 8-17	**406**	I

NUMBERS

6:22-27	**18**	ABC
11:4b-15	**407**	I
25-29	**137**	B
12:1-13	**408**	I
13:1-2, 25—14:1, 26-29, 34-35	**409**	I
20:1-13	**410**	I
21:4-9	**252**	I, II
24:2-7, 15-17a	**187**	I, II

DEUTERONOMY

4:1-2, 6-8	**125**	B
1, 5-9	**239**	I, II
32-40	**411**	I
32-34, 39-40	**165**	B
5:12-15	**86**	B
6:2-6	**152**	B
4-13	**412**	I
7:6-11	**170**	A
8:2-3, 14b-16a	**167**	A
10:12-22	**413**	I
11:18, 26-28, 32	**85**	A
18:15-20	**71**	B
26:4-10	**24**	C
16-19	**229**	I, II
30:10-14	**105**	C
15-20	**220**	I, II
31:1-8	**414**	I
34:1-12	**415**	I

JOSHUA

3:7-10a, 11, 13-17	**416**	I
5:9a, 10-12	**33**	C
24:1-13	**417**	I
1-2a, 15-17, 18b	**122**	B
14-29	**418**	I

JUDGES

2:11-19	**419**	I

6:11-24a etc.

6:11-24a	**420**	I
9:6-15	**421**	I
11:29-39a	**422**	I
13:2-7, 24-25a	**195**	I, II

RUTH

1:1, 3-6, 14b-16, 22	**423**	I
2:1-3, 8-11; 4:13-17	**424**	I

1 SAMUEL

1:1-8	**305**	II
9-20	**306**	II
20-22, 24-28	**17**	C
24-28	**198**	I, II
3:1-10, 19-20	**307**	II
3b-10, 19	**65**	B
4:1-11	**308**	II
8:4-7, 10-22a	**309**	II
9:1-4, 17-19; 10:1a	**310**	II
15:16-23	**311**	II
16:1-13	**312**	II
1b, 6-7, 10-13a	**31**	A
17:32-33, 37, 40-51	**313**	II
18:6-9; 19:1-7	**314**	II
24:3-21	**314**	II
26:2, 7-9, 12-13, 22-23	**81**	C

2 SAMUEL

1:1-4, 11-12, 19, 23-27	**316**	II
5:1-7, 10	**317**	II
1-3	**162**	II
6:12b-15, 17-19	**318**	II
7:1-5, 8b-12, 14a, 16	**11** B; **200**	I, II
4-17	**319**	II
18-19, 24, 29	**320**	II
11:1-4a, 5-10a, 13-17	**321**	II
12:1-7a, 10-17	**322**	II
7-10, 13	**93**	C
15:13-14, 30; 16:5-13a	**323**	II
18:9-10, 14b, 24-25a, 30—19:3	**324**	II
24:2, 9-17	**325**	II

1 KINGS

2:1-4, 10-12	**326**	II
3:4-13	**328**	II
5, 7-12	**109**	A
8:1-7, 9-13	**329**	II
22-23, 27-30	**330**	II
41-43	**87**	C
10:1-10	**331**	II
11:4-13	**332**	II
29-32; 12:19	**333**	II
12:26-32; 13:33-34	**334**	II
17:1-6	**359**	II
7-16	**360**	II
10-16	**155**	B
17-24	**90**	C
18:20-39	**361**	II
41-46	**362**	II
19:4-8	**116**	B
9a, 11-16	**363**	II
9a, 11-13a	**115**	A
16b, 19-21	**99**	C
19-21	**364**	II
21:1-16	**365**	II
17-29	**366**	II

2 KINGS

2:1, 6–14   367 II
4:8–11, 14–16a   97 A
  18b–21, 32–37   250 I, II
  42–44   110 B
5:1–15a   237 I, II
  14–17   144 C
11:1–4, 9–18, 20   369 II
17:5–8, 13–15a, 18   371 II
19:9b–11, 14–21, 31–35a, 36   372 II
22:8–13; 23:1–3   373 II
24:8–17   374 II
25:1–12   375 II

2 CHRONICLES

24:17–25   370 II
36:14–16, 19–23   32 B

EZRA

1:1–6   449 I
6:7–8, 12b, 14–20   450 I
9:5–9   451 I

NEHEMIAH

2:1–8   457 I
8:1–4a, 5–6, 7b–12   458 I
  2–4a, 5–6, 8–10   69 C

TOBIT

1:3; 2:1a–8   353 I
2:9–14   354 I
3:1–11a, 16–17a   355 I
6:10–11; 7:1, 9–17; 8:4–9a   356 I
11:5–17   357 I
12:1, 15, 20   358 I

ESTHER

4:17, n; p–r; aa–bb, gg–hh   227 I, II

1 MACCABEES

1:10–15, 41–43, 54–57, 62–64   497 I
2:15–29   500 I
4:36–37, 52–59   501 I
6:1–13   502 I

2 MACCABEES

6:18–31   498 I
7:1–2, 9–14   156 C
  1, 20–31   499 I

JOB

1:6–22   455 II
3:1–3, 11–17, 20–23   456 II
7:1–4, 6–7   74 B
9:1–12, 14–16   457 II
19:21–27   458 II
38:1, 8–11   95 B
  1, 12–21; 40:3–5   459 II
42:1–3, 5–6, 12–16   460 II

PROVERBS

3:27–34   449 II
8:22–31   166 C
9:1–6   119 B
21:1–6, 10–13   450 II
30:5–9   451 II
31:10–13, 19–20, 30–31   157 A

ECCLESIASTES

1:2–11   452 II
2:21–23   114 C
3:1–11   453 II
11:9–12:8   454 II

SONG OF SONGS

2:8–14   197 I, II

WISDOM

1:1–7   491 I
  13–15; 2:23–24   98 B
2:1a, 12–22   248 I, II
  12a, 17–20   134 B
  23—3:9   492 I
6:1–11   493 I
  12–16   154 A
7:7–11   143 B
  22—8:1   494 I
9:13–19   129 C
11:22—12:2   153 C
12:13, 16–19   106 A
13:1–9   495 I
18:6–9   117 C
  14–16; 19:6–9   496 I

SIRACH

1:1–10   341 I
2:1–13   342 I
3:2–6, 12–14   17 ABC
  19–21, 30–31   126 C
4:12–22   343 I
5:1–10   344 I
6:5–17   345 I
15:16–21   76 A
17:1–13   346 I
  20–28   347 I
24:1–4, 12–16   19 ABC
27:5–8   84 C
27:33—28:9   130 A
35:1–15   348 I
  15b–17, 20–22a   150 C
36:1–2a, 5–6, 13–19   349 I
42:15–26   350 I
44:1, 9–13   351 I
47:2–13   327 II
48:1–15   368 II
  1–4, 9–11   186 I, II
51:17–27   352 I

ISAIAH

1:10, 16–20   231 I, II
  10–17   389 II
2:1–5   1 A; 175 I, II
4:2–6   175 I, II
5:1–7   139 A
6:1–8   388 II
  1–2a, 3–8   75 C

7:1–9   390 II
  10–14   10 A; 196 I, II
8:23b—9:3   67 A
9:1–6   14 ABC
10:5–7, 13–16   391 II
11:1–10   4 A; 176 I, II
22:19–23   121 A
25:6–10a   142 A; 177 I, II
26:1–6   178 I, II
  7–9, 12, 16–19   392 II
29:17–24   179 I, II
30:19–21, 23–26   180 I, II
35:1–10   181 I, II
  1–6a, 10   7 A
  4–7a   128 B
38:1–6, 21–22, 7–8   393 II
40:1–11   182 I, II
  1–5, 9–11   5 B; 21 C
  25–31   183 I, II
41:13–20   184 I, II
42:1–7   257 I, II
  1–4, 6–7   21 ABC
43:16–21   36 C
  18–19, 21–22, 24b–25   80 B
45:1, 4–6   145 A
  6b–8, 18, 21b–25   189 I, II
48:17–19   185 I, II
49:1–6   258 I, II
  3, 5–6   64 A
  8–15   246 I, II
  14–15   82 A
50:4–9a   259 I, II
  4–7   38 ABC
  5–9a   131 B
52:7–10   16 ABC
  13—53:12   40 ABC
53:10–11   146 B
54:1–10   190 I, II
  5–14   41 ABC
55:1–11   41 ABC; 21 B
  1–3   112 A
  6–9   133 A
  10–11   103 A; 225 I, II
56:1, 6–7   118 A
  1–3a, 6–8   191 I, II
58:1–9a   221 I, II
  7–10   73 A
  9b–14   222 I, II
60:1–6   20 ABC
61:1–3a, 6a, 8b–9   260 I, II
  1–2a, 10–11   8 B
62:1–5   13 ABC; 66 C
  11–12   15 ABC
63:16b–17, 19b; 64:2b–7   2 B
65:17–21   244 I, II
66:10–14c   102 B
  18–21   123 B

JEREMIAH

1:1, 4–10   397 II
  4–5, 17–19   72 C
2:1–3, 7–8, 12–13   398 II
3:14–17   399 II
7:1–11   400 II
  23–28   240 I
11:18–20   249 I, II
13:1–11   401 II
14:17–22   402 II
15:10, 16–21   403 II
17:5–10   233 I, II

54–58	405 I, II	
14:1–12	406 I, II	
13–21	112 A; 407 I, II	
22–36	407, 408 I, II	
22–33	115 A	
15:1–2, 10–14	408 I, II	
21–28	118 A; 409 I, II	
29–37	177 I, II	
16:13–23	410 I, II	
13–20	121 A	
21–27	124 A	
24–28	411 I, II	
17:1–9	25 A	
10–13	186 I, II	
14–20	412 I, II	
22–27	413 I, II	
18:1–5, 10, 12–14	414 I, II	
12–14	182 I, II	
15–20	127 A; 415 I, II	
21—19:1	416 I, II	
21–35	130 A; 238 I, II	
19:3–12	417 I, II	
13–15	418 I, II	
16–22	419 I, II	
23–30	420 I, II	
20:1–16a	133 A; 421 I, II	
17–28	232 I, II	
21:1–11	37 A	
23–27	187 I, II	
28–32	136 A; 188 I, II	
33–43, 45–46	234 I, II	
33–43	139 A	
22:1–14	142 A; 422 I, II	
15–21	145 A	
34–40	148 A; 423 I, II	
23:1–12	151 A; 231, 424 I, II	
13–22	425 I, II	
23–26	426 I, II	
27–32	427 I, II	
24:37–44	1 A	
42–51	428 I, II	
25:1–13	154 A; 429 I, II	
14–30	157 A; 430 I, II	
31–46	160 A; 224 I, II	
26:14—27:66	38 A	
14–25	259 I, II	
28:1–10	41 A	
8–15	261 I, II	
16–20	58 A; 165 B	

MARK

1:1–8	5 B	
7–11	21 B; 209 I, II	
12–15	23 B	
14–20	68 B; 305 I, II	
21b–28	71 B; 306 I, II	
29–39	74 B; 307 I, II	
40–45	77 B; 308 I, II	
2:1–12	80 B; 309 I, II	
13–17	310 I, II	
18–22	83 B; 311 I, II	
23—3:6	86 B	
23–28	312 I, II	
3:1–6	313 I, II	
7–12	314 I, II	
13–19	315 I, II	
20–35	89 B	
20–21	316 I, II	
22–30	317 I, II	
31–35	318 I, II	
4:1–20	319 I, II	
21–25	320 I, II	
26–34	92 B; 321 I, II	
35–41	95 B; 322 I, II	
5:1–20	323 I, II	
21–43*	98 B; 324 I, II	
6:1–6	101 B; 325 I, II	

7–13	104 B; 326 I, II	
14–29	327 I, II	
30–34	107 B; 328 I, II	
34–44	213 I, II	
45–52	214 I, II	
53–56	329 I, II	
7:1–13	330 I, II	
1–8, 14–15, 21–23	125 B	
14–23	331 I, II	
24–30	332 I, II	
31–37	128 B; 333 I, II	
8:1–10	334 I, II	
11–13	335 I, II	
14–21	336 I, II	
22–26	337 I, II	
27–35	131 B	
27–33	338 I, II	
34—9:1	339 I, II	
9:2–13	340 I, II	
2–10	26 B	
14–29	341 I, II	
30–37	134 B; 342 I, II	
38, 43, 45, 47–48	137 B	
38–40	343 I, II	
41–50	344 I, II	
10:1–12	345 I, II	
2–16*	140 B	
13–16	346 I, II	
17–30*	143 B	
17–27	347 I, II	
28–31	348 I, II	
32–45	349 I, II	
35–45*	146 B	
46–52	149 B; 350 I, II	
11:1–10	37 B	
11–26	351 I, II	
27–33	352 I, II	
12:1–12	353 I, II	
13–17	354 I, II	
18–27	355 I, II	
28b–34	152 B; 241, 356 I, II	
35–37	357 I, II	
38–44*	155 B; 358 I, II	
13:24–32	158 B	
33–37	2 B	
14:1—15:47	38 B	
12–16, 22–26	168 B	
16:1–7	41 B	
9–15	266 I, II	
15–20	58 B	

LUKE

1:1–4	69 C	
5–25	195 I, II	
26–38	11 B; 196 I, II	
39–45	12 C; 197 I, II	
46–56	198 I, II	
57–66	199 I, II	
67–79	200 I, II	
2:1–14	14 ABC	
15–20	15 ABC	
16–21	18 ABC	
22–40*	17 B	
22–35	202 I, II	
36–40	203 I, II	
41–52	17 C	
3:1–6	6 C	
10–18	9 C	
15–16, 21–22	21 C	
23–28	210 I, II	
4:1–13	24 C	
14–22a	215 I, II	
14–21	69 C	
16–30	431 I, II	
16–21	260 I, II	
21–30	72 C	
24–30	237 I, II	

31–37	432 I, II	
38–44	433 I, II	
5:1–11	75 C; 434 I, II	
12–16	216 I, II	
17–26	181 I, II	
27–32	222 I, II	
33–39	435 I, II	
6:1–5	436 I, II	
6–11	437 I, II	
12–19	438 I, II	
17, 20–26	78 C	
20–26	439 I, II	
27–38	81 C; 440 I, II	
36–38	230 I, II	
39–45	84 C	
39–42	441 I, II	
43–49	442 I, II	
7:1–10	87 C; 443 I, II	
11–17	90 C; 444 I, II	
19–23	189 I, II	
24–30	190 I, II	
31–35	445 I, II	
36—8:3*	93 C	
36–50	446 I, II	
8:1–3	447 I, II	
4–15	448 I, II	
16–18	449 I, II	
19–21	450 I, II	
9:1–6	451 I, II	
7–9	452 I, II	
11b–17	169 C	
18–24	96 C	
18–22	453 I, II	
22–25	220 I, II	
28b–36	27 C	
43b–45	454 I, II	
46–50	455 I, II	
51–62	99 C	
51–56	456 I, II	
57–62	457 I, II	
10:1–12, 17–20	102 C	
1–12	458 I, II	
13–16	459 I, II	
17–24	460 I, II	
21–24	176 I, II	
25–37	105 C; 461 I, II	
38–42	108 C; 462 I, II	
11:1–13	111 C	
1–4	463 I, II	
5–13	464 I, II	
14–23	240 I, II	
15–26	465 I, II	
27–28	466 I, II	
29–32	226, 467 I, II	
37–41	468 I, II	
42–46	469 I, II	
47–54	470 I, II	
12:1–7	471 I, II	
8–12	472 I, II	
13–21	114 C; 473 I, II	
32–48*	117 C	
35–38	474 I, II	
39–48	475 I, II	
49–53	120 C; 476 I, II	
54–59	477 I, II	
13:1–9	30 C; 478 I, II	
10–17	479 I, II	
18–21	480 I, II	
22–30	123 C; 481 I, II	
31–35	482 I, II	
14:1, 7–14	126 C	
1–6	483 I, II	
1, 7–11	484 I, II	
12–14	485 I, II	
15–24	486 I, II	
25–33	129 C; 487 I, II	
15:1–32	132 C	
1–10	488 I, II	

31b–34   26 B
31b–39   482 I
35, 37–39   112 A
9:1–5   115 A; 483 I
10:8–13   24 C
11:1–2a, 11–12, 25–29   484 I
13–15, 29–32   118 A
29–36   485 I
33–36   121 A
12:1–2   124 A
5–16a   486 I
13:8–10   127 A; 487 I
11–14a   1 A
14:7–12   488 I
7–9   130 A
15:4–9   4 A
14–21   489 I
16:3–9, 16, 22–27   490 I
25–27   11 B

1 CORINTHIANS

1:1–9   428 II
1–3   64 A
3–9   2 B
10–13, 17   67 A
17–25   429 II
22–25   29 B
26–31   70 A; 430 II
2:1–5   73 A; 431 II
6–10   76 A
10b–16   432 II
3:1–9   433 II
16–23   79 A
18–23   434 II
4:1–5   82 A; 435 II
6b–15   436 II
5:1–8   437 II
6b–8   42 ABC
6:1–11   438 II
13c–15a, 17–20   65 B
7:25–31   439 II
29–31   68 B
32–35   71 B
8:1b–7, 11–13   440 II
9:16–19, 22b–27   441 II
16–19, 22–23   74 B
10:1–6, 10–12   30 C
14–22   442 II
16–17   167 A
31—11:1   77 B
11:17–26, 33   443 II
23–26   39 ABC; 169 C
12:3b–7, 12–13   63 BC
4–11   63 A; 66 C
12–30*   69 C
12–14, 27–31a   444 II
31—13:13*   72 C; 445 II
15:1–11   75 C; 446 II
12–20   447 II
12, 16–20   78 C
20–26, 28   160 A
35–37, 42–49   160 A; 448 II
45–49   81 C
54–58   84 C

2 CORINTHIANS

1:1–7   359 I
18–22   80 B; 360 I
3:1b–6   83 B
4–11   361 I
15—4:1, 3–6   362 I
4:6–11   86 B
7–15   363 I
13—5:1   89 B
5:6–10   92 B
14–17   95 B

14–21   364 I
17–21   33 C
20—6:2   219 I, II
6:1–10   365 I
8:1–9   366 I
7, 9, 13–15   98 B
9:6–11   367 I
11:1–11   368 I
18, 21b–30   369 I
12:1–10   370 I
7–10   101 B
13:11–13   164 A

GALATIANS

1:1–2, 6–10   87 C
6–12   461 II
11–19   90 C
13–24   462 II
2:1–2, 7–14   463 II
16, 19–21   93 C
3:1–5   464 II
7–14   465 II
22–29   466 II
26–29   96 C
4:4–7   18 ABC
22–24, 26–27, 31—5:1   467 II
5:1–6   468 II
1, 13–18   99 C
16–25   63 B
18–25   469 II
6:14–18   102 C

EPHESIANS

1:1–10   470 II
3–14*   104 B
3–6, 15–18   19 ABC
11–14   471 II
15–23   472 II
17–23   58 ABC
2:1–10   473 II
4–10   32 B
12–22   474 II
13–18   107 B
3:2–12   475 II
2–3a, 5–6   20 ABC
8–12, 14–19   171 B
14–21   476 II
4:1–6   110 B; 477 II
1–13*   58 B
7–16   478 II
17, 20–24   113 B
30—5:2   116 B
32—5:8   479 II
5:8–14   31 A
15–20   119 B
21–33   480 II
21–32   122 B
6:1–9   481 II
10–20   482 II

PHILIPPIANS

1:1–11   483 II
4–6, 8–11   6 C
18b–26   484 II
20c–24, 27a   133 A
2:1–11   136 A
1–4   485 II
5–11   486 II
6–11   38 ABC
12–18   487 II
33–8a   488 II
3:8–14   36 C
17—4:1*   27 C; 489 I
4:4–7   9 C

6–9   139 A
10–19   490 II
12–14, 19–20   142 A

COLOSSIANS

1:1–8   433 I
9–14   434 I
12–20   162 C
15–20   105 C; 435 I
21–23   436 I
24—2:3   437 I
24–28   108 C
2:6–15   438 I
12–14   111 C
3:1–11   439 I
1–5, 9–11   114 C
1–4   42 ABC
12–21   17 ABC
12–17   440 I

1 THESSALONIANS

1:1–5b   145 A
1–5, 8b–10   425 I
5c–10   148 A
2:1–8   426 I
7b–9, 13   151 A
9–13   427 I
3:7–13   428 I
12—4:2   3 C
4:1–8   429 I
9–11   430 I
13–18*   154 A; 431 I
5:1–6, 9–11   432 I
1–6   157 A
16–24   8 B

2 THESSALONIANS

1:1–5, 11b–12   425 II
11—2:2   153 C
2:1–3a, 14–17   426 II
16—3:5   156 C
3:6–10, 16–18   427 II
7–12   159 C

1 TIMOTHY

1:1–2, 12–14   441 I
12–17   132 C
15–17   442 I
2:1–8   135 C; 443 I
3:1–13   444 I
14–16   445 I
4:12–16   446 I
6:2c–12   447 I
11–16   138 C
13–16   448 I

2 TIMOTHY

1:1–3, 6–12   355 II
6–8, 13–14   141 C
8b–10   25 A
2:8–15   356 II
8–13   144 C
3:10–17   357 II
14—4:2   147 C
4:1–8   358 II
6–8, 16–18   150 C

TITUS

1:1–9   491 II
2:1–8, 11–14   492 II
11–14   14 ABC

APPENDIX III: TABLE OF RESPONSORIAL PSALMS AND CANTICLES

I. RESPONSORIAL PSALMS

Psalm 1   78, 185, 220, 233, 344, 464, 469, 476, 479, 497, 549, 595, 598, 652, 674, 739, 808

Psalm 2   212, 267, 283, 879

Psalm 3   323, 498

Psalm 4   47, 360

Psalm 5   365, 378, 437

Psalm 6   793

Psalm 7   249

Psalm 8   166, 264, 306, 330, 472, 753, 884, 904

Psalm 9   394, 412, 465, 502

Psalm 10   302

Psalm 11   340

Psalm 12   481, 636

Psalm 15   108, 125, 337, 372, 449, 498, 537, 739

Psalm 16   41, 46, 99, 158, 261, 300, 361, 364, 418, 441, 513, 534, 546, 583, 619, 651, 664, 721, 739, 777, 824, 845, 859

Psalm 17   156, 250, 384, 447, 455, 499

Psalm 18   148, 152, 255, 327, 412

Psalm 19   29, 41, 69, 105, 137, 174, 224, 310, 341, 352, 380, 399, 458, 468, 495, 542, 561, 590, 641, 643, 657, 666, 684, 686, 727, 748, 782, 816, 829, 840, 845, 849, 854, 874

Psalm 21   310, 421

Psalm 22   38, 53, 174, 324, 486, 766, 924, 971

Psalm 23   31, 49, 107, 142, 160, 172, 177, 251, 328, 421, 493, 510, 516, 535, 565, 578, 659, 677, 700, 721, 739, 749, 753, 758, 766, 772, 787, 798, 824, 869, 978, 997, 1013, 1019

Psalm 24   10, 196, 318, 320, 434, 477, 478, 491, 503, 524, 667, 777, 813

Psalm 25   3, 23, 68, 136, 174,187, 199, 238, 355, 356, 793, 829, 997, 1013, 1019, 1024

Psalm 26   378

Psalm 27   27, 59, 67, 174, 179, 243, 257, 271, 327, 363, 432, 458, 487, 488, 753, 758, 762, 793, 813, 829, 845, 854, 859, 879, 1013

Psalm 28   443

Psalm 29   21, 336

Psalm 30   41, 48, 90, 98, 190, 244

Psalm 31   40, 85, 232, 274, 323, 367, 527, 536, 596, 639, 692, 696, 715, 965, 971

Psalm 32   77, 93, 325, 333, 347, 471, 753

Psalm 33   25, 41, 52, 117, 146, 165, 197, 262, 272, 339, 350, 371, 385, 429, 430, 433, 445, 471, 476, 743, 803, 813, 997

Psalm 34   33, 116, 119, 122, 150, 174, 188, 225, 248, 269, 270, 338, 359, 369, 370, 379, 492, 515, 517, 529, 533, 540, 550, 552, 554, 570, 574, 591, 597, 604, 607, 609, 631, 660, 678, 699, 715, 739, 753, 758, 787, 793, 798, 803, 808, 813, 849, 978, 997

Psalm 36   398

Psalm 37   321, 331, 342, 387, 435, 492, 518, 547, 560, 579, 589, 672, 693, 727

Psalm 40   64, 65, 120, 307, 314, 318, 422, 443, 474, 514, 545, 548, 566, 584, 602, 637, 656, 687, 694, 721, 813, 859, 978, 982, 991

Psalm 41   80

Psalm 42   41, 237, 279, 484, 753, 762, 793, 798, 1013, 1019

Psalm 43   41, 237, 279, 453, 753, 762, 793, 798, 1013, 1019

Psalm 44   308

Psalm 45   439, 622, 681, 709, 733, 813, 854

Psalm 46   245, 671, 703

Psalm 47   58, 174, 295, 296, 316

Psalm 48   326, 372, 390

Psalm 49   343, 344, 447, 904

Psalm 50   88, 231, 311, 335, 348, 377, 379, 389, 395, 400, 500

Psalm 51   22, 35, 41, 132, 174, 219, 221, 226, 242, 321, 322, 366, 387, 408, 410, 418, 422, 753, 894, 950

Psalm 52   433

Psalm 54   134, 436

Psalm 55   342, 971

Psalm 56   314, 448

Psalm 57   289, 315

Psalm 59   403

Psalm 60   371

Psalm 61   762

Psalm 62   82, 437, 469

Psalm 63   96, 124, 154, 174, 352, 603, 753, 762, 793, 813, 1013

Psalm 65   103, 362, 762, 914

Psalm 66   55, 102, 174, 275, 276, 415, 753

Psalm 67   18, 57, 118, 191, 281, 406, 829, 874, 919

Psalm 68   126, 297, 298, 299, 479

Psalm 69   94, 105, 259, 390, 405, 406, 460, 485, 971

Psalm 71   72, 195, 258, 358, 397, 586, 634, 793

Psalm 72   4, 20, 174, 176, 193, 194, 213, 214, 215, 889, 899

Psalm 74   376

Psalm 77   411

Psalm 78   113, 309, 397, 416, 638, 787, 978

Psalm 79   230, 349, 374, 402, 459

Psalm 80   2, 12, 139, 186, 316, 386, 884, 940

Psalm 81   86, 241, 333, 405, 407

Psalm 82   493

Psalm 84   17, 330, 400, 404, 441, 507, 703, 772, 813, 819, 845, 859

Psalm 85   5, 104, 115, 174, 181, 189, 315, 362, 382, 396, 420, 424, 474, 864, 884, 889, 899, 940, 954

Psalm 86   106, 222, 324, 463, 793, 960

Psalm 87   280, 456

Psalm 88   456, 457

Psalm 89   11, 13, 97, 200, 260, 282, 309, 312, 317, 319, 370, 543, 555, 581, 588, 611, 626, 670, 673, 682, 688, 721, 753, 772, 835

Psalm 90   114, 129, 143, 334, 354, 428, 452, 454, 559, 793, 904, 909

Psalm 91	24, 174, 353, 383, 650
Psalm 92	84, 92, 808
Psalm 93	161, 268, 341, 388
Psalm 94	336, 391, 484
Psalm 95	28, 71, 127, 141, 174, 236, 240, 308, 410, 508, 703, 819
Psalm 96	14, 66, 145, 182, 202, 203, 204, 288, 351, 425, 426, 431, 504, 520, 526, 541, 544, 571, 617, 635, 655, 665, 683, 721, 766, 772, 829, 849, 874
Psalm 97	15, 61, 305, 368, 429, 466, 614, 697
Psalm 98	16, 56, 144, 159, 174, 205, 206, 207, 284, 294, 317, 348, 365, 430, 434, 467, 470, 489, 505, 580, 679, 689, 777, 829, 874
Psalm 99	361, 403
Psalm 100	51, 91, 174, 208, 290, 350, 435, 444, 448, 473, 506, 772, 813, 864, 869, 884, 954
Psalm 101	444
Psalm 102	252, 338, 392, 408, 455, 793, 935
Psalm 103	30, 60, 79, 81, 83, 130, 170, 174, 183, 235, 301, 325, 345, 346, 364, 377, 391, 402, 511, 523, 557, 563, 739, 749, 793, 803, 864, 950, 960, 997, 1013
Psalm 104	21, 41, 62, 63, 174, 329, 331, 766, 914
Psalm 105	17, 234, 254, 263, 307, 373, 385, 386, 388, 392, 466, 472, 488, 496
Psalm 106	247, 332, 334, 374, 381, 401, 409, 419, 721
Psalm 107	95, 423, 884, 914, 924, 929
Psalm 108	482
Psalm 110	169, 311, 313, 319, 512, 558, 568, 690, 721, 772, 787, 829, 845, 978
Psalm 111	312, 347, 368, 445, 446, 461, 465, 483
Psalm 112	73, 339, 353, 354, 367, 487, 490, 496, 539, 594, 599, 616, 618, 623, 630, 645, 676, 695, 739, 803, 854, 884, 924
Psalm 113	135, 415, 442, 467, 564, 627, 709, 864, 945, 985
Psalm 114	416
Psalm 115	285, 380, 384
Psalm 116	26, 39, 131, 168, 278, 305, 337, 363, 393, 442, 772, 787, 798, 978, 991
Psalm 117	87, 123, 277, 463, 519, 525, 532, 556, 577, 593, 612, 663, 685, 721, 766, 772, 829, 874, 1013
Psalm 118	41, 42, 43, 44, 45, 50, 174, 178, 265, 266, 446, 819, 869, 971
Psalm 119	76, 109, 229, 273, 328, 335, 343, 345, 357, 360, 373, 381, 407, 414, 431, 450, 451, 460, 468, 477, 494, 495, 497, 501, 522, 567, 600, 608, 610, 625, 633, 648, 675, 727, 782, 819
Psalm 121	147, 359, 762, 929
Psalm 122	1, 162, 174, 175, 287, 450, 478, 489, 703, 819, 869, 884, 889, 1013
Psalm 123	101, 355, 793, 829, 854, 879, 884, 940
Psalm 124	389, 475, 538, 562, 575, 576, 592, 620, 698, 715, 879
Psalm 125	6, 36, 149, 449, 480, 528, 551, 553, 585, 605, 615, 640, 642, 644, 646, 654, 662, 715, 753, 919
Psalm 126	884, 909
Psalm 128	17, 140, 157, 332, 356, 375, 424, 427, 480, 658, 739, 803
Psalm 130	34, 89, 174, 228, 462, 470, 894, 950, 1013
Psalm 131	151, 485, 486, 582, 624, 632, 649, 669, 691, 739

Psalm 132	320, 329, 369, 606, 621
Psalm 135	382
Psalm 136	174, 394, 417
Psalm 137	32, 375, 457
Psalm 138	75, 111, 121, 227, 292, 647, 945
Psalm 139	426, 427, 440, 459, 462, 491, 587
Psalm 141	346
Psalm 143	793, 1013
Psalm 144	313, 453, 482, 502
Psalm 145	54, 100, 110, 112, 133, 153, 174, 184, 246, 286, 340, 383, 428, 432, 436, 438, 439, 481, 490, 629, 661, 766, 787, 798, 803, 945, 978
Psalm 146	7, 70, 128, 138, 155, 357, 366, 404, 423, 494
Psalm 147	19, 74, 167, 180, 209, 216, 239, 349, 413, 483, 782, 787, 978
Psalm 148	293, 413, 521, 530, 569, 628, 733, 803, 854, 1019
Psalm 149	210, 217, 291, 351, 425, 438, 452, 500
Psalm 150	440, 499

II. OLD TESTAMENT CANTICLES

Exodus 15:1–18	41, 395, 396
Deuteronomy 32:1–43	401, 411, 414, 419, 420
1 Samuel 2:1–10	198, 306, 573, 709
1 Chronicles 29:10–13	326, 501, 703, 945
Tobit 13:1–9	358, 451, 929
Judith 13:18–19	531, 613, 709, 1002
Isaiah 12:1–6	9, 21, 41, 171, 417, 475, 572, 985, 997
Isaiah 38:10–20	393, 793, 935
Jeremiah 31:10–14	256, 399, 409, 454, 869
Daniel 3:52–56	164, 253, 398, 503
Daniel 3:57–88	504, 505, 506, 507, 508
John 2:2–8	461

III. NEW TESTAMENT CANTICLES

Luke 1:46–55	8, 376, 601, 653, 680, 709, 1002
Luke 1:68–79	322, 464, 473

TABLE I

PRINCIPAL CELEBRATIONS OF THE LITURGICAL YEAR
1999–2025

Year	LECTIONARY CYCLE		Ash Wednesday	Easter	Ascension Thursday	Pentecost
	Sunday	Weekday				
1999	A	I	17 Feb	4 Apr	13 May	23 May
2000	B	II	8 Mar	23 Apr	1 June	11 June
2001	C	I	28 Feb	15 Apr	24 May	3 June
2002	A	II	13 Feb	31 Mar	9 May	19 May
2003	B	I	5 Mar	20 Apr	29 May	8 June
2004	C	II	25 Feb	11 Apr	20 May	30 May
2005	A	I	9 Feb	27 Mar	5 May	15 May
2006	B	II	1 Mar	16 Apr	25 May	4 June
2007	C	I	21 Feb	8 Apr	17 May	27 May
2008	A	II	6 Feb	23 Mar	1 May	11 May
2009	B	I	25 Feb	12 Apr	21 May	31 May
2010	C	II	17 Feb	4 Apr	13 May	23 May
2011	A	I	9 Mar	24 Apr	2 June	12 June
2012	B	II	22 Feb	8 Apr	17 May	27 May
2013	C	I	13 Feb	31 Mar	9 May	19 May
2014	A	II	5 Mar	20 Apr	29 May	8 June
2015	B	I	18 Feb	5 Apr	14 May	24 May
2016	C	II	10 Feb	27 Mar	5 May	15 May
2017	A	I	1 Mar	16 Apr	25 May	4 June
2018	B	II	14 Feb	1 Apr	10 May	20 May
2019	C	I	6 Mar	21 Apr	30 May	9 June
2020	A	II	26 Feb	12 Apr	21 May	31 May
2021	B	I	17 Feb	4 Apr	13 May	23 May
2022	C	II	2 Mar	17 Apr	26 May	5 June
2023	A	I	22 Feb	9 Apr	18 May	28 May
2024	B	II	14 Feb	31 Mar	9 May	19 May
2025	C	I	5 Mar	20 Apr	29 May	8 June

TABLE II

WEEKS IN ORDINARY TIME: 1999–2025

Year	LECTIONARY CYCLE Sunday	Weekday	WEEKS IN ORDINARY TIME before Lent Number of Weeks	Ending	after Easter Season Beginning	Week Number	First Sunday of Advent
1999	A	I	6	16 Feb	24 May	8	28 Nov
2000	B	II	9	7 Mar	12 June	10	3 Dec
2001	C	I	7	27 Feb	4 June	9	2 Dec
2002	A	II	5	12 Feb	20 May	7	1 Dec
2003	B	I	8	4 Mar	9 June	10	30 Nov
2004	C	II	7	24 Feb	31 May	9	28 Nov
2005	A	I	5	8 Feb	16 May	7	27 Nov
2006	B	II	8	28 Feb	5 June	9	3 Dec
2007	C	I	7	20 Feb	28 May	8	2 Dec
2008	A	II	4	5 Feb	12 May	6	30 Nov
2009	B	I	7	24 Feb	1 June	9	29 Nov
2010	C	II	6	16 Feb	24 May	8	28 Nov
2011	A	I	9	8 Mar	13 June	11	27 Nov
2012	B	II	7	21 Feb	28 May	8	2 Dec
2013	C	I	5	12 Feb	20 May	7	1 Dec
2014	A	II	8	4 Mar	9 June	10	30 Nov
2015	B	I	6	17 Feb	25 May	8	29 Nov
2016	C	II	5	9 Feb	16 May	7	27 Nov
2017	A	I	8	28 Feb	5 June	9	3 Dec
2018	B	II	6	13 Feb	21 May	7	2 Dec
2019	C	I	8	5 Mar	10 June	10	1 Dec
2020	A	II	7	25 Feb	1 June	9	29 Nov
2021	B	I	6	16 Feb	24 May	8	28 Nov
2022	C	II	8	1 Mar	6 June	10	27 Nov
2023	A	I	7	21 Feb	29 May	8	3 Dec
2024	B	II	6	13 Feb	20 May	7	1 Dec
2025	C	I	8	4 Mar	9 June	10	30 Nov

TABLE III: ORDER OF THE SECOND READINGS
FOR SUNDAYS IN ORDINARY TIME

Sunday	Year A	Year B	Year C
2	1 Corinthians, 1–4	1 Corinthians, 6–11	1 Corinthians, 12–15
3	"	"	"
4	"	"	"
5	"	"	"
6	"	"	"
7	"	2 Corinthians	"
8	"	"	"
9	Romans	"	Galatians
10	"	"	"
11	"	"	"
12	"	"	"
13	"	"	"
14	"	"	"
15	"	Ephesians	Colossians
16	"	"	"
17	"	"	"
18	"	"	"
19	"	"	Hebrews, 11–12
20	"	"	"
21	"	"	"
22	"	James	"
23	"	"	Philemon
24	"	"	1 Timothy
25	Philippians	"	"
26	"	"	"
27	"	Hebrews, 1–10	2 Timothy
28	"	"	"
29	1 Thessalonians	"	"
30	"	"	"
31	"	"	2 Thessalonians
32	"	"	"
33	"	"	"

TABLE IV: ORDER OF THE GOSPEL READINGS
FOR SUNDAYS IN ORDINARY TIME

Sunday	Year A Matthew	Year B Mark	Year C Luke
Baptism of Lord	3:13–17	1:7–11	3:15–16, 21–22
2	[John 1:29–34]	[John 1:35–41]	[John 2:1–11]
3	4:12–23	1:14–20	1:1–4; 4:14–21
4	5:1–12	1:21–28	4:21–30
5	5:13–16	1:29–39	5:1–11
6	5:17–37	1:40–45	6:17, 20–26
7	5:38–48	2:1–12	6:27–38
8	6:24–34	2:18–22	6:39–45
9	7:21–27	2:23—3:6	7:1–10
10	9:9–13	3:20–35	7:7–17
11	9:36—10:8	4:26–34	7:36—8:3
12	10:26–33	4:35–41	9:18–24
13	10:37–42	5:21–43	9:51–62
14	11:25–30	6:1–6	10:1–12, 17–20
15	13:1–23	6:7–13	10:25–37
16	13:24–43	6:30–34	10:38–42
17	13:44–52	[John 6:1–15]	11:1–13
18	14:13–21	[John 6:24–35]	12:13–21
19	14:22–23	[John 6:41–51]	12:32–48
20	15:21–28	[John 6:51–58]	12:49–53
21	16:13–20	[John 6:60–69]	13:22–30
22	16:21–27	7:1–8, 14–15, 21–23	14:1, 7–14
23	18:15–20	7:31–37	14:25–33
24	18:21–35	8:27–35	15:1–32
25	20:1–16	9:30–37	16:1–13
26	21:28–32	9:38–43, 45, 47–48	16:19–31
27	21:33–43	10:2–16	17:5–10
28	22:1–14	10:17–30	17:11–19
29	22:15–21	10:35–45	18:1–8
30	22:34–40	10:46–52	18:9–14
31	23:1–12	12:28–34	19:1–10
32	25:1–13	12:38–44	20:27–38
33	25:14–30	13:24–32	21:5–19
34	25:31–46	[John 18:33–37]	23:35–43

TABLE V: ORDER OF SUNDAY READINGS

FIRST SUNDAY OF ADVENT

YEAR A	YEAR B	YEAR C
Isaiah 2:1 – 5	Isaiah 63:16b – 17, 19b; 64:2b – 7	Jeremiah 33:14–16
Romans 13:11 – 14a	1 Corinthians 1:3 – 9	1 Thessalonians 3:12 — 4:2
Matthew 24:37 – 44	Mark 13:33 – 37	Luke 21:25 – 28, 34 – 36

SECOND SUNDAY OF ADVENT

YEAR A	YEAR B	YEAR C
Isaiah 11:1 – 10	Isaiah 40:1 – 5, 9 – 11	Baruch 5:1 – 9
Romans 15:4 – 9	2 Peter 3:8 – 14	Philippians 1:4 – 6, 8 – 11
Matthew 3:1 – 12	Mark 1:1 – 8	Luke 3:1 – 6

THIRD SUNDAY OF ADVENT

YEAR A	YEAR B	YEAR C
Isaiah 35:1 – 6a, 10	Isaiah 61:1 – 2a, 10 – 11	Zephaniah 3:14 – 18a
James 5:7 – 10	1 Thessalonians 5:16 – 24	Philippians 4:4 – 7
Matthew 11:2 – 11	John 1:6 – 8, 19 – 28	Luke 3:10–18

FOURTH SUNDAY OF ADVENT

YEAR A	YEAR B	YEAR C
Isaiah 7:10 – 14	2 Samuel 7:1 – 5, 8b – 12, 14a, 16	Micah 5:1 – 4a
Romans 1:1 – 7	Romans 16:25 – 27	Hebrews 10:5 – 10
Matthew 1:18 – 24	Luke 1:26 – 38	Luke 1:39 – 45

CHRISTMAS, VIGIL MASS

YEARS ABC: Isaiah 62:1 – 5; Acts 13:16 – 17, 22 – 25; Matthew 1:1 – 25 (18 – 25)

CHRISTMAS, MIDNIGHT MASS

YEARS ABC: Isaiah 9:1 – 6; Titus 2:11 – 14; Luke 2:1 – 14

CHRISTMAS, MASS AT DAWN

YEARS ABC: Isaiah 62:11 – 12; Titus 3:4 – 7; Luke 2:15 – 20

CHRISTMAS, MASS DURING THE DAY

YEARS ABC: Isaiah 52:7 – 10; Hebrews 1:1 – 6; John 1:1 – 18 (1 – 5, 9 – 14)

HOLY FAMILY

YEAR A	YEAR B	YEAR C
Sirach 3:2 – 6, 12 – 14	Genesis 15:1 – 6; 21:1 – 3	1 Samuel 1:20 – 22, 24 – 28
Colossians 3:12 – 21	Hebrews 11:8, 11 – 12, 17 – 19	1 John 3:1 – 2, 21 – 24
Matthew 2:13 – 15, 19 – 23	Luke 2:22 – 40 (22, 39 – 40)	Luke 2:41 – 52

JANUARY 1: MARY, MOTHER OF GOD

YEARS ABC: Numbers 6:22 – 27; Galatians 4:4 – 7; Luke 2:16 – 21

SECOND SUNDAY AFTER CHRISTMAS

YEARS ABC: Sirach 24:1 – 2, 8 – 12; Ephesians 1:3 – 6, 15 – 18; John 1:1 – 18 (1 – 5, 9 – 14)

EPIPHANY

YEARS ABC: Isaiah 60:1 – 6; Ephesians 3:2 – 3a, 5 – 6; Matthew 2:1 – 12

BAPTISM OF THE LORD

YEAR A	YEAR B	YEAR C
Isaiah 42:1 – 4, 6 – 7	Isaiah 55:1 – 11	Isaiah 40:1 – 5, 9 – 11
Acts 10:34 – 38	1 John 5:1 – 9	Titus 2:11 – 14; 3:4 – 7
Matthew 3:13 – 17	Mark 1:7 – 11	Luke 3:15 – 16, 21 – 22

FIRST SUNDAY OF LENT

YEAR A	YEAR B	YEAR C
Genesis 2:7 – 9; 3:1 – 7	Genesis 9:8 – 15	Deuteronomy 26:4 – 10
Romans 5:12 – 19 (17 – 19)	1 Peter 3:18 – 22	Romans 10:8 – 13
Matthew 4:1 – 11	Mark 1:12 – 15	Luke 4:1 – 13

SECOND SUNDAY OF LENT

YEAR A	YEAR B	YEAR C
Genesis 12:1 – 4a	Genesis 22:1 – 2, 9a, 10 – 13, 15 – 18	Genesis 15:5 – 12, 17 – 18
2 Timothy 1:8b – 10	Romans 8:31b – 34	Philippans 3:17 — 4:1; (3:20 — 4:1)
Matthew 17:1 – 9	Mark 9:2 – 10	Luke 9:28b – 36

THIRD SUNDAY OF LENT

YEAR A	YEAR B	YEAR C
Exodus 17:3 – 7	Exodus 20:1 – 17 (20:1 – 3, 7 – 8, 12 – 17)	Exodus 3:1 – 8a, 13 – 15
Romans 5:1 – 2, 5 – 8	1 Corinthians 1:22 – 25	1 Corinthians 10:1 – 6, 10 – 12
John 4:5 – 42 (4:5 – 15, 19b – 26, 39a, 40 – 42)	John 2:13 – 25	Luke 13:1 – 9

FOURTH SUNDAY OF LENT

YEAR A	YEAR B	YEAR C
1 Samuel 16:1b, 6 – 7, 10 – 13a	2 Chronicles 36:14 – 16, 19 – 23	Joshua 5:9a, 10 – 12
Ephesians 5:8 – 14	Ephesians 2:4 – 10	2 Corinthians 5:17 – 21
John 9:1 – 41 (9:1, 6 – 9, 13 – 17, 34 – 38)	John 3:14 – 21	Luke 15:1 – 3, 11 – 32

FIFTH SUNDAY OF LENT

YEAR A	YEAR B	YEAR C
Ezekiel 37:12 – 14	Jeremiah 31:31 – 34	Isaiah 43:16 – 21
Romans 8:8 – 11	Hebrews 5:7 – 9	Philippians 3:8 – 14
John 11:1 – 45 (11:3 – 7, 17, 20 – 27, 33b – 45)	John 12:20 – 33	John 8:1 – 11

PASSION (PALM) SUNDAY

PROCESSION:

YEAR A	YEAR B	YEAR C
Matthew 21:1 – 11	Mark 11:1 – 10	Luke 19:28 – 40

MASS:
YEARS ABC: Isaiah 50:4 – 7; Philippians 2:6 – 11

YEAR A	YEAR B	YEAR C
Matthew 26:14 — 27:66; (27:11 – 54)	Mark 14:1 — 15:47; (15:1 – 39)	Luke 22:14—23:56; (23:1 – 49)

HOLY THURSDAY

YEARS ABC; Exodus 12:1 – 8, 11 – 14; 1 Corinthians 11:23 – 26; John 13:1 – 15

GOOD FRIDAY

YEARS ABC; Isaiah 52:13 — 53:12; Hebrews 4:14 – 16; 5:7 – 9; John 18:1 — 19:42

EASTER VIGIL

YEARS ABC; Genesis 1:1 — 2:2 (1:1, 26–31a); 22:1–18 (22:1–2, 9a, 10–13, 15–18); Exodus 14:15 — 15:1; Isaiah 54:5–14; 55:1–11; Baruch 3:9–15, 32 — 4:4; Ezekiel 36:16–17a, 18–28; Romans 6:3–11

YEAR A	YEAR B	YEAR C
Matthew 28:1–10	Mark 16:1–7	Luke 24:1–12

EASTER SUNDAY

YEARS ABC; Acts 10:34a, 37–43; Colossians 3:1–4 or 1 Corinthians 5:6–8; John 20:1–9 (Evening: Luke 24:13–35)

SECOND SUNDAY OF EASTER

YEAR A	YEAR B	YEAR C
Acts 2:42–47	Acts 4:32–35	Acts 5:12–16
1 Peter 1:3–9	1 John 5:1–6	Revelation 1:9–11a,
John 20:19–31	John 20:19–31	12–13, 17–19,
		John 20:19–31

THIRD SUNDAY OF EASTER

YEAR A	YEAR B	YEAR C
Acts 2:14, 22–33	Acts 3:13–15, 17–19	Acts 5:27b–32, 40b–41
1 Peter 1:17–21	1 John 2:1–5a	Revelation 5:11–14
Luke 24:13–35	Luke 24:35–48	John 21:1–19; (21:1–14)

FOURTH SUNDAY OF EASTER

YEAR A	YEAR B	YEAR C
Acts 2:14a, 36–41	Acts 4:8–12	Acts 13:14, 43–52
1 Peter 2:20b–25	1 John 3:1–2	Revelation 7:9, 14b–17
John 10:1–10	John 10:11–18	John 10:27–30

FIFTH SUNDAY OF EASTER

YEAR A	YEAR B	YEAR C
Acts 6:1–7	Acts 9:26–31	Acts 14:21b–27
1 Peter 2:4–9	1 John 3:18–24	Revelation 21:1–5a
John 14:1–12	John 15:1–18	John 13:31–33a, 34–35

SIXTH SUNDAY OF EASTER

YEAR A	YEAR B	YEAR C
Acts 8:5–8, 14–17	Acts 10:25–26, 34–35, 44–48	Acts 15:1–2, 22–29
1 Peter 3:15–18	1 John 4:7–10	Revelation 21:10–14, 22–23
John 14:15–21	John 15:9–17	John 14:23–29

ASCENSION THURSDAY

YEAR A	YEAR B	YEAR C
Acts 1:1–11	Acts 1:1–11	Acts 1:1–11
Ephesians 1:17–23	Ephesians 4:1–13, (4:1–7, 11–13)	Hebrews 9:24–28; 10:19–23
Matthew 28:16–20	Mark 16:15–20	Luke 24:46–53

SEVENTH SUNDAY OF EASTER

YEAR A	YEAR B	YEAR C
Acts 1:12–14	Acts 1:15–17, 20a, 20c–26	Acts 7:55–60
1 Peter 4:13–16	1 John 4:11–16	Revelation 22:12–14, 16–17, 20
John 17:1–11a	John 17:11b–19	John 17: 20–26

PENTECOST SUNDAY

YEAR A	YEAR B	YEAR C
Acts 2:1–11	Acts 2:1–11	Acts 2:1–11
1 Corinthians 12:3b–7, 12–13	Galatians 5:16–25	Romans 8:8–17
John 20:19–23	John 15:26–27; 16:12–15	John 14:15–16, 23b–26

TRINITY SUNDAY

YEAR A	YEAR B	YEAR C
Exodus 34:4b – 6, 8 – 9	Deuteronomy 4:32 – 34, 39 – 40	Proverbs 8:22 – 31
2 Corinthians 13:11 – 13	Romans 8:14 – 17	Romans 5:1 – 5
John 3:16 – 18	Matthew 28:16 – 20	John 16:12 – 15

BODY AND BLOOD OF CHRIST

YEAR A	YEAR B	YEAR C
Deuteronomy 8:2 – 3,14b – 16a	Exodus 24:3 – 8	Genesis 14:18 – 20
1 Corinthians 10:16 – 17	Hebrews 9:11 – 15	1 Corinthians 11:23 – 26
John 6:51 – 58	Mark 14:12 – 16, 22 – 26	Luke 9:11b – 17

SECOND SUNDAY IN ORDINARY TIME

YEAR A	YEAR B	YEAR C
Isaiah 49:3, 5 – 6	1 Samuel 3:3b – 10, 19	Isaiah 62:1 – 5
1 Corinthians 1:1 – 3	1 Corinthians 6:13c – 15a, 17 – 20	1 Corinthians 12:4 – 11
John 1:29 – 34	John 1:35 – 41	John 2:1 – 11

THIRD SUNDAY IN ORDINARY TIME

YEAR A	YEAR B	YEAR C
Isaiah 8:23b — 9:3	Jonah 3:1 – 5, 10	Nehemiah 8:2–4a, 5–6, 8–10
1 Corinthians 1:10 – 13, 17	1 Corinthians 7:29 – 31	1 Corinthians 12:12 – 30;
Matthew 4:12 – 23 (4:12 – 17)	Mark 1:14 – 20	(12:12 – 14, 27)
		Luke 1:1 – 4; 4:14 – 21

FOURTH SUNDAY IN ORDINARY TIME

YEAR A	YEAR B	YEAR C
Zephaniah 2:3; 3:12 – 13	Deuteronomy 18:15 – 20	Jeremiah 1:4 – 5, 17 – 19
1 Corinthians 1:26 – 31	1 Corinthians 7:32 – 35	1 Corinthians 12:31 —
Matthew 5:1 – 12a	Mark 1:21 – 28	13:13 (13:4 – 13)
		Luke 4:21 – 30

FIFTH SUNDAY IN ORDINARY TIME

YEAR A	YEAR B	YEAR C
Isaiah 58:7 – 10	Job 7:1 – 4, 6 – 7	Isaiah 6:1 – 2a, 3 – 8
1 Corinthians 2:1 – 5	1 Corinthians 9:16 – 19, 22 – 23	1 Corinthians 15:1 – 11
Matthew 5:13 – 16	Mark 1:29 – 39	(15:3 – 8, 11)
		Luke 5:1 – 11

SIXTH SUNDAY IN ORDINARY TIME

YEAR A	YEAR B	YEAR C
Sirach 15:15 – 20	Leviticus 13:1 – 2, 44 – 46	Jeremiah 17:5 – 8
1 Corinthians 2:6 – 10	1 Corinthians 10:31 — 11:1	1 Corinthians 15:12, 16 – 20
Matthew 5:17 – 37 (5:20 – 22a, 27 – 28, 33 – 34a, 37)	Mark 1:40 – 45	Luke 6:17, 20 – 26

SEVENTH SUNDAY IN ORDINARY TIME

YEAR A	YEAR B	YEAR C
Leviticus 19:1 – 2, 17 – 18	Isaiah 43:18 – 19, 21 – 22, 24b – 25	1 Samuel 26:2, 7 – 9, 12 – 13, 22 – 23
1 Corinthians 3:16 – 23	2 Corinthians 1:18 – 22	1 Corinthians 15:45 – 49
Matthew 5:38 – 48	Mark 2:1 – 12	Luke 6:27 – 38

EIGHTH SUNDAY IN ORDINARY TIME

YEAR A	YEAR B	YEAR C
Isaiah 49:14 – 15	Hosea 2:16b, 17b, 21 – 22	Sirach 27:4 – 7
1 Corinthians 4:1 – 5	2 Corinthians 3:1b – 6	1 Corinthians 15:54 – 58
Matthew 6:24 – 34	Mark 2:18 – 22	Luke 6:39 – 45

NINTH SUNDAY IN ORDINARY TIME

YEAR A	YEAR B	YEAR C
Deuteronomy 11:18, 26 – 28, 32	Deuteronomy 5:12 – 15	1 Kings 8:41 – 43
Romans 3:21 – 25a, 28	2 Corinthians 4:6 – 11	Galatians 1:1 – 2, 6 – 10
Matthew 7:21 – 27	Mark 2:23 — 3:6	Luke 7:1 – 10

TENTH SUNDAY IN ORDINARY TIME

YEAR A	YEAR B	YEAR C
Hosea 6:3 – 6	Genesis 3:9 – 15	1 Kings 17:17 – 24
Romans 4:18 – 25	2 Corinthians 4:13 — 5:1	Galatians 1:11 – 19
Matthew 9:9 – 13	Mark 3:20 – 35	Luke 7:11 – 17

ELEVENTH SUNDAY IN ORDINARY TIME

YEAR A	YEAR B	YEAR C
Exodus 19:2 – 6a	Ezekiel 17:22 – 24	2 Samuel 12:7 – 10
Romans 5:6 – 11	2 Corinthians 5:6 – 10	Galatians 2:16, 19 – 21
Matthew 9:36 — 10:8	Mark 4:26 – 34	Luke 7:36 — 8:3 (7:36 – 50)

TWELFTH SUNDAY IN ORDINARY TIME

YEAR A	YEAR B	YEAR C
Jeremiah 20:10 – 13	Job 38:1, 8 – 11	Zechariah 12:10 – 11; 13:1
Romans 5:12 – 15	2 Corinthians 5:14 – 17	Galatians 3:26 – 29
Matthew 10:26 – 33	Mark 4:35 – 41	Luke 9:18 – 24

THIRTEENTH SUNDAY IN ORDINARY TIME

YEAR A	YEAR B	YEAR C
2 Kings 4:8 – 11, 14 – 16a	Wisdom 1:13 – 15; 2:23 – 24	1 Kings 19:16b, 19 – 21
Romans 6:3 – 4, 8 – 11	2 Corinthians 8:7, 9, 13 – 15	Galatians 5:1, 13 – 18
Matthew 10:37 – 42	Mark 5:21 – 43 (5:21 – 24, 35b – 43)	Luke 9:51 – 62

FOURTEENTH SUNDAY IN ORDINARY TIME

YEAR A	YEAR B	YEAR C
Zechariah 9:9 – 10	Ezekiel 2:2 – 5	Isaiah 66:10 – 14c
Romans 8:9, 11 – 13	2 Corinthians 12:7 – 10	Galatians 6:14 – 18
Matthew 11:25 – 30	Mark 6:1 – 6	Luke 10:1 – 12, 17 – 20 (10:1 – 9)

FIFTEENTH SUNDAY IN ORDINARY TIME

YEAR A	YEAR B	YEAR C
Isaiah 55:10 – 11	Amos 7:12 – 15	Deuteronomy 30:10 – 14
Romans 8:18 – 23	Ephesians 1:3 – 14 (1:3 – 10)	Colossians 1:15 – 20
Matthew 13:1 – 23 (13:1 – 9)	Mark 6:7 – 13	Luke 10:25 – 37

SIXTEENTH SUNDAY IN ORDINARY TIME

YEAR A	YEAR B	YEAR C
Wisdom 12:13, 16 – 19	Jeremiah 23:1 – 6	Genesis 18:1 – 10a
Romans 8:26 – 27	Ephesians 2:13 – 18	Colossians 1:24 – 28
Matthew 13:24 – 43 (13:24 – 30)	Mark 6:30 – 34	Luke 10:38 – 42

SEVENTEENTH SUNDAY IN ORDINARY TIME

YEAR A	YEAR B	YEAR C
1 Kings 3:5, 7 – 12	2 Kings 4:42 – 44	Genesis 18:20 – 32
Romans 8:28 – 30	Ephesians 4:1 – 6	Colossians 2:12 – 14
Matthew 13:44 – 52 (13:44 – 46)	John 6:1 – 15	Luke 11:1 – 13

EIGHTEENTH SUNDAY IN ORDINARY TIME

YEAR A	YEAR B	YEAR C
Isaiah 55:1 – 3	Exodus 16:2 – 4, 12 – 15	Ecclesiastes 1:2; 2:21 – 23
Romans 8:35, 37 – 39	Ephesians 4:17, 20 – 24	Colossians 3:1 – 5, 9 – 11
Matthew 14:13 – 21	John 6:24 – 35	Luke 12:13 – 21

NINETEENTH SUNDAY IN ORDINARY TIME

YEAR A	YEAR B	YEAR C
1 Kings 19:9a, 11 – 13a	1 Kings 19:4 – 8	Wisdom 18:6 – 9
Romans 9:1 – 5	Ephesians 4:30 — 5:2	Hebrews 11:1 – 2, 8 – 19
Matthew 14:22 – 23	John 6:41 – 51	(11:1 – 2, 8 – 12)
		Luke 12:32 – 48 (12:35 – 40)

TWENTIETH SUNDAY IN ORDINARY TIME

YEAR A	YEAR B	YEAR C
Isaiah 56:1, 6 – 7	Proverbs 9:1 – 6	Jeremiah 38:4 – 6, 8 – 10
Romans 11:13 – 15, 29 – 32	Ephesians 5:15 – 20	Hebrews 12:1 – 4
Matthew 15:21 – 28	John 6:51 – 58	Luke 12:49 – 53

TWENTY-FIRST SUNDAY IN ORDINARY TIME

YEAR A	YEAR B	YEAR C
Isaiah 22:19 – 23	Joshua 24:1 – 2a, 15 – 17, 18b	Isaiah 66:18 – 21
Romans 11:33 – 36	Ephesians 5:21 – 32	Hebrews 12:5 – 7, 11 – 13
Matthew 16:13 – 20	John 6:60 – 69	Luke 13:22 – 30

TWENTY-SECOND SUNDAY IN ORDINARY TIME

YEAR A	YEAR B	YEAR C
Jeremiah 20:7 – 9	Deuteronomy 4:1 – 2, 6 – 8	Sirach 3:17 – 18, 20, 28 – 29
Romans 12:1 – 2	James 1:17 – 18, 21b – 22, 27	Hebrews 12:18 – 19, 22 – 24a
Matthew 16:21 – 27	Mark 7:1 – 8, 14 – 15, 21 – 23	Luke 14:1, 7 – 14

TWENTY-THIRD SUNDAY IN ORDINARY TIME

YEAR A	YEAR B	YEAR C
Ezekiel 33:7 – 9	Isaiah 35:4 – 7a	Wisdom 9:13 – 19
Romans 13:8 – 10	James 2:1 – 5	Philemon 9b – 10, 12 – 17
Matthew 18:15 – 20	Mark 7:31 – 37	Luke 14:25 – 33

TWENTY-FOURTH SUNDAY IN ORDINARY TIME

YEAR A	YEAR B	YEAR C
Sirach 27:33 — 28:9	Isaiah 50:5 – 9a	Exodus 32:7 – 11, 13 – 14
Romans 14:7 – 9	James 2:14 – 18	1 Timothy 1:12 – 17
Matthew 18:21 – 35	Mark 8:27 – 35	Luke 15:1 – 32 (15:1 – 10)

TWENTY-FIFTH SUNDAY IN ORDINARY TIME

YEAR A	YEAR B	YEAR C
Isaiah 55:6 – 9	Wisdom 2:12, 17 – 20	Amos 8:4 – 7
Philippians 1:20c – 24, 27a	James 3:16 — 4:3	1 Timothy 2:1 – 8
Matthew 20:1 – 16a	Mark 9:30 – 37	Luke 16:1 – 13 (16:10 – 13)

TWENTY-SIXTH SUNDAY IN ORDINARY TIME

YEAR A	YEAR B	YEAR C
Ezekiel 18:25 – 28	Numbers 11:25 – 29	Amos 6:1a, 4 – 7
Philippians 2:1 – 11 (2:1 – 5)	James 5:1 – 6	1 Timothy 6:11 – 16
Matthew 21:28 – 32	Mark 9:38 – 43, 45, 47 – 48	Luke 16:19 – 31

TWENTY-SEVENTH SUNDAY IN ORDINARY TIME

YEAR A	YEAR B	YEAR C
Isaiah 5:1 – 7	Genesis 2:18 – 24	Habakkuk 1:2 – 3; 2:2 – 4
Philippians 4:6 – 9	Hebrews 2:9 – 11	2 Timothy 1:6 – 8, 13 – 14
Matthew 21:33 – 43	Mark 10:2 – 16 (10:2 – 12)	Luke 17:5 – 10

TWENTY-EIGHTH SUNDAY IN ORDINARY TIME

YEAR A	YEAR B	YEAR C
Isaiah 25:6 – 10a	Wisdom 7:7 – 11	2 Kings 5:14 – 17
Philippians 4:12 – 14, 19 – 20	Hebrews 4:12 – 13	2 Timothy 2:8 – 13
Matthew 22:1 – 14 (22:1 – 10)	Mark 10:17 – 30 (10:17 – 27)	Luke 17:11 – 19

TWENTY-NINTH SUNDAY IN ORDINARY TIME

YEAR A	YEAR B	YEAR C
Isaiah 45:1, 4–6	Isaiah 53:10–11	Exodus 17:8–13
1 Thessalonians 1:1–5b	Hebrews 4:14–16	2 Timothy 3:14 — 4:2
Matthew 22:15–21	Mark 10:35–45 (10:42–45)	Luke 18:1–8

THIRTIETH SUNDAY IN ORDINARY TIME

YEAR A	YEAR B	YEAR C
Exodus 22:20–26	Jeremiah 31:7–9	Sirach 35:12–14, 16–18
1 Thessalonians 1:5c–10	Hebrews 5:1–6	2 Timothy 4:6–8, 16–18
Matthew 22:34–40	Mark 10:46–52	Luke 18:9–14

THIRTY-FIRST SUNDAY IN ORDINARY TIME

YEAR A	YEAR B	YEAR C
Malachi 1:14b — 2:2b, 8–10	Deuteronomy 6:2–6	Wisdom 11:22 — 12:2
1 Thessalonians 2:7b–9, 13	Hebrews 7:23–28	2 Thessalonians 1:11 — 2:2
Matthew 23:1–12	Mark 12:28b–34	Luke 19:1–10

THIRTY-SECOND SUNDAY IN ORDINARY TIME

YEAR A	YEAR B	YEAR C
Wisdom 6:12–16	1 Kings 17:10–16	2 Maccabees 7:1–2, 9–14
1 Thessalonians 4:13–18 (4:13–14)	Hebrews 9:24–28	2 Thessalonians 2:16 — 3:5
Matthew 25:1–13	Mark 12:38–44 (12:41–44)	Luke 20:27–38 (20:27, 34–38)

THIRTY-THIRD SUNDAY IN ORDINARY TIME

YEAR A	YEAR B	YEAR C
Proverbs 31:10–13, 19–20, 30–31	Daniel 12:1–3	Malachi 3:19–20a
1 Thessalonians 5:1–6	Hebrews 10:11–14, 18	2 Thessalonians 3:7–12
Matthew 25:14–30 (25:14–15, 19–21)	Mark 13:24–32	Luke 21:5–19

THIRTY-FOURTH OR LAST SUNDAY IN ORDINARY TIME

YEAR A	YEAR B	YEAR C
Ezekiel 34:11–12, 15–17	Daniel 7:13–14	2 Samuel 5:1–3
1 Corinthians 15:20–26, 28	Revelation 1:5–8	Colossians 1:12–20
Matthew 25:31–46	John 18:33b–37	Luke 23:35–43

TABLE VI: DATES OF ALL SUNDAYS AND FEASTS, 1999–2013

Sunday/Feast Day	1999 Year A	2000 Year B	2001 Year C
1st Sunday of Advent	November 29, 1998	November 28, 1999	December 3, 2000
2nd Sunday of Advent	December 6, 1998	December 5, 1999	December 10, 2000
Immaculate Conception, December 8	Tuesday	Wednesday	Friday
3rd Sunday of Advent	December 14, 1998	December 12, 1999	December 17, 2000
4th Sunday of Advent	December 20, 1998	December 19, 1999	December 24, 2000
Christmas, December 25	Friday	Saturday	Monday
Holy Family	December 27, 1998	December 26, 1999	December 31, 2000
Mary, Mother of God, January 1	Friday	Saturday	Monday
Epiphany	January 3, 1999	January 2, 2000	January 7, 2001
Baptism of the Lord	January 10, 1999	January 9, 2000	January 8, 2001*
2nd Sunday in Ordinary Time	January 17	January 16	January 14
3rd Sunday in Ordinary Time	January 25	January 23	January 21
4th Sunday in Ordinary Time	January 31	January 30	January 28
Presentation of the Lord, February 2	Tuesday	Wednesday	Friday
5th Sunday in Ordinary Time	February 7	February 6	February 4
6th Sunday in Ordinary Time	February 14	February 13	February 11
7th Sunday in Ordinary Time	_____	February 20	February 18
8th Sunday in Ordinary Time	_____	February 27	February 25
9th Sunday in Ordinary Time	_____	March 5	_____
Ash Wednesday	February 17	March 8	February 28
1st Sunday of Lent	February 21	March 12	March 4
2nd Sunday of Lent	February 28	March 19	March 11
3rd Sunday of Lent	March 7	March 26	March 18
4th Sunday of Lent	March 14	April 2	March 25
5th Sunday of Lent	March 21	April 9	April 1
Passion (Palm) Sunday	March 28	April 16	April 8
Joseph, Husband of Mary, March 19	Friday	March 20+	Monday
Annunciation, March 25	Thursday	Saturday	March 26+
Holy Thursday	April 1	April 20	April 12
Good Friday	April 2	April 21	April 13
Easter Sunday	April 4	April 23	April 15
2nd Sunday of Easter	April 11	April 30	April 22
3rd Sunday of Easter	April 18	May 7	April 29
4th Sunday of Easter	April 25	May 14	May 6
5th Sunday of Easter	May 2	May 21	May 13
6th Sunday of Easter	May 9	May 28	May 20
Ascension	May 13	June 1	May 24
7th Sunday of Easter	May 16	June 4	May 27

+ This solemnity has been transferred to this date.   * This feast is celebrated this year on a weekday.

Sunday/Feast Day	1999 Year A	2000 Year B	2001 Year C
Pentecost	May 23	June 11	June 3
Trinity Sunday	May 30	June 18	June 10
Body and Blood of Christ	June 6	June 25	June 17
Sacred Heart	June 11	June 30	June 22
9th Sunday in Ordinary Time	_____	_____	_____
10th Sunday in Ordinary Time	_____	_____	_____
11th Sunday in Ordinary Time	June 13	_____	_____
12th Sunday in Ordinary Time	June 20	_____	_____
Birth of John the Baptist, June 24	Thursday	Saturday	Sunday
13th Sunday in Ordinary Time	June 27	July 2	July 1
Peter and Paul, Apostles, June 29	Tuesday	Thursday	Friday
Independence Day, July 4	* *	Tuesday	Wednesday
14th Sunday in Ordinary Time	July 4	July 9	July 8
15th Sunday in Ordinary Time	July 11	July 16	July 15
16th Sunday in Ordinary Time	July 18	July 23	July 22
17th Sunday in Ordinary Time	July 25	July 30	July 29
18th Sunday in Ordinary Time	August 1	_____	August 5
Transfiguration, August 6	Friday	Sunday	Monday
19th Sunday in Ordinary Time	August 8	August 13	August 12
Assumption, August 15	Sunday	Tuesday	Wednesday
20th Sunday in Ordinary Time	_____	August 20	August 19
21st Sunday in Ordinary Time	August 22	August 27	August 26
22nd Sunday in Ordinary Time	August 29	September 3	September 2
Labor Day	September 6	September 4	September 3
23rd Sunday in Ordinary Time	September 5	September 10	September 9
Triumph of the Cross, September 14	Tuesday	Thursday	Friday
24th Sunday in Ordinary Time	September 12	September 17	September 16
25th Sunday in Ordinary Time	September 19	September 24	September 23
26th Sunday in Ordinary Time	September 26	October 1	September 30
27th Sunday in Ordinary Time	October 3	October 8	October 7
28th Sunday in Ordinary Time	October 10	October 15	October 14
29th Sunday in Ordinary Time	October 17	October 22	October 21
30th Sunday in Ordinary Time	October 24	October 29	October 28
31st Sunday in Ordinary Time	October 31	November 5	November 4
All Saints, November 1	Monday	Wednesday	Thursday
All Souls, November 2	Tuesday	Thursday	Friday
32nd Sunday in Ordinary Time	November 7	November 12	November 11
Dedication of St. John Lateran, November 9	Tuesday	Thursday	Friday
33rd Sunday in Ordinary Time	November 14	November 19	November 18
Christ the King	November 21	November 26	November 25
Thanksgiving	November 25	November 23	November 22

* * When Independence Day falls on Sunday, the special Votive Mass texts are not used.

Sunday/Feast Day	2002 Year A	2003 Year B	2004 Year C
1st Sunday of Advent	December 2, 2001	December 1, 2002	November 30, 2003
2nd Sunday of Advent	December 9, 2001	December 8, 2002	December 7, 2003
Immaculate Conception, December 8	Saturday	December 9, 2002[+]	Monday
3rd Sunday of Advent	December 16, 2001	December 15, 2002	December 14, 2003
4th Sunday of Advent	December 23, 2001	December 22, 2002	December 21, 2003
Christmas, December 25	Tuesday	Wednesday	Thursday
Holy Family	December 30, 2001	December 29, 2002	December 28, 2003
Mary, Mother of God, January 1	Tuesday	Wednesday	Thursday
Epiphany	January 6, 2002	January 5, 2003	January 4, 2004
Baptism of the Lord	January 13, 2002	January 12, 2003	January 11, 2004
2nd Sunday in Ordinary Time	January 20	January 19	January 18
3rd Sunday in Ordinary Time	January 27	January 26	January 25
4th Sunday in Ordinary Time	February 3	_____	February 1
Presentation of the Lord, February 2	Saturday	Sunday	Monday
5th Sunday in Ordinary Time	February 10	February 9	February 8
6th Sunday in Ordinary Time	_____	February 16	February 15
7th Sunday in Ordinary Time	_____	February 23	February 22
8th Sunday in Ordinary Time	_____	March 2	_____
9th Sunday in Ordinary Time	_____	_____	_____
Ash Wednesday	February 13	March 5	February 25
1st Sunday of Lent	February 17	March 9	February 29
2nd Sunday of Lent	February 24	March 16	March 7
3rd Sunday of Lent	March 3	March 23	March 14
4th Sunday of Lent	March 10	March 30	March 21
5th Sunday of Lent	March 17	April 6	March 28
Passion (Palm) Sunday	March 24	April 13	April 4
Joseph, Husband of Mary, March 19	Tuesday	Wednesday	Friday
Annunciation, March 25	April 8[+]	Tuesday	Thursday
Holy Thursday	March 28	April 17	April 8
Good Friday	March 29	April 18	April 9
Easter Sunday	March 31	April 20	April 11
2nd Sunday of Easter	April 7	April 27	April 18
3rd Sunday of Easter	April 14	May 4	April 25
4th Sunday of Easter	April 21	May 11	May 2
5th Sunday of Easter	April 28	May 18	May 9
6th Sunday of Easter	May 5	May 25	May 16
Ascension	May 9	May 29	May 20
7th Sunday of Easter	May 12	June 1	May 23
Pentecost	May 19	June 8	May 30

+ This solemnity has been transferred to this date.

Sunday/Feast Day	2002 Year A	2003 Year B	2004 Year C
Trinity Sunday	May 26	June 15	June 6
Body and Blood of Christ	June 2	June 22	June 13
Sacred Heart	June 7	June 27	June 18
9th Sunday in Ordinary Time	_____	_____	_____
10th Sunday in Ordinary Time	June 9	_____	_____
11th Sunday in Ordinary Time	June 16	_____	_____
12th Sunday in Ordinary Time	June 23	_____	June 20
Birth of John the Baptist, June 24	Monday	Tuesday	Thursday
13th Sunday in Ordinary Time	June 30	_____	June 27
Peter and Paul, Apostles, June 29	Saturday	Sunday	Tuesday
Independence Day, July 4	Thursday	Friday	* *
14th Sunday in Ordinary Time	July 7	July 6	July 4
15th Sunday in Ordinary Time	July 14	July 13	July 11
16th Sunday in Ordinary Time	July 21	July 20	July 18
17th Sunday in Ordinary Time	July 28	July 27	July 25
18th Sunday in Ordinary Time	August 4	August 3	August 1
Transfiguration, August 6	Tuesday	Wednesday	Friday
19th Sunday in Ordinary Time	August 11	August 10	August 8
Assumption, August 15	Thursday	Friday	Sunday
20th Sunday in Ordinary Time	August 18	August 17	_____
21st Sunday in Ordinary Time	August 25	August 24	August 22
22nd Sunday in Ordinary Time	September 1	August 31	August 29
Labor Day	September 2	September 1	September 6
23rd Sunday in Ordinary Time	September 8	September 7	September 5
Triumph of the Cross, September 14	Saturday	Sunday	Tuesday
24th Sunday in Ordinary Time	September 15	_____	September 12
25th Sunday in Ordinary Time	September 22	September 21	September 19
26th Sunday in Ordinary Time	September 29	September 28	September 26
27th Sunday in Ordinary Time	October 6	October 5	October 3
28th Sunday in Ordinary Time	October 13	October 12	October 10
29th Sunday in Ordinary Time	October 20	October 19	October 17
30th Sunday in Ordinary Time	October 27	October 26	October 24
31st Sunday in Ordinary Time	November 3	_____	October 31
All Saints, November 1	Friday	Saturday	Monday
All Souls, November 2	Saturday	Sunday	Tuesday
32nd Sunday in Ordinary Time	November 10	_____	November 7
Dedication of St. John Lateran, November 9	Saturday	Sunday	Tuesday
33rd Sunday in Ordinary Time	November 17	November 16	November 14
Christ the King	November 24	November 23	November 21
Thanksgiving	November 21	November 27	November 25

* * When Independence Day falls on Sunday, the special Votive Mass texts are not used.

Sunday/Feast Day	2005 Year A	2006 Year B	2007 Year C
1st Sunday of Advent	November 28, 2004	November 27, 2005	December 3, 2006
2nd Sunday of Advent	December 5, 2004	December 4, 2005	December 10, 2006
Immaculate Conception, December 8	Wednesday	Thursday	Friday
3rd Sunday of Advent	December 12, 2004	December 11, 2005	December 17, 2006
4th Sunday of Advent	December 19, 2004	December 18, 2005	December 24, 2006
Christmas, December 25	Saturday	Sunday	Monday
Holy Family	December 26, 2004	December 30, 2005[+]	December 31, 2006
Mary, Mother of God, January 1	Saturday	Sunday	Monday
Epiphany	January 2, 2005	January 8, 2006	January 8, 2007
Baptism of the Lord	January 9, 2005	January 9, 2006	January 7, 2007[+]
2nd Sunday in Ordinary Time	January 16	January 15	January 14
3rd Sunday in Ordinary Time	January 23	January 22	January 21
4th Sunday in Ordinary Time	January 30	January 29	January 28
Presentation of the Lord, February 2	Wednesday	Thursday	Friday
5th Sunday in Ordinary Time	February 6	February 5	February 4
6th Sunday in Ordinary Time	_____	February 12	February 11
7th Sunday in Ordinary Time	_____	February 19	February 18
8th Sunday in Ordinary Time	_____	February 26	_____
9th Sunday in Ordinary Time	_____	_____	_____
Ash Wednesday	February 9	March 1	February 21
1st Sunday of Lent	February 13	March 5	February 25
2nd Sunday of Lent	February 20	March 12	March 4
3rd Sunday of Lent	February 27	March 19	March 11
4th Sunday of Lent	March 6	March 26	March 18
5th Sunday of Lent	March 13	April 2	March 25
Passion (Palm) Sunday	March 20	April 9	April 1
Joseph, Husband of Mary, March 19	Saturday	March 20[+]	Monday
Annunciation, March 25	April 4[+]	Saturday	March 26[+]
Holy Thursday	March 24	April 13	April 5
Good Friday	March 25	April 14	April 6
Easter Sunday	March 27	April 16	April 8
2nd Sunday of Easter	April 3	April 23	April 15
3rd Sunday of Easter	April 10	April 30	April 22
4th Sunday of Easter	April 17	May 7	April 29
5th Sunday of Easter	April 24	May 14	May 6
6th Sunday of Easter	May 1	May 21	May 13
Ascension	May 5	May 25	May 17
7th Sunday of Easter	May 8	May 28	May 20
Pentecost	May 15	June 4	May 27

+ This solemnity has been transferred to this date.

Sunday/Feast Day	2005 Year A	2006 Year B	2007 Year C
Trinity Sunday	May 22	June 11	June 3
Body and Blood of Christ	May 29	June 18	June 10
Sacred Heart	June 3	June 23	June 15
9th Sunday in Ordinary Time	_____	_____	_____
10th Sunday in Ordinary Time	June 5	_____	_____
11th Sunday in Ordinary Time	June 12	_____	June 17
12th Sunday in Ordinary Time	June 19	June 25	_____
Birth of John the Baptist, June 24	Friday	Saturday	Sunday
13th Sunday in Ordinary Time	June 26	July 2	July 1
Peter and Paul, Apostles, June 29	Wednesday	Thursday	Friday
Independence Day, July 4	Monday	Tuesday	Wednesday
14th Sunday in Ordinary Time	July 3	July 9	July 8
15th Sunday in Ordinary Time	July 10	July 16	July 15
16th Sunday in Ordinary Time	July 17	July 23	July 22
17th Sunday in Ordinary Time	July 24	July 30	July 29
18th Sunday in Ordinary Time	July 31	_____	August 5
Transfiguration, August 6	Saturday	Sunday	Monday
19th Sunday in Ordinary Time	August 7	August 13	August 12
Assumption, August 15	Monday	Tuesday	Wednesday
20th Sunday in Ordinary Time	August 14	August 20	August 19
21st Sunday in Ordinary Time	August 21	August 27	August 26
22nd Sunday in Ordinary Time	August 28	September 3	September 2
Labor Day	September 5	September 4	September 3
23rd Sunday in Ordinary Time	September 4	September 10	September 9
Triumph of the Cross, September 14	Wednesday	Thursday	Friday
24th Sunday in Ordinary Time	September 11	September 17	September 16
25th Sunday in Ordinary Time	September 18	September 24	September 23
26th Sunday in Ordinary Time	September 25	October 1	September 30
27th Sunday in Ordinary Time	October 2	October 8	October 7
28th Sunday in Ordinary Time	October 9	October 15	October 14
29th Sunday in Ordinary Time	October 16	October 22	October 21
30th Sunday in Ordinary Time	October 23	October 29	October 28
31st Sunday in Ordinary Time	October 30	November 5	November 4
All Saints, November 1	Tuesday	Wednesday	Thursday
All Souls, November 2	Wednesday	Thursday	Friday
32nd Sunday in Ordinary Time	November 6	November 12	November 11
Dedication of St. John Lateran, November 9	Wednesday	Thursday	Friday
33rd Sunday in Ordinary Time	November 13	November 19	November 18
Christ the King	November 20	November 26	November 25
Thanksgiving	November 24	November 23	November 22

+ This solemnity has been transferred to this date.

Sunday/Feast Day	2008 Year A	2009 Year B	2010 Year C
1st Sunday of Advent	December 2, 2007	November 30, 2008	November 29, 2009
2nd Sunday of Advent	December 9, 2007	December 7, 2008	December 6, 2009
Immaculate Conception, December 8	Saturday	Monday	Tuesday
3rd Sunday of Advent	December 16, 2007	December 14, 2008	December 13, 2009
4th Sunday of Advent	December 23, 2007	December 21, 2008	December 20, 2009
Christmas, December 25	Tuesday	Thursday	Friday
Holy Family	December 30, 2007	December 28, 2008	December 27, 2009
Mary, Mother of God, January 1	Tuesday	Thursday	Friday
Epiphany	January 6, 2008	January 4, 2009	January 3, 2010
Baptism of the Lord	January 13, 2008	January 11, 2009	January 10, 2010
2nd Sunday in Ordinary Time	January 20	January 18	January 17
3rd Sunday in Ordinary Time	January 27	January 25	January 24
4th Sunday in Ordinary Time	February 3	February 1	January 31
Presentation of the Lord, February 2	Saturday	Monday	Tuesday
5th Sunday in Ordinary Time	_____	February 8	February 7
6th Sunday in Ordinary Time	_____	February 15	February 14
7th Sunday in Ordinary Time	_____	February 22	_____
8th Sunday in Ordinary Time	_____	_____	_____
9th Sunday in Ordinary Time	_____	_____	_____
Ash Wednesday	February 6	February 25	February 17
1st Sunday of Lent	February 10	March 1	February 21
2nd Sunday of Lent	February 17	March 8	February 28
3rd Sunday of Lent	February 24	March 15	March 7
4th Sunday of Lent	March 2	March 22	March 14
5th Sunday of Lent	March 9	March 29	March 21
Passion (Palm) Sunday	March 16	April 5	March 28
Joseph, Husband of Mary, March 19	March 31[+]	Thursday	Friday
Annunciation, March 25	April 1[+]	Wednesday	Thursday
Holy Thursday	March 20	April 5	April 1
Good Friday	March 21	April 10	April 2
Easter Sunday	March 23	April 12	April 4
2nd Sunday of Easter	March 30	April 19	April 11
3rd Sunday of Easter	April 6	April 26	April 18
4th Sunday of Easter	April 13	May 3	April 25
5th Sunday of Easter	April 20	May 10	May 2
6th Sunday of Easter	April 27	May 17	May 9
Ascension	May 1	May 21	May 13
7th Sunday of Easter	May 4	May 24	May 16
Pentecost	May 11	May 31	May 23
Trinity Sunday	May 18	June 7	May 30

Sunday/Feast Day	2008 Year A	2009 Year B	2010 Year C
Body and Blood of Christ	May 25	June 14	June 6
Sacred Heart	May 30	June 19	June 11
9th Sunday in Ordinary Time	June 1	_____	_____
10th Sunday in Ordinary Time	June 8	_____	_____
11th Sunday in Ordinary Time	June 15	_____	June 13
12th Sunday in Ordinary Time	June 22	June 21	June 20
Birth of John the Baptist, June 24	Tuesday	Wednesday	Thursday
13th Sunday in Ordinary Time	_____	June 28	June 27
Peter and Paul, Apostles, June 29	Sunday	Monday	Tuesday
Independence Day, July 4	Friday	Saturday	* *
14th Sunday in Ordinary Time	July 6	July 5	July 4
15th Sunday in Ordinary Time	July 13	July 12	July 11
16th Sunday in Ordinary Time	July 20	July 19	July 18
17th Sunday in Ordinary Time	July 27	July 26	July 25
18th Sunday in Ordinary Time	August 3	August 2	August 1
Transfiguration, August 6	Wednesday	Thursday	Friday
19th Sunday in Ordinary Time	August 10	August 2	August 8
Assumption, August 15	Friday	Saturday	Sunday
20th Sunday in Ordinary Time	August 17	August 16	_____
21st Sunday in Ordinary Time	August 24	August 23	August 22
22nd Sunday in Ordinary Time	August 31	August 30	August 29
Labor Day	September 1	September 7	September 6
23rd Sunday in Ordinary Time	September 7	September 6	September 5
Triumph of the Cross, September 14	Sunday	Monday	Tuesday
24th Sunday in Ordinary Time	_____	September 13	September 12
25th Sunday in Ordinary Time	September 21	September 20	September19
26th Sunday in Ordinary Time	September 28	September 27	September 26
27th Sunday in Ordinary Time	October 5	October 4	October 3
28th Sunday in Ordinary Time	October 12	October 11	October 10
29th Sunday in Ordinary Time	October 19	October 18	October 17
30th Sunday in Ordinary Time	October 26	October 25	October 24
31st Sunday in Ordinary Time	_____	_____	October 31
All Saints, November 1	Saturday	Sunday	Monday
All Souls, November 2	Sunday	Monday	Tuesday
32nd Sunday in Ordinary Time	_____	November 8	November 7
Dedication of St. John Lateran, November 9	Sunday	Monday	Tuesday
33rd Sunday in Ordinary Time	November 16	November 15	November 14
Christ the King	November 23	November 22	November 21
Thanksgiving	November 20	November 26	November 25

* * When Independence Day falls on Sunday, the special Votive Mass texts are not used.

Sunday/Feast Day	2011 Year A	2012 Year B	2013 Year C
1st Sunday of Advent	November 28, 2010	November 27, 2011	December 2, 2012
2nd Sunday of Advent	December 5, 2010	December 4, 2011	December 9, 2012
Immaculate Conception, December 8	Wednesday	Thursday	Saturday
3rd Sunday of Advent	December 12, 2010	December 11, 2011	December 16, 2012
4th Sunday of Advent	December 19, 2010	December 18, 2011	December 23, 2012
Christmas, December 25	Saturday	Sunday	Tuesday
Holy Family	December 26, 2010	December 30, 2011[+]	December 30, 2012
Mary, Mother of God, January 1	Saturday	Sunday	Tuesday
Epiphany	January 2, 2011	January 8, 2012	January 6, 2013
Baptism of the Lord	January 9, 2011	January 9, 2012[+]	January 13, 2013
2nd Sunday in Ordinary Time	January 16	January 15	January 20
3rd Sunday in Ordinary Time	January 23	January 22	January 27
4th Sunday in Ordinary Time	January 30	January 29	February 3
Presentation of the Lord, February 2	Wednesday	Thursday	Saturday
5th Sunday in Ordinary Time	February 6	February 5	February 10
6th Sunday in Ordinary Time	February 13	February 12	_____
7th Sunday in Ordinary Time	February 20	February 19	_____
8th Sunday in Ordinary Time	February 27	_____	_____
9th Sunday in Ordinary Time	March 6	_____	_____
Ash Wednesday	March 9	February 22	February 13
1st Sunday of Lent	March 13	February 26	February 17
2nd Sunday of Lent	March 20	March 4	February 24
3rd Sunday of Lent	March 27	March 11	March 3
4th Sunday of Lent	April 3	March 18	March 10
5th Sunday of Lent	April 10	March 25	March 17
Passion (Palm) Sunday	April 17	April 1	March 24
Joseph, Husband of Mary, March 19	Saturday	Monday	Tuesday
Annunciation, March 25	Friday	March 26[+]	April 8[+]
Holy Thursday	April 21	April 5	March 28
Good Friday	April 22	April 6	March 29
Easter Sunday	April 24	April 8	March 31
2nd Sunday of Easter	May 1	April 15	April 7
3rd Sunday of Easter	May 8	April 22	April 14
4th Sunday of Easter	May 15	April 29	April 21
5th Sunday of Easter	May 22	May 6	April 28
6th Sunday of Easter	May 29	May 13	May 5
Ascension	June 2	May 17	May 9
7th Sunday of Easter	June 5	May 20	May 12
Pentecost	June 12	May 27	May 19

+ This solemnity has been transferred to this date.

Sunday/Feast Day	2011 Year A	2012 Year B	2013 Year C
Trinity Sunday	June 19	June 3	May 26
Body and Blood of Christ	June 26	June 10	June 2
Sacred Heart	July 1	June 15	June 7
9th Sunday in Ordinary Time	————	————	————
10th Sunday in Ordinary Time	————	————	June 9
11th Sunday in Ordinary Time	————	June 17	June 16
12th Sunday in Ordinary Time	————	————	June 23
Birth of John the Baptist, June 24	Friday	Sunday	Monday
13th Sunday in Ordinary Time	————	July 1	June 13
Peter and Paul, Apostles, June 29	Wednesday	Friday	Saturday
Independence Day, July 4	Monday	Wednesday	Thursday
14th Sunday in Ordinary Time	July 3	July 8	July 7
15th Sunday in Ordinary Time	July 10	July 15	July 14
16th Sunday in Ordinary Time	July 17	July 22	July 21
17th Sunday in Ordinary Time	July 24	July 29	July 28
18th Sunday in Ordinary Time	July 31	August 5	August 4
Transfiguration, August 6	Saturday	Monday	Tuesday
19th Sunday in Ordinary Time	August 7	August 12	August 11
Assumption, August 15	Monday	Wednesday	Thursday
20th Sunday in Ordinary Time	August 14	August 19	August 18
21st Sunday in Ordinary Time	August 21	August 26	August 25
22nd Sunday in Ordinary Time	August 28	September 2	September 1
Labor Day	September 5	September 3	September 2
23rd Sunday in Ordinary Time	September 4	September 9	September 8
Triumph of the Cross, September 14	Wednesday	Friday	Saturday
24th Sunday in Ordinary Time	September 11	September 16	September 15
25th Sunday in Ordinary Time	September 18	September 23	September 22
26th Sunday in Ordinary Time	September 25	September 30	September 29
27th Sunday in Ordinary Time	October 2	October 7	October 6
28th Sunday in Ordinary Time	October 9	October 14	October 13
29th Sunday in Ordinary Time	October 16	October 21	October 20
30th Sunday in Ordinary Time	October 23	October 28	October 27
31st Sunday in Ordinary Time	October 30	November 4	November 3
All Saints, November 1	Tuesday	Thursday	Friday
All Souls, November 2	Wednesday	Friday	Saturday
32nd Sunday in Ordinary Time	November 6	November 11	November 10
Dedication of St. John Lateran, November 9	Wednesday	Friday	Saturday
33rd Sunday in Ordinary Time	November 13	November 18	November 17
Christ the King	November 20	November 22	November 24
Thanksgiving	November 24	November 25	November 26

+ This solemnity has been transferred to this date.

TABLE VII
COMMON RESPONSORIAL PSALMS FOR THE SEASONS

This table is a guide to the "Common Texts for Sung Responsorial Psalms" on pages 441–450. These texts for refrains (see page 441) and for seasonal responsorial psalms (see pages 441–450) are provided "in order that the people may be able to join in the responsorial psalm more readily" through the use of one text over several Sundays. (See the General Instruction of the Roman Missal, #36.) These psalms may replace the psalms given for individual Sundays in the lectionary.

ADVENT

REFRAIN FOR USE WITH ANY PSALM:

"Come, O Lord, and set us free."

COMMON PSALMS FOR ALL OR ANY PART OF ADVENT:

Psalm 25 (page 441):   *"To you, O Lord, I lift my soul."*

Psalm 85 (page 441):   *"Lord, show us your mercy and love."*

CHRISTMAS SEASON

REFRAIN FOR USE WITH ANY PSALM:

"Lord, today we have seen your glory."

COMMON PSALM FOR THE CHRISTMAS SEASON:

Psalm 98 (page 442):   *"All the ends of the earth have seen the saving power of God."*

COMMON PSALM FOR EPIPHANY:

Psalm 72 (page 442):   *"Lord, every nation on earth will adore you."*

LENT

REFRAIN FOR USE WITH ANY PSALM:

"Remember, O Lord, your faithfulness and love."

COMMON PSALMS FOR ALL OR ANY PART OF LENT:

Psalm 51 (page 443):   *"Be merciful, O Lord, for we have sinned."*

Psalm 91 (page 443):   *"Be with me, Lord, when I am in trouble."*

Psalm 130 (page 444):   *"With the Lord there is mercy, and fullness of redemption."*

COMMON PSALM FOR PALM SUNDAY THROUGH WEDNESDAY OF HOLY WEEK:

Psalm 22 (page 444):   *"My God, my God, why have you abandoned me?"*

EASTER VIGIL

COMMON PSALM AT THE EASTER VIGIL:

Psalm 136 (page 444):   *"God's love is everlasting."*

EASTER SEASON

REFRAIN FOR USE WITH ANY PSALM:

"Alleluia" (repeated at least twice).

COMMON PSALMS FOR ALL OR ANY PART OF THE EASTER SEASON:

Psalm 118 (page 445): *"This is the day the Lord has made;
let us rejoice and be glad."*

Psalm 66 (page 446): *"Let all the earth cry out to God with joy, alleluia."*

ON OR AFTER THE ASCENSION:

Psalm 47 (page 446): *"God mounts his throne to shouts of joy."*

ON PENTECOST:

Psalm 104 (page 446): *"Lord, send out your Spirit, and renew the face
of the earth."*

ORDINARY TIME

REFRAINS FOR USE WITH ANY PSALM OF PRAISE:

"Praise the Lord for he is good."

*"We praise you, O Lord, for all your works
are wonderful."*

"Sing to the Lord a new song."

REFRAINS FOR USE WITH ANY PSALM OF PETITION:

"The Lord is near to all who call on him."

"Hear us, Lord, and save us."

"The Lord is kind and merciful."

COMMON PSALMS FOR ALL OR ANY PART OF ORDINARY TIME:

Psalm 19 (page 447): *"Lord, you have the words of everlasting life."* or:
"Your words, Lord, are Spirit and life."

Psalm 27 (page 447): *"The Lord is my light and my salvation."*

Psalm 34 (page 448): *"I will bless the Lord at all times."* or:
"Taste and see the goodness of the Lord."

Psalm 63 (page 448): *"My soul is thirsting for you, O Lord my God."*

Psalm 95 (page 448): *"If today you hear his voice, harden not your hearts."*

Psalm 100 (page 449): *"We are his people, the sheep of his flock."*

Psalm 103 (page 449): *"The Lord is kind and merciful."*

Psalm 145 (page 449): *"I will praise your name for ever,
my king and my God."*

COMMON PSALM FOR THE LAST WEEKS OF ORDINARY TIME:

Psalm 122 (page 450): *"Let us go rejoicing to the house of the Lord."*

Also from Liturgy Training Publications:

Lectionary for Mass: The Sundays in Three Volumes
The Passion of Our Lord Jesus Christ prepared and with notes by George R. Szews
Guide to the Revised Lectionary by Martin Connell
Lectionary for Masses with Children: Ritual Editions
Lectionary for Masses with Children: Study Editions
Guide to the Lectionary for Masses with Children by Peter Mazar and Robert Piercy
Rite of Christian Initiation of Adults: Ritual Edition
Rite of Christian Initiation of Adults: Study Edition
Rito de la Iniciacion Cristiana de Adultos: Edicion Ritual
Rito de la Iniciacion Cristiana de Adultos: Edicion de estudio
Order of Christian Funerals: Ritual Edition
Order of Christian Funerals: Study Edition
Holy People, Holy Place: Rites for the Church's House by Thomas G. Simons
The Liturgy Documents: A Parish Resource, Volume I
The Liturgy Documents: A Parish Resource, Volume II
The Liturgy Documents Volume I on Disk for Windows
Los Documentos Liturgicos: Un recurso pastoral
Bishops' Committee on the Liturgy Newsletter: 1976 – 1980
Bishops' Committee on the Liturgy Newsletter: 1981 – 1985
Bishops' Committee on the Liturgy Newsletter: 1986 – 1990
Bishops' Committee on the Liturgy Newsletter: 1991 – 1995

Order from your bookstore or Liturgy Training Publications.